900 BIBLE QUESTIONS ANSWERED

900 BIBLE QUESTIONS ANSWERED

William L. Pettingill

Grand Rapids, MI 49501

900 Bible Questions Answered by William L. Pettingill.

Published in 1991 by Kregel Classics, an imprint of Kregel Publications, P. O. Box 2607, Grand Rapids, MI 49501. Kregel Classics provides trusted and time-proven publications for Christian life and ministry. Your comments and suggestions are valued.

Cover Design: Don Ellens

Library of Congress Cataloging-in-Publication Data
Pettingill, William L., 1866-1950.
[Bible questions answered]
900 Bible questions answered / William L. Pettingill.
p. cm.
Reprint. Previously published: Bible questions answered. Grand Rapids, MI: Zondervan Publishing House. c1979.
Includes Indexes.
1. Bible—Theology. 2. Bible. I. Title.
BS543.P45 1991 230—dc20 90-20615
CIP

ISBN 0-8254-3541-2 (paperback)

2 3 4 5 6 Printing / Year 97 96 95 94

Printed in the United States of America

CONTENTS

Preface 6
The Bible 7
God 19
The Father 22
The Son 25
The Holy Spirit 46
Creation 55
Man .57
Satan 59
Angels 64
Sin 66
Salvation 76
The Church 96
Ordinances of the Church . .114
The Gospel 124
The Kingdom 127
Israel 131
After Death 148
Heaven 154
Hell 158
Assurance 163
Eternal Security 165
Justification 178
Law and Grace 180
Grace 186
The Sabbath 187
The Crucifixion Day 191
The Resurrection 193
Questions on the Parables . .195
Christian Conduct 200
The Heathen World 220
Election 220
Faith 222
Regeneration 225
Repentance 227
Sanctification or Holiness . .228
Temperance 233
Prayer 234
Divine Healing 243
Marriage 247
Roman Catholicism 249
Antichristian Cults 251
The Future 260
People and Places 307
Miscellaneous 351
Subject Index 397
Scripture Index 405

PREFACE

When the Queen of Sheba visited the King of Israel "to prove him with hard questions" Solomon "told her all her questions: there was not any thing hid from the King which he told her not" (1 Kings 10:1-3). I have not always been able to answer all questions to the satisfaction of my questioners. Often I have had to resort to the frank reply, "I do not know." And yet it has been my privilege through the years, according to the testimony of some of God's children, to give them some help in the dissolving of their doubts and the solution of their problems.

The present volume presents an accumulation of questions and answers on Bible subjects, gathered in part from my personal correspondence files, and in part from my editorial work. For several years, while Dean of the Philadelphia School of the Bible and Editor of *Serving-and-Waiting*, its official organ, I conducted a "Question Box" in the magazine. For such matter as has been gathered from that source, grateful acknowledgment is hereby made. Beginning in 1928 I published a personal magazine called *Just a Word*, and much of the matter used in this book comes from its columns.

And, above all, I give thanks to God for the high and holy privilege of ministering in His Word among His beloved and blood-bought children. May it please Him to use this testimony for the glory of the name which is above every name, even the name of our Lord and Savior Jesus Christ!

"Blessing, and honor, and glory, and power, be unto Him that sitteth upon the throne, and unto the Lamb forever and ever!"

THE BIBLE

The Word of God

In what sense is the Bible the Word of God?

In Psalm 19, verses 7 to 9, there are six titles for the Scriptures, associated with six attributes and six effects. The Scriptures are defined as (1) the law of Jehovah; (2) the testimony of Jehovah; (3) the statutes of Jehovah; (4) the commandment of Jehovah; (5) the fear (that is, the reverence) of Jehovah, and (6) the judgments of Jehovah. There are ten such titles for the Word of God in Psalm 119. They are (1) the way; (2) the testimony; (3) the precept; (4) the commandment; (5) the saying; (6) the law; (7) the judgment; (8) the righteousness; (9) the statute, and (10) the word.

The expression "the law of Jehovah" has no particular reference to the commandments of Sinai; it is rather a generic term for the Scriptures. About all the Scriptures David had was the five books of Moses, and this collection of books is known throughout the Bible as the Torah or the Law. It is equivalent to our term, "the Scriptures."

Let it be noted that here are six definite propositions set forth concerning the Scriptures. Every one of these propositions is capable of demonstration; and indeed every one of them has been worked out to a satisfactory conclusion by millions of God's people throughout the ages. It is true that the law of Jehovah *is* perfect and complete, converting the soul; that the testimony of Jehovah *is* sure, making wise the simple; that the statutes of Jehovah *are* right, rejoicing the heart; that the commandment of Jehovah *is* pure, enlightening the eyes; that the fear of Jehovah *is* clean, enduring forever; and that the judgments of Jehovah *are* true and righteous altogether. That these things are so is just as certain as that two plus two makes four.

The Inspiration of the Scriptures

How are the Scriptures inspired?

Writing on *The Extent of Inspiration*, Dr. James H. Brookes says:

"It is a foolish objection often urged against the statements of the Bible upon this subject, that it permits the witness to testify for himself. Of course it does, and the testimony is unavoidable. The argument is not with the infidel, although even here it is perfectly fair to see what claims the book makes, and then to discover whether these claims can be substantiated. But the argument is with those who profess to believe the Bible as a whole, and therefore recognize the credibility of the witness. If a man whose reputation is unimpeached should be summoned to the witness stand, his testimony is to be received, even when it affects his own interests, and goes far, it may be, to establish his own side of the controversy. What then does the Bible itself say as to the extent of its inspiration?

"All Scripture is given by inspiration of God' (2 Tim. 3:16); or if the reading of the Revised Version be preferred, 'Every Scripture inspired of God is also profitable for teaching,' it only makes the affirmation the stronger, because it refers to every one of the sacred writings mentioned in the preceding verse, and comprising the Old Testament books which existed then precisely as we have them now. The testimony is not that the writers were inspired, but the writings; and writings are made up of words and the letters which form the words. Therefore the words are inspired, or God-breathed, including every inflection of the words, and every little particle. This must be so from the nature of the case, because if only the thoughts of the writers were inspired, and they were left to the haphazard and chance selection of words which weak, fallible, and for the most part illiterate men might choose to use in order to express their thoughts, it is obvious that we have no revelation at all. We can get at the thoughts of others only through their words, and if the words of the Scriptures were not the precisely prepared and suitable vehicle for the transmission of the thoughts of the writers, it is plain to any man of common sense that so far as we are concerned, the inspired thoughts would be of no value whatever.

"But happily we are not left to good-for-nothing human reasoning to settle this great question. It is the declaration of the Bible concerning all the Old Testament prophets and writers that 'holy men of God spake as they were moved by the Holy Spirit' (2 Peter 1:21), or as Alford renders it, 'men had utterance from God, being moved by the Holy Spirit,' or as the Revised Version has it, 'men spake from God, being moved by the Holy Spirit.' It is not that they thought, but they spake as they were moved by the Holy Ghost, often indeed uttering thoughts, the significance and scope of which they themselves did not understand, and often using words contrary to their own natural will and purpose, as we see from Num. 22:35-38; 1 Sam. 19:20-24; 1 Kings 13:11-22; John 11:49-52."

God Revealing Himself

Why should we believe that the Bible is from God?

Because it proves itself as God's revelation of Himself. We quote from Frederic Bettex:

Is there a God? Yes. Without Him the material and the spiritual world is an unintelligible chaos, without sense and purpose. This God must be a personal, living God; an impersonal God is no God; and a dead God is folly.

If this God of life created us, why is death in us? Because we have fallen away from Him. Is this God and our Creator nevertheless concerned about our temporal and eternal welfare? Yes. How can we know it? Only through a revelation on His part.

Has He given us such a revelation? Yes. He has at all times revealed himself to individuals through appearances, visions, and dreams, and to mankind as a whole through the written Word, the Bible, given to His servants.

What is the Bible therefore? A divine revelation. "Eye hath not seen, nor ear heard . . . God hath revealed them unto us by his Spirit." "The revelation of Jesus Christ, which God gave unto him, to show unto his servants the things which must shortly come to pass" (Rev. 1:1). "The mystery of Christ is revealed unto his holy apostles and prophets by his Spirit."

How did this revelation take place? In this manner, that the third person of the Godhead, the Holy Ghost, ever and ever enthused, filled, inspired a man, so that he could not do otherwise than speak and write what the Triune God wanted to impart to mankind through him. "Holy men of God spake as they were moved by the Holy Ghost" (2 Peter 1:21). "This Scripture must needs have been fulfilled, which the Holy Ghost by the mouth of David spake before" (Acts 1:16). "Behold, I have put my words in thy mouth" (Isa. 51:16; 59:21; Jer. 1:9).

Must a Christian believe the whole Bible? Yes. It is a unit, and man dare not select what he would believe, and what not. Whoever does not believe the Old Testament does not believe the New either. Paul testifies before Felix, "I believe all things which are written in the law and in the prophets" (Acts 24:14). Christ came into the world in order that "all things be fulfilled, which were written in the law of Moses, and in the prophets, and in the Psalms, concerning him" (Luke 24:44).

But cannot a man honor Christ, love Him, strive to follow Him, and call himself a Christian, without acknowledging His deity? No; that is self-deception. Thus man "maketh God a liar; because he believeth not the record that God gave of his Son" (1 John 5:10). And the end is terror. "If ye believe not that I am he, ye shall die in your sins" (John 8:24). Christ is the "king of aeons"; "He upholds all things by the word of His power" (Heb. 1:3). "He came of the fathers as concerning the flesh, who is over all, God blessed forever" (Rom. 9:5). This or nothing.

But where does reason come in? Nowhere.

Then why did God give us reason? For planting and building, buying and selling, marrying and being given in marriage.

Did God not give us reason also for the purpose of judging His Word? No. To want to judge the Bible by reason is unreasonable, since the Bible rests upon miracles, which reason cannot grasp. But if my reason is to be the criterion, and is able to tell me how much of the Bible I am to believe, then by equal right this must be true of every other man's reason; and if we listen to them all in succession, not a word of the Bible remains valid.

But must not human erudition and science prove valuable even in view of the Bible, and for Bible study? No. "I thank thee, O Father, Lord of heaven and earth, because thou hast hid these things from the wise and prudent" (Matt. 11:25).

What shall the Christian answer the scoffer who wants to prove to him that the Bible contains all kinds of mistakes, and errors, and contradictions, and things that are untenable? Nothing. He is not concerned about the reason of the faith that is in you (1 Peter 3:15), but about the expression of his own conceited wisdom in holy things. We are not to give that which is holy unto the dogs, and it does not pay to contend with a blind man concerning light and colors. On account of his faith in the Bible, the Christian must suffer to be considered a fool by the world.

Let us once for all abandon all hope of ever inventing a faith in the Bible that will find grace in the sight of the world, no matter whether it call itself Christian or godless. Just as the "wisdom of this world is foolishness with God," so the wisdom of God is and will remain foolishness with this world. If your faith in the Bible does not bring upon you the opposition, the more refined or the grosser mockery, the silent or the outspoken contempt and hatred of the world, the educated, and the scholars, you may know thereby that it is not the true faith. Or do you claim to be greater than your Master? He spoke "words of eternal life," "and they mocked Him."

Whoever had such faith in the Bible? Those who overcame the world by faith, the prophets, the apostles, the martyrs.

But why must such be the only correct, true, and Christian faith in the Bible? Because it is and was the faith of Christ.

A Complete Bible

Was any of the Bible left out when our Bible was translated (Rev. 22:19)?

No. We have a complete Bible.

The Canticles

What is the meaning of the phrase, "The Canticles"?

It is the name sometimes applied to the Song of Solomon. Its full name is given in the first verse of the first chapter, "The song of songs, which is Solomon's." In the Latin Vulgate the title is literally translated *Canticum Canticorum,* meaning "Song of Songs." The Song was read on the eighth day of the passover festival, the book being allegorically interpreted by the rabbis as having reference to the history of the exodus. The book has a twofold significance: first, it is "the expression of pure marital love as ordained of God in creation, and the vindication of that love as against both asceticism and lust—the two profanations of the holiness of marriage. The secondary and larger interpretation is of Christ the Son and His heavenly bride the Church" (Scofield).

The Septuagint

What is the Septuagint?

The word "septuagint" is from the Latin *septuaginta,* meaning "seventy"; and it is the name of a Greek version of the Old Testament books made between 280 and 130 B.C. It contains also the apocryphal books. According to a legend preserved in the so-called Letter of Aristeas, the translation was made at Alexandria in Egypt in 72 days by 72 learned Jews from Jerusalem (six from each of the twelve tribes) at the command of Ptolemy Philadelphus, about 270 years before Christ. It is the version used by the Greek church. The traditional 70 or 72 translators became known as "The Seventy," and their translation as The Septuagint.

Beginning of the New Testament

Where does the Old Testament end, and the New Testament begin?

According to the printer, the Old Testament ends with the book of Malachi, and the New Testament begins with the book of Matthew. But, strictly speaking, this is not true. John the Baptist was not a New Testament character, but the greatest of the Old Testament prophets, according to the Lord Jesus Himself (Matt. 11:11,12). The New Testament did not begin until the blood of Christ was shed. Just before going to the cross our Lord established the ordinance of the Lord's Supper. Taking the cup in His hand, He said, "This cup is the new testament in my blood" (1 Cor. 11:25). This was just after He had celebrated the last passover with His disciples. The New Testament began with the crucifixion of Christ, His resurrection and ascension into Heaven, and the descent of the Holy Spirit as recorded in the second chapter of Acts, in which chapter the New Testament Church had its birth.

Why Four Gospels

Why do we have four Gospels instead of one?

The reason for this is that it has pleased the Holy Spirit of Truth to present the Lord Jesus in four characters, corresponding to the four cherubim of Ezekiel and The Revelation. The first is like a lion, the second like a calf or ox, the third has a face as the face of a man, and the fourth is like a flying eagle. In Matthew the Lord Jesus is presented as the Lion of the tribe of Judah, the King of Israel. In Mark He is shown as the devoted Servant, toiling patiently according to His Father's will, and finally yielding up His life as a substitutionary sacrifice. This is the ox character, always ready for service.

In Luke He is presented as the Son of Man, representing a lost race and bearing its sins. John describes Him as the Son of God, who, like a flying eagle came from Heaven and returned to Heaven, the eternal God incarnate. Therefore we have four Gospel records instead of one. The Holy Spirit of Truth has been pleased to have it so and it is not for us to cut up His work and patch it together into "harmonies" or "interwoven Gospels." Let us rather take up these books reverently and separately as we have received them from Him, and let us seek to know His mind concerning them and the Person presented in them.

I have long believed that Matthew's Gospel is the most misunderstood book in the Bible. The reason for this is that the average reader looks into Matthew's Gospel and reads it without remembering that it is preeminently the Gospel of the Kingdom rather than the Gospel of the Grace of God. We look in vain in Matthew for any such statements of the way of salvation as we find on almost every page in the Gospel of John, which latter Gospel was written that men might believe that Jesus is the Christ the Son of God, and that believing, they might have life in His name (John 20:30,31). Matthew sets forth our Lord as the King preeminently, rather than as our individual Savior, and it is only as we remember these distinctions that these books become intelligible to us.

The Synoptics

Why are the books of Matthew, Mark and Luke called The Synoptical Gospels, and why is the book of John not in included?

The reason is that the first three Gospels present a synopsis of the life and work of our Lord, as John does not. "Synopsis" is really a Greek word, brought over into the English without change, and it is made up of *sin*, meaning "together," and *opsis*, meaning "view." The synoptics give a generally parallel view of our Lord's life and work, while John presents his facts from another perspective, keeping in view all the time his purpose, as stated In John 20:30,31, that the reader "might believe that Jesus is the Christ the Son of God," thus obtaining "life through his name."

Two Chapters Alike

Are there two chapters alike in the Bible?

Yes. The 19th chapter of 2 Kings and the 37th of Isaiah are practically identical.

Ignorance of Scriptures

Why are so many, even among God's people, ignorant of the Bible? The Bible is said to be the best seller of all books, and yet it seems to be that only one here and there among God's people knows much about the Bible. Can you explain this?

The answer is that God's people who generally at their conversion love the Bible and read it and study it, do not go on obeying it. There is a law of Revelation by which God reveals truth only so far as His child obeys it. When God reveals the truth, and the Christian obeys that truth, then God reveals more truth. So long as the Christian goes on submitting himself to the truth already revealed, God goes on revealing more truth. When the time comes that the Christian shrinks back from obeying that which God sets forth in His Word, that Christian stops loving the Word and stops understanding it. There is no use in saying, "I do not quite understand this, and I will set it aside and go on," for one cannot go on that way. The only way on is through that road which God has pointed out. You cannot go around it, you cannot go under it, you cannot go over it, but you must go through it, and you must be fair with God if you would grow in grace and in knowledge. It is a great tragedy that so many of God's people seem to be perfectly willing to go on in ignorance of His Word.

Adding to the Words of God

What does Revelation 22:18 mean?

Revelation 22:18 and 19 should be taken together, and the whole passage constitutes a solemn warning against tampering with the Book of the Revelation. Whoever does such a thing will suffer for it at the hand of God.

It ought to be added that the words in verse 19, "book of life," are incorrect, and the matter has been set right by the Revised Version which reads, "God shall take away his part from the *tree* of life," instead of the "*book* of life." No one's part is ever taken away from the *book* of life.

Why the Greek New Testament

Can you tell us why the Greek language was chosen for the first writing of the New Testament books?

A very interesting question. The probable answer is that God in His wisdom chose Greek as the medium of the New Testament message, because Greek was already a finished language and was almost universally employed throughout the world of that day. We ought to thank God that the Hebrew and Greek languages were employed for the original manuscripts of the Bible because both of these languages were already finished, and therefore subject to little or no change through the centuries that followed. If a new language had been employed such, for example, as English is now, it would have been a tragedy, because as the centuries came and went the language would be so changed as to make it unintelligible to modern readers. All this is just another sign of the immeasurable wisdom of God.

Principle of the Norm

I have heard reference made to "the principle of the norm in Bible study." Can you explain what is meant?

The principle of the norm is a familiar principle in the commercial world. There is a Bureau of Standards in Washington where may be found the standard yardstick, the pound weight, bushel measure, and so on, and all over this country these standards must be conformed to in obedience to law.

Just so, there are in the Bible standards or norms. Every doctrine of Scripture has its norm. That is to say, every doctrine of Scripture has some place in Scripture assigned to it where the Spirit of God gives us full information about that particular doctrine. For example, the norm of the doctrine of resurrection is the fifteenth chapter of 1 Corinthians; of the doctrine of faith, the eleventh chapter of Hebrews; for the doctrine of love, the thirteenth chapter of 1 Corinthians; of the doctrine of the glorious second coming of Christ, the twenty-fourth chapter of Matthew, and of the doctrine of the Rapture, or the catching away of the saved to meet the Lord in the air, the fourth chapter of 1 Thessalonians.

Much confusion would be avoided if the principle of the norm were always observed. To illustrate: If we were to listen to the Spirit of God as He unfolds the doctrine of the Rapture in the fourth chapter of 1 Thessalonians, we should stop talking about "a partial Rapture," or the catching away of only a certain few of God's born-again people. Here we are taught that those who are to be caught up include all "who sleep in Jesus," and all "who are alive and remain at His coming." The doctrine of the Rapture is frequently mentioned elsewhere in the New Testament, and every mention of it when interpreted in view of the principle of the norm will be made perfectly clear as conforming to that principle. It is only when we avoid the principle of the norm and build up our doctrine upon isolated passages independently of that principle that we come into trouble. The Bible is its own best commentary.

Question of Interpretation

Would you tell us the meaning of the words in 1 Corinthians 2:13, "comparing spiritual things with spiritual"? Does this mean that Paul in writing the New Testament searched through the Old Testament for material?

By no means. In this second chapter of 1 Corinthians Paul is setting forth the doctrine of the inspiration of the Scriptures, "the things which God hath prepared for them that love him" (verse 9). In the tenth verse he declares that these "things which God hath prepared for them that love him" have been revealed to him, in common with the other writers of the Scripture, by the Spirit of God who "searcheth all things, yea, the deep things of God." In verse 13 he says that these things thus revealed to him are transmitted by him, "not in the words which man's wisdom teacheth, but which the Holy Spirit teacheth; interpreting spiritual things to spiritual men" (R V., margin).

In other words, the Bible is written for those who love God and for none other. There is no use in anyone else even trying to understand the Scriptures, for "the natural man receiveth not the things of the Spirit of God: for they are foolishness unto him; neither can he know them, because they are spiritually discerned. But he that is spiritual discerneth all things, yet he himself is discerned of no man" (verses 14,15, literal translation).

It ought to be said in this connection that the Gospel of John is addressed primarily to unbelievers that they may be saved. It is written that men "might believe that Jesus is the Christ, the Son of God," in order that believing they "might have life through his name" (John 20:30,31). The Gospel of John, therefore, is the book which unbelievers should read to lead them to salvation; and after they are saved, then they have a share in the rest of the Scriptures which are "prepared for them that love" God.

Divisions in Psalm 119 and Lamentations

What is the meaning of the words in the intersections of the 119th Psalm?

They are the letters of the Hebrew alphabet, in their proper order; and in the original text each verse of the section bearing a certain letter begins with that letter. The Psalm is an "acrostic." The same thing is seen in the book of the Lamentations of Jeremiah. There are 22 letters in the Hebrew alphabet, and you will observe that each chapter in Lamentations has 22 verses, except chapter 3, which has 66 verses, or three times 22. The chapters containing 22 verses each begin each verse with a Hebrew letter, using all the letters of the alphabet in succession; and the third chapter has three verses for each letter.

Whose Is the Bible?

This question has been put to me, and I pass it on to you: If it be true that more space is given in the Bible to the restoration of Israel than to any other one theme, why is not the Bible more for the Jews than for us?

It is beyond question that the Bible is preeminently a Jewish book, and that it was written, first of all, for the Jews; as it is written, "To them were committed the oracles of God" (Rom. 3:2). The Gospel itself is "to the Jew first" (Rom. 1:16). It is only "through their fall," or through their failure to receive the Gospel, that "salvation is come unto the Gentiles, for to provoke them [that is, the Jews] to jealousy" (Rom. 11:11). Moreover, it is only through their future salvation as a nation that universal blessing is to reach the Gentile world. "For if the casting away of them be the reconciling of the world, what shall the receiving of them be, but life from the dead?" (Rom. 11:15).

Interpretation

Someone made the statement that no passage of Scripture can have more than one true and right interpretation. If this is so, how are we to know what is that true and right interpretation?

No passage of Scripture can have two interpretations which conflict with each other. I am sure that many passages on prophecy have a local application as well as a broader one, but that is another matter.

Italicized Words

What is the meaning of italics in our Bible? I have been asked the meaning of this and every explanation I offer is rejected. I should like very much to have your word on it.

Words printed in italics in the English Bible are usually words supplied by the translators "to make sense." That is to say, there are no words in the original which are represented by these supplied words, but the translators have supplied them, believing them to be needed to convey the idea intended by the writer. They ought to be carefully watched, for very often they confuse the sense instead of clearing it.

Literal or Figurative

Is the Bible always to be understood literally?

I answer by quoting from Dr. C. I. Scofield. He says there is a difference between the historical and the prophetical portions of the Word of God. Of the Historical Scriptures he says: "These are (1) literally true. The events recorded occurred. And yet (2) they have (perhaps more often than we suspect) an allegorical or spiritual significance. Example, the history of Isaac and Ishmael (Gal. 4:22-31). Who can doubt that the narrative portions of Scripture abound in spiritual analogies? For example, the story of Mephibosheth (2 Sam. 9:1-13); of Isaiah's cleansing (Isa. 6:1-8), etc. It is then permitted—while holding firmly the historical verity—reverently to spiritualize the historical Scriptures."

Continuing, Dr. Scofield says of the Prophecies: "Here we reach the bound of absolute literalness. Figures are often found in the prophecies, but the figure invariably has a literal fulfillment. Not one instance exists of a 'spiritual' or figurative fulfillment of prophecy. Since God has invariably fulfilled prophecy with exact literalness, this rule for the interpretation of unfulfilled prophecy is established by God Himself. Jerusalem is always Jerusalem, Israel always Israel, Zion always Zion. But the inspired rule given in 2 Peter 1:20 must ever be obeyed by the student of prophecy: 'Knowing this first, that no prophecy of the Scripture is of any private interpretation.' In other words, no prophecy is to be interpreted by itself, but must be collated with all the other prophetic utterances on that subject. The sum total of all revelation concerning any subject is the true doctrine of Scripture upon that subject. A further caution forms the golden rule of Scripture interpretation—study the context. Simply to read what precedes and what follows any passage will, in most cases, clear up its difficulties."

An illustration of the statement, "Figures are often found in the prophecies, but the figure invariably has a literal fulfillment," follows: "It would be, perhaps, more accurate to say, the thing figured, or the meaning hidden in the figure, has a literal fulfillment. For instance, in the 37th chapter of Ezekiel the prophet sees a vision of a valley full of dry bones. Then as he views the bones, he sees them covered with flesh and skin; and they stand up, an exceeding great army. This is the figure. Verses 11 to 14 explain the figure. These bones are the whole house of Israel, and the meaning of the new life given to the bones is explained to be a future restoration of Israel to their own land—the land of Palestine. The thing figured by the vision of the valley of dry bones will be literally fulfilled. Israel will be literally brought back to her own land, according to verses 11-14. Then follows the figure of the two sticks that become one stick in the hand of the prophet. That is explained to mean a future reunion of the ten-tribe kingdom with Judah and Benjamin. There shall no more be two nations, but one nation, like the one stick made out of the two sticks, and that will be literally fulfilled. In other words, we have but to ascertain the meaning of the figure, and we have then something that in the plan of God will be fulfilled literally."

The Scriptures of Our Lord's Time

1. During His earthly ministry did the Lord Jesus have the Old Testament books just as we have them?

2. Did He have and quote from other books not now included in the canon?

3. Do we find quotations in the New Testament from all the books now found in the Old Testament?

1. The Scriptures of our Lord's time upon earth were the same 39 books as are now included in the Old Testament, though they were not arranged in the same order. They were grouped in three parts or sections: (1) The Law; (2) The Prophets; and (3) The Psalms; and this was in our Lord's mind when He used the language of Luke 24:44; His endorsement covered the whole body of Old Testament books.

2. Doubtless our Lord knew of the many writings claiming to be inspired, but I am not aware that He quoted from any but the recognized canonical book.

3. Not from all of them, but from very many of them, and particularly from those books which latterly have been the object of severe criticism on the part of those who deny inspiration; for example, Deuteronomy, Isaiah, Daniel, Jonah, etc. Our Lord Himself and the apostolic writers gave special endorsement to those books which have been attacked by the enemy.

The Roman Catholic Bible

Is the Catholic Bible in any respect like the Protestant Bible?

The Roman Catholic Bible is a translation from the same manuscripts as the Protestant Bible. The translation is not fair in some places, however. The Roman Catholic Bible includes certain Apocryphal books between the Old and New Testaments which are discarded by the Protestant churches. The Roman Catholic Bible is called the Douay Version and may be purchased at any bookstore where religious books are sold.

Apparent Contradictions

I have always been accustomed to believe in the truth of the Holy Scriptures, from beginning to end. But now I find a difficulty. For instance: 2 Samuel 23:8 says that the Tachmonite slew 800 men at one time. In 1 Chronicles 11:11, where he is called "the Hachmonite," the number of men he slew is reduced to 300. One of these statements is not true.

Again, compare 1 Samuel 28:6 and 1 Chronicles 10:14. You cannot believe both.

These are just samples and it is not important that we believe either of these accounts. But Jesus Christ said, "The scripture cannot be broken." Then what is scripture?

These are very obviously instances of copyists' errors. It is only the original manuscripts that are inerrant. Yet it is truly wonderful how free from error even the translations are, for there is no error even in them that affects any vital doctrine.

An Interpolation

I have heard it said that the latter part of Romans 8:1 should be

omitted; that is, the words, "who walk not after the flesh, but after the Spirit." But how may we know that these words should be omitted? Who says so? and by what authority do they say so? And if they should be omitted, why are they not omitted from the English Bible itself?

There is no dispute among textual critics about it: they all agree that the verse should read simply, "There is therefore now no condemnation to them which are in Christ Jesus," and that the remainder of the verse as found in the common English version is an interpolation, which should be omitted. Evidently, some copyist thought the statement as it stood was "just too good to be true" and therefore tried to improve upon it. The interpolated words are not found in the ancient manuscripts, and they are omitted from the revised edition of the English Bible, as indeed they should be.

A Valuable Book

Which book, apart from the Bible, has been the greatest blessing to you?

Without hesitation I answer, *Rightly Dividing the Word of Truth*, by Dr. C. I. Scofield. It is only a little book, but I personally know of many Christian workers who declare that they got their first intelligent understanding of the Word of God through this little book; and this also is my own personal testimony.

GOD

The Trinity

When Jesus went to Heaven, were there then two persons called God in Heaven who could talk, walk, etc.?

Yes, there were not only two, but three such Persons, the Father, the Son and the Holy Spirit. And all of them could certainly talk, walk, etc. The Trinity is a fact, even though it is a mystery. We are not called upon to explain it.

The Mystery of the Trinity

I have been asked the question concerning "God the Father, God the Son and God the Holy Ghost." Are we to think of these as three separate persons, or as one?

Without controversy great is the mystery of the Trinity. For my own part I never use the expressions referred to, that is, "God the Father, God the Son, and God the Holy Ghost." This would seem to imply not only three persons, but also three Gods. While without doubt the Father is God, and the Son is God, and the Holy Spirit is God, yet there are not three Gods, but only three persons in one God. Of course all this is quite beyond our comprehension and yet it is the plain teaching of the Scriptures. It sometimes appears that a single passage of Scripture will have reference to all three persons of the Godhead. For example, in the baptism of our Lord as recorded in Matthew 3:16,17, the Father is heard speaking out of Heaven, the Son is standing there in the water, and the Spirit of God descends like a dove and abides upon Him.

In the very first sentence of the Bible, "In the beginning God created the heaven and the earth," the Trinity is suggested in the fact that the name "God" or "Elohim" in the Hebrew is a plural noun, while the verb "created" is a singular verb. Thus we have an intimation that in some mysterious fashion God is three and God is one. The same principle is demonstrated also in Genesis 1:26, where God says, "Let us make man in our image," etc. This plural pronoun indicates the Trinity; but in the 27th verse we read that God created man in (not "their" but) "his" own image, "In the image of God created he him; male and female created he them."

It is related of a half-witted boy that when he applied for admission to the membership of a certain church and was asked for his confession, he could only say, as he held up his three fingers: "Three in one and one in three, and the one in the middle died for me." Perhaps that is as profound as any other statement of the Trinity, and it may be as far as any of us could go in defining the wonderful mystery of the Godhead.

The Trinity and Unity of God

Will you be so kind as to explain how God can be one and three at the same time?

Such an explanation is impossible. We may believe what we cannot explain; we may apprehend what we cannot comprehend. It is clear that the Bible teaches the trinity and unity of God. It is intimated at least in the first verse of the Bible, Genesis 1:1, where "God" is a plural noun (which in the Hebrew indicates three or more persons) and the verb "created" is singular. "To one who receives with meekness the engrafted Word which is able to save our souls," says Edward Henry Bickersteth, "the Scriptures prove beyond contradiction that as the Father is God, so is Jesus Christ God, and so the Holy Spirit is God. This truth, however, must be combined with another, which is revealed with equal clearness and enforced with equal solemnity: 'I am Jehovah, and there is none else, there is no God beside me.' The combination of these truths establishes the doctrine of the holy Trinity, for these Three must together subsist in one infinite divine essence, called Jehovah or God; and as this essence must be indivisible, each of them must possess not a part or portion of it, but the whole fullness or perfection of the essential Godhead forming, in a unity of nature, One Eternal Jehovah, and therefore revealed by a plural noun as the Jehovah Elohim, which comprehends these Three; but with this solemn qualification, that the Jehovah Elohim is in truth but one Jehovah, a Triune God, Father, Son, and Holy Ghost."

God's Name Not Mentioned

Is there a book in the Bible which does not mention God by name?

Yes. In the book of Esther there is no mention of any of the names of God. Throughout the book, however, He reveals Himself most clearly by His mighty acts and His watchcare over His people.

Divine Titles Distinguished

Please tell us why the divine titles "Lord" and "God" are printed so differently in the Bible. Sometimes these words are found altogether in capital letters, and sometimes with only the first letter a capital. What is the reason for this?

The name Jehovah, which occurs over seven thousand times in the Hebrew Scriptures of the Old Testament, is preserved to us only six times altogether in our common English version. Elsewhere it is translated either "Lord" or "God." But when it is so translated, the word "Lord" or "God" is printed altogether in capital letters, LORD or GOD. Whenever you see either of these words printed in the Old Testament altogether in capitals you may know that it stands for the name Jehovah. When "Lord" is printed with only one capital letter it stands for Adonai which really means Lord or Ruler. When the word "God" is printed with only one capital letter it stands for the word Elohim which is the first name of Deity used in Scripture: "In the beginning God created the heaven and the earth" (Gen. 1:1). And sometimes, when you see "lord" with no capital letter, it applies to a human being; and "gods," without the capital, refers to heathen deities, except in one instance, where it applies to men (Ps. 82:6; John 10:34-36). The men called gods here seem to be the rulers and judges of the earth seen in Psalm 2 and Romans 13:1-7.

Seeing God

Beginning at Gen. 32:30 we have followed through references, as given by the Scofield Bible, to John 1:18, concerning men seeing God. We understand that sin and a knowledge of sin separates men from God. Yet the passages are not clear to me or to the class of which I am leader. Will you please explain?

The matter is explained for you in the final footnote on the page (1115) containing John 1:18, in which Dr. Scofield says: "The divine essence, God, in His own triune person, no human being in the flesh has seen. But God, veiled in angelic form, and especially as incarnate in Jesus Christ, has been seen of men."

A Consuming Fire

What is meant by the words of Hebrews 12:29, "our God is a consuming fire"?

Read the context, beginning at verse 25: "See that ye refuse not him that speaketh. For if they escaped not who refused him that spake on earth, much more shall we not escape if we turn away from him that speaketh from heaven," etc. God delights to save, and He will save those who listen to Him and receive His offered gift of eternal life, but He must, on account of His own righteousness, deal in righteous judgment with those who tread His Son under foot, making the blood of the covenant an unholy thing and doing despite unto the Spirit of grace. It is a fearful thing to fall into the hands of the living God (Heb. 10:28-31). Fire is a symbol of God's righteous wrath against sin.

God and War

Does God have anything to do with war?

Yes. It is written that the Lord Jesus at His second coming will "judge and make war" (Rev. 19). And even before His coming to judgment, though not before His coming for His own, He will send universal war among the nations. "Thus saith Jehovah of Hosts, the God of Israel; Drink ye and be drunken, and spue, and fall, and rise no more, because of the sword which I will send upon you. And it shall be, if they refuse to take the cup at thine hand to drink, then shalt thou say unto them, Thus saith Jehovah of Hosts, Ye shall surely drink. For, lo, I begin to bring evil on the city (Jerusalem) which is called by my name, and should ye be utterly unpunished: for I will call for a sword upon all the inhabitated of the earth, saith Jehovah of Hosts" (Jer. 25:27-29).

THE FATHER

Universal Fatherhood

A preacher whom I recently heard made a strong argument for the Universal Fatherhood of God, based on the 3rd chapter of Luke, the genealogy of Jesus being traced back to "Adam, which was the son of God." He also sought to enforce his argument by the words of Acts 17:28, "We are also his offspring." I reject his theory, but how can I answer it to others who like the idea of Universal Fatherhood and brotherhood?

There is no doubt that men are God's offspring in the sense indicated by the Scriptures cited. That is, we all came out of Adam, who came from the hands of God. But nothing is more clearly taught in the Scriptures than that since the Fall all men are "by nature the children of wrath," and that to become the children of God they must be born again. Just give this testimony to those "who like the idea of Universal Fatherhood and brotherhood," but don't bother to prove to them the truth of the testimony. Until they are born again they will not understand these things. The command under which we are working is not to prove the gospel, but to preach it.

Who May Call God Father?

Have unconverted men the right to call God their Father?

No. Please read John 8:42-44.

The Unchangeable God

In the Old Testament God is represented as a living person who talked and appeared to others. Is He so yet?

Yes, He has not changed, and doubtless He still talks and appears to folks. If not to folks on earth, certainly He talks and appears to folks in Heaven. There is not now the need that there was in the past that He should appear to those on earth, for they have His full revelation in His Word.

The God of Gods

How do you explain Deuteronomy 10:17, "For Jehovah your God is God of gods and Lord of lords"? Is there more than one God?

In 2 Corinthians 4:4 Satan is called the god of this age. The gods of the heathen world are said to be demons in 1 Corinthians 10:20. In addition to these there are doubtless many imaginary gods. But Jehovah is Sovereign over them all and in the absolute sense there is no god but He.

Gods Many and Lords Many

How do you explain 1 Corinthians 8:5,6? What does "gods many, and lords many" mean?

The passage itself answers your question. Beginning with the latter part of verse 4, it reads: "We know that an idol is nothing in the world, and that there is none other God but one. For though there be that are called gods, whether in heaven or in earth (as there be gods many, and lords many) but to us there is but one God, the Father, of whom are all things, and we in him, and one Lord Jesus Christ, by whom are all things, and we by him. Howbeit there is not in every man that knowledge," etc.

God Is a Spirit

Why do we say God is a Spirit? If He has a body and can walk and talk, how can He be a Spirit?

We say God is a Spirit because the Book says so. The fact that He is manifested in a body, as was Jesus for over 30 years on earth, does not make Him any less a Spirit. Even men and women are spirits, though they have bodies.

His Name Shall Be Great

Do Psalm 113:3 and Malachi 1:11 speak of time or distance?

The expression is highly poetic and its meaning is that the time is coming when, forever after, God's name shall be great among the nations. That will be when the earth is "filled with the knowledge of the glory of the Lord, as the waters cover the sea."

The Rule and Righteousness of God

Please explain Matthew 6:33, "But seek ye first the kingdom of God, and his righteousness; and all these things shall be added unto you." While I have diligently studied the footnotes in the Scofield Reference Bible, I have not yet been able to ascertain (1) An exact definition of "the kingdom of God"; (2) who are included in the pronoun "ye" and "you"; (3) what "all these things" include, and (4) when "all these things shall be added unto you."

I should say that the Kingdom of God in the text referred to means the rule of God. Let this be the first consideration of God's children, that His rule should be without hindrance, in the individual life not only, but also in the world itself, and in the universe at large. Let this be the first thing in our program, and in our desires, and in our plans.

The pronouns "ye" and "you" may refer to anyone who complies with the conditions laid down. Of course, that would be only to a child of God, for no other can seek "first the Kingdom of God, and his righteousness." The "all these things" are the things referred to in the preceding verses, things to eat and things to drink and things wherewith to clothe us. Our Heavenly Father knows that we have need of all these things, and He will see to it that these things are supplied to those who seek first His rule and His righteousness.

The time when "all these things" shall be added to us remains in God's own will and purpose. Sometimes it pleases God to lead His children through times of privation for His own purposes. Meanwhile it is sure that "all things work together for good to them that love God, to them who are the called according to his purpose" (Rom. 8:28).

THE SON

Our Lord's Voluntary Humiliation

What is meant by the word of Philippians 2:7, where it is stated that our Lord Jesus Christ "made himself of no reputation"?

Many books have been written in an attempt to answer just this question. The Greek phrase translated, "made himself of no reputation" in the Authorized Version is translated by the Revisers, "emptied himself." Of course there in much mystery here. Let it suffice to say that the glorious Son of God took upon Himself such humiliation as to make Him an effectual High Priest who might be touched with the feeling of man's infirmities (Heb. 4:15). "Wherefore in all things it behooved him to be made like unto his brethren, that he might be a merciful and faithful high priest in things pertaining to God to make reconciliation for the sins of the people. For in that he himself hath suffered being tempted, he is able to succor them that are tempted" (Heb. 2:17,18).

The Firstborn of Creation

In Colossians 1:15, Christ is called "the firstborn of every creature;" and yet in the succeeding verse it is stated that "all things were created by Him." How can that be?

The words quoted from verse 15 should be translated "the Firstborn of all creation." He was never born, except in his incarnation; the word "firstborn" is positional and indicates that He is the Head over all creation.

The Ancestry of Jesus

Is the genealogy in Luke 3:23-38 that of Mary the mother of our Lord through Nathan? Who was Nathan? Does the Bible give us the names of Mary's parents? If Luke 3 gives Mary's genealogy, why is her name not mentioned? Is the genealogy of Matthew 1 that of Joseph through Solomon?

Nathan was a son of David and Bathsheba, and thus a full brother of Solomon (1 Chron. 3:5). Mary's father's name was Eli (or Heli; Luke 3:23). It is not mentioned elsewhere, but tradition also gives him this name, and gives Ann as Mary's mother's name. The father's name is given in the genealogy of Luke 3, because no women's names are mentioned in the table. The Matthew table gives Joseph's descent from David through Solomon. According to Jeremiah 22:24-30 this would prevent Joseph or his seed from occupying David's throne. Coniah (Jer. 22:24) is identical with Jechonias (Matt. 1:11,12). It is because Jesus was Mary's seed, "the seed of the woman" (Gen. 3:15), and not the seed of Joseph, that He is entitled to inherit the throne of David.

Our Lord's Birth

Is the doctrine that Jesus was born of a virgin mother really an important and vital part of the Christian faith?

Yes. His virgin birth is demanded by the Old Testament Scriptures and declared by the New Testament (Isa. 7:14; Matt. 1:18-25). And, besides, if He should prove to be the natural son of Joseph, He would be cut off from all right to the throne of David; for Joseph was of the seed of Coniah, and God declared in Jeremiah 22:24-30 that no descendant of Coniah could ever sit upon that throne. Joseph is shown in Matthew 1 to have descended from Jechonias, another form of Coniah's name, while Luke 3 shows that through His mother Mary the Lord Jesus descended from David, not through Solomon and Coniah, but through another son of David named Nathan. No one is a Christian who denies our Lord's virgin birth.

Was Jesus a Jew?

Please tell me whether Jesus was ever a Jew. My pastor recently stated from the pulpit that Jesus could never have been a Jew because His Father was divine.

The Lord Jesus was from eternity divine, but almost twenty centuries ago the divine Son of God became incarnate in human flesh and was born of a Jewish mother, and therefore became a Jew. He is still, in His human capacity, a Jew, and when He comes again it will be to establish His crown rights to the throne of His Jewish ancestor David (Luke 1:31-33).

Begotten of the Father

What does Hebrews 1:5 mean? Was the Son of God with the Father always, or was He begotten of the Father after "the beginning"?

The Son of God was not "begotten of the Father" in the sense that He ever began to be. He has "neither beginning of days, nor end of life" (Heb. 7:3), "whose goings forth have been from of old, from everlasting" (Mic. 5:2). The words of Hebrews 1:5, quoted from Psalm 2:7, "Thou art my Son; this day have I begotten thee," and the other words quoted from 2 Samuel 7:14, "I will be to him a father, and he shall be to me a son," do not disprove our Lord's eternity. The quotation from Psalm 2:7, "This day have I begotten thee," points to the day of His resurrection when He was begotten again from the dead (compare Col. 1:18; Acts 13:33). In Colossians 1:15, He is called, according to the King James Version, "the firstborn of every creature." A better translation would be "the firstborn of all creation." In Revelation 3:14 He is called, "the beginning of the creation of God." The meaning of these Scriptures is that He occupies the place in creation which belongs to the firstborn, that is, the head of the house. He is the Beginning and the Ending, and His position is "as a Son over his own house" (Heb. 3:6). Our Lord's full deity is shown in many Scriptures (see for example, the various quotations from the Old Testament applied to Him in the first chapter of Hebrews, and compare John 1:1-5 and Col. 1:16,17).

The Deity of Our Lord

How do we know that the Lord Jesus is God?

Our Lord's deity is proven as follows:

1. All the Old Testament names of God are merged in the Lord Jesus Christ.
2. The Lord Jesus received human worship.
3. He forgave sins.
4. He displayed omnipotent power.
5. He displayed omniscience.
6. He asserted His omnipresence.
7. The New Testament Scriptures assert the deity of the Lord Jesus.

Was Jesus Divine?

My daughter is teaching school, and some of the pupils asked her if she believed that Jesus was God. She told them "Yes," and she quoted such Scriptures as John 1:1-15. Then they asked her to explain John 14:28, "Ye have heard how I said unto you, I go away, and come again unto you. If ye loved me, ye would rejoice, because I said, I go unto the Father: for my Father is greater than I." They said that this verse proved that God was greater than Jesus, and they said that when Jesus was on earth He prayed to God in Heaven. How shall she answer this question?

The answer is in the incarnation of the Son of God, who thus became the Son of Man. The whole story is told in that wonderful paragraph beginning with the 5th verse of Philippians 2, "Let this mind be in you, which was also in Christ Jesus: who, being in the form (or position, or rank) of God, thought it not a thing to be retained by grasping to be equal with God: but made himself of no reputation, and took upon Him the form of a slave, and was made in the likeness of men: and being found in fashion as a man, He humbled himself, and became obedient unto death, even the death of the cross." Jesus, the man, certainly says of God, "My Father is greater than I," but Jesus, the Son of God, as such could never say such a thing.

The Eternal Christ

Was Jesus alive before He was born of Mary? Some tell us He was not, while Scripture tells us He was in the bosom of the Father from all eternity; and, in spite of John 1:1,2, they ask the question, if Jesus was the Word—was it Jesus who came to Jeremiah when Scripture states that the Word of the Lord came to Jeremiah; forgetting, I suppose, Hebrews 1:1?

There was never a time in the past eternity before His advent into the world that the Son of God was not alive. He is without beginning of days or end of life (Heb. 7:3). He is also the eternal Word of God, and it was He who dealt with Jeremiah and with all the Old Testament prophets. He has always been the revealer of God to men. This is the true meaning of John 1:18: "No man hath seen God at any time; the only begotten Son, which is in the bosom of the Father, He hath declared (or, revealed) Him."

The Everlasting Father

Why is the title, "the everlasting Father," applied to the Lord Jesus Christ in Isaiah 9:6?

It should be translated "the Father of the Ages," and refers to the fact that by Him the dispensations were programmed, or the ages planned (Heb. 1:2 and 11:3, Greek).

Till Shiloh Come

Please explain Genesis 49:10—"The scepter shall not depart from Judah, nor a lawgiver from between his feet, until Shiloh come; and unto him shall the gathering of the people be." Is it not true that the throne of David has been empty since the overthrow of Jerusalem by Nebuchadnezzar 2,500 years ago?

Yes, it is true that David's throne is unoccupied temporarily. But that does not mean that the scepter has departed from Judah. In God's reckoning the scepter is still in the hands of Judah, and in due time—when Shiloh comes—it will be revealed that Jesus of Nazareth is the promised Shiloh, "the blessed and only Potentate, the King of kings, and Lord of lords" (1 Tim. 6:15,16). Our Lord is of the tribe of Judah, and He is the rightful Heir to David's throne.

The word "Shiloh" means the Peacemaker, and points to the Prince of Peace (Isa. 9:6). The Ancient Versions, however, almost unanimously translate, "He to whom it belongs," thus reminding us of Ezekiel 21:27, "He whose right it is" (Compare Luke 1:31-33).

Messiah and Christ

What is the difference between Messiah and Christ?

There is no difference. Messiah and Christ are identical, Messiah being the Hebrew word and Christos the Greek word. To translate either of these words into English we must say, "the anointed one." In Old Testament times prophets, priests, and kings, were inducted into office by having oil poured upon them. Thus they became the anointed of the Lord. This oil was a type of the Holy Spirit (Zech. 6:1-6). The anointed one is the Christos, the anointing is the Chrisma. In this general sense there were many messiahs or anointed ones. But in the specific sense the Lord Jesus is *the* Messiah or Christ par excellence. He is distinctively the Christ of God (Luke 9:20). He is the Prophet and the Priest and King all in one. A prophet is one who speaks for God to men. A priest is one who appears before God for men. And a king is one who rules for

God over men. In His first advent nearly two thousand years ago the Lord Jesus functioned as the Prophet of God, speaking for God to men; in His present work at the right hand of the Majesty on High He functions as Priest, appearing before God for men; and when He comes again it will be to function as King, reigning for God over men.

King or Lord?

Is Jesus King or Lord? I have recently heard a statement from a theological professor that Jesus is Lord but will never be a King. Please explain this.

Our Savior is our Lord, and one day He will be manifested as "the blessed and only Potentate, the King of kings and Lord of lords" (1 Tim. 6:15; Rev. 19:16). The promise of God is that His Son will ascend the throne of David, reigning over the house of Jacob and over a kingdom that shall have no end (Luke 1:31-33).

"Our Elder Brother"

I have heard the Lord Jesus called "our elder Brother." I have never seen the phrase in the New Testament. If it is there please give me the place where I can find it. If not in the New Testament please give me the author of the phrase.

The phrase is not in the New Testament, and as to who originated it I cannot tell. I never use the expression myself, and am sorry to hear anybody use it, for to me it seems to lack in reverence toward our Lord. It is true that we are His brethren in the family of God if we are born again. And in Hebrews 2:12 it is declared that "He is not ashamed to call them brethren" who are the children of God by faith. It is good to have Him call us brethren, but let us leave that to Him, and let us remember that He is our Lord, and that we are to worship Him (Ps. 45:11).

The Genealogy of Mary

Is there any passage of Scripture in the Old Testament where the genealogy of Mary the mother of Jesus can be traced back to David?

Of course Mary is not mentioned in the Old Testament, but it is without controversy that the genealogy in Luke 3 is hers. Notice in verse 23 of that chapter that Joseph is spoken of as "the son of Heli"; but the words, "the son," are in italics, which means that they have been supplied by the translators and do not occur in the Greek text. This is the rule throughout Luke's genealogical table. Dr. Scofield's note on the passage in Luke is no doubt correct: "In Matthew, where unquestionably we have the genealogy of Joseph, we are told (1:16) that Joseph was the son of Jacob. In what sense, then, could he be called in Luke 'the son of Heli'? He could not be by natural generation the son of both Jacob and of Heli. But in Luke it is not said that Heli begat Joseph, so that the natural explanation is that Joseph was the son-in-law of Heli, who was, like himself, a descendant of David. That he should in that case be called 'son of Heli' ('son' is not in the Greek, but rightly supplied by the translators) would be in accord with Jewish usage (compare 1 Sam. 24:16). The conclusion is therefore inevitable that in Luke we have Mary's genealogy; and Joseph was 'son of Heli' because espoused to Heli's daughter. The genealogy in Luke is Mary's, whose father, Heli, was descended from David" (Scofield Reference Bible).

Emmanuel

Why does the Bible say in Matthew 1:23, "They shall call his name Emmanuel," and He was not called Emmanuel?

It is true that Jesus is not actually called Emmanuel in the Bible itself, but notice what Matthew says: "They shall call his name Emmanuel, which being interpreted is, God with us." Now, He has often been called "Emmanuel" by His people, and also "God with us." Therefore the prophecy is fulfilled.

A Popular Misconception

I have recently heard it said that the wise men of the East were not in the same scene as the shepherds at the time of our Lord's birth in Bethlehem. Can this be true?

Despite the popular misconception it must be answered that the statement you heard is true. If you will read the account of Luke 2:1-40 and compare it with Leviticus 12:1-8 you will see that at the time of our Lord's birth and the visit of the shepherds the holy family remained in or near Jerusalem for nearly six weeks, and then returned to Nazareth. Then if you will read the account of Matthew 1:18 to 2:23 you will find that the visit of the wise men was not to the stable where the Babe lay in a manger, but rather to a house where the young Child was. Then you will see that directly after the visit of the wise men, Joseph, being warned of God in a dream, was sent with Mary and her Child into Egypt where they remained until the death of Herod, following which they returned to Nazareth in Galilee. This must have been at least a year subsequent to the birth and the visit of the shepherds, and it might have been as much as two years, as may be suggested by the fact that Herod "sent forth, and slew all the children that were in Bethlehem, and in all the coasts thereof, from two years old and under, according to the time which he had diligently inquired of the wise men."

A Question of Time

Did the adoration of the shepherds in the stable at Bethlehem take place at the same time with the visit of the wise men from the East?

By no means. The adoration of the shepherds took place immediately after the birth of our Lord, but the visit of the wise men came certainly a year, and perhaps even two years later. In Luke 2, we learn that after the birth of the Child and the adoration of the shepherds, there came the circumcision when the Child was eight days old, and then came the days of the mother's purification which, according to the law, occupied 33 days (Lev. 12:1-14). It was at the end of the mother's days of purification that the offering was presented of "a pair of turtle doves, or two young pigeons" (compare Luke 2:24 with Lev. 12:8). Thus it appears that Joseph and Mary and the Child remained in Bethlehem after the birth for something like six weeks, after which they returned into Galilee, to their own city Nazareth (Luke 2:39), where "the child grew, and waxed strong in spirit, filled with wisdom: and the grace of God was upon him" (Luke 2:40).

In Luke 2:41 we read that "his parents went to Jerusalem every year at the feast of the passover." It was on one of these annual visits to Jerusalem, perhaps a year, or even two years, after the birth, that the visit of the wise men took place, the account of which we have in Matthew 2. The first verse of that chapter may be legitimately translated, "Now Jesus, having been born in Bethlehem of Judea in the days of Herod the king," etc. This visit of the wise men was followed immediately, not by Joseph and Mary and the Child returning to Nazareth, but rather by the flight of the holy family into Egypt, where they remained until the death of Herod, after which they returned again to Nazareth (Matt. 2:13-23).

Joseph and Mary's Children

Did Jesus have any blood brothers and sisters? Were there other children in the home of Joseph and Mary?

Yes. Strictly speaking, they were half-brothers and half-sisters, since Joseph, their father, was not the father of Jesus. The half-brothers are named, and the half-sisters are mentioned without naming them, in Matthew 13:55,56.

That these were really Mary's children is proven by Psalm 69:8, which Psalm is certainly Messianic. Compare verse 4 with John 15:25; verse 9 with John 2:17 and Romans 15:3; and verse 21 with Matthew 27:34, 48 and John 19:29,30; and then compare verse 8 with John 7:3-5, and note the words, "my brethren" and "my mother's children."

Mighty or Almighty

Will you please answer a question for me? I believe Jesus Christ was God in the flesh, but because of a question put to me I could not answer satisfactorily. In Isaiah 9 it is written that Jesus is "The mighty God" and it does not have the "Almighty" there. For that reason it was suggested that Jesus while here was not the "Almighty" but the "Mighty." Please explain.

This seems to be an attempt to make a distinction where there is no real difference. That Jesus is God, in the most absolute sense, there is no possible doubt to one who is subject to the Scriptures. Nor did He cease to be God during the days of His flesh. From everlasting to everlasting He is God. The opening verses of the Gospel of John and the Epistle to the Hebrews are quite enough to settle this matter for any yielded heart. "In Him dwelleth all the fullness of the Godhead bodily" (Col. 2:9).

Our Lord's Threefold Office

How did Christ offer Himself in His prophetic character, in His priestly character, and in His kingly character?

Our Lord exercised His prophetic office when He was here in the days of His flesh telling forth the message of God. This He did not only by His words, but also by His acts and in His own Person. The meaning of the word "prophet" is forthteller. He is now exercising His priestly office as He ministers at the right hand of the Majesty on high, making intercession for His people. He will show Himself in His kingly character at His Second Coming as "the blessed and only Potentate, the King of kings, and Lord of lords" (1 Tim. 6:15).

The Virgin Birth

Must we believe the virgin birth was necessary in order to separate Christ's humanity from the sinfulness which is the inheritance of all the race from Adam? For, after all, this only halved the matter. The influence of the mother exceeds that of the father during the period of gestation. Did she contribute of her sinful nature, or did God bar the transmission of sin from her to her son? And if so, why could not He bar the transmission from two human parents as well as one?

No doubt He could have done so, but the question is not what He could have done, but rather what He *did*. And according to the record, what He did was to create a body for His Son and place that body in the womb of a virgin, just as in the first creation He created a body for the first man and placed that body in the garden of Eden. "Why should it be thought. . . . incredible" that GOD should do these things? The real difficulty with those who reject the testimony of the Book as to the supernatural is that they have a wrong conception of who God is and what He can do.

The Temptation of Jesus

Was our Lord tempted because He was in the likeness of sinful flesh, in order that He could come to the aid of those that are tempted?

The record is that He was "made like unto his brethren, that he might be a merciful and faithful High Priest in things pertaining to God, to make reconciliation for the sins of the people. For in that he himself hath suffered being tempted, he is able to succor them that are tempted" (Heb. 2:17,18). But we must have a care lest we receive or convey a wrong definition of the word "tempted" as applied to Him. He was tested in all points like ourselves, sin excepted (Heb. 4:15). That is to say, He had no testing, or temptation, from indwelling sin. And yet He knows us altogether and is the never-failing resource of His people. "Let us come boldly unto the throne of grace, that we may obtain mercy, and find grace to help in time of need" (Heb. 4:16).

The Impeccability of Christ

Do you teach that the Lord Jesus could not have sinned? Where, then, was the temptation? Does not the Bible teach that He was tempted

just as we are tempted? And does it not say that He was a man of like passions with us?

No, it does not say that. You are confusing Him with Elijah, or Paul and Barnabas (James 5:17; Acts 14:15). Our Lord was indeed a Man, but unlike other men, He had no sin in Him. This explains the last clause of Hebrews 4:15, which really says, not "yet without sin," but "apart from sin." In our temptations there is enticement from indwelling sin; but He was never enticed that way, for there was in Him no indwelling sin. If it be objected that one who is unable to sin cannot really be tempted, it is sufficient to answer that temptation really means testing. And to say that our Lord could not be tempted would be like saying that pure gold could not be subjected to a test to determine its purity. Or that an impregnable fortress could not be attacked. Our Lord, despite this great difference between Himself and us, is nevertheless able to sympathize with us, for He knows what is in everyone of us, and on account of His love for us and our relation to Him as members of His body, He suffers with us when we suffer. If Jesus of Nazareth had failed under the test and yielded to the temptation of Satan, that would have proven, not that God in the flesh could sin, but rather that Jesus of Nazareth was not God in the flesh. Thank God for the wilderness test, and for the resultant demonstration that Jesus of Nazareth is indeed Immanuel, God with us! And again, if we say that the Lord Jesus could have sinned while upon earth, how can we deny that He might sin even now up in Heaven? May the thought be far from us! The Man at the Father's right hand is one with the Father, and neither with Him nor with the Father is there any variableness, or even the shadow of turning.

The Sinlessness of Christ

How did the virgin birth free Christ from the guilt of Adam's first sin? Does a child partake only of the nature of his father, and not at all of his mother, so that Christ, being conceived of the Holy Ghost, was born without the guilt of original sin, having no human father?

Our Lord's freedom from sin did not result from His virgin birth. Of course, it is true that a child partakes of its mother's nature as well as that of its father. But in this case the whole work was miraculous, and by the power of the Holy Spirit the Son of God was preserved from the taint of human sin. The same God who created a body for Adam and placed it in the garden of Eden also created a body for His Son and placed it in the womb of the virgin. See Hebrews 10:5.

This, however, is not to say that the doctrine of the virgin birth is unimportant. Indeed, it is vital to our faith. If Jesus had been begotten by Joseph then He never could ascend the throne of His father David, for in that case He would be not only of the house of David (which, of course, He must be in order to inherit the throne), but He would also be a descendant of Coniah the son of Jehoiakim whose seed is forever prohibited from occupying that throne (compare Jer. 22:24-30 with Jer. 23:5,6).

A Strange Command

What is the significance of our Lord's frequent command to those whom He healed, not to make His acts known? See Luke 8:56; Matthew 9:30, and similar passages.

On Matthew 16:20 Dr. Scofield has this enlightening note: "The disciples had been proclaiming Jesus as the Christ, that is, the covenanted King of a Kingdom promised to the Jews, and 'at hand.' The Church, on the contrary, must be built upon testimony to Him as crucified, risen from the dead, ascended, and made 'Head over all things to the Church' (Eph. 1:20-23). The former testimony was ended, the new testimony was not yet ready, because the blood of the new covenant had not yet been shed, but our Lord begins to speak of His death and resurrection (verse 21). It is a turning-point of immense significance."

Again, on Mark 8:22-26, he says: "Our Lord's action here is most significant. Having abandoned Bethsaida to judgment (Matt. 11:21-24), He would neither heal in that village, nor permit further testimony to be borne there (verse 26). The probation of Bethsaida as a community was ended, but He would still show mercy to individuals. Compare Rev. 3:20. Christ is outside the door of that church, but 'If any man hear my voice', etc." (*Scofield Reference Bible*).

Our Lord's Word to Caiaphas

To what time did our Lord refer, as concerning Caiaphas, in Matthew 26:64?

In reply to Caiaphas' words, "I adjure thee by the living God, that thou tell us whether thou be the Christ, the Son of God," the Lord Jesus said unto him, "Thou hast said: nevertheless I say unto you, Hereafter shall ye see the Son of Man sitting on the right hand of power, and coming in the clouds of heaven."

The reply of our Lord was addressed to Caiaphas officially and not personally. He was a representative of the nation of Israel, and the message is intended for the nation rather than the man himself. It will be fulfilled in due time at the Second Advent.

The Two Anointings

How many times, and by whom, was our Lord anointed? I refer to the anointing, or anointings, described in Matthew 26:7; Mark 14:3; Luke 7:37,38; John 11:2; 12:1-8.

There were two anointings, and they were separated from each other by about two years in time, and by the distance between Judea and Galilee in miles. There is nothing in common between them except that they both took place in the houses of men called Simon.

Simon was a common enough name, and it is not to be wondered at that two such men should be connected with these records. Luke alone tells us of the first anointing, in chapter 7:36-50. This incident took place early in our Lord's ministry while He was in Galilee. The woman who anointed His feet and wiped them with the hairs of her head is described as "a woman in the city, which was a sinner" (verse 37). This doubtless means that she was an impure woman. By some strange and inexplicable combination of circumstances there is a widespread notion that she was Mary Magdalene. Indeed, "Magdalene" has come to mean an unchaste woman. Of course it means nothing of the sort. Mary was called Magdalene because she came from Magdala, and there is no slightest intimation in the Scripture that she was a "sinner" in the sense of unchastity. Mary of Magdala had suffered from demon possession and had been wonderfully delivered by the Lord Jesus, but there is nothing in the Scripture records to indicate that she figures in the anointing described in Luke 7.

The second anointing took place two years later, when our Lord was about to be betrayed into the hands of sinners and crucified. This anointing is described in Matthew 26:6-13; Mark 14:3-9; John 12:1-8. It occurred "in the house of Simon the leper" (Matt. 26:6; Mark 14:3). This house was located in Bethany, according to all three of the writers. John tells us that this anointing took place at a supper which had been prepared for the Lord Jesus, and that at this supper "Martha served," and her brother "Lazarus was one of them that sat at the table with Him." He does not, however, tell us that it was in the home of Martha and Lazarus. There has been much conjecture as to the identity of "Simon the leper," but the record does not help us to identify him. It is not stated that "Simon the leper" was present at the supper, and we may safely assume that if this Simon were present, he was surely no longer a leper. No leprosy ever long remained in the presence of the Lord Jesus. The woman who did the anointing at this supper was Mary of Bethany, the sister of Martha and Lazarus.

Matthew and Mark tell us that Mary anointed our Lord's head, and from John we get the additional information that she also anointed His feet and wiped them with her hair. No contradiction is implied. Both His head and His feet were anointed. "The ordinary anointing of hospitality and honor," says Dr. Scofield, "was of the feet (Luke 7:38) and head (Luke 7:46). But Mary of Bethany, who alone of our Lord's disciples had comprehended His thrice repeated announcement of His coming death and resurrection, invested the anointing with the deeper meaning of the preparation of His body for burying. Mary of Bethany was not among the women who went to the sepulcher with intent to embalm the body of Jesus."

It is well to remember that our Lord was so pleased with Mary's act of devotion, growing out of her simple faith in His testimony concerning His coming death and resurrection, that He commanded His disciples, saying, "Wheresoever this gospel shall be preached in the whole world, there shall also this, that this woman hath done, be told for a memorial of her."

Our Lord's Nazarite Vow

I should like to know the meaning of the words of Matthew 26:29, "I will not drink henceforth of this fruit of the vine, until that day when I drink it new with you in my Father's kingdom."

The meaning will be clear if you will notice our Lord's words in verse 27, "Drink ye all of it," and again in the parallel Scripture, Luke 22:17, "Take this, and divide it among yourselves." He did not drink of the cup with His disciples, for His blood was not to be shed for Himself but for them. Compare the vow of the Nazarite (Numbers 6:3,4, 20).

Lifted Up from the Earth

What is the true meaning of our Lord's words in John 12:32, "And I, if I be lifted up from the earth, will draw all men unto me"?

The next verse answers your question: "This he said, signifying what death he should die" (verse 33). He was to die by being lifted up on a cross from the earth. His death was to be by crucifixion (compare Ps. 22:16; Isa. 53:7; John 3:14-16; 8:28; 18:31,32). Thus lifted up in death Christ drew all men unto Him and died for them all, bearing away their sins from before the face of God (1 John 2:1,2; Heb. 2:9). The sin question has therefore been disposed of, and disposed of righteously. Today the big question is not the sin question, but the Son question. What will you do with Jesus who is called Christ? Upon your answer to this question depends your fate for time and eternity. See 1 John 5:12.

Lifted Up from the Earth

Please explain John 12:32. Does the lifting up here indicate the exalting of the Lord Jesus in preaching?

No, it does not. "All men," even in the smallest communities, are not drawn to Christ by the most faithful preachers. The meaning of the passage is far different. Study the context, from the twentieth verse. Philip and Andrew approached the Lord with a request from certain Gentiles desiring to see Him. Now, observe carefully the strange effect upon our Lord of this unusual request. He was rarely so stirred as now.

There was apparently some strange significance attaching to this visit of the Gentiles which does not appear upon the surface. In verse 24 our Lord pictures Himself as a grain of wheat. Gentiles are desiring to see Him. It was a crisis in His ministry.

Apparently He did not show Himself to these Gentiles, and the reason was that He had no ministry for Gentiles, except to die for them. Like the corn of wheat which, unless it falls into the ground and dies, abides alone, but which if it dies, it brings forth fruit, so He must lay down His life. He must die for the world; men must be born again, and that could not be apart from His own death; the Son of Man must be lifted up (compare John 3:14).

The Lord Jesus here reaffirms His determination to yield up His life for the salvation of men. Christ according to the flesh could be of no benefit to the Gentiles; it must be Christ crucified and risen again (compare 2 Cor. 5:16 with 1 Cor. 1:23,24). In verses 25 and 26 of John 12 our Lord calls His disciples to a life of self-abnegation, and points out that this is the true path to glory. Notice, in verse 27, how our Lord is stirred.

"Now," says He, "is my soul troubled; and what shall I say?" Our Lord is questioning Himself, so to speak. What shall He say? Shall He say, "Father, save me from this hour"? Not so, for "for this cause came I unto this hour." This rather would He say, "Father, glorify thy name." It was a solemn reiteration of His devotion to His Father's will. He would drink of His Father's cup to the dregs. He would go on to death, even the death of the cross. And thus, instead of saving Himself, He would save others. Thus He would lead "many sons unto glory."

Our Lord's decision was greeted by the audible answer of the Father speaking out of Heaven, saying: "I have both glorified it, and will glorify it again." It was the Father's acceptance of His Son's devotion. This was the third and last time, during our Lord's earthly ministry, that the Heavens were thus opened for the Father to speak through them in approval of the Son (Matt. 3:17; 17:5).

To get the true meaning of this passage, we must be brought by the Holy Spirit into the very atmosphere of it. Hear the thrill in our Lord's voice as He says: "Now is the judgment (Gr. *crisis*) of this world: now shall the prince of this world (that is, Satan) be cast out" (verse 31).

And how was Satan to be cast out? Read the answer in verse 32: "And I, if I be lifted up from the earth, will draw all men unto me." The thirty-third verse explains precisely the meaning of the thirty-second: "This He said, signifying what death He should die." By His death on the cross, then, our Lord drew all men unto Himself. When His blood was poured out on Calvary He displaced the first Adam as the federal head of the race, drawing all men unto Himself. "One died for all, therefore all died" (2 Cor. 5:14, R.V.).

It is thus that our Lord is "the Savior of the world"—"the Savior of all men" (John 4:42). He is the Savior "specially of those that believe," but He is also, in a very true sense, the Savior of the whole race (1 Tim. 4:10). The race is not saved, but that is not because it has no Savior. "The Lamb of God, which taketh away the sin of the world" (John 1:29) tasted "death for every man" (Heb. 2:9). The world is not saved, but He died in order "that the world through Him might be saved" (John 3:17). Redemption was wrought for His enemies. "He is the propitiation for our sins: and not for ours only, but also for the sins of the whole world" (1 John 2:2).

The "Cup"

A statement that you made regarding the "cup" (Matt. 26:39-42; Mark 14:36; Luke 22:42) grieved me very much. I would not have written about it, but our pastor, too, used your definition, and caused disagreement in the class. It seems to me, in these days when Christ is humanized, the adversary is putting in his tactics. If Christ is God, which we all believe, how could Satan have taken His life? According to John 10:17,18, it is plain He laid His life down voluntarily, and took it up again. On the cross He cried with a LOUD voice, not like a weak man dying.

I am especially sorry to have you think that I am "humanizing" our Lord Jesus Christ, anymore than He is "humanized" by the New Testament itself. Is it not true that He was really human as well as really divine? And if that be true, and if He could be weary and hungry and thirsty, is it impossible for Him also to have known the sensation of fear?

It is easy to ask hard questions, and it is hard to answer them. None of us knows exactly what it means when we read in the Word of God that the eternal Son of God "emptied himself" in order to be our Savior. Evidently there were self-imposed limitations—self-imposed voluntarily—which our Lord assumed in His incarnation; but what those limitations were we do not fully know.

According to Hebrews 5:7, we read of our Lord, "who in the days of his flesh, when he had offered up prayers and supplications with strong crying and tears unto him that was able to save him from death, and was heard in that he feared." The 1911 Bible reads that He "was heard as to that which He feared." And in the margin it reads that He "was heard in respect to that which He feared."

This passage could mean nothing if it does not mean that our Lord feared, and that because of His fear He called upon His Father to save him from death, and that His prayer was answered or granted. That is the meaning of He "was heard." If the "cup" from which He prayed to be delivered was the death of Calvary, then His prayer was not granted; but if the "cup" from which He prayed to be delivered was His threatened death in the Garden, then His prayer was granted, for He did not die in the Garden. That He was threatened with death in the Garden might be indicated by the words, "My soul is exceeding sorrowful, even unto death" (Matt. 26:38).

In all this I know there are difficulties presented, but I have done the best I could with the difficulties. If my solution does not appeal to you, why then, of course, you are in no way bound to accept it. I think, however, that you might find it difficult to find a better solution that would meet all the points involved.

Crucifixion and Resurrection Dates

Will you please explain why the crucifixion and resurrection of Christ do not come in the same month and on the same day of the month each year?

The crucifixion of our Lord took place on the fourteenth day of the month Abib or Nisan, which corresponds almost exactly to our April. And therefore the fourteenth day of that month is the exact anniversary of the crucifixion. The resurrection took place on the first Sunday after the crucifixion. The general observance of "Easter" in our day is not according to the Word of God. The word "Easter" is found only once in the Bible (Acts 12:4), and even there it is a mistranslation of the Greek word, *pascha*, and the Revised Version has properly changed it to "passover." The name was originally applied to a spring festival in honor of the heathen Eastra or Ostara, the teutonic goddess of light and spring. About the eighth century the name was transferred by the Anglo Saxons to the Christian festival designed to celebrate the resurrection of Christ, and it comes "on the first Sunday after the first full moon after the spring equinox." Of course this is ridiculous, but it is true nevertheless.

Eloi, Eloi, Lama Sabachthani

What language do the words, "Eloi, Eloi, lama sabachthani," in Mark 15:34 come from? They were uttered by the Lord Jesus on the cross. Some have said that it was an unknown language, but that it was interpreted by the aid of the Holy Spirit.

The words are an English *transliteration* (not *translation*) of the Greek, which is the Greek transliteration of the Aramaic. This was the common vernacular at the time of our Lord's First Advent.

The Finished Work of Christ

In John 17:4 the Lord Jesus said that He had finished the work His Father had given Him to do. On the cross He said, "It is finished." Was the work He did after John 17:4 included in His work of redemption?

The work of redemption in the sense of atonement for our sins was completed on the cross of Calvary. But He did not stop working after He arose from the dead, and He is at work now. In His earth life He only "began to do and teach" (Acts 1:1). All His work then and now may he thought of as included in the great work of redemption. As a matter of fact, ever since God's rest was interrupted by man's sin He has been at work to redeem man from sin. In John 5:17 our Lord said: "My Father worketh hitherto, and I work."

And in this connection let us remember that the ministry of suffering appointed to many of the children of God is in order to "fill up that which is behind of the afflictions of Christ in my flesh for his body's sake, which is the church" (Col. 1:24).

There is, then, such a thing as the finished work of Christ and such another thing as the unfinished work of Christ. We rejoice in the completeness of His atoning work on the cross of Calvary. Let us also rejoice that one day there will be left nothing "behind of the afflictions of Christ," because His body then will have been completed, and the ministry of suffering will be over. Then

"From sorrow, toil, and pain,
And sin, we shall be free;
And perfect love and friendship reign
Through all eternity."

Our Lord's Brethren

Please tell me who are meant in the fifth verse of the seventh chapter of St. John: "For neither did his brethren believe in him."

The reference is to our Lord's brethren according to the flesh, that is, the other children of His mother Mary. There are those who deny that Mary had other children, but the Scripture is against them. In Matthew 12:46 reference is made to "his mother and his brethren"; in Matthew 13:55 four of His brethren are named, they were James and Joses and Simon and Judas, and in the 56th verse, His sisters are also mentioned.

Mark 6:3 is a parallel passage. There His brothers are again named and His sisters referred to. In John 2:12 we read that "he went down to Capernaum, he, and his mother, and his brethren, and his disciples." It is good to notice that in Acts 1:14 these brethren of our Lord appear as believers. Here it says that the apostles "all continued with one accord in prayer and supplication with the women, and Mary the mother of Jesus, and with his brethren." In 1 Corinthians 9:5 Paul mentions the brethren of the Lord in connection with Cephas and himself. And in Galatians 1:18,19 Paul speaks of his first visit to Jerusalem after his conversion when he went "to see Peter, and abode with him fifteen days. But other of the apostles saw I none, save James the Lord's brother."

It is true that the Greek word for "brethren" (*adelphoi*) is the word for "kinsman" or "relative" whether near or remote. On this account those who object to the teaching that Mary had other children than Jesus insist that wherever His brethren according to the flesh are mentioned, they are His cousins or relatives in some other sense than as the children of Mary.

All of this might be true were it not for a single verse in Psalm 69 where the Holy Spirit of truth has settled the matter. This is one of the confessedly Messianic Psalms, and the Lord Jesus is its constant theme. It is in this Psalm that we hear Him saying, "They gave me also gall for my meat; and in my thirst they gave me vinegar to drink" (verse 21; compare Matt. 27:34 and John 19:28-30). Even in the confessions of sin found in the Psalm it is our Lord who speaks, confessing our sins as His own, thus showing His full identification with us as He hung on the cross in our place. Now look at verses 7-9:

"Because for thy sake I have borne reproach; shame hath covered my face.

"I am become a stranger unto my brethren, and an alien unto my mother's children.

"For the zeal of thine house hath eaten me up (see John 2:17) and the reproaches of them that reproached thee are fallen upon me."

To those whose hearts are subject to the authority of the Word of God this is convincing. Mary had other children after the birth of the Lord Jesus, and the "brethren" of our Lord alluded to in the New Testament Scriptures we have been considering were His mother's children.

Anointing of Christ's Body

I believe that Christ was crucified on Wednesday, but will you please tell me why the women did not anoint the body on Friday, as I have never seen any explanation of why they waited until Sunday?

The obvious answer is that the women would not have been allowed access to the body of the Lord until after the three-day period, for which the Roman guard had been set. In other words, there were sixteen Roman soldiers set to guard the body from its incarceration in the tomb on Wednesday evening until the end of the third day following, which would be Saturday evening. Those soldiers would have seen to it that the body was not disturbed on Friday.

Making His Grave with the Wicked

What is the meaning of the words, "he made his grave with the wicked" (Isa. 53:9)? Did the tomb of Joseph of Arimathaea lie in the section of the Jewish cemetery assigned to criminals?

Evidently not. The tomb was Joseph's "own new tomb, which he had hewn out in the rock" (Matt. 27:60). And John tells us that "in the place where he was crucified there was a garden; and in the garden a new sepulcher, wherein was never man yet laid. There laid they Jesus" (John 19:41,42).

Isaiah 53:9 is translated by A. C. Gaebelein as follows: "Men appointed his grave with the wicked, but he was with the rich in his death, because he had done no violence, neither was there guile in his mouth."

Did Christ Descend into Hell?

Did Christ go to hell when He died?

No. The so-called Apostles' Creed, which of course the apostles never saw, is wrong in the statement that "He descended into hell." He descended into hades, which is often confused with hell in the current version of the Scriptures. "Sheol" is the Old Testament word and "hades" the New Testament word for the place of departed spirits. The lost are still there, and are suffering there, as is shown by the sixteenth chapter of Luke. Their final abode will be in the lake of fire, which is hell. Their awful fate is shown in Revelation 20:14,15, which says: "And death and hades were cast into the lake of fire. This is the second death. And whosoever was not found written in the book of life was cast into the lake of fire."

His Wound Stripes

What is meant by the words of Isaiah 53:5, "with his stripes we are healed"?

The meaning is the same throughout the verse, and it is that Christ died for our sins and that by faith the believer is saved through His blood. In 1 Peter 2:4 there is a divine unfolding of the meaning: "Who his own self bare our sins in his own body on the tree, that we, being dead to sins, should live unto righteousness: by whose stripes ye were healed." He is the only one in Heaven with wound stripes, and these wound stripes, unlike those of the returned soldiers, speak not of escape from death, but rather of His obedience "unto death, even the death of the cross."

On What Day Did Our Lord Rise?

How can we go on, insisting that the first day of the week is "the Lord's day" in view of the plain statement of Matthew 28 that it was on the Sabbath and before the first day of the week had begun, first the women came to the tomb and found it already empty, and were told by the angel, "He is not here: for he is risen, as he said"? This surely was on Saturday before sunset, and the weekly sabbath had not yet come to its end.

Presumably, were there no account given of the resurrection other than that provided by the inspired pen of Matthew, the idea of devoting the first day of the week to the commemoration of our Lord's victory over the grave would not have occurred to anyone. On the basis of his record of the event, there is, as I see it, not the slightest warrant for designating Sunday as the Lord's day.

I know, of course, that the descriptions of the resurrection presented by the other evangelists, and the accounts to be found in their writings regarding the various visits to the tomb which were made by different groups and by individuals at various times, seem to contradict Matthew's story. However, after having given much study to the whole matter, I am unable to discover any lack of harmony when Matthew's narration is used—as, it seems to me, it should be used—as the "norm" scripture. To my mind, there is no other way to avoid confusion regarding this important phase of truth, nor any other way of silencing those who so absurdly contend that Matthew's version, in its apparent conflict with those of the other inspired writers, shows the whole affair to have been a hoax and a delusion.

In considering the problem here presented, let us begin with a word touching the principle of the "norm," as mentioned by the questioner. In selecting a passage as the norm for any certain doctrine, a passage should be chosen which gives clear, full and unmistakable teaching concerning that doctrine, rather than an isolated verse which might be construed in more than one way if considered apart from its context and without regard to the teaching of Scripture elsewhere. Now, the time of the arrival of the women at the tomb, and other facts related to our Lord's resurrection, are clearly set forth in the other Gospels. Therefore we should use the other Gospels as the norm passages, rather than Matthew 28:1 whose exact meaning does not appear on the surface.

The solution of the problem we are discussing lies in a correct understanding of the Greek adverb *opse*, occurring in the Authorized Version and "late on" in the Authorized Revision. *Opse* is an adverb of Matthew 28:1 and translated "in the end of" in the Authorized time, which has two meanings, both of which are found in the Greek classics. One meaning is "late," and the other is "after a long time," or "long after." Godet cites classic passages in which *opse* means "after," as, for example, "after the Trojan war," "the mysteries being over," etc.

Whenever we come upon a word having two meanings, the context must determine which meaning is the correct one. In this instance, the verb translated "began to dawn" decides the question for us. The verb comes from a root meaning "light." It is in the form of a present participle in the locative case, and the locative case speaks of "time within which." Thus the women arrived at the sepulcher during the time when it was growing light. This decides which of the two meanings belonging to *opse* should be chosen. In this passage it means "after." Thayer's lexicon translates "the sabbath having just passed, after the sabbath," that is, "at the early dawn of the first day of the week," and adds, "an interpretation absolutely demanded by the added specialization of" the participle mentioned above.

Strong's Concordance defines *opse* as meaning "late in the day, or, by extension, after the close of the day."

The phrase, "began to dawn," etc., may be translated in numerous ways; "as it began to lighten toward the first day of the week," "as it grew toward daylight," "at the dawning toward the first day of the week," etc. The verb means "to grow toward dawn," "to begin to shine" or "to grow light." The root of the word is the Greek word meaning "light," and hence the primary, ordinary, usual meaning of the phrase signifies at the dawning toward the day-part of the first day of the week. This, then, is the preferred rendering, and it should be used unless the facts of the case determine otherwise.

The old Wycliffe translation reads: "Forsothe in the euenyng of the saboth, that scheyneth in the firste daye of the woke."

Tyndale has it this way: "The saboth daye at even, which dauneth the morowe after the saboth."

Anthony Purver's translation (London, 1764), renders it: "But in the night after the sabbath, at the dawning of the first day after it."

In the Book of the New Covenant (translator not named; London, 1838) it says: "And after the sabbath, when it began to dawn on the first day of the week."

The Syriac Peschito version makes it: "For the evening (end) of the sabbath, when the first (day) in the week was lightening."

Emphatic Diaglott: "Now after the sabbath, as it was dawning to the first day of the week."

F. W. Grant: "Now after the sabbath, as it began to dawn the first day of the week."

Overbury: "After the sabbath, as the first day of the week began to dawn."

Weymouth: "After the sabbath, in the early dawn of the first day of the week."

Fenton: "After the sabbaths, towards the dawn of the day following the sabbaths."

Woodruff: "After the sabbath, when the day began to dawn; on the first day of the week."

Campbell: "Sabbath being over, and the first day of the week beginning to dawn."

Noyes: "And the sabbath being over, as it began to dawn toward the first day of the week."

Newcome: "But after the sabbath, as it began to dawn toward the first day of the week."

Wakefield: "Now, after the end of the week, as the first day of the (next) week began to dawn."

Thomson: "Now the sabbath being over, at the dawn of the first day of the week."

Weekes: "Then after the sabbath, at the dawning toward the first day of the week."

Scarlett: "After the sabbath, in the dawn, toward the first day of the week."

Taylor: "And after the sabbath, as the first day of the week began to dawn."

Worsley: "Now after the sabbath, in the dawning towards the first day of the week."

Norton: "And the sabbath being over, in the dawn of the first day of the week."

Jamieson, Fausset and Brown: "After the sabbath, as it grew toward daylight."

These translations fit all the requirements, are literal according to Greek usage, fit the context, and harmonize with the other records.

Another strong argument for the first-day-of-the-week resurrection of our Lord is the typical one. In Leviticus 23 the calendar of the Feasts of Jehovah, the wavesheaf of the firstfruits, was to be waved before Jehovah "on the morrow after the sabbath" (v. 11). In 1 Corinthians 15:23 Paul interprets the type for us, identifying Christ as the firstfruits of the resurrection. It was "on the morrow after the sabbath" that Christ came from the tomb and showed Himself first to Mary of Magdala. He forbade her to touch Him until He had ascended to the Father, to be presented unto Him as the wave-sheaf of the firstfruits.

And so, the first day of the week is "the Lord's day." The Old Testament sabbath is gone, and we now assemble ourselves together to worship Him, rejoicing that, having been delivered up for our offenses, He rose again for our justification.

"Touch Me Not"

Why did Jesus say, "Touch me not" to Mary (John 20:17 & 27) while He invited Thomas to handle Him?

The answer is that as the wave sheaf of the firstfruits, He must, "on the morrow after the sabbath," be presented to God as a token and portion of the first resurrection, before anyone else should be permitted to touch Him. See Leviticus 23:9-14; 1 Corinthians 15:20-24. Between His appearing to Mary and His appearing later in the day to His other disciples, our Lord ascended into Heaven, fulfilling the type of the wave sheaf of Leviticus 23:9-14. As the firstfruits of the resurrection (1 Cor. 15:23), He must be presented before Jehovah to be accepted for us (Lev. 23:11). This must take place before His presentation to any other. Another type fulfilled was that of the Day of Atonement. Our Lord had accomplished His sacrifice and when He was seen by Mary, He was, as it were, on His way to enter into the presence of God to present there His own blood on our behalf (Heb. 9:11,12). All this, of course, must take place immediately upon His resurrection in order to perfectly fulfill the requirements of the typical Scriptures.

The Nail in a Sure Place

Will you please explain Isaiah 22:25?

To understand this verse the passage should be read beginning with verse 15 where God's judgment is pronounced against Shebna, who was to be displaced as treasurer by Eliakim the son of Hilkiah, of whom God says in verse 21: "I will clothe him with thy robe, and strengthen him with thy girdle, and I will commit thy government into his hand." The language of verses 22 to 24 has a double application, for it clearly looks forward to Christ (compare Rev. 3:7). But when you come to the 25th verse Shebna again comes into view as the one who supposes himself to be firmly fixed in his post as a "nail that is fastened in the sure place." In spite of his fancied security he is nevertheless to "be cut down, and fall; and the burden that was upon it shall be cut off: for Jehovah hath spoken it."

The Theophanies

Will you please state how the following passages are harmonized?

1 John 4:12 and 1 John 4:18, "No man hath seen God at any time"; and Exodus 24:10, "And they saw the God of Israel: and there was under his feet as it were a paved work of a sapphire stone, and as it were the body of heaven in his clearness." Exodus 24:11, "Also they saw God, and did eat and drink."

The words you quote are not found in 1 John: 4:18, but they occur in 1 John 4:12, and again in John 1:18, where the answer to your question is furnished by the remaining words of the verse: "The only begotten Son, which is in the bosom of the Father, he hath declared him," or "made him known"; literally, "led him forth," as in an introduction. The theophanies, or appearings of God in the Old Testament were preincarnate manifestations of our Lord Jesus Christ. Compare, for example, Isaiah 6:1-10 with John 12:37-41.

Christ After the Flesh

What is it to know Christ "after the flesh" (2 Cor. 5:16)?

It is to know Him as the man "in the flesh," or the unregenerate man, knows Him. Such knowledge of Christ is described by Dr. Scofield as "an intellectual belief in the historical Christ, which is distinct from 'believing on Him.' The latter implies trust, dependence. Intellectual belief does not bring salvation, as belief with trust does to those who truly, with the heart as well as the mind, believe."

THE HOLY SPIRIT

Ghost or Spirit

Is the Holy Ghost a Spirit?

Yes. The Holy Ghost is a Spirit—the Holy Spirit. Ghost and Spirit are the same word in the original text.

Baptism of the Holy Spirit

I belong to the Full Gospel Tabernacle in ________________, where I was converted. In what way do you believe in the baptism of the Holy Spirit? We abide by Acts 2—Pentecost. But I have never yet received the baptism, though four of my friends have, in a wonderful way. Please give me your opinion on the subject.

You are quite wrong in supposing that a born-again person may be without the baptism of the Holy Spirit. With regard to the person and work of the Holy Spirit in relation to believers the New Testament teaches:

1. In this present dispensation every Christian is born of the Spirit. The new birth is as truly a birth as is the old birth. We are children of our earthly parents by generation: and we are children of our heavenly Father by regeneration. This work of regeneration is the work of the Holy Spirit, whose instrumentality in bringing about the new birth is the incorruptible seed of the Word of God (John 3:1-7; 1 Peter 1:23-25; James 1:18; John 1:11-13).

2. Every Christian (by which is meant every born-again person) becomes at the moment of his new birth a member of the body of Christ. "We are members of his body, of his flesh, and of his bones" (Eph. 5:30). This union with Christ is the result of the baptism of the Holy Spirit. It is not true, therefore, as some would have us believe, that this baptism of the Holy Spirit is "a second work of grace" separated from regeneration by an interval of time. The baptism of the Holy Spirit is the experience not of some, but of all Christians. "For by (or, in) one Spirit are we all baptized into one body, whether we be Jews or Gentiles, whether we be bond or free; and have been all made to drink into one Spirit" (1 Cor.12:13; compare Eph. 4:4,5; Rom. 6:3; Gal. 3:27).

3. Every born-again person at the moment of his new birth receives the Holy Spirit into his own body, and ever afterward is indwelt by the Holy Spirit. This abiding with us forever is continuous and without a moment's intermission. We may grieve Him, we may resist Him, we may quench Him; but we cannot grieve Him away, nor can we drive Him away. To the carnal Corinthian

Christians the Holy Spirit through the apostle Paul wrote, saying: "What? know ye not that your body is the temple of the Holy Spirit, who is in you, whom ye have of God, and ye are not your own?" (1 Cor. 6:19; compare 1 Cor. 3:16; Rom. 8:8,9).

4. The Holy Spirit thus indwelling the believer becomes the believer's anointing; and as such He is our infallible Teacher, and Guide into all truth. This is in fulfillment of our Lord's promise in John 16:13. Every one of God's "little children" is thus made absolutely safe from the danger of apostasy. "Little children, it is the last time: and ye have heard that antichrist shall come, even now are there many antichrists; . . . But ye have an Unction from the Holy One, and ye know all things. I have not written unto you because ye know not the truth, but because ye know it, and that no lie is of the truth. . . . These things have I written unto you concerning them that seduce you. But the Anointing which ye have received of him abideth in you, and ye need not that any man teach you; but as the same Anointing teacheth you of all things, and is truth, and is no lie, and even as it hath taught you, ye shall abide in him" (1 John 2:18-27). The words "Unction" and "Anointing" represent the same word in the Greek (Chrisma), and it is easily seen that the reference is to the Holy Spirit, of whom oil is a frequently employed symbol in the Word of God (compare Zech. 4:1-6). All the anointings of prophets, priests and kings in the Old Testament were typical of the enduement of the Holy Spirit. It is good to have such a Teacher, and to be assured that by His power the promise is certain of fulfillment that we shall be kept from falling and presented faultless before the presence of His glory with exceeding joy (Jude 24).

5. The Holy Spirit who is our Anointing is also our Seal. In 2 Corinthians 1:21,22, it is written, "Now he which stablisheth us with you in Christ, and hath anointed us, is God; who hath also sealed us, and given the earnest of the Spirit in our hearts." He is thus the token to us of safety, and security, as well as of ownership and possession. We who have believed in the Lord Jesus Christ were, upon believing, "sealed with that Holy Spirit of promise, which is the earnest of our inheritance until the redemption of the purchased possession, unto the praise of his glory" (Eph. 1:13,14; compare 4:30).

6. Believers are exhorted to be filled with the Spirit (Eph. 5:18). Having been born of Him, and baptized into Christ in Him, having become in our bodies His temple, having received Him as our Anointing, and Seal, it is fitting that we should yield ourselves unto Him (Rom. 6:13), presenting to Him our bodies "a living sacrifice, holy, acceptable unto God," which is indeed our "reasonable service" (Rom. 12:1). When we thus yield ourselves to Him and permit Him to fill us He controls our lives and produces in us His own fruit, which is "love, joy, peace, longsuffering, gentleness, goodness, faithfulness, meekness, self-control" (Gal. 5:22,23).

This is the secret of effectiveness in the Christian life.

Praying for the Spirit

In Luke 11:13 our Lord said that the heavenly Father would "give the Holy Spirit to them that ask him." Are we to conclude from this

that the Christian must ask for the gift of the Spirit before he receives Him?

No. When the words of Luke 11:13 were spoken the Holy Spirit had not yet been bestowed upon the Church (John 7:39). Today we are in a new dispensation or order of things; and in this present order of things every saved person is (1) born of the Spirit through believing the Word (John 1:11-13; 3:3-8; James 1:18; 1 Peter 1:22-25); (2) baptized in the Spirit, and into the body of Christ (1 Cor. 12:13, R.V.; Rom. 6:3; Gal. 3:27); (3) anointed of the Spirit as his infallible Teacher (1 John 2:20-27); (4) sealed by the Spirit as the earnest of his inheritance until the day of redemption (2 Cor. 1:21,22; Eph. 1:13,14; 4:30); and (5) indwelt by the Spirit (1 Cor. 6:19,20; Rom. 8:8-11).

In addition to all this the believer is commanded in Ephesians 5:18-21 to be also filled with the Spirit in order that the Spirit Who is the Holy Spirit of God may take full possession of him, and control his life, and bring forth His own fruit in the believer (Gal. 5:22,23).

The Personality of the Holy Spirit

Is it sinning against the Holy Spirit when one does not believe in His personality as the third person in the Godhead?

Yes, it is sinning against the Holy Spirit, and sinning against the Godhead generally, for in rejecting the testimony of Scripture as to the personality of the Holy Spirit one makes God a liar. But it should be added that this is not the sin against the Holy Spirit mentioned in Matthew 12:24-32; Mark 3:22-30 and Luke 11:14-20. The sin referred to there is the sin committed by those who said that the Lord "hath an unclean spirit" (Mark 3:30). This is the unpardonable sin.

The Witness of the Holy Spirit

Will you deal with the question of the witness of the Spirit in the light of Hebrews 10:15; 1 John 5:10; Romans 8:16? I notice one word in each of these Scriptures that seems to stand out prominently; namely, "to," "in" and "with." Will you stress the application of these three words in the light of their context?

The witness of the Holy Spirit to us, spoken of in Hebrews 10:15, is through the Word, whose Author He is, and which is cited in the next verse (16): "This is the covenant," etc., quoted from Jeremiah 31:33. The same passage is also quoted in Hebrews 8:10. Let us learn from this that all the Holy Spirit's testimony is according to His Word.

The witness of the Holy Spirit in us is an inward conviction of the truth as set forth in that same Word of God. It is not a mere "feeling" that we are saved; it is far more and better than feeling; it is an assurance, based upon the plain promises of Scripture. It results from believing "the witness of God which he hath testified of his Son." As it is put in John 3:33, "He that hath received his testimony hath set to his seal that God is true."

And the witness of the Holy Spirit with us is His testimony concerning the result of believing God. The Spirit of God at once communicates with the spirit of the believer and convinces him that he has now become God's child and heir.

All this is precious. How wonderful it is thus to come into communication and fellowship with "The Most High God, Possessor of Heaven and Earth," and to be assured of an eternal relationship to Him as His child and an eternal position in His household! Hallelujah!

The Birth and Baptism of the Holy Spirit

Please explain why the "birth" of the Spirit and the "baptism" of the Spirit are usually thought of, spoken of and taught as being one and the same operation. In John 20:22 Jesus breathed on the disciples and said unto them, "Receive ye the Holy Ghost." That was their birth of the Spirit, was it not? In Acts 2:4 they were all filled with the Holy Ghost. Was not this their baptism of the Spirit?

I have asked one or two learned theologians who frankly confess that they cannot differentiate the birth and the baptism. Why should they be thought identical? The dictionary defines them as separate and distinct, why should not we so separate them in our spiritual thought and practice?

While the birth and the baptism are simultaneous, they are by no means identical. By the birth we are brought into the family of God as new-born babes; by the baptism we are made members of Christ, "of his body, of his flesh, and of his bones."

We ought not to take the experience of the apostles and first disciples as the norm and pattern of our own experience. They were saved before the cross and before the New Testament advent of the Holy Spirit; we were saved long afterwards. In the present dispensation every believer (1) is born of the Spirit (John 3:3-7; James 1:18; 1 Peter 1:23-25); (2) is baptized by Him into the body of Christ (1 Cor. 12:12,13; Rom. 6:1-3; Gal. 3:27); (3) receives Him as the Anointing by whom we are to be led into the truth (1 John 2:20-27; John 14:16,17; 16:12-15); (4) is sealed by Him unto the day of redemption (2 Cor. 1:21,22; Eph. 1:13; 4:30); (5) and is indwelt by Him (1 Cor. 3:16; 6:19,20; Rom. 8:9). All of these things are true of every believer; but not every believer is filled with the Spirit. This we are commanded to be:

"Be not drunk with wine, wherein is excess; but be filled with the Spirit" (Eph. 5:18).

As we yield to Him He fills us, and as He fills us, He controls us and transfigures us "into the same image from glory to glory" (2 Cor. 3:18).

Baptism by Fire

What is meant by the baptism with fire, in Matthew 3:11 and Luke 3:17?

The reference is to the baptism of the Holy Spirit as our Energizer and Purifier. "Quench not the Spirit" (1 Thess. 5:9) means "Don't put out the fire."

The Transition Period

In the light of Acts 8:15-17, and Acts 19:2, are we to believe in the baptism of the Holy Spirit as distinct from His incoming at regeneration?

No. Acts 8:15-17 belongs to the transition period while the gospel was passing from Jews to Gentiles. Up to the time when the gospel went fully over to the Gentiles the gift of the Holy Spirit seems to have waited until after water baptism (Acts 2:38); but beginning with the meeting in the house of Cornelius the Holy Spirit's coming upon believers was immediate, and preceded water baptism (Acts 10:44-48). The Ephesian "disciples" of John the Baptist were not Christians when Paul met them. Paul preached Christ to them and rebaptized them, using "the name of the Lord Jesus"; and, perhaps because there might have been some doubt as to the risen Christ's approval of his action without a visible manifestation, the visible manifestation was given. But the doctrine of Holy Spirit baptism for this Church age is unmistakably set forth in 1 Corinthians 12:12,13. We are all baptized by the one Spirit into the body of Christ. This means that every believer, when he believes, is at once baptized by the Holy Spirit "into Jesus Christ" (Rom. 6:2,3; Gal. 3:27).

The Holy Spirit at Samaria

Please explain why the believers at Samaria failed to receive the Holy Spirit upon believing. What was the difference between their case and that of the Hebrew believers at Pentecost in the second chapter of Acts?

The record is found in Acts 8:14-17: "Now when the apostles which were at Jerusalem heard that Samaria had received the Word of God, they sent unto them Peter and John, who, when they were come down, prayed for them, that they might receive the Holy Ghost: (For as yet he was fallen upon none of them: only they were baptized in the name of the Lord Jesus.) Then laid they their hands on them, and they received the Holy Ghost."

The difference between the case at Samaria and that at Jerusalem lay in the fact that no apostles were present at Samaria. The preacher was not Philip the apostle, but Philip the deacon or evangelist. It was necessary that apostles should be present, especially Peter, to whom was given authority in Matthew 16:19 to act as spokesmen for the absent Christ.

Since or When

Please explain Paul's question, addressed to "certain disciples" at Ephesus, "Have ye received the Holy Ghost since ye believed?" (Acts 19:2). Does this indicate or imply that the believer does not receive the Holy Spirit until some time subsequent to regeneration?

No. The correct reading is given in the Revised Version: "Did ye receive the Holy Spirit when ye believed?" Something was obviously wrong with these "certain disciples," and this provoked the apostle's question. It developed, as shown by the context, that these were "disciples," not of Christ, but of John the

Baptist. Therefore Paul preached Christ to them, and they believed, were rebaptized, and received the Holy Spirit in visible manifestation, as had been the case with the Jews in Acts 2, and with the Samaritans in Acts 10. The reception of the Holy Spirit is not "a second blessing" or "a second work of grace," for "if any man have not the Spirit of Christ (meaning the Holy Spirit of God, as shown by the context), he is none of his" (Rom. 8:8-11; compare 1 Cor. 6:19).

Filled with the Holy Spirit

Do you teach "death to self" as the only means of experiencing a complete filling of the Spirit? Is this not the meaning of Romans 12:1,2, and 1 Thessalonians 5:22,23?

Every believer is filled with the Holy Spirit exactly in the degree that he yields himself to God as one who is alive from the dead, and his members as instruments of righteousness unto God. To yield himself fully he must reckon himself dead indeed unto sin, but alive unto God through Jesus Christ our Lord (Rom. 6:11-13). "Yield" in this passage and "present" in Romans 12:1 are the same word in the Greek Testament. The Thessalonian passage cited calls us to separation as to our walk. "Sanctify" means to set apart, that is, to separate. As we yield ourselves unto God we are separated unto Him, and therefore separated from everything contrary to Him.

The Holy Spirit Striving with Man

Please explain the first part of Genesis 6:3: "My Spirit shall not always strive with man." I am anxious to know. Our pastor has told some dreadful stories about God leaving man never to return. I know that we should not grieve the Holy Spirit.

The whole verse should be read: "And Jehovah said, My Spirit shall not always strive with man, for that he also is flesh: yet his days shall be an hundred and twenty years." This period of probation was for the world of men before the flood of Noah's day. There is nothing here to indicate that the Spirit of God leaves man "never to return." Yet it is a dangerous thing to reject His pleadings. There is no time assured to any man but now.

A Distinction with a Difference

As the Holy Spirit will be taken out of the world at Christ's second coming, how can unbelievers be converted during the millennium?

There is no statement in Scripture that the Holy Spirit will be taken out of the world. He is omnipresent, and therefore, cannot be absent from any place at any time. In 2 Thessalonians 2:7 the Scripture testifies that He will be taken out of the way as the restrainer of iniquity. There is a real difference between being taken out of the world and being taken out of the way.

Led by the Holy Spirit

What do you mean by saying, "being led by the Holy Spirit"?

The Holy Spirit of God seeks to guide every child of God in even the smallest details of life. He indwells every believer (1 Cor. 6:19), and is perfectly able to make a willing child hear His voice. He may speak through the Word, or through circumstances, or by the still, small voice. His leading is never contrary to the Word, of course. But that does not mean that the way to be led by Him is to shut one's eyes and then open the Bible and put a finger on a verse with the eyes still shut, expecting guidance to come that way. The Spirit leads through the Word by the plain teaching of the Word, and when that does not fully reveal His will He will find other ways of communicating His will to those who really desire to know it in order to obey it. "For the eyes of Jehovah run to and fro throughout the whole earth to show himself strong in the behalf of them whose heart is perfect toward him" (2 Chron. 16:9).

The Omnipresent Holy Spirit

How can there be salvation after the Church is raptured and the Holy Spirit is taken away?

There is no Scripture which teaches that the Holy Spirit will be taken away from the earth at the Rapture, but rather He is to be "taken out of the way" as the Restrainer of the working of lawlessness (2 Thess. 2:7). From that time the Holy Spirit, who is ever omnipresent, will be still here, but here in the same sense as He was here before His coming in Acts 2 for the work of gathering out a people for the name of the Lord.

Grieving Away the Holy Spirit

Is it possible for a child of God to grieve away the Holy Spirit?

No. We may indeed grieve Him (Eph. 4:30), but we cannot grieve Him away. We may resist Him (Acts 7:51), but once He comes to dwell in our bodies He comes to abide forever (1 Cor. 6:19; compare John 14:16). We may quench Him (1 Thess. 5:19), but He will never leave us nor forsake us. Having begun a good work in us He "will perform it until the day of Jesus Christ" (Phil. 1:6).

Blaspheming the Holy Spirit

What is the sin against the Holy Spirit?

The answer to your question about the sin against the Holy Spirit is found in Mark 3:30. It was "because they said, he hath an unclean spirit," that He uttered the words of solemn warning just preceding. They were in effect calling the Holy Spirit of God the unclean spirit of Satan. All the light we have upon the subject is in Matthew 12:24-29; Mark 3:22-30 and Luke 11:14-23. The practical lesson for us seems to be that we ought to distinguish carefully every religious work, as to whether it has behind it the Holy Spirit of God or the unclean spirit of Satan. And while we must not judge persons we are called upon to judge their works, the test always being the Word of God.

The Laying on of Hands

Please explain Acts 8:12-17. When a man believes in the Lord Jesus

Christ as his personal Savior he receives the Holy case of the Samaritans, did it also require the layin

The reason the Holy Spirit did not respond in Acts was not present. According to Matthew 16:19 Peter was the ap man for the risen Christ, and so he had to be present, first, in the chapter of Acts when the Jews first heard the gospel; then in the eighth chapter when the Samaritans were to be let in; and then in the fourteenth chapter when the Gentiles were to receive the message. After his three keys were used, that was the end of it.

Tarrying Ten Days

Why did the disciples have to wait ten days in Jerusalem for the Holy Spirit to come upon them? What about those who died in the interval of the ten days?

The ten days' waiting was needed to fulfill the Pentecostal type of Leviticus 23. In verses 9 to 14 of that chapter there is the type of the wave-sheaf of the firstfruits which was fulfilled in the resurrection of our Lord. Verses 15 to 21 give the type of the firstfruits fulfilled in the formation of the New Testament Church in Acts 2. This, according to the type, must take place on the morrow after the seventh sabbath following the wave-sheaf offering. That is, it must be fifty days between the offering of the wave-sheaf and the offering of the firstfruits. The word "Pentecost" is the Hebrew word for fiftieth, and therefore the antitype must be delayed until "the day of Pentecost was fully come." As for those who died in the interval of the ten days, if there were such, their salvation was in no way affected, but they missed being included in the New Testament Church.

The Unity of the Spirit

Please define "the unity of the Spirit."

The word "unity" occurs but three times in the English Bible, and in all these three occurrences it refers to the same thing—the unity of the body of Christ established and maintained by the Holy Spirit. The word first appears in Psalm 133, where this unity is likened to "the precious ointment upon the head" of the high priest, reaching even "to the skirts of his garments." The reference is unmistakable. Our Lord Jesus, anointed with the Holy Spirit as "the oil of gladness" above His fellows (Ps. 45), is presented typically as the Head over all things to the Church which is His body (Eph. 1:22,23). The other two uses of the word "unity" are in Ephesians 4. In verse 3 we are exhorted to "keep the unity of the Spirit," and then this "unity of the Spirit" is analyzed for us: it consists of seven fundamental truths to which we are to hold; they are (1) one body, (2) one Spirit, (3) one hope, (4) one Lord, (5) one faith, (6) one baptism, and (7) one God and Father. These are the true "Christian fundamentals," and they are the proper and Scriptural basis for all Christian fellowship. Then follows the mention of gifts bestowed by the risen Lord upon His body for its upbuilding, "till we all come in the unity of the faith, and of the

-ledge of the Son of God, unto a perfect man, unto the measure of the -ture of the fullness of Christ" (verse 13). The "perfect man" referred to is Christ as He shall be when His Church is completed and manifested as His Body, "the fullness of him that filleth all in all."

A Question about Tongues

Is it true that speaking with tongues is an indispensable sign of having been baptized with the Holy Spirit?

No, it is not true. During the formation of the New Testament this sign generally accompanied the baptism of the Holy Spirit; but, like other spectacular signs, this sign was withdrawn as the New Testament approached completion.

In 1 Corinthians 14, where the whole question of tongues is treated in detail, it is forbidden to speak in tongues in the absence of an interpreter (verse 28). The baptism of the Holy Spirit is simultaneous with regeneration, as are also the anointing, the sealing and the indwelling of the Holy Spirit (see John 3:3-8; 1 Cor. 12:12,13; Rom. 6:3; Gal. 3:27; 1 John 2:20-27; 2 Cor. 1:21,22; Eph. 1:13; 4:30). And in addition to all these we are commanded to be filled with the Spirit, which filling is not like the others, once for all, but should be often repeated. Indeed. we are filled with the Spirit continuously so far as we are yielded to Him.

The Gift of Tongues

1. **Did Paul have the gift of "divers kinds of tongues" (1 Cor. 14:18)?**
2. **If 1 Corinthians 14:22 is true, why do we not have that gift today?**

1. Yes.

2. Because it has pleased the Lord to withdraw it. Even in apostolic times its exercise was forbidden in the absence of an interpreter (1 Cor. 14:28).

Tongues and the Holy Spirit

There is a sect in our town calling itself "The Four-Square Gospel" and teaching that we must speak in tongues or else we are not sealed with the Holy Spirit. Is this true?

No, it is not true. Every believer is sealed at the moment he believes. "Now he which stablisheth us with you in Christ, and hath anointed us, is God; who hath also sealed us, and given the earnest of the Spirit in our hearts" (2 Cor. 1:21,22). "In whom ye also trusted, after that ye heard the word of truth, the gospel of your salvation: in whom also after that ye believed (having also believed, R.V.), ye were sealed with that Holy Spirit of promise, which is the earnest of our inheritance until the redemption of the purchased possession, unto the praise of his glory" (Eph. 1:13,14). "And grieve not the Holy Spirit of God, where by ye are sealed unto the day of redemption" (Eph. 4:30). These Scriptures show plainly that the sealing of the Holy Spirit is the common possession of all believers.

CREATION

God's Perfect Creation

Does Genesis 1:2 teach that God really created the earth "without form and void"?

No. Indeed it is definitely denied elsewhere in Scripture that He did so. The primal creation is described in the first verse, and the second verse tells of the effect of some great catastrophe which occurred afterwards, leaving the earth without form and void. The second verse may be properly translated, "And the earth became without form and void." The Hebrew word *hayetha* translated "was" in our common version, is often translated "became" elsewhere in Scripture.

The Gap Between Genesis 1:1 and 2

What proof is there to confirm the theory, advanced by Dr. Scofield and others, of an indeterminate gap between the first and second verses of Genesis 1?

The date of Genesis 1:1 is unrevealed. Beginning with the second verse we are told of a replenishing of the earth, following some great catastrophe between the first and second verses, which is not recorded. The Hebrew word *hayetha*, translated "was," is many times rendered "became" elsewhere in Scripture. The Scriptural evidence in favor of this rendering in connection with the waste and desolate condition of the earth is well set forth in Pember's *Earth's Earliest Ages*, to which you are referred. Rotherham translates Genesis 1:2 as follows: "Now the earth had become waste and wild, and darkness was on the face of the roaring deep, but the Spirit of God was brooding on the face of the waters." And in a note on the words "waste and wild" he says: "Hebrew *tohu wobohu*. Evidently an idiomatic phrase, with a play on the sound ('assonance'). The two words occur together [elsewhere] only in Isaiah 34:11 and Jeremiah 4:23; examples which favor the conclusion that here also they describe the result of previous overthrow." *The Companion Bible* has this note on the word translated "without form" or "waste": "Not created tohu (Isa. 45:18), but became *tohu* (Gen. 1:2; 2 Peter 3:5,6). 'An enemy hath done this' (Matt. 13:25, 28, 39. Compare 1 Cor. 14:33)."

The questions you ask would require almost a volume to answer in detail. Whether or not God *could* have created the rocks with fossils in them need not be discussed here, for the evidence shows that He did not so create them. The fossils are so numerous and can be so well identified with known forms of life that we have no hesitation in making that assertion. However, it does not follow that interpretations of the fossils are necessarily correct. We will state, however, that "the gap theory" no more implies a second creation after the primeval ruin than does the reconstruction of the earth after the deluge. The act described in verse one is the creation, the work of the six days, a reconstruction. If you will read George McCready Price's "New Geology" you will find that there is no scientific need to assume great gaps or long periods in geology. He claims, and other noted geologists agree with him, that there are many evidences of cataclysms in the geological records, and that such catastrophes as Noah's flood might account for both fossils and strata. He gives evidence to show that the uniformitarian theory of Lyell and Hutton is no longer unchallenged, and that the entire science of geology must be rewritten. It is true that scientists of the evolutionary school endeavor to laugh Price out of court; but he not only gives the results of his own investigations but also quotes from the best authorities in proof of them.

There are many truths of God's Word involving difficulties, and the same is true of every theory of science, as scientists themselves are ready to acknowledge. While "the gap theory" may not be without its difficulties, the same would be true of any other theory. Let us remember that the account in Genesis is only an outline, and that the geological record is also very fragmentary. Two outlines may present difficulties and even contain what appear to be contradictions. Were we to know all that is implied in the story of Creation as given through Moses, and were we also in possession of the whole history of which the record of the rocks gives merely an outline, we should find no difficulties and no contradictions. Scientists constantly ask us to have faith where absolute proof is not forthcoming. God also requires the same thing, but at the same time gives such strong evidence of the truth of His Word that faith itself is built upon certainty.

MAN

Created or Evolved

What is the testimony of Scripture to show that man is the direct creation of God?

There is no slightest intimation in the Bible that man is the product of evolution. Man was created by God and not evolved out of the mud. To those who bow to the authority of the Scriptures there is no doubt concerning this proposition. The revealed facts are thus outlined by Dr. Scofield:

1. Man was created, not evolved. This is (a) expressly declared, and the declaration is confirmed by Christ (Matt. 19:4; Mark 10:6) (b) 'an enormous gulf, a divergence practically infinite' (Harley) between the lowest man and the highest beast, confirms it; (c) the highest beast has no trace of God-consciousness the religious nature; (d) science and discovery have done nothing to bridge that 'gulf.'

2. That man was made in the 'image and likeness' of God. This 'image' is found chiefly in man's tri-unity, and in his moral nature. Man is 'spirit and soul and body' (1 Thess. 5:23). 'Spirit' is that part of man which 'knows' (1 Cor. 2:11), and which allies him to the spiritual creation and gives him God-consciousness. 'Soul' in itself implies self-conscious life, as distinguished from plants, which have unconscious life. In that sense animals also have 'souls' (Gen. 1:24). But the 'soul' of man has a vaster content than 'soul' as applied to beast life. It is the seat of his emotions, desires, affections (Ps. 42:1-6). The 'heart' is, in Scripture usage, nearly synonymous with 'soul.' Because the natural man is, characteristically, the soulual or psychical man, 'soul' is often used as synonymous with the individual, for example, Genesis 12:5. The body, separable from spirit and soul, and susceptible to death, is nevertheless an integral part of man, as the resurrection shows (John 5:28,29; 1 Cor. 15:47-50; Rev. 20:11-13). It is the seat of the senses (the means by which the spirit and soul have world-consciousness) and of the fallen Adamic nature (Rom. 7:23,24)."

Evolution

Can you give the names of any recognized scientists who discredit the theory of evolution?

Yes. Prof. William Bateson of England, perhaps the leading biologist of his day, has recently said that "while forty years ago the Darwinian theory was accepted without question, today scientists have come to a point where they are unable to offer any explanation for the genesis of species. There is no evidence of any one species acquiring new faculties but there are plenty of examples of species losing faculties. Species lose things but do not add to their possessions. Variations of many kinds, often considerable, we daily witness, but no origin of species."

Prof. N. S. Shaler, Harvard geologist, says: "It begins to be evident to naturalists that the Darwinian hypothesis is still essentially unverified."

The late Prof. Virchow, described as "the foremost chemist on the globe," said of evolution: "It is all nonsense. It cannot be proved by science that man descended from the ape or from any other animal; all real scientific knowledge has proceeded in the opposite direction. The attempt to find the transition from animal to man has ended in total failure. The middle link has not been found and never will be. It has been proved beyond doubt that during the past five thousand years there has been no noticeable change in mankind."

The Canadian geologist, Sir William Dawson, says: "The record of the rocks is decidedly against Evolutionists especially in the abrupt appearance of new forms. Every grade of life was in its highest and best estate when first introduced. Nothing is known about the origin of man."

Prof. Agassiz, one of the greatest of scientists, said: "The theory of the transmutation of species is a scientific mistake, mischievous in its tendency."

Lord Kelvin, greatest of modern scientists, says: "I marvel at the undue haste with which teachers in our universities and preachers in our pulpits are restating truth in the terms of evolution while evolution remains an unproven hypothesis."

Dr. Etheridge, the British Museum's famous expert in fossilology, says: "Nine-tenths of the talk of evolutionists is sheer nonsense. This museum is full of proofs of the utter falsity of their views."

There are many others, but these may suffice to show that the evolutionary theory is untrue. Dr. Marion Mc.H. Hull declares that the theory of evolution is destructive to the inspiration of the Bible, the fall of man, the deity and virgin birth of Christ, the atonement and regeneration, and continues: "Since the theory of evolution has been shown to be only a theory, since it has been shown to be discredited by scientists of highest repute, since it has been shown to be an unprovable theory, and since it has been shown to be destructive to the Word of God and the great doctrines of the Bible, why should we let it have a place in our thinking any more? Let us get back to the safe and sane position of a simple faith in the plain truth as expressed in the God-breathed Book, every letter of which is God-breathed, written by men who were inspired by God to set forth the truth without any error whatever. As for me and my house, we shall stand flat-footed on the Book, and accept it at its face value without question."

SATAN

Is there a Personal Devil?

Why do you believe Satan to be a real being?

For the same reason that I believe God to be a real being. The Word of God mentions Satan by name sixty-six times, and calls him the Devil thirty-four times. In every one of these one hundred mentions of him he is shown to be a personal being with personal attributes. Then, too, he is often mentioned in the Bible in places where his name is not used. But wherever he is mentioned in Scripture, whether with his name or without it, he is shown to be a mighty person who seeks to turn men away from the worship of the true God.

Why Study Satan?

Is it important for us to know about Satan?

It surely is of great importance that we should know who Satan is, and the Scriptures have not left us in the dark concerning him. It is quite the fashion nowadays to dispose of Satan as a bugaboo of the dark ages and to make him the butt of joke and ridicule. This casual attitude towards Satan is doubtless quite in keeping with his own plans, as the enemy of God and man; for if we can be deluded into thinking of him only as something unreal or unworthy of serious thought, it will leave us unarmed against his snares.

Satan is a person. There is not a single impersonal reference to him in the whole Bible. Personal names, personal pronouns, personal acts, personal planning and plotting, personal reasoning and scheming are all attributed to him and show him to be an actual person as truly as God is a person, as truly as men are persons. Satan is not merely an evil influence or an evil principle.

Satan is a person of great dignity (Jude 8,9). Originally created perfect, he fell from his high estate through pride. Doubtless he is the spiritual king of Tyre described in Ezekiel's prophecy (compare Ezek. 28:11-17 with John 8:44 and 1 Tim. 3:6). Unlike the fallen angels of Jude 6, he is not under restraint but "as a roaring lion, walketh about, seeking whom he may devour" (1 Peter 5:8).

Satan is not in hell. Though that awful place is especially for him and his angels (Matt. 25:41), and he will certainly be cast at last into the lake of fire (Rev. 20:10), his residence during the present age is chiefly in the heavenly realms where he has access to God's presence and accuses the saints before Him day and night (Job 1:6-12; Rev. 12:10). His ejection from heaven, described in Revelation 12:9, is yet future. The Lord Jesus spoke of the same event prophetically in Luke 10:18, and John 12:31. When Satan finally reaches hell it will be to suffer eternal torment. He will be "cast into the lake of fire and brimstone, where the beast and the false prophet are, and shall be tormented day and night forever and ever" (Rev. 20:10).

Meanwhile, Satan is now a ruler—the ruler of the host of wicked spirits in the heavenly realms, the prince of the power of the air, the prince of this world and the god of this age (Eph. 2:2; 6:12; John 12:31; 14:30; 2 Cor. 4:4).

Satan, the Church, and Israel

What is the meaning of Revelation 12:1-6 and 13-17?

The woman is Israel, "of whom as concerning the flesh Christ came" (Rom. 9:5). The sun is Christ in His character as the glory of Israel (Mal. 4:2).

The moon is the Church, shining with the reflected glory of the absent Sun. She is under the woman's feet as indicating Israel's prior position chronologically, and perhaps to remind us that "salvation is of the Jews" (John 4:22).

The dragon is Satan, and the seven heads and the horns and crowns speak of his position as the prince of this world, the god of this age, and the prince of the power of the air (John 12:31; 14:30; 2 Cor. 4:4; Eph. 2:2; compare Rev. 13:1-4).

The Man Child, of course, is Christ (compare verse 5 with Ps. 2:7-9). But it is the complete Christ, including "the Church, which is his body, the fullness (or completion) of him" (Eph. 1:22,23). He is the Head, and the church is the body. The Head and body united constitute the "one man" of Galatians 3:28, R.V.; the "perfect man" of Ephesians 4:13; and the "man child" of Revelation 12:5. The Man Child is now in process of birth, and the sufferings of Israel through the centuries of the present age have been labor-pains which must continue until the Church, "the fullness of the Gentiles, be come in" (Rom. 11:25). When the church is fully gathered out (Acts 15:14), then, the body of Christ having been completed, the Man Child fully born, it will immediately be "caught up unto God" (Rev. 12:5; 1 Thess. 4:16-18). It is this completion that Satan seeks to prevent. He is ever threatening the Man Child and would devour Him and His body if that were possible, which of course it is not, for greater is He that is in us than he that is in the world (1 John 4:4).

As soon as the Church is completed and caught up to meet the Lord, Israel will come under the special protection of God. The Great Tribulation which will constitute the latter half of the seven years of Daniel's seventieth week, enduring 1260 days or "a time, and times, and half a time" (one year, plus two years, plus half-a-year, making three and-a-half years), will be preeminently "the time of Jacob's trouble, but he shall be saved out of it" (Jer. 30:7; Rev. 12:6, 14).

Delivered unto Satan

Will you kindly explain 1 Corinthians 5:5?

In this verse the Apostle Paul commands the Corinthian Church to deliver one of its members who was guilty of uncleanness—"to deliver such an one unto Satan for the destruction of the flesh, that the spirit may be saved in the day of the Lord Jesus." The command is put into another form in verse 13: "Therefore put away from among yourselves that wicked person." There are at least two other instances in Scripture where children of God were given into Satan's hands temporarily. Job was thus "delivered unto Satan." This was God's response to Satan's taunting challenge (Job 1:9-12; 2:4-6). Evidently it was in order to show that God is able to sustain His people through any trial. The demonstration was complete, and the record of it has been of great help and comfort to God's people through the ages. Likewise Peter was given over to Satan for sifting as wheat, but he was warned of it and assured of his Advocate's prayer in his behalf—"that thy faith fail not" (Luke 22:31,32). And, indeed, our Lord Himself was thus turned over to Satan—driven by the Spirit into the wilderness to be tempted (Mark 1:12,13). It is good to note that the sinning Corinthian Christian was evidently brought to penitence by his experience with Satan and restored to the fellowship of the Church. This is indicated by the apostle's message in 2 Corinthians 2:6-11.

Satan and Heaven

Is the Devil in Heaven?

Satan is the prince of the power of the air, the prince of this world and the god of this age (Eph. 2:2; John 12:31; 2 Cor. 4:4). His casting out of heaven is yet future, our Lord's words in Luke 10:18 being predictive, and he still has access to God as the "accuser of the brethren" (Rev. 12:10). His final doom will be to be cast into the lake of fire, which is hell, but that is yet to be. See Revelation 20:10.

The Power of the Air

What is "the power of the air" of which Satan in the prince (Eph. 2:2)?

The Revised Version reads, "the prince of the powers of the air," and these powers are defined in Ephesians 6:12, R.V., as "the spiritual hosts of wickedness in the heavenly places." The powers of the air are the hosts of wicked spirits in the service of Satan. These are his spiritual agents, and in addition to these, he has human agents who "are false apostles, deceitful workers, transforming themselves into the apostles of Christ. And no marvel; for Satan himself is transformed into an angel of light. Therefore it is no great thing if his ministers also be transformed as the ministers of righteousness; whose end shall be according to their works" (2 Cor. 11:13-15).

Satan and His Body

Is there any Scripture to indicate that Satan is now without a body? Did he not have a body in Heaven before he fell?

Satan is probably the personage addressed as the spiritual King of Tyre in Ezekiel 28:11-19, and his description there indicates that originally he had a body which was beautiful almost beyond imagination. Whether he now has a body is not revealed in Scripture so far as I know. But he seems to have the power to appear in various forms.

Lucifer

Who Is Lucifer?

Lucifer is one of Satan's names. It appears but once in Scripture and even there the Revisers have changed it to "day star." (Read the whole passage, Isaiah 14:12-20.)

Beelzebub

Who is Beelzebub?

This is a name applied by our Lord to Satan as the prince of the demons (Matt. 10:25; 12:24, 27; Mark 3:22; Luke 11:15-19). A similar name, "Baal-zebub," is applied to the god of Ekron in 2 Kings 1:2-16.

Belial

Who is Belial?

It is a name applied to Satan in 2 Corinthians 6:15. The word signifies "worthlessness" or "wickedness" or "baseness." It occurs sixteen times in the Authorized Version of the Old Testament, but the Revisers have changed it every time to read, "wicked," "base," etc.

Abaddon and Apollyon

Who is "the angel of the bottomless pit" of Revelation 9:11?

He is Satan, and he is named here in Hebrew Abaddon, and in Greek Apollyon, both of which mean "destroyer."

The Binding of Satan

I understand that when the Millennial Kingdom is here, the thousand-year reign of Christ and His glorified saints, Satan will be bound. Is that correct?

Yes, that is correct. Revelation 20:1-3 is perfectly clear on this point: "And I saw an angel come down from heaven, having the key of the bottomless pit and a great chain in his hand. And he laid hold on the dragon, that old serpent, which is the Devil, and Satan, and bound him a thousand years, and cast him into the bottomless pit, and shut him up, and set a seal upon him, that he should deceive the nations no more, till the thousand years should be fulfilled."

Satan not Omniscient

When speaking of Satan, I have heard it said that he tempts us where we are weakest. If that is so, he must be all-knowing. Do you know of any text in the Bible that gives us light on this subject?

No. I am glad to believe, as I do believe, that although Satan is supernatural and superhuman, he is not all-knowing which would be omniscient. If he were not limited, then it could not be said: "Greater is he that is in you, than he that is in the world." I thank God that Satan cannot tempt us in any way without God's permission, and that with every temptation God Himself makes the means of escape (1 Cor. 10:13).

Satan's Limitations

Has Satan foreknowledge? If not, how did he know Jesus was the Son of God when it had been revealed to no one at the time?

When our Lord Jesus was born His divine Sonship was proclaimed by angels and shepherds and the wise men from the east. It surely could have been no secret, and Satan needed no foreknowledge to know that Jesus was the Son of God. Surely Satan was deeply concerned in the events around Bethlehem at the time. Though men might have forgotten the significance of these events, he remembered them.

Satan's Power

Does Satan have equal power with God?

It is never true that Satan has "equal power with God." Unquestionably God has delegated great power into Satan's hands, but it is always limited, and it is never in any sense equal to the power of God.

ANGELS

The Nature of Angels

Will you tell us something about the angels so frequently mentioned in Scripture?

Angels are mentioned about three hundred times in the Bible. There are at least three strong reasons why we should seek to know about them: (1) Because the Bible speaks about them so frequently; (2) because of their present ministry amongst us; (3) because we are to live with them throughout eternity.

The word "angel" means "messenger." The term is a designation of an office, rather than the description of a person. An angel might be one of the "sons of God"—heavenly, as for instance, the seraphim; or earthly, as the human prophets of God. In Malachi 3:1 the Lord Jesus is called "the Angel of the covenant;" and yet in Hebrews 1:5,6 and 2:16 we learn that the Lord Jesus never took on Himself the nature of angels.

The word "angels" is employed in seven senses in Scripture: (1) as referring to human messengers (2 Sam. 2:5; Luke 7:24); (2) for human messengers bearing a divine message (Hag. 1:13; Gal. 4:14); (3) for impersonal providences, as the "thorn in the flesh, the messenger (angelos) of Satan to buffet me" (2 Cor. 12:7); (4) for bishop or pastor of the churches (Rev. 2nd and 3rd chapters); (5) for demons without bodies, infesting the air and seeking to take possession of men (Matt. 12:24; 25:41); (6) for heavenly beings such as Jacob met on the way back home (Gen. 33:1,2); and (7) for one particular heavenly messenger, called distinctively "the angel of the Lord" (Ex. 3:2) which usually refers, without doubt, to our Lord Jesus Christ Himself in His preincarnate manifestation or theophanies.

Fallen Angels

Who or what are the fallen angels?

There are two classes of fallen angels mentioned in Scripture: (1) "The angels which kept not their first estate [place], but left their own habitation," are "chained under darkness," awaiting judgment (2 Peter 2:4; Jude 6; 1 Cor. 6:3; John 5:22). (2) The angels who have Satan (Gen. 3:1; Rev. 20:10) as leader. The origin of these is nowhere explicitly revealed. They may be identical with the demons (Matt. 7:22). For Satan and his angels everlasting fire is prepared (Matt. 25:41; Rev. 20:10).

Angels or Men?

Do you believe that the angels referred to in 2 Peter 2:4, and Jude 6, may be those who are called "sons of God" in Genesis 6:2?

No, I do not believe that the "sons of God" of Genesis 6:2 are angels. I agree with Dr. Scofield that it was a matter of the marriage of believers and unbelievers, which has always been, and still is, the curse of God's people.

The Archangel

I recently heard a preacher refer to Gabriel as the archangel. Was he right in this?

The title of archangel is applied in Scripture only to Michael (Jude 9). The word "archangel" occurs elsewhere only once. In 1 Thessalonians 4:16 we read of "the voice of the archangel." Notice that it says, "the archangel," and not "an archangel." The prefix "arch" means "first," and it would seem that there could not be two first angels. And yet Michael is referred to in Daniel 10:13 as "one of the chief princes." In Daniel 10:21 he is referred to as "Michael your (that is, Israel's) prince." In Daniel 12:1 he is referred to as "the great prince which standeth for the children of thy people," that is, Israel, Daniel's people. In Revelation 12:7 we read that "there was war in heaven: Michael and his angels fought against the dragon; and the dragon fought and his angels." This again seems to put Michael in the place of leadership over the angels of heaven as their archangel.

The name Gabriel occurs four times in Scripture: Daniel 7:16; 9:21; Luke 1:19, 26. The same Gabriel who ministered to Daniel came also over five hundred years later and ministered to Zacharias the father of John the Baptist, and to Mary the virgin mother of our Lord.

Angels of the Churches

Who were thc angels of the seven Churches of the second and third chapters of the Revelation?

The word "angel" means "messenger"; and these "angels of the churches" were doubtless messengers from the churches sent to visit John in his exile on Patmos, and it was by their hands that John returned his message to the churches. In this sense anyone is an angel to the church who bears a message from God to the church.

SIN

The Fall of Man

Please explain the clauses, "in sorrow shalt thou eat of it all the days of thy life," in Genesis 3:17; also "the man is become as one of us," in verse 22 of the same chapter. My pastor says this latter clause proves that the "fall" was up instead of down.

The Revised Version gives the true meaning of the clause referred to in Genesis 3:17. Verses 16 and 17 are given by the Revision as follows:

"Unto the woman he said, I will greatly multiply thy pain and thy conception; in pain thou shalt bring forth children; and thy desire shall be to thy husband, and he shall rule over thee. And unto Adam he said, Because thou hast hearkened unto the voice of thy wife, and hast eaten of the tree, of which I commanded thee, saying, Thou shalt not eat of it: cursed is the ground for thy sake: in toil shalt thou eat of it all the days of thy life."

Sin had brought with it what the 8th of Romans calls "the bondage of corruption," with its attendant evils.

As to the second clause referred to in your inquiry, it should not be read by itself. "Knowing good and evil" is not the same thing as "knowing the difference between good and evil." In 2 Corinthians 5:21 it is written that the Lord Jesus "knew no sin," but that does not mean that He was ignorant concerning sin, or that He did not know the difference between good and evil. Adam and Eve by the fall—and it was a fall and not an "elevation"—came to know sin as being its victims and in bondage to it. There is no comfort for evolutionists in that dreadful fact.

Man's Downfall

Since Adam was created in "the image of God" how do you account for the presence of "cave men," which is proved historically? I have been asked this question and am at a loss to explain it. Did man during the centuries degenerate into cave men and then become civilized again?

Yes. There is no proof of the existence of men before Adam. The first chapter of Romans depicts the awful career of man beginning with the knowledge of God and going downward to the awful bottom. Up from this bottom many have come back to the knowledge of God again, and some have become His children through the new birth.

Sin and Satan

Is sin always caused by the attacks of Satan?

Sin is not always the result of Satan's attacks. Even during the Millennium when Christ will be here on the throne and when Satan is restrained for a thousand years, there will yet be sin; so much so, that, at the end of the thousand years when Satan is released, he finds it possible to muster a tremendous army of rebels against the Lord. Sin is a part of man's make-up, and it is inseparable from him in this life. It is no doubt true that as he becomes more intimate with God, he will become more sensitive to sin and will, therefore, find in himself far more sin than he ever before dreamed was there.

What Is Sin?

Is an act of disobedience to the Lord's command, always a sin that needs confession although committed through thoughtlessness or weakness?

Surely! All coming short of the glory of God is sin whether in thought, or word, or deed; and sin, whether we are conscious of it or not, should be confessed, and we should judge ourselves for it. In the Levitical economy the offerings were for sins done unwittingly or in ignorance. Presumptuous sins were punished. Contrast Leviticus 4:1,2, 13, etc., with Leviticus 10:1,2, and Job 1:5.

Presumptuous Sins

What are the presumptuous sins referred to in: "Keep back thy servant from presumptuous sins and let them not have dominion over me" (Ps. 19:13)?

The Old Testament divides sins into two classes. First, sins done in ignorance, or unwittingly. Second, sins committed wittingly or knowingly. For the former class the bloody offerings were provided, but for presumptuous sins there was no such provision, and they must be punished. See, for example, Leviticus 22:14; Joshua 20:3-5.

Imputation Illustrated

I recently heard it said in public that the doctrine of imputation was illustrated in the Epistle of Philemon. Will you explain this?

It is quite true. When Paul in this Epistle asks Philemon to receive his runaway slave Onesimus, he says: "If he hath wronged thee, or oweth thee ought, put that on mine account; I Paul have written it with mine own hand, I will repay it." This is a perfect illustration of the doctrine of imputed righteousness. It is as if the Son of God had said before the foundation of the world concerning our sins, "Put it to mine account, I will repay it." And the righteous God agreed to that arrangement, and, imputing our sins to the Lord Jesus on the cross of Calvary, He was thus able righteously to impute unto us all the virtues of Christ. The death on Calvary of the infinite Son of God was of sufficient value in the sight of God to constitute the ransom price for all our sins. As it is written in 2 Corinthians 5:21, "He hath made him to be sin for us, who knew no sin; that we might be made the righteousness of God in Him."

Sin, Righteousness and Judgment

Will you please explain John 16:3, the last two parts?

The ministry of the Holy Spirit toward the world is to convince men of sin, of righteousness and of judgment. The "sin" referred to is the sin of the rejection of the Son of God: "Of sin, because they believe not on me" (verse 9). The "righteousness" is the righteousness of Christ Himself who, in His absence will be represented here by the Holy Spirit. "Of righteousness," says Christ, "because I go to my Father, and ye see me no more." He claimed to be the Son of God, and, in proof of this claim, He purposed to send the Holy Spirit from Heaven into the world. When the Holy Spirit came therefore, His coming was a demonstration of the righteousness of the claims of the Son of God. The Son Himself is absent from the world so far as His visible body is concerned. But the presence of the Holy Spirit here is positive proof that the Son of God went where He said He was going when He left His disciples on the Mount of Olives.

The "judgment" of which the Spirit of God was to reprove or convince the world was the judgment of Satan: "Of judgment, because the prince of this world is (or, hath been) judged." Satan is under the judgment of God though the time of his execution is not yet come. In John 12:31 our Lord said: "Now is the judgment of this world: now shall the prince of this world be cast out." And then as if explaining His meaning He said in the next verse, "And I, if I be lifted up from the earth, will draw all men unto me." His lifting up from the earth was about to take place on the cross for "this he said, signifying what death he should die" (verse 33). The cross of Calvary was the scene of the most tremendous battle of the ages. It was there that the Son of God, "through death," defeated "him that had the power of death, that is, the devil" (Heb. 2:14). In due time Satan will meet his doom in the Lake of Fire (Rev. 20:10). Meanwhile we are to remember that he is a defeated foe, and we are not to be afraid of him. "Submit yourselves therefore to God. Resist the devil, and he will flee from you" (James 4:7).

The Unpardonable Sin

What is the unpardonable sin referred to in Matthew 12:31,32?

Let us study the context, beginning with verses 22 and 23: "Then was brought unto him one possessed with a demon, blind, and dumb: and he healed him, insomuch that the blind and dumb both spake and saw. And all the people were amazed, and said, Is not this the son of David?" It was plain that this work was supernatural and superhuman. The Pharisees, not willing to attribute it to the Spirit of God, declared that Jesus had an evil spirit—that He cast out demons by Beelzebub the prince of demons, that is, by Satan himself. Replying to this, the Lord Jesus shows the absurdity of supposing Satan arrayed against Satan. It was not likely that the prince of the power of the air should be fighting against his own forces. How, then, should his kingdom stand? And what had they to say about the exorcists among themselves—were they, too, casting out demons by Beelzebub? Jesus had not been so foolish as to attempt to rob the strong man—that is, Satan—without first binding him. The very first act of His ministry was to overcome this "strong man" in the wilderness, and now He was spoiling his house. The lines were sharply drawn and the fight was on. "He that is not with me is against me; and he that gathereth not with me scattereth abroad" (Matt. 12:30). To ascribe to the devil the work of the Holy Spirit of God was a most terrible act of blasphemy which should never be forgiven (Matt. 12:31,32). This, then, is "the unpardonable sin"—to charge the Lord Jesus Christ with acting by the power of Satan—to accuse the Holy Spirit of God with being the unclean spirit of Satan! Mark very plainly states that Jesus uttered this warning, "because they said, He hath an unclean spirit" (Mark 3:30). Their cup of iniquity was full to overflowing and He lifted up His voice against them. "Either make the tree good, and its fruit good," said He, "or make the tree corrupt, and its fruit corrupt: for the tree is known by its fruit. Ye offspring of vipers, how can ye, being evil, speak good things? For out of the abundance of the heart the mouth speaketh. The good man out of his good treasure bringeth forth good things: and the evil man out of his evil treasure bringeth forth evil things. And I say unto you, that every idle word that men shall speak they shall give account thereof in the day of judgment. For by thy words thou shalt be justified, and by thy words thou shalt be condemned" (Matt. 12:33-37).

The unpardonable sin should not be confused with the "sin unto death" of 1 John 5:16,17. The "sin unto death" is a sin committed by a child of God which brings upon him physical death under the chastening hand of his faithful heavenly Father. There were instances of this "sin unto death" in the Corinthian Church (1 Cor. 11:30-32).

The Unpardonable Sin and Eternal Security

Can a man or woman who has been born again, say ten years ago, get into the place where he or she can commit the unpardonable sin and be lost?

A man who *has been born again* cannot commit the "unpardonable sin" and get lost. A man who receives the Lord Jesus Christ as his personal Savior, accepting His finished work as his only hope of salvation, cannot get lost for Jesus Himself said in John 10:27,28: "My sheep hear my voice, and I know them, and they follow me: and *I give unto them eternal life*; and *they shall never perish, neither shall any pluck them out of my hand.*" Saved and *safe* is the man who puts himself under the shelter of the shed blood of the Lord Jesus Christ, and neither Satan, angels, nor principalities can pluck out of God's hand the man who has placed his trust in His only begotten Son.

The Sin unto Death

What is the "sin unto death?"

The "sin unto death" and the "sin not unto death" of 1 John 5:16,17 are to be understood in the light of the doctrine taught in 1 Corinthians 11:31,32. Physical death is sometimes a judicial penalty from God visited upon His saved people for unconfessed, unjudged sin. When a Christian falls into sin, his salvation indeed is not jeopardized, but his fellowship with God is interrupted. The way back into fellowship is through confession (1 John 1:9). If God's child, in such circumstances, refuses to confess, the Father is forced to chasten him. The Corinthian Christians were in just such a case. They had been disorderly in the observance of the Lord's Supper by eating the bread and drinking the cup of the Lord unworthily, that is, in an unworthy manner. They were thus guilty of the body and blood of the Lord (1 Cor. 11:27). They refused to examine themselves, in order that they might so eat of the bread and drink of the cup as to please God (verse 28). They continued to eat and drink unworthily, eating and drinking judgment unto themselves, not discerning the Lord's body (verse 29). For this cause, many were weak and sickly among them and many had fallen asleep; that is to say, they had died under the chastening hand of God. They were still saved, but physical death had been visited upon them in chastening (verse 30). Had they judged themselves, they would not have been judged by Him (verse 31), but since they had compelled Him to judge them, they had been chastened of the Lord that they should not be condemned with the world (verse 32). Condemnation is impossible for those who are in Christ Jesus (Rom. 8:1, R.V.). They have already been condemned in the person of their Substitute and put to death on the cross of Calvary. Now, since they have become God's children by the new birth, they can never again be brought under condemnation, but they may be chastened even unto physical illness or physical death.

Moses sinned unto death (Deut. 32:48-52); Achan committed a sin unto death (Josh. 7:16-26); and Ananias and Sapphira committed a sin unto death (Acts 5:1-11).

Inbred Sin

What does the Bible teach in regard to inbred sin?

The Bible teaches that sin, meaning the old self life in the believer, remains there until the believer goes to Heaven. It is unchanged and unchangeable. Along with the old sin nature is the new nature which comes in at the new birth, and thus the indwelling Spirit of God is working in the believer. Just so far as the believer is yielded to the Holy Spirit, the Holy Spirit controls the believer's life and walk.

Sin and Selfishness

Is sin merely selfishness? Is there selfishness in unbelief, malice, or hatred of God? Would you mind explaining this to me?

Underneath all these things is self usurping the place belonging to God. It is men living unto themselves instead of unto Him who died for them and rose again. See 2 Corinthians 5:14,15. And yet selfishness and sin are not precisely synonymous terms. Selfishness is lust which, having conceived, bringeth forth sin (James 1:15).

The Sin of Adultery

What does God's Word teach concerning adultery? If a man commits adultery, is he then in God's sight separated from his wife? Does adultery in God's sight end the marriage relationship? Would it be right for the adulterer to live with his wife again?

There is no teaching in Scripture that the sin of adultery automatically frees the adulterer from his or her marriage vows. The marriage relationship is not so easily annulled in the Word of God. Yes, it would be right for the guilty man to live with his wife again if she is willing to forgive and receive him. Under the law of Moses, adultery was a capital crime. In Leviticus 20:10, it is written of "the man that committeth adultery with another man's wife, even he that committeth adultery with his neighbor's wife, the adulterer and the adulteress shall surely be put to death."

Sin and No Sin

Please explain to me 1 John 3:9.

The apparent conflict between 1 John 1:8 and 1 John 3:9 has ever been a source of perplexity to Christian interpreters. In the former verse John writes: "If we say that we have no sin, we deceive ourselves, and the truth is not in us." In the latter verse the same writer says: "Whosoever is born of God doth not commit sin; for his seed remaineth in him: and he cannot sin, because he is born of God."

Many and devious are the attempts to reconcile this apparent contradiction. Eradicationists take special delight in 1 John 3:9. One of these, a young man, accosted this editor during some meetings down in the Virginia peninsula, saying, "May I ask you a question?"

"Certainly."

"Please give me your interpretation of 1 John 3:9."

"I will do that, after you have given me your interpretation of 1 John 1:8."

"No, I want you to tell me the meaning of 1 John 3:9."

"But, you see, 1 John 1:8 comes before 1 John 3:9. Let us deal with this first, and then we will come to your verse."

The young man turned away sorrowfully and with apparent pity for us. Of course, he would say that by an experience called a second work of grace, the old nature had been eradicated from him and that he could no longer sin. But, looked at squarely, if the verse proves what he claims it proves, it proves too much. For it is not speaking merely of persons who have received a second work of grace, it includes all who have been born of God. The so-called "Holiness" people cannot claim the language as applying exclusively to them.

A common interpretation applies the statement of 1 John 3:8 to the new nature in the believer. We are told that what is meant by the verse is that when a Christian falls into sin it is the old nature that is at work for the new nature, since it is "created in righteousness and true holiness," cannot sin. Of course, that is all true enough, and it is elsewhere taught in the Word of God: "If then I do that which I would not, I consent unto the law that it is good. Now then it is no more I that do it, but sin that dwelleth in me" (Rom. 7:16,17). But this interpretation will not do for 1 John 3:9. It is excluded by the language of the succeeding verse which says: "In this the children of God are manifest, and the children of the devil." Whatever the sin may be that is referred to in the ninth verse, it is something that is manifest to those looking on, and it is something that cannot be done by a born-again person.

Then there are those who apply the language of 1 John 3:9 to the believer's standing as contrasted with his state. When one is born again he is brought into a standing which never afterwards varies: he is "accepted in the Beloved." His sin, and also his sins, have all been imputed to Christ, and now the righteousness of Christ is imputed to him. He enters into the blessedness of a man unto whom God imputeth righteousness without works, saying, "Blessed are they whose iniquities are forgiven, and whose sins are covered. Blessed is the man to whom the Lord will not impute sin" (Rom. 4:5-8).

The doctrine of imputation is a doctrine that is beautiful and true. There is a wonderful illustration of its working in Numbers 23:21 where God says that "He hath not beheld iniquity in Jacob, neither hath he seen perverseness in Israel." He saw His people only under the blood which, according to His reckoning, had already been shed "from the foundation of the world" (Rev. 13:8). Thus, by what someone has called "the higher ethic of the cross," the righteous God was able to impute His own righteousness unto His sinning people (2 Cor. 5:19, 21).

But this interpretation of 1 John 3:9 must also be rejected in view of the language of verse 10: "In this the children of God are manifest, and the children of the devil." The believer's standing is not something which is made manifest to the on-looker, and the "sin" of 1 John 3:9 is a matter affecting the believer's testimony. It is something that no believer can do.

Yet another, and, perhaps, even more common, interpretation tells us that the sin referred to in our verse is a continuous act or habit of life and that the born-again person does not go on sinning. Some of the private translators of the New Testament have substituted the word "practice" for the word "commit." Mr. Darby, for instance, makes the verse read: "Whoever has been begotten of God does not practice sin, because his seed abides in him, and he cannot sin, because he has been begotten of God." The Rotherham translation reads: "Whosoever hath been born of God is not committing sin, because a seed of him within him abideth; and he cannot be committing sin, because of God hath he been born;" and in a footnote Mr. Rotherham says: "The tense shows continuance." All of this interpretation is freely conceded, but it is difficult to see how it helps any toward a solution of our problem. The statement still stands that the Born Again person "cannot be committing sin," or "cannot sin." The full force of the statement is that the regenerate person is not able to do the thing here called sin.

And yet there stands the statement of 1 John 1:8: "If we say that we have no sin, we deceive ourselves, and the truth is not in us."

We recently met a pastor in western Pennsylvania who declared that neither he nor any member of his church ever sins. That would be glorious if it were only true. But it is plain from the Word of God that he is deceiving himself, and, what is even worse, he is helping to deceive those who are under his shepherdly care. Happily the children of God generally are laboring under no such delusion.

Several years before Dr. Scofield went to be with the Lord, this editor said to him: "I see that you have adopted the word 'practice' in the margin of your Reference Bible relating to the third chapter of First John. But, Doctor, how does that help matters any? When you consider that any coming short of the glory of God in thought or word or deed is sin, is it not true that we all do practice sin?"

"Alas! alas! so we do," replied the Doctor.

It is only to those who are ignorant of God's righteousness that the idea ever occurs that they may be able to establish their own righteousness (Rom. 10:3). We are all practicing sin, and that continually.

What, then, is the true explanation of 1 John 3:9? "Sin" as referred to in this verse must be different from "sin" as found in 1 John 1:8; and, whatever the sin of 1 John 3:9 is, it is something that cannot be committed by a regenerate person.

The key to our problem is found, as we believe, in the Revised rendering of the fourth verse of the chapter.

In the Authorized Version the verse reads: "Whosoever committeth sin transgresseth also the law: for sin is the transgression of the law."

That there is something wrong with this translation is evident from the fact that the New Testament clearly teaches that the believer is "not under the law, but under grace" (Rom. 6:14); and "sin is not imputed when there is no law" (Rom. 5:13) "for where no law is, there is no transgression" (Rom. 4:15).

In the Revision 1 John 3:4 reads: "Everyone that doeth sin doeth also lawlessness; and sin is lawlessness."

Now, if the whole paragraph, beginning with this verse, be read in view of the definition of sin given here, we shall see what the Holy Spirit of truth evidently had in mind when the paragraph was written.

No born-again person will be guilty of sin in the sense of lawlessness.

Lawlessness at its root is the denial of any rule over one's life.

It is to say that even God has no right to control the life of His child.

It is to say, "I will not have this Man to rule over me." It is anarchy. This was the sin of the Antinomists of the dark ages. Indeed, antinomianism is suggested in the word for lawlessness, which is *anomia*.

There is a vast difference between disobedience and lawlessness. One may disobey the will of God, while at the same time acknowledging God's will to be right and that it ought to be obeyed.

It was a renewed heart that spoke in Romans 7:22 saying, "I delight in the law of God after the inward man;" even while admitting that there was another law at work within that heart, warring against the law of the mind, and bringing God's child into captivity to the law of sin which was in his members. He was disobeying God's will, but he was not claiming the right to disobey it. He was striving to obey it, and in his failure he cried out, "O wretched man that I am! who shall deliver me from the body of this death?" (verse 24).

Another illustration of this truth is found in the case of an Old Testament believer, who, when his sin was brought home to him, cried out, saying: "Against thee, thee only, have I sinned, and done this evil in thy sight: that thou mightest be justified when thou speakest, and be clear when thou judgest" (Ps. 51:4). Wisdom is justified of all her children, and so also is God justified of His.

No matter how backslidden a child of God may be, he never boasts of his backsliding nor claims the right to backslide. He remains a child of God all the time, and he is wretched even while living in disobedience to God's Word and will.

Assuming for a moment that we have come upon the key to our mystery, let us now paraphrase the passage, 1 John 3:4-10, making use of the key:

"Whosoever committeth sin committeth also lawlessness; and sin is lawlessness. And ye know that he was manifested to take away our sins; and in him is no lawlessness. Whosoever abideth in him is never lawless: whosoever is lawless hath not seen him, neither known him . . . He who is lawless is of the devil; for the devil was lawless from the beginning. . . . Whosoever is begotten of God is never lawless; for his seed remaineth in him; and he cannot be lawless because he is begotten of God. In this the children of God are manifest, and the children of the devil."

This is the true meaning of John's language in this same Epistle, chapter 2:3-6: "And hereby we do know that we know him, if we keep his commandments. He that saith, I know him, and keepeth not his commandments, is a liar, and the truth is not in him."

Let us not think of "commandments" here as applying to Moses' law to Israel from Sinai. "John uses 'commandments,' says Dr. Scofield, "(1) in the general sense of the divine will, however revealed, 'his word' (verse 5); and (2) especially of the law of Christ (Gal. 6:2; 2 John 5). See, also, John 15:10-12" (*Scofield Reference Bible*).

"But whoso keepeth his word, in him verily is the love of God perfected (that is, brought to fruition, or to its intended end): hereby know we that we are in him. He that saith he abideth in him ought himself also so to walk, even as he walked."

How did He walk with reference to the Word and will of His Father? We know that He always did the will of His Father, that it was His delight to do His will, His meat to do the will of Him that sent Him.

What a wonderful work it is that God has wrought in His people. Not only has He delivered them from the penalty of sin and removed the Law so that it can no longer sting them to death (1 Cor. 15:56,57; 2 Cor. 3:7-11); but He has also wrought within them a new creation, which ever causes them to look up to

Him, crying, Abba, Father, confessing His Lordship over their lives and delighting in the accomplishment of His will in them.

And one day, praise God, we shall come to the end of the road, where we shall be presented faultless before the presence of His glory with exceeding joy.

"To the only wise God our Savior, be glory and majesty, dominion and power, both now and ever. Amen."

SALVATION

God's Sovereignty, Election, and Man's Responsibility

Did God create some to be lost, or does His Word teach that He knew some or certain ones would be lost when He gave them life, or did God give certain ones life knowing that they would be lost? Is it not right for us to inquire into these things?

It is no doubt right for us to inquire into these things, but let us be careful to confine our inquiry to the Word of God and let us not be led off into inferences which may lead us far astray. There is no doubt that God's absolute sovereignty is clearly taught in the Word of God, and just as clearly is man's responsibility also taught in the Word. Our difficulty comes when we seek to "harmonize" these two doctrines. Such a task seems to be beyond the power of the human mind. Let us believe all that God has said on the subject and be content to wait for further light as to the harmony between these things. We may depend upon it that "the Judge of all the earth" will "do right." Let us preach to men as if everything depended upon them, and then let us pray to God for them as if everything depended upon God.

I quote here from a personal letter received from Dr. C. I. Scofield in reply to a question about election:

You know of course the two antagonistic views of the Calvinists and Arminians. You state correctly the hyper-Calvinistic view, that God in His sovereign wisdom elected certain persons to be saved and doomed certain others to be damned, and the Arminian view that God has put before all men the possibility of salvation and has left them to elect blessing or cursing. As usual, where parties have been formed in the church of God upon doctrine, the truth is compounded of both views. It is not true, as the Arminians say, that election takes effect only in the will of the sinner. Such passages as Ephesians 1:4 cannot be explained by saying they simply teach the foreknowledge of God. On the other hand, there is no biblical warrant for the hyper-Calvinistic doctrine of reprobation. It is in the Calvinistic theology and inference from their doctrine of election. If God has chosen of His own good will without any cause moving Him thereto, certain persons to be saved, they argue that He has necessarily left certain other persons to be damned.

As a general thing I am exceedingly shy of inferential doctrines. I fancy our reasons break down at precisely that point. The things that are revealed are for us and our children, but the secret things belong to God. The truth about election seems to be simply this: God elects to be saved all who are in Christ (see Eph. 1:4 and kindred passages). And he offers fairly and in good faith a place "in Christ" to whosoever will. In other words, the election which is in the Biblical idea indistinguishable from predestination (though some theologians try to make a distinction), is to position rather than salvation. It stands connected with sonship rather than with redemption.

The emphasis in the writings of Paul, where the great predestination passages are found, is upon the greatness of the position into which we of this dispensation have been brought, having predestinated us unto the adoption of children. Now this, as you readily see, is a very different thing from being predestinated unto salvation (Eph. 1:5). To the same effect, the great passage in Romans 8:29: "For whom he did foreknow he also did predestinate to be conformed to the image of his Son, that he might be the firstborn among many brethren."

The subject, of course, is full of difficulty, and yet I cannot but believe that most of the difficulty grows out of the misrepresentation of the nineth chapter of Romans. If one only sees that Romans 9,10 and 11 form, not a continuation of the apostle's argument from the eighth chapter onward, but a parenthesis in which the apostle takes up at length the relation of Judaism to Christianity; so that troublesome nineth chapter has not to do with individual salvation but national election, the contrast being not between the saved and the lost but between Israel and the Gentiles; then I believe a most fruitful source of confusion on this important subject is eliminated.

I note your deprecation of teaching which puts God in the position of arbitrary dealing. There is no doubt, dear brother, that many passages of Scripture bearing upon the sovereignty of God leave difficulties in the mind. In other words, the Scriptures do not turn aside to vindicate the dealings of God. Here is the sphere of faith. Faith says, "I do not understand, but I believe that God always does right and some time I shall know the precise connection between His righteousness and His seemingly arbitrary dealings. In the meantime I trust."

As to the question of prayer for the conversion of the unsaved, I can only say we enter there upon a sphere of faith alone. God tells us to pray and love prompts us to pray. Prayer for the unsaved is putting the unsaved in a very special way into the hands of God; and I do not believe any good ever comes to us from speculating upon prayer.

Salvation and the Dispensations

I understand from your teaching concerning the dispensations into which time is divided, that in each dispensation there is a new test, and that under each of these tests man fails and comes into judgment. In the dispensation of innocence, for example, the test was obedience of the injunction concerning the tree of knowledge, and man failed to meet the test, resulting in his expulsion from Eden. Then, under the dispensation of law the test was obedience of the commandments of Sinai; man again failing, and the captivities resulted. Now, will you please tell us what was the relation between the dispensational test

and the way of salvation? In other words, was obedience, which would be good works, the way of salvation under the dispensations preceding the present dispensation of grace?

No. Salvation has always been, as it is now, purely a gift of God in response to faith. The dispensational tests served to show man's utter helplessness, in order to bring him to faith, that he might thrust himself upon God and be saved by grace through faith plus nothing. The law was Israel's schoolmaster (rather, guide) unto Christ, that the people might be justified by faith. But now that faith has come, even Israel is no longer under the guide (Gal. 3:24,25).

Salvation in Past Dispensations

Will you please tell me how the Jews were saved before the death of Christ? I know, of course, that they were saved by looking forward as we look backward, but I will thank you to go into some details.

Old Testament believers were saved exactly as New Testament believers are saved. As appears from the form of your question, you are familiar with the principle of retroaction in connection with the death of Christ on the cross. He died for those who had lived before, as well as for those who have lived since. This principle is set forth in Romans 3:25; Hebrews 9:15. The Gospel of salvation by grace through faith is not a new thing contrary to the Old Testament Scriptures, but is only a newly or more fully revealed thing. Adam and Eve, Noah and Abraham, Moses and David, and all the Old Testament saints were saved on account of the blood of Jesus just as truly as we are thus saved.

The Just Shall Live by Faith

Please explain verses 2-4 of the second chapter of Habakkuk.

Habakkuk 2:2-4 is a very important passage. The prophet had given a testimony to Jehovah in 1:12-17, and in 2:1 he awaits Jehovah's answer, saying, "I will stand upon my watch, and set me upon the tower, and will watch to see what he will say unto me, and what I shall answer when I am reproved."

Then came the reply:

"And Jehovah answered me, and said, Write the vision, and make it plain upon tables (tablets), that he may run that readeth it. For the vision is yet for an appointed time, but at the end it shall speak; because it will surely come, it will not tarry. Behold, his soul which is lifted up is not upright in him: but the just shall live by his faith."

The vision, which occupies the entire chapter, has three elements: (1) The sins of Israel will be judged (vs. 5-15); (2) God's purpose to fill the earth with the knowledge of His glory will be ultimately accomplished (14); and (3), meanwhile, "the just shall live by faith" (compare Rom 1:17; Gal. 3:11; Heb. 10:37,38).

Grades of Offering

Please explain the different grades of offering under the Old Covenant. For example, in the first chapter of Leviticus, we are told that

one might make a burnt-offering of the cattle, of the herd, of the flock, or he might bring fowls, as turtle-doves or young pigeons. What in the significance of all this?

It was a provision for the poor who could not bring an expensive offering. It is one of the proofs of our Lord's earthly poverty that when Joseph and Mary presented the Child at the temple they brought an offering, and their offering was neither a bullock nor a sheep, but "a pair of turtle-doves, or two young pigeons" (Luke 2:24). Thus we see "the grace of our Lord Jesus Christ, that, though he was rich, yet for your sakes he became poor, that ye through his poverty might be rich" (2 Cor. 8:9).

But there was another significance to these grades of offering. They typify the degrees of apprehension among God's people as to the value of the one sacrifice offered at Calvary. Some of us estimate the value of the blood far more highly than others of us, and those who have a high estimate of the value of the blood devote themselves more fully to the service of God than the others of us, and those who have a high estimate of the value of the blood devote themselves more fully to the service of God than others. That is to say, they bring a larger offering than the others.

The three grades of offering appointed to believers are found in Romans 12:1,2 where we are besought to present our living bodies to God, and in Hebrews 13:15,16 where we are exhorted to "offer the sacrifice of praise to God continually"; and "to do good, and to communicate (that is, to share what we have with others): for with such sacrifices God is well pleased."

The believer who properly evaluates the sacrifice of Calvary says from his heart:

"Were the whole realm of nature mine,
That were an offering far too small.
Love so amazing, so divine,
Demands my soul, my life, my all."

Salvation in the Present Time

Please explain Romans 3:25.

The passage teaches that the death of Christ was for believers past and future. That is to say, the work of Christ on the cross had in view those who should live afterward, and also those who had lived before the cross was set up. There is a second showing forth here. The supplied words, "I say," in both the King James Version and the Revision, spoil the sense. Paul is not merely repeating in verse 26 what he has already said in verse 25: he is saying something new. Rotherham's reading of the passage (verses 25,26) clears up the matter:

"Whom God hath set forth as a propitiatory covering, through faith in his blood, for a showing forth of his righteousness, by reason of the passing-by of the previously committed sins, in the forbearance of God—with a view to a showing forth of his righteousness in the present season, that he might be righteous even when declaring righteous him that hath faith in Jesus."

Here is the great triumph of the Gospel. God Himself is justified, and He succeeds in justifying sinful men! By the Gospel God's righteousness is shown as to the past; His righteousness is shown as to "the present time"; and His righteousness is shown in His justification of those who, on their own merits, are only unrighteous! Surely, this is a wonderful salvation, and He is a wonderful Savior!

Adoption

What is meant by the phrase, "the adoption of sons" (Gal. 4:5)?

A similar expression is found in Ephesians 1:5 where we read that God has "predestinated us unto the adoption of children." The Greek word for "adoption" is ***huiothesia***, which means "placing as a son." It does not have the same meaning as our English word "adoption" in modern usage. In olden times a boy was not called a son until he came of age; and then he was proclaimed as his father's son and heir, in a ceremony called "huiothesia."

God does not adopt those who are not His children already. Adoption is a word of position rather than of relationship. When a man is born again he becomes by that birth a child of God, and then God places him in the position of full sonship in his house. The Holy Spirit indwelling the believer assures him of this new position as a present experience. The full manifestation of this wonderful position, however, awaits the second coming of our Lord when the believer will receive his transformed body; and it will be made manifest to principalities and powers in the heavenly places that he is indeed a son of God. This is stated in Romans 8:23 where we read that we wait "for the adoption, to wit, the redemption of our body."

Children and Sons

Could you explain the first part of Galatians 4, concerning sonship? Are not all Christians sons of God?

The contrast is between the status of Jewish believers before the death and resurrection of Christ, and that of all believers, whether from among Jews or Gentiles, afterwards. In the old dispensation, believers were in the position of minor children and under the law, but in the new dispensation, believers —all of them—are in the position of full grown sons, free from the law and in partnership and fellowship with the Father. The "elements of the world" (verse 3) are the commandments of Sinai (compare verses 9 and 21 and Col. 2:20). The law was an elementary "child-guide unto Christ," that they might be justified by faith. But after faith came they were delivered from the old "child-guide," being no longer under law, but under grace (Gal. 3:23-25; Rom. 6:14). In Galatians 3:25 the word "children" should read "sons." The whole matter is worked out in the fourth chapter.

If Ye Continue

What shall we say of the words, "if ye continue," in Colossians 1:23, and "if we hold . . . steadfast unto the end," in Hebrews 3:14? What of those who do not thus continue?

Those who do not continue prove thereby that they are not really saved at all; "for if they had been of us, they would no doubt have continued with us" (1 John 2:19).

The Needle's Eye

What is meant by the words of the Lord Jesus in Matthew 19:24, "It is easier for a camel to go through the eye of a needle, than for a rich man to enter into the kingdom of God"? Does it refer to the Needle's Eye Gate in the wall of Jerusalem, through which a camel cannot go except when he is without a load and on his knees?

No, that is not His meaning. He meant to teach that it is impossible for a rich man to enter into the Kingdom of God. But, thank God, what is impossible for man is possible with God; and the way He saves a rich man is to make the rich man see that his riches are not his at all, but God's. The rich man, like any other man, must come as a helpless, hopeless, naked and undone sinner, and receive the unspeakable gift of God, which is eternal life through Jesus Christ our Lord (Rom. 6:23).

Inability to Believe

Is it ever impossible for a man to believe the gospel?

Yes, it is possible for one to come to the place where he is unable to believe. In John 12:39 it is declared of certain people that "they could not believe." And the reason given is in the words quoted from Isaiah 6: "He hath blinded their eyes, and hardened their hearts; that they should not see with their eyes, and understand with their hearts, and be converted, and I should heal them." It is tragically possible for people to trifle with God and the Word of God so long that their hearts become hardened, and they are unable to believe. The Word of God itself, unless it is believed and obeyed, becomes a snare, and through it the human heart becomes hard and callous.

It is vital to remember that God never reveals any truth to a man except to have that man obey the truth. If a man goes on obeying, God goes on revealing, but if a man disobeys and keeps on disobeying the time comes when God no longer reveals truth to him, and his eyes are blinded and his heart is hardened. In 2 Thessalonians 2:10-12 we read of "them that perish because they received not the love of the truth, that they might be saved. And for this cause God shall send them strong delusion, that they should believe a lie: that they all might be damned who believed not the truth, but had pleasure in unrighteousness." This is solemn language and we do well to take heed unto it.

Without God and Without Hope

I have a very dear friend who is fine in every respect, but he does not believe in God. He is 20 years old, and calls himself a Deist. Is there any hope for him? He says he believes in the laws of nature. Please tell me of a passage in the Bible that might mean the salvation of a really fine character.

The answer is that there is no such thing on the earth as "a really fine character." The Bible testifies that "there is no difference, for all have sinned and come short of the glory of God" (Rom. 3:22,23). Your friend, who "calls himself a Deist" and "does not believe in God" is in awful peril, for he makes God a liar, he treads underfoot the Son of God, making the blood of the covenant an unholy thing, and does despite or insult to the Spirit of grace (Heb. 10:29). He is not in danger of being lost, but he is already lost. He is "condemned already because he hath not believed in the name of the only begotten Son of God" (John 3:18). He is without Christ, without God, and without hope, unless he turns to the Lord, confessing himself as a helpless and lost sinner, and receiving the Son of God as his Savior and Lord (John 1:11-13).

Universal Redemption

If, as you teach, the sins of the whole world were laid on Jesus as He died on the cross, why is not the whole world saved?

The whole world would be saved if salvation were only forgiveness, or even justification (Rom. 5:18,19). But salvation is life; and the world is lost because it will not come to Him who offers life (John 5:39,40; Rom. 5:21; 6:23). The Bible certainly does not teach universal salvation, but it just as certainly teaches universal redemption. The blood was shed for all men (1 John 2:1,2; Heb. 2:9; 1 Tim. 4:10).

Mystery of the New Birth

Can you explain the new birth?

No. The second birth is a mystery, and so is the first birth. No one is able to explain either of them. We know only that in the first birth certain causes produce certain effects, and that in the second birth certain causes produce certain effects. The second birth is a birth, no less than the first. And just as one must be born in order to enter into the natural life, so, "except a man be born again, he cannot enter into the Kingdom of God" (John 3:1-8). This new birth is "of the Spirit," through the Word (James 1:18); and it is unto life eternal, since the Word is incorruptible seed, which "endureth for ever" (1 Peter 1:22-25).

Assurance of Salvation

How do you know you are saved, and what do you do if you doubt your salvation?

I know I am saved because of the testimony of the Word of God. I have confessed with my mouth Jesus as Lord, and I have believed with my heart that God hath raised Him from the dead, and His Word says that whosoever does those two things shall be saved (Rom 10:9,10). Then, too, there are many tests laid down in the Word of God by which we may determine whether we are saved. What is your attitude toward the Bible itself? If you are saved, the Bible speaks to your heart, and you hear in it the voice of your Father, and the call of your Shepherd. Then, too, if you are saved you have a peculiar affection for others who are saved. "We know that we have passed from death unto life, because we love the brethren" (1 John 3:14). There is no need for anyone to remain in doubt about his salvation. See 1 John 5:13.

Must One Hear the Gospel to Be Saved?

Can a person who never heard the Gospel but has read it from the Bible or from a tract, be saved if he or she believes on the Lord Jesus Christ?

Certainly. Believing the Gospel is what saves. And whether it be heard or read is not important. The great thing is to believe it. It is true generally that "faith cometh by hearing, and hearing by the Word of God" (Rom. 10:17), but certainly that would not hinder a person who is totally deaf from being saved because he could not hear the Gospel. It is written in Romans 10:9,10, "that if thou shalt confess with thy mouth," etc., but that would not hinder a dumb man without the power of speech, from being saved. There are other ways of confessing besides with the mouth. "By grace are ye saved through faith" (Eph. 2:8).

The Believer's Assurance

Please comment for us on Isaiah 32:17.

Isaiah 32:17 reads: "And the work of righteousness shall be peace; and the effect of righteousness quietness and assurance forever." It is a splendid statement of the believer's assurance and the ground for it. The believer is assured of salvation because of the work of righteousness wrought out for him on the cross of Calvary by the Lord Jesus when He died for our sins according to the Scriptures. He was "delivered up for our offenses, and was raised again for our justification" (Rom. 4:25), and this justification is our righteousness, and the effect of this righteousness is "quietness and assurance forever." The believer is saved by grace through faith plus nothing. And whoever is saved is safe forever.

Not Cast Out

Just what is the meaning of the words of our Lord in John 6:37, "him that cometh to me I will in no wise cast out"? Did He mean that those who came would surely be received? Or is there some further meaning?

There is indeed "some further meaning," and it is precious. Of course, all who come to Him He will surely receive, but that is not His meaning here. Please read the words you have quoted, together with the three verses immediately following them:

"Him that cometh to me I will in no wise cast out. For I came down from heaven, not to do his own will, but the will of Him that sent me. And this is the Father's will which hath sent me, that of all which he hath given me I should LOSE NOTHING, but should raise it up again at the last day. And this is the will of Him that sent me, that every one which seeth the Son, and believeth on him may have everlasting life: and I will raise him up at the last day."

The teaching here is that, once He gets us, He will never lose us: the life He gives is everlasting, and can never stop. Those whom He saves are forever safe.

The Way Back to God's Fellowship

I was saved at the age of 19, and I never doubted that God intended that I should one day preach the gospel. But I fell into deep sin, and I have felt myself to be accused of God—very much so. His displeasure has been unmistakable. It is hard for me to see how a man could ever be just like he was after such defilement, even though he should repent and be forgiven. It will be my lasting regret. I remember your having stated in an article that "backsliding is always attended by immeasurable loss." That is certainly true, as I can well testify. If I had gone ahead with God I would be a thousand times better off today. I am in the dark, and doubts and perplexities have multiplied. Can you help me?

Please let me thank you for writing me of your trouble. It is well that you are troubled, for it would be too bad if God permitted an estranged child to be happy out of His fellowship. You are having the experience of the prodigal son who could not thrive on hog food and longed for his father's house.

But, my dear brother, you must stop walking in unbelief, for that is the worst kind of sin you could commit in God's sight. When He says that "if we (that is we, His children) confess our sins, He is faithful and just to forgive us our sins, and to cleanse us from all unrighteousness" (1 John 1:9), He means just that, and it is for us to believe Him, and to receive with joyful assurance the forgiveness He so freely gives. If we fail to do this, we are denying the value of the blood of Calvary, which God says "cleanseth us from all sin" (1 John 1:7).

Count on His faithfulness, and rejoice in sins forgiven, and then go to work to testify of His goodness, and tell others about His readiness to save. "He that winneth souls is wise." Get your eyes off yourself, and exert yourself to get others saved, and then you may expect your Heavenly Father to restore unto you the joy of His salvation.

Forgiveness

Can a true Christian hold a grudge? In the Lord's prayer it says "forgive us our trespasses as we forgive," etc. Do we not have to forgive before we can expect forgiveness?

A truly regenerated person may fall into a backslidden state, and be out of fellowship with his Father; and while in that state he may do many sinful things, even "hold a grudge." The so-called Lord's prayer, given to Jewish disciples under law, does not give the basis of forgiveness in this day of grace. You will find the true basis for us in Ephesians 4:32, "forgiving one another, even as God, for Christ's sake, hath forgiven" us. Of course, a backslidden Christian, so long as he walks in sin, whether holding a grudge or something else, loses his fellowship with God, his joy, his testimony and his fruitfulness. The way back for him is to confess and forsake his sin. "If we (that is, we Christians) confess our sins, he is faithful and just to forgive us our sins, and to cleanse us from all righteousness" (1 John 1:9).

Retroactive Atonement

Is it true that the death of Christ on Calvary was retroactive in its effects?

Yes. In God's plan of redemption, His Son was reckoned as "the Lamb slain from the foundation of the world" (Rev. 13:8), and it was by His blood, already in God's reckoning shed on Calvary, that Old Testament believers were saved. Their sins were imputed to Christ beforehand. This is the meaning of Romans 3:25, where we read that God set forth His Son as "a propitiation through faith in his blood, to declare his righteousness in the remission of sins that are past through the forbearance of God"; and also of Hebrews 9:15, which shows that on the cross the Son of God died "for the redemption of the transgressions that were under the first testament."

Grace for Grace

What is the meaning of John 1:16: "And of his fullness have all we received, and grace for grace"?

This verse contains a truly wonderful statement. The thought is that when one is born again he receives the Lord Jesus Christ as the unspeakable gift of God; "of his fullness have all we received." When we receive Christ we receive "of his fullness." In Colossians 2:9,10, it is written: "For in him dwelleth all the fullness of the Godhead bodily. And ye are complete in him, which is the head of all principality and power."

At the moment of the new birth all this fullness becomes the possession of the believer. This does not become manifest all at once, nor indeed will it be fully manifest until the believer is finally presented "faultless before the presence of his glory with exceeding joy" (Jude 24). When one is born again he becomes at once a son of God, "and it doth not yet appear what we shall be: but we know that, when he shall appear, we shall be like him; for we shall see him as he is" (1 John 3:1,2).

"We shall be like him," and this will be true in the most absolute sense; we shall be like Him, and in us every beauty of His adorable Person will be duplicated. This is the meaning of the clause, "grace for grace." The Reviser's marginal rendering is "grace upon grace." The preposition rendered "for" or "upon" might even more literally be rendered, "corresponding to." Thus we should read, "And of his fullness have all we received, and grace corresponding to grace." Every grace in Him will be reflected in us, just as in the mirror every detail of one's face is reflected. This is the goal awaiting us at the end of our course. What a wonderful Savior!

The Spirit and the Letter

What does Paul mean in Romans 2:29 when he says: "But he is a Jew, which is one inwardly; and circumcision is that of the heart, in the spirit and not in the letter; whose praise is not of men, but of God"? My difficulty is with the phrase, "in the spirit, and not in the letter."

You will find a similar expression in Romans 7:6 where Paul writes: "But now we are delivered from the law, that being dead wherein we were held; that we should serve in newness of spirit, and not in the oldness of the letter." "The letter" is the law of Moses to which the believer is dead and from which he is forever free, while "the spirit" signified the relation of the believer to Christ through the new life received in his new birth.

This matter will be cleared up even further by a study of 2 Corinthians 3, where Paul presents a series of contrasts between the law and the gospel, and where Paul declares that he is a minister of the new covenant, "not of the letter, but of the spirit; for the letter killeth, but the spirit giveth life" (verse 6). In verse 7 he speaks of the law, that is, the letter which killeth, is "the ministration of condemnation," while the gospel is called, "the ministration of righteousness."

The law utterly condemns the best man in the world, while the gospel utterly justifies the worst man in the world who believes it. In verse 11 Paul declares that the law which was glorious is "done away," while the gospel which is even more glorious "remaineth." "The contrast," says Dr. Scofield, "is not between two methods of interpretation, literal and spiritual, but between two methods of divine dealing: one through the law, the other through the Holy Spirit." In 2 Corinthians 3:18 the ministry of the Holy Spirit in the life of the believer is wonderfully set forth in these words: "But we all, with open face beholding as in a glass the glory of the Lord, are changed, into the same image from glory to glory, even as by the Spirit of the Lord."

Why Men Are Lost

Three fine young married men worked in a bank. None of them was a member of any church. One day a bandit robbed the bank and murdered the three young men. The bandit was captured and sentenced to death. Prior to his death, a preacher talked to him and he was converted. He died with the church's blessing. Then said the lecturer, "You tell me this murderer swung off the gallows into everlasting glory and looked down from the safe battlements of glory and saw in the place of pain below the three men he had shot down in their unregenerate state?" Would you explain the fallacy in this reasoning?

The three bank clerks, if they were lost, were lost because they had persistently rejected the gift of God which is eternal life. They hadn't killed anyone, but they had done that which is much worse; they had trodden under foot the Son of God, making the blood of the covenant an unholy thing, and doing despite unto the Spirit of grace (Heb. 10:29). The murderer, if he was saved, was saved because Christ had died for his sins and he had believed on Him unto salvation. "Whosoever will may come."

The Peril of Rejecting Christ

What is the meaning of 2 Peter 2:20?

It is a warning to those who know the way of salvation and still reject it. The three verses, 20 to 22, should be read together: "For if after they have escaped the pollutions of the world through the knowledge of the Lord and Savior Jesus Christ, they are again entangled therein, and overcome, the latter end is worse with them than the beginning. For it had been better for them not to have known the way of righteousness, than, after they have known it, to turn from the holy commandment delivered unto them. But it is happened unto them according to the true proverb, The dog is turned to his own vomit again; and the sow that was washed to her wallowing in the mire." There is no conceivable way for a dog or a hog to become a sheep except to be born again. And so there is no conceivable way for a sinner to become a child of God except to be born again. It is not enough to know the gospel. The gospel must be believed and obeyed.

A Christian

What is a Christian, and how does a man become a Christian?

A Christian is a born-again person. The Church of God is made up of all those, and only those, who are born again, born from above by grace through faith in the Lord Jesus Christ. The way to become a Christian is to receive the Lord Jesus Christ as one's own personal Savior. There is no other way. Receiving Christ is what the New Testament means by believing on Christ. This is shown by John 1:11-13, where the phrase, "as many as received him," is made equivalent to "them that believe on his name."

May Small Children Be Converted?

Please inform us about the conversion of small children. Is it true that they may be really converted?

It depends upon what you mean by "small." Of course, it is impossible for a babe in arms to be converted, but many eminent men have become intelligent and powerful Christians who were converted at a very early age. Isaac Watts was born again at the age of nine years, Jonathan Edwards at seven and Robert Hall at twelve. I myself am personally acquainted with thorough-going Christians who were born again as young as five years of age. But such cases are exceptional. Care should be taken, for instance, in the present child evangelism movement, lest the children "raise the hand" or "come forward" to please a much-loved teacher, when there may have been no change whatever in the children's hearts toward God. But care must be taken, too, in the case of older folks. We have all seen them coming forward when "the doors of the church" were opened and have seen them received into the membership with what seemed very superficial examination. Well, let us take it right home, and take heed to the exhortation, "Examine yourselves, whether ye be in the faith." And let us remember also the words of Matthew 18:3: "Except ye be converted and become as little children, ye shall not enter into the kingdom of heaven."

How Children Are Saved

Do you think that children of unbelieving parents, dying before they reach the age of accountability, are lost? I always thought they would go to Heaven, but some time ago a minister said they would be lost, and gave Psalm 58:3 as his reason. What do you think?

Psalm 58:3 says: "The wicked are estranged from the womb: they go astray as soon as they be born, speaking lies." Children are sinners, and therefore they need salvation. Since Jesus died for all, He died for the children whether their parents are believers or unbelievers. And such children, dying before the age of accountability, are under the blood and saved by the blood.

Watch for Your Children's Salvation

I have a problem that is worrying me a lot these days. I have one child, a girl, that I have given Bible instructions to since she was old enough to understand. I taught her the meaning and use of prayer, so I know many times in her grade school days when she was 8 or 9 years, she has told me how she asked God to help her solve many problems. When she was about 14 years there was much talk about our ancestors being monkeys, but she said, "No one can make me believe that." I was so happy about her and felt sure she was going to grow up to be a servant of God and to help in His work. When she was about 16 years a change came over her and when I mention anything about the Bible it seems to annoy her and she seems to have lost interest. Do you think that she was really saved at that early age and that God will in some way bring her back?

But did you ever definitely tell your child the way of salvation, and seek to lead her to receive the Lord Jesus Christ as her personal Savior? From all you tell me, she may have never been saved at all. Let us be more thorough and watchful, lest we fail to lead our children aright.

Children in the Kingdom

Is there any Scriptural foundation for the teaching that there will be infants and other children taking part in the first resurrection and that they will reign with Christ a thousand years?

I am convinced that unaccountable children are saved by the blood of Christ and that they will participate in the first resurrection and the Rapture. But I have no light upon the question as to what their part will be in the Kingdom.

Children in the Rapture

What Scriptural light is there as to the effect of the Rapture of the Church on children who have not reached an accountable age? Is there any difference between children of saved and unsaved parents in that event?

I know of no Scripture bearing directly upon your question. I have no doubt that all who die in infancy, whether children of saved or of unsaved parents, are saved through the blood of Christ. Since the Rapture is a deliverance from the terrible judgments of the Great Tribulation, I am satisfied that all infants, since they are in a state of safety at the time of the Rapture, will be taken away with the Church. Yet I speak reservedly for I am afraid of purely inferential doctrines and of conclusions based upon implications only.

The Case of a Child Born Dead

Has God told us whether a still-born infant has a living soul? What does the Bible say to a mother whose baby never breathed?

The fact that the child "never breathed" after birth does not alter the fact that it certainly lived in the mother's womb before birth. It therefore had a living soul and spirit, as well as a living body, in the prenatal state, and is safe in Him who died for us all, and who said of little children, "Of such is the kingdom of God" (Mark 10:14).

Called and Chosen

Will you please give the meaning of the last part of Matthew 20:16— "for many be called, but few chosen"?

The clause referred to is found also in Matthew 22:14, and in both instances it relates to a Parable of the Kingdom. In the case you cite the question is one of rewards rather than of Salvation. "Many are called to work in God's Vineyard," says Archbishop Trench, "but few retain that humility, that entire submission to the righteousness of God, that utter abnegation of any claim as of right on their own part, which will allow them in the end to be partakers of His reward." And Mr. Spurgeon, writing upon the Parable of the King's Son, said: "Those who were 'called' included the rejecters of the King's invitation; who, by their refusal, proved that they were not 'chosen.' Even amongst those who accepted the invitation there was one who was not 'chosen,' for he insulted the King in His own palace, and showed his enmity by his disobedience to the royal requirements. There were, however, 'chosen' ones; and sufficient to fill the festal hall of the great King, and to render due honor to the wedding of His Son. Blessed are all they that shall sit down at the Marriage Supper of the Lamb! May the writer and all his readers be amongst that chosen company, and forever adore the distinguishing grace of God which has so highly favored them!"

Many Called, but Few Chosen

It is said by some that Christ taught a distinct separation or class condition of His followers in saying, "Many are called but few are chosen," and that this is emphasized in the Parable of the Ten Virgins. In this they teach that the wise virgins are the Spirit-filled, and only they will be caught up in the Rapture—all others must pass into the Tribulation. Does not this savor of the spirit of Seventh-Day Adventists who claim that they alone are the 144,000?

In the above Parable is not the expression positive that the foolish "took no oil" in their vessels? Can the word "vessels" possibly refer to the body in distinction from the spirit?

The Parable of the Ten Virgins has no direct reference to Christians of any "class"; it refers to professing Jewish disciples of the Great Tribulation period, some of them true believers and some mere professors, "having not the Spirit" (Jude 19; compare Rom. 8:9 and context).

The "vessels" of the Parable are unquestionably the bodies (See 1 Cor. 6:19,20).

Any teaching is mischievous which divides born-again ones into "classes." The Spirit of Truth is always careful to preserve in His teaching the unity of the body. The Rapture is for all who belong to the Lord, and He "knoweth them that are his."

Saved by His Life

What is meant by the words in Romans 5:10, "We shall be saved by his life"? I supposed we were saved by the death of Christ rather than by His life.

It is true that we are saved by His death on Calvary, but we are kept saved by His life in resurrection power. This is the argument throughout the passage to which you refer, Romans 5:8-10: "God commendeth his love toward us, in that, while we were yet sinners, Christ died for us. Much more then, being now justified by his blood, we shall be saved (kept safe) from wrath through him. For if, when we were enemies, we were reconciled to God by the death of his Son, much more, being reconciled, we shall he saved (kept safe) by his life."

This is the teaching of Hebrews 7:25: "Wherefore he is able also to save them to the uttermost that come unto God by him, seeing he ever liveth to make intercession for them." And this is the meaning of our Lord's assuring words in John 14:18: "Because I live, ye shall live also." Without His resurrection, His death on the cross would have been merely death.

Saved with Difficulty

In 2 Peter 1:11 we read of the "abundant entrance," yet in 1 Peter 4:18 he writes that the righteous are scarcely saved. What is the explanation of this seeming discrepancy?

The phrase "scarcely saved" means "saved with difficulty." Our salvation was God's most difficult problem, for it involved His justice as well as His mercy. How could He righteously reckon righteous those who were unrighteous? He "found a ransom," and by the death of His Son, that Son Himself being a willing sacrifice, God found a way, "that he might be just, and the justifier of him which believeth in Jesus" (Rom. 3:26) This is the marvel and the triumph of the gospel.

The Case of Cornelius

Was Cornelius a saved man before he sent for Peter? The words of Acts 11:14 would seem to indicate that he was not.

You are quite right; but Cornelius sought after God and was found of Him. His salvation came through hearing and believing the Gospel at Peter's mouth.

The Drawings and Desires of God

In John 6:44, will you please make it clear that God draws, and desires that all should be saved?

John 6:44 says only that no man can come to the Son unless the Father draw him, and he will be raised up at the last day. But it is clear, from other Scriptures, that God desires that all men should be saved and come to the knowledge of the truth (1 Tim. 2:4). He is "long-suffering to us-ward, not willing that any should perish, but that all should come to repentance" (2 Peter 3:9). This verse by no means clears up the relation between the doctrines of divine sovereignty and human freedom, both of which are Bible doctrines and true. The true attitude of faith is to believe them both and then to follow the old Pastor's example who said: "I pray for my people as if everything depended upon God, and then I preach to them as if everything depended upon them." That is a good rule to follow.

The Gift of God

In Ephesians 2:8 it says: "For by grace are ye saved through faith; and that not of yourselves: it is the gift of God." To what does the pronoun "it" refer? Is it grace? Some have thought it was faith. One man thought it meant salvation. What would you interpret it to mean?

There may be some question as to precisely what is referred to here as being "the gift of God"; but it is certain that the "grace," the "faith," and the "salvation," are all included in "the gift of God" which is "eternal life in Christ Jesus our Lord" (Rom. 6:23, R.V.).

Thou and Thy House

I have a family of persistent unbelievers with as strong a set of wills as probably exist. They will sometimes listen to the Word in obdurate silence and utmost indifference, but never yield an inch. I have faith that constant prayer will effect what would be nothing short of a miracle in their case. Is there any practical consolation to be had in Acts 16:31? Was that invitation specific only to the jailer and "his"

family, or can I also take it? Even then, how can it be taken literally? Each one must make "his own" peace with God through Jesus Christ, and not one for another—so wherein does this promise count? I am sorely tried.

The language of Acts 16:31, taken by itself, is capable of two constructions: either, "Believe on the Lord Jesus Christ, and thou shalt be saved, and (by reason of thy belief) thy house also shalt be saved" or, "Believe on the Lord Jesus Christ, and thou shalt be saved; and this is true not only for thee, but it is also true that if thy house believe on the the Lord Jesus Christ, it too shalt be saved." The context shows that the latter construction is correct. For the preachers "spake unto him the word of the Lord, *and to all that were in his house*," with the result that the jailer "rejoiced, believing in God *with all his house*." Of course, each person had to believe for himself. Keep right on with your praying to God for your own house, and keep on in your faithful testimony, leaving it all with Him who knows all about it and "judgeth righteously."

How Shall We Escape?

Is Hebrews 2:3 for the saved or the unsaved?

It is for the unsaved. The saved *are* saved just because they have not neglected "so great salvation."

Salvation for Murderers

Is a person who commits murder forever lost, regardless of repentance after?

Salvation is freely offered to sinners who come to God through Jesus Christ His Son. David was a murderer, but God forgave him and received him. Whosoever will may come.

Adam's Salvation

Can you tell us whether or not Adam was saved? And will you kindly give some Bible reasons for your answer?

I have no doubt that Adam was saved. The fact that he called his wife's name Eve (meaning living or life-giver), "because she was the mother of all living" (Gen. 3:20), proves that he believed the promise of God with reference to the coming Redeemer who should be the Seed of the woman.

Salvation and Rewards

If after a number of years of faithful service a Christian should stumble, does he lose his reward for the work that has been done previously? Kindly give Scriptures pointing out your answer.

Salvation is a gift, and rewards are earned by works. Salvation is a present possession, and rewards are a future attainment. God is not unfaithful nor forgetful and will certainly reward His faithful servants for every faithful service. On the other hand, He is sure to faithfully chasten those whom He loves and who are in need of chastening. We may depend upon the Judge of the whole earth to do right. Read 1 Corinthians 3:11-15; 11:31,32; 2 Corinthians 5:10; Hebrews 12:1-11.

Rewards

Will there be rewards in Heaven, or only in the Millennium?

Both.

Degrees of Rewards

Are there differences in rewards for believers?

Yes. Read 1 Corinthians 3:11-15. Rewards are to be distinguished from salvation. Salvation is a free gift while rewards are earned by works. Salvation is a present possession while rewards are a future attainment.

Crowns

What is the significance of crowns in the Scriptures, such as the crown of glory, etc.?

Salvation and rewards are carefully distinguished in Scripture and crowns are rewards. Salvation is a gift, while rewards are earned by works. Salvation is the believer's present possession, while rewards await the judgment seat of Christ (1 Cor. 3:11-15). There are five crowns offered for rewards: (1) The crown of rejoicing, for faithfulness in service (1 Thess. 2:19,20; Phil. 4:1); (2) the crown of righteousness, for faithfulness in testimony (2 Tim. 4:8); (3) the crown of life, for faithfulness under trial (James 1:12; Rev. 2:10); (4) the crown of glory, for faithfulness in suffering (1 Peter 5:4; Heb. 2:9); (5) the crown incorruptible, for faithfulness in the exercise of self-control in the race for Christ's approval (1 Cor. 9:24-27).

Salvation of Unitarians and Roman Catholics

How can a Unitarian who denies the atonement, who teaches salvation by character instead of grace, and who counts the blood of Jesus Christ of no more importance when it was shed upon the cross than when it was flowing through His veins be saved? How about Hebrews 9:22? How about the book of Galatians, which was written especially to show the evils of the admixture of law and grace?

How can a Roman Catholic be saved, who counts the word of the priest of greater import than the Word of God, and who believes that when, in the confessional, the priest raises his hand and says, "I absolve thee," his sins are forgiven without ever going to Christ Himself?

Unitarianism is non-Christian, and so also is Roman Catholicism. Yet I have no doubt that there are individuals in both these communions who, in spite of the system with which they are connected, are nevertheless believers on the Lord Jesus Christ as the Son of God and as God incarnate; and, of course, if there are such, they are saved.

I remember a dear old man I once knew in Pennsylvania who was related to the Hicksite Quakers, and the Hicksite Quakers, as you know, are Unitarians. I was invited by this man to teach a weekly Bible class in his home which I did for quite a long time; and although he continued even to his death with the Hicksite Friends, yet he confessed to me that he believed in the Lord Jesus Christ and worshiped Him as God in the flesh.

Training has much to do with these things. Let us thank God that He knows those who are His. And no matter what their relation may be to this or that or the other group, nevertheless, if they are born again they belong to Him.

How to Tell

Since the Bible is so easy to understand that even a wayfaring man or a fool shall not err therein (Isa. 35:8), how can men of God differ so much in the exposition of the Scriptures? Is it possible for both to be filled with the Holy Spirit? How can we tell which is right?

The answer to your question is in the second chapter of the First Epistle of John. Every child of God has the Holy Spirit dwelling within him, and he must study the Word of God for himself under the Spirit's guidance and not be guided by any man. Read especially verses 20 to 27.

Walking in the Flesh

Please explain Romans 8:12-14.

There will be no difficulty at all in understanding these verses if you will see that in this chapter walking in the flesh is simply an unsaved man trying to get saved through his own efforts. The whole argument of Romans 8 hinges on the question as to whether one is truly saved or not. The word "brethren" in verse 12 might present a difficulty, but I do not think it does. Paul is addressing his argument to a Christian church, but the argument itself is upon the question as to how men are saved. Salvation comes not through walking after the flesh and seeking by fleshly efforts to make oneself presentable to God, but rather through walking after the Spirit, that is, giving up all self efforts and depending only upon the Spirit of God to accomplish the work including regeneration and all that follows.

It is Possible

Is it possible for the regenerate man to walk in the flesh? We read in many of the Epistles of a whole list of sins which are of the flesh, and it is declared that all they which do such things shall not enter into the Kingdom of God.

It is, alas, quite possible for the believer to walk in the flesh for the flesh in the believer is unchanged. It is exactly the same as the flesh in an unbeliever. By the flesh, of course, is meant the old nature, born of Adam, which remains unchanged and unchangeable until we are changed into the Lord's image at His coming.

Meanwhile, if we walk in the flesh, God will chasten us for He is a faithful

Father. The reference to "those which do such things" is to the natural man who is not born again. We must interpret these passages in the light of the general teaching of Scripture on the subject.

Sincerity in Error

I know some people that are holding to erroneous beliefs concerning the Bible and salvation, and I am interested in this question: Will such people, when they are perfectly sincere, be lost just because they hold such teachings?

Saul of Tarsus was sincere when he held erroneous belief regarding salvation, but he was lost until he received the Lord Jesus Christ as his own personal Savior. Sincerity is a good thing if it is directed in the right way, but sincerity in error is dangerous. Salvation does not lie in that direction: "for by grace are ye saved through faith."

Repentance and Salvation

What place has repentance in salvation? Should we tell people to repent of their sins to be saved?

The Gospel of John is the Holy Spirit's Gospel Tract, written that men might believe that Jesus is the Christ the Son of God; and that believing they might have life through His name (20:31). And it does not mention the word "repentance." But that is only because repentance is a necessary part of saving faith. Strictly speaking, the word repentance means "a change of mind." It is by no means the same thing as sorrow (2 Cor. 7:10). Since it is not possible for an unbeliever to become a believer without changing his mind, it is therefore unnecessary to say anything about it. The only thing for a man to do to be saved is to believe on the Lord Jesus Christ: and to believe on Him is the same thing as receiving Him (John 1:11-13).

THE CHURCH

The Church's Mission

What is the Church's relation to Christ and to the world?

The Church is the body of Christ and also His bride. In Ephesians 2:10 the Church is called His workmanship, His masterpiece, His poem (Gr. *poiema*). It is a wonderful statement. The Church is God's masterpiece, His handiwork. In it He has fully expressed Himself; into it He has poured Himself; to it He has devoted Himself; and when it is finished, His glory shall be upon it. In the meantime we are "created in Christ Jesus" for a purpose which is "unto good works." And good works are those works "which God hath before ordained that we should walk in them." Children of God are engaged in a good work only when they are walking in the path which he has before ordained (afore prepared, R.V.) that we might walk in it. To do any other work is to be doing an evil work.

The mission of the Church in the world is one of the most misunderstood of subjects. Most people suppose that the Church is in the world to reform it and improve it and to "make the world a better place to live in." Such an idea is foreign to the Biblical conception of God's purpose in putting the Church into the world.

The Church's business in the world is to complete itself. At first thought, that seems to be far from the truth for it appears to present a selfish program which must of necessity be contrary to the mind of God. But when it is remembered that in order for the Church to complete itself it must win from the world and bring to God those who are to be members of the Church which is the body of Christ, it is seen that the mission of the Church is not selfish after all but, rather, most unselfish.

The mission of the Church is set forth briefly in Ephesians 4:12 where it is declared that the purpose of the risen Lord's ministry gifts is "for the perfecting of the saints for the work of the ministry, for the edifying of the body of Christ." But we must read this verse with care. It is not, as is so often said of it, a threefold statement. It is not for the perfecting of the saints; then, for the work of the ministry; and, finally, for the edifying of the body of Christ. It is rather a single statement. Christ's purpose in the bestowal of His gifts is, in a word, the edifying of His body, the church; and in order to achieve this end He must have ministry, that saints must be perfected, or trained; and, in order that the saints may be perfected or trained, certain men have been gifted by the Holy Spirit, and then they themselves have been given by the risen Christ to

His Church. The Revision is a great improvement: "For the perfecting of the saints, unto the work of ministering"; and so is the 1911 Bible: "For the perfecting of the saints unto the doing of service." And always with this end in view: the edifying (that is, the building up, the upbuilding, the completion) of the body of Christ, which is the Church.

According to the 13th verse all this is to go on "till we all come in the unity of the faith, and of the knowledge of the Son of God, unto a perfect Man, unto the measure of the stature of the fullness of Christ."

"Unto perfect manhood," or "unto perfect womanhood" is not at all the meaning of the phrase. It is this: God is now at work making a Man. How long it took to make the first man we may not know; but for nearly two thousand years He has been at work making the new Man. That Man is Christ. His body is the Church. Whenever a sinner is converted to Him, a new member is added to His body, and the body is that much nearer completion. This work is to go on until the last sinner to be converted in this dispensation is turned unto God, and then the perfect Man will be complete having arrived at "the measure of the stature of the fullness of Christ." The Man-child is not yet fully born; the moment he is fully born he will be "caught up unto God, and to His throne" (1 Thess. 4:16-18; Rev. 12:5).

A Perfect Man

In several of your addresses which I have heard and in your writings, commenting upon Ephesians 4:23, you have said that "God is now making a Man." This has reference to the church which is Christ's body, and commonly called also His bride. How can the Church be a Man, and it still be a bride? or do you believe that the new Jerusalem is the bride, and the present-day church the body?

The new Jerusalem is the appointed abode of the glorified church (Eph. 5; Rev. 21). I have at no time said, whether in public address or in my writings, that the Man now in process of making is the church. This Man is made up of the church as a body and Christ Himself as the Head. The church is His body, and also His bride, as taught clearly in Ephesians 5:25,26. The matter is explained by the quotation in Ephesians 5:30,31 of the words of Adam in Genesis 2:23,24. Adam was not complete in his body without Eve, who was bone of his bones and flesh of his flesh. And yet she was also his bride. The church is Eve's antitype.

The Unity of the Body

I notice that the Revised Version omits the word "broken" from 1 Corinthians 11:24, making it read, "This is my body which is for you." Please tell us if this is the correct rendering.

Yes, it is the correct rendering, and it is much to be preferred. The Holy Spirit of Truth, both in plain teaching and in type, has been careful throughout the Scriptures to preserve the unity of the body of Christ.

The passover lamb in Exodus 12, of course, was a type of the Lamb of God which takes away the sin of the world. The lamb's body was not permitted to be broken, so far as its bones were concerned. The flesh was to be eaten, and "if the household be too little for the lamb" the flesh might be shared with the neighbors; but "in one house shall it be eaten; thou shalt not carry forth ought of the flesh abroad out of the house; neither shall ye break a bone thereof" (verses 4, 46).

Again, as our Lord's body hung on the cross, it was another type of the Church which is His body (Eph. 1:22,23); therefore it was not suffered that any bone of that body should be broken (John 19:31-37).

Thus it appears that the word "broken" should not be used in connection with the Lord's Supper. The body was given for us, but it was not broken.

In Ephesians 5:30 we are told that we who are born again are "members of his body, of his flesh, and of his bones." How good it is to know that "He keepeth all his bones, not one of them is broken" (Ps. 34:20).

The Church Both Body and Bride

How can the Church be the bride of Christ if she is His body (Eph. 1:22,23)?

It is easier to ask "how" than to answer "how." These are not matters to be explained by human reasoning, but rather matters to be received by faith. They are not matters of logic, but rather matters of revelation. That the Church is both the body and bride of Christ is the plain teaching of Ephesians 5:25-33, where, in verse 31 there is a reference to Genesis 2:24, comparing the Church to Eve as a type. Eve was taken out of Adam, and therefore they were one flesh. His body was not complete without her, and she was also his bride.

The Bride of Christ

A friend of ours is quite certain that Israel is the bride of Christ, while I believe that the church is His bride. She thinks that the bride will go through the Great Tribulation, but that the church will not. In talking with her I should like to be a little clearer on a few things myself. Revelation 21:9,10 says that the New Jerusalem is the bride, and Hebrews 12:22,23 states that the church and the New Jerusalem are the same. Why do the twelve gates of the New Jerusalem bear the names of the twelve tribes of Israel?

The bride of Christ is the church (Eph. 5:25-33); this passage settles the question for me. It is true that the church is built upon the foundation of the apostles and prophets (Eph. 2:20), and therefore it is quite fitting that the foundation stones of the New Jerusalem should bear the names of the twelve apostles of the Lamb. Then, too, we are never to be allowed to forget that "salvation is of the Jews" (John 4:22), and therefore the names of the twelve tribes of Israel are associated with the gates of the eternal city. The church, which is the bride, will not pass through the Great Tribulation, for she is delivered from the wrath to come (1 Thess. 1:9,10).

Sun Worship and Sunday Worship

Can you show me what Bible difference there is between sun worship and Sunday worship?

I am not sure that I understand your question. I do not know of anyone who practices such a thing as Sunday worship. Sun worship consists in the worship of the sun, but what you call Sunday worship is the worship of God on Sunday. There is a vast difference between worshiping a day and worshiping on a day.

Ordination

What Scriptural ground is there for the "ordination" of preachers?

There are four New Testament passages referring to laying on of hands in connection with an action corresponding to ordination. The word itself in its ecclesiastical sense does not occur in the New Testament. "Ordained" in Acts 14:23 should read "elected" or "appointed," as in the Revised Version. In Acts 6 it is shown that the seven deacons after being chosen by the multitude were appointed to office by the apostles with prayer and the laying on of hands. The "prophets and teachers" at Antioch set apart Barnabas and Saul for their missionary work by laying their hands on them with fasting and prayer (Acts 13). In 1 Timothy 4:14 and 2 Timothy 1:6 the gracious gift which was in Timothy is said to have come with the laying on of hands of the presbytery (that is, a body of elders), with which Paul himself seems to have been associated. The words, "Lay hands suddenly on no man," of 1 Timothy 5:22 are also supposed by many to refer to the act of ordination.

Ordained Ministers and Their Functions

Can no one but an ordained minister serve at the communion table?

The Scripture makes no such regulation or restriction. Man "has sought out many inventions," and one of the worst of these is the distinction between so-called clergy and laity. The Bible knows nothing of this.

Disagreeing with Paul

I recently heard of a woman preacher who said that Paul was "a crusty old bachelor" and that this was the reason he objected to woman's leadership in the church. Was she right?

No. To begin with, Paul was probably not a bachelor but a widower; for while he had not a wife during his apostolic ministry, it is evident that he had previously been a member of the Sanhedrin, and its membership was confined to married men. But whether Paul was a bachelor or not is relatively unimportant. The vital point to remember is that Paul was a fully authorized apostle of Christ, and folks who talk about disagreeing with Paul's teaching in the New Testament Epistles should remind themselves that those Epistles are God's own Word. Their controversy, therefore, is not with Paul, but with God Himself. Take heed how you hear, and what you do about it! Every Christian woman should be eternally grateful for the position to which she is elevated in the New Testament Church, and she ought to be careful not to seek the position of leadership denied her, lest she grieve and quench the Spirit of God.

The Preacher's Program

Just what is the business of a preacher? I mean, what is he supposed to do who is set apart for the office or work of a pastor? Being myself a pastor, I am sometimes confused, when I see what is expected of me by my church and by the community in which I am located. Just what is my job?

It is little wonder that you are confused, for there is a very general misconception of what the preacher's duties really are. But if you are subject to the Word of God there need be no confusion concerning your "job," as you put it. Let me commend to you the preacher's program, as given by the risen Lord to His servant Paul when He Himself "ordained" him. You will find it in Acts 26:16-18: "I have appeared unto thee for this purpose, to make thee a minister and a witness both of these things which thou hast seen, and of those things in the which I will appear unto thee, delivering thee from the people, and from the Gentiles, unto whom now I send thee, to open their eyes, and to turn them from darkness to light, and from the power of Satan unto God, that they may receive forgiveness of sins, and inheritance among them which are sanctified by faith that is in me."

I can think of no higher appointment than this, and it is the appointment of every minister of Christ. Let him apply himself, first and last and all the time, to this mighty task, and he will find himself fully occupied.

Administration of the Ordinances

Yesterday I was thrust through with the accusation of modernism because, forsooth, I said that our present act of ordination had nothing to do with the administration of the ordinances; that it was purely a matter of denominational order, and not of New Testament legislation. I should greatly value your exposition of this controverted question.

I agree with you perfectly that there is no connection whatever between "our present act of ordination" and "the administration of the ordinances." Perhaps I will go even further than you and say that it is not even "a matter of denominational order" any more than it is one "of New Testament legislation." I consider it an impertinence for any denomination to set barriers about "the administration of the ordinances," and to say who may and who may not administer the Lord's Supper or baptism. It is perfectly clear to me that any believer has a right to baptize another believer and to minister the bread and wine at the Lord's table.

Clergy and Laity

Would you say that there is no difference in God's sight between a

group of believers who gather together as simple members of the body of Christ, with no humanly chosen head, but who seek to allow the Holy Spirit to minister through whom He will; and another group of believers who appoint a man to minister to them and call themselves by some other name than simply "church" or "gathering?" Where does God authorize men to appoint a man to minister to them? Have we not then clergy and laity (Nicolaitanism), which God says He hates (Rev. 2:15).

There should be no such thing in the church as clergy and laity. We teach, and hold tenaciously to, the doctrine that all the born-again ones, wherever they may be, are a common brotherhood of priests unto God. We do recognize the office of bishop (or pastor, or elder) and also that of deacon which is according to the New Testament; and it is contrary to the New Testament for any group of believers to ignore these two offices in the Church. As for Nicolaitanism, there is just as much chance for it in the one meeting you speak of as in the other; and, indeed, I have seen very much of it in meetings which were said to be gatherings simply unto the Lord's name. I thank God that I, too, with Him, hate Nicolaitanism; and if I am guilty of it in any way, I do not know it.

Gowned Ministers and Vested Choirs

What is your opinion of a vested choir and a gown on a minister? Would you wear one? If not, why not?

I am not enthusiastic over vestments in church services. But my objection to "a gown on a minister" is very much greater than my objection to "a vested choir." You ask whether I would wear a pulpit gown, and if not, why not? My answer is that I would not, and the reason is that I object to anything that smacks of priestcraft and implies that the preacher is of a different class or order from other Christians. The distinction between "clergy" and "laity" is entirely unscriptural. The Church is made up of a common brotherhood of believers constituting one common priesthood. Therefore the preacher or pastor is no more a priest than any other member of the body of Christ. This is the basis of my objection to a gowned preacher. The matter of a vested choir is more a matter of personal taste, but in my judgment it is a relic of ritualism which ought to have no place in the New Testament Church.

Joining the Church

May I ask a triplicate question? Not that I am personally in doubt, but I want the clarifying influence of your knowledge and understanding of the Scriptures.

1. Is not the church the "body of Christ?" And if so, is there any consistency in the unregenerate "joining the church"?

2. Since, as we believe, there are many instances of individuals joining the church who show no valid evidence of new birth, who is to blame ?—the church, the individual joining, the pastor receiving him, or "all" of them?

3. Do such persons "actually" become "members" of the church (the body of Christ) by having their names enrolled on a church record?

1. The church of God is the body of Christ, made up of regenerate persons only, and it is an abomination for an unregenerate person to join even a local church.

2. To receive an unregenerate person into the membership of a local church is a crime against God, against the church universal, against the local church itself, and against the person thus received. The blame must rest upon the church receiving such a person, and the pastor who acts in behalf of the church, more than upon the person himself, for he is ignorant of the whole matter and therefore does not understand the nature of his act. Some people have a long score to settle in this regard.

3. Of course, no one can become a member of the church which is Christ's body who is not born again. Enrollment on church records does not count unless one is also registered in Heaven.

The Church of Christ

Please explain why you sometimes say "church of Christ"? I cannot find it in the Bible. There is only one church spoken of in the Bible and that is the church of God. All other names are man's make-up.

Maybe so. But it is difficult to understand why any one should object to calling the church by the name of Christ, since He is Head over all things unto it, and it is His body and bride. While it is true that the expression, "the church of Christ," in that form, is not scriptural, yet in Romans 16:16, Paul uses it in the plural, saying, "The churches of Christ salute you." And these are the same churches which, in 1 Corinthians 11:16; 1 Thessalonians 2:14 and 2 Thessalonians 1:4, he calls "the churches of God."

Church Discipline

What is meant in Matthew 18:18 by the words, "Whatsoever ye shall bind on earth shall be bound in heaven: and whatsoever ye shall loose on earth shall be loosed in heaven"?

It is our Lord's authorization of discipline in the then future church; verses 15-19 should be read together; and the same authorization is found in John 20:22,23. Under this authorization the church has a right to exclude a member who is living in sin and refusing to confess it and judge himself. In 1 Corinthians 5 the Apostle Paul insists upon the exercise of such discipline "in the name of our Lord Jesus Christ" and "with the power of our Lord Jesus Christ, to deliver such an one to Satan for the destruction of the flesh, that the spirit may be saved in the day of the Lord Jesus" (verses 4,5). The sinning member was a child of God, but he was out of fellowship and therefore must be excluded from the fellowship of the Lord's people until he is brought to self-judgment (see 1 Cor. 11:31,32). Our Lord's words to Peter in Matthew 16:19 refer to a quite a different matter. The pronouns "thee" and "thou" are singular rather than plural as in the other passages, and here our Lord is delivering to Peter the keys which he used in Jerusalem (Acts 2), Samaria (Acts 8), and Caesarea (Acts 10), admitting Jews, Samaritans and Gentiles into the Kingdom of Heaven.

Head Covering

I should like to know your teaching on head covering (1 Cor. 11).

The teaching of the chapter referred to is that women ought not to attend the assembly with bare heads, and that men ought not to cover their heads when attending the assembly. It is purely a question of Christian order and whether the Lord's people are willing to submit themselves to the Word of God. Headship in the assembly is vested in the man, and woman is given in the assembly a place of subjection. Christian women ought not to complain of this, for the same New Testament which gives them this place of subjection in the Church, has delivered them from social slavery wherever it has gone, and it has given them a place of exaltation unknown where the gospel has not been preached.

Gifts from the Lost

Should gifts from the unsaved be received for the Lord's work?

No. How can they be acceptable unto God when He so plainly declares that they that are in the flesh "cannot please God" (Rom. 8:8)? How can an offering be acceptable to God coming from one "who hath trodden under foot the Son of God, and hath counted the blood of the covenant, wherewith he was sanctified, an unholy thing, and hath done despite unto the Spirit of grace" (Heb. 10:29)? "The sacrifice of the wicked is an abomination" (Prov. 21:27). In the beginning of the Church dispensation the gospel workers "went forth taking nothing of the Gentile" (3 John 7), and that is the only proper course for today.

"For the Destruction of the Flesh"

The words in 1 Corinthians 5:5: "To deliver such an one unto Satan for the destruction of the flesh," seem to me to be everything but clear as regards the action on the part of the church assembly at Corinth. What is the literal meaning? In other words, what did the assembly do when it did this?

It merely voted to exclude the offending member from fellowship in the assembly and at the Lord's table until he should be brought to repentance and restored to fellowship with God. And from 2 Corinthians 2:5-11 and 7:8-16 it would seem that precisely this result was brought about. It is a great pity that in our day church discipline is so generally a lost art.

Woman's Ministry in the Church

I wish you would discuss the question, should women teach men or preach to them? Just what privileges should they have in the churches? 1 Timothy 2:11-14; 1 Corinthians 14:33-37.

In answer to your question, I am passing on to you an article by Dr. Harry

A. Ironside, who says: "It is very easy to become one-sided in regard to scriptural doctrines and principles. One would seek to preserve the golden mean and recognize the breadth of scripture as well as its clearly defined limitations. I do not see how anyone desiring to be subject to the Word of God can refuse the plain definite instruction in regard to woman's place in the assembly as set forth in 1 Corinthians 14, and 1 Timothy 2. When the assembly is gathered together in a scriptural way then a woman's place is one of silence so far as ministry is concerned, and also I take it so far as public prayer goes. She recognizes the headship of the man through whom Christ speaks to His Church, which is aptly pictured by the subject woman. This is no slight upon the woman. It is simply the recognition of her proper place in nature. In the new creation there is neither Jew nor Gentile, male nor female, but all are one in Christ Jesus. But this does not alter our natural standing as men and women living in this world. Outside of the assembly of God other conditions prevail which are not necessarily governed by the passages referred to. First Corinthians 11 is, to my mind, utterly unintelligible unless it indicates a sphere of more or less publicity where women in the company of men are at liberty under certain conditions to pray and prophesy. Such liberty, however, needs to be carefully guarded lest it develop into license and the woman aspire to a place which God in His wisdom would shield her from.

"The blatant feminism of the present day is one of the signs of the end-times. It is but one symptom of the lawlessness of the closing days of the dispensation. Christian women should be the last to encourage anything of this kind.

"As some have raised the question as to the right of a woman to teach a Bible class or instruct in a school where both sexes are present, I should say that this has nothing whatever to do with the prohibitions mentioned above. Such a class or school does not constitute an assembly of God. It is a voluntary arrangement in which people agree to go together for instruction and help. If they choose to sit under a woman teacher, she certainly could not be charged with usurping authority. Priscilla evidently took precedence over her husband in the instruction of Apollos, and he, though an eloquent man and mighty in the Scriptures, was not too proud to learn from her. To teach in an authoritative way is forbidden the woman. To instruct in a class while maintaining her womanly character is quite in keeping with the doctrine of Scripture.

"There is another point, however, which it is well to keep in mind. When things had all gone wrong in Israel, and men had proven recreant to their trust, God raised up a woman judge and gave to Deborah a place quite contrary to the orderly condition of things. We need not be surprised if in the present confusion of Christendom (when men have failed so wretchedly to maintain the truth of God) He raises up a host of holy women to hold aloft the banner of truth which has fallen from the hands of unfaithful men.

"Some years ago, Dr. H. H. Snell, an English Bible teacher of repute, was walking along a busy street with a brother in the Lord, when their attention was attracted to two women who were conducting a street meeting, giving out the Gospel to a great throng of both sexes. The unnamed brother, a rigid stickler as to the letter of the Word, turned to the Doctor and said, 'What a disgusting thing to see those women so forgetful of their place as to be preaching in public!' The venerable Dr. Snell replied, 'My brother, it is because you and I are not there that God is using them.'"

We also append herewith Dr. Scofield's statement on the subject of woman's ministry:

"There is no verse which says a woman must not preach. Three things are forbidden to women: (1) They must not interrupt meetings where the Holy Spirit is at work, by asking questions (1 Cor. 14:23-35); (2) A woman must not 'teach.' The word *didaskein* here means, as defined by Thayer, 'to deliver didactic discourses'—that is, to teach doctrinally by authority,—as we would say, dogmatically. It is the same word used by the apostle of himself in 1 Timothy 2:7. A woman must not set herself up as an authority in matters of doctrine, like an apostle (1 Tim. 2:12); (3) A woman must not be put in a place of authority in the church, such as the office of elder would be (1 Tim. 2:12,13). The ordination of women is an abomination. It should be remembered that two great principles govern the relation of subordination in marriage (Gen. 3:16; 1 Tim. 2:13). The second is like, but has special reference to marriage as a type. The wife is to be in subjection to her husband 'as the church is unto Christ.' It is obvious that 1 Corinthians 14:34,35, relates to married women, as also do 1 Timothy 2:12 and Ephesians 5:24. The prohibition to 'teach' is, however, general. 'I suffer not a woman to teach (authoritatively)!' So far all is negative. What a woman clearly may do is (1) to 'prophesy' (1 Cor. 11:5; Acts 21:9). The gift of prophecy is not exclusively nor even chiefly foretelling, but forthtelling—speaking to edification, and exhortation, and comfort (1 Cor. 14:3). Such speaking, therefore, is permissible to women. A word as to covering the head in 1 Corinthians 11:5: Nothing could be more contrary to the whole spirit of this dispensation than to use the casual mention of an ancient custom in a Greek city as fastening a legal and, so to speak, Levitical ceremonial upon Christians in all ages. The point is that 'the head of the woman is the man.' It is the divine order. The angels know this. To them any inversion of that order would be disorder. In Corinth a shorn or 'uncovered' head in the presence of men was a badge of harlotry, and a harlot is not only a woman who sells her body, but she is a woman who has thrown off the restraints of subordination—of the divine order. In a mixed assembly, therefore, a spiritually-minded and Biblically-taught Christian woman who speaks or prays would do so in a modest and womanly manner, keeping her place in the divine order. It will be obvious, therefore, that, within the limits expressly fixed, and with the spirit of modesty and subordination, a Christian woman may exercise a wide and varied ministry. (2) She may teach, in any sense not involving dogmatic declaration of doctrine; (3) she may speak 'to edification and comfort;' (4) she may also pray (1 Cor. 11:5); and, (5) since 'him that heareth' is commanded to say 'Come,' she may evangelize."

Christian Giving

If a Christian is in a peculiar place of financial distress and receives

a gift of money to be used specifically for relief from that position, is it his duty to tithe that particular sum?

Tithing is an Old Testament law rather than a New Testament rule of giving. Under the Law the Israelites were commanded to give not merely one-tenth, but much more. First, there was the tithe (that is, one-tenth) of all produce as well as of all flocks and cattle, which was claimed by Jehovah, and which was paid in kind, or if redeemed one-fifth of its value was added. The Levites received this tithe, and they in turn paid one-tenth of it to the High Priest. Then there was a second additional tithe of field produce alone, used for celebrating the sacred feasts each first and second year at Shiloh or Jerusalem, and every third year at home with a feast to the Levites, the stranger, the fatherless and the widows. Some writers claim that there was also a third tithe for the support of the poor, though this is denied by others, who hold that the second tithe on every third year was shared by the Levites with the poor.

All this tithing was required. It must be done to obey the Law. These tithes included the Israelite's taxes. Whatever he desired to bring as freewill offerings must be added to these required offerings.

The New Testament plan of giving is in 1 Corinthians 16:2 and 2 Corinthians 9:7: "Upon the first day of the week let every one of you lay by him in store, as God hath prospered him;" and "Every man according as he purposeth in his heart, so let him give; not grudgingly, or of necessity: for God loveth a cheerful (Greek, 'hilarious') giver."

It goes without saying that Christians should give as much under grace, or even more, than the Israelites were required to give under the Law. But it is always to be a matter of the heart—"according as he purposeth in his heart." Otherwise the giving will be done "grudgingly, or of necessity," which is hateful to God; for He "loveth a hilarious giver."

All this is not to say that Christians ought to give in a haphazard and slipshod way: far from it! Our giving should be systematic, regular, proportionate—"as God hath prospered" us—and spontaneous, with a glad heart. Such giving brings delight to the heart of our Father.

And He promises to remunerate us for our giving and in due proportion to our giving. What else can the words of 2 Corinthians 9:6, 8, 11 mean? "But this I say, He which soweth sparingly shall reap also sparingly; and he which soweth bountifully shall reap also bountifully . . . And God is able to make all grace abound toward you; that ye, always having all sufficiency in all things, may abound to every good work: . . . being enriched in everything to all bountifulness, which causeth through us thanksgiving to God."

Touching the specific point raised in your question, no one can decide for you. All depends upon precisely what one may have promised to God in the matter of tithing. If one's covenant with Him includes the tithing of gifts as well as of general funds, then one must fulfill one's vow. But, even in such an event, it would be altogether too bad if he did it grudgingly or unwillingly. The heart is the thing. "For if there be first a willing heart, it is accepted according to that a man hath, and not according to that he hath not" (2 Cor. 8:12).

Tithing

How may I prove tithing belongs to the present dispensation of grace?

You cannot prove that tithing belongs to the grace dispensation for it does not so belong. It is a good thing to give proportionately as God prospers (1 Cor. 16:2), and it certainly ought to be considered a high privilege to give to God under grace as much as His people were commanded to give under law; but tithing is not laid down in the New Testament as a Christian obligation. The doctrine of Christian giving is found clearly set forth in the 8th and 9th chapters of 2 Corinthians: (1) We must first give our own selves unto the Lord (8:5); (2) our giving proves the sincerity of our love (8:8); (3) we ought to give whatever we have promised to give (8:10,11); (4) if there be first a willing mind it is accepted according to what we have and not according to what we have not (8:12); (5) if we give sparingly we shall reap sparingly (9:6); (6) let us give as we purpose in our hearts, not grudgingly or of necessity: for God loves a cheerful giver (9:7); the Greek word for "cheerful" is hilarious; God loves a hilarious giver; (7) God takes account of our giving and is both able and willing to see that all grace shall abound toward us who give with willing hearts (8:8-11); and, finally, let it be remembered that we can never give beyond His giving (8:9; 9:15).

The Limit of Giving

Are tithes the limit of Christian giving?

By no means. Tithing is not the principle of Christian giving at all, though many Christians practice tithing. The 8th and 9th chapters of 2 Corinthians contain the norm of the doctrine of Christian giving.

Dipping into the Tithe

Do you think I should be doing right to use part of my one-tenth in getting a better education? I should like to have a better education. I went only to sixth grade and had to quit at the age of 11 years. After I set aside the one-tenth I don't have enough left for an education as there are four of us to support.

The setting aside of the tithe is purely a matter of liberty, but after it is devoted to the Lord's work specifically it is better to use it that way. Pray to your Heavenly Father for guidance as to whether He would have you use a part of the tithe to get a better education.

Christian Giving

Please explain 2 Corinthians 9:6: "He that soweth sparingly shall reap also sparingly; and he that soweth bountifully shall reap also bountifully." Does this mean that if we give money for God's work He will increase our financial income?

I do not believe so. It is true that in Luke 6:38 our Lord said: "Give, and it shall be given unto you; good measure, pressed down, and shaken together, and running over, shall men give into your bosom. For with the same measure that ye mete withal it shall be measured to you again." But this word is found in connection with our Lord's teaching concerning the kingdom which is to be set up in the earth on His return. In that day the King Himself will see to it that men shall treat each other equitably and righteously. We all know that it is not so today, and that no man may trust other men to treat him fairly just because he treats them fairly. I am reminded of a child of God who was famous for his liberal support of Christian missions. He endorsed another man's paper for $150,000, and was robbed of it all. Such instances might be multiplied indefinitely. The children of God must await the setting up of the kingdom before they may expect righteous treatment from their fellow men.

In the meantime, nevertheless, the law of agriculture applies in the matter of Christian giving. Paul was discussing Christian giving when he wrote, in Galatians 6:6-8, "Let him that is taught in the word communicate unto (or, share with) him that teacheth in all good things. Be not deceived; God is not mocked: for whatsoever a man soweth, that shall he also reap. For he that soweth to his flesh shall of the flesh reap corruption; but he that soweth to the Spirit shall of the Spirit reap life everlasting."

"Life everlasting." This is the harvest. Everlasting life is God's free gift to the believer, but the believer, through his giving, may reap a rich harvest of everlasting life for others, who by his giving may hear the gospel and live by it. The harvest is a spiritual harvest; it is "of the Spirit." But it is sure. It may be delayed. It may not be gathered here, but it will certainly be gathered there.

Raising Money for the Church

Will you kindly give your belief and opinion of churches holding Sunday picnics and having stands at county fairs, etc., to raise money for the Church?

Any method employed to raise money for the Church is unscriptural which ignores the following principles laid down in the Word of God:

1. To be acceptable to God, the offering must come from His own people and not from the unsaved. The unsaved can do nothing to please God (Rom. 8:8). "Without faith it is impossible to please him" (Heb. 11:6; compare 2 Cor. 8:5).
2. It must be a free-will offering (2 Cor. 9:7).
3. It must be brought cheerfully. The Greek word for "cheerful" in 2 Corinthians 9:7 is "hilarious!"
4. It must be proportionate in view of the giver's ability (1 Cor. 16:1,2; 2 Cor. 8:12).

It is a shameful thing for the bride of Christ to pose as a beggar before an ungodly world.

Selling Books in the Church

Is it right to sell books in the church? And if so, should they be sold

on Sunday? Is it not written, "Make not my Father's house a house of merchandise," and "Remember the Sabbath day to keep it holy"?

It is so written. The former of these quotations comes from John 2:16, and the words were spoken by the Lord Jesus when He drove the sellers of sheep and oxen from the temple.

The second quotation is from one of the ten commandments given to Israel at Sinai. The record is in Exodus 20, and the fourth commandment says: "Remember the sabbath day, to keep it holy. Six days shalt thou labour, and do all thy work: but the seventh day is the sabbath of Jehovah thy God: in it thou shalt not do any work, thou, nor thy son, nor thy daughter, thy manservant, nor thy maidservant, nor thy cattle, nor thy stranger that is within thy gates: for in six days Jehovah made heaven and earth, the sea, and all that in them is, and rested the seventh day: wherefore Jehovah blessed the sabbath day, and hallowed it" (verses 8-11).

It is so written. But what is written in these two Scriptures has nothing to do with selling books in a church building, nor with selling these books on Sunday.

1. The temple in Jerusalem was God's appointed place for the worship of Israel. It was not a meeting-house, but rather a house where the people brought their offerings as provided by the law of Moses. It came to an end with the destruction of Jerusalem in 70 A.D.

The New Testament church is not a building at all, but consists of the people of God, redeemed by the blood of Christ, and is free from the law. The meeting-house is not the church, but rather the people who meet from time to time, not forsaking the assembling of themselves together. In the meeting-house the Word of God is preached, and the people contribute money to support the ministry of the Word. There is no more reason why they should not buy in the meetinghouse good books expounding the Word. Indeed, there is no better place for such sale than a Christian meeting-house.

2. Sunday is not the sabbath. There was never a sabbath but Saturday, the seventh day of the week; and the notion that the sabbath was changed by our Lord from Saturday to Sunday is utterly without foundation. The sabbath was a part of the law, which was in force only "till the seed should come to whom the promise was made" (Gal. 3:19), that is, from Moses to Christ, a period of about fifteen hundred years. The law was Israel's schoolmaster to bring them to Christ, "that they might be justified by faith." But after that faith is come, even Israel is no longer under a schoolmaster" (Gal. 3:25). The law was a ministration of condemnation and death, and is done away in Christ (2 Cor. 3:7-11). The sabbath was never given to man until the law was issued from Sinai and then only to Israel (Neh. 9:13,14). The Gentiles have never had it (Rom. 2:14). Under the law, all work was forbidden on the Sabbath, that is, on Saturday; and for picking up some sticks on that day a man was stoned to death by God's command (Num. 15:32-36).

From all this it appears that to sell good Christian literature in a church building is perfectly acceptable, and that Sunday, when more Christians gather than on any other day, is the best day to sell it.

In this connection it ought to be said that while Sunday is not a sabbath, it is nevertheless a precious day that ought to be carefully guarded by the Christian. It is not to be observed, like the sabbath, as a day of enforced idleness; but rather as a day of high privilege, presenting extraordinary opportunity to gather in the Lord's name and to make Him known to others. It is well that by civil law the first day of the week is set aside for rest, for it has been clearly demonstrated that man needs to rest from his usual labors once a week, and that he can produce more in six days if he has such rest than in seven days without it.

The Institutional Church

Is it scriptural for the church to construct buildings provided with modern appliances for amusement and recreation, for the purpose of interesting young folks in the church in order that they may become Christians and members of said church?

Enormous sums of money are expended for the construction of such buildings and the conduct of great "plants" to be employed as indirect means for reaching the masses and making them Christians. If one-half of the money expended in huge church "plants" were devoted to actual evangelization, the work of God would prosper in a much greater degree than under all the indirect methods invented by man. This applies also to the work of foreign missions where so frequently the efforts of the missionaries are toward extraneous by-products rather than the work of preaching the Gospel of grace. May God deliver us all from this grievous error!

Denominations

Does God want the mischief done by denominations continued under the name of interdenominations?

Certainly not, for God is not the author of mischief. How long He may allow the present state of things to continue is not revealed. We only know that the end of it all will be sure. Those who are truly His own by the new birth will be gathered to Him in the Rapture of 1 Thessalonians 4:13-18 and the remaining mass of profession will be spewed out of His mouth (Rev. 3:14-16).

Legalism and Schism

Give the distinction between the legalism of those who sought to put Gentile believers under the law of Moses, and those who were "of Christ."

There is little or no relation between these two classes. The legalists in their ignorance of the gospel of the grace of God sought to set up the Law of Moses as the rule of the believer's life. The sufficient answer to legalism is the epistle to the Galatians, and in that epistle the curse of God is pronounced upon any preacher who proclaims the false gospel of legalism.

Those who spoke of themselves as "of Christ" (1 Cor. 1:12) were a faction in the Corinthian Church as truly as those who spoke of themselves as "of Paul," or "of Apollos," or "of Cephas." They were all guilty of schism, and the "of Christ" party were as guilty as the others. Indeed, it may be that they were more guilty than the others for it is more than likely that through a professed adherence to Christ, they were seeking to set aside the apostolic authority of Paul. Frequent allusions to such objectors to his authority are found in both of the Corinthian epistles.

"We discover," says Dean Alford, "very plain signs of an influence antagonistic to the apostle having been at work in Corinth. Teachers had come, of Jewish extraction (2 Cor. 11:22), bringing with them letters of recommendation from other churches (2 Cor. 3:1), and had built on the foundation laid by St. Paul (1 Cor. 3:10-15) a worthless building on which they prided themselves. These teachers gave out themselves for apostles (2 Cor. 11:13), rejecting the apostleship of Paul (1 Cor. 9:2; 2 Cor. 10:7,8), encouraging disobedience to his commands (2 Cor. 10:1, 6), and disparaging in every way his character and work for the gospel. It is probable that these persons were excited to greater rage against St. Paul by the contents of the first Epistle; for we find the plainest mention of them in the second."

Will the Church be Divided in Heaven?

Does the Bride of Christ include the whole Church, or only "the overcomers"?

The bride includes all those who are born again during this dispensation, and of course that means the whole church. It is unscriptural and mischievous to teach that the church will be divided in heaven, and that only a select company of particularly "holy" people will constitute the bride. It was not to such, but to the Corinthians (carnal, and yet Christians), that the Holy Spirit said, "I have espoused you to one husband, that I may present you as a chaste virgin to Christ" (2 Cor. 11:2). The conclusive doctrine of the bride of Christ is found in Ephesians 5:25-33, and the words of verse 32 leave no ground for doubt on the point raised in your question: "This is a great mystery: but I speak concerning Christ and the church"—not a part of the church, but "the church." The whole church, therefore, constitutes the Bride of Christ.

And who are "the overcomers"? They are simply *believers*; all believers are overcomers, all who are truly born again. "For whatsoever is born of God overcometh the world: and this is the victory that overcometh the world, even our faith. Who is he that overcometh the world, but he that believeth that Jesus is the Son of God" (1 John 5:4,5). These are the overcomers addressed in the letters to the churches in the second and third chapters of the Revelation. And how do they overcome? It is "by the blood of the Lamb, and by the word of their testimony" (Rev. 12:11).

The church of the living God is one, and its unity will be manifested in the ages to come, without faction or schism, without flaw or imperfection, "not having spot, or wrinkle, or any such thing. . . . holy and without blemish" (Eph. 5:27).

Organism and Organization

I find the following in "The Soul Winners' Testament": "Do not

become confused by the many false teachings (2 Peter 2:1; Matt. 15:9; 2 Tim. 3:13; 2 Thess. 2:3). The true Church is composed of regenerated individuals who are born into Christ, being an organism and not an organization." I should appreciate very much your explanation of the words "organism" and "organization," also "the true Church."

The difference between an "organism" and an "organization" is the difference between life and death. Our own human bodies are organisms, but you would hardly call them organizations. Just so the church of God is not an organization like a lodge or club or society of individuals, but it is an organism, being the body of Christ; and all its members, that is to say, all who are truly born again, and only such, are members of the real church—members of Christ's body, of His flesh and of His bones (Eph. 5:30).

Bishop, Elder and Pastor

What is the difference a bishop, a pastor and an elder?

These titles are applied interchangeably to the same person in the New Testament churches. The word "bishop" (Greek, *episcopos*) means "overseer"; "elder" (*presbuteros*) meant originally an elder man. It refers to the man, while "bishop" refers to his office. Pastor, of course, means "shepherd." See 1 Peter 5:1-5.

The Minister's Title

Should we or should we not call a minister "Reverend"?

There are some ministers who like to be called "Reverend," and there are other ministers, like myself, who prefer not to be called by that title. The word "reverend" occurs only once in the Bible; in Psalm 111:9, speaking of God, it says: "Holy and reverend is his name"; and the meaning of the word, according to Strong's Concordance, is "dreadful, frightful, terrible." I should much prefer some other epithet. Strictly speaking, and in conformity with Scripture instead of common usage, the minister should be called "Pastor" or "Elder." And, best of all, if he is born again, you may call him "Brother." For one might become a minister, and be called Pastor, or Elder, or Bishop, or Reverend, even Doctor, without being saved at all; but in order to be a brother he must be born again.

The Great Commission in Mark

Will you please explain the meaning of Mark 16:15-18? Is this the Great Commission for the church?

Since this question is a confusing one to many readers, we gladly answer it here. First, let us quote the passage in full:

"15. And he said unto them, Go ye into all the world, and preach the gospel to every creature.

"16. He that believeth and is baptized shall be saved; but he that believeth not shall be damned.

"17. And these signs shall follow them that believe; in my name shall they cast out demons; they shall speak with new tongues;

"18. They shall take up serpents; and if they drink any deadly thing, it shall not hurt them; they shall lay hands on the sick, and they shall recover."

It is perfectly clear that "these signs" do not now "follow them that believe." Mark's gospel, like Matthew's and Luke's, is primarily a kingdom book, and I am satisfied that none of them contains the Church's marching orders—not even the so-called "Great Commission" of Matthew 28:18-20. The fact that in the Acts all water baptism was in the name of the Lord Jesus and not that of the Trinity shows that the apostles were not working under the Matthew commission. To be sure, we are to preach the gospel to every creature but what gospel? The only gospel known to the synoptics was the gospel of the kingdom. Our gospel of the grace of God is found among the four evangelists only in John. The "Great Commission" of the church is in Acts 1:8, as amplified and exemplified by the apostolic practice as recorded in the whole book of Acts; as, for example, 10:47,48; 19:4,5 (compare Col. 3:17). Doubtless the "Great Commissions" of Matthew and Mark will be fulfilled after the church is completed and removed, for then it is that "this Gospel of the Kingdom shall be preached in all the world" (Matt. 24:14).

ORDINANCES OF THE CHURCH

Baptism and the Lord's Supper

Is it true, as taught in some quarters, that baptism and the Lord's Supper were temporary, and that they are not intended for the New Testament Church? What was Peter's relation to the Church?

No, it is not true. These two ordinances were given to the Church for the entire period of this dispensation. Baptism was practiced long after the "period of transition" so much spoken of by those who would have us believe that the ordinance was not given for us of the present time; indeed, it has never been suspended by any considerable portion of the Church, but has gone on till this day. Peter was, without doubt, the apostle to the Jews, but nevertheless he was sent by the Holy Spirit to open the door to the Gentiles when the first sermon to Gentiles was to be preached (Acts 10), and when his Gentile hearers believed the gospel and received the Holy Spirit, Peter, speaking with apostolic authority, "commanded them to be baptized in the name of the Lord." The apostle to the Gentiles was Paul, and in a Gentile city, Ephesus (Acts 19:1-5), finding "certain disciples" who were ignorant of the gospel, he preached Christ unto them and then re-baptized them—"they were baptized in (into) the name of the Lord Jesus." The manifestations which followed showed that what had been done in His name was approved by the risen Christ Himself, for "when Paul had laid his hands upon them, the Holy Spirit came on them, and they spake with tongues, and prophesied." There is nothing here or elsewhere to indicate that baptism was a temporary arrangement for that time and that we are to have nothing to do with it. As to the Lord's Supper, the words of 1 Corinthians 11:26, "till he come," ought to settle the matter. It is a memorial feast which is to be observed, in obedience to His Word, until we see His face. The Word is perfectly clear on these things. "Be not carried away by every wind of doctrine."

The Scriptural Order

Should unbaptized Christians partake of the Lord's Supper?

The proper order as pictured in the two ordinances is death, burial, resurrection, and then nourishing the new life by feeding upon Christ.

The Lord's Supper

A question has come up in our church with regard to the use of wine at the Lord's table. Some contend for grape juice, and others for

the fermented wine. One man will not commune because we use grape juice. I should like to have your opinion on this matter.

In the Church where I was pastor for twenty years and am still a member, we use unfermented grape juice and unleavened bread on the Lord's table.

This use is in keeping with the fact that leaven is a type of evil in the Word of God (and fermentation is only another form setting forth the same principle) and therefore we feel that anything typifying the flesh and blood of our Lord Jesus Christ ought to be free from fermentation or leaven.

However, I should not make a test of fellowship along this line. It is one of the things in which we may give each other liberty. "Let every man be fully persuaded in his own mind."

The Lord's Supper Again

What is the meaning of 1 Corinthians 11:20: "When ye come together therefore into one place, this is not to eat the Lord's supper"?

The literal reading would be, "Ye cannot eat the Lord's supper." They were going through the form of eating the Lord's supper, but they were not really eating the Lord's supper at all, but rather turning it into a disgraceful orgy. In the 17th verse he tells the Corinthians that whenever they had a meeting they came "together not for the better, but for the worse." That is to say, every meeting they had did more harm than good. We fear this may be true concerning many such meetings in these days.

The Equality of the Priesthood

If a minister is not "regularly ordained" does he have the right to serve at communion?

There is nothing in Scripture which restricts the right to serve at the Lord's Supper to ordained ministers. I know of nothing to prevent any believer thus serving at the table. The present day prevailing custom of dividing the equal brotherhood of worshiping believer-priests into "clergy" and "laity" is without a shred of authority in the Word of God.

This Is My Body

Do you believe in the real presence of Christ's body and blood in the Sacrament of Holy Communion? Does He not distinctly say: "Take, eat, this is my body"? and "Take, drink, this is my blood"?

No, I do not believe in the doctrine of transubstantiation. When our Lord said, "This is my body," He could not have meant it literally because at that moment His body was seated at the table; and, similarly, the wine in the cup could not have been really His blood, for His blood was yet in His veins. The only reasonable conclusion is that the bread and wine *represented* His body and blood. It is as if I should say of a picture on a wall, "This is my father."

Discerning the Body

Please explain 1 Corinthians 11:29: "For he that eateth and drin-

keth unworthily, eateth and drinketh damnation to himself, not discerning the Lord's body."

Let us first read the verse in the better translation of the American Revised Version: "For he that eateth and drinketh, eateth and drinketh judgment unto himself, if he discern not the body." The word "damnation" is exceedingly unfortunate here. There is no such thing possible as damnation for a believer. The people rebuked in this passage were believers, notwithstanding the fact that they were walking in the flesh and displeasing God in connection with their celebration of the Lord's Supper.

The whole passage beginning with the verse 17 should be considered. The apostle accuses the Corinthian Church of disorderliness in connection with the observance of the Lord's Supper. In verses 23-25 he gives simple instructions as to how the Supper should be eaten, and in verse 26 he gives the purpose of the Supper, which is to "show the Lord's death till he come."

Then beginning at verse 27 he speaks of the sinfulness of an unworthy observance of the ordinance. Here, too, it is better to read from the Revised Version: "Wherefore whosoever shall eat the bread or drink the cup of the Lord in an unworthy manner, shall be guilty of the body and the blood of the Lord. But let a man prove himself, and so let him eat of the bread, and drink of the cup."

We have already quoted verse 29. Verse 30 says: "For this cause many among you are weak and sickly, and not a few sleep." This means, of course, that on account of their sinful observance of the Lord's Supper God had sent among them in chastening, an epidemic of weakness and sickliness, and in many cases this weakness and sickness had resulted fatally: "not a few" had died under the chastening hand of God. Then in verse 31 (and here the Authorized Version is better) he says: "For if we would judge ourselves, we should not be judged. But when we are judged, we are chastened of the Lord, that we should not be condemned with the world."

Now to go back to your question concerning the verse 29. These believers who were eating and drinking in an unworthy manner were bringing upon themselves judgment from the hand of a faithful Father, because they were not discerning the Lord's body.

All believers are members of the Lord's body (Eph. 5:25), and except we discern His body in His members when we gather together with them at the Lord's Table, though we may go through the form of eating the Lord's Supper, we are not really eating the Lord's Supper at all. This is the point in verse 20: "When ye come together therefore into one place, this is not to eat the Lord's Supper," or as the Revised Version puts it, "When therefore ye assemble yourselves together, it is not possible to eat the Lord's Supper." They thought they were eating the Lord's Supper; they were going through the form of eating the Lord's Supper; but they were not really eating the Lord's Supper at all. They were failing to discern the true significance of the Supper and failing to discern the Lord's body in it all.

There may be some relation between all this and our Lord's revelation of Himself to the Emmaus disciples in Luke 24:13-32. While He talked with them by the way their hearts burned within them, as He opened to them the Scriptures, but they did not know Him until they saw Him breaking bread. It was then that they discerned Him and His resurrection body. And it is particularly true of a really Scriptural observance of the Lord's Supper that we discern Him in the breaking of bread.

The History of Baptism

Is there anything in Church history to indicate that the Church in the first and second century ignored or set aside believer's baptism by immersion in water? In Acts we read that when a person believed on the Lord Jesus he was baptized in water. It seems to me that all believers were baptized in the early Church. I believe that Romans 6:3,4; Galatians 3:27; and Colossians 2:12 can mean nothing else than baptism in water; but Bible teachers today say these three Scriptures do not mean water baptism at all.

How did infant baptism come in?

The early Church knew nothing of any baptism other than believer's baptism by immersion in water. It was not until late in the twelfth century that even the Roman Catholic Church considered any other baptism valid.

I think there is real ground for honest difference of opinion as to whether Romans 6:3,4; Galatians 3:27; and Colossians 2:12, refer to water baptism. For myself I believe that Romans 6:3 refers to the baptism of the Holy Spirit, and that the fourth verse refers to water baptism. But I am perfectly certain that water baptism, by immersion of believers only, is required in the New Testament. This is not to say that it is a saving ordinance, which I do not believe.

Infant baptism came in through the doctrine of baptismal regeneration when people began to believe water baptism to be necessary to salvation. Then they began to baptize infants and sick people and so on, and since they could not always immerse them, they took to pouring or sprinkling water upon them.

Baptism and Circumcision

Did baptism take the place of circumcision? If so, why is there no mention of a child being baptized in the New Testament?

No. There is no relation between circumcision and baptism, except that both are a symbol of death to the flesh. Baptism has the added significance of resurrection out of death (Col. 2:11,12). As for infant baptism, it is utterly unscriptural.

Baptism and Circumcision

Does infant baptism take the place of circumcision in this dispensation?

I will let Dr. Scofield answer this question:

The whole question of circumcision in relation to the Gentile believers in Christ in this dispensation came up before the council at Jerusalem, described in the 15th chapter of Acts. The thought of the Jewish believers in Christ was a very natural one. If the Jews must, in order to have the benefit of the Abrahamic covenant, receive circumcision, it naturally seemed to them that much more the Gentiles must receive the sign of the covenant if they were to share in its blessings. But the decision of the council at Jerusalem was that the Gentile converts did not need circumcision, and there is not in all that discussion a single hint of the notion that baptism takes the place of circumcision as a sign for Christians in this age. There is a theological teaching that as the Jews had circumcision in order to enter the Abrahamic covenant, so the Christian has baptism for the same purpose; but there is not one syllable of Scripture connecting baptism with the Abrahamic covenant. It is purely and only a theological concept. Baptism was a new ordinance instituted for believers of this age, as a public witness to identification with Christ (*Dr. C. I. Scofield's Question Box*, page 15).

No Salvation Through Baptism

Can we be saved through baptism? The teaching in one of our churches here is that a child or infant can be saved through baptism. They claim that God plants His Spirit within the soul of the child, and that this is the new birth as recorded in John 3:5; and that at confirmation this baptism is renewed, and this is the spiritual birth, or rather conversion.

Such teaching is unscriptural. The only water baptism known to Scripture is the immersion of a person after he has believed and is saved. In other words, an unsaved person ought not to be baptized at all. But a saved person ought to be baptized as a matter of obedience and testimony. The teaching that baptism at any time is a means of salvation is Satanic; and as for confirmation, multitudes have gone through that ceremony and have come out simply confirmed sinners.

All these things are the inventions of the enemy to befog the simple truth that salvation is always by grace through faith plus nothing. Ephesians 2:8-10 puts the matter in exactly the right order. Our salvation is by grace through faith, and that not of ourselves: it is the gift of God: not of works, lest any man should boast. It is a new creation "unto good works" indeed, but the good works are to follow salvation rather than precede it.

Baptism and Salvation

1. Does water baptism in any way add to salvation, or does it in any way enter into it? I cite Ephesians 2:8,9. Are we saved by faith through the blood of Christ from our original sin only, and are we obliged to atone through water baptism for those sins that have been committed from childhood until Christ was accepted?

2. What is meant, and what weight has water baptism in the phrase, "He that believeth and is baptized shall be saved"?

3. What does the word "water" mean in the phrase, "born of water and of the Spirit" (John 3:5)?

4. Is the phrase "baptized into Christ" (Gal. 3:27) water baptism or spiritual?

5. Is there remission of sins in Christian baptism as there was in John's baptism? Peter referred to it in his sermon (Acts 2:38).

1. Water baptism does not in any way add to our salvation, nor does it in any way enter into it. We are saved by faith and by grace through faith, and on the ground of the shed blood of Christ; and this, not only from our "original sin," but from "all sin, and from all our sins." The teaching that water baptism in any way atones for our sins is unscriptural.

2. The expression, "He that believeth and is baptized shall be saved" (Mark 16:16), doubtless has to do with the Kingdom age rather than the Church age. Notice the context: "But he that believeth not shall be damned. And these signs shall follow them that believe; in my name shall they cast out demons; they shall speak with new tongues; they shall take up serpents; and if they drink any deadly thing, it shall not hurt them; they shall lay hands on the sick, and they shall recover." These signs do not follow faith in the Lord Jesus Christ in this present age. They are Kingdom signs. When Peter preached on the day of Pentecost and was asked by his hearers what they should do, he answered, "Repent, and be baptized every one of you in the name of Jesus Christ for the remission of sins, and ye shall receive the gift of the Holy Ghost. For the promise is unto you, and to your children, and to all that are afar off, even as many as the Lord our God shall call" (Acts 2:38,39). By these words he did not mean to include Gentiles, but only Jews who were afar off as well as those who were present on that occasion. Up to that time it seemed that the Holy Spirit did not come upon believers until after water baptism had been accomplished. But when you come to Acts 10, where the gospel goes to the Gentiles, the order is reversed, for it was while Peter spoke that "the Holy Spirit fell on all them which heard the word." Then Peter asked, "Can any man forbid water, that these should not be baptized, which have received the Holy Spirit as well as we? And he commanded them to be baptized in the name of the Lord" (Acts 10:44-48). From that time on, as seems apparent, baptism followed salvation rather than preceded it.

3. "Water" in John 3:5 is a reference to the Word of God. The same imagery is employed in Titus 3:5 (Compare Eph. 5:25-27, James 1:18, 1 Peter 1:23).

4. The phrase "baptized into Christ" (Gal. 3:27), refers to the "one baptism" by which in the "one Spirit" the believer is baptized at the moment of regeneration into the "one body," that is, the body of Christ (Compare 1 Cor. 12:12,13, R.V.; Eph. 4:4-6).

5. There is no remission of sins in Christian baptism (I have already referred to Acts 2:38). Christian baptism has its place in the Christian life, and is a matter for the Christian's obedience; but to make it a means of salvation is to violate the teaching of Scripture and muddle the gospel of grace.

The Greek Words for Baptism

Will you please show us precisely what the Greek words mean which relate to the doctrine of water baptism?

The most frequent word relating to water baptism is *baptizo*. This word is translated "Baptist" once, "baptize" 9 times, "baptizing" 4 times, "baptizest" once, "baptizeth" twice, "baptized" 61 times, "wash" once, and "washed" once, making 80 times in all.

Baptisma occurs 26 times, and is translated "baptism" 22 times, "baptisms" once, "washing" twice, and "washings" once.

Baptismos occurs 4 times, and is translated "baptisms" once, "washing" twice, and "washings" once.

Baptistes occurs 14 times, and is translated "Baptist" 13 times, and "Baptist's" (possessive) once.

Bapto occurs 3 times, and is translated "dip" once and "dipped" twice.

Embapto occurs 3 times, and is translated "dipped" once, and "dippeth" twice.

The total is 130 times, and in every instance its meaning is to immerse, submerge, bury out of sight. No authority on New Testament Greek will dispute this statement. It so occurs that none of the Greek Lexicons or Dictionaries is the work of immersionists, and yet all agree that the words actually employed in the New Testament for baptism have the meaning we have here indicated.

We recall a warm discussion between two Presbyterian ministers, one of whom (and perhaps both) had been experiencing some uneasiness on the subject of baptism. Finally one said to the other: "Look here now. Here is one text where *'bapto'* is used and it cannot mean 'immerse.'"

"What is that?" asked his friend.

"In Luke 16:24. Here *'bapto'* is translated 'dip.' Now you know it does not mean that Lazarus was to immerse his whole hand in water."

"Ah," said the friend, who had been contending for 'immerse,' "thank you for that fine bit of evidence for my contention. Of course, Lazarus was not asked to immerse his hand, or even his finger; but he was wanted to immerse the 'tip' of his finger in the water. Tell me, how else could he 'dip' it in water?"

There was no answer for this, and it is unanswerable.

The Formula in Baptism

In view of Matthew 28:19, why do we find all through The Acts that believers were baptized in the name of the Lord Jesus only? Is the form in Matthew the correct one for the present time?

In the Revised Version, Matthew 28:18-20 reads: "And Jesus came to them and spake unto them, saying, All authority hath been given unto me in heaven and on earth. Go ye therefore, and make disciples of all the nations, baptizing them into the name of the Father and of the Son and of the Holy Spirit: teaching them to observe all things whatsoever I commanded you: and lo, I am with you always, even unto the end of the world." This we would call "The Kingdom Commission." Of course, we are well aware that it is often spoken of as "the Great Commission" of the Church, but we are convinced that this is an error. It would be a strange thing to find the Church's commission in the Kingdom Gospel.

Then, too, if we look into The Acts of the Apostles we shall find that it was not this Matthew commission under which the apostles worked. In the first place, they did not preach the Gospel of the Kingdom, which is the only Gospel known to Matthew, and which is the proclamation that "the kingdom of heaven is at hand." They preached rather the Gospel of individual salvation by the grace of God, through faith, on the ground of the shed blood of the Son of God, and this Gospel is not found anywhere in Matthew. Let it be observed also that the baptisms of The Acts are not "into the name of the Father and of the Son and of the Holy Spirit," but rather "into the name of the Lord Jesus" (Acts 2:38; 8:16; 10:48; 19:5). The commission under which the apostles wrought was that of Acts 1:8: "But ye shall receive power, after that the Holy Spirit is come upon you: and ye shall be witnesses unto me both in Jerusalem, and in all Judea, and in Samaria, and unto the uttermost part of the earth." The name of the Lord Jesus is in this day and dispensation the name which is above every name, and whatsoever we do in word or deed is to be done in the name of the Lord Jesus, giving thanks to God and the Father through Him (Col. 3:17). The Kingdom commission will come into force after the Church is gathered out, and then God will raise up a great company of evangelists out of Israel who will go everywhere with the Gospel of the Kingdom as a testimony unto all nations, and then shall come the end of the Great Tribulation period, and then shall come the Son of Man in the clouds of heaven with power and great glory to set up the promised Kingdom upon earth (Matt. 24:14).

The Baptism of Our Lord

I wish you would explain why the Lord Jesus was baptized. I heard a man who claims to be a preacher say some time ago that "Jesus was baptized because He had sinned."

But He had not sinned, nor did He ever sin, for in Him there was no sin (1 John 3:5). He Himself gave the reason for being baptized when He said to John in Matthew 3:15, "Suffer it to be so now: for thus it becometh us to fulfill all righteousness." The pronoun "us" includes all believers, for He had us all in mind. In His baptism the means of salvation is set forth in a picture. He fulfilled all righteousness for us when He died and was buried and rose from the dead. Baptism symbolizes all that, and when a believer submits himself for baptism, and is buried as a dead man, and then raised up as in resurrection, he is proclaiming his faith in Christ's death, burial and resurrection as the means by which he is saved.

Baptism for the Dead

Please explain 1 Corinthians 15:29,30: "Else what shall they do which are baptized for the dead, if the dead rise not at all? why are they then baptized for the dead? And why stand we in jeopardy every hour?" Is it true that there was in Paul's day a custom among Christians of baptizing a living believer in behalf of a dead unbeliever?

No, there was no such custom. And had there been one it is impossible to conceive of Paul mentioning it without condemning it. The teaching of the passage is this: If there is to be no victorious end of the warfare in which we are engaged why go on with it, and why continue the work of recruiting for soldiers? Believers are dying continually and thus thinning the ranks. Why go on seeking to fill up the ranks? Why go on baptizing more converts to take the room of these who have died, if there be no resurrection? It is only because we know that there is victory at the end that we must go on with the work.

Foot Washing

What is the teaching of John 13:14, "If I then, your Lord and Master, have washed your feet; ye also ought to wash one another's feet"? Is it meant to teach us to be humble?

The teaching of John 13 is to be understood in the light of the 7th verse: "Jesus answered and said unto him, What I do thou knowest not now; but thou shalt know hereafter." Simon Peter certainly understood that there was a great lesson in humility here, but there was something else he did not yet understand. Then there are the words in verses 10 and 11: "Jesus saith to him, He that is washed needeth not save to wash his feet, but is clean every whit: and ye are clean, but not all. For he knew who should betray him; therefore said he, Ye are not all clean." That certainly did not mean that Judas Iscariot had a dirtier body than the others, but only that there was this difference between Judas Iscariot and all the others: the others were true believers, but Judas Iscariot was not. They were clean every whit in the sense that they had been born again, but they needed daily to have their walk cleansed from defilement and so do we all.

Washing One Another's Feet

Please explain your belief in regard to feet washing, whether you believe it is intended for God's children of today.

I do not believe that washing one another's feet was intended as a permanent ordinance for the Church. The key to the true meaning of John 13:1-17 is the 7th verse: "What I do thou knowest not now; but thou shalt know hereafter." In the same discourse, at chapter 14:25,26, our Lord said: "These things have I spoken unto you, being yet present with you. But the Comforter, which is the Holy Spirit, whom the Father will send in my name, he shall teach you all things, and bring all things to your remembrance, whatsoever I have said unto you." And again, at 16:12,13, He said: "I have yet many things to say unto you, but ye cannot bear them now. Howbeit when he, the Spirit of truth, is come, he will guide you into all truth . . . he will show you things to come . . . he shall receive of mine, and shall show it unto you."

From all this I gather that Simon Peter and his fellow-apostles were to look under the surface for the true significance of our Lord's action in washing their feet, and await its interpretation by the Holy Spirit. This interpretation by the Holy Spirit is found, as I believe, in Galatians 6:1: "Brethren, if a man be overtaken in a fault, ye which are spiritual, restore such an one in the spirit of meekness; considering thyself, lest thou also be tempted." To wash one another's (already clean) feet in a public service is a small matter and easy as compared with cleansing a sinning saint's walk "with the washing of water by the Word."

THE GOSPEL

What Is the Gospel?

Will you tell us what is meant by the expression "the Gospel"?

Sometimes the phrase is used to indicate one of the four first books of the New Testament, as the Gospel of Matthew, of Mark, of Luke, or of John. The word Gospel means good news. In his Reference Bible, four forms of the Gospel are distinguished by Dr. Scofield as follows:

1. The Gospel of the Kingdom. This is the good news that God purposes to set up on the earth, in fulfillment of the Davidic Covenant (2 Sam. 7:16), a kingdom, political, spiritual, Israelitish, universal, over which God's Son, David's heir, shall be King, and which shall be, for one thousand years, the manifestation of the righteousness of God in human affairs. See Matthew 3:2.

Two "preachings" of this Gospel are mentioned, one past, beginning with the ministry of John the Baptist, continued by our Lord and His disciples, and ending with the Jewish rejection of the King. The other is yet future (Matt. 24:14), during The Great Tribulation, and immediately preceding the coming of the King in glory.

2. The Gospel of the grace of God. This is the good news that Jesus Christ, the rejected King, has died on the cross for the sins of the world, that He was raised from the dead for our justification, and that by Him all who believe are justified from all things. This form of the Gospel is described in many ways. It is the Gospel "of God" (Rom. 1:1) because it originates in His love; "of Christ" (2 Cor. 10:14) because it flows from His sacrifice, and because He is the lone Object of Gospel faith; of "the grace of God" (Acts 20:24) because it saves those whom the Law curses; of "the glory" (1 Tim. 1:11, 2 Cor. 4:4) because it concerns Him who is in the glory, and who is bringing the many sons to glory (Heb. 2:10); of "our salvation" (Eph. 1:13) because it is the "power of God unto salvation to every one that believeth" (Rom. 1:16); of the "uncircumcision" (Gal. 2:7) because it saves wholly apart from forms and ordinances; of "peace" (Eph. 6:15) because through Christ it makes peace between the sinner and God, and imparts inward peace.

3. The everlasting Gospel (Rev. 14:6). This is to be preached to the earth-dwellers at the very end of the Great Tribulation and immediately preceding the judgment of the nations (Matt. 25:31). It is neither the Gospel of the kingdom, nor of grace. Though its burden is judgment, not salvation, it is good news to Israel and to those who, during the tribulation, have been saved (Rev. 7:9-14, Luke 21:28; Ps. 96:11-13; Isa. 35:4-10).

4. That which Paul calls, "my Gospel" (Rom. 2:16). This is the Gospel of the grace of God in its fullest development, but includes the revelation of the result of that Gospel in the outcalling of the Church, her relations, position, privileges, and responsibility. It is the distinctive truth of Ephesians and Colossians, but interpenetrates all of Paul's writings.

There is "another Gospel" (Gal. 1:6; 2 Cor. 11:4) "which is not another," but a perversion of the Gospel of the grace of God, against which we are warned. It has had many seductive forms, but the test is this: it invariably denies the sufficiency of grace alone to save, keep, and perfect, and mingles with grace some kind of human merit. In Galatia it was law, in Colosse fanaticism (Col. 2:18, etc.). In any form its teachers lie under the awful anathema of God.

"My Gospel"

Was the Kingdom of God which Paul preached different from the Gospel of grace which he declared as "my Gospel"? If so, wherein?

Paul's message, called by him "my Gospel," included the truth about the Kingdom of God, both in its present mystery form and in its future manifestation. His "Gospel" was the whole body of revelation for this dispensation, comprising the origin, calling and destiny of the Church of God. It is true that those who receive the Lord Jesus Christ in this present age are at once translated into the Kingdom of God; but it is also true that all such are in the Church which is the body of Christ. These things are by no means identical; the Church is a far different thing from the Kingdom; although, of course, since Christ is King in the Kingdom and Head of the Church, the Kingdom and the Church have much in common.

Paul's Gospel

What was distinctive in "the Pauline gospel"? Did not the other apostles preach the same gospel that Paul preached?

Yes, all the apostles preached the same gospel. But it was through Paul that the full body of Church truth was revealed. It is not found in the Old Testament, nor in Matthew, Mark or Luke. See Ephesians 3:1,2 and 2 Peter 3:15,16.

The Dispensation of the Gospel

In 1 Corinthians 9:16,17 Paul said that necessity was laid upon him to preach the Gospel. If he did it willingly he would receive a reward, and if not, then a dispensation of the Gospel was committed unto him. What did he mean by this "dispensation of the Gospel"?

The Revisers have changed the word "dispensation" to "stewardship." Verses 17 and 18 in the Revision read: "For if I do this of mine own will, I have a reward: but if not of mine own will, I have a stewardship entrusted to me. What then is my reward? That, when I preach the gospel, I may make the gospel without charge, so as not to use to the full my right in the gospel." The obvious meaning is that Paul was made a steward of the good news of God, and whether he preached the good news willingly or not, he was still under obligation to preach it, and he must give an answer to God for the way he discharged that obligation. Happily, in his case, he preached the Gospel with all his heart and of his own free will, and therefore a reward awaited him. There is a solemn lesson in all this for every Christian. The Gospel is committed to every one of us as a stewardship, and it is required of stewards that they be faithful (1 Cor. 4:2).

THE KINGDOM

The Great Commission

In Matthew 28:19,20, it says: "Go ye therefore, and teach all nations . . . Teaching them to observe all things whatsoever I have commanded you," etc. Now the question is this: if Matthew said that the things and teachings told in his book were to be taught to all nations, how does it come that you say some of the truths taught are not for the Christians of this dispensation, but rather for the Jews? If He commanded that all His teachings be observed and taught to all nations, why does not Matthew 24:29-31 apply to Gentile Christians? He was then speaking to believers who afterward became pillars of the Church.

I have long been convinced, and have taught that the Great Commission of Matthew 28:19,20 is primarily applicable to the Kingdom rather than to the Church. If this were kept in mind we should not fall into confusion regarding our marching orders, which are found in Acts 1:8, with details in the Epistles to the Churches. The Matthew commission will come into force for the Jewish Remnant after the Church is caught away.

Kingdom Laws

Please explain Matthew 5:40, "And if any man will sue thee at the law, and take away thy coat, let him have thy cloak also."

The primary application of these precepts in the Sermon on the Mount is to the Millennial Kingdom; for the Sermon on the Mount consists of a code of laws for the administration of that Kingdom. In that day the King will reign in righteousness, and the poor, the meek, will receive righteous judgment (Isa. 11:3-5). Stolen coats and cloaks will be quickly restored to their rightful owners in that day. But the Kingdom and the Church, though by no means identical, have many things in common; and the words of Matthew 5:40 might well be placed also in 1 Corinthians 6:6-8, so far, at least, as they apply to lawsuits between believers. As for other lawsuits, one would generally be getting off cheap if the cost amounted to no more than the price of a coat and a cloak. It is a good thing therefore if the matter can be "settled out of court."

The Kingdom in Mystery and Manifestation

1. John the Baptist preached that the Kingdom of Heaven was at hand, and so did our Lord. Was this Kingdom that they preached the

same thing that we call the thousand years' Millennial reign of Christ on earth?

2. If so, will any unsaved or unbelievers enter this reign with Christ?

3. In John 3:3, Christ tells Nicodemus that except a man be born again he cannot see the Kingdom of God. Is this Kingdom of God the Millennium?

4. And is the Kingdom of God spoken of in Luke 19:11 identical with the other two aforesaid Kingdoms?

5. Am I right in contending that there will be no unsaved people entering this Kingdom? Our Lord said it was prepared for those on His right hand from the foundation of the world (Matt. 25:34).

1. Yes, the Kingdom offered by John the Baptist and our Lord was the same as that which will be established at the Second Advent and endure for a thousand years before merging into the eternal state.

2. No. When the Kingdom is finally established under His reign there will be no unsaved ones in the Kingdom. But during the period of the Millennium many will be born and among these not all will be born again. This explains Satan's success at the end of the thousand years in gathering a vast host of rebels against the Lord (Rev. 20:7-9).

3. No. The Kingdom of God in its mystery or unseen form is already here, and every born-again believer is in it.

4. The Kingdom of God referred to in Luke 19:11 is the Kingdom in manifestation. Strictly speaking, the Kingdom of Heaven in manifestation will come first when the Son of God will establish the reign of Heaven upon earth. This is the Millennium. The Kingdom of God will immediately follow the Millennium (1 Cor. 15:24).

5. As shown by answer No. 2, I agree with you as to the Kingdom when first established in manifestation.

The New Offer of the Kingdom

Did Christ give the Jewish nation another chance in the first few chapters of The Acts to have the Kingdom set up?

Yes. In Acts 3:17-21 the offer is found. "The appeal here," says Dr. Scofield, "is national to the Jewish people as such, not individual as in Peter's first sermon (Acts 2:38-39). There those who were pricked in heart were exhorted to save themselves from (among) the untoward nation; here the whole people is addressed, and the promise to 'national' repentance is 'national' deliverance: 'and he shall send Jesus Christ' to bring in the times which the prophets had foretold. The official answer was the imprisonment of the apostles, and the inhibition to preach, so fulfilling Luke 19:14" (*Scofield Reference Bible*).

The Keys of the Kingdom of Heaven

Please explain Matthew 16:19, "And I will give into thee the keys of the kingdom of heaven and whatsoever thou shalt bind on earth shall be bound in heaven: and whatsoever thou shalt loose on earth shall be loosed in heaven."

Notice that in this verse, as in the 18th, the pronouns are singular. "Thee" and "thou" cannot apply to the whole company of apostles. If the others were included the pronouns would be "ye" and "you." The passage here must not be confused with Matthew 18:18, which deals with Church discipline. Here in 16:19 Peter alone is in view. Observe also that the keys are not to Heaven, but rather to the Kingdom of Heaven.

The act of Christ in delivering the keys of the Kingdom of Heaven into Peter's hands, with authority to bind or loose, will become clear if we are careful to search for its meaning only in the Scriptures themselves. The Lord Jesus was about to leave the earth, to be absent for a long time. It was necessary that the King, before His departure, should make it known who could enter the Kingdom and upon what conditions. The New Testament had not yet been written. He here selects Peter, His first convert, to speak for Him in this regard.

If we carefully trace Peter's movements after his Lord's departure, we shall find that it is he and he alone who opened the doors of the Kingdom of Heaven. There were three of these keys received by Peter from the Lord Jesus' hands. The first was used on that great day of Pentecost, when Peter was the spokesman and when he opened the doors of the Kingdom to the people of Israel. "The promise is unto you," said he, "and to your children, and to all that are afar off, even as many as the Lord our God shall call" (Acts 2:39; compare Dan. 9:7). To be sure, the other disciples also preached on that day, but Peter had to be present and approving. He was the chief spokesman.

Again, after the persecution that arose in connection with the death of Stephen, Philip went to Samaria and preached to the Samaritans. But, though many believed the Word, the Holy Spirit fell on none of them. "Now when the apostles that were at Jerusalem heard that Samaria had received the Word of God, they sent unto them Peter and John: who, when they were come down, prayed for them, that they might receive the Holy Spirit, for as yet it was fallen upon none of them: only they had been baptized into the name of the Lord Jesus. Then they laid their hands on them, and they received the Holy Spirit" (Acts 8:14-17, R.V.). This was Peter's second key. He had now opened the doors of the Kingdom to the Jews and the Samaritans.

The third and last key was used in Acts 10, to open these doors to the Gentile world. Cornelius, the Roman centurion, was commanded by an angel of God to send to Joppa for Peter; and Peter, by the vision of the great sheet, was shown that even the unclean Gentiles were no longer unclean, for God had cleansed them. Peter went to the house of Cornelius and preached the Gospel to those assembled there.

Peter was not the apostle to the Gentiles; that was Paul's office, and Paul was converted in the preceding chapter. But Peter, the apostle to the circumcision, must be the first to take the Gospel to the uncircumcision, for Peter had the keys. In each of these three instances, God showed, by the visible descent of the Holy Spirit upon the hearers, that what Peter was doing upon the earth was ratified in Heaven.

Never again was there any use for keys to the Kingdom, for the doors were wide open, so that all who would might come. In the case of the Ephesians, who had received only John's baptism (Acts 19), Peter's presence was not needed, for he had already opened the Kingdom to 'all' Gentiles.

ISRAEL

The Chosen People

Why did God choose Israel to be a special people unto Himself?

He says it is because He loved them, but just why He loved them He has not revealed. In Deuteronomy 7:6-8 He says: "For thou art a holy people (that is, a separate people people set apart) unto Jehovah thy God: Jehovah thy God hath chosen thee to be a special people unto himself, above all people that are upon the face of the earth. Jehovah did not set his love upon you, nor choose you, because ye were more in number than any people; for ye were the fewest of all people: but because Jehovah loved you, and because he would keep the oath which he had sworn unto your fathers, hath Jehovah brought you out with a mighty hand, and redeemed you out of the house of bondmen, from the hand of Pharaoh king of Egypt."

From this we learn that God loved them because He loved them. That is about as far as love can go in explaining itself. He loved them because He loved them; and it was because of His oath that He delivered them from slavery.

There is a most amazing passage in this connection in Deuteronomy 32:8,9, which we quote: "When the Most High divided to the nations their inheritance, when he separated the sons of Adam, he set the bounds of the people according to the number of the children of Israel. For Jehovah's portion is his people; Jacob is the lot of his inheritance."

God's eternal purpose is to bless the world through Israel. Already He has done so in measure, for "salvation is of the Jews" (John 4:22), but the fullness of future blessing is indicated in the wondrous promise of Isaiah 27:6—"He shall cause them that come of Jacob to take root: Israel shall blossom and bud, and fill the face of the world with fruit."

The Hebrew Nation

Did the Hebrew nation include all the descendants of Abraham (which would include that of the four sons by Keturah), or are the Hebrews and the descendants of Isaac, the chosen people, identical?

Only the Israelites, the descendants of Jacob, are called Hebrews in the Scriptures.

Promises to Israel

Can all the promises to the Jew in the Old Testament be claimed by the Gentiles or the Church by faith?

There are many who do claim them as applying to the Gentiles and the Church, but there is no ground for such a claim. God is not through with Israel. His chosen people are at this present time in a place of rejection and darkness, but this is not to be forever. "For I would not, brethren, that ye should be ignorant of this mystery lest ye should be wise in your own conceits; that blindness in part is happened to Israel, until the fullness of the Gentiles be come in. And so all Israel shall be saved: as it is written, There shall come out of Zion the Deliverer, and shall turn away ungodliness from Jacob: for this is my covenant unto them, when I shall take away their sins" (Rom. 11:25-27).

The Hebrew Feasts

Will you please tell us how many feasts were held during one year in the Old Testament?

In the calendar of feasts in Leviticus 23, seven feasts are mentioned. They were: Passover, Unleavened bread, Firstfruits, Pentecost, Trumpets, Atonement, Tabernacles. In the wilderness, before Israel had entered the land of promise, the order was different (see Ex. 23:16).

This Generation

What did Jesus mean when He said, "This generation shall not pass, till all these things be fulfilled" (Matt. 24:34)?

He meant that the people of Israel who were the generation of Jacob, that is, his family, his descendants, should be preserved as a people until all these things should be fulfilled. The Greek word 'genea' is defined by the Lexicons as meaning "race, kind, family, stock, breed." Dr. Scofield points out "that the word is used in this sense here is sure because none of 'these things,' that is, the world-wide preaching of the Kingdom, the Great Tribulation, the return of the Lord in visible glory, and the regathering of the elect, occurred at the destruction of Jerusalem by Titus, A. D. 70. The promise is, therefore, that the generation—nation, or family of Israel—will be preserved unto 'these things'; a promise wonderfully fulfilled to this day" (*Scofield Reference Bible*).

Israel and the Church

1. The Church is spoken of as the Bride of Christ, to sit upon His throne and share the glorious reign of righteousness during the Millennial age. A Jewish lady remarked to a Christian: "We (the Jews) worship the FATHER," as though that were the source for them of greater power than that of the Son. It made me think of what the prophet wrote of Israel when God said, "I have married you (Israel)." Is there any sense in which Israel, redeemed, will occupy the throne of God and supersede in power the position of the Church?

2. Then again: "Christ, our passover, is sacrificed for us." The Passover lamb and the lamb of atonement were two different things for Israel. Were the two merged in one for the Church on Calvary?

1. No. The Bride will occupy the highest possible place, on the throne with

the King, ruling over the nations. Israel, however, will be exalted above the nations, "the head and not the tail." Israel is the unfaithful wife of Jehovah, but she will be won back to her Husband. That, however, will in no wise affect the Church's position as the Bride of the Lamb. A restored wife cannot be called either a bride or a virgin, both of which terms are applied to the Church (Eph. 5:25-33; Rev. 21:2; 22:17; 2 Cor. 11:2).

2. Yes; and even for Israel the Lamb of God was the Antitype of both the Old Testament types.

Israel and the Land

Was there ever a time in the history of the Israelites when they actually took possession of the entire "promised land"?

No. In the days of Solomon the land was put under tribute, perhaps in its entirety, but this by no means fulfills the promise of God with reference to Israel's occupation of the whole land. This will be accomplished in connection with our Lord's second advent.

The Tabernacle of David

What is meant by the tabernacle of David (Acts 15:16)? I read in the Old Testament about the tabernacle of Moses and the temple of Solomon, but where is there such a thing as the tabernacle of David?

The tabernacle of David is the same thing as the house of David, meaning his dynasty as king over Israel. The words of James in Acts 15:13-18 constitute one of the dispensational mountain peaks of Scripture. His comments were delivered at a meeting in Jerusalem, called for the purpose of deciding the relation of the Christian to the law of Moses. There it was decided that the Christian is free from the law. This speech of James cleared the atmosphere for those who were perplexed about the new thing which had come in, called the Church of God, and they wondered what had become of the promises of God concerning the Kingdom, which promises are so often found in the Old Testament Scriptures.

James showed that everything was proceeding according to the word of prophecy. God is now visiting the Gentiles to take out of them a people for His name, and after this the Lord "will return, and will build again the tabernacle of David, which is fallen down; and I will build again the ruins thereof, and I will set it up; that the residue of men might seek after the Lord, and all the Gentiles, upon whom my name is called, saith the Lord, who doeth all these things. Known unto God are all his works from the beginning of the world." James was quoting a passage from Amos 9:11-15 as an epitome or summary of "the words of the prophets" generally. As soon as the Church of God is completed the Lord will return, and He will set His hand again to the establishment of the throne of David and the fulfillment of all the prophecies concerning that throne.

Turning now to the Old Testament Scriptures you will find in Psalm 78:60-72 a most significant passage referring to our question. In verses 60 to 64 the sufferings of Israel under the chastening hand of God are recounted. And in verses 65 to 70 we read: "Then the Lord awaked as one out of sleep, and like a mighty man that shouteth by reason of wine. And he smote his enemies in the hinder parts: he put them to a perpetual reproach. Moreover he refused the tabernacle of Joseph, and chose not the tribe of Ephraim: but chose the tribe of Judah, the mount Zion which he loved. And he built his sanctuary like high palaces, like the earth which he hath established for ever. He chose David also his servant, and took him from the sheepfolds: from following the ewes great with young he brought him to feed Jacob his people, and Israel his inheritance. So he fed them according to the integrity of his heart; and guided them by the skillfullness of His hands."

Then in Isaiah 16 the promise is written that "In mercy shall the throne be established: and he shall sit upon it in truth in the tabernacle of David, judging, and, seeking judgment, and hasting righteousness" (verse 5). In Isaiah 33:20-24 it is written: "Look upon Zion, the city of our solemnities: thine eyes shall see Jerusalem a quiet habitation, a tabernacle that shall not be taken down; not one of the stakes therefore shall ever be removed, neither shall any of the cords thereof be broken. For the Lord is our judge, the Lord is our lawgiver, the Lord is our king; he will save us. And the inhabitant shall not say, I am sick: the people that dwell therein shall be forgiven their iniquity."

And finally there is the passage in Amos already referred to, chapter 9, verses 11-15: "In that day will I raise up the tabernacle of David that is fallen, and close up the breeches thereof; and I will raise up his ruins, and I will build it as in the days of old: that they may possess the remnant of Edom, and of all the nations, which are called by my name, saith the Lord that doeth this. Behold, the days come, saith the Lord, that the plowman shall overtake the reaper, and the trader of grapes him that soweth seed; and the mountains shall drop sweet wine, and all the hills shall melt. And I will bring again the captivity of my people of Israel, and they shall build the waste cities, and inhabit them; and they shall plant vineyards, and drink the wine thereof; they shall also make gardens, and eat the fruit of them. And I will plant them upon their land, and they shall no more be pulled up out of their land which I have given them, saith the Lord thy God."

A Double Sign

What is the significance of the fact that at each end of their wilderness experience the children of Israel passed through a body of water, first the Red Sea and afterward the Jordan river?

Your question is new to me, and interesting. It may be that the passage through the Red Sea speaks of the death and burial and resurrection of Christ, and the believer's death and burial and resurrection in Christ, delivering him from the penalty of sin; and that the passage through Jordan typifies the believer's death to the world and his resurrection to a separated and fruitful life. It is a mistake to think of Canaan as a type of heaven. There was fighting in the promised land as well as in the wilderness, but the difference was that in the land there was generally triumph over the enemy instead of defeat as in the wilderness.

Our Debt to Israel

What is meant by "Salvation is of the Jews"?

The words were spoken by our Lord as He taught the woman of Samaria, as related in the 4th chapter of John. The woman had raised a question touching the rival claims of Jews and Samaritans. "Our fathers," said she, "worshiped in this mountain (Gerizim, Deut. 27:12); and ye (Jews) say, that in Jerusalem is the place where men ought to worship."

Our Lord's reply was: "Woman, believe me, the hour cometh, when ye shall neither in this mountain, nor yet at Jerusalem, worship the Father. Ye worship ye know not what: we know what we worship: for salvation is of the Jews. But the hour cometh, and now is, when the true worshipers shall worship the Father in spirit and in truth: for the Father seeketh such to worship him. God is a Spirit: and they that worship him must worship him in spirit and in truth" (John 4:20-24).

The declaration that "salvation is of the Jews" suggests our immeasurable debt to Israel. All that we have worth having has come to us through the Jews. Our Bible is a Jewish Book, and our Savior is a Jewish Savior. Let us never forget it, nor let us forget to pray for God's chosen people. It is true that for the present they are, as a nation, in the place of rejection; but "even so then at this present time also there is a remnant according to the election of grace" (Rom. 11:5), and some Jews are getting saved.

As for the nation as such, "blindness in part is happened to Israel, until the fullness of the Gentiles be come in" (Rom. 11:25). The blindness is neither complete (it is only "in part"), nor is it final (it is only "until" the Church is completed). In due time, we know, God will again reveal Himself to His ancient covenant people. Already He has brought them back to their own land. He is now in the process of turning them unto Himself. Then shall come the universal blessing for which the world waits. "He shall cause them that come of Jacob to take root: Israel shall blossom and bud, and fill the face of the world with fruit" (Isa. 27:6; compare Jer. 31:31-34; 32:37-41). Scriptures on this point might be multiplied almost indefinitely.

The Fullness of the Gentiles

What is meant by "the fullness of the Gentiles" in Romans 11:25?

It is an expression referring to the people to be gathered out from the Gentiles for the Lord's name in this present dispensation (Acts 15:14). This people from among the Gentiles, being united with the remnant according to the election of grace gathered out from Israel, constitute the Church of God which is the body of Christ, "the fullness of him that filleth all in all" (Eph. 1:22,23; 4:13).

Believing Jews and Gentiles are thus united by the blood of Christ, "who hath made both one, and hath broken down the middle wall of partition between us; having abolished in his flesh the enmity, even the law of commandments contained in ordinance; for to make in himself of twain one new man, so making peace" (Eph. 2:14,15).

When this body of Christ shall have been completed, then the fullness of the Gentiles will have come in. After this, God will take up Israel again, the Redeemer will return in His second coming, and will turn away ungodliness from Jacob; for this is His covenant unto them, when He shall take away their sins (Romans 11:25-27). And then will come the universal blessing for which the world waits. "He shall cause them that come of Jacob to take root: Israel shall blossom and bud, and fill the face of the world with fruit" (Isaiah 27:6).

The Children's Crumbs

When it is convenient I would like you to explain Mark 7:27,28.

The Syro-Phoenician woman was a Gentile, and the Lord Jesus had come to minister to Israel, and His rejection by Israel was not yet complete. The Jews were the "children" and the Gentiles had no more claim upon Him than the dogs of the street had upon the home of one who did not own them. See the fuller and parallel account of the incident in Matthew 15:21-28, and Dr. Scofield's footnote, saying: "For the first time the rejected Son of David ministers to a Gentile. It is a precursive fulfillment of Matt. 12:18. Addressed by a Gentile as Son of David, He makes no reply, for a Gentile has no claim upon Him in that character (Matt. 2:2; Eph. 2:12). Addressing Him as 'Lord,' she obtained an immediate answer. See Rom. 10:12,13."

The Children's Bread

Will you kindly explain the meaning of Matthew 15:26,27, where it speaks of the children's bread. I heard it explained that wherever "the children's bread" was mentioned in the Bible it meant healing. Is that true? Also, kindly state your views on divine healing and the anointing with oil. Is it for us Gentiles of today?

The Canaanitish woman of Matthew 15:21-28 is a type of the Church of God. In response to her heart's desire this woman is richly blessed with more than she asks or thinks, and by her example she teaches us a great lesson of humble faith. It will not be forgotten that this woman was a Gentile, and not only a Gentile, but a Canaanite, a representative of that race which was under God's peculiar curse. "Thou shalt drive out the Canaanites"—this was the word to Israel upon their entering the land of Canaan. The promise of Zechariah 14:21, looking forward to the restored land and restored Temple worship, says, "In that day there shall be no more a Canaanite in the house of Jehovah of hosts." But grace is without any limit and overleaps all obstacles. Through Israel's failure, this despised outcast received the blessing of the Lord that made her rich.

It is at first a most astonishing thing to see the Lord Jesus refusing to respond to this woman's cry of need. It is so unlike Him, whose ears are always open to the slightest call upon His name. But He cannot answer her. She is calling upon Him as the Son of David; and so He is, but as such—as Son of David—He has nothing to do with a Canaanite.

"Then came she and worshiped him saying, Lord, help me," etc. (verses 25-28).

She had now dropped the Jewish title, "Son of David"—this was His name as Israel's King. "Lord, help me!" was her cry, and it is not in His heart to resist that call. The Bread of Life belonged first to the children of the household, that is, to the Jews. If it has come to the Gentiles, it is still true that "salvation is of the Jews," and it is still for the Jews—"to the Jew first." What we have received is just that which was first offered to the children and rejected by them, and it has fallen to us from the Master's table. And even these crumbs are for those only who are willing to stoop down to take them—for those only who are ready to humble themselves and take the place of the dogs, deserving nothing, earning nothing, meriting nothing (see Rom. 11:11-27).

Divine healing is of course always possible to God. Whenever He desires to heal, He is perfectly able to do so. And sometimes it is His plan to do so. The anointing with oil of James 5 is a symbolic picture of the work of the Holy Spirit. Whether it be directly applicable to present day Christians or not is a question upon which there is much difference of opinion among enlightened teachers. But it is always true that "the prayer of faith shall save the sick." And wherever the prayer of faith is found God will surely answer it, and "raise him up." But it ought to be said that the prayer of faith is a gift from God, and it cannot be prayed except He inspire it. When it is His will to heal He will give the prayer of faith, and when it is not His will to heal He will withhold it. The proper attitude of the believer is to desire the will of God above healing and above everything else. That is why our Lord Himself prayed, "Nevertheless, not my will, but thine, be done."

All Israel

Is it actually stated in the Word of God that every Jew living at our Lord's return will be converted and become a missionary like Paul?

It is not stated in the Word of God that every Jew living at the time of our Lord's return will be converted and become a missionary like Paul. Before the Kingdom is actually set up there is to be a judgment of Israel, in which the rebels will be sifted out and prevented from entering into the land of Israel. The Scripture regarding this judgment is in Ezekiel 20:33-38, which reads:

"As I live, saith the Lord GOD, surely with a mighty hand, and with a stretched out arm, and with fury poured out, will I rule over you: And I will bring you out from the people, and will gather you out of the countries wherein ye are scattered, with a mighty hand, and with a stretched out arm, and with fury poured out. And I will bring you into the wilderness of the people, and there will I plead with you face to face. Like as I pleaded with your fathers in the wilderness of the land of Egypt, so will I plead with you, saith the Lord GOD. And I will cause you to pass under the rod, and I will bring you into the bond of the covenant: And I will purge out from among you the rebels, and them that transgress against me: I will bring them forth out of the country where they sojourn, and they shall not enter into the land of Israel: and ye shall know that I am the LORD."

It is true that in the Kingdom at the beginning of the millennial reign of our Lord all the Israelites included therein will be saved.

Every Jew

Does Romans 11:25,26 teach that every Jew will be saved?

No; but rather that the whole nation—all the Jews then living—will be turned to the Lord when the Kingdom is set up. It has no reference to Israelites who live in the meantime and reject the way of salvation. (read Jer. 31:31-34; Rom. 2:28,29; 9:6; Ezek. 20:33-38).

Israel and Judah

You say of our Lord that "Israel should have known Him, for He fulfilled their Scriptures." Is there not some confusion here? You certainly mean Judah when you say Israel, which the Bible does not. Israel never rejected the Savior, while Judah did.

It is true that the Bible sometimes makes a distinction between Judah and Israel. Indeed it very often does so. But it is not true that it always does so. It frequently uses the term "Israel" in a generic sense as including the whole nation—Judah, Benjamin, Levi and all the other tribes. Please note the following instances among others which you no doubt will find:

In Matthew 8:10 our Lord said He had not found so great faith, "no, not in Israel." In view of this, it would be difficult to substantiate your proposition that "Israel never rejected the Savior, while Judah did."

In Matthew 10:6 He sends His messengers only to "the lost sheep of the house of Israel." Now, since their ministry was confined to the land of Palestine, it is evident that these lost sheep of the house of Israel were the people then residing in the land and known as Jews. You certainly would not contend that the messengers were to hunt out those who had joined Judah from the lost ten tribes. Their ministry was to all the Israelites then in the land, and certainly a Jew is an Israelite.

In Luke 1:80 we read of John the Baptist that "the child grew, and waxed strong in spirit, and was in the deserts till the day of his shewing unto Israel." According to your contention this should read "Judah" instead of "Israel," since John the Baptist also confined his ministry to those who were then in the land.

In John 1:31 the Baptist says of his Lord that he "knew him not: but that he should be made manifest to Israel, therefore am I come baptizing with water." But our Lord was made manifest only to the Israelites then in the land, whom you would insist upon calling Jews, and to whom you would deny this term "Israel."

In John 3:10 our Lord calls Nicodemus "a master of Israel," though in verse 1 the record calls him "a ruler of the Jews."

It is true that Judas Iscariot was the only representative of the tribe of Judah among the apostles, and it is significant that it was he who sold his Master (also of the tribe of Judah) to His enemies, and it is also probably true that we ought to be more careful in making the distinction to which you refer. And yet I think you will agree that the distinction is not always made even in the Scriptures.

The Jews' Salvation

What do you think about the Jews' salvation (a)—as individuals; (b)—as a people?

The Scriptures teach that there is no difference between Jew and Gentile. As individuals, Jews are to be saved through the Gospel the same as Gentiles; as a nation, the people of Israel are set aside for the time being, "until the fullness of the Gentiles be come in." This is the same as saying, until the Church, which is the body of Christ, is completed. When that will be, no man can tell. It may be at any moment that the Church will be completed and be caught up to meet the Lord in the air.

Israel in Travail

What is the significance of the "woman in travail" in Micah 4:10?

It is Israel, the "daughter of Zion," as the verse says. The people of Israel are today "like a woman in travail," and because of their rejection of their Messiah nearly 2,000 years ago they are now given up to this suffering "until the time that she which travaileth hath brought forth" (Mic. 5:3). "Blindness in part is happened to Israel, until the fullness of the Gentiles be come in" (Rom. 11:25-27). The full number of Gentiles to make the church complete must be saved before this blindness is removed. In due time this will be accomplished, as is shown in Revelation 12:1-6, where the woman "travailing in birth" is Israel, and the "man child" is Christ, including "the church which is his body, the fullness of him that filleth all in all" (Eph. 1:22,23). All this means that there is a real and intimate relation between Israel's present sufferings and the building up of the church. It is a mystery, but it is no less real for that.

Israel's Resurrection

Some time, if convenient, will you please state when you think the "saved of Israel" arise from the dead? Would that be at the Rapture along with "the dead in Christ" or could it be in Daniel 12:1,2? I have never found any statement concerning it.

Whether Daniel 12:1,2 refers to a separate resurrection for Israel is a question often discussed, but never yet fully settled. But that every saved Israelite, dead and living, will participate in the Rapture is beyond reasonable question. The Rapture includes all those who "sleep in Jesus" or "the dead in Christ" along with all living believers.

Special Judgment for Israel

Is it true that there is a future separate judgment for the people of Israel?

Yes. This judgment is described in Ezekiel 20:33-38. We quote from the American Standard Revised Version:

As I live, saith the Lord Jehovah, surely with a mighty hand, and with a stretched out arm, and with wrath poured out, will I be king over you: and I will bring you out from the peoples, and will gather you out of the countries wherein ye are scattered, with a mighty hand, and with a stretched out arm, and with wrath poured out: and I will bring you into the wilderness of the peoples, and there will I enter into judgment with you face to face. Like as I entered into judgment with your fathers in the wilderness of the land of Egypt, so will I enter into judgment with you, saith the Lord Jehovah. And I will cause you to pass under the rod, and I will bring you into the bond of the covenant; and I will purge out from among you the rebels, and them that transgress against me; I will bring them forth out of the land where they sojourn, but they shall not enter into the land of Israel: and ye shall know that I am Jehovah.

The Remnant

In your book, *Israel—Jehovah's Covenant People*, page 69, you state, "The Church can never be caught up to her Lord until this elect Jewish Remnant is brought in." Several of us are mystified as to that statement. We had thought the Bible teaches that this Remnant shall be saved when our Lord delivers them at Armageddon. Of course Jewish believers entering the Church will be in the "Rapture." Why then do you indicate that this event will be dependent on, or rather, delayed by, them?

If you will read again the statement on page 69 of *Israel—Jehovah's Covenant People* you will see that the remnant referred to is the present remnant: "at this present time also there is a remnant according to the election of grace" (Rom. 11:5). This present time remnant is being added to the people being gathered out from the Gentiles for His name, and these will become one new man in Christ, constituting the Church, which is His body. This remnant must be gathered out, and the Church must be completed before the Rapture can take place. It seems to me that the statement is perfectly clear.

The Sealed Remnant

Does Revelation 7:4-8 mean that only 144,000 people will go to Heaven?

It doesn't say anything about going to Heaven. This Scripture describes certain ones who are sealed out of the tribes of Israel and certainly they are saved, but whether they themselves will go to Heaven is a question, for the future home of the people of Israel is, as I believe, the restored earth.

The Tribe of Simeon

To what extent does the tribe of Simeon figure in the kingdom of Israel as divided? Geographically they were located south of the kingdom of Judah, and they do not seem to be mentioned in the history if they belonged with the ten tribes of Israel.

The matter is in doubt. *Smith's Bible Dictionary* says: "What part Simeon took at the time of the division of the kingdom we are not told. The only thing which can be interpreted into a trace of its having taken any part with the northern kingdom are the two casual notices of 2 Chronicles 15:9 and 34:6, which appear to imply the presence of Simeonites there in the reigns of Asa and Josiah. On the other hand the definite statement of 1 Chronicles 4:41-43 proves that at that time there were still some of them remaining in the original seat of the tribe, and actuated by all the warlike lawless spirit of their progenitor. Simeon is named by Ezekiel (48:25), and the author of the Book of the Revelation (7:7) in their catalogues of the restoration of Israel."

Judah and Benjamin

In 1 Kings 12:20 we read, "There was none that followed the house of David, but the tribe of Judah only." Now, Benjamin followed the house of David. How is that explained?

In 1 Kings 11:29-32 the prophet Ahijah rends Jeroboam's new garment, and instructs him to take ten of the pieces, signifying by this (verse 31) that God would give ten tribes to him. Judah and Benjamin answer to the two remaining pieces of the rent garment. That Benjamin remained with Judah is shown by such passages as 1 Kings 12:21-23 and 2 Chron. 11:12. These two tribes were so closely united that in the passage you mention they are regarded as one. The tribe of Levi adhered to the house of David (2 Chron. 11:13,14), and many from other tribes were also included in Judah (1 Kings 12:17; 2 Chron. 15:9), but it was a matter of choice with these.

Joseph and Benjamin

I know that the history of Joseph is a wonderful prophecy of our Lord Jesus Christ; but I do not understand Genesis 45. What is its prophetic meaning, especially verses 1-4?

This is the point of transition between Joseph and Benjamin as a double or joint type of Christ. I again quote Dr. Scofield: "It is important to observe that Benjamin now becomes prominent. Joseph is peculiarly the type of Christ in His first advent, rejection, death, resurrection, and present exaltation among the Gentiles, but unrecognized of Israel. As the greater Benjamin, 'Son of sorrow,' but also 'Son of my right hand' (Gen. 35:18), He is to be revealed in power in the Kingdom. It is then, and not till then, that Israel is to be restored and converted. Typically, Genesis 45:1,2 anticipates the revelation prophetically described, Ezekiel 20:33-36; Hosea 2:14-23, at which time the Benjamin type of Christ will be fulfilled."

The Lost Tribes of Israel

Are the Jews who will be living at the time of the Great Tribulation to be the lost tribes of Israel?

The "lost tribes of Israel" are the ten tribes taken away in the Assyrian captivity in the days of King Hoshea of Samaria. These ten tribes have never returned and we do not know where they are. It is certain, however, that there is a remnant of them living somewhere, and they are, of course, known to God, and they are to be brought back and located as tribes in the land during the Millennium. See Ezekiel, chapters 37, 47 and 48.

Israelites and Jews

Are the words "Israel" and "Jew" used interchangeably in Scripture? I have recently read that the ten tribes have completely lost their identity in the nations, and that the only Jews known today are from the tribes of Judah and Benjamin. Is this correct?

"Israel" and "Jew" are sometimes used interchangeably in the Scripture and sometimes there is a distinction. Strictly speaking, "Jew" is a religious word, having to do with Judaism as a religious system. But the word is not always used, even in Scripture, in that strict sense.

In 1 Corinthians 10:32 the whole human race is divided into three classes, Jews, Gentiles and Christians, in which case the Jews certainly include all of Israel who have not become Christians. For certainly no Israelite is a Gentile.

But the teaching of Scripture is perfectly clear that the twelve tribes of Israel as such are to be gathered back to their own land, which is to be allocated among them, as tribes, in the Millennial Kingdom. See Ezekiel 48:1-7, 23-29. Also Jeremiah 23:5-8; Isaiah 11:12,13. Indeed there are many Scriptures on this subject which will leave no doubt in the minds of those who esteem the Word of God as the court of final appeal.

The Israel of God

Who constitute the Israel of God mentioned in Galatians 6:16?

The answer is found in Romans 4:12. The Israel of God consists of those Israelites "who are not of the circumcision only, but who also walk in the steps of the faith of our father Abraham." Again, in Romans 9:6-8 it is written that "they are not all Israel, which are of Israel; neither, because they are the seed of Abraham, are they all children: but, in Isaac shall thy seed be called. That is, they which are the children of the flesh, these are not the children of God: but the children of the promise are counted for the seed." Then, too, there is the statement of Romans 2:28,29: "For he is not a Jew, which is one outwardly; neither is that circumcision, which is outward in the flesh: but he is a Jew, which is one inwardly; and circumcision is that of the heart, in the spirit, and not in the letter; whose praise is not of men, but of God."

To speak of the Church as "the Israel of God" or as "Spiritual Israel" is an error. The "Spiritual Israel" is an Israel within Israel, just as in our day there is a true Church within the professing Church; but Israel and the Church should never be thought of as identical.

Israel's Restoration

Please explain Matthew 24:32 and Ezekiel 36:34.

It is agreed among enlightened Bible scholars that the fig tree is a symbol of the nation of Israel. In Luke 21:24, the Gentile rule over Jerusalem is set forth as a sign of "the times of the Gentiles." So in Matthew 24:32, in the parable of the fig tree, it is pointed out by our Lord that when the fig tree puts forth its leaves, that is, when Israel is aroused from her age-long slumber and begins to show signs of national reawakening and restoration, that will indicate that the end of the age is very near. The promise of Matthew 24:34 is that "this generation" (meaning the nation of Israel) "shall not pass till all these things be fulfilled." That is, God will not suffer the nation to be destroyed or to cease to exist as a nation until all these promises be accomplished.

The words of Ezekiel 36:34 refer to the time when the land of Palestine, which so long lay desolate, will again be made fruitful, for a testimony unto the Gentile nations "round about" (verses 35,36).

Israel's Restoration

Was not the return from the Babylonian captivity the fulfillment of the promises of Israel's restoration?

No. Please read Ezekiel 39:25-28; Amos 9:13-15; Zechariah 8:20-23; 14:1-9, 16; Romans 2:1-6, 13-15, 25-27.

The Blighted Fig Tree

Why did Jesus curse the fig tree, or expect to find fruit on it, when we are told, "the time of figs was not yet" (Mark 11:12-14)? Is this the same incident that is recorded in Matthew 21:19?

I understand that the two accounts are parallel and record the same event. Dr. Scofield says that "fig trees which have retained their leaves through the winter usually have figs also. It was still too early for new leaves or fruit." He also says that "the withered fig tree is a parabolic miracle concerning Israel (Luke 13:6-9). Compare Matthew 24:32,33, a prophecy that Israel shall again bud" (Scofield Reference Bible).

Jew and Gentile Alike

Does Acts 10:44-48 mean that henceforth the Gentiles were to have the same blessings as the Jews?

Certainly. "For he is our peace, who hath made both one, and hath broken down the middle wall of partition between us; having abolished in his flesh the enmity, even the law of commandments contained in ordinances; for to make in himself of twain one new man, so making peace; and that he might reconcile both (that is, Jew and Gentile) unto God in one body by the cross, having slain the enmity thereby: and came and preached peace to you that were afar off (that is, the Gentiles), and to them that were nigh (that is, the Jews). For through him we both have access by one Spirit unto the Father" (Eph. 2:14-18; compare also Rom. 4:9-12).

Jewish Sacrifices

Did the Jewish sacrifice of the lamb cease at the crucifixion in A.D. 30, or at the destruction of the temple by Titus in A.D. 70? Some teach

that after Jesus, the Lamb of God, was slain, the sacrifice of the Passover lamb ceased at once.

I think it is clear from the Epistle to the Hebrews that the sacrifices in the Temple continued until the destruction of Jerusalem, which was only about six years after that Epistle was written. See, for example, Hebrews 8:4,5; 10:1-3, 11.

The Jewish sacrifice of the lamb in the celebration of the Passover had to cease when the Temple was destroyed, for that was the only place it could be offered under the Law. The Passover which is now celebrated every year by them is without any lamb, and this in itself is a graphic fulfillment of the prophecy in Hosea 3:4,5. Here it is declared that for many days the children of Israel would be "without a sacrifice."

The Jews and Jerusalem

We hear much of the Jews these days going to rebuild and inhabit Jerusalem and set up a national government and rule their own land. Can we expect anything like this after reading Luke 21:24? Our Lord said, "Jerusalem shall be trodden down of the Gentiles, until the times of the Gentiles be fulfilled." Can Jerusalem prosper under the Jews before the Lord comes to reign over her?

Israel will never be sovereign in Jerusalem before Messiah's return to reign. But the Scriptures teach that Antichrist will enter into covenant with the Jews for seven years—Daniel's seventieth week—and that during the first half of that period they will build a temple in Jerusalem. Doubtless they will enjoy a period of prosperity under Antichrist's rule until he breaks his covenant "in the midst of the week" and brings upon them the horrors of the Great Tribulation.

The Temple of Solomon

I will be very grateful if you will take the trouble to explain the need for Solomon to employ so many thousands of men for so long a time to complete two comparatively small houses—the temple and his own palace.

It is difficult for us in these days of modern machinery and high-priced labor to appreciate the circumstances under which Solomon's building was done. There was no lack of labor, and he had many slaves. It was a gigantic task to hew the cedar and fir trees in the Lebanon mountains, bring them down to the sea, convey them in boats to Joppa, and then carry them up to Jerusalem. See 1 Kings 5:8,9; 2 Chronicles 3:16. Then let us remember that "the house, when it was in building, was built of stone made ready before it was brought thither: so that there was neither hammer nor axe nor any tool of iron heard in the house, while it was in building" (1 Kings 6:7). This means that there was much greater care taken with these stones and other parts of the building than is taken in these latter days of rush and turmoil.

The Temples of Zerubbabel and Herod

When and how was the temple of Zerubbabel destroyed, and when was Herod's temple erected?

It was in Passover time in B.C. 21 or 20 that Herod announced his intention of restoring the temple. There is no record that the temple had been utterly destroyed, but it had grown old, and Herod's plan was to rebuild it. According to Josephus the whole edifice was pulled down to its foundation and the new building erected on an enlarged scale. But the ruins still exhibit in some parts what seem to be the foundations laid by Zerubbabel and beneath them the more massive sub-structions of Solomon. Herod's temple itself was completed in about a year and a half, and the courts in about eight years, but further operations were carried on so slowly that the Jews reckoned forty-six years as the whole time consumed (John 2:20).

Herod's Temple

Where do you find in the Bible that the temple used in Christ's time was Herod's temple?

There is no mention in the Bible of Herod's temple under that name, but it is a matter of historic fact, which no one denies or doubts, that the temple standing during Christ's time was actually built by Herod the Great, and not by the returned remnant. There was a temple built by the returned remnant. This was begun under Zerubbabel in 534 B.C., and after a long intermission was resumed in 520 B.C. and completed in 516 B.C. under Darius Hystaspes. This second temple was gradually removed by Herod as he proceeded with the building or rebuilding of a temple designed to rival the first rather than the second. This work was commenced in B.C. 21 or 20. The temple itself was finished in about a year and a half and the courts in 8 years, but the subsequent operations were carried on so dilatorily that the Jews reckoned 46 years as the whole time consumed (John 2:20). It was in the courts of this temple that Jesus preached and healed the sick. It caught fire during the siege of Jerusalem under Titus A.D. 70 and was burned to the ground.

The Jewish Calendar

Please explain why the Jews celebrate their New Year in September instead of January 1; also why they place the creation 243 years nearer than our calendar makes it.

We pass on the statement of *The Encyclopedia Britannica* that according to the Jewish Calendar the creation of man . . .

> . . . is considered to have taken place 3760 years and 3 months before the commencement of the Christian era. The year is lunisolar, and, according as it is ordinary or embolismic, consists of 12 or 13 lunar months, each of which has 29 or 30 days. Thus the duration of the ordinary year is 354 days, and that of the embolismic is 384 days. In either case, it is sometimes made a day more, and sometimes a day less, in order that certain festivals may fall on proper days of the week, for their due observance. . . .
>
> As the Greek and Roman methods of computing time were connected with certain pagan rites and observances which the Christians held in abhorrence, the latter began at an early period to imitate the Jews in reckoning their years

from the supposed period of the creation of the world. The chronological elements on which both Jews and Christians founded their computations for determining this period were derived from the Old Testament narratives, which have been transmitted to us through three distinct channels. These are the Hebrew text of the Scriptures, the Samaritan text, and the Greek version known as the Septuagint. In respect of chronology, the three accounts are totally irreconcilable with each other; and no conclusive reason can be given for preferring any one of them to another. . . .

Des Vignoles, in the preface to his *Chronology of Sacred History*, asserts that he collected upwards of 200 different calculations, the shortest of which reckons only 3483 years between the creation of the world and the commencement of the vulgar era, and the longest 6984. The difference amounts to 35 centuries. It suffices, therefore, to point out that the so-called era of the creation of the world is a purely conventional and arbitrary epoch that, practically, it means the year 4004 B.C.—this being the date which, under the sanction of Archbishop Ussher's opinion, has won its way, among its hundreds of competitors, into most general acceptance. . . .

Before the departure of the Israelites from Egypt their year commenced at the autumnal equinox; but in order to solemnize the memory of their deliverance, the month of Nisan or Abib, in which that event took place, and which falls about the time of the vernal equinox, was afterwards regarded as the beginning of the ecclesiastical or legal year. In civil affairs, and in the regulation of the jubilees and sabbatical years, the Jews still adhere to the ancient year, which begins with the month Tisri, about the time of the autumnal equinox."

Israel in Her Own Land

What significance do you attach to the presence in Palestine today of millions of Jews?

The return within the twentieth century of millions of Jews to Palestine is one of the most momentous of the signs of the times. God's promise is written large in the Scriptures that one day the whole nation will return and will occupy all the land bounded by five great inland seas, the Mediterranean on the west, the Black Sea on the northwest, the Caspian Sea on the northeast, the Persian Gulf on the southeast and the Red Sea on the southwest. The land to be given to Israel reaches all the way back to the Euphrates River, and the people located in that land will be the most strategically located nation in the world.

But the gift of the land, as set forth in an Abrahamic covenant in the twelfth, thirteenth, fifteenth and seventeenth chapters of Genesis, is modified by predictions of three dispossessions and restorations. Genesis 15:13-16; Jeremiah 25:11,12; Deuteronomy 28:62-65; 30:1-3. Two of these dispossessions and restoration have already taken place. The nation is now in its third dispersion, from which it will be restore at the second coming of Christ to reign as King, according to God's covenant to David (Deut. 30:1-3; Jer. 23:5-8; Ezek. 37:21-25; Luke 1:31-33; Acts 1:11; 15:14-17; Rev. 22:20.)

Bene Israel

Who are the "Bene Israel"?

There is a tribe of approximately 15,000 people located in India called "The Bene Israel." They claim to be descended from Jacob. They have in their language certain words and phrases of Hebrew origin, and they have many Jewish customs and manners, though they do not practice "Yibom"; that is, they do not marry the widow of a deceased brother to raise up seed unto him. The Jews generally do not recognize their claim as Jews. It is believed by some that "Bene Israel" belongs to some Indian tribe converted to Judaism in early times.

Israel's Future Glory

Who or what is meant, in Zephaniah 3:19, by "that which is lame, and, that which was driven away"?

Israel is meant, and the whole paragraph, beginning with the verse 14, is a picture of her future glory. I quote from the Revision:

"Sing, O daughter of Zion; shout, O Israel; be glad and rejoice with all the heart, O daughter of Jerusalem. Jehovah hath taken away thy judgments, he hath cast out thine enemy, the King of Israel, even Jehovah, is in the midst of thee; thou shalt not fear evil any more. In that day it shall be said to Jerusalem, Fear thou not; O Zion, let not thy hands be slack. Jehovah thy God is in the midst of thee, a mighty one who will save; he will rejoice over thee with joy; he will rest in his love; he will joy over thee with singing. I will gather them that sorrow for the solemn assembly, who were of thee; to whom the burden upon her was a reproach. Behold, at that time I will deal with all them that afflict thee; and I will save that which is lame, and gather that which was driven away; and I will make them a praise and a name, whose shame hath been in all the earth. At that time will I bring you in, and at that time will I gather you; for I will make you a name and a praise among all the peoples of the earth, when I bring back your captivity before your eyes, saith Jehovah."

There are many similar promises in Scripture for the future glory of Israel. See, for example, Isaiah 62; Jeremiah 31:31-34; Zechariah 8:13-23; and Romans 11:25-27.

AFTER DEATH

Appointed to Die

Please explain Hebrews 9:27 which reads as follows: "And it is appointed unto men once to die, but after this the judgment."

It hardly needs explaining, for it means precisely what it says. Observe, it does not say that all men are thus appointed. Since we are assured in 1 Corinthians 15:51 that "we shall not all sleep," some of us are hoping to be excused from keeping this appointment.

Spiritually and Physically Dead

I should like to ask you to tell me what Jesus meant in Matthew 8:22, "Let the dead bury their dead"?

It means "Let the spiritually dead bury their physically dead." It should be read in relation to its context in the verses preceding.

How Is Death Abolished

If the Lord Jesus "hath abolished death," as stated in 2 Timothy 1:10, why is it that people, including Christians, go on dying?

There are three kinds of death: physical death, spiritual death, and the second death. Physical death is the least important of all. It is the separation of the body from the spirit and soul. Spiritual death is separation from God who is the source of all life. The second death is this spiritual death prolonged into eternity and in the lake of fire. Our Lord Jesus Christ has abolished spiritual and the second death for all who take their place under the shelter of His shed blood. And for these He has robbed even physical death of it terror, assuring them that if they should die they would be at once absent from the body and present with the Lord (2 Cor. 5:6-8). And finally even physical death will be abolished for believers, for we are assured that "we shall not all sleep" (1 Cor. 15:51); that is, we shall not all die. Some of us will be alive and remaining at the coming of our Lord (1 Thess. 4:13-18), and will therefore go to heaven without dying.

Hades Past and Present

Where do we get our authority for saying Paradise was beneath, in explaining Ephesians 4:8-10? Please explain fully with Scripture reference.

This question involves the study of the Greek word *"Hades"* and the Hebrew word *"Sheol."* Dr. Scofield's exposition of this subject is so good that we shall not try to improve upon it: *Hades*, "the unseen world," is revealed as the place of departed human spirits between death and resurrection. The word occurs, Matthew 11:23; 16:18; Luke 10:15; 16:23; Acts 2:27, 31; Revelation 1:18; 6:8; 20:13,14, and is the equivalent of the Old Testament 'Sheol.' The Septuagint invariably renders 'Sheol' by 'Hades.'

Hades before the ascension of Christ. The passages in which the word occurs make it clear that Hades was formerly in two divisions, the abodes respectively of the saved and of the lost. The former was called "Paradise" and "Abraham's bosom." Both designations were Talmudic, but adopted by Christ in Luke 16:22; 23:43. The blessed dead were with Abraham; they were conscious and were "comforted" (Luke 16:25) The believing malefactor was to be, that day, with Christ in "Paradise." The lost were separated from the saved by a "great gulf fixed" (Luke 16:26). The representative man of the lost who are now in Hades is the rich man of Luke 16:19-31. He was alive, conscious, in the full exercise of his faculties, memory, etc., and in torment.

Hades since the ascension of Christ. So far as the unsaved dead are concerned, no change of their place or condition is revealed in Scripture. At the judgment of the Great White Throne, Hades will give them up, they will be judged, and will pass into the Lake of Fire (Rev. 20:13,14). But a change has taken place which affects Paradise. Paul was "caught up to the third heaven . . . into Paradise" (2 Cor. 12:1-4). Paradise, therefore, is now in the immediate presence of God. It is believed that Ephesians 4:8-10 indicates the time of the change. "When he ascended up on high he led a multitude of captives." It is immediately added that He had previously "descended first into the lower parts of the earth," that is, the Paradise division of Hades. During the present Church-age the saved who have died are "absent from the body, and at home with the Lord." The wicked dead in Hades and the righteous dead "at home with the Lord," alike await the resurrection (Job 19:26; 1 Cor. 15:52).

Hell and the Grave

Please, does the word "hell" mean the grave every time it is mentioned in Holy Writ? Some of my friends insist upon this. If you can help me, please do so.

Your friends are wrong. The English translators have confused several words in both Testaments by translating them into the words "grave," "hell," etc. The awful truth about hell is found in our Lord's own words in Mark 9:42-48. Hell is the lake of fire, into which death and hades are to be finally cast, with all their occupants (Rev. 20:14,15).

Hades, Purgatory, Hell and Heaven

The Roman Catholics claim that everyone goes to Hell. In Acts 2:27 and Acts 2:34 I find some things I cannot understand. Please explain.

Does the spirit of everyone who dies go to The Father who gave it? Does this include the wicked as well as Christians ?

The Roman Catholic teaching is not that everyone must go into Hell, but that everyone must for a longer or shorter time go into Purgatory. This doctrine is based not upon Scripture, but upon the traditions of the church, which are without value to a believer in the Word of God.

"Hell" in Acts 2:27 should read "Hades." Our Lord's soul did not go into Hell, but it did go into Hades, which until His resurrection included the abode of the saved and that of the lost, though these were separated by "a great gulf fixed" and impassable (Luke 16:26). At His resurrection He took with Him to Heaven all the saved out of Hades, and since that time, the saved, at death, go immediately to be "with the Lord" in Heaven (Eph. 4:8-10; 2 Cor. 5:6-8).

It is only the saved whose spirits go to God. The lost go to their "own place" (Acts 1:25).

Sinning in Hell

Are we to understand from Revelation 22:11 that the lost will continue sinning in hell? If so, how can they sin in the bodies they will have then?

I can see no reason why the lost should not be able to sin as well "in the bodies they will have then" as in the bodies they have now. And doubtless they will go on sinning. Corruption never stops in its process. It goes on getting worse and worse. The language of the Revised Version in the verse you cite is exceedingly solemn: "He that is unrighteous, let him do unrighteousness still: and he that is filthy, let him be made filthy still: and he that is righteous, let him do righteousness still: and he that is holy, let him be made holy still"; and in the margin the word for "still" is always rendered "yet more"; indicating that the filthy will go on becoming filthier throughout the ages. May God forbid that any of my readers should end in such a fate!

The Lake of Fire

Where does the Bible state that the lake of fire is hell?

If you will read Mark 9:42-48; Matthew 25:41 and Revelation 20:14,15, I think you will be convinced that the lake of fire and hell are two names for the same place. (It should be noted that the word for "hell" in Rev. 20:14 should be translated "hades.")

Paradise

Jesus and the penitent thief went to Paradise, did they not? Where is Paradise? Do we all go to some place at death to be there temporarily, before we go to Heaven?

Paradise, before the resurrection of Christ, was a part of Hades; but after the resurrection of Christ it became a part of Heaven, for in 2 Corinthians 12:4 it is identified with "the third heaven." See Luke 16:19-26; Acts 2:25-27. In these passages "hell" should read "hades." See also Ephesians 4:7-10, which evidently marks the point of transition when Paradise and all its inhabitants were removed from Hades to Heaven.

A Question of Harmony

Will you please explain or harmonize the apparently conflicting statements, "today shalt thou be with me in paradise," with, "As Jonah was there three days and three nights in the whale's belly; so shall the Son of man," etc.?

Only the body of our Lord went into the grave. His soul and spirit went (with the dying thief) to Hades, which then included Paradise. After the resurrection, the Paradise section, so to speak, of Hades was removed to Heaven.

The Departed

Will you explain if after death the departed ones are perfectly conscious of where they are, and are the saved ones able to see and speak with our Lord? Please give the Scriptures which point out your answer.

The departed, both saved and unsaved, are perfectly conscious; and the saved are "absent from the body and at home with the Lord" (Luke 16:19-31; 2 Cor. 5:6-8, R.V.). That the saved are able to see and speak with the Lord with whom they are thus "at home" is beyond doubt. We are able to speak to Him even from here; surely those who are in His bodily presence will not be less privileged than we. See also Revelation 6:9-11 and 22:4.

The State of the Departed

Will you please tell us the state of those who have gone home to be with the Lord Jesus? Do they see and talk with our Savior, and do they walk around? When the unsaved are raised do they put on their old, vile, diseased and crippled bodies? The saved put on incorruptible bodies, but what about the unsaved?

The Scriptures do not give full light on all these questions. We are sure, however, that the saved who have gone on before are now absent from the body, and at home with the Lord (2 Cor. 5:8, R.V.). That they see the Lord seems to be clear from Matthew 18:10, where our Lord in speaking of little children says: "That in heaven their angels do always behold the face of my Father which is in Heaven." While they do not yet have their resurrection bodies, for "without us" they can "not be made perfect" (Heb. 11:40) that is, they with us, wait "for the adoption, to wit, the redemption of our body" (Rom. 8:23). Meanwhile, it is apparent from certain Scriptures, that pending the time when they shall have their resurrection body they even now have something corresponding to a body which enables them to communicate with each other and with their surroundings (Rev. 6:9-11; 7:9-17).

As to the resurrection bodies of the unsaved I have no light. That there is to be such a bodily resurrection for them is certain from Revelation 20:11-15, but the nature of those bodies is not described in Scripture.

The Bema

What is the Bema?

The Bema is "the judgment seat of Christ" referred to in 2 Corinthians 5:10, and related to the judgment of believers' works, which judgment is described in 1 Corinthians 3:11-15. At this judgment only the saved will appear, and it will be there that their rewards, if any, will be given to them. "If any man's work abide which he hath built thereupon (that is, upon the foundation 'which is Jesus Christ') he shall receive a reward (not salvation, for that is already his in the foundation, but a 'reward in addition to salvation'). If any man's work shall be burned, he shall suffer loss: but he himself shall be saved; yet so as by fire." God offers salvation to the lost and rewards to the saved. Salvation is a gift, in response to faith, while rewards are earned by works. Salvation is the believer's present possession, but rewards are a future attainment.

The Rich Man and Lazarus

What do you think the parable of the rich man and Lazarus teaches?

1. There seems to be no question of right and wrong; only rich and poor. The rich man was punished because he had been rich and the poor man was comforted. "Son, remember that thou in thy lifetime receivedst thy good things, and likewise Lazarus evil things: but now (therefore) he is comforted, and thou art tormented." And the preaching of Moses and the prophets, to whom he was referred, would not be the gospel of salvation by faith in Jesus Christ.

2. Again, it is said that this is not a parable but rather a statement of a fact, an occurrence. Then do you think that, although Heaven and Hell are "afar off" from each other, you can look over and converse from one to the other? I hope not.

1. It is not stated that "the rich man was punished because he had been rich," nor that the poor man was saved on account of his poverty. The facts are given, but why the rich man was punished or the poor man comforted is not explained. The implication, however, is sufficiently clear that the rich man was supremely selfish—all that could be said of him was that he dressed lavishly and fared sumptuously. God was not in his program, nor yet Lazarus, nor any one but himself. As for Lazarus, it may be significant that his name is given, being the Greek form of Eleazar—"helped of God." Certainly we may be sure that our Lord never intended this story to contradict all His teachings elsewhere on salvation by faith.

2. There is no indication of a parable here. Our Lord is telling a true history of what happened to two men who once lived and died. No parable of Scripture mentions any person's name. No, we shall not look into Hell from Heaven. As a matter of fact, Lazarus was not in Heaven, nor the rich man in Hell. Both of them were in Hades, though each in a separate part of Hades, and the two parts were divided by an impassable gulf. Since that time Lazarus has been transferred from Hades to Heaven. This change took place at our Lord's ascension, when "he led captivity captive," (Ps. 68:18, Eph. 4:8). The rich man will remain in Hades until after the Millennium, when "death and

Hades" shall be "cast into the lake of fire," which is Hell, the final abode of the lost. (Rev. 20:13,14).

The Valley and Land of the Shadow of Death

What is meant by "the valley of the shadow of death" (Ps. 23:4) and also, "the land of the shadow of death" (Isa. 9:2)?

By "the valley of the shadow of death" the psalmist evidently referred to the experience awaiting him when he should die. The same idea was in Job's mind when he said: "Are not my days few? Cease then, and let me alone, that I may take comfort a little, before I go whence I shall not return, even to the land of darkness and the shadow of death; a land of darkness, as darkness itself; and of the shadow of death, without any order, and where the light is as darkness" (Job 10:20-22). Such was the view of death held by the patriarch before God gave man a Bible. In Ps. 88:12 David called the place beyond the horizon "the land of forgetfulness."

The prophecy of Isaiah 9:1,2 was fulfilled in our Lord's visit to Galilee, as shown by Matthew 4:13-16, and there "the land of the shadow of death" seems to be identified with "Galilee of the Gentiles."

The fact is that men who are separated from God are constantly living in the shadow of death, being "through fear of death . . . all their lifetime subject to bondage" (Heb. 2:15). How good it is to know Him "who hath abolished death, and hath brought life and immortality to light through the gospel" (2 Tim. 1:10)! Those who know Him may truly say, "Yea, though I walk through the valley of the shadow of death, I shall fear no evil: for thou art with me; thy rod and thy staff they comfort me."

Annihilationism

The Seventh Day Adventists claim that the Annihilation of the wicked is taught in Malachi 4:1 by the words "that it shall leave them neither root nor branch." Is this claim true?

No. Annihilationism is a doctrine unknown to Scripture and opposed to it. The language of Amos 2:9 is similar. The destruction predicted in such Scriptures has nothing to do with the souls and spirits of men in the sense of annihilating them; it refers only to the wiping out of God's enemies from the earth.

Soul Sleeping

I have a friend who says that when a person dies his soul is sleeping until Christ come, and also that there is no Hell. What is the answer?

The answer is that your friend is poisoned with Russellism or some other doctrine contrary to Scripture. The Word of God teaches plainly enough, concerning both the saved and the lost, that they are perfectly conscious after death, that the saved dead are absent from the body and present with the Lord, that Heaven is the final abode of the saved, and Hell of the lost (Luke 16:19-31; 2 Cor. 5:6-8; Rev. 20:6, 12-15).

HEAVEN

The Place Called Heaven

Do you consider Heaven a place, say like a planet, somewhere?

Yes. Heaven is a place. I do not say it is "like a planet," but it is "somewhere." The Lord Jesus said He was going to prepare a place for us and that finally where He is we shall be also. It is necessary that Heaven should be a place, for otherwise the resurrected body of our Lord would be nowhere, and that is unthinkable. He sits on a real throne beside His Father in a real place in the highest of the Heavens, far above all other Heavens (Eph. 4:10).

Happiness in Heaven

How can I answer a question like this? If my mother was saved and I was not, could she be happy in Heaven without me?

Those who go to Heaven will certainly be happy there. Just how it could be worked out in the case you mention is not revealed, but it is perfectly clear that Heaven is a place of joy and gladness for all who get there. And how good it is to remember that all may go there who desire to do so, if only they go by the blood sprinkled way!

What It Is Like in Heaven

I had a little daughter who died at the age of six years. While with us, she always delighted in the worship of the family altar, the reading of the Word and prayer. She often talked of the pearly gates and the golden streets of Heaven, and I know she dearly loved the Lord. I believe she is now with Him, don't you? Now, I wonder if she is happy and content. Does she ever think of us, or has all earthly memory ceased?

Also, a dear young Christian woman has passed on leaving a family of small, helpless children. Can she feel content in Heaven when she thinks of these helpless loved ones? Or is the joy so great up yonder that earthly things are not considered? Does time seem long for those up yonder while their loved ones are still on earth? Does the dear Lord meet each of His children as each passes out of this life into eternity? Does a child of God feel Himself entirely at home and at peace as soon as he meets the Lord, or does he gradually get used to it?

I hope I have understood things aright that the departed spirit has a body up yonder which is received as soon as the body of clay is left.

How I wish I could answer all these questions coming from the warm and loving heart of a Christian mother! But not much is revealed in the Book of God concerning these details of the Heavenly state. It is probably better so, for if we knew all about it we should not be content to remain here a single hour. Paul was caught up into that realm, and on account of the abundance of the revelations he had to be given a thorn in the flesh to keep him from being too much puffed up (2 Cor. 12:7). We may rest assured that our dear ones in Heaven are perfectly happy and contented and at peace. And when we get there we shall find that, however rough the road may have been, "right was the pathway leading to this."

Who Will Go to Heaven?

What do the Scriptures teach about who will go to Heaven?

The Scriptures teach that the only way to Heaven is through a personal acceptance of the Lord Jesus Christ as Savior; He has opened the way to God by the shedding of His blood as our substitutionary sacrifice.

How We Shall See God

Shall we see the three Persons of the Godhead in Heaven?

I do not know, for it is not revealed in Scripture. Some students say we shall see only the Son, in whom "dwelleth all the fullness of the Godhead bodily" (Col. 2:9); but in various places in Scripture the Father is seen and also the Son (Dan. 7:13,14; Rev. 5:6,7, for instance); and I know of nothing in Scripture which would preclude the possibility of God manifesting Himself visibly in His three Persons. Anyway, we may depend upon it that if any when we get to Heaven, everything will be perfectly satisfactory (Ps. 65:4).

The Saved in Heaven

Do the souls of Christians at death go to Heaven and be at once with Christ? Do they see Him and talk with Him, and do they have bodies? Are they consciously with the Father and the Son and the saints who have preceded them to Heaven? Can they talk, sing, etc, in their present state?

Here are many questions in one, and the answer to all of them is "Yes." In 2 Corinthians 5:1-8 the matter is discussed, and it is there shown that the picture you draw is a true one. The saints, though now consciously in Heaven with Christ and the family of God, are not yet in their resurrected bodies; their mortal bodies remain in the graves till the Rapture (1 Cor. 15). But they are not unclothed or naked. Nor are they floating around as invisible spirits incapable of speech or action; nor are they asleep or unconscious. Revelation 6:9-11 mentions the souls of slain martyrs. They were seen, they heard, they spoke, and white robes were given them. All this is mystery, but it is true. Let us not worry about the explanation of these mysteries, but just go on believing what the Word says about them.

Our Loved Ones in Heaven

Is there any Scripture warrant for the belief, expressed by so many, that we shall meet our friends and loved ones in Heaven. There evidently will be no husbands or wives, and therefore no mothers or fathers.

We may be sure that we shall not know less in Heaven than we know here. 1 Corinthians 13:12 declares that we shall then see, not "darkly," but "face to face"; now we "know in part," but then we shall know even as we are known. We may confidently expect to know every person in Heaven, and they will all be "our friends and loved ones."

Gender in Heaven

I shall appreciate it very much if you will explain to me whether or not there are gender distinctions in Heaven. In Hebrews 1:4 there is a reference mark pertaining to the word "angels." They say it is always used in the masculine gender. Does this mean that all angels are men? If that is so, how would you speak of women who have passed into the Great Beyond?

Neither men nor women become angels when they go to Heaven. Angels are a separate and distinct order of beings. The old hymn which says, "I want to be an angel," is unscriptural, for human beings are never transformed into angels. It is true that the word "angels" is always used in the Bible in the masculine gender. Male and female, in the human sense, is never ascribed to angels; and in this sense there will be no gender distinctions, even among glorified saints in Heaven; for in Matthew 22:30 it is written that "in the resurrection they neither marry, nor are given in marriage, but are as the angels of God in Heaven" (see also Mark 12:25; Luke 20:34-36).

Knowing Each Other in Heaven

What proof have we that we shall know each other in Heaven?

That we shall know each other in Heaven is shown, as I believe, in 1 Corinthians 13:12. It is difficult to suppose that we shall know less in Heaven than we know here. "For now we see through a glass, darkly; but then face to face: now I know in part; but then shall I know even as also I am known."

No Denominations in Heaven

Could "In my Father's house are many mansions" mean "in my Father's house are many denominations"? I have never heard this interpretation until today when a friend said this is what she believes it means.

I am sorry to disagree with your friend. You may depend upon it that when we reach the Father's house we shall have no more of "denominations." Of course, in the Father's house now and here, there are many denominations; but that is not the meaning of the passage cited; namely, John 14:2.

Wives in Heaven?

What will a man do with two wives in heaven?

He will not have any wives in heaven, for the marriage relation ceases with life upon the earth. Your question is practically identical with one put to our Lord and answered by Him in Matthew 22:23-33: "The same day came to him the Sadducees, which say that there is no resurrection, and asked him, saying, Master, Moses said, If a man die, having no children, his brother shall marry his wife, and raise up seed unto his brother. Now there were with us seven brethren: and the first, when he had married a wife, deceased, and, having no issue, left his wife unto his brother: Likewise the second also, and the third, unto the seventh. And last of all the woman died also. Therefore in the resurrection whose wife shall she be of the seven? for they all had her. Jesus answered and said unto them, Ye do err, not knowing the scriptures, nor the power of God. For in the resurrection they neither marry, nor are given in marriage, but are as the angels of God in heaven. But as touching the resurrection of the dead, have ye not read that which was spoken unto you by God, saying, I am the God of Abraham, and the God of Isaac, and the God of Jacob? God is not the God of the dead, but of the living. And when the multitude heard this, they were astonished at his doctrine."

The True Tabernacle

What is meant by the true tabernacle (Heb 8:2)?

The true tabernacle is the tabernacle in Heaven, a pattern of which was shown to Moses in the holy mount, and after which the earthly tabernacle was modeled (Ex. 25:40; Heb. 8:5).

The New Heaven and New Earth

In Revelation 21 it speaks of a new heaven and a new earth. Are we to take this literally? Is there to be a complete new heaven and new earth, or just this old one cleaned off? In Isaiah 65:17 it says, "I create new heavens and a new earth." This has been discussed in our Bible class, and some think it should not be taken literally.

From Psalm 102:25,26, where we read that the present heavens and earth shall "perish," and "be changed," and from 2 Peter 3:5-13, where the former world, "being overflowed with water, perished" (verse 6), referring to the flood of Noah, it would seem that the new heavens and earth will be the old ones renovated, this time by fire rather than water.

HELL

The Reality of Hell

Do you believe in the biblical Hell, just as the Bible describes it?

Yes. Hell is a place as truly as Heaven is a place. Hades in the New Testament, and Sheol its Old Testament equivalent, are often mistranslated Hell, and this mistranslation tends to confuse the doctrine for English readers. But the Bible surely speaks of Hell. Not only is Hades or Sheol a place, but so also is Gehenna, Hell, the Lake of Fire, prepared for the Devil and his angels, and one day they shall be consigned to that awful place together with all those of the human race whose names are not found written in the Book of Life.

How?

If Hell is everlasting, how can those in Heaven now, or in the future, really be happy if they have relatives, such as father, mother, sister, brother or friend, who are in Hell while they are in Heaven? One would think they would remember these poor lost friends and relatives and often wonder whether God really will keep them there forever and ever. I cannot see how one could be happy in heaven, with this knowledge.

The easiest question to ask, and the hardest to answer, is "How?" The only answer I have to this question is "I do not know." God's ways are not as our ways, nor His thoughts as our thoughts; they are infinitely better and higher (Isa. 55:8,9). No one will be in Hell unless he or she has trodden under foot the Son of God, making His blood common and doing insult to the Spirit of Grace (Heb. 10:29). As for happiness in Heaven, those who find themselves there will be more concerned for the honor and glory of God than for the claims of human relationship. "Wisdom is justified of her children," and God is justified by them that are His.

Eternal Punishment

One of my Sunday school pupils recently came in contact with a Seventh Day Adventist who is visiting in our neighborhood and trying to start a work here. Of course, the question of eternal punishment was brought up, and the Adventist said that the wicked were annihilated in Hell. My friend told him that Revelation 20:10 says that Satan is cast into the Lake of Fire where the Beast and False Prophet are, and is tormented for ever and ever. The Adventist said that the "are" is in

italics because it has been put in the Sacred Writings by the translators, and it has no right to be there. Can such an argument be answered from Scripture?

It is true that the word "are" is supplied by the translators in the Authorized Version of Revelation 20:10. But the pronoun "they" has been omitted by the translators which is plainly in the Greek text. The presence of that pronoun "they" in the text makes it legitimate and necessary to supply the word "are." The Revised Version has the correct rendering of the verse: "And the devil that deceived them was cast into the lake of fire and brimstone, where are also the beast and the false prophet; and they shall be tormented day and night for ever and ever." The doctrine of annihilation, however, is in contradiction to the whole teaching of Scripture, and the answer to it does not need to be rested upon Rev. 10:10. The record of the rich man and Lazarus in Luke 16 (which is sometimes erroneously called a parable), and the testimony of our Lord in Mark 9:38-48, and many other Scriptures on the same subject, ought to be enough, and are enough, to satisfy any honest student of the truth of eternal conscious punishment.

The Second Death

Will you please explain Revelation 20:14 and Matthew 25:41? How can it be a second death if there is everlasting fire? Are the wicked annihilated entirely?

No. As Mr. Spurgeon says, annihilation would be "ended" punishment rather than "endless" punishment. Death never means cessation of existence, but only cessation of life, which is a different thing. God is the source of life, and the worst form of death is that spiritual death by which men are separated from Him. The duration of the punishment of the lost is proved to be endless by the use of the same words as are used to indicate the duration of the life of the saved: they are both *aionion*, translated eternal or everlasting. The same word is used also to denote the endlessness of the being and glory of God.

The Soul after Death

An advocate of no eternal torment seeks to prove to me that God's original sentence was death (Gen. 2:16,17), and that the condition of death is non-existence, or oblivion (Eccl. 3:19,20; 9:5,6, 10; Ps. 146:4). He also says that the Valley of Hinnom (Gr., Gehenna) was a place used by the Jews to destroy the waste of the city, and therefore typifies the complete destruction of the wicked (Ps. 145:20; Ps. 37:20; Rom. 6:23; Matt. 10:28; Heb. 2:14).

He tries to prove that eternal torment is a lie forced upon mankind by Satan, for Christ did not endure eternal torment in addition to dying (Rom. 6:23) to pay the penalty of our sins (1 Cor. 15:3,4, 22,23; 1 Tim. 2:5,6).

Knowing that God is merciful and just, and has no pleasure in the death of the wicked (Ezek. 33:11), how can I refute these statements?

I shall be very grateful for any light that you can give me on this subject.

The best answer I know to the questions you raise is furnished by Dr. C. I. Scofield, whose remarks I quote on the subjects of soul-sleeping and annihilation, from his Correspondence Course, under the subject of "Death":

Two errors concerning the biblical meaning of death require notice. The first is that physical death is the cessation of all consciousness until the resurrection of the body. This error is sometimes called "soul sleeping," and rests mainly upon a few Old Testament passages. For example: Psalm 88:10, "Wilt thou show wonders to the dead?" Psalm 115:17, "The dead praise not Jehovah, neither any that go down into silence;" Isaiah 38:18, "For the grave cannot praise thee; death cannot celebrate thee;" Ecclesiastes 9:5, "But the dead know not anything." It is said that the New Testament word "sleep" explains this unconsciousness. The answer is twofold:—

First. The Old Testament revelation was almost silent upon the future state. Doubtless the truly enlightened saint of the former dispensations dimly foresaw life after death, as in the case of Job (19:26), but even this dim apprehension was exceptional, and seems to have been by a special revelation. Abraham saw Christ's day and was glad (John 8:56). David foresaw the resurrection of Christ (Acts 2:29-31). The general fact is that the time for the unfolding of conditions beyond the grave had not come. It was reserved to Christ to "bring life and immortality to light through the gospel." It is not said that Christ brought life and immortality into *existence*, but into *revelation*. Life and immortality always existed. The grave, therefore, bounded the horizon of the Old Testament vision. Accordingly, speaking within the limits set to their knowledge, the Old Testament writers speak—and correctly for all time—of the grave (whether considered as the place of sepulture, or as Sheol in a wider sense as the intermediate state of the dead) as the place where the activities of life cease. If men are to serve or praise God, they must do it now. This is still true. Pending the first resurrection, the saintly "activities" cease; "They rest from their labors, and their works do follow them" (Rev. 14:13).

Secondly. But cessation of labor and cessation of consciousness are different facts. The New Testament, in which, rather than in the Old, we should expect to find every doctrine completed, leaves it beyond question that the dead, whether lost or saved, are separated from their bodies and are in full consciousness (Isa. 14:9-11; Mark 9:43-48; Luke 16:19-31; John 11:26; 2 Cor. 5:1-8; Phil. 1:21-23; Rev. 6:9-11).

The second error, variously called the annihilation or conditional immortality theory, affirms (with many variations of detail) that only the regenerate have immortality and that the unregenerate cease to exist. In some forms of this teaching the moment of physical death is held to be the moment of non-existence. Others hold that unconscious existence continues until the resurrection of the impenitent dead (Rev. 20:12,13). At that time consciousness is restored and the body raised for the act of judgment after which "the second death" ends both consciousness and existence.

These views rest upon the alleged meaning of such words as "perish" (John 3:15,16), "everlasting destruction" (2 Thess. 1:9), and "destroy" (2 Thess. 2:8). It is contended that these words imply cessation of being.

The first form of this error has already been met. The physical death of the unregenerate is neither annihilation nor unconsciousness. The rich man in Hades is intensely conscious. Lost souls in Sheol are fully aware of the advent of the fallen and doomed.

A very brief examination of the word alleged to imply extinction of being as the penalty of sin will suffice to show the baselessness of the contention. The Greek word *apollumi*, translated "perish" in John 3:15,16, is often used in the New Testament to describe a condition which renders impossible a normal or intended use, as the bottles into which new wine is put are said to "break, and the wine runneth out, and the bottles *perish*—are no longer fit for their intended use (Matt. 9:17). In the parallel passage, in Mark 2:22, the same word is rendered "marred." In Matthew 10:6; 15:24, the same word is rendered "lost." "Go rather to the lost sheep"; "I am not sent but unto the lost sheep." In Matthew 18:11, ". . . come to save that which was lost." In the parables of the Lost Sheep and of the Prodigal Son in Luke 15 the same word (translated "lost") is used of each. Certainly neither the sheep nor the son was "lost" or "perished" in the sense of annihilation.

The "destruction" of 2 Thessalonians 2:8 is that of the "man of sin," the "lawless one," and "beast" at the appearing of the Lord in glory. That this is not annihilation, nor even death, is manifest from Revelation 19:19,20, where it is said that the Beast was "cast alive" into a Lake of Fire. A thousand years afterward they are still there (Rev. 20:10). That this condition is unchangeable is shown from the words of duration, "for ever and ever," which are used to denote the eternal duration of God's own existence (Heb. 1:8; Gal. 1:5; Rev. 4:9,10; 10:6).—(*Scofield Correspondence Course*)

Eternity

Does the word "eternity" in the original writings occur once only?

"Eternity" is not a word of the original Bible languages. It is an English word, and it occurs once only—in Isaiah 57:15. The Hebrew word in this instance, "*ad*," is not the usual word for eternity. The ordinary word for eternity in the Old Testament is *olam* in some of its forms. Its Greek equivalent is *aion*, and this is the New Testament word for age, ages, or, in its adjective form—*aionion*—for eternal or endless. The same word is used to denote (1) the duration of the being and glory of God; (2) the duration of the life and bliss of the saved; and (3) the duration of the punishment of the lost. In Matthew 25:46 both "everlasting" and "eternal" represent *aionion* in the Greek.

No Second Chance

Will unsaved people who are dead have another chance?

The Bible teaches no such thing as "another chance" after death.

Eternal and Everlasting

I find in Young's Analytical Concordance under the word "eternal" forty-two references, and the translation shows the word "eternal" to mean age-lasting in such passages as John 3:15; 10:28; 17:3 and in the Epistles through to Jude. Likewise under the word "everlasting" I find that it is shown as age-lasting in the original twenty-five passages, some of which are John 3:16; 3:36; 5:24, etc. I have always used these passages to show the eternal security of the believer, but now I cannot, since it is only age-lasting. Will you kindly explain?

The Greek word for "eternal" and "everlasting" is *aionion*, and while it is true that various combinations of the word may be translated "for the age" or "unto the ages" or "unto the ages of the ages," it is the only way in Greek to say "eternal" or "everlasting." That it stands for endlessness is apparent from the fact that it is the word used for the being and glory of God, which without controversy is endless. The same word is used for the being and glory of God, for the security of the believer in Christ, and for the punishment of the lost.

Ecclesiastes and Immortality

I have three verses of Scripture which I should like you to explain: they are Ecclesiastes 9:5,6, 10. Do they refer in any way to the immortality of the soul?

No, they do not. The vision of Ecclesiastes is limited to those things that may be seen and known "under the sun"; which phrase is the key to the book. "Verse 10," says Dr. Scofield, "is no more a divine revelation concerning the state of the dead than any other conclusion of 'the Preacher' (Eccl. 1:1) is such a revelation. Reasoning from the standpoint of man 'under the sun,' the natural man can see no difference between a dead man and a dead lion (verse 4). A living dog is better than either. No one would quote verse 2 as a divine revelation. These reasonings of man apart from divine revelation are set down by inspiration just as the words of Satan (Gen. 3:4; Job 2:4,5) are so set down. But that life and consciousness continue between death and resurrection is directly affirmed in Scripture (Isa. 14:9-11; Matt. 22:32; Mark 9:43-48; Luke 16:19-31; 2 Cor. 5:6-8; Phil. 1:21-23; Rev. 6:9-11)."

ASSURANCE

Saved and Sure of It

You made a statement recently that has perplexed me somewhat. As nearly as I can recall, you said, "It is a wonderful thing to be saved and not know it, but it is much more wonderful to be saved and know it." Do I understand you to mean that there will be some who are actually saved and will be caught up at the Rapture who are not aware that they are saved? Can a man believe and not know that he does?

It is true that I made the statement in almost, if not quite, the the words you quote: "It is a wonderful thing to be saved and not know it, but it is much more wonderful to be saved and know it." I did not mean by those words, however, just what you thought I meant. What I had in mind was the fact that there are many dear children of God who have salvation but do not have assurance of that salvation. They believe on the Lord Jesus Christ. They have received Him as their Savior. They are born again. They have salvation, and are perfectly safe; but on account of a lack of teaching they have not rested in the fact that the work is done. They need what the New Testament calls "the full assurance of faith," "the full assurance of understanding," and "the full assurance of hope."

Knowing When We Are Saved

Must every saved person know the time and the place, and when and where he was saved?

Not necessarily. It is an error to insist that unless we know precisely when and where we were saved we are not saved at all. When an outbreaking hardened sinner is born again, of course he knows the time and place; but, happily, there are many saved in childhood and youth. In many cases the outward change is too slight to be seen by human eyes. This lack of outward change does not mean that there is no great change in such cases. The change indeed is miraculous, and God sees it and knows all about it. None of us remembers his first birth, but the fact that we are here proves that we have been born. The great thing to know is that we are now in Christ, and if we are in Him we need not worry about when and where we get there.

Knowing Our Destination

Do you think people know just before they die where they are going? I have heard of them telling where they were going. What do you think?

I should not like to wait until just before I die to know where I am going. I have known for a long time exactly where I am going, and it is the privilege of all of God's people to know this thing. The First Epistle of John was written to those who believe on the name of the Son of God that they may know that they have eternal life (1 John 5:13); and of course since we know that we have eternal life we know where we are going. We know that the moment we are "absent from the body" we shall be "at home with the Lord" (2 Cor. 5:8, R.V.).

As to vision given to those about to die, I can well believe that it is often true that God's children are permitted to see into the world beyond. It is said that Mr. Moody during his dying moments had such a vision, and of course the same thing is said of many others.

Sure of Heaven

I listened to a prayer meeting address recently given by a pastor starting with the words, "We can never be sure of Heaven until we are there." This address was directed against the doctrine of the believer's security. The text used was Romans 2:7, and the speaker stated that only those Christians "who by patient continuance in well doing seek for glory and honor and immortality" will eventually inherit eternal life. He insisted that Christians must be persistent and must "hold on" if they would finally reach Heaven. I should greatly appreciate your exposition of this verse.

The verse must be interpreted in the light of its context. There are four principles of judgment enumerated in Romans 2:1-16: namely, (1) "according to truth" (2); (2) "according to his deeds: to them who by patient continuance," etc., (6 and 7); (3) "there is no respect of persons with God" (11); and (4) "according to my gospel" (16). Under the first three of these principles there would be no hope for any sinner, but under the fourth principle there is assured hope for anyone who may take his place under the shelter of the shed blood of the Son of God. In other words, the pastor's text had nothing to do with the pastor's sermon or with his theme. The believer's eternal security rests upon ample grounds in the Word of God and cannot be questioned by anyone who understands the principle of salvation by grace.

ETERNAL SECURITY

Can the Saved Be Lost?

Is it possible for a truly born-again one to be lost?

It is by no means possible for a truly born-again one to be lost (John 10:27-30).

Once Saved Always Saved

A Bible teacher in one of his talks said that a man once saved was always saved. He proved it by Bible verses entirely to my satisfaction. I am a college student and am trying to get some of my close college friends to see the thing as clearly as I do. Will you please send me some verses and reasons to prove this point?

In connection with this subject it is well to remember that: Salvation is a *gift*.

It is received through *faith alone*. A man can *do* nothing either to save himself or to keep himself saved; if he could, then salvation would be at least in part by works which the Word of God emphatically denies.

It is by *grace*, absolutely independent of any merit on the part of the recipient. It cannot be merited in any slightest degree, otherwise it would not be by grace.

When a man receives Jesus Christ as his personal Savior, he is born of God, he becomes a child of God. This is not a figure of speech, but an actuality, and having been born he cannot be unborn.

The life which the believer receives is eternal life. In God's reckoning the believer is already seated with Christ in Heaven.

See Romans 6:23; 8:29-39; John 1:12,13; 3:15,16, 18, 36; 5:24; 6:39,40; 10:27-30; Acts 10:43; 16:31; Romans 1:16; 3:21-26; chapter 4; 10:8-10; Galatians chapter 3; Ephesians 2:1-10; Colossians 3:1-4; 1 Peter 1:3-5; 1 John 5:1-13, etc. These passages could be added to almost indefinitely.

Is the Backslider Lost?

In your teaching of the Parable of the Prodigal Son you said that both the prodigal and his elder brother were saved but out of fellowship. If saved, they must be safe also. Do you mean that if the prodigal had died during his wanderings he would have gone to Heaven? What is the spiritual state of a backslider? Hebrews 10:29 seems to be a contradiction of your statement. I always supposed that the lesson to be drawn from the story of the prodigal son is the forgiveness of God.

Your supposition is right. But "the forgiveness of God" has many aspects. For example, a sinner who turns to God receives forgiveness of sin, but so also does a sinning saint who turns to God from his sinning and is thus restored to fellowship. In your question concerning the Parable of the Father and His Two Sons, you are confusing symbols with the things symbolized. The statement to which you refer was that "the men symbolized are both saved, and both are backsliders. That is, they are children of the Father, but out of fellowship." You now ask whether we "mean that if the prodigal had died during his wanderings he would have gone to Heaven." If you mean to ask whether the backslidden Christian (who is symbolized by the prodigal), if he should die during the period of his backsliding, would yet go to Heaven, the answer is Yes. For a backslidden Christian is still a Christian and is still a child of God, though he be out of fellowship. A case in point is furnished by the 11th chapter of 1 Corinthians. In the latter part of that chapter there is a discussion of the disorderly conduct of the Lord's Supper by the Corinthian Church. This had become so grievous that God had been compelled to exercise discipline by visiting His people with sickness and even death, for many of them had actually died under His hand. That is to say, they were backslidden and they died during their backsliding. And yet they went to Heaven, as is shown by verses 30-32: "For this cause many are weak and sickly among you, and many sleep. For if we would judge ourselves, we should not be judged. But when we are judged, we are chastened of the Lord, that we should not be condemned with the world." Backsliding is attended by immeasurable loss. But salvation is a gift whose keeping is not committed to those who are saved. The same God who saves them keeps them.

Hebrews 10:29 has no application to a saved man. The 26th verse speaks of those who "sin wilfully" after having received (not salvation, but) "the knowledge of the truth." Many a man has the knowledge of the truth but refuses to walk in the truth. He knows that Jesus is a Savior, and yet he rejects Him. Now, in the 29th verse he is described as one "who hath trodden under foot the Son of God, and hath counted the blood of the covenant, wherewith he was sanctified, an unholy thing, and hath done despite unto the Spirit of grace." This is not a backslidden Christian, but a rebellious and blasphemous unbeliever.

All confusion on this question would disappear if we once learned that salvation is by grace. Grace is favor, and is independent of merit, of deservings, or of works; it is "the gift of God."

Difficult to Determine

In James 5:19,20 is the one erring from the truth a believer who is backslidden, and is his salvation from the death of backsliding?

The Epistle of James like that to the Hebrews is addressed "to the twelve tribes which are scattered abroad," and it has the Jews particularly in mind. Whether the "brethren" of James 5:19 are the writer's brethren in the racial sense or in an evangelical sense is difficult to determine. And whether he is here speaking of a backslidden Christian or a lost sinner is a question concerning which equally devout and godly writers differ. In either case the passage is somewhat obscure, and the rule may be well applied here, "Never use an if to contradict a Verily, verily I say unto you." It is clear from Scripture elsewhere that a backslidden saint may be chastened even unto physical death (1 Cor. 11:30-32). And on the other hand it is clear from Scripture that the unsaved sinner, unless he gets saved, will finally be cast into the Lake of Fire which is the second death (Rev. 20:15; 21:8).

Forgiveness

If a Christian backslides or commits some sin, must he go before the church to make confession, or may he go to God in secret and confess to Him and have forgiveness? I recently heard a minister say that if public confession was not made, God would send severe chastisement.

It depends much upon the character of the sin and backsliding. If the sin was against the church, then confession ought to be made to the church as well as to God. If it was against an individual or individuals, confession should be made to him or them. The confession of 1 John 1:9 is confession to God; but in James 5:16 it is written, "Confess your faults one to another."

Eternal Security and Backsliding

Does the doctrine or theory of eternal security imply that Christians cannot become backsliders ?

No; there is no such implication. Christians (meaning truly born-again persons) may backslide, and, alas, most of us do so more or less frequently. But there is a vast difference between the backsliding of a believer and the apostasy of a mere professor. The apostate is described in 1 John 2:18,19. He goes out from us, but in doing so he proves that he was never of us.

The Certainty of Eternal Life

Will you please explain the clause, "for in them ye think ye have eternal life" in John 5:39? It is the word "think" which is not clear to me.

If you will read the passage in the Revised Version your difficulty will clear up. Our Lord was speaking to His enemies among the Jews who sought to kill Him for blasphemy (verse 18). It is to these enemies He said, "Ye search the Scriptures, because ye think that in them ye have eternal life; and these are they which bear witness of me; and ye will not come to me, that ye may have life" (39,40). There is no uncertainty about the believer's possession of eternal life. Please turn to John 6 and read verses 37 to 40, and let your heart rejoice in the certainty of eternal life: "All that the Father giveth me shall come to me; and him that cometh to me I will in no wise cast out" (37). Now notice what follows: "For I came down from heaven, not to do mine own will, but the will of him that sent me. And this is the Father's will which hath sent me, that of all which he hath given me I should lose nothing, but should raise it up again at the last day. And this is the will of him that sent me, that every one which seeth the Son, and believeth on him, may have everlasting life: and I will raise him up at the last day." Nothing could be more satisfying than these words of our precious Lord, assuring His people who believe in Him that they are already in possession of that life which cannot end.

The Believer's Eternal Security

Please tell me what you think of eternal security. I believe in eternal security myself, but I have met so many who do not.

The question as to whether a truly saved man may ever be lost is the question raised here. Great controversies have resulted from the wide divergence of opinion among God's people regarding it. But for one who really understands the Gospel of the grace of God there is no possibility of doubt as to the eternal safety of the Christian. No man can convince another by arguing over isolated passages of Scripture. Taken in their proper connection, all the statements of Scripture dealing with the subject are in perfect harmony. They all teach that since the saved man has been saved by the grace, that is the unmerited favor, of God; since salvation is a gift which he has received by faith; since he never began to deserve it and therefore he cannot keep it by deserving it; and since, even to the end of his earthly life, he must go on coming short of the glory of God which would forfeit his salvation if it were forfeitable; therefore, if any man is ever finally saved at all, it must be by God's power and not by any of his own meritorious works or deservings.

If we could see the Lord Jesus here, in the flesh and visible to our mortal sight; and we were given the privilege of putting the question to Him; and we should ask Him, saying, "O thou blessed Lord Jesus, who hath loved us and washed us from our sins in thine own precious blood, wilt thou not tell us, once and for all, whether we are always in danger of losing our salvation, as some of our teachers insist? Is it possible that one who is really born anew and becomes God's child, may after all be lost?" And suppose He should reply, saying: "My sheep hear my voice, and I know them, and they follow me: and I give unto them eternal life," would that be enough? And suppose He should continue, saying, "And they shall never perish," would that be sufficient? And suppose He should still go on, and say, "Neither shall anyone pluck them out of my hand. My Father, which gave them me, is greater than all; and no one is able to pluck them out of my Father's hand. I and my Father are one." Would that be satisfactory?

Well, He has been here, and said all that, and it is on record in John 10:27-30, and there is nothing in all Scripture that, rightly understood in the light of the context, disputes His statement here in the least particular.

The writer has a dear friend who said to another while they were arguing about this doctrine: "You remind me very much of my son who, while a very small boy, went with me for his first ride in a boat. He had never seen a boat before, and he was greatly interested in it and in the big water in which we were floating. He saw no such danger in that water as I saw, and during the whole trip I was carefully and firmly holding onto him with my hand lest he should fall or jump overboard and be drowned."

"Well," replied his friend, "that's all right, and I see that no one can get us out of God's hand, but we can jump out of His hand if we will, just as your boy could have wriggled out of his coat and jumped into the water."

"But," was the reply, "I was not holding the coat; I was holding the boy; and I saw to it that he could not get out of my hand even if he wanted to. Supposing you should succeed in getting out of God's hand, and staying out, then what would be the result? Would you perish?"

"Certainly."

"But, brother, don't you see that the Lord has covered just that point? He says, 'and they shall never perish.'"

"Why," exclaimed the other, "so He did. I never thought of it that way. O, how wonderful that is! The Lord has said I shall never perish! That lifts a tremendous burden from my heart which I have been bearing for twenty years."

Once in Grace Always in Grace

Please explain the teaching called "once in grace always in grace." Just how far can Christian people indulge in worldly things and feel safe on this statement? Or, in other words, is there any limit to what Christian people may do so long as they are willing to confess their wrong doing and ask for forgiveness? Kindly make this plain, as I am afraid some have a mistaken idea of this saying.

All confusion on the subject of eternal security would disappear from your mind if only you could become clear on the meaning of grace. Salvation is by grace through faith and not by works. We are not saved because we are good, nor are we lost because we are bad. A man who is truly born again is safe forever, and is as sure of Heaven as if he had already been there ten thousand years. He may fall into sin, and, since the flesh in the believer has not been changed a bit and is as corrupt as ever, he may do very evil things. David, for example, was guilty of adultery and murder after he became saved. But David was forgiven and restored to God's fellowship even after doing such terrible things. He suffered greatly, however, as a result of his sins, and every child of God will suffer as the result of the sins he commits.

If a sinning saint refuses to confess his sin then God must deal with him. In 1 Corinthians 5 there is an instance of this kind. Here was a man who was living in openly sinful relation with "his father's wife" (verse 1)—evidently his stepmother. By apostolic authority this man was excluded from the fellowship of the Corinthian church, "to deliver such an one unto Satan for the destruction of the flesh, that the spirit may be saved in the day of the Lord Jesus" (verse 5). The apostolic command was, "Therefore put away from among yourselves that wicked person" (verse 13). It is evident from 2 Corinthians 2 that by this drastic method the sinning Christian was brought to repentance and confession, for in that chapter Paul says: "Ye ought rather to forgive him, and comfort him, lest perhaps such an one should be swallowed up with overmuch sorrow. Wherefore I beseech you that ye would confirm your love toward him. . . . To whom ye forgive any thing, I forgive also: for if I forgave any thing, to whom I forgave it, for your sakes forgave I it in the person of Christ: lest Satan should get an advantage of us: for we are not ignorant of his devices" (2 Cor. 2:7-11).

The question is often raised as to what would happen to a sinning Christian if he should die before being brought to repentance and confession. Happily we have an answer for that also in the New Testament Scriptures. The Corinthian Christians had fallen into sin in connection with the celebration of the Lord's Supper. This is discussed in 1 Corinthians 11:17-34. These sinning Christians had not been brought to repentance as yet, and some of them on this account had become weak and sickly, and some had died under the chastening hand of God. "For as often as ye eat this bread, and drink the cup, ye proclaim the Lord's death till he come. Wherefore whoever shall eat the bread or drink the cup of the Lord in an unworthy manner, shall be guilty of the body and the blood of the Lord. But let a man prove himself, and so let him eat of the bread, and drink of the cup. For he that eateth and drinketh, eateth and drinketh judgment unto himself, if he discern not the body. For this cause many among you are weak and sickly, and not a few sleep. But if we discerned ourselves, we should not be judged. But when we are judged, we are chastened of the Lord, that we may not be condemned with the world" (1 Cor. 11:26-32, R.V.). You see, it is when we refuse to judge ourselves that we bring the chastening hand of our God upon us in judgment, and then we are chastened, "that we may not be condemned with the world." There is no possibility of a child of God coming under the condemnation of God though he may be so chastened as even to be visited with physical death.

Reconciling Scripture

How do you reconcile 1 Corinthians 9:27 and Hebrews 6:4-6 with the doctrine of the eternal security of the saints (John 10:28,29)?

There is no need to "reconcile" Scripture, for it is always harmonious in all its parts. The passages you cite have no bearing upon the doctrine of eternal security. The word "castaway" in 1 Corinthians 9:27 is translated "rejected" in the Revised Version. The Greek word is *adokimos*. The same word is used in 2 Timothy 2:15 without the negative prefix and is there translated "approved." Its meaning in 1 Corinthians 9:27, therefore, is disapproved. What Paul feared was that he might fail in securing his Lord's approval upon his services. His salvation is not in question at all. Compare 1 Corinthians 3:11-15; 11:31,32.

In order to understand the teaching of Hebrews 6:4-6 it is necessary to study the context. Beginning at the 10th verse of the 5th chapter the Lord Jesus is referred to as "called of God an high priest after the order of Melchisedec. Of whom we have many things to say, and hard to be uttered, seeing ye (the Hebrews) are dull of hearing. For when for the time ye (the Hebrews) ought to be teachers, ye (Hebrews) have need that one teach you (Hebrews) again which be the first principles of the oracles of God; and are become such as have need of milk, and not of strong meat. For every one that useth milk is unskillful in the word of righteousness: for he is a babe. But strong meat belongeth to them that are of full age (full growth, R.V.), even those who by reason of use have their senses exercised to discern both good and evil."

Then comes the exhortation of the opening verses of the sixth chapter, in which the writer calls upon his Hebrew brethren, who have not yet received Christ although they have come to a knowledge of Him, beseeching them to declare themselves openly for Christ. The Old Testament was their elementary school, their kindergarten, the place of first things or principles. The time had now come for graduation from the primer grade. The law was their schoolmaster unto Christ that they might be justified by faith (Gal. 3:24). He writes now to them saying, "Therefore leaving the principles of the doctrine of Christ, let us go on unto full growth (the same Greek word as in the preceding verse is translated "full age"); not laying again the foundation of repentance from dead works, and of faith toward God, of the doctrine of baptisms, and of laying on of hands, and of resurrection of the dead, and of eternal judgment." All these are Old Testament doctrines even including "the doctrine of baptisms" (compare Mark 7:3,4 in the Greek). The apostle is exhorting the Hebrews to go on unto Christ to whom all these doctrines pointed. "And this will we do, if God permit. For it is impossible for those who were once enlightened (as the Hebrews had been) and have tasted of the heavenly gift, and were made partakers of (literally, companions, those who go along with) the Holy Ghost, and have tasted the good word of God (this had come to them through the ages by the prophets), and the powers of the coming age (these were the miracles they had witnessed), if they shall fall away, to renew them again unto repentance; seeing they crucify to themselves the Son of God afresh, and put him to an open shame."

There is nothing here which speaks of a born-again person losing his salvation. If it referred to such, then it would prove that one who had thus lost his salvation could never again be saved. "It is impossible (not difficult, not improbable, but impossible) . . . to renew them again unto repentance." This proves too much for those who would use it to set aside the doctrine of the believer's security, but when it is applied to Hebrews, and especially to those Hebrews living at the time the Epistle was written, it all becomes perfectly clear. It teaches that there is no salvation for any unless they receive the Lord Jesus Christ and put themselves under the shelter of His shed blood. This, of course, is true for all time.

Paul's Fear

Kindly explain what Paul meant by his fear that he might become a castaway (1 Cor. 9:27).

The word for "castaway" is *adokimos* and means "disapproved." Paul was speaking of his service and not of his salvation (compare 1 Cor. 3:11-15 and 11:31,32).

Enduring to the End

Kindly explain Matthew 10:22; 24:13 and Mark 13:13.

In each of these verses our Lord is quoted as saying, "He that endureth to the end shall be saved." The "end" to which He was referring in each case was the same end, that is, the end of the Great Tribulation period just preceding His coming to judgment. This is true even in Matthew 10:22; for, as Dr. Scofield well says on that chapter, "The scope of verses 16-23 reaches beyond the personal ministry of the twelve, covering in a general sense the sphere of service during the present age. Verse 23 has in view the preaching of the remnant in the Tribulation, and immediately preceding the return of Christ in glory. The remnant then will not have gone over the cities of Israel till the Lord comes" (*Scofield Reference Bible*). The word about enduring to the end is a note of encouragement for His suffering witnesses in that awful day of trial.

"Ye Think Ye Have"

What is meant by "think" in John 5:39? May not we who believe KNOW whether we are saved?

Indeed we may, and we should. The Revised Version makes a much needed correction here. Verses 37-40 read as follows: "And the Father that sent me, he hath borne witness of me. Ye have neither heard his voice at any time, nor seen his form. And ye have not his word abiding in you: for whom he sent, him ye believe not. Ye search the scriptures, because ye think that in them ye have eternal life; and these are they which bear witness of me; and ye will not come to me, that ye may have life."

The First Epistle of John was written expressly "that ye may know that ye have eternal life, even unto you that believe on the name of the Son of God" (5:13, R.V.).

Discipline and Eternal Security

When convenient, would you please give an explanation of Ezekiel 3:17-21, especially the latter part of the 19th, 20th and 21st verses? Should they be applied to the Church? This passage has been used to prove that a believer may become a lost soul by failing to warn the unsaved.

This passage and other similar ones in the Old and New Testaments refer to discipline rather than to eternal life. The death referred to is not spiritual death but physical which is sometimes visited by God upon His people as chastening and discipline for their sins. This doctrine is clearly set forth in 1 Corinthians 11:27-32. Here were people who had sinned against God in relation to the Lord's Supper, and they were chastened, some with sickness and others with death. But all this was that they "should not be condemned with the world" (verse 32). The word rendered "damnation" in verse 29 has been properly changed by the Revisers to "judgment." It is not possible for believers to come under condemnation, though it is possible for them to come under the chastening hand of God, sometimes even to the extent of physical death.

Working Out Our Own Salvation

Please explain Philippians 2:12. How can we work out our own salvation? Does not this passage conflict with the thought of the sixth verse of the first chapter?

In Philippians 1:6 the apostle writes: "Being confident of this very thing, that he which hath begun a good work in you will perform it until the day of Jesus Christ." Your confusion is natural if you think of "salvation" in 2:12 as referring to the believer's eternal welfare. That it does not refer to this is evident when we remember that the Epistle is addressed to those who are already saved, to "the saints in Christ Jesus" (1:1). The word "salvation" in 1:19 evidently relates to Paul's hope of being delivered from prison and being permitted to visit his Philippian friends (compare the context, particularly 1:25,26). "Deliverance" is a perfectly good translation of the Greek word for "salvation," and it may denote temporary as well as eternal deliverance. I am convinced that in Philippians 2:12 it signifies temporary deliverance. The Philippian church was depending too much upon Paul, and felt helpless in his absence to conduct its affairs or to solve its problems. In its perplexity Paul is appealed to through Epaphroditus' visit to the apostle in Rome. In writing to them in reply, the apostle directs the attention of the Philippian believers to the presence of God with them, who was as able to deliver them from difficulty in Paul's absence as in his presence. Therefore let them work out their *own* deliverance with fear and trembling, for though Paul was not with them, *God* was there, even dwelling in and with them, and working among them, both to will and to do that which would please Him. The preposition translated "in" is frequently rendered "among" in the New Testament. This interpretation is in keeping with the context which cannot be said of the interpretation usually given.

Saved and Safe

If a saved man cannot get lost, what do Luke 9:62; Hebrews 3:12-14; 6:4-6; 10:26-39; 12:15; 1 Peter 5:8; 2 Peter 2:20,21; 3:17 and Revelation 22:19, mean?

Luke 9:62 has no bearing on the doctrine. There is no indication that the man addressed was a born-again man. Hebrews 3:12-14 is a warning against *unbelief* (see verse 19). Like all these hortatory passages in Hebrews it had in mind Hebrews particularly who still supposed they could be saved through Judaism without believing God's testimony concerning His Son. The things mentioned in Hebrews 6:4-6 are not the "things that accompany salvation" (see verse 9). In Hebrews 10:26 read "sin-offering" for "sacrifice for sins." The Hebrews were warned against supposing that the temple sin-offering could avail for them now that the Son of God had offered Himself in their behalf; if they sinned willfully in rejecting Him they must be lost. Hebrews 12:15 is along the same line: let no man suppose that there is salvation any other way than by "the grace of God." 1 Peter 5:8 is a warning against yielding to Satan; it does not apply to the question we are considering. 2 Peter 2:20,21 should be read with verse 22. These professors may look like sheep but in reality they are only dogs and swine needing to be born again before they could have the sheep nature. To know the way of righteousness is not enough: salvation is only for those who do not "turn from the holy commandment delivered unto them," namely, to believe on God's Son Jesus Christ (John 3:18). 2 Peter 3:17 is an exhortation to steadfastness; it has no hint that any child of God is in danger of being lost. Revelation 22:19 has no suggestion that a child of God would or could do the thing forbidden. If you want to know the truth about the believer's security, go to some Scripture where the doctrine is really taken up and discussed, as, for example, John 10:27-30. The saved man is forever safe.

The Vine and the Branches

Please explain John 15:2, 6: "Every branch in me that beareth not fruit he taketh away. . . . If a man abide not in me, he is cast forth as a branch, and is withered; and men gather them and cast them into the fire, and they are burned."

The Scripture you quote has long presented a very real difficulty to students of the Word, and is a favorite passage with the Arminian commentators, for they insist that it proves the possibility of a truly saved man being lost. On the other hand, the Calvinists are much troubled by it, and among them there is no consensus of opinion.

Suppose we say that these words teach the possibility of a truly regenerate man being lost after all, what shall we then do with the great body of Scripture which teaches the exact opposite? No prophecy of Scripture is of any *by-itself* interpretation (2 Peter 1:10). We must not interpret any single passage so as to make it flatly contradict all that Scripture elsewhere says upon the subject.

There is, for example, no room for doubt as to the meaning of our Lord Jesus' words in John 10:27-30. He declared that His sheep *have* eternal life, and that "they shall *never* perish."

Then, too, the whole fabric of the Gospel rests upon the doctrine of grace, and grace is unmerited favor; by it the whole thought of salvation by works is excluded. If a believer sins—and what believer does not sin?—his fellowship is suspended, his communion with God is interrupted, but his salvation is not jeopardized, nor is his restoration to God's fellowship by means of being "saved again," but it is through confession. "If we confess our sins, he is faithful and just to forgive us our sins, and to cleanse us from all unrighteousness" (1 John 1:9). But what if the sinning believer refuses to confess his sins, what then? The answer is in 1 Corinthians 11:31,32: "If we would judge ourselves, we should not be judged. But when we are judged, we are *chastened* of the Lord, that we *should not be condemned* with the world." This chastening may take the form of weakness, or sickness, or even death, as shown by the context, but it is chastening, and not condemnation. "Whom the Lord loveth he chasteneth," but condemnation is impossible for the believer (John 5:24; Rom. 8:1, R.V.; Heb. 12:6).

On the other hand, what shall we say to the words, "Every branch in me that beareth not fruit he taketh away"? Some writers tell us that this taking away is the result of chastening, as in 1 Corinthians 11:30 "many sleep"; that is, many in the Corinthian church had died on account of unconfessed sin. "They are taken away as branches, though not lost" (*Malachi Taylor*). This might be an acceptable explanation were it not for the terrible words of verse 6 of this chapter, "Men gather them, and cast them into the fire, and they are burned."

Others, and this is a large class of writers, tell us that these severed branches were never really in the vine at all, except by outward appearance; that they are *professing* Christians. Dean Alford, for example, says that they "are made members of Christ by baptism," the vine being "*the visible church here*, of which Christ is the *inclusive* Head: the vine *contains* the branches; hence the unfruitful, as the fruitful, are 'in me,'" that is, in Christ. This is hardly satisfactory when one remembers that the words we are studying are words from the mouth of the Lord Himself, who spake as other men never spake, and all of whose words are pure words.

Still other writers insist that the unfruitful branches are the people of Israel, who indeed are described in Romans 11 as natural branches cut off from the good olive tree. But this interpretation also fails, for the dispensational cutting off is really national rather than individual. Israel as a nation is cut off; "blindness in part is happened to Israel" for the time being, "until the fullness of the Gentiles be come in" (Rom. 11:25-27). Yet whenever an individual Jew believes in the Lord Jesus Christ he is received on the same footing as other believers. "God hath not cast away his people which he foreknew" (Rom. 11:2).

By still other writers we are taught that what we have here is a parable of service, and that it is not to be interpreted as applying to salvation. These writers emphasize the words "as a branch" in the 6th verse, and they tell us that a man might be cast forth as a branch, that is, that he might be a rejected servant, without having his salvation endangered. But there is nothing said in the parable about service; the whole theme is fruit-bearing; and there is a vast difference between service and fruit-bearing, though no one will deny the real connection between them. Believers are "created in Christ Jesus unto good works" (Eph. 2:10), and this is service; but fruit is not works. "The fruit of the Spirit is love, joy, peace," etc. (Gal. 5:22, 23). These are not things that a Christian is called upon to do, nor are they things that he *can* do. They are the effect of yielding, rather than of working.

Great light is shed upon our problem when we consider the comprehensive scope of our Lord's atoning work. There is a sense in which Christ, by His work on the cross, displaced Adam as the federal head of the race. In God's reckoning Christ died for all, and in Him all died. The purpose of His death was "that they that live should no longer live unto themselves, but unto him who for their sakes died and rose again" (2 Cor. 5:15, R.V.). This is the true meaning of our Lord's mysterious words in John 12:32, "And I, if I be lifted up from the earth, will draw all men unto me. This he said, signifying what death he should die." Lifted up on the cross, He drew all men unto Him and died in their room and stead.

In this federal sense, the race is reckoned as in Him. In 1 Corinthians 15:22 it is written, "As in Adam all die, even so in Christ shall all be made alive." And this includes not only the saved, who are to "be raised incorruptible" (verse 52), but also "the rest of the dead," who must be raised to receive their final doom (Rev. 20:5,12-15). Through Adam's sin "judgment came unto all men to condemnation; even so through one act of righteousness (that is, by the righteous act of Christ on the cross) the free gift came unto all men to justification of life. For as through the one man's disobedience the many were made sinners, even so through the obedience of the one shall the many be made righteous" (Rom. 5:18,19, R.V.).

Not all men are saved, and yet the sacrificial death of Jesus cannot be limited in its effects to believers. While the Scriptures do not teach universal salvation, they surely do teach universal redemption. Christ was "the Lamb of God, which taketh away the sin of *the world*" (John 1:29) . When He died on the cross, it was in the divine purpose "that he by the grace of God should taste death for every man" (Heb. 2:9). He "is the Savior of all men, specially of those who believe" (1 Tim. 4:10). "Those that believe" are saved, while those that reject are lost; but it remains true that even those who are lost have a Savior, for He "is the Savior of all men." He is truly "the propitiation for our sins: and not for ours only, but also for the sins of the whole world" (1 John 2:2).

Mr. Spurgeon, preaching on this 2nd verse of John 15, says: "Both the persons described in the text were in Christ: in Christ in different senses it is plain, because the first persons were not so in Christ as to bring forth fruit. Consequently, as fruit is that by which we are to judge a man, they were not in Christ effectually, graciously, influentially, or so as to receive the fruit-creating sap. If they had brought forth fruit, their fruitfulness would have been a sign that they were in Christ *savingly*. Who will venture to say that a man who yields no fruit of righteousness can be really a Christian? Yet they were in Christ in some sense or other." He then goes on to express the opinion that the rejected branch had been in Christ only as a matter of outward profession. He is quite right in saying that they were "in Christ in some sense or other," but he is not clear as to their exact position. Hengstenberg well remarks that "what is spoken of is the unfruitful branches actually being *in Christ* the vine, and not their thinking themselves or others thinking them, to be so."

Take the case of little children. We all believe that little children, until "the age of accountability," whenever that may be—and God knows when it comes—are saved; but *why* are they saved? Surely it is not because they are good, for they are not good. They are sinners and "by nature the children of wrath"; and yet they are saved because they are included in the redemptive work of Christ on the cross of Calvary. He died for them, because He died for all, and they are safe under the blood until they have reached the place where they are morally responsible before God. When "the age of accountability" arrives, then the individual must personally believe on the Lord Jesus Christ or be lost. If he believes, he abides in Christ, is born again, and becomes the possessor of eternal life; and he shall never perish. If, on the other hand, he rejects the Savior, "he is cast forth as a branch and is withered." If he goes on rejecting and finally rejects, he will be cast into the fire and burned.

There are those who insist that a believer always retains freedom of the will to depart from the faith just as he was free to accept or reject salvation in the beginning. But this is false reasoning. A child of God has no more "freedom of the will" to cease to be God's child than has the child of any other father to set aside such a relationship. A child of God may be a disobedient child, but he remains a child, and for his disobedience he must reckon with a faithful Father who will deal with him as with a son and not a bastard (Heb. 12:8).

"Thanks be unto God for His unspeakable gift!"

JUSTIFICATION

Just Persons

Who were the "just persons" in Luke 15:7?

They were non-existent, imaginary persons. Of course, there are no persons who are righteous except those who are justified by faith. But the Pharisees and scribes of verse 2 imagined themselves to be "just persons, which need no repentance." Our Lord's Parable of the Lost Sheep was intended to teach them otherwise, and to show them that the publicans and sinners of verse 1, whom they considered hopeless, were the cause of great joy in Heaven, because they repented, while the religious leaders—the Pharisees and scribes—were themselves the hopeless ones because they refused to repent.

The Two Justifications

Since God declares His own righteousness that has real value before Him (Rom. 3:26), and imputes that same righteousness, or accounts it, to the ungodly, justifying him (Rom. 4:5), how can you reconcile the statements of Romans 4:2-4 with James 2:14, 21,22, 24, 26?

There is no discord between the two passages. Paul is discussing the sinner's justification "before God" (Rom. 4:2), while James is occupied with the believer's justification before men—"show me" and "ye see" are his key-words (verses 18 and 24). God looks upon the heart and sees the faith there, and that faith is counted unto us for righteousness. This is when we first believe, and it is justification by faith. It is this justification "before God" that saves us, and it is "without works." It may be a long time afterwards that we are able to demonstrate our faith in the sight of men, so that they may be shown, or made to see, that we are truly born again. It is true that both Paul and James cite Abraham in their arguments, and both point to Genesis 15:6; but James quotes in this connection the words, "and he was called the friend of God." God called Abraham His friend in Isaiah 41:8, but Jehoshaphat also called Abraham a friend of God in 2 Chronicles 20:7. He was justified in the sight of men as well as "before God."

But James cites another Scripture. He points to Genesis 22:12. There was an interval of forty years between Abraham's believing the Lord in Genesis 15 and his offering up of Isaac on the altar in Genesis 22, and during all that forty years Abraham was a saved man. In brief, Paul in Romans 4 is occupied with our salvation, while James is concerned about our testimony. There is no disagreement between them. It was Paul who in another place wrote that "in Jesus Christ neither circumcision availeth any thing, nor uncircumcision; but faith which worketh by love;" and again, "ye were sometimes darkness, but now are ye light in the Lord: walk as children of light" (Gal. 5:6; Eph. 5:8).

LAW AND GRACE

Death to the Law

Was the law of Sinai ever given to the Gentiles? Was it not given exclusively to Israel? If so, how can it be said that any one has died to the law except a Jewish believer?

The law of Sinai was issued only to Israel. That nation was carefully taken out of Egypt and in a separated place in the wilderness it received the law through Moses. In Romans 2:14 it is twice stated that the Gentiles have not the law. And in Romans 6:14 it is plainly declared that the Christian, whether he be formerly a Jew or a Gentile, is "not under the law, but under grace."

Read Romans 2:14,15, as given in the Revised Version: "For when Gentiles that have not the law do by nature the things of the law, these, not having the law, are a law unto themselves; in that they show the work of the law written in their hearts, their conscience bearing witness therewith, and their thoughts one with another accusing or else excusing them." The thought here is that the Gentiles who have not the law have a conscience which bears witness in agreement with the moral principles of the law, and which testifies against them when they do the things forbidden in the law. They have no written document of the revelation of God's decrees such as was given to Israel. But God has written these decrees in their moral essentials upon the Gentiles' hearts.

In Galatians 2:16-21 the definite article before the word "law" is omitted, for the apostle there is dealing with a principle. Literally he writes that "a man is not justified by works of law," and "by works of law shall no flesh be justified." And in verse 19 he says, "I through law died unto law, that I might live unto God." And again, "if righteousness is through law, then Christ died for nought."

Thus we see that all believers, Gentiles as well as Jews, have died to law-keeping as a principle and have been brought into the realm of grace where, since there is no law, sin cannot have dominion over them (Rom. 6:14).

The Decalogue

Is the Decalogue for this dispensation?

No. It was a temporary covenant, given only to Israel, and was "added" (to the Abrahamic covenant) "till the Seed (Christ) should come to whom the promise was made." "Before faith came" Israel was "kept under the law, shut up unto the faith which should afterwards be revealed. Wherefore the law was" Israel's "schoolmaster to lead" them "unto Christ, that" they "might be justified by faith. But after that faith is come" even they "are no longer under a schoolmaster" (Gal. 3:19-25). As for the Gentiles, they have never had the law (Rom. 2:14). And as for the Christian, he is "not under the law, but under grace" (Rom. 6:14).

Free from the Law

The believer is "dead" to sin, to the Law, to the world (Gal. 6:14), legally, judicially, but not experimentally; and the Law has nothing to do with my standing before God, my acceptance in Christ; but is needed to regulate my state, my walk through this world. Is this right?

Not entirely. The New Testament declares that "the law is not made for a righteous man"; and if you have been justified by faith that is precisely what you are—"a righteous man." The Law of Sinai has no direct bearing upon the Christian, though it is a part of the Scripture given by inspiration and is profitable for instruction in righteousness (2 Tim. 3:16). It is not, however, the believer's rule of life any more than it is his means of life. In fact, he does not come to Mount Sinai at all (Heb. 12:18-24). In Christ the Law is "done away" (2 Cor. 3:1-11); and the promise is that "sin shall not have dominion over you: for ye are not under the law, but under grace" (Rom. 6:14). The Law was a temporary covenant—Israel's "schoolmaster unto Christ," that they "might be justified by faith. But after that faith is come," even Israel is "no longer under a schoolmaster" (Gal. 3:19-25). The believer's means of life is Christ, his rule of life is Christ, and his life is Christ (2 Cor. 3:18; Col. 3:1-4). "Stand fast therefore in the liberty wherewith Christ hath made us free, and be not entangled again with the yoke of bondage" (Gal. 5:1).

Our Moral Obligations

Although those who have been redeemed are no longer under the law, aren't they still obligated to keep the Ten Commandments, in that they do not steal, kill etc.?

The Ten Commandments did not make it wrong to steal and kill. It was just as wrong to do these things *before* the Law of Sinai was issued as afterward. The Christian is not under the Law of Sinai at all, but the New Testament gives him his rule of life, which is to obey the Lord Jesus Christ in all things. It is a new law of love, written in the believer's heart through the new birth. Under this new rule, "let him that stole steal no more"; "lie not one to another"; "love one another." The Christian lives under what has been called "the expulsive power of a new affection."

Commandments

In 1 John 5:2 and 3 the word "commandments" is used three times. Is John referring to the Ten Commandments? I have a friend who claims that he endeavors to obey the commandments out of love to the Lord Jesus. If I tell him that no man has ever kept the Law, excepting

the Lord Jesus, and no man ever will, he quotes Philippians 4:13. Believing the entire body of Scripture from Genesis to Revelation, he admits and believes that justification comes by faith alone. Furthermore, he claims that the Ten Commandments are written not with ink, but by the Spirit of the living God upon his heart (2 Cor. 3:3). He states that I have nine of them written on my heart, but have failed to let the Spirit of God write the fourth one there. He admits that the believer is not under the Law and that love is the believer's rule of life, and the believer should, therefore, out of a heart of love remember the sabbath day to keep it holy.

How would you handle the situation? I imagine your answer will be that the Law was never given to the Gentile or the Church and therefore there is no sabbath to be observed by the believer. Kindly give me further information.

The man who claims that the Ten Commandments are the commandments referred to in 1 John 5:2,3, has the burden of proof upon him. There is nothing there to show it, and certainly God has many other commandments besides the Ten Words of Sinai which He gave to Israel and only to Israel. It is surely a strange state of mind that would lead a man to use the 3rd chapter of 2 Corinthians to prove that we are under the Law of the commandments, since that is precisely the chapter which declares that the Law (and not the ceremonial Law either, but the so-called moral Law, "written and engraven in stones") is "done away" and "abolished" (verses 11, 13).

One needs only to read the Epistle to the Galatians, which is so largely devoted to this question, to find, unless he is absolutely closed against conviction, that the Law of Sinai was a temporary covenant given for temporary purposes "till the Seed should come to whom the promise was made" (Gal. 3:19). If it were not true that the Law was done away in Christ, sin should certainly "have dominion" over "us," but that dominion is now impossible for the very reason that we "are not under the law, but under grace" (Rom. 6:14).

As for the sabbath, it was done away with the rest of the commandments, and though we do have the Lord's Day as the gracious gift of the risen Christ to us, it is a misnomer to refer to it as the sabbath. Those who do so are guilty of putting the new wine of the Gospel into the old wineskins of Judaism. The result is that the wineskins break, and the wine is spilled, and what we have left is neither Judaism nor Christianity, but a sorry hodgepodge, lacking both the terror of Law and the freeness of grace.

The Child Conductor

Please explain how the Law is our schoolmaster to bring us unto Christ (Gal. 3:24).

The words "our" and "us" refer to Israelites rather than to us. In studying this passage we should be careful to observe the pronouns. Paul, who wrote the Epistle to the Galatians, was a Hebrew, and had therefore been under the Law of Moses until he became a Christian. As for the Gentiles, they have never had the Law, as we are told twice in one verse (Rom. 2:14). The word translated "schoolmaster" really means child-conductor. In the eastern household, this was a servant, a part of whose duty it was to conduct the child from the home to school, day by day. The point in the passage is that after conducting the child to school, the child-conductor had nothing more to do with the child. The Law of Moses was a child-conductor for the Hebrews to bring them to Christ that they might be justified by faith. But since faith has come, even the Hebrews "are no longer under a child-conductor" (verse 25). In the 26th verse, the pronoun is changed from the first person to the second. In the Galatian churches the people were mostly from the Gentiles, and since it was true for Gentile Christians as well as Hebrew Christians that they had been saved by faith, the apostle says: "For ye are all the children of God by faith in Christ Jesus." The Spirit of God had baptized them into Christ, and in this new relationship "there is neither Jew nor Greek, there is neither bond nor free, there is neither male nor female: for ye are all one in Christ Jesus. And if ye be Christ's, then are ye Abraham's seed, and heirs according to the promise" (verses 27-29). Childhood and heirship are not matters of Law, but of promise.

Gentiles and the Law

In Romans 2:14, I read that the Gentiles "have not the law." How and where did the Gentiles get the Law, if they had any, and how were they benefited by the Law, not offering sacrifice? In Galatians 3:23, who is meant by the word "we" in the expression "we were kept under the law," by the word "our" in verse 24, "the law was our schoolmaster," and the words "them" and "we" in Galatians 4:5? How does Ephesians 2:12 connect with these passages?

It is true that in Romans 2:14 it is twice declared that the Gentiles have not the Law. In Galatians 3:23 the word "we" refers to Hebrews, the writer being one of them. In the 24th verse the word "our" has the same reference. The Law was Israel's schoolmaster unto Christ, that they might be justified by faith. But after that faith is come, even they are no longer under the schoolmaster. Please notice that in verse 26 the pronoun is changed from the first to the second person plural, and all the way to the end of the chapter the second personal pronoun is used because the people addressed were all believers in Christ in the New Testament sense, whether Hebrews or Gentiles. In Galatians 4:5 the words "them" and "we" have the same allusion. The reference is to Israelites who under the old covenant, if they were believers, had the relation of minor children in the family, but who, under the new covenant, are put in the place of sonship. Notice again how the pronoun is changed at the 6th verse from "we" to "ye."

The Law was never given to any but to Israel.

Ephesians 2:12 confirms all this. The Gentiles, being aliens from the commonwealth of Israel, were, in consequence, strangers from the covenant of promise as well as from all other covenants. They had no hope. They were without God in the world.

As to your question, "How and where did the Gentiles get the Law, if they had any, and how were they benefited by the Law, not offering sacrifice?" my answer is, that they never had the Law. The Law was given to Israel for a particular and temporary purpose, and it is now done away (2 Cor. 3).

Why Folks Die

Please explain Romans 5:13, "For until the law sin was in the world: but sin is not imputed when there is no law. "

Here we have to go to the Revised Version. In the 5th chapter of Romans it is explained how it was that although there was no law until Moses, yet people died. Death is the wages of sin, but, as Romans 5:13 says, "sin is not imputed when there is no law. Nevertheless death reigned from Adam to Moses, even over them that had not sinned after the similitude of Adam's transgression, who is the figure of him that was to come." The answer is in the 12th verse, "Wherefore, as by one man sin entered into the world, and death by sin; and so death passed upon all men, for that all sinned." Not "have sinned." That word "have" does not belong in the text. The teaching here is that although men were not under law between Adam and Moses, yet they had all been under law in Eden—a law with the death penalty attached: "In the day that thou eatest thereof thou shalt surely die." Adam and Eve sinned, and because they sinned they died. And all men were in Adam, and sinned in him, and therefore they die. Thus it is that death passed upon all "for that all sinned."

This same principle is seen operating in Hebrews 7 where it is declared in verses 9 and 10 that "Levi also, who receiveth tithes, paid tithes in Abraham. For he was yet in the loins of his father, when Melchisedec met him." The context shows that when the apostle says "Levi" he includes the whole order of the Levitical or Aaronic priests. The teaching is that the Levitical priests, all the priests who descended from Aaron, were inferior to Melchisedec; and that this was shown in the fact that when Melchisedec and Abraham met, as recorded in Genesis 14, and Melchisedec received tithes from Abraham, and Abraham paid tithes to Melchisedec, Levi and Aaron and all their descendants in the priestly family paid tithes to Melchisedec on that day because they were still in the loins of their father when Melchisedec met him.

And don't forget that this principle is seen again in the cross; for we are assured that in the reckoning of God we were in Christ on that cross, that we were crucified with Him, buried with Him, made alive together with Him, raised up together with Him, and are already seated together with Him in Heaven. Hallelujah!

How to Convince a Sinner

1. When a person rejects the gospel, is he put back under the law?

2. If not, how can we convince him that he is a sinner and that he is lost?

3. How did man become a sinner in the first place? Was it by his disobedience of the law of Eden—"thou shalt not eat thereof"?

1. No. There is no law to put him under, for the law was done away in Christ (2 Cor. 3:7-11). The law was given to Israel only, and it was temporary, lasting only from Moses to Christ, being added to the Abrahamic covenant of promise "until the Seed (Christ) should come to whom the promise was made" (Gal. 3:19).

2. The testimony of John 16:7-11 should be sufficient. Men are lost sinners "because they believe not on" the Lord Jesus as their Savior. Their sin, the sin which condemns them, is in refusing to believe "in the name of the only begotten Son of God" (John 3:18). In rejecting Him they make God a liar (1 John 5:10).

3. No. Man did not become a sinner by sinning. He sinned because he was a sinner. God made him a free agent, able to choose between believing God or believing Satan. God told man that the forbidden fruit would kill him. Satan denied it, and man, believing Satan, became a sinner. And because he was a sinner he disobeyed God and died. So it is today. Man is not made a sinner by his sins, but he sins because he is a sinner. In the gospel, however, ample provision is made for the sinner and for his sins. Christ died for our sins not only, but He died for us. He died, not only for the wrong things we have done, but also for the wrong things we are. "Hallelujah! What a Savior!"

GRACE

What Is Grace?

What is grace?

Grace is favor. We often say "unmerited favor," which is tautological. Favor to be favor, must be unmerited. Grace is gift, and salvation is by grace because it is God's gift to anyone who is willing to take it. "It is of faith, that it might be by grace; to the end the promise might be sure to all the seed" (Rom. 4:16); it could not be sure to anyone if it were otherwise. "And if by grace, then is it no more of works: otherwise grace is no more grace. But if it be of works, then is it no more of grace: otherwise work is no more work" (Rom. 11:6). Praise God for salvation by grace!

Falling from Grace

What is falling from grace? Is it losing one's salvation?

No. The only reference in the Bible to falling from grace is in Galatians 5:4, where Paul declares that those who were turning to law-works for saving or keeping them had "fallen from grace." It is an error to apply this expression in any other way.

Love to God and Man

Do any Christians love their neighbors as themselves, and is it possible to love God with all the heart, and all the soul, and all the strength?

I would say that the Law thus epitomized in Luke 10:27 is God's yardstick to show us how very short we come of His righteous requirements and of His glory. Of course, it is quite impossible even for Christians, since they still have in them the old nature along with the new nature, to measure up to God's perfect standards. It is good, however, to remember that, while we are unable to do these things in and of ourselves, God is working in us both to will and to do of His good pleasure and has promised to present us one day faultless before the presence of His glory with exceeding joy.

THE SABBATH

Not Changed but Abolished

Why do Christians generally keep the first day of the week as the Sabbath instead of the seventh as the Lord commanded? Where in the Bible do we get authority to change God's Law?

There is no such authority, and the Law has not been changed, but it has been abolished. Strictly speaking, it is unscriptural to speak of any day as the "Christian Sabbath." The first day of the week is doubtless "the Lord's Day" referred to in Revelation 1:10, but that does not make it the Sabbath. The Bible knows no weekly Sabbath but Saturday. If Christians were under the Law at all, they would be obliged to keep the Saturday Sabbath. But they are not under the Law; they are under grace (Rom. 6:14). The Law was given to Israel as a schoolmaster to bring them to Christ that they might be justified by faith. But now that faith is come, even they are no longer under the schoolmaster (Gal. 3:23-25). As for the Gentiles, they never had the Law (Rom. 2:14). The Law of Sinai, "written and engraven in stones," was a temporary covenant, a "ministration of death" and "condemnation," which is now "done away" (2 Cor. 3:7-11; compare Rom. 7:1-4). Sunday, or the Lord's Day, is a weekly celebration of the resurrection of our Lord from the dead.

The Temporary Covenant

You say that "The law of Sinai, written and engraven in stones, was a temporary covenant, a ministration of death and condemnation which is now done away." Also you say "it is unscriptural to speak of Sunday as the Sabbath."

In that connection I should like to ask a couple of questions.

1. Is Westcott & Hort's Greek New Testament true to the original manuscripts? If so, and I have always heard that it is, then there is scriptural authority for the change of the Sabbath, for Matthew 28:1 says: "At the end of the sabbath (ton Sabbaton), as it began to dawn toward the first or chief of the sabbaths (ton Sabbaton), came Mary Magdalene and the other Mary to see the sepulcher."

2. Is the Sermon on the Mount a manual of arms for the Christian now or only in Christ's Millennial reign? If now, then practically everyone of the moral commandments such as the ten commandments, though not the ceremonial, is reiterated and enlarged rather than abrogated in the Sermon on the Mount.

While we live under grace and not under Law, yet it seems to me from Christ's statements that the moral part of the Law is enlarged and glorified though the ceremonial part is done away.

Maybe I am wrong and I should like your opinion on the matter.

1. Westcott and Hort's Greek New Testament is undoubtedly a very reliable work. But your difficulty arises from the fact that the Greek word in the New Testament (*any* Greek New Testament) is the same for "sabbath" as for "week." This is true of the Old Testament Hebrew also. Whether "sabbath" or "week" is meant in any particular case must be determined by the context. Westcott and Hort do not translate into English; if they did they would doubtless render Matthew 28:1 exactly as the Authorized and Revised Versions have done.

2. The Sermon on the Mount applies directly to the Kingdom age rather than to this one. But it is true that even in the New Testament Epistles all the principles of the moral Law are reiterated and insisted upon. But the Sabbath law is purely ceremonial, though found in the heart of the so-called moral Law. The distinction between that and ceremonial Law is artificial and arbitrary. We are not under Law at all, whether moral or ceremonial. This is not to say that we are free to be immoral. The thing is that instead of putting us under an external Law God has wrought in our hearts a desire to please Him and obey Him.

Believing the Word

You say, "The righteous requirement of the Law is fulfilled in believers because they have stopped trying to keep the Law and have accepted the Lord Jesus Christ as their Savior." Do you teach that grace gives license to violate the Ten Commandments? The seventh day Sabbath is included in "the righteous requirement of the Law," (Rom 8:4). It cannot mean some modified Law with the Sabbath left out for at that time the New Testament was not written.

A minister here claimed that Colossians 2:14-17 included the Ten Commandments, and especially the seventh day Sabbath, but the Seventh Day Adventists take the position that this passage refers only to the ceremonial Law.

1 John 3:4 says that "sin is the transgression of the law," and Paul says, "for by the law is the knowledge of sin" (Rom. 3:20), and then he quotes from the Law about which he is speaking, "Thou shalt not covet" (Rom. 7:7), thus showing that he has reference to the Ten Commandment law, and that is the Law that says, "the seventh day is the Sabbath." Now, if the willful violation of that Law is sin, then we should observe the Sabbath, for the violation of it is sin.

There is no need whatever of confusing this matter if we will just believe what the New Testament says about it. Trying to keep the Law is what Romans 8 means by walking in the flesh. We Gentiles were never under the Law anyway, and it is a purely academic question with us whether Colossians 2:14-

17 refers to the ceremonial Law only or to the whole Law. When Paul says that it "was against us," he is referring to himself as a former Jew who had been under the Law. In reading Colossians and Galatians and the other Epistles, we should be very careful to distinguish between the pronouns. Look, for example, at Galatians 3:19-29, and see how carefully Paul changes from "we" to "ye" in verses 25 and 26.

1 John 3:4 does not really say, "Sin is the transgression of the law," but rather, "Sin is lawlessness," that is to say, it is denial of any authority over us. The correction is made in the Revised Version.

In 2 Corinthians 3 the Law, "written and engraven in stones," is said to be a "ministration of condemnation" and "a ministration of death," as contrasted with the Gospel, which is a ministration of justification and a ministration of life. And the Law is said to be "done away in Christ." (Omit the italicized words; they are not in the text at all.)

Read the Epistle to the Galatians and believe what it says, and you will be led out of all difficulty about our relation to the Sabbath. There has not been a Sabbath in 1900 years for, strictly speaking, the Sabbath came to an end when the present dispensation began. We have, however, a Lord's Day, which is a precious heritage unto us and which ought to be carefully preserved. It is a mistake to refer to it as a Sabbath, for it is nothing of the kind except as the laws of our states have made it a civil Sabbath. As such, of course, it is of inestimable blessing in the industrial world and ought to be carefully prized and protected from invasion so that our people may have an opportunity to obey the command which bids them not to forsake the assembling of themselves together.

The Sabbath

What are your views on the Sabbath? Is the Seventh Day Adventist's charge concerning its change justified? or do they stick too much to the letter?

That is not the trouble. The Seventh-dayists have departed from the letter. The Sabbath was never changed, and on this point they are right; but the Sabbath was abolished, and on this point they are wrong. The Sabbath was a part of the Law, which "is done away in Christ." Read (and believe) the third chapter of Second Corinthians, as well as the Epistles to the Romans and Galatians, and you will see that we are not under the Law at all, but under grace; and that what we now have is not the Sabbath at all, but the Lord's Day, which is an entirely different institution. Don't tell a Seventh-dayist that the Sabbath was changed, for it was not; but tell him the Sabbath is displaced by the Lord's Day, and you will be telling him the truth.

The Sabbath and the Lord's Day

Is there anything in the Old Testament enjoining or commanding the Sabbath to be used as a day of worship? The fourth commandment makes no mention of worship; only the cessation of all work.

That is all. The Sabbath was a day of enforced idleness. Our Lord's Day has nothing in common with it except that it comes once a week and is dedicated peculiarly to God. To speak of the "Christian Sabbath" is confusion. The Sabbath was an institution of the old covenant, which is "done away" (2 Cor. 3). Let us rejoice that we are "free from the law" even as to Sabbaths (Rom. 6:14; Col. 2:16) but let us rejoice also in the privileges of the Lord's day, which offers so many opportunities for the united worship and service of God.

The Sabbath in the Millennium

In explaining the Sabbath question you say that the Sabbath will be again observed in the Kingdom age. Please state reasons for said observance, and why it should be so in the Millennium.

The statement was based upon the Scripture cited in connection therewith, namely, Isaiah 66:23. It is clear that the verses preceding the verse must relate to the Kingdom age; and the verse itself says: "And it shall come to pass, that from one new moon to another, and from one sabbath to another, shall all flesh come to worship before me, saith Jehovah." Likewise, in Zechariah 14:16, it is written that "it shall come to pass, that every one that is left of all the nations which came against Jerusalem shall even go up from year to year to worship the King, Jehovah of hosts, and to keep the feast of tabernacles." As for the purpose in the mind of God in restoring the Sabbath during the Millennial age, it has not been revealed to us. It may be in order that on a certain set day there may be the assembly of God's people before Him. Unless some day is agreed upon, such an assembly would manifestly be impossible. That is true even of our own Lord's Day, the first day of the week. The Spirit of God seems to have led His people from the very beginning of the New Testament to set apart the first day of the week as a day on which to assemble in the name of the risen Lord. That does not make it a Sabbath, of course, and it is not a Sabbath; but a return to the weekly Sabbath in the Kingdom age might serve the purpose I have mentioned.

THE CRUCIFIXION DAY

What Day of the Week?

On what day of the week was our Lord crucified?

To us it is perfectly obvious that the crucifixion was on Wednesday. The general impression that the crucifixion took place on Friday is doubtless due to the fact that it occurred on the day before the sabbath, and it has been generally assumed that the sabbath referred to was the weekly sabbath, which, of course, came on Saturday.

But there were many sabbaths in the Hebrew calendar beside the fifty-two weekly sabbaths of the year; and the sabbaths by which the feast of Passover and unleavened bread was begun and ended were reckoned as peculiarly sacred sabbaths. "In the first day ye shall have an holy convocation: ye shall do no servile work therein. But ye shall offer an offering made by fire unto Jehovah seven days: in the seventh day is an holy convocation: ye shall do no servile work therein" (Lev. 23:7,8).

The passover always fell on the 14th day of Abib (Lev. 23:5); and of course this would be on a different day of the week each successive year. All the evidence on the subject of the day of our Lord's crucifixion seems to lead to the conclusion that the feast began that year on Thursday—and "that sabbath day was an high day" (John 19:31)—and that the crucifixion was on the day before, which would be Wednesday.

The Jewish day began at 6 P.M., instead of midnight. The body of our crucified Lord was placed in the tomb just before 6 P.M. on Wednesday, which was the beginning of Thursday. It remained there through Thursday (night and day), Friday (night and day), and Saturday (night and day), and was raised from the dead just as Sunday was beginning (Matt. 28:1), or what we now would call Saturday evening about 6 o'clock. Thus the entombment endured through three days and three nights, fulfilling our Lord's own prediction in Matthew 12:40.

No one saw the resurrection of our Lord. The record shows that when the disciples visited the tomb immediately after the weekly sabbath had ended, that is, on Saturday night, they found the tomb empty.

Again—The Crucifixion Day

I have a problem which you might help me with, if you will. You stated that the crucifixion of our Lord took place on Wednesday, basing the statement on Matthew 12:40 and other passages. This is reasonable, but even more often is the resurrection referred to as on

the third day. Remembering that the Jews reckoned their days from evening to evening, if Christ were crucified on Wednesday, the resurrection would be on at least the fourth day after. I believe in the verbal inspiration of the Scriptures, and hence believe that there must be some explanation, although I do not understand it.

It is true that the resurrection day is often referred to as the third day. But it is also referred to as "after three days" (Mark 8:31) "within three days" (Mark 14:58) "in three days" (John 2:19) and after "three days and three nights" (Matt. 12:40).

I, too, believe in the verbal inspiration of the Scriptures, and our problem is to find the harmony between all these expressions.

That harmony, as I believe, is to be looked for in connection with idiomatic expression. You know that there is such a thing as usage, and as some one has said, "Any usage is good usage if there be enough of it." In our English language we fall into usage which at first seems to be entirely contrary to grammar, and yet we go on using expressions which finally find their place in our English dictionaries because the usage becomes so common.

Now, then, if it can be found that "on the third day" was an expression used among the Jews as equivalent to "within three days" or "in three days" or "after three days and three nights," then our problem is solved. And I think there is just such a solution to be found in the Word of God itself. Please look at Esther 4:16 where Queen Esther is quoted as saying: "Go, gather together all the Jews that are present in Shushan, and fast ye for me, and neither eat nor drink three days, night or day." Now look at the first verse of chapter 5: "Now it came to pass on the third day, that Esther put on her royal apparel, and stood in the inner court of the king's house." You see here the expression "on the third day" is equivalent to "after three days and three nights."

Now look again at 2 Chronicles 10:5, where Rehoboam said: "Come again unto me after three days." And yet in the 12th verse it reads: "So Jeroboam and all the people came to Rehoboam on the third day, as the king bade, saying, Come again to me on the third day." Here you will see that "after three days" is the exact equivalent, according to the Hebrew usage and idiom, of "the third day."

Now, does not this warrant us in saying that the expression in Matthew 12:40, "So shall the Son of Man be three days and three nights in the heart of the earth" is to be regarded as equivalent to the language of Luke 24:21, "Today is the third day since these things were done"?

THE RESURRECTION

Christ the Firstfruits

How can we reconcile 1 Corinthians 15:20 with the record in Matthew 27:52 that there was a resurrection of some of the saints at the time of Christ's crucifixion?

There is no such record in Matthew 27:52 or elsewhere. Verse 53 carefully states that it was "after his resurrection."

Saints Raised at Christ's Resurrection

Please explain Matthew 27:52,53, "many bodies of the saints which slept arose, and came out of the graves after his resurrection, and went into the holy city, and appeared unto many." I have had these verses explained in the light of Ephesians 4:8, but I do not feel that Ephesians 4:8 explains them.

I know nothing about this passage, Matthew 27:52,53, except just what it says. I am unable to trace any connection between this passage and Ephesians 4:8.

It ought to be noted that the resurrection of these saints was not at the time of the crucifixion, but "after his resurrection." How many there were of these, or whether they went back into their graves, or what became of them, I do not know. It is one of the mysteries that I expect to have cleared up when we get to Heaven.

The Resurrection Bodily

In His resurrection did the Lord Jesus actually come forth bodily from the dead?

Yes. Otherwise there was no resurrection at all. Our Lord predicted His bodily resurrection in John 2:18-22. Look at His words there recorded, and consider them. They are either true or false. If they are false, then He either knowingly or ignorantly told a falsehood; and in either case He could be no one's Savior. Make no mistake in supposing the doctrine of the resurrection of Christ to be unimportant. It is a vital part of our faith, and without it there is no faith worth mentioning. See how Paul deals with it as a basic doctrine in 1 Corinthians 15.

The Napkin and the Linen Clothes

Please explain John 20:7: "And the napkin that was about his head, not lying with the linen clothes, but wrapped together in a place by itself."

The explanation is that the linen clothes still lay where they had been while the Lord's body was yet in them, with the same convolutions as when surrounding the body, while the napkin had been carefully folded and placed by itself in a separate place. All this showed that a miracle had taken place, and when John "saw" it he "believed. For as yet they knew not the scripture, that he must rise again from the dead" (verses 8,9).

Lazarus and Christ

Would you please tell me what is the difference between the resurrection of Lazarus (John 11:33-44) and the resurrection of Jesus Christ?

I am not sure that I understand the full purport of your question. Of course, we know nothing about the resurrection of Lazarus except what is written in John 11. There was certainly a vast difference between it and the resurrection of our Lord. Our Lord was raised from the dead with a glorified body. And it was on account of His death and resurrection that we are assured of a glorious resurrection. There is no indication that Lazarus was raised with a glorified body. Whether he died again or was taken to heaven with the body with which he was raised is not told us in Scripture. But the presumption is very strong that he went through death the second time, since there is no indication that his body was glorified when he was raised at Bethany.

QUESTIONS ON THE PARABLES

The Unjust Steward

In the parable of Luke 16:1-8, it is difficult to understand how the unjust steward could be commended by our Lord. Please explain.

But the unjust steward was not commended by our Lord. It was *his* lord who commended him. Notice that the word lord is not printed with a capital L. It is the steward's employer who commended him. To me the matter has offered no difficulty. I can easily understand how the unjust steward's master might appreciate the shrewdness of the man and for that commend him in spite of the fact that he had suffered a financial loss through the steward's crookedness. It is not stated that his master approved of his act but only that he commended him. This commendation was on account of his foresight in providing for the future even in temporal things. Of course, the lesson of our Lord in giving the parable is perfectly obvious. We ought to provide for the future in eternal things. The teaching is made clear by the key-verse, the 9th, as rendered in the Revised Version: "And I say unto you, Make to yourselves friends by means of the mammon of unrighteousness; that, when it shall fail, they may receive you into the eternal tabernacles." In these words our Lord clearly advises us to use our money to send folks to Heaven, so that when we reach there they may welcome us.

Unrighteousness and Everlasting Habitations

Will you kindly give me light on Luke 16:8,9? How can the friends of unrighteousness receive anyone "into everlasting habitations"?

That, of course, would be impossible. But you have not read the parable carefully. Read it again. The mammon of unrighteousness is money. The word "mammon" comes from the Greek *mammonas*, Latin *mammona*, Aramaic *mamona*, and its meaning is riches. Since riches are worshiped by the unrighteous world, *mammon* is called by our Lord the mammon of unrighteousness. The parable referred to in your question teaches us what use we are to make of money. We should use it to send people to Heaven. The Revisers have corrected the translation to make it read: "Make to yourselves friends by means of the mammon of unrighteousness; that when it (that is, the mammon, or money) shall fail, they (the friends) may receive you into the eternal tabernacles." The Word of God says that "he that winneth souls is wise" (Prov. 11:30); and also that "they that be wise shall shine as the brightness of the firmament; and they that turn many to righteousness as the stars forever and ever" (Dan. 12:3). What joy it will be for soul-winners to greet in Heaven those whom they have helped to send there!

Pounds and Talents

What is the difference between the Parable of the Pounds and the Parable of the Talents (Luke 19:11-27; Matt. 25:14-30)?

There is a difference between these parables, although there are many points of similarity also. The emphatic lesson in the Parable of the Talents seems to be that the Lord's return will be a test of professed service. In the Parable of the Pounds the great point emphasized is the postponement of the kingdom as it says in the 11th verse that he "spake a parable, because he was nigh to Jerusalem, and because they thought that the kingdom of God should immediately appear."

The Prodigal Son

In the Parable of the Prodigal Son, does the son represent the sinner or a backslider?

He represents a backslidden child of God restored to fellowship with the Father through confession of his sins, in agreement with the promise of 1 John 1:9. This same is true of all the three parables of Luke 15—The shepherd recovering his wandering sheep, the woman (representing the Church) recovering her lost coin, and the father recovering his sinning boy. None of these—the sheep, the coin, the boy—was "lost," except in the sense that each of them was out of place. The sheep belonged to the shepherd all the time, but was out of the fold where his other sheep were gathered. The coin belonged to the woman all the time, and all the time was *in the house*, but it was out of its proper place, perhaps, as some have suggested, adorning her person as part of a necklace or bracelet. The wandering boy belonged to his father all the time, but was out of his fellowship and away from his house. It is a beautiful chapter on the doctrine of restoration to the Father's communion of those who have "sinned against heaven, and in His sight."

The Meaning of Leaven

What does leaven mean?

Leaven is a Bible symbol of evil working under cover. Any good concordance will show you every occurrence of the word leaven in the Bible and will prove the truth of what we have said. See, for example, Exodus 12:15-20; Leviticus 2:11; Matthew 16:6; Mark 8:15; 1 Corinthians 5:5-8; Galatians 5:8,9.

The Significance of Leaven

Please explain why leaven is included in the Pentecostal offering (Lev. 23:17), in view of your teaching that leaven always typifies evil. Also explain the Parable of the Leaven in Matthew 13:33.

Leaven in Scripture is uniformly a symbol of evil or corruption, and it is so employed in the Pentecost type. Jews and Gentiles, both evil and corrupt, are yet saved through faith, and are "accepted in the beloved" on account of His shed blood. Please observe that in the ritual of Pentecost (Lev. 28:15-21) the two wave-loaves were presented with bloody offerings.

In the Parable of the Leaven, the woman is the apostate church, mingling with the pure meal of the Word of God (which is His appointed food for the household of faith) the leaven of false doctrine. The three measures of meal may speak of the threefold division of the professing church—Protestant, Roman Catholic, Greek Catholic. Each has a measure of meal, but in each the meal is so poisoned by corrupt doctrine and practice as to make it a menace to the children of God. The leavening process goes on till the whole lump becomes corrupt. The end will be for the Lord Himself to spew the disgusting mixture out of His mouth (Rev. 3:14-16).

The Hid Treasure and the Pearl

Please give the interpretation of the Parable of the Hid Treasure (Matt. 13:44), and also that of the Pearl (Matt. 13:45,46).

The treasure is Israel, now hidden in the field which is the world. The Man who in His joy goes and sells His all and buys the field is the Lord Jesus. He bought the field by giving His precious blood on Calvary, and therefore not only by creation but also by redemption, "the earth is Jehovah's, and the fullness thereof; the world, and they that dwell therein" (Ps. 24:1). One day the treasure will be brought forth and "Israel shall blossom and bud, and fill the face of the world with fruit" (Isa. 27:6). That will be when He has turned away ungodliness from Jacob, and the promise of Exodus 19:5,6 and Psalm 135:4 will be fulfilled: "If ye will obey my voice indeed, and keep my covenant, then ye shall be a peculiar *treasure* unto me above all people: for all the earth is mine: and ye shall be unto me a kingdom of priests, and an holy nation. For Jehovah hath chosen Jacob unto himself, and Israel for his peculiar *treasure*." The pearl of great price is the Church. The Man is again the Lord Jesus. The price is His blood (Eph. 1:14; 1 Cor. 6:19,20 and 1 Peter 1:18,19).

The Ten Virgins

What do you think of the Parable of the Ten Virgins (Matt. 25:1-13)? Some say that all believers will be taken away when the Church or the body is raptured. But it seems to me that some Christians will be left here for the Tribulation. I should like to have your opinion.

The coming of the Bridegroom here is not at the Rapture of the Church. Such a thing is not to be sought for in Matthew. It is rather His return with His Bride at the close of the Great Tribulation (see chapter 24:29,30). It is "the revelation of the Lord Jesus from heaven with the angels of his power in flaming fire, rendering vengeance to them that know not God, and to them that obey not the gospel of our Lord Jesus: who shall suffer punishment, even eternal destruction from the face of the Lord and from the glory of his might, when he shall come to be glorified in his saints and to be marveled at in all them that believed in that day" (2 Thess. 1:7-10, R.V.).

In the ancient Syriac New Testament as well as the Latin Vulgate, the first verse of our chapter reads: "Then may the kingdom of heaven be shadowed forth by ten virgins, who took their lamps and went out to meet the bridegroom and bride" (see John 3:29). The word "marriage" in verse 10 should read "marriage feast" (see R.V.). The actual marriage will have already taken place in Heaven.

The virgins are professing Jewish disciples during the King's absence and just preceding His return. It is not like the Holy Spirit to present the Church under a plural figure; He is too jealous for the unity of the body of Christ. In 2 Corinthians 11:2 the Church is seen as "a chaste virgin," not a company of virgins. Again, in Psalm 45, the Church is seen as the Queen, the King's Bride; while the Jewish disciples are seen as "the virgins her companions that follow her." Likewise, the Jewish remnant is seen twice in The Revelation as a company of virgins (7:4; 14:3,4). The Bride will certainly appear with her Bridegroom when He is manifested, but she is not typified by the virgins in the parable.

The lamps or torches are the Word of God in a type (Ps. 119:105; 2 Peter 1:19).

The going forth of the virgins is their outward profession of loyalty to the coming King. They all "went forth."

The oil is a type of the Holy Spirit (Zech. 4). Five of the virgins had oil in their vessels with their torches. So every regenerate person has the Holy Spirit indwelling his body as well as the Word of God in his hands. We have this treasure in earthen vessels (2 Cor. 4:7; 1 Cor. 6:19). The foolish virgins took no oil. They were "none of his" (Rom. 8:9), for though they had a form of godliness they denied the power thereof (2 Tim. 3:5).

All boasting is excluded by the humiliating statement of the 5th verse—"While the bridegroom tarried, they all slumbered and slept," wise and foolish together, showing the failure of the flesh, and reminding us of our Lord's agonized question in the garden (Matt. 26:40).

The scene which follows the midnight cry is very pitiful. There is a great trimming of lamps signifying, in the figure, a frantic searching of the Word of God at a time when it will be too late; a great longing for the oil of God, even a willingness to buy at any cost, but it is all in vain, for while they went, the Bridegroom came and the door was shut. There is much prayer—"Lord, Lord, open to us!" but He knows them not for they are not among "them that are his" (2 Tim. 2:19). Surely there is need for the exhortation of verse 13, "Watch, therefore!" (Compare Luke 12:35,36.)

The Wheat and the Tares

In the parable of Matthew 13:24-30, is the Kingdom of Heaven, spoken of there, the Church or the world? Are the wheat and the tares the people in the Church or in the world? My pastor teaches that it refers to the Church. To me it seems it cannot be so, according to the

Word which teaches that the true Church is the body of Christ. How can wheat and tares be together in it? They can't be.

You are right: "They can't be." The answer to your question is in the 38th verse of the same chapter: "The field is the world." This parable is often used as an argument against the exercise of church discipline, because of the words in verse 30, "Let them both (the wheat and the tares) grow together until the harvest." But the parable is not talking of the church, either the true Church which is the body of Christ, or of the professing church. "The field is the world."

CHRISTIAN CONDUCT

Christians and Ambition

Is it inconsistent for a Christian to be ambitious?

No. But he should not be selfishly ambitious. In 2 Corinthians 5:9 the Apostle Paul told of his ambition. Literally rendered, the verse reads: "Wherefore we are ambitious, that whether at home (in the body) or absent (from the body and present with the Lord) we may be well-pleasing unto Him."

Christians and Worldliness

Do you think that one who is born again will do worldly things?

Yes, if he is walking in the flesh and out of fellowship with God. In such a case he loses his joy and his fruit and his testimony, and the way back for him is indicated in 1 John 1:9: "If we (the children of God) confess our sins, he is faithful and just to forgive us sins, and to cleanse us from all unrighteousness."

Seeking Another's Wealth

What is the meaning of 1 Corinthians 10:24: "Let no man seek his own, but every man another's wealth"? It doesn't sound good to me. It seems to teach covetousness as a duty, whereas elsewhere in Scripture we are warned against covetousness as idolatry.

It is unfortunate that the verse has been translated as we find it in the Authorized Version. The Revised Version reads: "Let no man seek his own, but each his neighbor's good." The whole chapter consists of an exhortation against doing anything that would cause a weak brother to stumble. The exhortation begins at the first verse of the eighth chapter and continues to the end of the tenth chapter, including indeed the first verse of chapter 11 which reads, "Be ye imitators of me, even as I also am of Christ" (R.V.).

The question discussed throughout the passage is whether a Christian should eat meat which had been offered in sacrifice to idols. Those who were strong in the faith saw no harm in eating such meat, but those who were weak were further weakened by it, and so Paul says in 10:23-29: "All things are lawful; but all things are not expedient. All things are lawful; but all things edify not. Let no man seek his own, but each his neighbor's good. Whatsoever is sold in the shambles, eat, asking no question for conscience sake; for the earth is the Lord's and the fullness thereof. If one of them that believe not biddeth you to a feast, and ye are disposed to go; whatsoever is set before you, eat, asking no question for conscience sake. But if any man say unto you, This hath been offered in sacrifice, eat not, for his sake that showed it, and for conscience sake: conscience, I say, not thine own, but the other's" (R.V.).

The matter is summed up in the 32nd and 33rd verses of the chapter and the first verse of chapter 11: "Give no occasion of stumbling, either to Jews or to Greeks, or to the church of God: even as I also please all men in all things, not seeking mine own profit, but the profit of the many, that they may be saved. Be ye imitators of me, even as I also am of Christ."

The same question is discussed in Romans 14 and 15, and it is summed up in Romans 14:21: "It is good not to eat flesh, nor to drink wine, nor to do anything whereby thy brother stumbleth." It is a good rule and a rule which every Christian should follow.

Creed and Conduct

What effect does Scriptural faith in the eternal security of the believer have upon the believer's attitude toward sin?

Your question is raised twice by Paul. In Romans 5:20, he says that "where sin abounded, grace did much more abound," and in 6:1-3, he says: "What shall we say then? Shall we continue in sin that grace may abound? God forbid. How shall we that died to sin, live any longer therein? Know ye not, that so many of us as were baptized into Jesus Christ were baptized into his death?" At the moment of his regeneration, the believer becomes a member of the body of Christ and partakes of the life of Christ, and this is because of the death of Christ in his behalf. Being joined to Christ, he is joined to the death of Christ, and receives from that union the life of Christ (Rom. 6:11). He is exhorted to reckon himself to have died indeed unto sin, but to be living unto God through Jesus Christ our Lord.

Then in 6:14,15 your question is raised again: "For sin shall not have dominion over you; for ye are not under the law, but under grace. What then? Shall we sin, because we are not under the law, but under grace? God forbid." This is the language of every renewed heart. Paul goes on to say: "Know ye not, that to whom ye yield yourselves servants to obey, his servants we are to whom ye obey; whether of sin unto death, or of obedience unto righteousness?" It is a warning against sin and a warning which the true believer will heed. Having died with Christ, he now lives in Him and for Him.

The case is beautifully stated in Galatians 2:20, R.V.: "I have been crucified with Christ; and it is no longer I that live, but Christ liveth in me: and that life which I now live in the flesh I live in faith, the faith which is in the Son of God, who loved me, and gave himself up for me."

We recently heard of two sisters who became Christians at the same time. They had been prominent members of what is sometimes called "fashionable society," and within a few days after their salvation they received an invitation to attend a social function, as they had been accustomed to do. To this they replied, saying, "We thank you very much for your kind invitation, but we died last Thursday night."

Compromising with the World

What were the compromises proposed by Pharaoh when God demanded that he should let His people go to worship Him in the wilderness? And what is the spiritual significance of these compromises?

Pharaoh first proposed that instead of separating from Egypt the people of Israel should sacrifice to God in the land of Egypt itself. Egypt is a type of the world, and God's people are called upon to separate from the world and the ways of the world in order to worship Him. Pharaoh is a type of Satan, who is the prince of this world, and who seeks to induce God's people to remain in a fellowship with the world. He tells them it is all right to be a Christian, but why separate from the world in order to do it?

Moses' answer is most significant: "It is not meet to do so; for we shall sacrifice the abomination of the Egyptians to Jehovah our God: lo, shall we sacrifice the abomination of the Egyptians before their eyes, and will they not stone us?" (Ex. 8:25,26). It so happened that the very things that the Egyptians worshiped were the things which the Israelites offered upon their altars. The Egyptians worshiped animals. The Israelites killed these animals and burned them upon their altars of burnt-offering. The significance of this is plain. Christians cannot really worship God while in fellowship with the world, for the things the world prizes most highly are the very things that Christians sacrifice in order to have real fellowship with God.

The second compromise was, "Ye shall not go very far away" (Ex. 8:27,28). Moses had said: "We will go three days' journey into the wilderness." And Pharaoh said: "I will let you go, that ye may sacrifice to Jehovah your God in the wilderness; only ye shall not go very far away." This is just a modification of the first compromise. It said: "Separate from the world if you must, but do not be too unworldly." The three days' journey demanded by Moses may point to the three days of our Lord's entombment. Surely, the sepulcher of our Lord should be a line of demarcation and separation from the world for God's people.

The third compromise is found in Exodus 10:8-11. Here Pharaoh proposed that the grown-up people should go into the wilderness, leaving their children in Egypt. This compromise is the one to which many of God's dear people submit, having an ambition that their children should be prosperous and popular. They do not take their children with them into the life of separation. Moses' answer to this third compromise was: "We will go with our young and with our old, with our sons and with our daughters, with our flocks and with our herds will we go; for we must hold a feast unto Jehovah."

The fourth compromise lies in Exodus 10:24-26, where Pharaoh proposed that the Israelites go into the wilderness, leaving their flocks and herds behind. This is equivalent to saying to believers: "Separate from the world as far as you like, only leave your property behind." Moses' answer was most significant: "Our cattle also shall go with us; there shall not an hoof be left behind; for thereof must we take to serve Jehovah our God; and we know not with what we must serve Jehovah, until we come thither." Just so! Christians cannot even know how to fully serve Jehovah until they have taken all their property and put it into His hands to use it as He may please. All we have and all we are came from Him and belongs to Him! Until we come to this position of devotion we have not really begun to worship God at all.

A New Creation

Can you help me in connection with 2 Corinthians 5:17? I am sure that I have been born again and am therefore a new creature, but I cannot say that in me "old things are passed away," or that in me "all things are become new." Please help me if you can.

I do not wonder that you are troubled. I only wonder that more of God's children are not troubled by the usual interpretation of this verse. When you were born again you received a new nature from God. But you did not get rid of the old nature. In every believer there are two natures: first, that which is natural, and second, that which is supernatural.

The first comes through the natural birth, and the second comes through the supernatural birth. The first nature is bad, and incurably so. The second nature is good, and absolutely so. The old nature can do nothing to please God. The new nature can do nothing to displease God. And this state of things must go on until we are transfigured into the image of our adorable Lord. Meanwhile though we are truly saved who have been born again, none of us can really say that within us old things are passed away, and all things are become new.

If you will look at the Revised Version you will see that this verse reads: "Wherefore if any man is in Christ, he is a new creature: the old things are passed away; behold, they are become new." But in the margin it reads: "Wherefore if any man is in Christ, there is a new creation: the old things are passed away; behold, they are become new." If we look at the statement of this verse objectively instead of subjectively I think we will understand it. Paul is speaking of the change that has come over everything from the new standpoint of the believer. Everything is different to him from what it once was.

If you look at a valley from the valley itself you may not see much of it, and it may be uninteresting, but if you go to the top of a mountain and look down over the valley it looks like a brand new valley to you. Everything is different.

It is just like that in the case of a born-again sinner. He has been taken up from the valley, so to speak, to the hill top, and from the new point of view everything is new. The creation itself is new, the old things are passed away, and all things have become new. Things look different to him, things sound different to him, things taste different to him, things feel different to him, and things smell different to him. All things are become new, "and all things are of God who has reconciled us to himself through Christ, and given unto us the ministry of reconciliation" (verse 18).

How to Drink

What did our Lord mean by the words, "If any man thirst, let him come unto me and drink" (John 7:37)? How may we drink?

You may find your answer in the context. See verse 38,39: "He that believeth on me, as the scripture hath said, out of his belly shall flow rivers of living water. (But this spake he of the Spirit, which they that believe on him should receive; for the Holy Ghost was not yet given; because that Jesus was not yet glorified.)" Drinking is believing—believing "as the scripture hath said" —believing the testimony of the Word of God concerning His Son. And those who thus drink, who thus believe, receive the Holy Ghost; for since the Son of God has been glorified the Holy Ghost has been given; and from those who thus drink, and drink deeply, out from them there flow rivers of living water. This is a beautiful picture of a normal Christian, living in touch with God and becoming a channel of blessing to others!

Standing and State

Please define the difference between the believer's standing and state.

The believer's standing has to do with his position in Christ, and his state has to do with his actual spiritual condition. The moment a man believes on the Lord Jesus Christ and is born again he enters into a position in grace as a result of the work of Christ. He is accepted in the beloved. However weak he may be, however ignorant, however fallible, his standing in Christ never varies. He has the same relationships in the family of God as the most illustrious saint. He is a child of God. He is accepted in the beloved as a full-grown son of God. He is a priest in a brotherhood of priests, and is assured that in this standing he will be eternally preserved.

On the other hand, his walk may be very far below his position, his state very far below his standing. And all the work of the Holy Spirit of God who indwells him is in order to bring his state up to his standing. He is already a saint, and he is called upon to walk as becometh a saint. The matter is put into a single sentence in Ephesians 5:8, where we read: "Ye were sometimes darkness, but now are ye light in the Lord: walk as children of light."

Separation

Does "Come out from among them, and be ye separate"' (2 Cor. 6:17) apply to us in this age? Does it mean to leave churches that are modernistic?

The exhortation in 2 Corinthians 6:17 certainly does apply to the present age, but its application is sometimes very difficult. God will guide His child, however, in every case if His child is willing to do His will when it is revealed to him.

The Unequal Yoke

Please explain 2 Corinthians 6:14—"Be ye not unequally yoked together with unbelievers." I have a friend who insists that by this passage of Scripture we are commanded to withdraw from membership in the church.

Your friend is entirely wrong in his interpretation of the Scripture cited. How could Paul have advised the Corinthian Christians to come out from the church which he himself had only recently organized? The whole paragraph in which the text is included is an exhortation to separation, not from the professing church, but from fellowship with unbelievers. "Be ye not unequally yoked together with unbelievers." The exhortation is just as timely today as ever. It forbids, for example, the marriage of believers with unbelievers; it forbids membership in lodges and clubs and other human organizations made up in part of Christians and in part of non-Christians; it forbids business partnerships with unbelievers; it forbids any yoking together of believers with unbelievers for a common purpose.

Of course, this principle may apply even in the case of a membership in some churches. In the awful apostasy of these last days there are churches, and many of them, alas! which have become hopelessly separated from God and the truth of God in all their testimony. Destructive critics occupy their pulpits, ungodly men who deny the Lord that bought them. They have turned away from the truth and turned unto fables. They bring reproach upon the Lord Jesus by denying His virgin birth, and by denying the need and efficacy of His blood atonement. In such a case, I do not think a believer ought to hesitate a single moment. He certainly should come out from among them and be separate.

It is quite another thing to hold, with your friend, that 2 Corinthians 6:17 means that we are to come out from the church and not belong to any church.

May the Lord give us all the abundant grace and wisdom that we need in these days to keep our feet in His path while we wait for His Son from Heaven!

Lawfulness and Expediency

In 1 Timothy 4:4 we read that "every creature of God is good, and nothing to be refused, if it be received with thanksgiving." Would that give a man freedom to drink a glass of wine, or smoke a cigar once in a while? Is that an actual sin? Or does it come under the head of things not expedient? Would it keep a man from the Rapture?

Suppose we put along with the verse you quoted this other word from Paul in Romans 14:21: "It is good neither to eat flesh, nor to drink wine, nor any thing whereby thy brother stumbleth, or is offended, or is made weak." And again, his word in 1 Corinthians 8:13: "Wherefore, if meat make my brother to offend, I will eat no flesh while the world standeth, lest I make my brother to offend." It cannot possibly be a question of lawfulness, for the Christian is "not under the law, but under grace" (Rom. 6:14). Of course it follows that "all things are lawful for me, but all things are not expedient: all things are lawful for me, but all things edify not" (1 Cor. 10:23). No, a Christian will not be kept from the Rapture by these things, but he may be kept from the approval of his Lord. Every Christian—by which I mean every born-again person—will be included in the Rapture, for the Rapture is part of our salvation, and our salvation is all of grace; but many a Christian will "suffer loss" at the Judgment Seat of Christ, though "he himself shall be saved; yet so as by fire" (1 Cor. 3:15). "Wherefore we are ambitious, that, whether at home or absent, we may be well pleasing unto him" (2 Cor. 5:9).

Making a Difference

Please explain Jude 22,23, especially the words, "making a difference."

This is a warning against the defilement which may attend one's efforts to win souls. See to it that you do not, in your zeal for rescuing others, enter into fellowship with them in their evil ways. The "making a difference" is explained by the context: some are to be won by compassion, and others must be snatched out, so to speak, from the fire. The Holy Spirit will give wisdom for all this, but His guidance will never be contrary to the written Word. That is the safe guide.

Avoiding Offenses

What is meant by Paul's words in Romans 14:16, "Let not then your good be evil spoken of?" How far can we apply this to the Christian of today? Am I to cease from doing what I believe to be right because some unsaved person says it is evil? I cannot see it that way.

The text referred to is in the midst of Paul's discussion on the question as to whether meat might be eaten by Christians which had been offered to idols. The same question is discussed in 1 Corinthians 8.

The point is that the Christian should do all in his power to avoid giving occasions of stumbling to the weak. This, of course, cannot be done altogether for there are some who stumble very easily. But, so far as it lies in our power, we should avoid even the exercise of our liberty if, by so doing, we can avoid giving offense to God's weaker children. The whole matter is beautifully summed up by Paul himself in Romans 14:21, "It is good neither to eat flesh, nor to drink wine, nor any thing whereby thy brother stumbleth, or is offended, or is made weak." And again in 1 Corinthians 8:13, "Wherefore, if meat make my brother to offend, I will eat no flesh while the world standeth, lest I make my brother to offend."

Personal Adornment

Will you please explain 1 Timothy 2:9? Do you believe that it is wrong for Christian women to wear ear bobs and flashy rings and necklaces?

No Christian, whether man or woman, should dress flashily. We should dress in such a way as not to attract attention to ourselves. There is danger at both ends of the line. There are Christians who make themselves conspicuous by their extreme plainness, and some of them make a form of "no form," thus placing themselves, and seeking to place others, under bondage. A similar passage is in 1 Peter 3:1-4.

Card-Playing, etc.

Is it wrong for a Christian to play cards, attend theater, etc.?

The 8th chapter of 1 Corinthians meets all your problems and will solve them if you approach the chapter in a spirit of submission. That chapter discusses the question as to whether a Christian should eat meat which had been offered in sacrifice to idols. Some said, Yes, and others said, No. Paul declares that while there is liberty to eat the meat, yet if our eating gives offense to a weaker brother we are to desist. For "if meat make my brother to offend, I will eat no flesh while the world standeth, lest I make my brother to offend" (verse 13).

The same question is discussed in the 14th chapter of Romans, and the same conclusion is reached: "It is good neither to eat flesh, nor to drink wine, nor any thing whereby thy brother stumbleth, or is offended, or is made weak" (verse 21).

First Corinthians 10:31 reads, "Whether therefore ye eat, or drink, or whatsoever ye do, do all to the glory of God." Let this test be applied to questionable things, and it will soon become evident whether or not they are expedient for a child of God.

Carnal Christians

Will Christians who walk in the flesh inherit Heaven?

If you mean by "Christians" those who have been born again, the answer is, Yes. All born-again persons will "inherit Heaven." But carnal Christians will lose much of blessing for their carnality, both here and hereafter (1 Cor. 3:11-15; 11:30-32).

The Cost of Discipleship

Just what is the meaning of Luke 14:26? It reads: "If any man come to me, and hate not his father, and mother, and wife, and children, and brethren, and sisters, yea, and his own life also, he cannot be my disciple."

The verse should be read in relation to its context. In the Parable of the Great Supper, verses 16 to 24, those who "with one consent began to make excuse" pleaded various reasons for rejecting the invitation. One of them had "bought a piece of ground" which he "must needs go and see." Another had "bought five yoke of oxen" which he must "go to prove." And yet another said, "I have married a wife, and therefore I cannot come." This makes our Lord's language in the 26th verse intelligible. If any man come unto Him he must count the cost of discipleship, and he must hate anything or anyone coming between him and his Lord. Whether it be "a piece of ground," or "five yoke of oxen," or even "a wife." Dr. Scofield's footnote is informing. He says: "All terms which define the emotions or affections are *comparative*. Natural affection is to be, as compared with the believer's devotedness to Christ, as if it were hate. See Matthew 12:47-50 where Christ illustrates this principle in His own person. But in the Lord the natural affections are sanctified and lifted to the level of the divine love (compare John 19:26,27; Eph. 5:25-28)." (*Scofield Reference Bible.*)

Our Appointed Portion

Is there any definite promise in the New Testament that our God will prosper His sons and daughters in this world's goods, any more than He would the unsaved? What about Christians driving sharp bargains with God?

No real Christian will think of "driving sharp bargains with God." And our appointed portion in this world is not worldly prosperity, but rather world-hatred, world-persecution and affliction. "In the world ye shall have tribulation" (John 16:33). "We must through much tribulation enter into the kingdom of God" (Acts 14:22). "The world knoweth us not because it knew him not" (1 John 3:1). These Scriptures, which might be multiplied indefinitely, are not threats, but promises. It is as true now as when it was written that "all that will live godly in Christ Jesus shall suffer persecution" (2 Tim. 3:12).

Confession and Forgiveness

A Bible teacher recently said: "An unconfessed sin is an unforgiven sin." I know that the Lord Jesus Christ took all my sins upon Him and died on the cross in my place. I know also that any sin in my life interferes with my fellowship with Him, and that not until confession of that sin can fellowship be restored. But can it be possible that, because I do not name a sin such a sin is unforgiven, when at the close of each day I merely ask forgiveness for the defilement of that day, without making mention of each separate sin?

It is going too far to say that "an unconfessed sin is an unforgiven sin" if by confession is meant the specific naming of each particular sin. Many—perhaps most—of our sins are sins of ignorance. We have a distorted view of sin and righteousness, else we should know that we are always coming short of the glory of God, which is sin. On the other hand, there is no promise of forgiveness for the *asking*; it is rather, "if we *confess* our sins, he is faithful and just to forgive us our sins" (1 John 1:9). We are on safe ground when we confess our sins and judge ourselves before God. It is not so much a question of naming the sins, though we ought not to shrink from naming them so far as we know them, it is rather a question of our heart's attitude before Him with reference to our sins. He desires "truth in the inward parts" (Ps. 51:6). "For thus saith the high and lofty One that inhabiteth eternity, whose name is Holy; I dwell in the high and holy place, with him also that is of a contrite and humble spirit, to revive the spirit of the humble, and to revive the heart of the contrite ones" (Isa. 57:15).

A Matter of Confession

Some years ago one sinned against the wife of a man. It was never

confessed to the wife, but was confessed to God. The one who sinned feels that it would be a reproach to the cause of Christ if public confession were made. If confession were never made, would it bar the one who confessed to God out of the pearly gates? Would you advise a public confession to the wife to be made?

Admission to "the pearly gates" is not determined in the way you suggest; entrance to Heaven depends solely upon whether one is born again. It is difficult to give advice in the case you mention. There are times when such a confession as you suggest would do far more harm than good. God will guide a willing child and show him what to do.

Ordinance of the Red Heifer

Will you please tell us the meaning of "the ashes of an heifer sprinkling the unclean," in Hebrews 9:13?

We need to look at the full statement of verses 13 and 14: "For if the blood of bulls and of goats, and the ashes of an heifer sprinkling the unclean, sanctifieth to the purifying of the flesh: how much more shall the blood of Christ, who through the eternal Spirit offered himself without spot to God, purge your conscience from dead works to serve the living God?" The reference is to the ordinance of the red heifer in Numbers 19, and I can do no better than to refer you to Dr. Scofield's exposition of this type:

"The red heifer: Type of the sacrifice of Christ as the ground of the cleansing of the believer from the defilement contracted in his pilgrim walk through this world, and illustration of the method of his cleansing. The order is: (1) The slaying of the sacrifice; (2) the sevenfold sprinkling of the blood, typical public testimony before the eyes of all of the complete and never-to-be-repeated putting away of all the believer's sins as before God (Heb. 9:12-14; 10:10-12); (3) the reduction of the sacrifice to ashes which are preserved and become a memorial of the sacrifice; (4) the cleansing from defilement (sin has two aspects—guilt and uncleanness) by sprinkling with the ashes mingled with water. Water is a type of both the Spirit and the Word (John 7:37-39; Eph. 5:26). The operation typified is this: The Holy Spirit uses the Word to convict the believer of some evil allowed in his life to the hindering of his joy, growth, and service. Thus convicted, he remembers that the guilt of his sin has been met by the sacrifice of Christ (1 John 1:7). Instead, therefore, of despairing, the convicted believer judges and confesses the defiling thing as unworthy a saint, and is forgiven and cleansed (John 13:3-10; 1 John 1:7-10).

How to Know God's Will

How may I find out what the will of God is for me?

In general the will of God for all of us is written in 1 Thessalonians 5:16-18, "Rejoice evermore. Pray without ceasing. In everything give thanks: for this is the will of God in Christ Jesus concerning you."

But this does not give particular guidance to the child of God who is seeking to know what God would have him to do.

It is the part of wisdom to set ourselves to the task of finding out the will of God, "proving what is acceptable unto the Lord. . . . See then that ye walk circumspectly, not as fools but as wise, redeeming the time, because the days are evil. Wherefore be ye not unwise, but understanding what the will of the Lord is" (Eph. 5:10-17).

In Colossians 1:9-12 the sevenfold apostolic prayer for God's children begins with the petition that they "might be filled with the knowledge of his will in all wisdom and spiritual understanding."

In Romans 12:1,2, the necessary steps are set forth by which any child of God may ascertain what the will of the Lord is:

1. "Present your bodies a living sacrifice, holy, acceptable unto God, which is your reasonable service."
2. "Be not conformed to this age."
3. "Be ye transformed."

The transformation is to be "by the renewing of your mind," and this is the work of the Holy Spirit through the Word of God (Titus 3:5-7; 2 Cor. 3:18).

And the result of this process is that the one who has gone through it step by step proves "what is that good, and acceptable, and perfect, will of God."

But let no one start out in this process until he has definitely decided to do the will of God when he knows it. Of course this is involved in the first step, for no one can really present his living body to God in absolute surrender and yieldedness whose will is not already submitted to God.

According to His Purpose

In Romans 8:28 we note that all things work together for good to them who are the called according to His purpose. But just what does it mean, "called according to His purpose"?

His purpose is explained in the twenty-ninth verse: "For whom He did foreknow, He did also predestinate to be conformed to the image of His Son, that He might be the firstborn among many brethren." Surely, all things which tend toward such a consummation must work together for good. And when we get to the end of the road, no matter how rugged it may have been, we shall sing: "Right was the pathway leading to this."

Conscience

Is it right to follow the dictates of our conscience? I contend that the Word of God is the Christian's guide.

I quite agree with you that "the Word of God is the Christian's guide," and that it is by no means safe to "follow the dictates of our conscience," except when our conscience is enlightened by the Word of God itself.

The Safe Guide

To what extent does God speak to us through our conscience, and to what extent can we rely on it?

Since man is a sinful creature, his conscience is a very unsafe guide. Even after regeneration, it is not possible to rely with confidence upon the guidance of one's conscience. Sometimes the conscience is "weak," and therefore, easily "defiled" (1 Cor. 8:7). Then in 1 Timothy 4:2, people are spoken of whose conscience is "seared with a hot iron." In Titus 1:15, people are referred to whose "mind and conscience is defiled." In Hebrews 9:14, believers are exhorted to keep their eyes upon the blood of Christ, so that it may "purge your conscience from dead works to worship the living God." In Hebrews 10:22, worshipers are exhorted to draw nigh, remembering that their hearts have been "sprinkled from an evil conscience." In a word, the only safe guide for any of us is the Word of God. We may always depend upon it to lead us in the right path.

Conscience an Unsafe Guide

Do you think it always possible to obey one's conscience? I know it is our duty, but is it possible always to do it?

Conscience is not always right and is therefore an unsafe guide. The Scriptures speak of an *evil* conscience (Heb. 10:22); a *weak* and *defiled* conscience (1 Cor. 8:7-12); and a "conscience *seared with a hot iron*" (1 Tim. 4:2); as well as of a *purged* conscience (Heb. 9:14); a *pure* conscience (1 Tim. 3:9; 2 Tim. 1:3); a *good* conscience (1 Tim. 1:5, 19; 1 Peter 3:16, 21) and a conscience *void of offense* (Acts 24:16).

Thus it is seen that the conscience is variable and therefore untrustworthy. It is only when it is enlightened and sensitive to the Word of God that conscience may be safely followed.

If by your question you mean to ask whether it is possible during this life to achieve sinlessness, my answer is, No. And yet we must not therefore excuse ourselves when we sin but rather confess our sins and judge ourselves before God (1 John 1:1-9); for only thus may we be kept in His fellowship and joy and be fruitful in His service.

The Responsibility of Following

Do you think it right to refuse to follow leaders that seem to be trying to control your every thought and all your gifts? It seems to me the budget plan upon which many of our churches are working is very materialistic. Soul saving is left out entirely. The main purpose seems to be to get funds, pay the leaders big salaries, and stint the missionary efforts. It seems like Ephesians 6:12, "spiritual wickedness in high places," also a political ring. If one refuses to fall in line one is almost considered a heretic.

Followers are responsible, in a measure, as well as leaders, and it certainly is as wrong to follow false leadership as it is to be a false leader. Let every believer remember that he himself is a priest with immediate access to God and immediate responsibility for not leading falsely, but the follower who submits to false leadership must also answer for that. "We must obey God, rather than men."

"Judge Not"

Please explain Matthew 7:1: "Judge not, that ye be not judged."

This command is generally misunderstood. For example, it is frequently urged as an argument against Church discipline of any kind. But the Church has received from her Lord and His accredited apostles most explicit directions to guide her in the exercise of judgment. In Matthew's Gospel itself our Lord gave instruction for the guidance of the then future Church in this matter, in chapter 18, verses 15-20. These instructions cannot be obeyed without the exercise of judgment, first on the part of the individual in determining that his brother has sinned against him, and then on the part of the assembly in deciding whether the aggrieved member has judged rightly.

Again, in the specific case of a member of the Corinthian church who was living in open and flagrant sin, the Spirit wrote by the apostle, in 1 Corinthians 5:9-13, expressly commanding the church to judge the man and exclude him from its fellowship. "Put away the wicked man from among yourselves." In the next chapter the apostle upbraids the believers for going to law before the unrighteous, and declares that matters in dispute ought to be brought before the church instead of the courts. "Dare any of you," he asks, "having a matter against his neighbor, go to law before the unrighteous, and not before the saints? Or know ye not that the saints shall judge the world? and if the world is judged by you, are ye unworthy to judge the smallest matters? Know ye not that we shall judge angels? how much more, things that pertain to this life? If then ye have to judge things pertaining to this life, do ye set them to judge who are of no account in the church? I say this to move you to shame. Is it so, that there cannot be found among you one wise man who shall be able to decide between his brethren, but brother goeth to law with brother, and that before unbelievers. Nay, already it is altogether a defect in you, that ye have lawsuits one with another. Why not rather take wrong, why not rather be defrauded?" (1 Cor. 6:1-8, R.V.).

A careful examination of Jesus' command, "Judge not, that ye be not judged," together with its context, will reveal its meaning. He never intended that His disciples should set aside all use of judgment, but rather that they should not apply to others any judgment which they would be unwilling to have others apply to them. We may and we must judge that which is openly and manifestly evil, and separate ourselves from it. We may and we ought to exercise the discernment God has given to us, as to outward acts; but there we must stop, for we can know nothing as to the inward motives.

To the same Corinthian church, which he commanded to judge and to put away the openly sinful and wicked man, Paul wrote, in 1 Corinthians 4:5, saying, "Judge nothing before the time, until the Lord come, who will both bring to light the hidden things of darkness, and make manifest the counsels of the hearts; and then shall each man have his praise from God." Here was a matter involving hidden things of darkness and counsel of the hearts. In such matters we are forbidden to judge, for we can know nothing of any man's heart motives. God is able to look upon the heart, but man may look only upon the outward appearance.

We are, however, commanded to judge ourselves, for we know our own hearts well enough to know that many an outward action which looks fair enough to our brethren is after all selfish and sinful. When we are honest enough with ourselves to judge ourselves, it is a healthful exercise. But often we excuse ourselves and refuse to use righteous judgment; and then God is compelled to deal with us. As it is written: "If we would judge ourselves, we should not be judged. But when we are judged, we are chastened of the Lord, that we should not be condemned with the world" (1 Cor. 11:31,32). This judging of ourselves will keep the "beams" from our own eyes and help us the better to remove the "motes" from our brother's eyes. For the heir of the Kingdom is not commanded, either here or elsewhere, to permit his brethren to go on in sin or error without seeking to deliver them. It is only that in order thus to serve them, he must himself have the single eye. Thus the apostle exhorts the Christian church in Galatians 6:1,2, R.V.: "Brethren, even if a man be overtaken in any trespass, ye who are spiritual, restore such a one in a spirit of gentleness; looking to thyself, lest thou also be tempted. Bear ye one another's burdens, and so fulfill the law of Christ."

Keeping in the Love of God

How can a Christian keep himself in the love of God (Jude 21)?

We are kept in the love of God by obedience. This is emphasized in John 15:10: "If ye keep my commandments, ye shall abide in my love; even as I have kept my Father's commandments, and abide in his love."

Christians and Warfare

Keeping in mind that our Lord said, "Blessed are the peacemakers," and commanded us to love our enemies, to do good to those that hate us, etc., should a Christian go to war to kill his enemies and friends also, when commanded by the government to do so?

It is the duty of the Christian to be obedient to the powers that be, for these powers are ordained of God, and they bear not the sword in vain (Rom. 13). Warfare is not a Christian institution, and neither is civil government a Christian institution, for there was civil government and there was warfare carried on by God's people before Christ came to the earth at all. Civil government, while not a Christian institution, is nevertheless a divine institution and is a gift of God, for which we should be continually thanking Him, for any government is far better than no government which is anarchy.

The Christian Church is to be conducted on the principle of grace, but civil government is to be conducted upon the principle of justice. The government is commanded of God to govern and in order to govern He has commissioned it to use force. The foundation of civil government is in the covenant of God to Noah, and is recorded in Genesis 9:1-6. In that covenant God established the principle of capital punishment: "Whoso sheddeth man's blood (that is, in murder), by man shall his blood be shed."

If we say that no Christian should have any part in civil government, then, of course, we must go on and say that no Christian should hold government office. Not only should he not enlist in the army, even if commanded to do so, not only must he not be a sheriff or a policeman or a constable, but neither may he be a school teacher, because the schools are conducted by government. None of us would be willing to live where there was no government, no policemen, no constables, no courts, no jails.

In the Old Testament times God often conducted warfare, using one nation against another, and sometimes even using heathen nations to scourge His own people Israel. In Judges 3:1,2, it is stated that certain nations were left in Canaan "to prove Israel by them, even as many of Israel as had not known all the wars of Canaan; only that the generations of the children of Israel might know, to teach them war, at the least such as before knew nothing thereof." Who can deny that Moses was commissioned of God, and Joshua after him, to conduct warfare? And as for David, the man after God's own heart, he was a man of war, and he declared in Psalm 144:1 that Jehovah taught his hands to war, and his fingers to fight.

The Christian is a citizen not only of heaven, but he is also a citizen here, and he is commanded of God to submit himself to earthly governments. It is his duty to obey the government in everything, except where the government commands him to do something that God has expressly forbidden. In such a case he may disobey the government and suffer the consequences, whatever they may be. Compare Acts 4:18-20.

Stay-at-Home Christians

What do you think of professing Christians sitting at home on Sunday and listening to sermons over the radio or television, instead of attending church where the Gospel is preached?

God's Word commands: "And let us consider one another to provoke unto love and to good works: *not forsaking the assembling of ourselves together*, as the manner of some is; but exhorting one another: and so much the more, as ye see the day approaching" (Heb. 10:24,25). Every Christian who is fortunate enough to belong to a church where the Gospel is preached in all its fullness ought by all means to attend the services of that church. It is surely contrary to the Word of God to forsake the assembling of ourselves together. Of course if you are unable to get to church that is another matter.

What May Christians Eat?

Will you please tell me how people get the idea that they may eat anything, when God has said that certain foods are unclean unto us, and for us not to eat it? For instance, swine flesh or pork? If you can find any place in the New Testament where He says we may eat pork I wish you would please tell me.

It is true that under the law of Sinai, issued to the Israelites in the wilderness, pork was declared as unclean, for though the swine parts the hoof it does not chew the cud. In order for food to be clean under the law of Moses it must come from an animal with a parted hoof that chews the cud (Lev. 11:1-8).

But all that is done away in the New Testament. In Mark 7 our Lord said: "Do ye not perceive, that whatsoever thing from without entereth into the man, it cannot defile him; because it entereth not into his heart, but into the belly, and goeth out into the draught, purging all meats?" (18,19). The Revised Version here reads: "This he said, making all meats clean." And in 1 Timothy 4 we are warned against those who would command us "to abstain from meats, which God hath created to be received with thanksgiving of them which believe and know the truth. For every creature of God is good, and nothing to be refused, if it be received with thanksgiving: for it is sanctified by the word of God and prayer" (1 Tim. 4:1-5).

Eating Again!

Do the instructions given to Israel in the eleventh chapter of Leviticus in regard to the eating of certain meats apply to the Church? Is it wrong for a Christian to eat meat, especially pork?

No, to both questions. See 1 Timothy 4:1-5.

Shall We Become Vegetarians?

Please explain Romans 14:21. Does it mean that we should abstain altogether from eating flesh? Did Paul have reference to the flesh offered to idols?

In Romans 14 and 1 Corinthians 8 the apostle discusses the question of whether Christians should eat flesh which had first been offered in sacrifice to idols. The churches were divided on the subject, one party claiming that the Christian is free from all such regulations, and the other party insisting that it was sinful to eat meat which had been offered to idols.

While agreeing that the Christian is not under bondage in such things, Paul nevertheless exhorted those who were strong in the faith to bear the infirmities of the weak and not to please themselves (Rom. 15:1). To avoid causing a weaker brother to stumble, Paul would eat no flesh so long as the world stood (1 Cor. 8:13). In our day there is no such question immediately before us as to whether we should eat flesh which has been offered in sacrifice to idols. But there are many other questions involving the same principle. All things are lawful for us, but not all things are expedient (1 Cor. 6:12). A splendid rule for every Christian to follow concerning any proposed course of action is to ask whether it will please God. Unless the answer is Yes, the safe way is to turn back from such proposed action and walk with Him in the narrow way. "Wherefore also we are ambitious, whether at home or absent, to be well pleasing unto him" (2 Cor. 6:9, R.V., margin).

The Sin of Worry

What do the words "take no thought" mean in Matthew 6:25?

They mean "don't worry." The whole passage (verses 25-34) shows the folly and sin of worry. The same teaching is found in Philippians 4:6,7. If we trust our Heavenly Father we will cast all our care upon Him, for He careth for us (1 Peter 5:7).

Should Christians Vote?

What does the Bible teach about a child of God voting? Please give me some light on the subject.

There is no direct statement in the Bible about whether or not a Christian should vote. The Bible does teach, however, that civil government is one of God's gifts to the race, and that makes civil government a divine institution. The ultimate form of civil government will be an absolute monarchy when the Man now at God's right hand will come back to earth to ascend the throne of His father David and to reign as "the blessed and only Potentate, the King of kings, and Lord of lords" (1 Tim. 6:15).

Meanwhile there are many different forms of civil government in the world. In this country we are living under a representative republic, and it is our privilege to choose our representatives.

Some Christians feel that since we are citizens of Heaven we cannot be at the same time citizens of any nation in this world. But this is a mistake. We are citizens and the responsibility is upon us. In my judgment, every Christian ought to look upon voting as a civic duty, and he ought to do his utmost to see to it that the right kind of representatives are put in office.

The Mysteries of Insanity

A neighbor of mine became mentally ill and is now confined in a hospital for the insane. Before this happened he gave strong evidence of having been truly saved, but now he is boisterous in profanity. Will you please explain this?

It is one of the mysteries of mental illness that often a child of God will become profane or even obscene in his conversation. The probable explanation is that in his case the old nature, being no longer under control, manifests itself freely. This old nature is called in the Word of God "the flesh," or "the natural man." At regeneration the old nature is by no means changed. It remains the same thing all the time, but a new nature comes in, abiding together with the old nature in the believer. The believer is exhorted not to walk in the flesh, not to yield to the old nature, not to give "the old man" an opportunity to manifest itself, but rather to walk in the Spirit and to mortify the deeds of the flesh.

In the case of your neighbor, if he has truly been born again, you may depend upon his heavenly Father to take care of him, even during his mental sickness, and to finally present him faultless before the presence of his glory with exceeding joy. This is what the blood of Christ does for us.

THE HEATHEN WORLD

The Universal Light

Please explain John 1:9: "That was the true Light, which lighteth every man that cometh into the world."

The meaning is that the Lord Jesus Christ is the Light not only of those to whom the Gospel has come, and by whom it is believed, but He is the Light of the world in a universal sense. In John 8:12 He says: "I am the Light of the World: he that followeth me shall not walk in darkness, but shall have the Light of life." It is true that only those who have received Him come to realize that "the darkness is past, and the true Light now shineth" (1 John 2:8); but that does not alter the fact that in a world-wide sense "the light of the knowledge of the glory of God in the face of Jesus Christ" has been shed abroad, and the judgment under which the human race rests is that "light is come into the world, and men loved darkness rather than light, because their deeds were evil" (John 3:19). The first chapter of Romans gives testimony to the fact that even those who have not heard the Gospel have nevertheless had witness borne to them through the works of God in the material universe. "Because that which may be known of God is manifest in them; for God hath showed it unto them. For the invisible things of him from the creation of the world are clearly seen, being understood by the things that are made, even his eternal power and Godhead; so that they are without excuse" (verses 19,20). This is often called "the light of nature." But what is meant by nature? The Word of God teaches us that it was the Son of God who created all things, and in whom all things hold together, and who upholdeth all things by the Word of His power (Col. 1:16,17; Heb. 1:3). The sun and the moon and the stars, then, are the work of His fingers (Ps. 8:3), and He set them in the heavens to "let them be for signs" (Gen. 1:14). The light proceeding from these "signs" has its origin in His own person. There is no light apart from Him. Thus it is that He is "the true Light, which lighteth every man that cometh into the world."

The Crisis of the World

Please explain the words, "the judgment of this world," in John 12:32.

There are two ways to transfer a word from one language to another: (1) by translation, and (2) by transliteration. The Greek word for "Judgment" is *crisis*. By transliteration we would read, "Now is the crisis of this world." It was surely a crisis, for again the Lord Jesus was deciding to die for us. Read the context, verses 20-33.

The Unevangelized

Will you please explain the position of the heathen world where the Gospel has not been preached? Is there any possibility of salvation in such a case?

Your question is answered in Romans 1, where it is declared that sufficient revelation is vouchsafed to the heathen, even the unevangelized heathen, to leave them without excuse before God (verse 20). No one can justly be held as "without excuse" unless there be a way out for him. Many millions of Gentiles were born and died during the days before the first Advent of Christ, and to these no missionary was ever sent except in such isolated instances as the mission of Jonah to Nineveh.

When the Son of God died on Calvary He was a propitiation (an atonement) for "the sins of the whole world" (1 John 2:2). No man is ever lost except through his own fault; the way of salvation is to follow the light given to him in the revelation of God. In Romans 2:6 it is declared that "every man" will be judged "according to his deeds." These deeds certainly include his reception or rejection of God as He is revealed, whether by "the invisible things of him from the creation of the world" showing "his eternal power and Godhead" (Rom. 1:20), or by the preaching of the Gospel through the mouth of a missionary. It is a good thing in connection with such a question as this to remember that "the Judge of all the earth," who knows the hearts of all men and is able to measure every man's responsibility, may be depended upon to "do right" (Gen. 18:26; Rom. 3:6).

Without Excuse

What is the future state of those who have died without an opportunity to accept Christ? When, and on what basis, will they be judged?

The answers to these questions are found in Romans 1 and 2. Even the unevangelized heathen are "without excuse," for "that which may be known of God is manifest in them; for God hath shewed it unto them." Two things are revealed unto them, and by them "clearly seen, being understood by the things that are made, even his eternal power and Godhead" (1:19,20). It is their duty to worship God, even though the Gospel has not been reached to them. The principles of judgment are four; namely (1) "according to truth" (2:2); (2) "to every man according to his deeds" (2:6); (3) without "respect of persons" (2:11); and (4) "according to my (Paul's) Gospel" (2:16).

Now, according to Paul's Gospel, and all the apostles agree with Paul's Gospel, the Lord Jesus tasted death for every man, and is thus the Savior of all men (Heb. 2:9; 1 Tim. 4:10). The failure of the unevangelized heathen to hear the Gospel does not alter the fact that they were included in the atonement wrought by Christ when on the cross. He died for all, the Lamb of God taking away the sin of the world (John 1:29). We may not know positively that any among the unevangelized heathen have really worshiped the true God according to the light given them, but neither can it be positively affirmed that such a thing is impossible. It is possible, else they would not be "without excuse."

And yet, even in such a case, salvation would not be apart from Christ, but rather *through* Christ, who "is the propitiation for our sins: and not for ours only, but also for the sins of the whole world" (1 John 2:2).

Meanwhile let us remember that we are commissioned and commanded to preach the Gospel to the uttermost part of the earth. The practical question with us is not what will happen to the unevangelized heathen but what may happen to the Christian Church if it fails to evangelize them.

ELECTION

God's Sovereignty and Man's Responsibility

Did God create some to be lost, or does His Word teach that He knew some or certain ones would be lost when He gave them life, or did God give certain ones life knowing that they would be lost? Is it not right for us to inquire into these things?

It is no doubt quite right for us to inquire into these things, but let us be careful to confine our inquiry to the Word of God and let us not wander into inferences which may lead us far astray. There is no doubt that God's absolute sovereignty is taught, and clearly taught, in the Word of God, and just as clearly is man's responsibility also taught in the Word. Our difficulty comes when we seek to "harmonize" these two doctrines. Such a task seems to be beyond the power of the human mind. Let us believe all that God has said on the subject and be content to wait for further light as to the harmony between these things. We may depend upon it that "the Judge of all the earth" will "do right." Let us preach to men as if everything depended upon them, and then let us pray to God for them as if everything depended upon God.

Election and Foreknowledge

If you have the space I would appreciate an explanation of the difference between "election" and "foreknowledge."

The meaning of election is "choice." And foreknowledge is simply "to know beforehand." The relation between these two doctrines is clearly stated by Dr. Scofield in his *Reference Bible*: "The divine order is foreknowledge, election, predestination. That foreknowledge determines the election or choice is clear from 1 Peter 1:2, and predestination is the bringing to pass of the election. Election looks back to foreknowledge; predestination forward to the destiny." But Scripture nowhere declares what it is in the divine foreknowledge which determines the divine election and predestination. The foreknown are elected, and the elect are predestinated, and this election is certain to every believer by the mere fact that he believes (1 Thess. 1:4,5).

Election and Free Grace

Will you please give me light on Romans 8:15-18? I cannot connect this Scripture with 1 Peter 3:9.

The relation between God's sovereignty and elective purpose on the one hand and free grace and human responsibility on the other has perplexed the commentators throughout the ages. The best course is to believe all that God says and wait for Him to make it plain. God insists upon His sovereignty and also upon man's responsibility. Believe both and preach both, leaving the task of "harmonizing" with Him.

Predestination

Recently the subject of predestination came up in our Sunday school, and later the pastor said from the pulpit that his God was not One who would predestinate people. There are different things that God has done for His people which our minister says He has not done and would not do. What would you think of him?

It is folly, to say nothing worse, to deny that there is such a doctrine in the New Testament. Your pastor's attention ought to be called to Romans 8:29,30 and Ephesians 1:5, 11. It would be far more honest for him to say that he does not understand the doctrine than to deny that there is such a doctrine. Predestination is that active exercise of the will of God by which He brings to pass certain results determined beforehand to be done. There is much of mystery about it, but that gives us no reason for denying that such a thing is taught in the Word of God.

Again—Predestination

We have become involved in a discussion on the subject of predestination, that is, as to whether our lives are mapped out for us from the beginning, or whether we are responsible for what happens in the course of our lives. I shall appreciate any information you may be able to give.

The whole question of the sovereignty of God and the responsibility of man is one which has perplexed theologians throughout the history of the Church. It is enough to say that while these two doctrines are taught in the Bible we are nowhere taught how to find the harmony between them. Perhaps it is too great for our minds to grasp. At any rate, it is good to remember that faith does not walk by sight, and can only function in the dark. Faith does not ask to know all about God, but faith believes all that God has said. There is no question as to the fact of God's elective plan. In 1 Peter 1:2 it is declared that God's election is according to His foreknowledge, but Scripture nowhere tells us what it is in God's foreknowledge which determines His divine choice. The connection between His foreknowledge and His electing grace is an unrevealed relation. See Deuteronomy 29:29.

FAITH

Living Faith

Is it necessary only to have a faith which recognizes Christ as Savior, or a faith which lives in Him and for Him?

The answer to this question is in the second chapter of James. Saving faith is living faith. In Romans 4 Paul describes justification before God. James in James 2 describes justification before men. Justification before God is accomplished instantly upon the exercise of living faith in the Word of God and the Son of God; but justification before men must await outward demonstration before men can know whether one really believes. We are saved by faith alone, but no man is saved by that faith which abides alone. Saving faith is living faith, as Paul puts it to the Galatians when he says that "in Jesus Christ neither circumcision availeth any thing, nor uncircumcision; but faith which worketh by love."

Saving Faith

In presenting God's plan of salvation to the sinner, is it scriptural to say one must confess Christ to be saved? There are many references in God's Word that by believing on the Son, Jesus Christ, one has everlasting life. I believe one will and should confess after he has believed, but many emphasize the confession as the way to be saved. Will you please show me from God's Word which a sinner must do?

It is true that belief is the sole condition of salvation. But what is belief? The Word of God shows belief to be far more than, and far different from, a mere intellectual assent to a set of propositions about Jesus of Nazareth. In John 1:11,12 believing on His name is seen to be the same thing as receiving Him. Therefore no one who has not received Him has really believed on His name. In Romans 10:9,10 receiving Him takes the form of confessing with the mouth while believing in the heart. And in Matthew 10:32 and Luke 12:8 our Lord makes receiving and confessing a public matter: It is to be "before men." Summing it all up, I should reply to your question that what a sinner must do to be saved is to believe in his heart that Christ died for his sins according to the Scriptures, that is to receive Him as his own personal Savior; and as there is opportunity the saved sinner should give testimony by open confession of Jesus as his Lord before men.

What Is Believing?

What is involved in "believeth that Jesus is the Christ" in 1 John 5:1?

Believing "that Jesus is the Christ" is equivalent to believing in Him as the Christ described in the Old Testament and revealed in the New; and believing "in him" or "on his name" means to receive Him as one's own personal Savior (John 1:12,13).

How Made to Believe?

How can those who laugh at Christians be made to believe?

It is impossible for us to make any one believe the Gospel. That is the work of the Holy Spirit (John 16:7-11). It is for us to testify, and pray for them, and leave the results with God.

Believing and Understanding

Is it possible for a person to be truly saved without knowing it?

Without question, there are multitudes of God's children who have definitely received the Lord Jesus Christ as their personal Savior, and yet are in uncertainty as to whether they are really saved. This comes, of course, from a lack of clearness as to what the Gospel is. It is good to know that a man is saved by *believing* the Gospel rather than by *understanding* it. It takes a long time for even the most spiritually intelligent among God's people to comprehend the beauties of the doctrine of grace, but their salvation does not rest upon their apprehension of these things. At the moment when they take the Lord Jesus as their Savior they receive with Him the gift of God which is eternal life, and His testimony concerning them is, "I give unto them eternal life; and they shall never perish, neither shall any one pluck them out of my hand" (John 10:28). First John is written for the express purpose of assuring believers of their eternal salvation (5:13).

Faith as a Grain of Mustard Seed

How are we to understand the Lord's saying in Matthew 17:20: "If ye have faith as a grain of mustard seed, ye shall say unto this mountain, Remove hence to yonder place; and it shall remove; and nothing shall be impossible unto you"? And in Luke 17:6: "If ye had faith as a grain of mustard seed, ye might say unto this sycamine tree, Be thou plucked up by the root, and be thou planted in the sea; and it should obey you"? I have always been puzzled over this "faith as a grain of mustard seed," and it seems hard to believe that the Savior in these passages means just what He says. I suppose Paul, in 1 Corinthians 13:2, may refer to this saying when he says, "and though I have all faith, so that I could remove mountains"; though the "all faith" of the Epistle doesn't sound as if it could be the same as the "faith as a grain of mustard seed" of the Gospels.

The point of our Lord's words appears when we observe that as recorded by Luke they were brought forth by the petition of the disciples, who said to the Lord, "Increase our faith." Think of that for a moment. It was equivalent to saying, "We wish we had greater confidence in thee; we wish thou wouldst help us to believe thou art honest and dependable and telling the truth." There was no answer for that but to remind these men that what they needed was not an increase of faith, for they had no faith to increase. A mustard seed is a small thing but it is *alive*; and faith, to be real, must be, not necessarily large, but *living*. This is the argument of James 2:14-17.

Never doubt that Jesus means just what He says. Faith is cooperation with God essentially, and no one who knows God at all can doubt His ability to remove mountains. Indeed, that is precisely what He will do one day, and doubtless it will be in response to the prayer of "faith as a grain of mustard seed" (see Zech. 14:4).

REGENERATION

Born from Above

A certain man in our church is quite a student of the Scriptures. He claims we are not born again until the Lord comes. He says that "born again" in John 3:33, means "born from above," and quotes Galatians 4:22-31, especially verse 26. He claims that this does not take place until the Lord comes. I am afraid this will cause confusion. He gave me John 3:12 as the reason why I could not see it his way.

It is true that the new birth is from above, but it is also true that the new birth takes place here and now the moment we receive the Lord Jesus Christ as our own personal Savior. According to James 1:18 God has already begotten us with the word of truth. According to 1 Peter 1:22,23, we have already been born again, "not of corruptible seed, but of incorruptible, by the Word of God, which liveth and abideth forever."

Do not let anybody worry you about a thing like this, for the Word of God is perfectly clear on the subject.

Born of Water and Spirit

What is the meaning of John 3:5, "Except a man be born of water and of the Spirit, he cannot enter into the kingdom of God"? Four explanations are given of the birth "of water": (1) that it refers to water baptism; (2) that it means the Word of God; (3) that it relates to the Holy Spirit, as in John 4:10-15; and (4) that it points back to the first birth, sometimes described as a "water birth." Which of these interpretations is correct?

The second is correct. Water baptism cannot be meant, for that would make water baptism an essential to salvation, which would contradict all the teaching of the Word of God elsewhere, as well as that of our Lord Himself. Water baptism is a duty and a privilege, but it is not a procuring cause of salvation. The third explanation indicated cannot be the true one, for the birth "of the Spirit" is mentioned in the same verse by our Lord. And the fourth explanation is also aside from the point, for though there be those who call the physical birth a "water birth," as a matter of fact it is nothing of the kind.

The second explanation really explains, and is in keeping with, the testimony of Scripture elsewhere on the subject. The water is a symbol of the Word of God, and the new birth is of the Word and of the Spirit, for the Holy Spirit uses the Word in bringing it about. In John 7:37-39 the double type is again found. The water is the Word of God, supplied and applied by the Spirit of God; the drinking of the water is believing on Christ "as the Scripture hath said." In John 3:10 our Lord rebuked Nicodemus, "a teacher in Israel," because he knew "not these things," for the same figure is employed in the Old Testament Scriptures, and Nicodemus should have been familiar with that fact (see, for example, Ezek. 36:25-27). In the New Testament the symbol is frequently used (see Titus 3:5-7; James 1:18; 1 Peter 1:22,23; Eph. 5:25,26; John 7:37-39).

Growing into a Christian

Is it possible for a child to grow into relationship with the Father and be a genuine Christian without having known when the change took place?

Your question is somewhat complicated. Children do not "grow into relationship with the Father." No one becomes a Christian without being born from above. Yet it is possible for a child to be born again "without having known when the change took place."

Reformation and Regeneration

Please make it plain why the *Scofield Reference Bible* states that Luke 11:24 refers to self-reformation and not to a born-again one.

It cannot refer to a born-again person, because regeneration is by no means the casting out of an unclean spirit and leaving the "house" empty. When a person is born again the Holy Spirit moves into the "house" and ever after abides there (1 Cor. 6:19; 2 Cor. 1:21,22; Eph. 1:13,14; 4:30; 1 John 2:20-27).

SANCTIFICATION OR HOLINESS

Instantaneous or Progressive?

Is sanctification instantaneous or progressive?

It is both. In its positional sense it is instantaneous (Heb. 10:10; 1 Cor. 1:2; 6:11). In its experiential sense it is progressive (John 17:17; 1 Thess. 5:23). The end of the process is indicated in 1 John 3: "We shall be *like him.*"

In, Of and By

I wish that you would please write and tell me what difference you see in the phrases "sanctified in Christ Jesus" (1 Cor. 1:2) and "sanctification of the Spirit" (1 Peter 1:2).

All sanctification is through the Holy Spirit, even the sanctification "by God the Father" (Jude 1), and the sanctification which has to do with our position in Christ Jesus. The word "sanctification" means separation or holiness, and the doctrinal meaning of the word is to be set apart for God. According to the teaching of Scripture the Christian is sanctified positionally, "through the offering of the body of Jesus Christ once for all" (Heb. 10:9,10). And he is sanctified experientially as he goes on in the Christian life apprehending the truth (John 17:17). Positional sanctification is instantaneous and applies to all believers alike. Experiential sanctification is progressive, varying according to the yieldedness of the believer. The end of this process will come when we are presented without fault in His own image and before the presence of His glory with exceeding joy (1 John 3:2; Jude 24,25).

By One Offering

Will you kindly give me a little light on Hebrews 10:10? If I understand it correctly, we are sanctified (or set apart) through the offering of His body once. Does this mean that Christ was offered once for all, or are we sanctified or set apart once for all? Can we be set apart more than once?

The word "once" in the text referred to has to do with the one offering on Calvary as contrasted with the many offerings under the Levitical covenant.

There is a sanctification which is *instantaneous* and *complete* for every believer from the moment he believes. He is instantly set apart by the reckoning of God and given the place of sonship in the Father's house, but in sonship he occupies a position in the family as being "in Christ."

Then there is a sanctification which is *progressive*. By this instantaneous sanctification the believer is made a saint (that is, a sanctified person, a holy person, a set apart person); and by *progressive* sanctification the saint becomes more and more saintly, his condition being brought nearer to his position, his state approaching more and more nearly his standing.

Then there is an *ultimate* sanctification which will be accomplished when the saint is separated from all sin and presented faultless before God's presence with exceeding joy, shining in the kingdom of his Father and in the perfect image of the Son.

Sanctification by Contact

Please explain the meaning of 1 Corinthians 7:14,15.

These verses read as follows: "For the unbelieving husband is sanctified by the wife, and the unbelieving wife is sanctified by the husband: else were your children unclean; but now are they holy. But if the unbelieving depart, let him depart. A brother or a sister is not under bondage in such cases: but God hath called us to peace."

The teaching here is sanctification by contact. The unbelieving husband of a Christian wife or the unbelieving wife of a Christian husband is sanctified by contact with the believing partner, and this sanctification extends to their children. (The word for "holy" is identical with that for "sanctified.") That this sanctification is not salvation is shown by the sixteenth verse: "For what knowest thou, O wife, whether thou shalt save thy husband? or how knowest thou, O man, whether thou shalt save thy wife?"

Sanctification is separation or being set apart. It never means sinlessness, and sometimes, as in this case, it does not even include salvation. Israel as a nation is sanctified, but it is not saved. Jerusalem as a city is sanctified—often called "the holy city"—but it is not saved. It is set apart by God for special purposes and put in a peculiar relation to Himself.

The unbelieving husband of a Christian woman, or the unbelieving wife of a Christian man, is set apart in a peculiar class in the reckoning of God, as are also the children of these mixed marriages. God is particularly interested in them; and what father would not be interested in his own sons' wives, and daughters' husbands, and grandchildren?

Under the old covenant, whatsoever should touch a sanctified altar was itself sanctified by this contact, and whatsoever should touch a sanctified person was sanctified itself by this contact (Ex. 29:37; 30:29). Our Lord made reference to this sanctification by contact in His teaching in Matthew 23:17-19.

It ought to be added that Paul's teaching in 1 Corinthians 7:14,15 does not give warrant for the putting on of the unequal yoke in marriage; it only deals with those who, having been married before conversion, find themselves bearing the unequal yoke. The apostle teaches that in such a case if the unbelieving partner is willing to go on in the marriage relationship then the believer should also go on, and in such a case the believer is assured of God's solicitous interest in them and their children. It is a delightful illustration of our God's gracious interest in our welfare and that of those related to us.

The Second Blessing

Will you tell me what the Scripture teaches about the second blessing? Our pastor thinks that we receive the Holy Spirit after we have been saved, that it is separate from our salvation. If he is right, we are wrong, as we believe that when we were born again we received the Spirit, and that He will never leave us. Please tell us what you think about it.

The "second blessing" doctrine, so called, is contrary to Scripture. The teaching of the New Testament is that all believers have the Holy Spirit dwelling in them (1 Cor. 3:16; 6:19; 12:12,13); but it also exhorts all believers to "be filled with the Spirit" (Eph. 5:18). It may be that your pastor refers to this *filling* as a second blessing.

Sinlessness

How can Christians have victory over sin? The Bible says, "Be ye therefore perfect, even as your Father which is in heaven is perfect," and it seems impossible to be perfect and sinless in this world.

Victory over sin is one thing and sinless perfection is another. The latter is not attainable so long as we are in the body, but the former is the Christian's privilege, and should always be his aim. "I beseech you therefore, brethren, by the mercies of God, that ye present your bodies a living sacrifice, holy, acceptable unto God, which is your reasonable service. And be not conformed to this world: but be ye transformed by the renewing of your mind, that ye may prove what is that good, and acceptable, and perfect, will of God" (Rom. 12:1,2).

Holiness and Perfection

Please explain Hebrews 12:14, and give the best text to offset the "perfection" theory.

Hebrews 12:14 is an exhortation to "follow peace with all men, and holiness, without which no man shall see the Lord." Holiness is not the same thing as perfection. Holiness is separation, and so also is sanctification, which is an exactly synonymous word with holiness, both coming from the same Greek word. The Epistle to the Hebrews consists in general of an appeal to Hebrews who were convinced that Jesus was the Messiah, but who hesitated to confess Him as such. The verse you cite is in line with this appeal, and the writer is calling upon his Hebrew brethren to separate themselves and walk in the path set before them, confessing Jesus as Lord (compare Rom. 10:9,10). Our holiness or sanctification is Christ Himself (1 Cor. 1:30) and therefore we are called saints, which means sanctified or holy persons, set apart unto God—"sanctified through the offering of the body of Jesus Christ once for all" (Heb. 10:10). As for perfection, we are on our way to that, and meanwhile, in our standing before God, our Lord has by His one great offering "perfected forever them that are sanctified," including, of course, every believer (Heb. 10:14). As to our walk, we should seek to have it conform to our position so far as that may be possible in the energy of the Holy Spirit.

Holiness and Sinlessness

Do the Scriptures teach holiness in the flesh?

"The flesh" can never be holy, and "they that are in the flesh cannot please God" (see Rom. 8:8,9). If you mean to ask whether a state of sinlessness can be attained while we are yet in the natural body, the answer is, No. And yet that fact must not be used as an excuse for sin. As a speaker once put it, "You need not be so afraid of perfection; for none of us ever got near enough to *perfection* to catch the *infection*." While we are always prone to sinning, let us not forget that we are called, not to uncleanness, but to holiness (1 Thess. 4:7).

Seven Questions on Holiness

1. Is it possible to be perfect in experience as we are perfect in position? If not, what should we do with that command in Leviticus 19:2: "Ye shall be holy: for I the LORD your God am holy?"

2. Is there a stage in holiness reached where a man will not wilfully sin (1 John 3:9; Matt. 5:48; 1 John 3:6; 5:18; Deut. 18:13; 1 Kings 8:61)?

3. When God asks us to be "perfect," what does He really mean by that word "perfect"?

4. Can we come into the same state of holiness possessed by Adam and Eve before they fell?

5. Does the Christian in this life ever experience that degree of holiness whereby the carnal nature is eradicated and temptation to him is no more from within, but only from without?

6. Is it possible to live without known sin; and is it probable that such a person lives; and has there ever been a living example excepting Christ?

7. In the different planes of "progressive sanctification" is there ever a highest plane reached by man, where he is more delivered from the attacks of Satan and thus less liable to commit sin? Or as man progresses in sanctification does the attack of Satan become more subtle and does he keep presenting new temptations whereby the Christian is more liable to fall?

Your questions remind me of an instance in my own experience a few years ago. A young woman friend of mine about to be graduated from college sent me a long list of questions. They were supposed to be hard questions, but they were all "old stuff," and I had answered them over and over again at various times, but here they were again. My answer to her was that her trouble was "an attitude of mind," and that even if I should answer all her questions she would still have as many left when I got through as when I began.

One of the best books I know on the subject of Holiness is Harry Ironside's *Holiness: The False and the True*. Mr. Ironside used to be a Salvation Army officer, and it was during that time that he went through the so-called experience of "sanctification," when he believed that the old nature had been eradicated and that he was no longer subject to temptation.

To answer your seven questions:

1. *Perfection* is not quite the same thing as *holiness*, although they are sometimes used synonymously. I should say that sinless perfection is not possible in this life. Nevertheless we must continually aspire unto it, and so far as it is possible we must be holy as Jehovah our God is holy.

2. This question is difficult to answer by a Yes or No. Sin is coming short of the glory of God. I suppose no real Christian "wilfully" desires to do that. But whether the goal is ever attained amongst us, I cannot tell.

3. The word "perfect" means exactly what it seems to mean to the average reader. It is really sinlessness, but I have already answered this question in answer No. 1.

4. Holiness is not the correct way to describe the state of Adam and Eve before the fall. They were innocent, but they had not yet been tested. It is quite impossible for any one who has known what sin is to come into the same state possessed by Adam and Eve before they fell.

5. The Scriptures certainly do not teach that the carnal nature is ever eradicated, or that the believer can ever get to the place where his temptation is wholly from without and not from within. Romans 7:18 is always true so long as we are here in the flesh at all. Of course, in the technical sense, no Christian is in the flesh (Rom. 8:9), but that is not the meaning of the expression in Romans 7:18.

6. I have known many persons who claim to be living without known sin; but I have never yet seen a satisfactory definition of "known sin." When you remember that any coming short of the glory of God is sin it is hard to think of our living for a moment in the absence of sin, or even known sin.

7. Sin is not always the result of Satan's attacks. Even during the Millennium, when Christ will be here on the throne, and when Satan is restrained for a thousand years, there will yet be sin—so much so that at the end of the thousand years when Satan is released he will find it possible to muster a tremendous army of rebels against the Lord. Sin is a part of man's make-up, and it is inseparable from him in this life. It is no doubt true that as he becomes more intimate with God he will become more sensitive to sin, and will therefore find in himself far more sin than he ever before dreamed was there; but it is also true that in such a case there will be ever-increasing victory over sin.

Eradication

Is eradication taught in the Bible?

No. Not until we are changed into the image of Christ will sin be eradicated. The Scriptures do not teach that the believer can ever, in this life, get to the place where his temptation is wholly from without and not from within. The language of Romans 7:18, "For I know that in me (that is, in my flesh) dwelleth no good thing," is always true so long as we are here in the flesh at all. Of course, in the technical sense no Christian is in the flesh (Rom. 8:9), but that is not the meaning of the expression in Romans 7:18.

TEMPERANCE

Our Lord's Position as to Wine

Please comment on Christ's miracle at Cana in turning water into wine. Was the wine fermented?

Of course a question like this is difficult to answer. The only way to solve the problem is to search the Scriptures. The Bible is the Word of God and so is Christ the Word of God, and there can be no disagreement between them; therefore our Lord's attitude toward wine must be that of the Scriptures. The Scriptures testify that "He causeth the grass to grow for the cattle, and herb for the service of man: that he may bring forth food out of the earth; and wine that maketh glad the heart of man. and oil to make his face to shine, and bread which strengtheneth man's heart" (Ps. 104:14,15); but He warns men that the gladness from the wine, the shining from the oil, and the strengthening from the bread are only temporary and cannot permanently satisfy (Isa. 55:1,2; John 6:27).

There is nothing to satisfy man's real longing that comes from the vine-tree of the earth, however. "From the kernels even to the husk" (Num. 6:4). He Himself is the True Vine of Heaven (John 15:1), and "He satisfieth the longing soul, and filleth the hungry soul with goodness" (Ps. 107:9; Isa. 55:1). His Word warns His people against fellowship with winebibbers and gluttons (Prov. 23:20), and declares that "it is not for kings to drink wine, nor for princes strong drink; lest they drink, and forget the law, and pervert the judgment of any of the afflicted" (Prov. 31:4,5).

Wine may be good for medicinal purposes (Prov. 31:6,7; 1 Tim. 5:23), but there is great danger that it may be used to excess, and it is far better to be filled with the Holy Spirit than to be drunken with what men call "ardent spirits" (Eph. 5:18).

I do not pretend to know the nature of the wine furnished by our Lord at the wedding of Cana, but I am satisfied that there was little resemblance in it to the thing described in the Scriptures of God as biting like a serpent and stinging like an adder (Prov. 23:29-32). Doubtless, rather, it was like the Heavenly fruit of the vine that He will drink new with His own in His Father's Kingdom (Matt. 26:29). No wonder the governor of the wedding feast at Cana pronounced it the best wine kept until the last. Never before had he tasted such wine, and never did he taste it again.

Christians and Prohibition

Why should a Christian concern himself with the enactment or enforcement of laws for the regulation or prohibition of the liquor traffic? Isn't his citizenship in Heaven? What right has the government to interfere with one's personal liberty in the matter of what should be eaten or drunk?

The Christian is surely a citizen of Heaven, but he is also a citizen here, and he has no right to shirk the responsibility thereby involved. And he ought to thank God every day of his life for the divine gift of human government, for without it he could not long survive. Any government is better than anarchy, and "the powers that be are ordained of God" (Rom. 13:1). Consider what would be the result if every Christian in the world should refuse to exercise the right of franchise or to hold public office. Even a schoolteacher is a public office-holder. What would happen to our children if every Christian schoolteacher should quit that office and turn it over to an enemy of Christ?

As to your question of "personal liberty," the answer is that no person is at liberty to do anything that threatens the well-being of society. The government certainly has a right to regulate the eating and drinking of its citizens if to do so is to help preserve the government itself from destruction. Preservation of itself is necessary to the government, so that it might function in the preservation of order. The drug traffic has long threatened the very existence of all government. And, since the Christian is a citizen and subject to the powers that be, he ought to help in every proper way to bring about the enactment and enforcement of such laws as are necessary to preserve the government and enable it to effectually function in its divinely appointed task. The Noahic Covenant of Genesis 9:1-6 has never been abrogated or modified, and is still in full force as the Magna Charta of Human Government.

PRAYER

Who May Pray

You say that until the sinner has received Christ he cannot enter into God's presence even to pray; and again you say that Cornelius the centurion was saved through hearing and believing the gospel from Peter. But in Acts 10:2 we read that Cornelius "prayed to God always," and, in verse 4, that his prayers and alms had come up for a memorial before God, and yet he was not saved until Peter entered his house and told him words whereby he and his house might be saved (Acts 11:14). Now if God does not hear the prayer of an unsaved man how can all this be understood?

It is quite true that Cornelius was heard before he was really saved. But his case is quite different from the sinner to whom I referred as being unable to pray. There is a vast difference between a man who has never heard the gospel and another man, who having heard it has rejected it, and yet believes that he may enter into God's presence and pray. He who despised Moses' law died without mercy under two or three witnesses: of how much worse punishment, do you suppose, shall he be thought worthy, who has trodden under foot the Son of God, and has counted the blood of the covenant, wherewith he was sanctified, an unholy thing, and has done despite unto the Spirit of grace? For we know him who said, "Vengeance belongeth unto me, I will recompense, saith the Lord. And again, The Lord shall judge his people. It is a fearful thing to fall into the hands of the living God" (Heb. 10:30-31).

Successful Prayer

I have been giving much thought to the subject of prayer, and it seems to me there are no less than seven requisites, if one would be certain of receiving the thing prayed for. If I am wrong, I most sincerely desire to be set right; if I am correct, I should like confirmation. The seven are: 1. Faith, believing (Matt. 21:22; Mark 11:24; Heb. 11:6). 2. "Abide in me, and my words abide in you" (John 15:7). 3. According to His will (John 9:31; 1 John 5:14,15). 4. In His name (John 14:13,14). 5. With thanksgiving (Phil. 4:6). 6. With forgiveness (Mark 11:25,26). 7. Without wrath (1 Tim. 2:8).

Instead of seven requisites for successful prayer, I should rather say that the one requisite is set forth in various ways in Scripture.

What I mean is that we cannot be abiding in Christ and having His Word abiding in us and then pray without faith, or contrary to His will, or without thanksgiving or forgiveness, or with wrath toward anyone.

In Ephesians 6 we are told to pray "in the Spirit." This is just another way of putting the same thing. But whenever we pray in the Spirit we are fulfilling all the other conditions.

The same thing is true with regard to the words "in His name." This is not a mere formula to be put on the end of a prayer, for the formula might be used without the prayer being in His name at all. As a matter of fact, we cannot pray in His name and in the Spirit except we are praying for something to which He would sign His own name.

The Proper Posture for Prayer

I have often wondered which way is the most pleasing to God, concerning prayer. Should one always pray down on his knees, or will God hear our prayer in any way, standing up or sitting down, with our hands folded and head bowed? Or, is it because our prayer is a true prayer right from the heart?

The attitude of one's heart is what really matters. The bodily attitude varies widely in connection with Bible prayers. The most frequently mentioned posture is standing. In Genesis 17:17,18, Abraham "fell on his face" and prayed; in Genesis 18:22,23, he stood and prayed. Abraham's servant, in Genesis 24:11-13, stood "at the well of water" and prayed. After the battle of Ai, Joshua "fell to the earth upon his face" and prayed (Josh. 7:6-9). Samson prayed standing between the pillars in the Philistine temple at Gaza, and asked for strength to destroy that temple, and God answered (Judg. 16:28). In 2 Samuel 7:18, David "sat before the Lord" and prayed. In 1 Kings 19:4 Elijah "sat down under a juniper tree" and prayed. In 2 Kings 20:2 Hezekiah prayed in his bed with his face turned toward the wall. Ezra (9:5,6) knelt to pray. Nehemiah (2:3,4) "shot the bird on the wing" in prayer, standing before the king and the king's mother. Later, in Jerusalem (9:4,5) he stood in prayer and had the congregation stand. Daniel (6:10) knelt in prayer three times a day when his life was threatened for it. Jonah (2:1) prayed "out of the fish's belly."

In Gethsemane our Lord "fell on his face" and prayed. He also prayed from the cross. So did the penitent thief. Stephen (Acts 7:59,60) knelt down in the middle of his prayer. Saul of Tarsus prayed from the ground as he lay in the middle of the Damascus road (Acts 9:4,5). After he had become the great apostle Paul, in Ephesians 3:14, he wrote, "I bow my knees unto the Father of our lord Jesus Christ." Let us avoid formalism in prayer, and let us "draw near with a true heart" when we pray.

The Disciples' Prayer

Should believers pray the prayer the Lord Jesus taught His disciples as given in Matthew 6:9-13?

I believe this prayer would be more properly designated the disciples' prayer.

Of course, there are many petitions in the prayer which a Christian may properly offer. But the prayer is not in the name of Christ, which is the true basis for all Christian prayer (John 14:13,14; 16:23-27). And it has one petition which no instructed believer since the crucifixion and resurrection of Christ can properly offer, namely, "forgive us our debts, as we forgive our debtors." This is on the principle of righteousness, but it is not on the principle of grace. I believe that in the Christian dispensation the believer is already forgiven according to the riches of God's grace (Eph. 1:7; 4:32; Col. 2:13; 1 John 2:12), and the measure of his forgiveness from God is by no means according to the measure of his forgiveness toward others. The true principle of forgiveness under grace is stated in Ephesians 4:32, "And be ye kind one to another, tenderhearted, forgiving one another, even as God for Christ's sake hath forgiven you."

It is true that there is another sense in which the believer must from time to time seek forgiveness in addition to the general forgiveness connected with his eternal salvation. When the believer falls into sin his *fellowship* with God is interrupted, and in 1 John 1:9, we are told that "if we confess our sins, he is faithful and just to forgive us our sins, and to cleanse us from all unrighteousness." But even here there is nothing said about our forgiveness toward others as being the measure of our forgiveness from God.

It goes without saying that an unforgiving spirit toward other believers is faulty and that it in itself is so sinful as to interrupt our communion with our Father. But He distinctly tells us that the way for us to obtain forgiveness from Him is to confess our sins unto Him.

In a word, this so-called Lord's prayer is upon Kingdom ground rather than upon Church ground. It is the privilege of the Christian, who, by the grace of God, has been made a New Testament priest, to draw near to his Father in the Holy of Holies and speak freely to Him in prayer in the name of the Lord Jesus, fully expecting to receive that for which he prays.

Unceasing Prayer

How can we "pray without ceasing"?

We "pray without ceasing" when we are constantly in the attitude of yieldedness, and desire to know and to do the will of God. There is danger that, having uttered our prayer to God, we may forget it and fail to look for the answer. We are "always to pray, and not to faint" (Luke 18:1).

Delay is Not Denial

Why did our Lord delay His going to Bethany in response to the cry of Mary and Martha when their brother, Lazarus, was about to die?

The natural inference from His delay would be that He did not love His Bethany friends, but the real reason for His delay was the other way around: it was *because* He loved them. Look at the record in John 11:5,6: "Now Jesus loved Martha, and her sister, and Lazarus. When he heard therefore that he was sick, he abode two days still in the same place where he was." The delay was not because he loved them not, but because He loved them. If He had gone to them at once Lazarus could not have died, for no one ever died in His presence; and it was necessary that Lazarus should die in order that God and His Son might be glorified in his resurrection. So instead of having a sick brother *healed*, these sisters had a dead brother *raised* from the dead. Let us learn from all this that though the answers to our prayers may not come as promptly as we desire, yet delay does not mean denial. The delay is because He loves us.

Praying for the Unsaved

Have we any direct Scripture that commands us to pray for sinners; that is, for their salvation?

In 1 Timothy 2:1 we are commanded to pray for "all men," and in verses 3 and 4, we are told that "this is good and acceptable in the sight of God our Savior; who will have all men to be saved, and to come unto the knowledge of the truth." It would seem therefore that this is practically a direct command to pray for the salvation of sinners. Indeed, intercession for sinners seems to be particularly committed to us, for in John 17:9 the Lord Jesus distinctly says: "I pray not for the world, but for them which thou hast given me; for they are thine." Therefore if the world is to be prayed for we must do it. It is really marvelous how little we pray, when we remember how much is promised to us in answer to prayer. May God teach us all how to pray!

Praying Through

What do people mean who talk about "praying through"? I cannot find it in the Word, unless it occurred Jacob wrestled with the angel and prevailed, or where the importunate one because of his insistence was answered. It puzzles me, because the ones who talk it so much as absolutely necessary are so inconsistent in their lives. Does not the Scripture say, "If we ask anything according to his will, he heareth us?"

There is much folly among God's own dear people relating to the subject of prayer, and I think I understand why you are troubled. It is a mistake to suppose that we shall be heard for our much speaking, and yet there is much teaching on prayer which tends to encourage that kind of thing as pleasing to God. Our Heavenly Father loves to have His children come to Him in their need, and, as you yourself have intimated, the promises concerning prayer are perfectly plain and simple.

Too little attention has been paid to the new teaching on prayer given by our Lord just before His betrayal and crucifixion. In John 14:12-14 and 16:23-27 He declared that the open sesame of prayer was now to be His own name. "Hitherto have ye asked nothing in my name: ask, and ye shall receive, that your joy may be full" (16:24).

What is it to ask in His name? It is far more than saying, "This I ask in Jesus' name," or "for Jesus' sake." Too many prayers bear that label when the thing asked for is wanted, not for His sake at all, but for the sake and the pleasure of the one bringing the petition. No prayer can really be in Jesus' name which Jesus Himself would refuse to sign, and to use His name in such a prayer is forgery.

In John 15:7 Jesus' name is not mentioned, but whoever prays while abiding in Him and having His Word abiding in him is praying in Jesus' name even if he does not mention the name.

And so also with the words "in the Spirit" in Ephesians 6:18. Whoever prays in the Holy Spirit is praying in Jesus' name whether he says so or not. And he is praying "according to" God's "will" (1 John 5:14,15). All these Scriptures we have cited are but various statements of the same condition of successful prayer. No prayer is ever denied which is presented in the name of the Lord Jesus. If it comes from one who is abiding in Christ and has the words of Christ abiding in him, and is prayed in the Holy Spirit, according to the will of God, how, indeed, could such a prayer be denied?

Our God loves to be inquired of. He loves to be trusted. "Let us therefore come boldly unto the throne of grace, that we may obtain mercy, and find grace to help in time of need" (Heb. 4:16).

Commanding God

What kind of a sin would you call it when people command God to do a certain thing?

I should call it a presumptuous sin, to say the very least. And I should say that it approaches blasphemy.

Again—Commanding God

You will remember answering a question not long ago as to whether it was right to command the Lord. I thought at the time of a passage which reads, "Concerning the work of my hands command ye me." Where it is to be found I do not know, but somewhere in the Old Testament. Perhaps the party who suggested it to the one who wrote you might like to hear from you on the passage, as well as I myself.

Thank you for reminding me of the passage, which you will find in Isaiah 45, verse 11: "Thus saith Jehovah, the Holy One of Israel, and his Maker, Ask me of things to come concerning my sons, and concerning the work of my hands command ye me." This is a gracious word from our God. Yet it does not mean what is often meant by those who teach that in prayer we have a right to command God, in the sense of demanding from Him what is asked, without regard as to whether the thing asked is according to His will. It was against this teaching that the former answer was directed.

The Intercession of Moses

Please explain Exodus 32:32,33.

In this passage Moses appears as the intercessor for his people. So earnest was he in his pleading for them that he was willing to be lost himself if only his people might be saved. The same spirit is seen in Acts 7:60; Romans 9:3, and preeminently in Luke 23:34.

Prayer and Promise

Is the promise of Revelation 3:10 the response to the prayer of Matthew 6:13?

The prayer of Matthew 6:13 and the promise of Revelation 3:10 are not quite parallel. The prayer, which reads literally: "Deliver us from the wicked one," is more general than the promise. The promise, as I understand it, has to do with the Great Tribulation, and is a pledge on the part of the risen Christ to take His Church out of the scene before the judgment of the great Tribulation bursts upon the earth. Read Revelation 3:10 in the Revised Version, which changes "temptation" to "trial."

Prayer for an Unsaved Brother

Is there some Scripture to show that an unsaved brother, if prayed for continually, will be saved before he dies, even though he may have many tribulations?

I do not know of any Scripture which absolutely guarantees that an unsaved brother will be saved in answer to our prayers. The words "and thy house" in Acts 16:31 give no such promise, as I have shown elsewhere in this book. If that were true we could by praying for the whole world expect the salvation of the world in answer to our prayers. The thing for us to do is to commit the matter to God and trust only in Him.

Prayer for Unbelievers

I heard a certain Bible teacher say that there was not one word of Scripture which showed that Jesus Christ or the Holy Spirit prayed for the unbeliever. He did not mention God, the first person of the Trinity. Is he correct in this? How about Luke 23:34, "Father, forgive them; for they know not what they do"?

I doubt not that the Bible teacher to whom you refer was speaking of the words of our Lord Jesus in prayer to the Father in John 17, when He said in verse 9: "I pray not for the world, but for them which thou hast given me; for they are thine." I do not know of any place in Scripture where we are taught that our Lord Jesus prays for the world. But I know that we ourselves are commanded to pray for all men (1 Tim. 2:1).

Negative Answers to Prayer

Is it not true that God answers by withholding from us the things we ask for, just as truly as when He gives us our desires?

In 2 Corinthians 12:8,9 God refused to grant Paul's petition for the removal of a "thorn in the flesh, the messenger of Satan." This, of course, is a negative answer to prayer. But the general principle of prayer is that whatever we ask we shall receive. The prayer, however, must be in the name of the Lord Jesus;

it must come from one who is abiding in Him and having His Word abiding in the petitioner; it must be in the Holy Spirit, and it must be according to the will of God (John 14:12-14; 15:7; 16:23-27; Eph. 6:18; 1 John 5:14,15). When Paul discovered that he was praying against the will of God, he stopped praying and at once began glorying in his infirmities, for when he was weak then he was strong.

How to Pray

Should prayer be only to the Father through the Son? Is there any Scripture that teaches us we should pray to Jesus? Is it wrong to ask the Holy Spirit for guidance or help?

From our Lord's new teaching on prayer in John 16:23-27 it would seem that, strictly speaking, our prayer should be addressed to the Father in the name of the Son. Yet I would be slow to say that it is wrong to pray directly to the Lord Jesus or to the Holy Spirit. See John 14:13,14. Our Father God is very kind to us, and it is good to remember that the Holy Spirit helps our infirmity, particularly with regard to prayer. See Romans 8:26, Revised Version.

Again—How to Pray

When I pray if I address my prayer to the Father I do not feel any nearness to the Lord Jesus, and if I address the Lord Jesus the Father becomes less distinct and real. This has bothered me all my life. I have never seen any clear instruction concerning it.

I cannot understand your difficulty about prayer. When it is remembered that the Father and the Son are one it is quite impossible to get near the One and be far from the other. The Lord's own instruction about prayer is clearly set forth in John 16:23-27. See also John 14:23: "If a man love me, he will keep my words: and my Father will love him, and we will come unto him, and make our abode with him." This surely makes both the Father and the Son, as well as indeed the Holy Spirit, so very near to the child of God.

"Speak to Him thou for He hears,
And Spirit with spirit can meet—
Closer is He than breathing,
And nearer than hands and feet."

May Unsaved Persons Pray?

Should unsaved people pray to God, excepting the prayer, "God be merciful to me a sinner"?

Strictly speaking, unsaved persons may not pray at all. The publican was not an unsaved sinner praying for salvation, but a member of the Commonwealth of Israel praying for mercy. Until the sinner has received Christ he cannot enter into God's presence even to pray. The only thing for him to do is to receive Christ, and then he may pray and obtain an answer.

How to Pray in War Time

How should one pray for our country when at war, and also for our boys who are on the front fighting?

Pray that God may cause the wrath of man to praise Him and that He may restrain the remainder of wrath (Ps. 76:10).

The Right to Pray

Will you tell me if the Bible teaches that an unsaved person may pray?

The Scriptures clearly teach that prayer is a priestly privilege, and that only those may pray who have entered "into the holiest by the blood of Jesus." Every Christian is a priest, and as such he has free "access by faith into this grace wherein we stand." How can one expect to be heard in prayer "who hath trodden under foot the Son of God, and hath counted the blood of the covenant, wherewith he was sanctified, an unholy thing, and hath done despite unto the Spirit of grace? . . . It is a fearful thing to fall into the hands of the living God" (Heb. 10:29-31).

Should Little Children Pray?

Is there any Scripture to show that we should teach our children to pray? I have a sister who belongs to an assembly of Christians which says that it is not Scriptural to teach children to pray.

Little children who have not reached the age of accountability, where they are able to intelligently believe the Gospel and to receive the Lord Jesus as their own personal Savior—and who are therefore, of course, unable to reject the Lord—are in a place of safety under the blood, since Christ died for the sins of the whole world. I should certainly teach such little children to pray. But when they have reached the age of accountability and have rejected the Lord Jesus Christ as their Savior and are thus rejecting the Son of God and making the blood of the covenant an unholy thing, and doing despite to the Spirit of grace, they certainly have no right to pray, and it is wrong to teach them that they have such a right.

Prayer and Fasting

In Matthew 17:21 it reads: "Howbeit this kind goeth not out but by prayer and fasting." Does this mean for Christians now to fast? Would we have more faith if we fasted often? Are our prayers more apt to be answered with fasting when praying?

The verse to which you refer has been entirely omitted from the Revised Version, as well as the words, "and fasting," in the parallel verse, Mark 9:29. It would be easy to get on legal ground in this matter of fasting. We certainly ought not to look upon either fasting or prayer as a matter of merit, and suppose that by either or both of them we can make ourselves more presentable to God. It may well be that a believer will be so absorbed in his prayers as to even forget to eat, or to lose all appetite for eating. That would be one thing. But to deliberately set about it to fast, with the idea that by so doing we might induce our reluctant Father to answer our prayers, would be quite another thing. Our Father delights to answer prayer, and He loves to be trusted. Let us not erect a second Sinai in the place of our Heavenly Zion (Heb. 12:18-24).

Fasting

So far as I can discover, "fasting" is not (really) mentioned in all the Epistles from Romans to Revelation inclusive, and as the Epistles embrace all the law and order for the Church, we are, therefore, not expected to do it. Or to put it in another way, it is in no way essential to prevailing prayer. In the Authorized Version "fasting" is mentioned in 1 Corinthians 7:5; 2 Corinthians 6:5; 2 Corinthians 11:27. The Revised Version omits it from 1 Corinthians 7:5, and Weymouth omits it from 1 Corinthians 7:5, and translates it "hunger and thirst" in 2 Corinthians 6:5; and "frequent fastings" in 2 Corinthians 11:27. But in Conybeare's translation "fasting" does not occur at all. Could you tell us how these differences come about? What part of it is due to a difference in the text of various manuscripts and how much of it is due to a difference in translation of the same Greek words?

Some groups appoint special days of fasting and prayer. But in the study of the life of George Müller, the subject of fasting is never mentioned so far as I can find, and I feel very well satisfied that he did not fast. But Mr. Müller moved heaven and earth by prayer to feed thousands of orphans for many, many years, and he himself said, when he was ninety-one years old, that "his prayers had saved tens of thousands of souls." If these things are so, why fast?

The reason some translators have omitted "fastings" from 2 Corinthians 6:5 and 11:27 is evidently because of a difference of opinion among them as to the meaning of the word, some believing that Paul is speaking of involuntary hunger, and others believing that he refers to voluntary hunger. Dean Alford retains the word "fastings" in each case, and says that it cannot refer to involuntary hunger because in 2 Corinthians 11:27, "fastings" are distinguished in the catalogue (of Paul's sufferings) from "hunger and thirst." I think there is no question as to the manuscript authority for the word being included in both the passages mentioned.

It is evident, therefore, that Paul sometimes fasted voluntarily, but it is equally evident that he never imposed fasting upon the churches as a matter of duty. "Let every one be fully persuaded in his own mind."

The Revised Version is doubtless correct in omitting "fasting" from Matthew 17:21; Mark 9:29; Acts 10:30 and 1 Corinthians 7:5.

DIVINE HEALING

Is It in the Atonement?

Is divine healing in the atonement?

Certainly, divine healing is in the atonement. So, also, is our eternal residence in Heaven in the atonement; but we have not yet reached Heaven. We are still on the earth, and we are still in bodies which are subject to "the bondage of corruption," for "we wait for the adoption, to wit, the redemption of our body." The redemption of our body is a part of the redemption wrought out for us on the cross of Calvary, and is therefore in the atonement. But we wait for it nevertheless. We have not yet entered into it. Our entire inheritance, which "is incorruptible, and undefiled, and that fadeth not away," is in the atonement, but for the time being it is "reserved in heaven for us," while we down here are "kept by the power of God through faith unto salvation ready to be revealed in the last time."

No one can believe more than I in the power of God to heal, or in His willingness to heal when it is according to His plan and purpose; but I deny, and I have the authority of the Word of God for denying, that divine healing is in the atonement in the same way that salvation is in the atonement, and that it may therefore be demanded and expected in response to faith in every case. I have seen men healed in response to prayer and faith, and I myself have more than once anointed persons for healing; and in some cases I have seen them healed, and in other cases have seen them go on in the suffering until they died. But in each case I believed, and still believe, that God's will was perfectly done; done by those who suffered unto death, as well as by those and in those who were healed promptly in answer to prayer.

The Prayer of Faith

I once heard a God-fearing man, who is as well read in the Bible as the average layman, say that "the days of miracles are past." Qualifying on the term miracle: I mean a miracle such as a man or woman, who by prayer heals and cures himself of an illness. My argument or side of the subject being that a man or woman who is ill and whose faith is great enough, can, through prayer, cure himself of an illness. This has been accomplished to the writer's knowledge, and it is in my opinion a miracle. The other man says that he does not believe a man can cure an illness in this manner, and that miracles belong to the days of the apostles. Will you please give your opinion on the above in detail?

When it is said that "the days of miracles are past," it is generally meant that we no longer live in the days when such spectacular miracles are performed as were performed, for instance, in the days of our Lord and His apostles. We do not now hear of men being raised from the dead, or water being turned into wine, or of any other such miracles as He and they performed. The healing of a sick man may be miraculous, but it is hardly in the class I have referred to. During the time when the New Testament was being written, and until it was completed the spectacular gifts continued, though toward the end of the period referred to they gradually disappeared; and now that the New Testament is completed God calls upon His people to walk by faith rather than by sight. It is still true that "the prayer of faith shall save the sick," but no one can pray the prayer of faith unless it be given to him to pray. Sometimes it is God's will to heal, and sometimes it is not. The proper attitude of faith is to be submissive under His hand, seeking His will as the very best thing for His child at all times.

He Bare Our Griefs

1. Would you please explain to me why the word "griefs" in Isaiah 53:4 is rendered "disease" and "sickness" in Deuteronomy 7:15; 28:61; 1 Kings 17:17; 2 Kings 1:2; 8:8; 2 Chronicles 16:12; 21:15, and why the word translated "sorrows" is rendered "pain" in Job 33:19?

2. And please explain why "disease" could mean "spiritual disease" when He "healed all that were sick" in Matthew 8:16,17.

3. And also explain why it is not in the atonement.

1. The reason the words are translated as indicated is that this is their correct translation.

2. Spiritual disease is not the meaning; it is physical disease, bodily sickness. Our Lord bore the griefs and sickness of His people by healing all who came to Him. But this was not done in the atonement on the cross.

3. Bodily healing for the believer is in the atonement in the ultimate sense, just as exemption from death is in the atonement. But we have not received all that was wrought out for us in the atonement. Believers still get sick and die, because the time has not arrived for us to enter upon our full inheritance which is "reserved in heaven" for us (1 Peter 1:4). Until then we have the Holy Spirit dwelling in us as "the earnest of our inheritance until the redemption of the purchased possession" (Eph. 1:14). Meanwhile we, who thus "have the firstfruits of the Spirit, even we ourselves groan within ourselves, waiting for the adoption, to wit, the redemption of our body" (Rom. 8:23).

May We Demand Healing?

Is it true, as some teach, that we may demand and expect bodily healing in response to faith and without the use of medicine, just as we may expect salvation that way? What do you say about James 5:14,15?

Bodily healing is not on the same basis as salvation; we still wait "for the adoption, to wit, the redemption of our body" (Rom. 8:23); and we must not expect any healing when it is, as it sometimes is, contrary to God's will (2 Cor. 12:7-9). And even when God's will is to heal, we have no right to "demand" that God shall heal "without the use of medicine." It sometimes pleases Him to bless the use of medicine, and sometimes it pleases Him to heal directly without such means. James (like Hebrews, 1 and 2 Peter, and Jude) is primarily a Hebrew-Christian Epistle, and doubtless the promise of James 5:14,15 will find its fullest accomplishment in the Kingdom age; but we need not limit its application. It is always true that "the prayer of faith shall save the sick," but "the prayer of faith" cannot be prayed unless God bestows it. God will give it whenever it is His will to heal. When it is not His will to heal, the yielded believer will say Amen, and rejoice in his thorn in the flesh, even as Paul did.

Healed by His Stripes

Does the word in 1 Peter 2:24, "by whose stripes ye were healed," apply to bodily healing?

No. The words are quoted from Isaiah 53:5 and have nothing to do with the healing of the body. Of course, God is able to heal, with or without means. Sometimes it pleases Him to heal with means and sometimes without them. But on the other hand, it is sometimes contrary to His will that there should be healing at all. And it is the proper attitude of faith to submit oneself unto Him, and to know that His will is best.

Is It for this Dispensation?

In the light of Hebrews 13:8; Matthew 8:17; Isaiah 53:4,5; 1 Peter 2:24,25; Galatians 3:13; and Deuteronomy 28, can it be Scripturally proven that divine healing was not meant for our own dispensation? Is our commission the same as He gave to His disciples in Luke 9:2? If not, why not?

The passages you cite say nothing about "our dispensation." Without doubt, divine healing is meant for this dispensation in so far as it may please God to grant it; but it must not be forgotten that we have not yet entered into all that was bought for us at the cross. Only the firstfruits of our inheritance have come to us in the person of the Holy Spirit, and we are "waiting for the adoption, to wit, the redemption of our body" (Rom. 8:23).

As to your question, "Is our commission the same as He gave to His disciples in Luke 9:2? If not, why not?" This is certainly not the commission under which we are supposed to work. Have you ever noticed the contrast between Luke 9:3 and Luke 22:36? These two commissions are very different. Do you try to work under either of them, and if so, which one? And if you are to work under either of them who is to choose which one? You confuse things and fail to rightly divide the Word of truth, and this leads to trouble always. We are not sent to preach the Kingdom nor the Gospel of the Kingdom, but rather the Gospel of personal salvation by grace through faith.

Healing the Sick

Please explain Mark 16:18, the last clause, where it says, "they shall lay hands on the sick, and they shall recover."

It is clear from a reading of the whole passage in Mark 16 that we have here Kingdom truth rather than Church truth. The signs that were to follow continued to be present during the interval after our Lord's ascension when the Kingdom was still being offered to Israel and while God was stretching out His hands to a disobedient and gainsaying people. After the formation of the Church and as the New Testament Scriptures neared completion the spectacular gifts were largely removed, and since that time they have been exceptional rather than the rule. It is altogether likely that after the Church is completed and caught out, these signs may be revived in connection with the preaching of the Gospel of the Kingdom in all the world as a testimony unto all nations before the end of the Great Tribulation and the Second Coming of Christ to earth (Matt. 24:14).

Healing without Saving

Christ healed the man who was blind from birth, and shortly afterwards healed his soul. Did Christ ever heal without saving also?

Not to my knowledge. Compared with salvation, bodily healing is a small thing. The sinning believer of 1 Corinthians 5 was sentenced by apostolic command to be delivered "unto Satan for the destruction of the flesh, that the spirit may be saved in the day of the Lord Jesus" (verse 5). This is not to say that all bodily suffering is the immediate result of sin (see John 9:2,3); sometimes it results from very different causes (see 2 Cor. 12:7). But, after all is said and done, bodily affliction, as compared with the future glory of the saved, is a small thing (2 Cor. 4:16-18).

MARRIAGE

Regulations as to Marriage

Please explain 1 Corinthians 7:14,15, 39.

In verses 14 and 15 the subject is that of a mixed marriage, in which, after two unbelievers have married, one of them has been saved. Let them not separate, but remain together; that is, if the unbeliever in the case is willing. "For the unbelieving husband is sanctified by the wife, and the unbelieving wife is sanctified by the husband: else were your children unclean; but now are they holy (or *sanctified*, the same word). But if the unbelieving depart, let him depart," etc.

Here are persons sanctified who are not saved. "For what knowest thou, O wife, whether thou shalt save thy husband? or how knowest thou, O man, whether thou shalt save thy wife?" (verse 16).

"Sanctified" means "set apart," and the teaching here is that the unsaved husband of a saved wife, or the unsaved wife of a saved husband, or the unsaved children of such a union, are sanctified, or set apart, as in a separate class, by reason of their relation to each other; just as under the Old Testament anything coming into contact with the altar was sanctified by that contact (Matt. 23:17-19; compare Ex. 30:29).

The 39th verse of 1 Corinthians 7 teaches that marriage is dissolved only by death, and that after the death of her husband a widow may marry again, but "only in the Lord"—that is, only to one who is "in the Lord." She might have been the wife of an unsaved man before, though being herself saved after she had married him; but now she must not again be "unequally yoked" to an unbeliever (compare 2 Cor. 6:14 to 7:1).

May Cousins Marry?

Is it against the teachings of the Bible for cousins to marry?

There is no Bible teaching upon the subject of the marriage of cousins. Under the Levitical code marriages were forbidden within a certain degree of consanguinity or affinity, but even then the marriage of cousins was not forbidden (see Lev. 18:1-30). Under the new covenant, the matter is not touched upon except indirectly in 1 Corinthians 5:1 where the church was rebuked for tolerating a situation where one of its members had "his father's wife," evidently meaning his step-mother. The all important marriage law of the New Testament is, "Be ye not unequally yoked together with unbelievers" (2 Cor. 6:14). Marriage for Christians should be "only in the Lord" (1 Cor. 7:39). Of course, the marriage of persons so closely related as to make such marriage incestuous is properly forbidden by civil laws.

Marriage and Divorce

1. Do you think it is right according to God's Word for a married person to seek a divorce? You know that in taking the marriage vow one swears to love, honor, etc., until death do part. Give me Scriptures on this, please.

2. Then is it right for a divorced person to marry again? Can a person who is saved or regenerated do such a thing? I think that nothing but trouble and sorrow will follow. My mother divorced my father and married again, and though her second husband was a fine man, she was not truly happy.

The whole question of marriage and divorce is a most solemn one. And it is one to which God's people should give earnest heed in these awful days of laxness along these lines.

1. There are circumstances, undoubtedly, when it is necessary and wise and Scriptural for a married couple to separate. And that is all that the word "divorce" really means: it is division. There is no thought of remarriage involved in the word itself. This matter of separation under certain conditions is covered in principle in 1 Corinthians 7:10-16.

2. Under the Law of Moses, remarriage of divorced persons was authorized in certain circumstances (Deut. 24:1-4). But on this our Lord Jesus said in Matthew 19:8,9: "Moses because of the hardness of your hearts suffered you to put away your wives: but from the beginning it was not so. And I say unto you, Whosoever shall put away his wife, except it be for fornication, and shall marry another, committeth adultery: and whoso marrieth her which is put away doth commit adultery." In this passage our Lord implies that one may put away his wife if she is guilty of fornication, that is, he may separate from her. But even here it is doubtful whether the husband is justified if "he shall marry another" while his first wife is yet living.

In Mark 10:1-12, which is a parallel account, no exception whatever is noted: "Whosoever shall put away his wife, and marry another, committeth adultery against her. And if a woman shall put away her husband, and be married to another, she committeth adultery" (11,12). Again in Luke 16:18 He says: "Whosoever putteth away his wife, and marrieth another, committeth adultery: and whosoever marrieth her that is put away from her husband committeth adultery."

In view of all these Scriptures on the subject it seems clear that the marriage relation cannot be dissolved except through death; and as one who is authorized to perform marriage ceremonies I have always refused to officiate where either of the parties to the marriage has been divorced and the former partner was yet living. I have also always refused to officiate in the marriage of a believer to an unbeliever (2 Cor. 6:14 to 7:1).

ROMAN CATHOLICISM

Catholics and Heaven

Will Catholics go to Heaven?

All born-again folks will go to Heaven, whether Roman Catholics or Protestants. And all are born again who confess Jesus as Lord and believe in their hearts that God hath raised Him from the dead. This involves a definite reception of the Lord Jesus as one's personal Savior (Rom. 10:9,10; John 1:11,12).

Celibacy

When did the church of Rome (Catholic) first forbid the priests to marry?

The Encyclopedia Britannica has an article on "Celibacy" which will give you the history of the whole matter. The first proposal that celibacy should be required in candidates for the priesthood was in the second Council of Carthage, A.D. 251. But it was much later that the rule was made binding upon all priests in the Roman church. Perhaps the decree of Pope Gregory VII, in A.D. 1074, marked the time when no priest could be a married man, and that ordination should be refused to those who would not promise to live in perpetual celibacy.

Did Paul Teach Celibacy?

Will you please give your interpretation of 1 Corinthians 7? Did Paul advocate celibacy, or not?

Paul advocated celibacy in this chapter, but evidently it was only "for the (then) present distress" (verse 26), and not for all time. In 1 Timothy 4:1-3 he particularly warns against the teaching of those "forbidding to marry." Also, in Hebrews 13:4 (R.V.) he writes, "Let marriage be had in honor among all, and let the bed be undefiled." (If the Pauline authorship of Hebrews be questioned, it is still the Word of God.) We may conclude therefore that the rule still holds good that is is not good for man to be alone (Gen. 2:18).

The Papacy and the Kingdom

If the Pope or the Roman Catholic wants to live in or under the reign of Jesus as Lord and Master and King, will he not have to give up all formality of worship and bigotry? Do the Roman Catholics

accept the Lord Jesus as their only Savior and Master, and depend upon His atoning blood for their salvation?

The Pope, or any other Romanist, may be saved on the same ground and by the same means as any other lost sinner. Doubtless many adherents of the Papacy will find salvation, but this will be in spite of, rather than because of, the system to which they belong. But all this is true also of much that is called Protestantism. Romanists generally put their faith in Mary and Joseph or some other "saint," rather than depending only upon the blood of the Son of God; and Protestants, frequently, if not so generally, put their dependence upon the false testimony of some Modernist messenger of Satan, rather than in the plain promises of the Scripture. "From such turn away."

ANTICHRISTIAN CULTS

Swedenborgianism

Who are the Swedenborgians and what do they teach?

This is a religious sect that follows the teachings of Emmanuel Swedenborg, who organized in London in 1787 what he called the Church of the New Jerusalem. They regard the universe as a whole, the outward world being the counterpart of the inner and spiritual. They hold that beneath the literal meaning of the Bible is the spiritual meaning, open to those having inner discernment. According to their teaching, justification is not by faith alone, but that "whoever fears God and works righteously" shall be saved. God is one, and the real trinity is in Christ. The last judgment has already taken place, and the New Jerusalem has already descended in the form of the New Church. They deny physical resurrection, and teach that at death men's eyes are opened to the spiritual world of which they are already a part, and they are drawn to heaven or hell by their own "affinities." Angels, according to this sect, are the spirits of departed human beings. Of course, all this is decidedly anti-scriptural, and therefore false.

British Israelism

What is British-Israelism?

British or Anglo-Israelism is the teaching that the British and other English-speaking people are the "lost tribes of the house of Israel," and that the people known as Jews are set aside, having no share in the promises of blessing for "Israel." The sect once had a vast body of literature, and a large following in Great Britain and Canada, as well as smaller followings in America and other countries. It is nevertheless contrary to Scripture. "Israel" and "Jews" are words used interchangeably in the Bible, and the promise of future glory is for the people called by these names, and not for Britain or America. These promises name the Jew in Zechariah 8:23 and Israel in Romans 11:25-27, to cite only two examples out of many.

Astrology

A person purporting to belong to the American Academy of Astrologers was consulted with regard to my future, having in hand data only as regarded my correct name, and the exact date of my birth. This was all without solicitation, and to the credit of this person be it said that, on the strength of such a small amount of information, a

great deal was spoken regarding my habits of thought and action which I knew to be exactly as had been stated. Furthermore, I know it to be a fact that very specific happenings regarding another person took place precisely as the astrologer had prophesied, and several years after the prophecies had been given. Could you enlighten me with a Bible message on this subject?

Modern astrology, like spiritism, may have supernatural elements, for Satan is supernatural, and it is one of his favorite devices to get God's people interested in supernatural things apart from God and His Word. "And when they shall say unto you, Seek unto them that have familiar spirits, and unto wizards that peep, and that mutter: should not a people seek unto their God? for the living to the dead? To the law and to the testimony: if they speak not according to this Word, it is because there is no light in them" (Isa. 8:19,20).

Buchmanism, or Oxford Group Movement

Please, sir, what is this thing called "Buchmanism"?

This thing called "Buchmanism" is also variously called "the Oxford Group Movement," "First Century Christianity," "the Groups" and "the Fellowship." The first name mentioned is from the name of its leader, Frank Buchman. Its dangers are pointed out by a former adherent, Pastor Harold T. Commons, as follows:

In my early Christian experience in Williams College (1923-1927), I was actively associated with the Group for over three years, taking part in many "house parties." I came to know all the leaders of the Group intimately, including Frank Buchman, Sam Shoemaker, Sherry Day, Ray Purdy, Cleve Hicks, Ken Twichell, Louden Hamilton, Sciff Wishard, Howie Blake, Charles Haines and many others, a list too long to name. I have been a close observer of the workings of the movement for over eight years, and feel that I can speak with authority. After three years on "the inside" I finally severed my connection with the Group out of loyalty to my Lord, for I realized that it is actually far removed from real New Testament Christianity.

At first acquaintance it seems to be what its name indicates, a revival of first century apostolic Christianity—emphasizing personal evangelism, guidance for daily living, the reality of sin and the necessity for a clean break with sin, etc.—all of which seems like real true Christianity with the dynamic behind it which is so often lacking in our modern churches. This is what makes it appeal to so many Christians. It seems so practical and vital. If the above things were built on the right foundation I would support the movement one hundred percent. But here is the trouble.

1. The movement cares not what a man believes but how he lives. This is salvation by works instead of by grace through faith. The New Testament teaches that without correct belief the best moral character in the world will not inherit eternal life (John 3:3).

2. The movement shares the fundamental fallacy of mysticism—an experimental religion. Everything is based upon experience. And experience can

never be a trustworthy foundation for religion, despite the popular belief to the contrary. Satan can give one all kinds of experiences. Revelation alone, as we have it in God's infallible Word, is the only sure foundation.

3. Both Modernists and Fundamentalists, believers and unbelievers, are welcomed into the Fellowship on the basis of a common experience of sin, confession and surrender. No questions are asked as to belief. And while some claim to be Fundamentalists, doctrine is never mentioned and there are many open Modernists in their ranks.

4. This doctrinal weakness or indifference is further illustrated by the lack of Bible teaching and instruction in the Word characteristic of the house parties. While it is recommended that the Bible be read during "quiet times," there is very little real Bible study, and no instruction as to the way of salvation, justification by faith, or any of the cardinal truths of redemption.

5. There is much stress laid on "surrender." But in all the talk of surrender there is no mention made of an atonement for sin. This is something entirely foreign to the New Testament, which stresses from beginning to end the substitutionary death of Christ and His blood shed on the Cross for our sins, for "without shedding of blood there is no remission of sin." In this respect Buchmanism differs not a whit from Mohammedanism, the very heart and core of which is surrender of the will to God without an atonement. In all the meetings of the Group I have ever attended or heard about there has never been any mention of the blood of Christ in its expiatory character.

6. It follows from this that the "changed lives" of the Group are nothing more than moral conversions, in no sense corresponding to the New Birth of the New Testament, which designates the passing of a soul from death to life by the acceptance of Christ's atoning work on the Cross. Anything that omits God's one remedy for sin (1 John 1:7) leaves the human soul still guilty before God regardless of how many moral conversions the person may have gone through.

(Note: Frank Buchman's Five "Cs" for the sinner supposedly cover the whole ground. They are: Conviction, Contrition, Confession, Conversion and Continuance. Every one of these is possible on a purely moral basis—know you are a sinner, feel sorry for your sins, confess them, turn away from them and continue on the new way. But if, in addition to all this, there is no faith in the blood of Christ and no acceptance of the Lord Jesus Christ as personal Substitute and Savior, then the guilt of sin still remains and the soul is unsaved.)

7. Then, while rightfully stressing the reality of sin, the method of open and public confession of sins is a very questionable procedure. It produces the desired psychological effect in the meeting, but it incites undue emotionalism, and also tends to lower the standards and to produce a sort of fellowship on the basis of sin that seems to me very undesirable. Specific sins, after continued open confession, seem not quite so terrible as they were at first. I well remember a statement of one of the leaders that "the fellowship of sinners is more real than the fellowship of saints."

8. Finally, their idea of "guidance" is false to Scripture. All Christians be-

lieve in God's guidance and being led of the Holy Spirit to make right choices and decisions. But the practice of the groups in sitting down with paper and pencil in hand and letting the mind go absolutely blank, and then writing down whatever flashes across the mind as God's orders for the day, is beyond anything promised or sanctioned in Scripture. Indeed, this "passivity" of mind is a very perilous condition to be in, for it is precisely at such moments that Satan gains control and does his devilish work. This is one of the fundamental errors of the mysticism that pervades the movement. True guidance comes through the Word of God, through God-given conviction after prayer and through circumstance.

Many truly born-again Christians have become attracted to the movement because of its deceptive appearance and its use of many old familiar terms and orthodox expressions. Many others have seen its fundamental errors and have either never gone into it or else have severed their connection with it as soon as possible. My prayer is that this frank testimony will enable many others to see that Buchmanism is another one of the many counterfeits and delusions of the "latter days" (1 John 4:1; 2 Peter 2:1,2; 1 Tim. 4:1; 2 Tim. 4:3).

Christadelphianism

Are Christadelphians Christians?

Christadelphians deny the Trinity and teach the doctrine of annihilation, although they profess to believe in Jesus as a Savior from sin. I could not class such as Christians. I cannot understand how one could be a Christian who denies the deity of Christ, or who teaches a doctrine so contradictory to the Scriptures as the doctrine of annihilationism.

Christian Science

What is wrong with the teachings of "Christian Science"?

Plenty. Eddyism, falsely called Christian Science, is neither Christian nor scientific, but is a fabrication of falsehood. It denies the personality of God, the doctrine of the Trinity and the deity of Christ. It declares there is no evil, and of course denies the need of salvation through the blood of the cross. Sin is only imaginary, "the error of mortal mind." The evil spirits cast out by the Lord Jesus were only "false beliefs." The Comforter bestowed by Christ is not the Holy Spirit but "Divine Science." And all this, plus much more of the same kind, is put forth as exposition of the Holy Scriptures! Christian Science, falsely so called, should be shunned as a pestilence.

Masonry

Can a man be a Christian and be a member of the Masonic fraternity?

No doubt many Christians are at the same time Masons. And doubtless many of these occupy these two positions conscientiously. But if you ask whether this is consistent and according to the Word of God I should have to say, No. Freemasonry and the lodge system generally constitute an enormous Unitarian religious organization. I say "Unitarian," because it is by no means necessary, in order to become a member of these lodges, for a man to confess Jesus Christ as "God manifest in the flesh." But according to the Word of God, one who does not thus receive the Lord Jesus and worship Him as God is an unbeliever. And the Word of God is emphatic in its insistence against any such alliance with unbelievers as is made necessary by fellowship in the lodge.

"Be ye not unequally yoked together with unbelievers: for what fellowship hath righteousness with unrighteousness? and what communion hath light with darkness? And what concord hath Christ with Belial? or what part hath he that believeth with an infidel? And what agreement hath the temple of God with idols? for ye are the temple of the living God; as God hath said, I will dwell in them, and walk in them; and I will be their God, and they shall be my people. Wherefore come out from among them, and be ye separate, saith the Lord, and touch not the unclean thing; and I will receive you, and will be a Father unto you, and ye shall be my sons and daughters, saith the Lord Almighty. Having therefore these promises, dearly beloved, let us cleanse ourselves from all filthiness of the flesh and spirit, perfecting holiness in the fear of God" (2 Cor. 6:14-7:1).

The Mormon Fraud

Will you please tell me what is the generally accepted theory, among Protestant Christians and those who have studied the matter, of the "Book of Mormon" and the plates? Is it nothing but deception, or what?

The whole system of Mormonism is a fraud. This is shown by its direct contradiction of Scripture and by its subtle and deceptive use of Scripture. The Mormon preacher and teacher and literature use Scripture terminology in an unscriptural way and thus seek to turn the testimony of the Bible against itself.

Modernism

Is Modernism a form of Christianity?

By no means. Modernism, parading under the name of Christ, is anti-Christian in all its teachings. It denies the inspiration of the Scriptures, teaches that if man ever fell he fell upward instead of downward, and is now evolving upward; it denies blood redemption; it has no place for the new birth, declaring that God is the Father of all men and that all will be saved eventually. It teaches that there is no such place as Hell and no such thing as eternal punishment. In short, there is nothing in common between the Christianity taught in the Scriptures and the teaching of Modernism, which has become so widespread in schools of all grades throughout Christendom so called, as well as in many places included in so called heathendom. Beware of Modernism, for it eats away at the core of Christianity like a cancer.

The Poison of Modernism

Why are so many preachers modernists, and why do even some

denominational colleges teach evolution? How are we parents to know where to send our young men and women to college?

As to why so many preachers are modernist, and why even some denominational colleges teach evolution, my only answer would be, "An enemy has done this." As to your third question, as to how parents are to know where to send your young men and women to college, my answer is that you should know before sending them anywhere. Inquire carefully, from the colleges themselves, and from those who can inform you reliably. A modernistic school or college, or a modernistic church, should be shunned like poison, for they are synagogues of Satan, every one of them, and if you subject your children to their poisonous teachings, God will surely hold you responsible.

New Thought

Will you please explain the movement called "New Thought"?

"New Thought" is described by one of its own advocates as "the right understanding of the nature and power of the mind." The same writer says of it that "the reality of an infinite, eternal and intelligent energy, principle or substance, perceptibly active everywhere and always in the phenomena we call life, is its basic principle." Dr. Frank S. Weston of Toronto describes "New Thought" as "a scheme of self-salvation through the exercise of one's own will." Prof. James of Harvard University says that "one of its doctrinal sources is the Four Gospels, another Emerson, another Berkleyan idealism, another spiritism with its message of law and progress, another the optimistic popular science evolution, and, finally, Hinduism has contributed a stain." The Bible is set aside as a source of authority, and there is no place in the system for the blood of the Lamb of God. It is pernicious and poisonous.

Russellism—a Sect of Many Names

What is the International Bible Students' Association?

It is Millennial Dawnism under another name. It is also called Jehovah's Witnesses. It is made up of the followers of the late "Pastor Russell," and it is well to give it a wide berth, for most of its teachings are contrary to the Word of God.

The Errors of Russellism

Judge Rutherford, the Russellite leader, claimed that there is no Hell or place of torture; it means the grave or death. That folks, when they die, are just sleeping, as how could there be a resurrection if they were in Heaven or Hell? No doubt you have read his books or know something about them. Do those who die, whether Christians or not, just sleep (of course in the body), and does the soul float somewhere in space, asleep until the resurrection? Then he teaches that finally all will be saved, as God is just and full of love and wants all men to be saved. Is this true? I was always taught, and believe, that those who die in Christ go to a place prepared for them. Heaven, I suppose, is

not for us until after the coming of Christ; but where are the souls of the saved and unsaved after death and until Christ's coming? Will you please point out somewhat in detail the wrong doctrines of Russellism?

Those who die in Christ are immediately in Heaven, being "absent from the body" and "present with the Lord" (2 Cor. 5:8). Prior to our Lord's death and resurrection, the saved were in the Paradise section of Hades, but when He ascended up on high He took them with Him into Heaven (Luke 16:23, R.V.; 23:43; Eph. 4:8-10; 2 Cor. 12:2-4). The lost are in Hades, awaiting their judgment at the Great White Throne (Luke 16:19-31, R.V.; Rev. 20:11-15, R.V.). Both the saved and the lost are conscious. There is no truth in the teaching either of soul-sleeping or of annihilationism.

Russellism denies the deity of Christ, teaching that Jesus was a created being. It also denies the incarnation, declaring that Jesus was nothing more than "a perfect human being." It practically denies also the atonement, robbing it of its power by declaring that it was "as a human being" that "He gave Himself a ransom for men." This language is quoted literally from Russell's writings. He says also "it was His flesh, His life as a man, His humanity, that was sacrificed for our redemption." Russellism also denies the resurrection of the body of Christ, declaring that the body was never resurrected, that "we know nothing about what became of it," and that it was "supernaturally removed from the tomb because if it had remained there it would have been an obstacle to the faith of the disciples." Russell also says "whether it was dissolved into gases or whether it is still preserved somewhere as a grand memorial of God's love no one knows." Russell also taught that Christ is now only a spirit, with no humanity whatsoever, thus denying our Lord's high-priestly intercession, for it is only as "the man Christ Jesus" He can be the "one mediator between God and men" (1 Tim. 2:6). Russellism also teaches the annihilation of the wicked dead. Indeed, it declares that death itself is annihilation. Russell says that "death is a period of absolute unconsciousness—more than that, it is a period of absolute non-existence." But he also says that the wicked dead are to be recreated in order to receive their final judgment, which will be total and eternal non-existence. This, of course, is a denial of the doctrine of eternal punishment. In a word, Russellism is utterly and absolutely unscriptural from beginning to end, and is made up of Satanic heresies.

A Russellite Heresy

Where are the dead between death and resurrection? I mean both saved and unsaved. I accept Dr. Scofield's explanation in Luke 16, but there are some erroneous teachings from our pulpits today that there are none in Heaven, and Russellism has taught it through its books.

There is not very much use in trying to catch up with Russellism. The Word of God is clear enough that the dead, both saved and lost, are conscious, the saved being in the conscious bliss of the presence of God, and the lost being in conscious torment in Hades. You speak of your acquaintance with the Scofield Bible on this point, and I think that there is nothing to be added.

A Russellite's Question

A Russellite asked me, saying, "Where would he go when he died?" and also asked, "Where is Heaven, and where is Hell, now?" What answer would you make, knowing their teaching of annihilation after death?

Where a Russellite, or any other person, goes after death depends altogether upon what he has done before death about the Lord Jesus. If he is in Christ when death comes, then he will at once be absent from the body and present (or, "at home") with the Lord (2 Cor. 5:8). If he dies out of Christ, he will surely find his place in Hell, in "the fire that never shall be quenched: where their worm dieth not, and the fire is not quenched" (Mark 9:42-48). These words are from the mouth of the Son of God, whose authority will not be questioned by any who have found shelter under His shed blood. The Russellites' "teaching of annihilation after death" has nothing to do with the case, for it is contrary to the plain teaching of Scripture.

Spiritism

What is the teaching of Spiritualism or Spiritism?

Spiritism is the better name for this cult, which is a dangerous one. Its central aim is to hold communication with the dead. It denies the fall of man, the evil of sin, the need of blood redemption, the deity of our Lord Whom the Spiritists describe as "a Jewish religious enthusiast who came to an untimely death"; it declares there is no Hell, no resurrection and no judgment. Spiritism substitutes faith in demons for faith in God; and it substitutes also a pretended new revelation for the Word of God. It teaches that "whatever is is right; evil does not exist; evil is good; a lie is the truth intrinsically; it holds a lawful place in creation; it is a necessity; vice and virtue too are beautiful to the eyes of the soul; virtue is good and sin is good; murder is good; murder is a perfectly natural act. That which is natural is divine, for God is the author of nature, and every murder that was ever committed had a divine necessity for being wrought, and is good." That may be enough to show the evil of Spiritism. It is the Devil's lie.

Unitarianism

What is the distinctive error of Unitarianism?

Unitarianism emphasizes the Unity of God and denies the doctrine of the Trinity. Of course, that means that Christ is not deity, and this shows that Unitarianism is anti-Christian. But Unitarianism is by no means confined to the Unitarian denomination; it is the central sin of Modernism, and is essentially a lie. "Who is a liar but he that denieth that Jesus is the Christ? He is antichrist, that denieth the Father and the Son. Whosoever denieth the Son, the same hath not the Father" (1 John 2:22,23). "I am the way, the truth, and the life; no man cometh unto the Father but by me" (John 14:6).

Unity

Please tell your readers something about the Unity movement.

According to the editor of the Unity magazine, the movement is decidedly unscriptural. In a letter to a subscriber who had stopped his subscription, the editor wrote: "We do not believe in a vicarious atonement, if by this you mean that Jesus Christ suffered on the cross for our sins and because of this act of His alone we are free. However, that is not the vital point in the Unity teaching. The teaching is based on the importance of man being continually conscious of the indwelling Christ." Of course, it is perfectly obvious that this editor is not speaking of the Christ of God revealed in the Scriptures of the Old and New Testaments, but of a Christ of his own imagining and devising.

Continuing, the editor wrote: "We do not believe in eternal punishment in hell-fire as the penalty for man's sins." But evidently our Lord Jesus believed in such a place, "where their worm dieth not, and the fire is not quenched" (Mark 9:42-48).

And, further, from the editor: "We believe and teach that Jesus Christ opened the way to eternal life and perfection for man. We believe that He did this by dying to all that pertains to the mortal, a work that culminated in His apparent (note that word) death on the cross."

Unity is a system of healing, and therefore it catches many followers who magnify the healing of the body above the gift of God which is eternal life. It is clearly the work of Satan (see 2 Thess. 2:9-12).

Universalism

Is Universalism true to the Scriptures?

No. Universalism teaches universal salvation. It tells us that all men, angels, demons, even Satan himself, will ultimately be saved. This makes the death of Christ a farce, and negates many of His own teachings, as for example, Mark 9:43-48; Luke 16:22-31, as well as the teaching of Scripture elsewhere as to the doctrine of eternal punishment. "To the law and to the testimony: if they speak not according to this word, it is because there is no light in them" (Isa. 8:20).

THE FUTURE

Order of Events

Will you kindly give us a simple outline of the order of events in God's revealed program for the future?

The first thing in order is the completion of the Church. Then comes the Rapture, that is the catching up of the saved to meet the Lord. This catching up will be the beginning, in Heaven, of the Day of Christ, continuing for the seven years of Daniel's Seventieth Week, during which will take place the judgment of believers' works at the bema or judgment seat of Christ to determine their rewards, and the marriage supper of the Lamb. Meanwhile, on the earth, the Beast and False Prophet will be manifested, and during the latter half of the seven years the Great Tribulation will take place. This will end with the battle of Armageddon, which will be immediately followed by the glorious Second Coming of Christ to earth to set up His millennial Kingdom. This will endure for a thousand years (the word Millennium means one thousand years) and will be followed by the eternal state and the final manifestation of the Kingdom of God. The great thing for us to remember in connection with all this is that the Rapture is an ever imminent event, which may take place at any moment of any day or any night. Keep looking up.

No General Judgment

When is the general judgment?

There is no such thing in the Scriptures as a general judgment. There are seven judgments, as follows:

1. The judgment of our sins. On the cross of Calvary, according to God's reckoning, in the person of our Substitute, we died for our sins. Therefore we who have believed unto salvation will never come into judgment for our sins (John 5:24, R.V.; 2 Cor. 5:19-21; Gal. 3:13).
2. The judgment of self. This should be going on constantly. When the children of God judge themselves, when they confess their sins, they are freely forgiven. But when they fail to do so they are chastened (1 Cor. 5:1-5; 2 Cor. 2:5-7; 1 John 1:9; 1 Cor. 11:31,32; Heb. 12:7).
3. The judgment of believers' works at the judgment seat of Christ, to determine, not their salvation, but their rewards (1 Cor. 3:11-15; 2 Cor. 5:9,10).
4. The judgment of living nations at our Lord's Second Advent, for their treatment of His brethren in Israel (Matt. 25:31-46).
5. The judgment of Israel (Ezek. 20:33-44; Ps. 50).

6. The judgment of the lost dead, at the close of the Millennium (Rev. 20:11-15).

7. The judgment of angels (1 Cor. 6:3; 2 Peter 2:4; Jude 6).

No General Resurrection

When is the general resurrection?

There is no general resurrection in Scripture. The first resurrection, spoken of also as the resurrection of the just, the resurrection of life, etc., is before the Millennium, and the second resurrection, the resurrection of judgment, when the lost will be raised from the dead to meet their final doom, will be after the Millennium. The first resurrection is in three parts, including the resurrection of Christ as the firstfruits (1 Cor. 15:20-23); the resurrection of the saints referred to in Matthew 27:52,53; the resurrection of the saved dead at the Rapture (1 Thess. 4:13-18) and the resurrection of the Great Tribulation martyrs (Rev. 20:4-6). This corresponds to the type of Leviticus 23:9-22, the firstfruits, the harvest and the gleanings.

Resurrection and Life

In John 11:25,26 do you understand that we have reference to the two classes of believer, those who have died in Christ and those who are alive and remain, at His coming to catch them away to meet Him in the air? Also, is not the same thought expressed in 1 Corinthians 15:51-54?

Yes, to both questions. On that day He will be revealed as "the resurrection and the life"—the "resurrection" to those who have died in the faith: "though they die" (R.V.), "yet shall they live"; and the "life" to those who have not fallen asleep. The former will be "raised incorruptible" and the latter will be changed, receiving bodies like His own, "this mortal" putting on immortality.

Definitions

Please define the words "millennium," "pre-millennialism," "post-millennialism," "pro-millennialism" and "a-millennialism."

"Millennium" is from the two Latin words "*mille*" (thousand) and "*annum*" (year), and it refers to the thousand years during which the Lord Jesus will reign in person when He returns to the earth. The expression, "thousand years," found six times in the twentieth chapter of The Revelation, refers to this Kingdom period.

"Pre-millennialism" is the teaching that the return of Christ will precede the thousand-year reign.

"Post-millennialism" holds that the Second Coming of Christ will not take place until after the whole world is converted and there has been a thousand years of peace and righteousness on the earth.

The "pro-millennialists" ("pro" meaning "for") tell us that though they do not know whether there will be a millennium or not, if there is one, they are for it!

"A-millennialism" (the Greek prefix: "a" meaning "no") denies that there is to be a millennium.

Our Lord's Premillennial Coming

Is the Second Coming of Christ before or after the Millennium?

I believe it is before. There can be no manifestation of the Kingdom in the absence of the King.

Premillennialism

What Bible authority do the premillennialists have for believing that the Rapture will take place prior to the Millennium?

Luke 17:34-37 seems to describe events that would fit the Rapture, "one shall be taken, and the other left," etc., but in the Scofield Bible the passage appears to be interpreted as referring to the Day of the Lord, Armageddon, etc. What is your opinion about this?

According to the postmillennial program the world must be converted and prepare to welcome the Lord Jesus Christ upon His return; but according to the New Testament program He comes back in a time of spiritual darkness, declension and apostasy, and "all the tribes of the earth mourn" and flee from before His face. Then, too, we are taught in the Word of God to watch and wait and look for His return, which would be manifestly impossible if we knew that His coming could not be for over a thousand years.

As to your second query, it is true that the language referred to—"one shall be taken, and the other left"—would fit in with the Rapture; but it is just as true that it would fit in with the Revelation of the Son of God from Heaven at the end of the Great Tribulation. The only difference is that at the Rapture the one taken would be taken up to meet the Lord in the air, and the other left to go through the judgments of the Great Tribulation; while at the Second Coming of Christ to the earth the one taken would be taken away in judgment, and the other left to go into the Millennial Kingdom. There is no detailed teaching about the Rapture of the Church until we come to the Epistles of Paul. It is a part of the great body of truth hidden in God through the ages until Paul came on the scene (Eph. 3:1-7).

One Taken and the Other Left

Does our Lord in Matthew 24:40-42 and Luke 17:34-36 refer to the Rapture, when the saved shall be caught up to meet Him in the air and the unsaved left here for the horrors of the Great Tribulation?

No. It is true that at the Rapture the saved shall be taken and the unsaved left; but these Scriptures refer to the Second Coming of Christ to the earth as Son of Man to "judge and make war" (Rev. 19:11). That this is so will become evident if the context is examined in either passage cited. Then, wherever His saved ones are found with the unsaved, whether in bed or at work, the unsaved will be taken away by death in judgment while the saved will be left to enter the Kingdom and share in its glories.

Why Called the Rapture

What is the meaning of the word "rapture" and why is it applied to the coming of our Lord for His people?

The word comes from a Latin root, *rapto*, which signified "caught up" or "snatched away." The word is used in the Latin Vulgate in 1 Thessalonians 4:17.

How Many in the Rapture?

We often hear the Rapture spoken of as "the Rapture of the Church." Will the Rapture include others besides the New Testament Church?

You will find the answer to your question in that standard passage on the Rapture (1 Thess. 4:13-18). All "who sleep in Jesus," and all "the dead in Christ" refer to the same company, and that company includes all the saved of all the ages, for no one has ever been saved except through the blood of the Lord Jesus Christ. All these, "the dead in Christ," and the living who are in Christ, will be caught up to meet the Lord in the air. How wonderful it is that those who have already been saved and gone on to be with the Lord will on that day come forth out of heaven with Him into the air! Without us they cannot be made perfect, for we belong to them, and they belong to us (Heb. 11:40; 12:23).

They must have their resurrection bodies, like unto the glorious body of their Savior. And on that day they will come to receive their bodies, and then we which are alive and remain and are in Christ shall be caught up together with them, having, of course, our own glorified bodies (1 Cor. 15:51-58). And so all the redeemed of all the ages will be gathered about the pierced feet of their Lord in the air, and then led by Him up through the heavens to the place of the throne of God, and be presented by the Son to His Father, saying, "Behold, I and the children which thou hast given me."

What a gathering that will be! Lord haste the day! Keep looking up!

No Partial Rapture

Is there to be a partial Rapture, or will there be Christians left here to pass through the Great Tribulation?

There will be no partial Rapture; that is to say, not just a part of those who have been truly saved up to that day, but all of them will be caught up, and will not pass through the Great Tribulation. They have been delivered from the wrath to come (1 Thess. 1:9,10). And they are not appointed unto wrath, but to obtain salvation through our Lord Jesus Christ who died for them, that, whether they wake or sleep, they should live together with him (1 Thess. 5:9,10). The Great Tribulation is a judgment upon God's enemies, and the Church, which is the body of Christ, will never be subjected by a righteous God to such a judgment.

Nearing the End

Do you think we are very near the end of the age? I am studying

the book of The Revelation, and it is wonderful. But how near are we to the end? Can you tell? I should love to know. Would you not?

Yes, I certainly should love to know. I am indeed convinced that we are very near the end-time. The presence of millions of Jews in their own land, the revival of the Roman empire now in progress before our eyes, and the settlement of "the Roman question" by which the Pope receives recognition as an independent sovereign—all these and many other signs are calculated to stir our hearts and keep us looking up. But let us remember that while the Second Advent of Christ to the earth is related to signs and times, we are appointed to look for an event which is signless and timeless, and may occur at any moment; namely, our Lord's coming into the air to take us unto Himself. "The Lord is at hand."

The Setting of the Time

Considering God's cycle of perfection or cycle of completeness in the number 7, why would it be improper to consider that man's age or man's week would be completed at the end of 6000 years, and that the Lord's day or Sabbath would be the Millennium of 1000 years? Is the definite time element the objection?

Yes, the time element is the objection. God's people are always brought to confusion when they become wise above what is written and try to figure out the exact time of the successive events in God's program. "The things that are revealed belong unto us" (Deut. 29:29), and that should be enough for us. "The Lord is at hand!" Therefore, keep looking up!

Signs of His Coming

Do you see any more vivid signs of His coming this year than you saw at this time last year?

There are things now in sight, more vividly than last year, which may, or may not, be signs of His coming to the earth to set up His Kingdom. But we are not to be occupied with signs and times and events; rather, we are to be always waiting for the Son of God from Heaven to catch us up to meet Him in the air. This is a signless and timeless event, which may transpire at any moment of any day or any night. Keep looking up.

Date Setting

What about the practice of setting dates for our Lord's return? Can it be said that the world is sufficiently evangelized for us to expect His return now?

I have no sympathy with the practice of figuring out dates for our Lord's return, for I consider such practice an unwarrantable attempt to pry into the secrets of God. Then, too, if we should succeed in figuring out the date for our Lord's return to earth to set up His Kingdom, we should know, as I believe, the date of His coming for His people when they shall be caught up to meet Him in the air. That would be mischievous, for it would destroy the blessed hope as a daily incentive in the Christian life. It is God's purpose that His people should be continually "looking for that blessed hope," and this would be quite impossible if we knew the date. As to the evangelization of the world, there is no Scripture teaching that this will be completed before the Rapture of the saints. The words of Matthew 24:14 have to do rather with the Second Coming of Christ to the earth to set up the Kingdom. There are many things to transpire before that event, but the Rapture is a signless and timeless event and is always imminent; that is to say, it may take place at any moment.

A Mischievous Practice

Have we the right to set dates in regard to Israel; for example, regarding the "seven times" of Leviticus 26 and Daniel 4:23? Some have made this to be 2520 years.

All such date-setting is mischievous and contrary to the warnings of Scripture. If the rule you mention be applied to Leviticus 26, it must be applied to four verses in that chapter (18, 21, 24, 28), and thus we should have four times 2520, or 10,080 years on our hands. As for Daniel 4:23, the direct application of the "seven times" is perfectly apparent: the king was to be insane and bereft of his throne and kingdom for seven years. And that is the way it turned out (verses 33,34).

Our Present Hope

What difference does it make whether Christ appears before the Millennium or after the Millennium?

The difference is that if His coming is to be delayed a thousand years and more it could not possibly be a present and blessed hope. It is a great thing to know that He may come for us at any moment and it is upon this ever-present possibility that the Word of God bases its exhortations for every Christian grace. "Every man that hath this hope in him purifieth himself, even as he is pure" (1 John 3:1-3).

The Next Thing

Did Paul expect Christ to return during his lifetime? Does not the Word of God teach that there must be a falling away first and the man of sin revealed before that great and notable event takes place?

Paul taught that Christ's coming in the air for His people might occur at any moment, and taught the Church to be looking for that great event as possible at any time. The falling away and the revelation of the man of sin are to precede Christ's Second Coming to the earth to set up His Kingdom, but nothing is slated to precede His descent into the air to catch away His people unto Himself. That is the next thing in the revealed program.

At Any Moment

How can our Lord's return be expected, and liable to occur at any moment, when the condition precedent to His return as set forth in Matthew 24:14 has not yet been fulfilled?

Matthew 24:14 has no reference to our Lord's return for His Church. When it says that the "gospel of the kingdom shall be preached in all the world for a witness unto all nations; and then shall the end come," its meaning, as shown by the context, is that after the Church has been caught up to meet the Lord in the air there will be a remnant of Israel turned to the Lord, and these will begin to preach the Gospel of the Kingdom ("Repent: for the kingdom of heaven is at hand"), giving warning of the soon coming of the King. This is the Gospel of the Kingdom and not the Gospel of our salvation. The Kingdom Gospel will be preached to all nations during the absence of the Church with her Lord and before the end of "the Great Tribulation."

The "Eagle Saints"

Do you think the few "eagle saints" (Matt. 24:28) will be called first in the Rapture? If so, when do you think the full Church of the dead and alive (1 Thess. 4:16,17) will be caught up?

There is no thought of saints, "eagle" or otherwise, in Matthew 24:28. The Rapture will not be piecemeal, but all at once, including all the saved, "dead and alive," who will be caught up to meet the Lord in the air. The teaching of a partial Rapture is based upon inferences from Scriptures rather than upon the Scriptures themselves. Shun it.

Those Left Behind

Will those left on earth when the Rapture occurs be conscious of the fact that this or that one of their loved ones, or of persons whom they knew, is gone, just as one living is conscious that another has died?

It is unthinkable that all the born-again ones in the world should be caught away and leave the others unconscious of the fact of their departure. Of course they will be conscious of that fact. Whether the Rapture itself will be witnessed by those not participating in it is another question. Many profound Bible students believe in a secret Rapture, and hold that even the shout of our Lord and the voice of the archangel and the trump of God will be unheard except by those who are caught away. Whether this position is the true one I am not prepared to say, for I have never yet found conclusive proof either for or against it.

The Rapture and the Second Advent

Are the Rapture and the Second Advent identical?

By no means. They are often confused, but they are separated from each other by all the events of Daniel's seventieth week of seven years, including the reign of the Beast and the horrors of the Great Tribulation. The Rapture (or catching-up) is described in 1 Thessalonians 4:13-18, and the Second Advent is described in Matthew 24:29-31; Revelation 19:11-16, and elsewhere. The Rapture is frequently spoken of as a phase or an aspect of the Second Advent. It is better to consider them separately. Each of them is a tremendous event. A great point of contrast between them is that the Second Advent, when our Lord comes as Son of man to judge and to make war, must be preceded by many things; but the Rapture, when He comes into the air to call us up to Him there, is a timeless and signless event which is always imminent and may take place at any moment.

Rightly Dividing the Word

You say that the Rapture is not mentioned in the Synoptic Gospels. I had supposed that Matthew 24:36-44; Mark 13:32-37; Luke 21:34-36, referred to the Rapture. If you do not think so, kindly tell me how you interpret these passages.

The passages cited apply to the Second Coming of Christ to the earth rather than to His coming into the air to catch away His people. In the words, "One shall be taken, and the other left," the meaning is that the one shall be taken away in judgment, while the other is left to participate in the Kingdom about to be set up on earth.

Between the Rapture and the Revelation

What is considered the length of the period of time between the Rapture of the saints and the return of the Lord as King of the Jews? I notice that Dr. Seiss estimates it at 77 years.

I am convinced that the interval between the Rapture and the Revelation will be seven years. The seventieth week of Daniel (Dan. 9:24-27) is all that remains of the Times of the Gentiles in the Word of prophecy. If the saints were caught up today, the final week of the seventy weeks of Daniel would immediately begin to run its course. The latter half of that week will constitute the Great Tribulation. And at the end of it the Son of Man will come in the clouds of Heaven with power and great glory to set up the Kingdom of Heaven upon earth.

The Imminent Rapture

Please give the references that teach that the Rapture comes before the Tribulation.

The Great Tribulation is "the wrath to come," from which the believer is delivered by the Rapture (1 Thess. 1:9,10). He is not appointed unto wrath, but to obtain salvation through our Lord Jesus Christ, who died for him, that, whether he wakes or sleeps, he should live together with Him (1 Thess. 5:9,10). The plagues of vials constitute the last series in the plagues making up or completing the wrath of God (Rev. 15:1; 16:1). The Great Tribulation is "the hour of trial, that hour which is to come upon the whole world, to try them that dwell upon the earth," and the children of God, because they have kept the word of His patience, will be kept from that hour of trial (Rev. 3:10, R.V.). The Rapture is ever imminent, and it may take place at any moment of any day or any night.

Partial Rapture

I know you do not believe in a partial or graded Rapture. But I am puzzled about the meaning the Holy Spirit desires to make known in Philippians 3:11, and the context. Do not, also, those "accounted worthy" in Luke 20:35; 21:36; and 2 Thessalonians 1:5, have reference to the same people, time and event as Philippians 3:11?

In Philippians 3 Paul is showing his "trial balance," so to speak. There had been a day when he was relying upon his record as "circumcised the eighth day, of the stock of Israel, of the tribe of Benjamin, an Hebrew of the Hebrews; as touching the law, a Pharisee; concerning zeal, persecuting the church; touching the righteousness which is in the law, blameless" (5,6).

These things he had counted as "gain" or "profit" or "assets"; but he had now come to see that they should be counted "loss for Christ." Instead of assets they were liabilities, and instead of making him solvent they made him bankrupt. He was better off without them than with them, therefore he had counted "all things but loss for the excellency of the knowledge of Christ Jesus" his Lord: he gave all these things up in order that he might "win Christ"; and along with winning Christ he came into possession of "the righteousness which is of God by faith," together with the knowledge of Christ, "and the power of his resurrection, and the fellowship of his sufferings, being made conformable unto his death," and a part in the first resurrection, that is, "the resurrection from among the dead." There was no uncertainty about all this. It is only that he gave up his old account in order to take over the new account, all of which is included in the gift of God which is eternal life in Christ Jesus our Lord.

As to the other Scriptures you quote, of course, you must recognize that none of us can be counted worthy of anything, except for our worthiness in Christ, since we are accepted in the Beloved. The Rapture is a part of our salvation, and salvation is always a matter of grace and not of merit or works.

Who Will Be Caught Up?

Will all believers be raptured when Jesus comes into the air for His saints, or only those who are "ready"?

All the saved will be caught up. The Rapture is a part of our salvation, and our salvation is an absolute gift. Those to be caught up are "the dead in Christ" and those (in Christ) who are "alive and remain" until His coming (1 Thess. 1:9,10; 4:13-18).

Together with Them

Shall we meet our loved ones and know them when we are caught up to meet Christ?

Yes. Note the words "together with them" in 1 Thessalonians 4:17, and compare 1 Corinthians 13:12.

Who Will Hear the Shout?

In 1 Thessalonians 4:16 it says that the Lord will descend with a shout, with the voice of the archangel, and with the trump of God: and the dead in Christ shall rise first. Now how is it possible that no one in the world can hear and know what is taking place?

I am not at all sure that "no one in the world can hear and know what is taking place." There are those who teach that the Rapture will be secret and that the noise will be heard only by those to be caught up; but I have never been convinced of the truth of that teaching.

Why Should We Watch?

What does Mark 13:35-37 mean? If everybody who loves God, or has loved Him, and believed in Him, has eternal life and is caught up, why does He say, "Watch"? To what does it refer?

The exhortations to watchfulness for the Lord's return which are found in the Synoptic Gospels (Matthew, Mark and Luke) have reference to the Second Coming of Christ to the earth at the end of the Great Tribulation to set up the Kingdom and to bring in the Millennium. There is no teaching about the Rapture of the saved until you get into Paul's Epistles. These exhortations in the Gospels are for the teaching of those who shall be upon earth, having turned to the Lord during the absence of the Church, following the Rapture and preceding the Second Advent to earth when "his feet shall stand in that day upon the mount of Olives, which is before Jerusalem on the east" (Zech. 14:4).

When we read the Epistles of Paul, however, and are taught the doctrine of the Rapture of the saved we also are told to be constantly looking for Him. The first thing Paul wrote was the first Epistle to the Thessalonians, and in this he says in the first chapter that the believers had "turned to God from idols to serve the living and true God; and to wait for his Son from heaven, whom he raised from the dead, even Jesus, which delivered us from the wrath to come" (1 Thess. 1:9,10).

This is the normal attitude of the believer. If believers have not this attitude they miss the blessedness that always accompanies the blessed hope in its practical effect upon the daily life. But there is no teaching that any Christian will be left behind and left out of the Rapture because he is not looking for it. It is a blessed thing to know that all members of the body of Christ (that includes every truly born-again one) will go up to meet Him when He calls, and will "ever be with the Lord" (1 Thess. 4:17).

Professing Christians Left Behind

Would you kindly explain what will happen to professing Christians who are left behind at the Rapture?

The same thing will happen to them as to others left behind. They must await the terrible sufferings of the Great Tribulation, unless indeed they should die before the Great Tribulation begins.

A Question of Trumpets

1. When or about when did the sixth trumpet of Revelation sound, and what outstanding events of history did it announce?

2. Are the seventh trumpet of Revelation 11:15 and the "trump of God" (1 Thess. 4:16) and the "last trump" of 1 Corinthians 15:52 all one and the same, or are they three separate and distinct trumpets sounding at different times?

1. The whole series of trumpets in The Revelation is yet future and will follow the catching away of the Church which is marked at Revelation 4:1 in the symbolic rapture of John in response to the call of the risen Christ to "come up hither!"

2. No, the seventh trumpet of Revelation 11:15 is by no means identical with "the trump of God" of 1 Thessalonians 4:16, or "the last trump" of 1 Corinthians 15:52. As indicated in the answer to your first question, the seventh trumpet of Revelation is the end of a series of trumpets marking the trumpet judgments of the Great Tribulation, following the catching away of the Church. "The trump of God" of 1 Thessalonians 4:16 and "the last trump" of 1 Corinthians 15:52 are identical. They are not angelic trumpets at all, but "the trump of *God*." This will precede all the other trumpets, and it is for the sound of this "trump of God" that we are now waiting. We may hear it at any moment, and when we do hear it we shall be caught together with the sleeping saints "to meet the Lord in the air: and so shall we ever be with the Lord. Wherefore comfort one another with these words."

The Last Trump

I wish to inquire about "the last trump" of 1 Corinthians 15:52. The reference is to the first resurrection or the Rapture of the Church. A very good Bible student recently called our attention to the word "last" and recalled at the same time the trumpet of The Revelation. That does not look like the Church being taken away before the Great Tribulation of The Revelation. Will you kindly explain the meaning of the word "last" in this connection?

There is no need of confusion between the seven angelic trumpets of The Revelation and the last trump of 1 Corinthians 15:52. For according to 1 Thessalonians 4:16, the trumpet that shall sound at the first resurrection will not be a trumpet of angels at all, but "the trump of God," which is a very different matter. I suppose it is called "the last trump" because it signals the last great event in the earthly career of the Church, when she will be delivered out of the earth and brought forever into the presence of her Lord.

Trumpet and Trumpets

Is there any relation between the trumpet of 1 Corinthians 15:52 and the trumpets of Leviticus 23:24?

I do not think there is any connection between the trumpet of the Rapture and the trumpets of Leviticus 23. As I understand the trumpets of Leviticus 23, they refer to the regathering of Israel at the end of the age.

Hearing the Trump

Will those living, both in Christ and out of Christ, hear the trump of God spoken of in 1 Thessalonians 4:16,17?

There is much difference of opinion among teachers on this point, many enlightened expositors insisting that the Rapture will be secret, with no one hearing the sound but those who are caught up to meet the Lord in the air. For my own part, I have never been able to agree with them. The shout of the Lord Himself, the voice of the archangel, and the trump of God, taken together, will surely make a tremendous noise, and that will make it embarrassing for those who don't believe in noise in connection with the things of God. Many of God's dear children will participate for the first time in a noisy open-air meeting, and they will like it. I see nothing in the record to show that none of the noise will be heard by the unsaved. In any event, our departure, whether secret or not, will constitute such a testimony as the world has not had since the beginning of time. "Amen. Even so, come, Lord Jesus!"

Prophetic Parallelisms

I should be thankful if you could give the parallelism between John 11:25,26 and 1 Corinthians 15:52,53, as I have endeavored to do but am unable.

The parallelism between John 11:25,26 and 1 Corinthians 15:52,53 is perfectly obvious. Martha had referred to "the resurrection at the last day" (verse 24). And at once our Lord draws a picture of what shall take place at the time of that resurrection. He is "the resurrection," and therefore by Him "the dead shall be raised incorruptible." He is also "the life," and therefore by Him "we," the living who remain at His coming, "shall be changed." He that believes in Him, though meanwhile he may die, "yet shall he live," the corruptible and corrupting body being raised in incorruptibility (so the Greek). As to those living when He returns, and believing in Him, they shall "never die" at all. The parallelism is too exact to be accidental.

Paul as a Pattern

Please explain 1 Timothy 1:16, where Paul speaks of being a "pattern."

It is believed to mean that his own conversion is a pattern of the final conversion of the nation of Israel. He was brought to Christ by a visible manifestation of His glory, and in the same manner will the nation be brought to Him. At His Second Advent to earth every eye shall see Him, and they shall look upon Him whom they have pierced, and they shall mourn for Him, as one mourneth for his only son, and shall be in bitterness for Him, as one that is in bitterness for his first-born (Zech. 12:10; John 19:36,37).

Old Testament Saints and the Bride

What are the Old Testament saints called in the Kingdom age, if the Church only is the Bride?

John the Baptist was an Old Testament saint, and he called himself "the friend of the bridegroom." Perhaps all the Old Testament saints should be so designated. It is probable that Jewish believers are meant by the expression in Psalm 45:14, "The virgins her companions that follow her shall be brought unto thee." It is plain from Ephesians 5:25-33; 2 Corinthians 11:2 and other Scriptures that the New Testament Church is the Bride.

The Twenty-four Elders

Who are represented by the twenty-four elders in Revelation 4:4?

The verse reads literally: "And round about the throne were four and twenty thrones: and upon the thrones I saw four and twenty elders sitting, clothed in white raiment: and they had on their heads crowns of gold." In Revelation 5:8 the elders are seen, "having every one of them harps, and golden vials full of odors, which are the prayers of the saints." Thus it is seen that these elders are crowned and enthroned, and that also they have vials full of odors or incense. This means that they are both kings and priests. Then their number is twenty-four, and that is the number of the courses in the Levitical priesthood (1 Chron. 24). It is evident that these elders represent the enthroned Church of God when she will be associated with her Lord, reigning over the kingdom and sharing His glory. The Church is made up of kings and priests unto our God (Rev. 1:6).

The Woman of Revelation 12

Who is the woman of Revelation 12, clothed with the sun, and the moon at her feet, and with a crown of twelve stars; who, being with child, crieth in travail to be delivered?

The woman is a type of the nation of Israel, "of whom as concerning the flesh Christ came." The sun symbolizes the eternal Christ Himself, who was, even before His incarnation as man, from everlasting to everlasting, "over all, God blessed forever" (Rom. 9:4,5). The moon is the Church, reflecting the glory of the absent Lord, as the physical moon reflects the glory of the absent sun. The twelve stars are the twelve tribes, or the twelve apostles, or both. The Man Child is the Christ of God, including, however, His completed "church, which is his body, the fullness (or completeness) of him that filleth (or completes) all in all" (Eph. 1:22,23). The dragon is Satan, who seeks to hinder the full birth and development of Christ's body. As soon as the body is completely born it will be "caught up unto God, and to his throne" (compare 1 Thess. 4:16,17).

The Marriage Supper of the Lamb

Where will the marriage supper of the Lamb take place?

The marriage supper of the Lamb takes place in Heaven between the Rapture of the saints and their return with the Lord at the end of the Great Tribulation. The coming of the Bridegroom described in Matthew 25:1-13 is not His coming for His Bride at the Rapture, but rather His coming with her at the close of the Great Tribulation as set forth in Matthew 24:29,30. Compare 2 Thessalonians 1:7-10, R.V. In the *Ancient Syriac New Testament* as well as the *Latin Vulgate* the first verse of Matthew 25 reads: "Then may the kingdom of heaven be shadowed forth by ten virgins, who took their lamps and went out to meet the bridegroom and the bride"; and in our own Revised Version the tenth verse of the same chapter reads that "while they went to buy, the bridegroom came; and they that were ready went in with him to the marriage feast: and the door was shut"—not to the marriage, but to the marriage feast. The marriage had already taken place in Heaven.

The Rapture and the Tribulation

Does the language of Mark 13:36, "Lest coming suddenly he find you sleeping," mean that the sleeping ones were those who were not watching for Him? Verse 37 says: "And what I say unto you I say unto all, Watch." Would not that "all" include the Christians who will be in the Rapture, as well as the Tribulation saints? Could it not mean that only those who watch or look for Him will be in the Rapture, as Hebrews 9:28 would indicate by the words, "them that look for him"? Then there is Luke 21:36, "Watch ye therefore, and pray always, that ye may be accounted worthy to escape all these things that shall come to pass, and to stand before the Son of man." Surely, those words, "worthy to escape," mean to escape the Tribulation sorrows, so it must mean for the Raptured saints. Are all the "watch" verses meant for the Tribulation saints?

Your confusion arises from your failure to distinguish between things that differ. The doctrine of the Rapture is not unfolded at all in the Synoptic Gospels—that is, Matthew, Mark and Luke; and indeed is only hinted at in John's Gospel, for even in John 14 it is not fully explained, and the language there would be unintelligible to us except for Paul's exposition of it in 1 Thessalonians 4, 1 Corinthians 15 and elsewhere.

The "coming of the Son of man" is the actual Second Coming of Christ to earth at the end of the Great Tribulation—and this is the coming set forth in the Gospels. The exhortations to "watch" are intended for believers who shall be here in the end-time, having turned to the Lord during Daniel's seventieth week, in the latter half of which period the Great Tribulation is located. Hebrews 9:28 also points to our Lord's "revelation from heaven" in His actual Second Advent to earth, rather than to the Rapture. The Rapture is unfolded in the Church and Pastoral Epistles of Paul, and in all of these we are taught to watch and wait and look for, not the Second Advent of our Lord Jesus Christ to the earth, but to that timeless and signless event which must precede His Second Advent by at least the period of Daniel's seventieth week of seven years, and is ever imminent. In other words, the Second Advent must be preceded by various events prophesied in the Word of God, including the Rapture, the rise of Antichrist, the Great Tribulation, etc. None of these things is predicted to take place before the Rapture, for the Rapture is the next thing on the page of Holy Writ and may take place at any moment.

Before the Rapture

Will the rebuilding of the temple be begun and the Antichrist revealed before the Rapture of the Church?

Not necessarily. Of course, the rebuilding of the temple might begin at any time, and would probably begin at once if the Jews were in total control of Jerusalem; but the Antichrist cannot be revealed before his time, for the Holy Spirit is withholding his revealing until the Church is completed and gathered out (2 Thess. 2:3-8). There are no prophetic events to precede the Rapture. The coming of the Lord for His own is a timeless and signless event, and we are to be expecting Him constantly, for He may come at any moment.

The Antichrist

Will the antichrist be a resurrected person?

I do not know. There are teachers who hold that the antichrist will be a reincarnation of Judas Iscariot, but that can only be a matter of suggestion or conjecture; it can be nothing else. There is no proof for such a position. Those who argue for this position point out that Judas Iscariot is called "a devil," and a "son of perdition" in the Word of God (John 6:70; 17:12). And it is written that Satan entered into Judas Iscariot, and also that Satan dwells in and acts through the antichrist (John 13:27; Rev. 13:2). But there are many sons of perdition and many men of sin, and many who yield themselves to Satan. Therefore I end my answer as I began it: I do not know.

Salvation after the Rapture

I heard a man say that if sinners did not accept the Gospel and Christ's free gift of salvation now, before Christ comes for His own, they would be eternally lost; it would be their last chance. Is that so, or it is true that some who have refused Christ as Savior may live on into the days after the Rapture, and may then accept Christ and become true Christians, even though they must suffer the trouble and distress of the Great Tribulation period? I heard the above statement made and I did not agree with the speaker at the time. Later I was questioned as to this, and I promised to write and ask you concerning this matter. Please explain.

I know that there are godly teachers who hold that none will be saved after the Rapture of the saved, who have before the Rapture heard and rejected the

Gospel. This teaching is based chiefly upon the language of the first and second chapters of 2 Thessalonians In verses 6-9 of chapter 1 it is written: "Seeing it is a righteous thing with God to recompense tribulation to them that trouble you; and to you who are troubled rest with us, when the Lord Jesus shall be revealed from heaven with his mighty angels, in flaming fire taking vengeance on them that know not God, and that obey not the gospel of our Lord Jesus Christ: who shall be punished with everlasting destruction from the presence of the Lord, and from the glory of his power."

Then in the second chapter at the tenth verse it speaks of certain ones "that perish; because they received not the love of the truth, that they might be saved. And for this cause God shall send them strong delusion, that they should believe a lie: that they all might be damned who believed not the truth, but had pleasure in unrighteousness."

Some teachers insist that this shows that those who have rejected the Gospel before the Rapture will not have a chance to be saved after the Rapture. I cannot see that their position is tenable on the basis of these chapters, or any others. So far as I can see, the matter is not revealed. We are not shown here whether these people's rejection of the truth is before the Rapture or after it. I should not like to teach that those who reject the Gospel now will certainly have an opportunity afterward to hear and believe it; nor am I ready to teach definitely that they certainly will not have such an opportunity. I do not dogmatize about these matters, for I hold that they are among the unrevealed things, and that it is a mistake to teach positively what is not positively revealed in the Scriptures. But, in any event, let us remind ourselves that none of us can know whether we shall even live until the Rapture. Now is the accepted time and now is the day of salvation. No one knows what a day will bring forth. Therefore let us preach the Word to the lost and seek their salvation while the door is still surely open to them.

Let it be added that there are some people who are constantly accusing us in this connection of preaching the doctrine of a "second chance." This is a false accusation. The doctrine of a second chance is the teaching that man will have a chance to be saved after death. Of course, that is an unscriptural and mischievous doctrine which we do not believe at all. Every man's eternal destiny will be fixed here in this life, and not after death.

The Kingdom Commission

Will Matthew 28:19 have a more literal fulfillment in a future dispensation?

I believe so. The Jewish age has seven years (Daniel's seventieth week) to run after the Church is caught away. A Jewish remnant will turn to the Lord at that time and will be His evangelists, preaching the Gospel of the Kingdom in all the world as a witness to all nations before the end of the period shall come (Matt. 24:14).

Position of the Raptured

Will you please tell me what will be the Millennial position of those

who have fallen asleep in Jesus, and those alive and remaining at His coming, who are caught up to meet Him in the air?

We have the assurance in 1 Thessalonians 4:17 concerning the dead in Christ and the living in Christ who are caught away at the Rapture that they shall "ever be with the Lord." Therefore wherever He is they will be. Then in Revelation 5:8-10 the Church, represented by the twenty-four elders, sings a song of praise to Him who has "made us unto our God kings and priests: and we shall reign on the earth." From these and other Scriptures it is evident that the Church will be associated with her Lord in His Millennial rule. "Do ye not know that the saints shall judge the world? . . . Know ye not that we shall judge angels?" (1 Cor. 6:2,3). The Church as the Bride of Christ will be Queen in the Kingdom when it is set up on the earth; and the Church as the body of Christ can hardly be thought of as separated from Him after He has taken her unto Himself without "spot, or wrinkle, or any such thing" (Eph. 5:25-33).

Who Will Have Part in the Rapture?

I recently became acquainted with a preacher of the Gospel, who is sincere, and true to the Scriptures in most of his teaching. He says, however, that the five foolish virgins were believers who were not ready when the Lord came, and therefore were not caught up at the Rapture.

He claims that only those who are looking for our Lord's return will be caught up at the Rapture, basing his argument on Hebrews 9:28.

He says that servants who act as those mentioned in Matthew 24:48-51; 25:24-30, will not share in the marriage supper of the Lamb, and therefore will not be a part of His Bride. Can you give me any light on these Scriptures?

It is a great mistake to read anything into Matthew which belongs to this present age. Matthew is Jewish and Kingdom from beginning to end, and says nothing about our Gospel or of Church truth. The wise and foolish virgins are all Jews, half of whom are born again during the Tribulation period, and all of whom are professing believers. The return of the Lord mentioned there is not His coming *for* the Church, but His coming *with* the Church at the end of Daniel's seventieth week.

Hebrews 9:28 also should be applied to the same thing. Its reference is not to the Rapture of the Church, but to the Second Coming of Christ to the earth.

The same thing applies to the questions about Matthew 24:48-51 and 25:24-30. They do not touch the subject of salvation by faith of those who believe during the present dispensation.

Nothing is more clearly taught in the Epistles than that every Christian is a member of the Bride of Christ, and that every Christian will be caught up at the Rapture. This is a part of our salvation, and salvation is never a matter of rewards or deservings, but only of grace.

Preachers after the Rapture

When all true believers are caught away at the Rapture, who will be left as witnesses during the Great Tribulation period to win souls for Christ? Will the Gospel be preached by those who knew the message of salvation but failed to accept, for instance, preachers and laymen who were merely professing Christians and who could not be claimed by Christ as His own? I know that the 144,000, God's chosen remnant of Israel, will be missionaries during that time, but who will preach in the churches, and who will teach the unsaved youths in our Sunday schools?

In "our" Sunday schools? What do you mean by "our" Sunday schools? We are not going to have any Sunday schools here after we are taken away at the Rapture. No doubt there will be Sunday schools and churches and services, but I think we need not speculate about that. The 144,000 will begin their work of evangelizing at once, and, no doubt, many Gentiles will then be saved as well as many Jews, so that there will be many people to preach in the churches and teach in the Sunday schools. This, of course, will be during the first half of Daniel's seventieth week and before the beginning of the Great Tribulation.

Another truth not generally understood is in 2 Thessalonians 2:7, "For the mystery of lawlessness doth already work: only there is one that restraineth now, until he be taken out of the way." "He," no doubt, means the Holy Spirit; and people have asked how anyone can be saved after the Holy Spirit is taken away? But the record does not say that the Holy Spirit will be taken away, but only that He will be taken "out of the way," which is a very different matter. He will still be here, but He will be taken out of the way as the restrainer of lawlessness.

This may be illustrated by a traffic policeman. At one moment he is standing in the center of a street restraining, say, the north-and-south-bound traffic. A moment later he is doing something else and has ceased to restrain the north-and-south-bound traffic, but he has not been entirely removed from the scene. Likewise, the Holy Spirit, who "came," in Acts 2, for a peculiar purpose, was already here. He is omnipresent, and therefore is never absent from any place. But He came on that day of Pentecost in a new manifestation; and He now continues the work He then began, that of gathering out a people for the body and Bride of Christ; and when this work is done His work will change, but He will still be here, and He will go on saving men and women in great numbers, as the Word of God distinctly shows (See Rev. 7:14, R.V.).

"The Lord Is at Hand"

What does "imminent" mean as applying to the Second Advent of Christ? If the Second Coming is imminent, just how imminent is it? It seems to be the consensus among many Christian writers that Christ may come NOW, at any time; that is, they seem to think that He will come within the next century. It seems to me that this has been taught

in every age, and yet century after century has rolled around, and still the Lord does not appear in the upper heavens. What is your interpretation of this?

The word "imminent" describes perfectly our Lord's coming into the air for His people. It is always imminent. This word "imminent" indicates that the great event for which we wait may take place at any moment; it is ever impending. We are appointed to "look" for it, and to "wait" for it, as something that might transpire at any time.

The Second Coming of Christ is something different. When He comes the second time it will be *to the earth* that He will come, and not *into the air*. There are many things that must transpire before His Second Coming to the earth *with* His people, but there is nothing in prophecy to transpire before His coming into the air for His people. We do not teach that He must come at once, nor even "within the next century"; but that it is the normal attitude of the Christian who has "turned to God from idols," and is serving "the living and true God" to be continually waiting "for His Son from heaven" (1 Thess. 1:9,10).

His coming for His saints is signless and timeless. There are signs, however, at present, evidently pointing to the end of the age and His coming to the earth, which coming will be later than His coming for His people by the period of seven years constituting "Daniel's Seventieth Week." These signs seem to be multiplying in these days, and therefore the heart of the believer is quickened in the glad expectation of His soon coming to take us to be with Himself. "Even so, come, Lord Jesus!" "The Lord is at hand!" Keep looking up!

"If by Any Means"

Did Paul in Philippians 3:10,11 mean to imply that he might miss the first resurrection altogether?

Not at all. Paul here follows the method of Romans 7, and gives his past experience, telling how he felt when stricken down on the Damascus road. He saw the utter worthlessness of all his attainments in "the Jews' religion" (Gal. 1:13,14). Counting all these but "dung," he turned from them to Christ, in order to obtain seven things: (1) acceptance in Christ, to "be found in him"; (2) the righteousness of God, not his own righteousness by law works, "but that which is through the faith of Christ, the righteousness which is of God by faith"; (3) a personal acquaintance with Christ—"that I may know him"; (4) a personal experience, not formal, but mighty—to know "the power of his resurrection"; (5) a share in His afflictions—"the fellowship of his sufferings"; (6) conformity to Christ's death—"being made conformable unto his death"; and (7) a share in the first resurrection—"the earlier resurrection, which is from among the dead" (*Rotherham's Translation*).

All these seven things are wrapped up in the little clause "that I may win Christ" in verse 8. The word for "win" is really "gain" as in verse 7. Having given up his own "righteousness, which is of the law," and having thus won Christ, all the rest followed as a matter of course. There was no doubt about

Paul's part in the first resurrection any more than about his part in "the righteousness which is of God by faith." The first resurrection and the Rapture connected therewith are as truly included in the Christian's salvation as is justification by faith. And since salvation, from start to finish, is by grace, it follows that every saved person will be raised in the first resurrection and "caught up to meet the Lord in the air," as surely as that every saved person *is* saved and that his salvation is by grace through faith, and "not of works, lest any man should boast."

Resurrection

Will there not be two resurrections of the saved—one at the Rapture, and one of the Tribulation saints, at the Second Coming of Christ? Would you teach that both are included in the first resurrection, but seven years apart?

I have no doubt that the first resurrection includes, first, the resurrection of our Lord Himself nearly two thousand years ago; second, the resurrection of the saved at the Rapture; and third, the resurrection of the Tribulation saints at the Second Coming of our Lord to the earth. This corresponds with the type of Leviticus 23, where the harvest is seen in three parts: the wave-sheaf of the firstfruits, the main harvest, and the gleanings.

A Resurrection of Jews

Please explain Daniel 12:2,3. What resurrection is referred to in these verses?

There is much difference of opinion among enlightened students of prophecy as to the point here raised. G. H. Pember's comment is interesting. He says: "The time of the end, in which the events predicted in the last six verses (of chapter 11) are to occur, will also witness other marvels. For Michael, the great Prince appointed by God to preside over the destinies of Israel, will arise from his comparative inactivity; and, as we learn from the Apocalypse, his first action will be to drive Satan and his angels out of the heavenly places, and to cast them down to the earth. Then a loud voice will be heard, saying: 'Woe for the earth and for the sea: because the devil is gone down unto you, having great wrath, knowing that he hath but a short time!' And so there will follow upon the earth that appalling Tribulation to which the prophets so often refer—a time of trouble such as never was since there was a nation, God's last mighty sifting before the Advent of His Christ. But, when it has passed by, glory shall come: for then, at length, Daniel's people, the children of Abraham, shall be delivered—that is to say, such of them as shall be found written in the Book of God's Remembrance, not having been cut off from their people through transgression. Nor will the glorious deliverance be confined to the living: there will also be a resurrection of dead Israelites, in which many from among those who sleep in the dustland shall awake, but by no means all. For it appears that of Israelites also, as well as of Christians, there will be a first or select resurrection, before the establishment of the Millennial Kingdom."

Pember paraphrases verse 2 thus: "And many of them that sleep in the dust-formed ground shall awake: these"—that is to say, those who awake—"shall be for eternal life; but those"—that is, the remainder of the sleepers, who do not awake—"for shame and eternal contempt." This exposition agrees with that of Saadiah the Gaon and Ibn Ezra, two celebrated Rabbis of the tenth and twelfth centuries.

Attaining unto the First Resurrection

If it be true that all the saved will be raised and caught up at the same time, how shall we understand Paul's word in Philippians 3:11; Hebrews 9:28; 11:35 and 2 Timothy 4:8? I believe all who keep their faith unto the end (as Paul did and as it is taught in Revelation 2:13 and 3:8, 10) will be raptured together. Why should Paul have troubled himself that "by any means" he "might attain unto the resurrection from the dead"? And what will happen to those saved ones who though loving their Savior the Lord Jesus Christ did not love His coming, so they are not ready? And what would be that "better resurrection," if there is only one good resurrection?

There is nothing in the Scriptures you quote or elsewhere in the Bible to contradict the teaching that all members of the body of Christ will be resurrected and raptured at the same time together. In Philippians 3:11 the "if" by no means implies a doubt that Paul would have a part in the first resurrection; it only speaks of the object he had in mind in giving up the things of Judaism it was in order that he might win Christ and be found in Him and have a part in the first resurrection. Now that he had given up all these things and had ceased to have confidence in the flesh and was worshiping God in the Spirit and rejoicing in Christ Jesus, surely there was no doubt left in his mind that he should share in the resurrection from amongst the dead.

Hebrews 9:28 has no reference to the Rapture whatever. It points to the actual Second Coming of Christ to the earth with His people rather than to His coming into the air for them.

Hebrews 11:35 is like Philippians 3:11. The ancient believers refused temporary deliverance from suffering in order that they might have a part in the better resurrection. Having thus made their choice, there is no doubt even by implication of their participation in that resurrection.

In 2 Timothy 4:8 the Rapture is not in mind; it is rather a question of rewards for those who "love his appearing."

The whole matter becomes clear when we remember that the Rapture is not a matter of rewards, but it is a part of our salvation. Indeed it is called "salvation" in Romans 13:11; 1 Thessalonians 5:9 and perhaps also 1 Peter 1:5. Salvation is a matter of grace only, however, and never a matter of works. How could any one expect to deserve or merit a part in the first resurrection? That, of course, would be quite impossible, but since it is part of our salvation, which is a gift from God through Jesus Christ our Lord, we may look hopefully toward it and joyfully anticipate our part in it. "Wherefore comfort one another with these words."

The Resurrection Body

It has been my belief that the bodies raised when Christ comes will be the same bodies which the saints had during their life here. Of course, I believe that these bodies will be changed the same as the bodies of living saints. But from 1 Corinthians 15:36,37 it seems that I may be wrong. The kernel of grain which is sown is not the kernel which is gathered at the harvest. However, the same body of Christ was raised, and even the nail prints will be visible when He comes again. If the same bodies are raised, as I am inclined to believe from 1 Corinthians 15:52 and 1 Thessalonians 4:16, can you tell me the meaning of 1 Corinthians 15:36,37?

Your question about the resurrection brings up a great mystery. It is true that the wheat which grows up from a kernel of grain sown in the ground is not precisely the kernel that was sown. And yet in a sense it is, nevertheless, the same body in another form. To my mind, there is no doubt that the Scriptures teach that our Lord rose from the dead in the body with which He went into the grave, except that that body was fashioned anew into a body of glory, instead of a body of humiliation, and that the same thing will occur in our own cases (Phil. 3:20,21).

The Resurrection Body of the Unbeliever

In the study of the resurrection body of the believer, I am struck with the absence of revelation on the resurrection body of the unbeliever. With what body does the unbeliever come forth in the resurrection? Can you give us at least the main Scriptures on this subject?

The only thing I know about the resurrection body of the unbeliever is that it is raised for judgment at the end of the Millennium. I do not know of any fuller light on the subject. Of course, there can be no resurrection which is not bodily, for the body is the thing that dies at the time of physical death. Resurrection therefore must be of the body whether of the saved or the unsaved.

The Great Tribulation

Is the Great Tribulation a dispensation?

No, the Great Tribulation is not exactly a dispensation, in the generally accepted meaning of that term. The dispensation of grace will not really close until the end of the Great Tribulation and the beginning of the dispensation of the Kingdom, at the coming back to earth of our Lord Jesus Christ.

Salvation during the Great Tribulation

Will anyone be saved during the Great Tribulation?

Yes. Read Revelation 7:9-17. The literal rendering of verse 14, adopted in the Revised Version, is "These are they that come out of the great tribulation, and they washed their robes, and made them white in the blood of the Lamb."

The Years of the Tribulation

Do you think that the seven years of Tribulation are going to be years as we count them 365 days to the year?

The years of the Great Tribulation will be three-and-a-half years, being the latter half of Daniel's seventieth week (Dan. 9:24-27). The Bible year is always 360 days, consisting of twelve months of 30 days each. Therefore the three-and-a-half years of the Great Tribulation will last exactly 1,260 days (Rev. 11:3).

Refuge in Petra

Where in the Bible are we told that Petra, in Palestine, is to be the refuge of the Jews in the last days?

Petra is not mentioned by name in the Bible. Many Bible students, however, believe that God will prepare a refuge in Petra for Israel in the time of the Great Tribulation. In Isaiah 43:19 it is written: "Behold, I will do a new thing. . . . I will even make a way in the wilderness, and rivers in the desert." It is clear that the symbolic woman of Revelation 12 is Israel, and in verse 6 we read of the woman fleeing into the wilderness, "where she hath a place prepared of God," and where she is fed and protected for the period of three and a half years (compare also verse 14). The formation of Petra seems designed for just such protection. The late William E. Blackstone, author of *Jesus Is Coming*, deposited in the caverns of Petra a large number of Bibles enclosed in strong boxes for the guidance of Israel during the time of their trial.

Out of the Great Tribulation

I am not sure of anyone being saved during the Great Tribulation except the 144,000 Jews that are sealed by the angel (Rev. 7:1-8). The next scene (verses 9-17) seems to me to be a heavenly scene and the redeemed host seen there to be Christians who come out of great tribulation as all real Christians do. I note you have misquoted verse 14, as you say, "These are they that come out of the great tribulation," when it really says, "These are they which came out of great tribulation."

No, we did not misquote the passage. It is true that in our common version the definite article "the" is omitted before the words "great tribulation," but you will find it there in the Revised Version. Indeed, the Greek text is even more decisive, for there it reads, "out of the tribulation, the great one."

Preachers in the Great Tribulation

Who will preach during the Great Tribulation?

From all that the Scriptures have to say upon the subject it seems clear that the Gospel of the Kingdom is to be preached during the Great Tribulation by a saved remnant out of Israel, numbering 144,000. They are to deliver their message "in all the world for a witness unto all nations," before the end of the Great Tribulation and the coming in glory of the Son of Man (Matt. 24:14; Rev. 7:1-17).

The 144,000

Who are the 144,000 sealed ones in the seventh chapter of Revelation?

They are Israelites, who will turn to God in the last days. Twelve thousand from each tribe, they are undoubtedly the evangelists who in that day, after the Church of God has been completed and caught up to her Lord, will preach the gospel of the Kingdom to the nations (Matt. 24:14). The result of their preaching is seen in the remaining portion of Revelation 7: "These are they that come out of the great tribulation" (verse 7, A.R.V.). Not merely "out of great tribulation," but "out of the tribulation, the great one" (so the Greek). These 144,000 are to be sealed. This will be necessary, for no Jew now knows for certain his tribe, but the divine sealers will know.

Saints in the Great Tribulation

Who are the saints mentioned in Revelation 13:7?

They are those who turn to God during the Great Tribulation. The same company is seen in Revelation 7:14, which, literally interpreted, reads: "These are they who come out of the tribulation, the great one, and have washed their robes, and made them white in the blood of the Lamb."

The Church and the Tribulation

Is there any Scriptural evidence that the Church will pass through tribulation or the Great Tribulation?

Tribulation is the appointed portion of the Church as it passes through this world. "In the world ye shall have tribulation: but be of good cheer; I have overcome the world" (John 16:33). There is nothing more clearly shown to us than "that we must through much tribulation enter into the kingdom of God" (Acts 14:22). But the Scripture is perfectly plain in its teaching that the Church will not pass through the Great Tribulation of the end-time. The Great Tribulation is to be a visitation of God's wrath upon a rebellious world. It is unthinkable that God will pour out His wrath upon those who by His Son have been delivered from the wrath to come (Ps. 2:5; 1 Thess. 1:9,10). Again, since in the person of our Substitute we have already borne the full measure of God's wrath when Christ died on the cross, the righteous God cannot righteously subject us to that wrath a second time. And yet again, since we have become members of the body of Christ, it would be subjecting Him a second time to the wrath of God.

The Church and the Tribulation

Have we any clear teaching from the Word of God that the "saints" or "Church" will go through the first three-and-a-half years of the Tribulation?

Speaking strictly according to the Scriptures, there is no such period as the first three-and-a-half years of the Tribulation. I know that, by some, the seven years of Daniel's seventieth week are divided into two parts, the first part being "the Tribulation" and the latter part being "the Great Tribulation"; but the Bible does not so divide it. Doubtless there will be much tribulation in the whole period, but the Tribulation and the Great Tribulation are the same thing in Scripture.

There will be saints on earth during the entire period, but they will be those who have become saved since the Rapture.

The Church will not pass through, nor into, any part of the seven years. She is appointed to serve God and to wait for His Son; and not until He comes and takes her unto Himself "in the air" can the seven years begin at all.

Gog and Magog

What is the meaning of the expression, "Gog and Magog," as used in the Bible?

The words to which you refer are found in Ezekiel 38 and 39 and Revelation 20:7-9. In Ezekiel 38:2,3 it reads: "Son of man, set thy face against Gog, the land of Magog, the chief prince of Meshech and Tubal, and prophesy against him, and say, Thus saith the Lord Jehovah: Behold, I am against thee, O Gog, the chief prince of Meshech and Tubal."

The Revised Version reads: "Son of man, set thy face toward Gog, of the land of Magog, the prince of Rosh, Meshech, and Tubal, and prophesy against him, and say, Thus saith the Lord Jehovah: Behold, I am against thee, O Gog, prince of Rosh, Meshech and Tubal."

Gog is the prince, and Magog is the land. "Rosh" is Russia and Meshech and Tubal are just another way of saying Moscow and Tobolsk, which are among the chief cities of Russia, one of them being its capital. The descendants of Magog, who was a son of Japheth (Gen. 10:2), settled in northeastern Europe, and their territory includes what we now call Russia. Ezekiel 38 and 39 describe a terrible conflict yet to take place between Russia and her allies on one side, and certain other nations on the other side in a contention for the possession of the land of Palestine. As Dr. Scofield puts it, "The whole prophecy belongs to the yet future 'day of Jehovah' (Isa. 2:10-22; Rev. 19:11-21), and to the battle of Armageddon (Rev. 16:14; 19:19), but includes also the final revolt of the nations at the close of the kingdom-age (Rev. 20:7-9)" (*Scofield Reference Bible*).

The Two Witnesses

Will not the two witnesses of Revelation 11:3-12 begin their ministry at the opening of the seventieth week of Daniel 9:27?

My view of the matter of the two witnesses is that their preaching is to take place during the latter half, rather than the former half, of Daniel's seventieth week. That is to say, I believe they will preach during the Great Tribulation proper, and that their resurrection and rapture will take place along with the rest of the Tribulation saints at the Second Coming of our Lord to earth.

Who are They?

Who are the two witnesses of Revelation 11:3-12?

If one considers the prediction of Malachi 4:5 along with our Lord's word in Matthew 17:11 (compare Mark 9:11-13), it is believed that one of the two witnesses of Revelation 11:3-12 is Elijah. There is a great deal of disagreement among New Testament exegetes as to the identity of the second witness. Some believe that it will be Moses, others believe that it will be Enoch, but there is no plain statement in the Word of God as to the matter. Therefore we must say that we do not know. This is one of the things to be revealed when we shall know as we are known.

The Seventy Weeks of Daniel

Please explain Daniel's seventy weeks (Dan. 9:20-27). There seem to be three divisions: (1) sixty-two weeks; (2) seven weeks; and (3) one week. Verse 26 especially is the one we desire to have discussed.

Your analysis is correct, except that the order is (1) seven weeks, or seven sevens, meaning forty-nine years, during which the city of Jerusalem was restored; (2) threescore and two weeks, or sixty-two sevens, meaning four hundred and thirty-four years, reaching down to the day when Messiah rode into His capital as the Prince, on the day of the so-called triumphal entry; and (3) the final seven of years, or Daniel's seventieth week. Please note that there is an interval between the second and third divisions, during which interval certain things are to occur. These events are "after the threescore and two weeks," as the first phrase of verse 26 should be rendered.

The things to occur during the interval are (1) the crucifixion of the Messiah, who is "cut off, but not for himself"; (2) the destruction of Jerusalem and the temple by the Roman army—the people of the coming prince, that is, the Man of Sin. The fact that it was a Roman army that destroyed Jerusalem in A.D. 70 proves, as is indicated elsewhere, that the Man of Sin, the last Gentile ruler, will be a Roman Emperor. His end shall be with a flood of the indignation and wrath of God (2 Thess. 2:8; Rev, 19:20). From A.D. 70 the age will be a troublous one, as the remainder of verse 26 shows. Literally, it reads: "and unto the end wars and desolations are determined." The final seven years—Daniel's seventieth week—is described in verse 27. It will begin when the Church, having been completed, is taken away to meet the Lord in the air (1 Thess. 4:13-18). The Man of Sin, described in verse 26 as "the prince that shall come," will be manifested as the Emperor of Rome. I believe that he will enter into alliance with the Jews then in the land of Palestine, confirming his covenant with "many," or the majority, for one seven of years. When the seven years period is half gone, that is, when three-and-a-half years have elapsed, he will break his covenant, forbid the further worship of Jehovah, and substitute the worship of himself and his image on pain of death.

The worship of the Emperor—"the abomination of desolation" (Matt. 24:15)—will be the state religion. This is explained circumstantially in Revelation 13. All men, everywhere, will be compelled to receive the Emperor's sign—

"the mark of the beast"—upon their hands or foreheads, and those who refuse to submit will find themselves universally boycotted, so "that no man might buy or sell, save he that had the mark, or the name of the beast, or the number of his name" (Rev. 13:17).

As a result of this state of things the world will be plunged into the Great Tribulation. The Jews will be the chief sufferers—it is "the day of Jacob's trouble" (Jer. 30:7), but the whole world will be involved (Dan. 12:1; Matt. 24:21). It is the visitation of the wrath of God (Ps. 2:5; 1 Thess. 1:9,10; 5:9; Rev. 3:10). It will last three-and-a-half years, "forty and two months" (Rev. 11:2); "twelve hundred and sixty days," which is three-and-one-half years of 360 days each, the length of the prophetic year throughout Scripture (Rev. 11:3).

Multitudes will turn to the Lord during that awful period of judgment (Rev. 7:14—"These are they which came out of the Tribulation, the Great one"—so the Greek reads). The Great Tribulation will be brought to an end by the Second Advent to earth of the Lord Jesus as Son of man, to "judge and to make war" (Rev. 19:11), and to subdue His enemies and set up the promised Kingdom of Heaven upon earth, restoring the throne of David and occupying it as King of kings and Lord of lords. And "He which testifieth these things saith, Surely, I come suddenly! Amen. Even so, come, Lord Jesus."

United States in Prophecy

Does the United States figure in prophecy?

I am not sure whether the United States is specifically mentioned in prophecy, although there are those among Bible students who believe that the language of Isaiah 18:1 applies to America as "the land shadowing with wings, which is beyond the rivers of Ethiopia." Of course, from the standpoint of the prophet in Jerusalem America would be beyond the rivers of Ethiopia, but for myself, I am doubtful as to this being a reference to the United States.

But in Revelation 13 it is clearly shown that the last Gentile ruler, who shall then be occupying the throne of the Roman empire, will reign temporarily over all the world; for it is written that power is to be given him "over all kindreds, and tongues, and nations" (verse 7). This would, of course, include the United States of America.

The Three Frogs

Are we living in the period indicated by the three frogs of Revelation 16:13,14; and if so are the three frogs personified in Hitler, Mussolini and Stalin, or in the three phases of public life and spirit, namely fascism, communism and the papacy?

The "three unclean spirits like frogs" of Revelation 16 appear between the sixth and seventh vials, or bowls of God's wrath during the Great Tribulation, and these bowl judgments cannot begin until the Church is completed and removed from the earth (Rev. 3:10). These "spirits like frogs" are described in the passage mentioned as "the spirits of demons, working miracles, which go forth unto the kings of the earth and of the whole world, to gather them to the battle of that Great Day of God Almighty," that is, Armageddon. The scene is yet future.

"Days" of Daniel 12

Please explain what is meant by the Daniel 12:11 and 12. What is the taking away of the daily sacrifice? And what is "the abomination that maketh desolate"? And what is meant by the 1290 days and the 1335 days?

The abomination of desolation is the image of the antichrist which will be set up in the temple in Jerusalem during the seven years constituting the "seventieth week of Daniel" (Dan. 9:27; 11:31; 12:11; Matt. 24:15; 2 Thess. 2:4; Rev. 13:14-18). There are three periods of "days" dating from the abomination. These periods are thus described by Dr. Scofield:

First—Twelve hundred and sixty days to the destruction of the beast (Dan. 7:25; 12:7; Rev. 13:5; 19:19,20). This is also the duration of the Great Tribulation (compare Dan. 12:4, note).

Second—Dating from the same event is a period of 1290 days, an addition of thirty days (Dan. 12:11).

Third—Again forty-five days are added and with them the promise of verse 12. No account is directly given of that which occupies the interval of seventy-five days between the end of the tribulation and the full blessing of verse 12. It is suggested that the explanation may be found in the prophetic descriptions of the events following the battle of Armageddon (Rev. 16:14; 19:21). The beast is destroyed, and Gentile world-dominion ended, by the smiting of the "Stone cut out without hands" at the end of the 1260 days, but the scene is, so to speak, filled with the debris of the image which the "wind" must carry away before full blessing comes in (Dan. 2:35). (*Scofield Reference Bible.*)

Which Beast Is the Antichrist?

I have before me as I write, a copy of the *Scofield Reference Bible*, and desire to ask you a question or two regarding a footnote on page 1342. In footnote 3, Dr. Scofield says that the Antichrist is "the Beast out of the earth" of Revelation 13:11-17, and the "False Prophet" of Revelation 16:13, etc. Is this your view of it? If your answer be "Yes," then I must begin my study of the Antichrist question all over.

But I may say that if Dr. Scofield is correct in this, a good many expositors are wrong. Samuel J. Andrews, in his *Christianity and Anti-christianity*, page 62, says that the Beast symbolizes Antichrist—but the Beast he refers to is the Beast from the sea (page 62, 11th line).

Moreover, the "man of sin" of 2 Thessalonians 2:3, who is generally believed to be identical with Antichrist in sitting in the temple of God, "showing himself that he is God," corresponds more nearly to the Beast of Revelation 13:6-8, from the sea, than to the Beast out of the earth whose chief function seems to be to bring about worship of the "first Beast" (see close of verse 12).

Finally, Dr. Scofield, saying that Antichrist is the Beast out of the earth and the False Prophet refers as to the latter to Revelation 16:13. That passage clearly shows that the Beast and the Prophet are not one but two personages: three frogs are produced, one from the devil, one from the Beast, one from the Prophet; and Revelation 19:20 is to the same effect.

It is true that Dr. Scofield applies the name Antichrist to the second Beast instead of the first Beast of Revelation 13. This was not always true. In former years he spoke of the first Beast, that is, the King, as the Antichrist. And, upon my inquiring about the change with reference to this matter, he said that the word "Antichrist" occurs only in the Epistles of John, and always refers to false prophets or teachers, rather than to a political ruler. Therefore he had changed his mind about the person to whom the term itself ought to apply, and he always afterward referred to the False Prophet as the Antichrist, and to the King as "the Beast." I am not saying that I agree with him in all this, for I do not; but this was his position for many years and up to the time he went to be with the Lord. As to the citations, Revelation 16:13; 19:20; 20:10, in the footnote referred to, you will see that in all of those places both the "Beast" and "False Prophet" are mentioned, and I suppose that is why he used those citations.

For myself, I still believe the King is the Antichrist, but it is generally my custom to refer to both of these personages in Revelation 13 by terms other than "the Antichrist." In order to avoid all confusion as to the one I am talking about, I speak of the first as the Beast King, and of the other as the False Prophet.

The Last Gentile Ruler

Will you please elucidate Daniel 11:37? I have been informed that "Elohim" is translated "God" and could quite correctly be translated "gods." The latter version would seem to imply that the last ruler will be a Gentile.

The Revised Version of Daniel 11:37,38 reads: "Neither shall he regard the gods of his fathers, nor the desire of women, nor regard any god; for he shall magnify himself above all. But in his place shall he honor the god of fortresses; and a god whom his fathers knew not shall he honor with gold, and silver, and with precious stones and pleasant things." It is true that "Elohim," the usual Hebrew word for God, is nevertheless plural, and may quite properly read "gods" where the context permits. It is also true that the last ruler of the world before our Lord's return to reign will be a Gentile, as is proved by the imagery of "the sea" in Revelation 13:1. By the same token the False Prophet of Revelation 13:11 will be an apostate Jew, for he comes up "out of the earth."

Future Concurrent Events

Is it likely that the Rapture, the beginning of Daniel's seventieth week, and the making of the covenant between Antichrist and the

many, may take place at the same time? If not, what, in your opinion, would hinder it?

I believe "that the Rapture, the beginning of Daniel's seventieth week, and the making of the covenant between Antichrist and the many, may take place at the same time." According to my view of dispensational truth, this is exactly the program.

The Son of Perdition

In John 17:12 and 2 Thessalonians 2:3 we find the expression, "the son of perdition." Have I any reason to believe that these expressions refer to the same person, or are they only similar expressions?

The first reference is to Judas, while the second one is to the Antichrist of the last days. There are teachers who hold that Judas will be reincarnated in the Antichrist, but the theory, as it appears to me, rests upon insufficient grounds in Scripture.

Mark of the Beast

I have often thought of the mark of the Beast that is to be in the hands and foreheads of his followers. It seems to me that the mark in the forehead will be hatred of the Jew in the mind, and the mark in the hand will be refusal to help him in his terrible trouble; that the hand and mind of the followers of the Beast will be against the Jew and in sympathy with the plot of the Beast against them, and that all who give sympathy or help to the Jew will be put to death. What is your opinion?

I am not able to agree with you as to the nature of the mark of the Beast. I believe that it will be a literal mark that can be seen by observers. Otherwise how could it be a mark that would enable the bearer to buy or sell?

Six Hundred Threescore and Six

What is the meaning of "666" in Revelation 13:18?

I am not sure that I know, though I have read many explanations. Seven is the number of divine completeness in the Word, and these sixes seem to me an indication of Antichrist's attempt, with Satan's help, but always without success, to imitate or duplicate the works of God. He often reaches six but never seven. Six is man's number. In The Revelation there are two opposing trinities, the trinity of God and the trinity of Satan. Three sixes speak of Satan's unavailing attempt, through the Beast and the False Prophet, to work the works of God.

Death Sought and Not Found

What is the meaning of Revelation 9:6, "And in those days shall men seek death, and shall not find it; and shall desire to die, and death shall flee from them"?

It means that in that day men will try to commit suicide and shall be unable to do so. It is the judgment of the fifth trumpet, and its punishment is far worse than death, but men will not be allowed to escape the punishment by taking their own lives. Let us thank God that through our Lord's death and resurrection we are delivered from the wrath to come, "For God hath not appointed us to wrath, but to obtain salvation by our Lord Jesus Christ, who died for us, that, whether we wake or sleep, we should live together with him" (1 Thess. 5:9,10).

The Oil and the Wine

Will you please give an explanation of Revelation 8:6, the last clause: "and see thou hurt not the oil and the wine"?

The scene is in the midst of the Great Tribulation. The Antichrist appears as the first seal is opened (verses 1,2); then follows war (3,4), and famine (5,6), in which there is a scarcity of the necessaries of life, such as wheat and barley, though the luxuries are untouched, such as oil and wine.

Russia and Rome in the End-Time

I have promised myself for several months to write and ask for your explanation of what is to me an enigma in the events described in Scripture as ushering in Christ's visible return to deliver the Jews. In Ezekiel 38 and 39 appears Gog with Magog & Co. (said to be Russia, Germany, Persia, etc.), sweeping down on Jerusalem when Christ intervenes to save His people. Magog & Co. seem to fill the entire picture, with no room for other antagonists. In Revelation the Beast and the False Prophet with their military forces (said to be those of the restored ten-kingdom Roman Empire) are the destructive power assailing Jerusalem when Christ breaks through the clouds to defend the Jews. Here again the Roman Empire picture seems complete in itself, with no room for other actors. Please try to harmonize these two pictures. I believe it will be helpful to many Bible readers.

Details may not be perfectly clear in all this, but one thing that is clear is that in the final siege of Jerusalem "all nations" will be gathered "against Jerusalem to battle" (Zech. 14:2). Russia and her allies evidently begin their campaign during the time of the Great Tribulation in the latter half of Daniel's seventieth week. But it is evident that when Armageddon comes, Russia and Rome, though at enmity with each other, make common cause against Israel, and are thus found side by side fighting against the Lord and His people.

The Abomination of Desolation

What is "the abomination of desolation, spoken of by Daniel the prophet" and referred to by the Lord Jesus in Matthew 24:15?

In reply to your question I give herewith Dr. Scofield's exposition of Daniel 7: "This repeats, with added details, the story of Nebuchadnezzar's vision of the Monarchy-Colossus. It is the story of the four universal Gentile Monarchies told again. The characteristic difference is, that the Colossus vision gives the outward seeming of the successive world-powers; the Beast vision their character. Authority vested in the Gentile is rapacious, selfish, cruel. The history of the world since Nebuchadnezzar is a history of wars. An ocean of human blood has been shed. The national symbol of every world-power today is a beast or bird of prey.

"The 'great sea' is, in Scripture imagery, always a symbol of the mass of mankind; (1) the lion-like beast, Nebuchadnezzar (the 'head of gold' of chapter 2); (2) the bear beast, Medo-Persia; (3) the leopard beast, the Grecian power of Alexander, divided into 'four heads' after his death; (4) the beast with iron teeth; here is the last, or Roman, world-power again. As in the case of the Colossus vision, the greater part of the Beast vision and of its interpretation is given to Rome and what comes of Rome, (Roman civil power, not the Papacy.) As the Colossus had ten toes, so the fourth Beast has ten horns. These are explained in verse 24 to be 'ten kings that shall arise.' Much ingenuity has been expended in identifying the ten (toes—horns) fragments of the former Roman Empire. This is useless, as the prophecy still awaits its fulfillment. It was not fulfilled at Christ's First Advent, for the Roman power was not then divided at all. Even the preliminary division into East and West had not taken place. But the image vision requires that the smiting of the Stone cut out without hands shall be upon the feet; just as, in the Beast vision the ten-horn form is followed by the Kingdom of the Ancient of Days.

"The ten Kings meant by the toes and horns are therefore future Kings who are to rule over the sphere anciently dominated by Rome, at the time when the Stone shall smite and the Kingdom of 'the saints of the Most High' shall be set up. 'A blind man ought to see that the action of the Stone is judgment, not grace. The times of the Gentiles end in wrath and ruin, and there succeeds them the visible Kingdom of God' (Prof. W. G. Moorehead). (5) The 'little horn,' verses 8, 24-26, is an eleventh King, who shall rise among the ten and overcome three of them. This 'little horn' is the terrible being described by Paul (2 Thess. 2:1-10) and by John (Rev. 13:1-8). It is he who, after overcoming three of the ten horns (Kings) of Daniel 7, is received as Emperor by the others, thus reviving the Roman or fourth Beast dominion in a federate form, as we learn from Revelation, and who, sitting 'in the temple of God, showing himself that he is God,' according to 2 Thess. 2:4, becomes thus the 'abomination of desolation spoken of by Daniel the prophet,' of Dan. 11:31 and 12:11, and of Matt. 24:15. (6) This 'little horn,' 'man of sin,' 'beast out of the sea,' prevails until the 'Ancient of Days' comes, 'and the time that the saints possess the Kingdom' (verses 21-27)."

Armageddon

Is Armageddon to be the actual scene of battle between Christ's forces and the evil powers on earth? It seems that some take the position that, on account of the Lord coming to the Mount of Olives, the battle will be in that vicinity, and that Armageddon is only the gathering place for the evil forces.

For answer to this question I quote from Dr. C. I. Scofield again. He says: "Armageddon (the ancient hill and valley of Megiddo, west of Jordan in the plain of Jezreel), is the appointed place for the beginning of the great battle in which the Lord, at His coming in glory, will deliver the Jewish remnant besieged by the Gentile world-powers under the Beast and False Prophet. Apparently the besieging hosts, whose approach to Jerusalem is described in Isaiah 10:28-32, alarmed by the signs which precede the Lord's coming (Matt. 24:29,30), have fallen back to Megiddo, after the events of Zechariah 14:2, where their destruction begins, a destruction consummated in Moab and the plains of Idumea (Isa. 63:1-6) This battle is the first event in 'the Day of Jehovah,' and is the fulfillment of the smiting-stone prophecy of Daniel 2:35" (*Scofield Reference Bible*).

Again—Armageddon

How long a time is there between the battle of Armageddon and the Millennium?

The judgments ushering in the Millennium will follow immediately after the battle of Armageddon (Zech. 14; Rev. 19).

After the Great Tribulation

Are we to live on earth with the Lord Jesus after the Great Tribulation?

After being caught up to meet Him in the air, we shall "ever be with the Lord" (1 Thess. 4:17) and wherever He is we are to be also throughout eternity. The promise is that we are to reign with Him on the earth, or over the earth. We are to share with Him His Millennial glory.

Before the Great Tribulation and After

Do I understand you to teach that the Lord will come before the Tribulation period and that afterward He will come the third time? I can find only two comings.

The Lord will not come back to the earth until after the Great Tribulation. But before He comes back to the earth—and indeed before any other event in revealed prophecy—He must fulfill the word of 1 Thessalonians 4:13-18, by coming, not to the earth, but into the air. Of His coming to the earth it is written that "his feet shall stand in that day upon the mount of Olives, which is before Jerusalem on the east," and that "the Lord my God shall come, and all the saints with thee" (Zech. 14:4,5).

Of His coming into the air it is written that "the Lord himself shall descend from heaven with a shout, with the voice of the archangel, and with the trump of God: and the dead in Christ shall rise first: then we which are alive and remain shall be caught up together with them in the clouds, to meet the Lord in the air" (1 Thess. 4:16,17). This is the event, ever imminent, possible at any moment, which is held before us in the Epistles of the New Testament as an incentive to holiness of walk and fruitfulness in service. Our place is plainly indicated for us: we are "to serve the living and true God; and to wait for his Son from heaven, whom he raised from the dead, even Jesus, which delivered us from the wrath to come" (1 Thess. 1:9,10).

Those that Look for Him

Please explain Hebrews 9:28, especially the words, "and unto them that look for him shall he appear the second time without sin unto salvation."

The text points to the Second Coming of Christ to the earth at the end of Daniel's seventieth week and of the Great Tribulation. It has a special reference to Hebrews, and it is to them particularly, or the believing remnant among them, that the Messiah will thus come when He appears the second time. It has no bearing upon the Rapture of the Church.

The Fate of the Lost at the Second Advent

What will become of the lost who are living at the Second Coming of Christ to the earth?

They "shall be punished with everlasting destruction from the presence of the Lord, and from the glory of his power" (2 Thess. 1:9).

The Carcass and the Eagles

What is the meaning of Matthew 24:28 and Luke 17:37?

In Matthew 24:28 our Lord said: "For wheresoever the carcass is, there will the eagles be gathered together"; and in Luke 17:37, "Wheresoever the body is, thither will the eagles be gathered together." He is speaking of His coming as Judge to deal with His enemies, and He employs the figure of the dead carcass, and the birds of prey finding it, to show how impossible it will be to escape His judgment in that day. It is apparent that He had Job 39:27-30 in mind: "Doth the eagle mount up at thy command, and make her nest on high? She dwelleth and abideth on the rock, upon the crag of the rock, and the strong place. From thence she seeketh the prey, and her eyes behold afar off. Her young ones also suck up blood; and where the slain are, there is she" (compare Rev. 6:15-17).

"With Me"

What does "with me" mean in Isaiah 63:3, "of the people, there was no man with me"? When He comes, the Church comes "with" Him, and it is composed of people from every tribe and nation.

I take it that the word, "of the peoples there was no man with me," simply refers to the fact that in His judgment upon His enemies He will be alone. I do not mean that the redeemed will not return with Him when He comes to judgment, but the judgment itself is His own work and not theirs.

Distinguishing Things that Differ

How do you fit 2 Peter 3:10 and John 14:2-4 into the program of the Lord's Second Coming?

They refer to two distinct events. John 14:2-4 refers to the Rapture, or catching away, of the saved, which may transpire at any moment; 2 Peter 3:10 refers to the Day of the Lord, which begins with the Lord's coming to judgment at the end of the Great Tribulation, and includes the whole thousand-year period called the Millennium, finally merging at the end of that period into the Day of God (compare 1 Cor. 15:28).

The Day of His Preparation

What is meant by the expression, "in the day of his preparation" in Nahum 2:3? I have an idea that "the day of his preparation" is the same time as the "last days" of 2 Timothy 3:1-5.

The expression refers primarily to the judgment upon Nineveh pronounced by the prophet Nahum about a hundred years before its fulfillment in the destruction of that city. It is doubtless a foreshadowing of the coming destruction of apostate Christendom; but it apparently goes beyond the Timothy passage and points to a time subsequent to the apostasy foretold there. The Timothy passage predicts the apostasy itself; the Nahum passage looks on to the punishment following the apostasy.

That Day

Please explain 2 Thessalonians 2:1-3.

The passage in 2 Thessalonians 2 is confused because of a mistranslation in the second verse, where "the day of Christ" should read "the day of the Lord." This day, that is to say, the "day of the Lord," which begins with the actual coming of the Lord to earth to put an end to man's day—that day cannot come until there first be the apostasy and the revelation of the man of sin. Before all that, however, must come the "day of Christ" in connection with His coming into the air to catch away His people. That is the thing for which we wait, and at that time we are to be delivered from the wrath to come by being removed from this scene entirely, and we shall be with the Lord until the judgment is over.

Day of the Lord

What is meant by the day of the Lord in 2 Thessalonians 2:2? I have supposed that the day of the Lord was the Great Tribulation before the Millennium, though in 2 Peter 3:10, it seems to refer to the time after the Millennium when the earth shall be completely destroyed. What, in the latter passage, is the relation between the first clause concerning the day of the Lord and the second clause concerning the destruction of the earth?

The day of the Lord does not include the Great Tribulation; that awful event is in the closing time of Man's day. The day of the Lord begins with the coming of the Lord to judge and to make war (Rev. 19:11). But it is an extended period reaching all the way through the Millennial reign of the Lord and finally merging into the day of God at the close of that period. This definition, I think, reconciles all the passages on the subject. Dr. Scofield's definition is as follows: "The day of Jehovah (called, also, 'that day,' and 'the great day') is that lengthened period of time beginning with the return of the Lord in glory, and ending with the purgation of the heavens and the earth by fire preparatory to the new heavens and the new earth (Isa. 65:17-19; 66:22; 2 Peter 3:13; Rev. 21:1). The order of events appears to be: (1) The return of the Lord in glory (Matt. 24:29,30); (2) the destruction of the Beast and his host, 'the kings of the earth and their armies,' and the false prophet, which is the 'great and terrible' aspect of the day (Rev. 19:11-21); (3) the judgment of the nations (Zech. 14:1-9; Matt. 25:31-46); (4) the thousand years, that is, the Kingdom age (Rev. 20:4-6); (5) the Satanic revolt and its end (Rev. 20:7-10); (6) the second resurrection and final judgment (Rev. 20:11-15); and (7) the 'day of God,' earth purged by fire (2 Peter 3:10-13)."

Three Prophetic Days

Please explain the difference between the "day of Christ," the "day of the Lord" and the "day of God."

The "day of Christ" is related to the Rapture of 1 Thessalonians 4:16-18 and the events transpiring in Heaven immediately following that event—the judgment of believers' works, the marriage supper of the Lamb, etc. (1 Cor. 1:8; 5:5; 2 Cor. 1:14; Phil. 1:6, 10; 2:16). The expression, "the day of Christ," occurs in 2 Thessalonians 2:2 according to the Authorized Version, but this is an error in translation which the Revised Version rightly corrects to "the day of the Lord."

The "day of the Lord" is an expression frequently found in the Old Testament, and the New Testament has it in Acts 2:20 (quoted from Joel 2:31); 1 Thessalonians 5:2; 2 Thessalonians 2:2, R.V.; 2 Peter 3:10. It is also called "that day" and "the great day." It begins with the Second Coming of Christ (not His coming into the air for His people, but His coming to the earth with them) and extends through the Millennium.

The "day of God" is the end and consummation of the "day of the Lord" (2 Peter 3:10-13; compare 1 Cor. 15:24).

The Times of the Gentiles

When will the times of the Gentiles end, and what will occur?

The times of the Gentiles will end when our Lord Jesus Christ comes to earth the second time at the end of the Great Tribulation, to dethrone the last Gentile King—the Antichrist of Revelation 13—and ascend the throne of His father David and begin His reign as "King of kings, and Lord of lords." Of course, the Rapture of the saved will precede all this by Daniel's seventieth week of seven years.

The New Jerusalem

What is the New Jerusalem?

It is the abode of the glorified Church, "the bride, the Lamb's wife," as she will be manifested in the age to come (Rev. 21).

The New Earth

What will be the purpose of "the new earth"?

It is believed by many enlightened teachers that the new earth will be the permanent home of redeemed Israel. The promise to Abraham was "that he should be the heir of the world" (Rom. 4:13).

Judgment of the Nations

In Matthew 25:31-46, are the sheep and the goat, the saved and unsaved that shall appear before the Son of Man at the judgment, there being only one great judgment day, as I have been taught? Also, in verse 32 it speaks of nations being separated one from another. It seems to me it must refer to individuals.

The judgment of Matthew 25 is one of many judgments, having but little in common, for example, with the judgment of the Great White Throne of Revelation 20:11-15, which occurs after the thousand years are finished (Rev. 20:7), while the judgment of Matthew 25 takes place at Christ's Second Advent before the Millennium (Matt. 25:31; Rev. 19:11-16; 20:4-6). There is a third group at the judgment of nations, called by the Judge "My brethren" (verse 40). These are believed to be the Jewish messengers who, during the Great Tribulation, shall preach the Gospel of the Kingdom "in all the world for a witness unto all nations." The basis of the judgment is the treatment accorded to these "brethren" and their message.

It is true that those judged are not groups, as nations, but individuals. The word for "nations" might as well be rendered "Gentiles."

David's Throne

Is it true that Jesus of Nazareth was the only living heir to David's throne in His day? Please give the reasons for this conclusion.

Yes. The heir to David's throne must be of David's lineage not only, but he must not be of the lineage of Jehoiachin, who was the last king in David's line to sit upon David's throne, and who was deposed by Nebuchadnezzar 600 years before Christ. Jehoiachin's uncle, Mattaniah, was enthroned in Jehoiachin's place, and his name changed to Zedekiah. Jehoiachin reigned only three months, but his brief reign was marked by terrible wickedness. His name appears as "Jeconiah" in 1 Chronicles 3:16 and Jeremiah 24:1. In Jeremiah 22:24-30 he is called "Coniah." This last cited passage is most important:

As I live, saith Jehovah, though Coniah the son of Jehoiakim king of Judah were the signet upon my right hand, yet would I pluck thee thence; and I will give thee into the hand of them that seek thy life, and into the hand of them whose face thou fearest, even into the hand of Nebuchadnezzar, king of Babylon, and into the hand of the Chaldeans. And I will cast thee out, and thy mother that bare thee, into another country, where ye were not born; and there shall ye die. But to the land whereunto they desire to return, thither shall they not return. Is this man Coniah a despised broken idol? is he a vessel wherein is no pleasure? wherefore are they cast out, he and his seed, and are cast into a land which they know not? O earth, earth, earth, hear the word of Jehovah. Thus saith Jehovah, Write ye this man childless, a man that shall not prosper in his days; for no man of his seed shall prosper, sitting upon the throne of David, and ruling any more in Judah (Jer. 22:24-30).

Here doubtless is to be found the key to the right understanding of the genealogical tables of our Lord Jesus Christ in Matthew and Luke. According to the Old Testament prediction, the Messiah must be the heir to the throne in the kingly line and really the seed of David without being descended as pertaining to the flesh from the wicked King Coniah. It seems impossible that this could be brought about, but again the integrity of the Word of God is shown.

Matthew gives the genealogy of Joseph, the foster father of Jesus, and this table shows that Joseph would have been the rightful King of Israel were it not for the prohibition against the seed of Coniah. Luke, on the other hand, gives the ancestry of Jesus through His mother, Heli being the father-in-law of Joseph.

A writer in *The Bible Student and Teacher* says:

In the genealogy in Luke, Joseph is called—as clearly and distinctly as is possible to do it in the Greek language—the son-in-law of Heli, making Mary the daughter of Heli, and the genealogy hers. The word *nomizeto* is derived from *nomos*, law. As used in Luke 3:23, it is translated in the Authorized Version, in connection with the context:

"Being (as was supposed) the son of Joseph, which was the son of Heli."

This mistranslation ("as was supposed") is perpetuated in the Revised Version. Now this is not at all the meaning of the word. It means, according to the dictionaries, "to be regarded or reckoned according to custom;" more strictly, "according to law." In this case the statement is made that Joseph was the son of Heli, according to Jewish law; that is, his son-in-law, to use the exact English phrase in its translation. Nothing could well be clearer than this.

On this point we find Wordsworth bringing out the meaning, as follows:

"As he was accounted by law (*nomos*). See Luke 4:22; John 6:42. This word *enomizeto* appears to intimate two things: first, that Jesus was not the son of Joseph by nature; and secondly, that he was son of Joseph by law. And therefore, although He was the promised Seed of the woman, His genealogy is traced through Joseph, who was united to Mary by the law of marriage, which God had instituted in Paradise; and He had a hereditary claim to the right of Joseph as son of David, and owed him filial obedience. See Matthew 1:1."

The translation of the words referred to in Luke 3:23, as found in Wilson's Emphatic Diaglott is: "as was allowed" instead of "as was supposed." Samuel Sharpe also translates "as was allowed." Murdoch's translation from the Syriac

Peshito Version reads, "And he was accounted the Son of Joseph the Son of Heli." This would tend to support the contention of the writer just quoted.

Mrs. T. C. Rounds has called attention to the fact that it is cited by Lightfoot from the Talmudic writings concerning "the pains of hell" that Mary, the daughter of Heli, was seen in the infernal regions suffering horrid tortures.

Commenting upon this citation, Mrs. Rounds says: This statement, while showing the animosity of the Jews toward the Christian religion, gives us the fact that Mary was, according to received Jewish tradition, the daughter of Heli, hence that it is her genealogy we find in Luke. From the fact that no woman's name could appear in the table, Joseph's name as son-in-law of Heli was taken instead, and the line of Mary traced through David, but, mark you, through Nathan his son. Joseph is also traced to David, but he comes from Solomon the King. He is, however, barred from the throne by Jeconiah, of whom it was written: "Write ye this man childless . . . no man of his seed shall prosper, sitting upon the throne of David" (Jer. 22:30), which was literally fulfilled.

In addition to all this there are many other points which show that Jesus of Nazareth was the only living heir to David's throne. He was the "Righteous Branch" to be raised up unto David, the King, who shall "reign and prosper, and shall execute judgment and justice in the earth." According to Jeremiah 23:5,6, He must be God in the flesh. He must be called "Jehovah Our Righteousness." Then according to Isaiah 9:6,7, He must be "the mighty God, the Father of the ages, the Prince of Peace." According to Micah 5:2, He must be the one "whose goings forth have been from of old, from everlasting." There was no other such heir to David's throne.

Again, He must be in a peculiar sense the Seed of the woman. This necessitated the virgin birth, and, of course, there was no other man in David's line or elsewhere who could fulfill these conditions.

David's Throne to Be Restored

Will David's throne be again set up?

Certainly. Nothing is clearer than that the throne of David will be literally re-established. "For unto us a Child is born, unto us a Son is given; and the government shall be upon his shoulder: and his name shall be called Wonderful, Counselor, The mighty God, The everlasting Father, The Prince of Peace. Of the increase of his government and peace there shall be no end, upon the throne of David, and upon his kingdom, to order it, and to establish it with judgment and with justice from henceforth even forever. The zeal of the Jehovah of hosts will perform this" (Isa. 9:6,7; see also Jer. 23:5-8; Luke 1:31-33; the passages are too numerous for citation). Well does the Scofield Reference Bible say: "The 'throne of David' is a phrase as definite, historically, as 'throne of the Caesars,' and as little admits of 'spiritualizing.'"

The Sure Mercies of David

I have been referred to Genesis 49:10 as illustrative of a prophecy that never has been and never could be fulfilled. What would you say?

Was there a recognized ruler over the house or tribe of Judah until the coming of Christ?

David and all his descendants who reigned, first over all Israel and then over the kingdom of Judah, were included in the tribe of Judah. David's line is traced through Solomon and Rehoboam and their successors reigning in Jerusalem until the fall of Jerusalem about 600 B.C. when Jehoiachin was sitting upon David's throne. Jehoiachin is otherwise known as Jechoniah or Coniah. He was repudiated together with all his seed in Jeremiah 22:24-30, but in Jeremiah 23:5,6, it was declared that a righteous Branch should be raised up unto the house of David, and a King should reign and prosper, and execute judgment and justice in the earth, his name being, "the LORD our Righteousness" (Jehovah-tsidkenu). That righteous Branch is Jesus of Nazareth, who is descended from David, not through Joseph's ancestor Coniah, but through Mary who was descended from David through his son Nathan, and whose genealogy is given in Luke 3. The genealogy of Matthew 1 is that of Joseph, and Coniah's name appears in the form of "Jechonias."

Hoshea or Messiah

How can we know that the prophecy of Isaiah 11:10,11 was not fulfilled in Hoshea's reign?

The proof that "that day" could not have referred to the time of King Hoshea lies in the fact that up to the very time of the overturning of the kingdom of Israel, when Hoshea sat upon the throne, and even to the very time of the overturning of David's own throne in Jerusalem, there had been no return of the remnant of God's people from Assyria. The terms of the promise are that "it shall come to pass in that day that the Lord shall set his hand again the second time to recover the remnant of his people," etc. Plainly this is an unfulfilled prophecy and must refer to a future time in which "He shall set up an ensign for the nations, and shall assemble the outcasts of Israel, and gather together the dispersed of Judah from the four corners of the earth."

The Kingdom in a Picture

Whatever could our Lord have meant when He said in Matthew 16:28, Mark 9:1 and Luke 9:27, that some of those standing with Him should never taste of death until they had seen "the Son of man coming in His kingdom," and "the kingdom of God with power"?

The key to the solution of your problem is found in 2 Peter 1:16-18. Within a few days after our Lord's declaration, the transfiguration scene took place as described in the verses immediately following His statement in all three of the Synoptic Gospels. The transfiguration was the Kingdom of God in a picture. By studying the picture we may know what the Kingdom of God will be like when it is finally set up upon the earth. In the center of the picture is Christ Himself, not now humiliated, but rather glorified. Then there is Moses, representing those participating in the Kingdom who have gone to heaven through death and then returned with the Lord at His second advent. Also, there is

Elijah, representing those in the Kingdom who have gone to heaven without dying and have returned with the Lord to share His glory and His reign. And finally there are Peter and James and John, not glorified, but in their natural bodies, representing the place of Israel in the future Kingdom.

The Knowledge of the Glory

Is there any significant difference between the promise of Isaiah 11:9 and that of Habakkuk 2:14? The former verse speaks of the knowledge of the Lord, and the latter speaks of the knowledge of the glory of the Lord.

The difference is indeed significant. Those who carefully study the Scriptures cannot fail to trace throughout the Book God's eternal purpose to one day fill the earth with the knowledge of Him and His glory, and to do this through His people Israel. When Israel rebelled against Him at Kadesh-Barnea, He threatened to destroy them and raise up from Moses a greater and mightier nation. Moses, however, interceded for them, and, in Numbers 14:20,21, God said: "I have pardoned according to thy word: but as truly as I live, all the earth shall be filled with the glory of the Lord." Israel's rebellion had only delayed the fulfillment of the divine purpose.

In Isaiah 11:9 it is shown that when the "Righteous Branch" of David's house (that is, Christ Himself) sets up His kingdom, then the earth will be filled with the knowledge of Him. Habakkuk's vision is an advance over that of Isaiah. In a degree, the knowledge of the Lord is now being spread abroad in the earth, but the knowledge of the glory of the Lord awaits His coming in glory to set up His kingdom. Meanwhile, we who have been justified by faith and have peace with God are rejoicing in hope of His glory (Rom. 5:1,2).

Millennial Glory

To what glory does Haggai 2:7 refer?

The verse reads: "And I will shake all nations, and the desire of all nations shall come: and I will fill this house with glory, saith Jehovah of hosts." The reference, unmistakably, is to the millennial glory connected with Messiah's return and reign.

Judah First

Please tell me where to find this passage, and give some explanation of it: "And God shall gather Judah first, lest Israel vaunt themselves against them."

There is no such passage; you are evidently confusing Judges 7:2 and Zechariah 12:7, and the latter passage is probably the one you have in mind, reading as follows: "The LORD also shall save the tents of Judah first, that the glory of the house of David and the glory of the inhabitants of Jerusalem do not magnify themselves against Judah." The application is to the end-time when the Lord Jesus will return to set up the Kingdom of David; He will deal so wisely with His people that "they shall be no more two nations, neither shall they be divided into two kingdoms any more at all" (Ezek. 37:22), and "he shall set up an ensign for the nations, and shall assemble the outcasts of Israel, and gather together the dispersed of Judah from the four corners of the earth. The envy also of Ephraim shall depart, and the adversaries of Judah shall be cut off: Ephraim shall not envy Judah, and Judah shall not vex Ephraim" (Isa. 11:12,13).

Reign of Christ

There is a repeated statement regarding Christ's reign that has puzzled me, and as yet I have found no satisfactory explanation. See 2 Samuel 7:10; Isaiah 9:7; Luke 1:32,33; Revelation 20:1-6, etc. It is the "forever" that I want in harmony with the "thousand years." If the throne of David is occupied by our Lord on earth forever, where does the thousand years come in? If in another sphere, after the Millennium, is it still the throne of David?

It is true that the reign of Christ will last for a thousand years, and also that it will last forever, even after the thousand years is over. The difference will be that the Kingdom will change in its form, so to speak, for at the end of the thousand years, Satan is to be cast into the Lake of Fire (Rev. 20:10), after which righteousness shall not only reign, but shall dwell forever.

The words of 1 Corinthians 15:24-28 do not intimate the end of Messiah's reign. Commenting upon these verses Dr. Scofield says: "Upon His return the King will restore the Davidic monarchy in His own person, regather dispersed Israel, establish His power over all the earth, and reign one thousand years (Matt. 24:27-30; Luke 1:31-33; Acts 15:14-17; Rev. 20:1-10). The Kingdom of Heaven, thus established under David's divine Son, has for its object the restoration of the divine authority in the earth, which may be regarded as a revolted province of the great Kingdom of God. When this is done (verses 24,25) the Son will deliver up the Kingdom (of Heaven, Matt. 3:2) to 'God, even the Father,' that 'God' (that is, the triune God, Father, Son, and Holy Spirit) 'may be all in all' (verse 28). The eternal throne is that 'of God and of the Lamb' (Rev. 22:1). The Kingdom age constitutes the seventh dispensation."

Millennial Conditions

Your teaching seems to indicate that during the Millennium the Church will be associated with Christ as His Bride in His reign over the earth. That would mean that people with glorified bodies would be mingling with and ministering to other people with natural bodies. How could that be?

I do not know how anything can be; but that this kind of thing is not impossible may be seen from the fact that the risen and glorified Christ did that very thing during the forty days of many infallible proofs between His resurrection and ascension. Never mind the "how" of these things. We have a God who can do great things, and we may depend upon Him to do whatever He undertakes.

Millennial Judgment

We have heard that all who sin during the Millennial period will be judged immediately by death. If this is the case, where will those come from whom Satan will gather together after he is loosed from the pit?

There is no clear teaching in the Bible that "all who sin during the Millennial period will be judged immediately by death," though some teachers have inferred such teaching from Psalm. 101:8, which, according to the Revised Version, says, "Morning by morning will I destroy all the wicked of the land or earth; to cut off all the workers of iniquity from the city of Jehovah"; and Isaiah 11:4, where it is written of the Millennial King that "with the breath of his lips shall he slay the wicked." But these are only inferences after all, and inferences are dangerous things in the building of Bible doctrines.

The Millennial Kings

Who are "the kings of the earth" in Revelation 21:24-26?

They are the co-rulers with Christ in the Millennial Kingdom. "Fear not, little flock; for it is your Father's good pleasure to give you the Kingdom."

During the Millennium

1. What Scriptural authority do you have for making the statement that there will be conversions during the Millennium?

2. Where in the Bible is it implied that there will be sinners during the Millennium, and that they will die during that period?

3. You say that probably no saints will die during the Millennium, or if they die, they will probably be immediately raised from the dead. Are these the ones who have accepted Christ after the first resurrection? I understand that those who are caught up to meet the Lord in the air have put on immortality, and death is swallowed up in victory as far as they are concerned.

4. What Scriptures deal with multitudes being born during the Millennium? I was under the impression that there would be no births during the Millennium.

In Isaiah 65:20, in a passage plainly referring to the Kingdom in manifestation, it is written that "there shall be no more thence an infant of days, nor an old man that hath not filled his days: for the child shall die an hundred years old; but the sinner being an hundred years old shall be accursed." This shows that there will be death and sin during the Millennium, and also a great lengthening of human life, so that a person who is a hundred years old will be considered a child; and one dying at that age without getting saved will be under a peculiar curse.

Though at the opening of the thousand years every soul admitted into the Kingdom is saved, there are to be accounted for the multitudes who will be born during the long period. These will be saved only if they believe on the Lord Jesus Christ and acknowledge Him, even as it is today. As Scofield says,

"The fact that the Kingdom age begins with a purgation of the nations does not imply that the descendants of those who are saved and enter the Kingdom will all be Christians. Some of the wickedest men in the world today are the sons of godly parents."

This accounts for the army of Satan gathered at the end of the thousand years to go against the Lord and His saints (Rev. 20:7-9). By the saints who may (or may not) die during the Millennium are meant those who have become saints during the Millennium, and not those caught away in the Rapture.

Our Residence during the Millennium

When Jesus comes back to this earth to sit on the throne of His father David, where will the Gentile Christians be?

The glorified Church, which will dwell in the new Jerusalem, is the Bride of the Lamb. But we have the assurance that where He is we shall be also. We shall therefore, I suppose, have access to both the heavenly Jerusalem and the new Jerusalem. We shall not be limited by being in earthly bodies and we will probably be surprised where we shall go in that day, and how.

Sin during the Millennium

With Satan and all his powers and principalities bound, why will people sin during the Millennium?

It is easy to answer your question about sin in the Millennium. There is no need for the presence of Satan in order to have sin in the flesh. Just let the flesh alone, and without any help it will certainly sin and do nothing but sin.

Sin and Death during the Millennium

Will there be sin in the Millennium, and temptation, and death, notwithstanding the binding of Satan?

Yes, there will be sin, temptation, and death during the thousand-years' reign of Christ, despite the fact that during the whole period Satan will be bound and confined to the bottomless pit. It is true that at the opening of the Kingdom age there will be none but born-again ones in the Kingdom. But these will doubtless beget many sons and daughters as the Kingdom age progresses, and these sons and daughters and their descendants must themselves be born again in order to be saved. Obedience to the will of the King will be enforced, but that all hearts will not be His is shown by the fact that, at the end of the Millennium, Satan, being loosed from his prison, finds it possible to gather an enormous army—the number of whom is as the "sand of the sea"—against "the camp of the saints" and "the beloved city" (Rev. 20:7-9).

The Kingdom age will be the final test of the flesh—the natural man—and under the most favorable environment, free from the machinations of Satan; and it will result, as all other tests have resulted, in the failure of man, and judgment from God. Isaiah 65 depicts Millennial conditions. In verse 17 there is in view the eternities after the Millennium has ended, but in verses 18-25 we see the Millennium itself. Verse 20 speaks of great longevity, but it also speaks of sin and death: "There shall be no more thence an infant of days, nor an old man that hath not filled his days: for the child shall die an hundred years old; but the sinner being an hundred years old shall be accursed." This is not the final state of man, for after the rebellion of Satan there will come the end of death itself (1 Cor. 15:26; Rev. 20:7-14; 21:1-4).

At the End of the Millennium

Where will Christ and His saints be during the time when Satan is loosed for a little season as mentioned in Revelation 20:3?

The matter is more fully referred to in Revelation 20:7-9. The name of Christ is not mentioned in this connection, but there is mention of "the camp of the saints," meaning, as I suppose, the gathering of the earthly saints who have turned to Christ during the Millennial reign. That they are located near Jerusalem is evident from the mention of "the holy city."

Our Lord's Subjects in the Millennium

Revelation 13:15 says that "the image of the beast should . . . cause that as many as would not worship the image of the beast should be killed." Revelation 19:21 says that "the remnant were slain with the sword of him that sat upon the horse." Now, if the Beast kills all the good people, and the Lord slays all the bad people, over whom will Jesus reign during the thousand years?

The statement of Revelation 13:15 is not that all who refuse to worship the Beast and his image should be killed, but only that to the second Beast there was given power to "cause that as many as would not worship the image of the beast should be killed." There is no record that he will execute that power upon everyone who thus refuses to worship. With reference to Revelation 19:21 I take it that "the remnant" refers only to the remnant of the armies gathered together to make war against the Lord (verse 19). Those armies certainly will not include all the people living on earth.

Death in the Millennium

Will any people die during the Millennium? And if so, are they immediately changed and taken into the Kingdom?

That there will be death for sinners in the Millennium is evident from Isaiah 65:20. What happens to one who is born again during the Kingdom age is not revealed, so far as I know.

Bloody Offerings in the Millennium

How can Ezekiel 43:21 be still awaiting fulfillment in view of the statement of Hebrews 10:8?

The final chapters of Ezekiel give a detailed description of bloody offerings to be resumed during the Millennium. It is evident that the purpose of these will be memorials, pointing backward to the "one sacrifice for sins forever" (Heb. 10:12) accomplished on Calvary. The bloody offerings of the past dispensation were memorials, pointing forward to that offering. In the incident of Melchizedek and Abram, there is an illustration of this principle. It represented the eating the Lord's Supper almost 2000 years before Calvary (Gen. 14:18), pointing forward to Calvary. We who are living now are eating the Lord's Supper pointing backward to Calvary. God would always be reminding His people of the fact that "the blood of Jesus Christ his Son, cleanseth us from all sin" (1 John 1:7).

Christ's Endless Kingdom

How can we reconcile Luke 1:33, where we are told that Christ's Kingdom shall have no end, with 1 Corinthians 15:24, where it is stated that there will be the end, when Christ shall relinquish His throne to the Father?

I suppose the answer is that even after He "shall have delivered up the kingdom to God, even the Father," Christ will continue as King by the decree of the Triune God, that He—the Triune God—"may be all in all" (verse 28). The eternal throne is that "of God and of the Lamb" (Rev. 22:1).

Future Generations

In Isaiah 65:20 it speaks of the child dying an hundred years old, also of "the sinner." If, as seems to be intimated, this verse refers to the time after the completion of the Millennium, I should like to ask if there is any other part of Scripture that teaches that there will be perpetual generations of people, some at least of whom will be sinners and will die? Perhaps the Scripture which says "there will be no more death" refers to saved ones? Is this speculation merely, or is there enough in Scripture about the matter to justify us in such inquiries? May speculations become detrimental to the Lord's interests?

There may be such danger in mere "speculations." But all that God has spoken of in His Book is "written for our learning" (Rom. 15:4), and we do well to study it carefully, taking heed meanwhile lest we be led into by-paths of mere speculation and become wise beyond what is written. I am satisfied that Isaiah 65:20 refers to conditions during the Millennium rather than afterwards. I believe, too, that, following the close of the Millennial period, and when the Kingdom shall have been turned over to the Father, "there shall be no more death." Further than this I have no light.

The Books and the Book

What are the books which are mentioned in Revelation 20:12, in connection with the judgment of the lost dead?

They are the records of those who are arraigned before the throne in that judgment. By these books it will be shown that all are guilty before God. Then another book is opened which is the book of life. And it is written that "whosoever was not found written in the book of life was cast into the lake of fire."

Judgment of the Wicked Dead

If the wicked dead are to be judged "according to their works" (Rev. 20:11-15) is their punishment in proportion to the goodness of their works? It seems that the punishment of all is the same, since they are all cast into the lake of fire, but then how is the judgment "according to their works"?

The judgment of the wicked dead is not "in proportion to the goodness of their works," for the very good reason that their works have no goodness (Rom. 3:12). The judgment will be according to what they have done with reference to the Christ of God. If they have heard the Gospel and rejected it, as so many people have done, and very often for some of them, their punishment will be far more severe than that of those who have never heard it at all. This is what I understand by the expression, "judged according to their works."

The Eternal Creation

Where is a place in the Bible where it says that all things shall pass away and there shall be a new heaven and a new earth? I believe it says, "Heaven and earth shall pass away." It has always puzzled me to know how Heaven can pass away when it is supposed to be eternal.

You are probably thinking of 2 Peter 3:5-13. From a careful reading of the passage, I think you will see that the present heaven and earth are to be changed into a new heaven and a new earth, as was the case in the time of the flood.

PEOPLE AND PLACES

An Apparent Discrepancy

I need an explanation of the apparent contradiction between 2 Kings 18:5 and 23:25. Each of these kings, according to the record, seems to be greater than the other.

The difference seems to be that Josiah's devotion was particularly "according to all the law of Moses." The revival under him was a Bible revival, in which the people were quickened in their desire to know the Scriptures and obey them.

Rahab the Harlot

Why did Joshua's spies go to a harlot's house? Why not some morally good house? Or did "harlot" have a different meaning in Bible times?

There has been no change in the meaning of the word "harlot." It may have been that Rahab was the only person in Jericho willing to receive the spies. In our day the Lord Jesus Himself is usually denied admission to what you call "morally good" homes. When He was here His enemies complained that He received sinners and ate with them (Luke 5:30-32). And in Matthew 21:31,32, He said to His critics: "The publicans and the harlots go into the kingdom of God before you. For John came unto you in the way of righteousness, and ye believed him not; but the publicans and the harlots believed Him: and ye, when ye had seen it, repented not afterward, that ye might believe him."

And consider how far the grace of God went in the case of Rahab. She not only has a place among the immortals of Hebrews 11 (verse 31), but she actually became an ancestress of the Lord Jesus according to the flesh (Matt. 1:5). The vital difference between Rahab and the "morally good" people in Jericho was that while she and they were all sinners, she was a believing sinner and they were unbelieving sinners. Therefore she was saved and they were lost.

How Elijah Obtained Water

Will you please explain how, after three and a half years of drought, the Prophet Elijah was able to find twelve barrels of water for drenching his sacrifice on Mount Carmel, as described in 1 Kings 18:33-35?

It has been pointed out that there are springs on Carmel which in modern times are never dry. Of course, these might have dried up after so long a time without rain. But it is certain that scarcely fifteen miles away from the scene on Carmel there is the Mediterranean sea, and, although its salt water is not good to drink, it would do very well in quenching any fire but the fire of God. To transport twelve barrels of water for fifteen miles would present no difficulty. In any event, the water was there, for the Word of God records the fact.

Dog and Hog

What is meant by the words of Matthew 7:6: "Give not that which is holy unto the dogs, neither cast ye your pearls before swine"? Who are the dogs, and who are the swine?

The dog and the hog were both unclean according to the Levitical law, and neither of them could be used for food or for sacrifice. Both words are used in 2 Peter 2:22 as figures of those who trifle with the Word of God. They are unsaved professors who have never been really born again. It is quite possible for them to avoid much of the world's pollution by mere contact with God's people, and then be entangled therein and overcome. It is better not to have known the way of salvation, than after they have known it to despise it and to turn away from the holy commandment delivered unto them. "But it happened unto them according to the true proverb, the hog is turned to his own vomit again; (Prov. 16:11), and the sow that was washed to her wallowing in the mire."

Casting Pearls Before Swine

What does it mean when it says don't cast your pearls before swine?

The Scripture referred to is Matthew 7:6, where our Lord says: "Give not that which is holy unto the dogs, neither cast ye your pearls before swine, lest they trample them under their feet, and turn again and rend you." Dogs are in Scripture a type of men who are openly unclean (compare Deut. 23:17,18, with Phil. 3:2,3 and Matt. 7:21-23). Swine are a familiar figure (2 Peter 2:22). They speak typically of those people who not only reject the Word of God but despise it. It may be that our Lord in using the figure was thinking of Proverbs 11:22, which says: "As a jewel of gold in a swine's snout, so is a fair woman which is without discretion."

Casting Out Devils

What do you understand is meant by "casting out devils" in the Bible? It says that Jesus would not let them speak, for they knew Him.

The phrase ought to read, "casting out demons." No one is really called a devil in the Bible except Satan and Judas. In John 6:70 Judas Iscariot is actually called a devil by the Lord Jesus Himself. The Greek word for "devil" is *diabolos*, which means adversary, and it is usually translated Satan. The demons are identical with the unclean spirits which sometimes took possession of men, and which were often cast out of men by the Lord Jesus. He forbade them to speak because He is somewhat particular about the source of any testimony. The devil and his emissaries are liars generally, and our Lord does not want the testimony of liars.

The Cave of Machpelah

There seems to be a discrepancy between the statement of Genesis 23:16-20, where Abraham is said to have purchased the field of Ephron, including the cave of Machpelah, and the statement of Genesis 33:19, that Jacob purchased the same field. If Abraham had bought the field for four hundred shekels of silver, why should Jacob buy the same field for one hundred shekels of silver? Was it not already his property?

The probable answer is that during the interval of 80 years between the two transactions the descendants of Hamor laid claim to the field, and that instead of asserting his title by inheritance Jacob repurchased the field. This is a perfectly natural supposition and disposes of any discrepancy between the two statements. See Genesis 49:29-32; 50:13; Joshua 24:32.

Abraham's Descendants

What is the difference between Hebrew, Israelite and Jew?

Hebrew is the racial name, Israel is the national name, and Jew the religious name for the descendants of Abram through Isaac and Jacob.

Abram and His Family

I had a question from an unbeliever the other day, with reference to Terah and Abram. The days of Terah were 205. Abram seems to have been born when Terah was 70 years old, and he left Haran when he, Abram, was 75 years old. The answer must be either that Abram left Haran before Terah died, contrary to the usual belief, or else he was born a good many years "after" Terah became 70, Nahor and Haran being his elders. It's not an important question of itself, but don't these people fling all sorts of puzzles at one?

They do, indeed. Let us see:

Haran was Terah's first-born son; Nahor, the second; and Abram the youngest; although Abram is named first in the record probably because he was the heir of the promises.

Haran was the father of Lot, Milcah and Iscah (Gen. 11:26-29). Milcah married her uncle Nahor and bore eight sons unto him, including Bethuel, the father of Rebekah who became Isaac's wife (Gen. 22:20-23).

Haran's second daughter, Iscah, the sister of Lot and Milcah, according to Jewish tradition, is identical with Sarai, who became Abram's wife (see Josephus—*Antiquities* 1:6, Section 5). This is quite possible, for there is no distinction in the Hebrew of the Old Testament between the words for daughter and granddaughter. If the Jewish tradition referred to is correct, then Sarai was the granddaughter of Abram's father, but not the granddaughter of his mother (Gen. 20:12). According to this understanding of the matter, Sarai became the wife of her uncle Abram, as her sister Milcah became the wife of her uncle Nahor.

Nahor, by the way, was named after Terah's father, the grandfather of Terah's three sons, Haran, Nahor and Abram.

The statement in Genesis 11:26 that, "Terah lived seventy years, and begat Abram, Nahor, and Haran," proves nothing as to the order of their birth. That Haran was the eldest of the three brothers is apparent from the fact that his brothers married his daughters, and that Sarai at the time of her marriage was only ten years younger than her Uncle Abram. When Abram, the youngest of the three brothers, was born, Terah was 130 years old, as appears from comparing Genesis 11:31 and 12:4 with Acts 7:2-4.

Experts in chronology agree that Abram's first call "when he was in Mesopotamia, before he dwelt in Charran (Haran)" (Acts 7:2), came to him in his sixtieth year; and the second call leading him out of Charran, "when his father was dead" (Acts 7:4) came, as we know, when he was 75 years old (Gen. 12:4). Abram's name, meaning "High father," was afterwards changed to Abraham, meaning, "Father of many nations"; and Sarai's name, meaning, "My princess," was changed to Sarah, meaning, "Princess," omitting the "my," since now she was to become not only a princess in a local and limited sense, but a mother of many nations, and therefore a sort of universal princess.

Abraham's Second Family

The Bible tells us that God performed a miracle upon the body of Abraham in order that Isaac might be born. But is it not true that Abraham begat other children after Isaac?

Yes, indeed. God did for Abraham "exceeding abundantly above" all that he asked or thought. After Sarah's death Abraham took another wife named Keturah and by her he fathered numerous children, whose names are given to us in Genesis 25:1-4. And here is a beautiful type. Sarah stands for "the mother of us all," that is, of all those who by grace through faith plus nothing have been born again and have become children of God and joint heirs with Christ, the antitype of Isaac (John 3:6-8; Gal. 4:26-29; Heb. 2:11-13; Heb. 1:2; Rom. 8:16,17). Keturah, who became Abraham's wife after the blessing had come through Isaac, may typify the future blessing coming to Israel as the natural seed of Abraham and as Jehovah's wife (Hos. 2:1-23; Deut. 30:1-9).

Was Moses Virgin Born?

Was Moses a virgin's son, as our Lord was? I have seen it so stated in a typical study comparing Moses as a type with Christ as the antitype.

No. All that was probably meant by the comparison was that Moses was adopted as the son of Pharaoh's daughter.

Moses' Disobedience

Can you explain Exodus 4:24,25 for me? It reads: "And it came to

pass by the way in the inn, that the Lord met him, and sought to kill him. Then Zipporah took a sharp stone, and cut off the foreskin of her son, and cast it at his feet, and said, Surely a bloody husband art thou to me."

The picture is clear. Moses had been yielding to his wife Zipporah, who objected to the circumcision of their son, which should have been done when he was eight days old. Moses is now responding to God's call for service, and yet God threatens to kill him in the way. Zipporah recognized the cause, and she herself, though reluctantly, circumcised the son, saying to Moses, "thou art a bloody husband unto me." The lesson for us is plain. The Lord Jesus is a bloody Husband unto us, and if we are to be used in God's service we must obey His Word.

Moses' Disobedience

In Exodus 4:24 whom did the Lord meet and seek to kill?

He threatened to kill Moses for his disobedience in failing to circumcise his son. From the record it appears that Moses had listened to his wife's protests during the years since the son was born, instead of obeying the commandment to circumcise the son when he was eight days old. See Genesis 17:9-14.

Moses' Parents

Who were the father and mother of Moses?

Moses' father's name was Amram, and his mother's, Jochebed (see Ex. 6:20).

The Body of Moses

What is meant by the contention between Michael and Satan about the body of Moses as referred to in the Epistle of Jude, verse 9?

When Moses died God buried him in a secret place unknown to man (Deut. 34:5,6). The suggestion comes from Josephus that this was because the children of Israel might have made an idol of Moses' body, had they known where it was. Of course we do not know whether this is true or not. In Matthew 17 Moses appeared with Elijah and the Lord Jesus on the mount of transfiguration, and that means Moses had his glorified body by that time. It is evident therefore that Michael had succeeded against Satan's opposition in recovering Moses' body from the tomb in order that it might appear on the mount.

The "Rabble"

Who constituted the "rabble" going up out of Egypt with the people of Israel in the Exodus (Num. 11:4-6)?

The mixed multitude ("rabble") consisted of Egyptians who went along with the children of Israel as they separated from Egypt, attracted no doubt by the miraculous character of Israel's deliverance. This rabble is a type of unconverted church members in our day. They join the churches, professing to be Christians, but without any real change of heart. They may be quite sincere in their profession at the moment, but sincerity will never take the place of regeneration.

This rabble then as now were the cause of weakness and division among the people of God. In Numbers 11:4-6 we read that "the rabble that was among them fell a lusting"; that is, they were not satisfied with the manna that God sent down from Heaven and desired the food of Egypt instead; "and the children of Israel also wept again, and said, Who shall give us flesh to eat? We remember the fish, which we did eat in Egypt freely; the cucumbers, and the melons, and the leeks, and the onions, and the garlic; but now our soul is dried away: there is nothing at all, beside this manna, before our eyes."

The manna was a type of Christ as God's appointed food for His people, the bread of Heaven. Unconverted church members of today, because they have lost their appetite for Christ as the bread of God, will turn to the things of the world, and will desire and demand that the things pleasing to the flesh be included in the work and way of the church. And because of their lusting after these things, such as extravagant buildings, ritualistic ceremonies, and "smooth things" from the mouth of the preachers, many of those who are unspiritual among God's real children are carried away also.

Decendants of Noah

I recently heard it stated that all the people now living upon the earth, white and black, red and brown and yellow, are descended from Noah. Is this true?

Yes. In the flood of Noah's time all human life was wiped off the face of the earth excepting Noah and his family. Only eight persons were saved from drowning. These were Noah and his wife and their three sons and their wives. The three sons were Sham, Ham and Japheth. The Genesis 10 tells about their descendants, and this chapter is esteemed by students of ethnology as the most important document in existence relating to that science. See Genesis 7:7; 9:18,19.

Jacob Not a Jew

If Jacob was a Jew, why was not Esau his twin brother a Jew also?

Neither Jacob nor Esau was a Jew, though both were Hebrews. Hebrew is a racial word, but Jew is a religious word, coming from the religion of Judaism. This religion was so named because from the tribe of Judah came the royal line and thus the leadership in the nation to which the religious system was given. The first occurrence of the word "Jew" in the Bible is in the plural—the Jews—in 2 Kings 16:6, and the first person called a Jew in the Scriptures was Mordecai, in Esther 2:5. We now call all Hebrews Jews, but, strictly speaking, as it is written in Romans 2:28,29, "he is not a Jew, which is one outwardly; but he is a Jew, which is one inwardly; and circumcision is that of the heart in the spirit, and not in the letter, whose praise is not of men, but of God."

Esau's Tears

In God's Word it is made plain that any sin is forgiven if truly repented of, but I would like you to explain Hebrews 12:16,17. Why was not Esau forgiven? It says he sought forgiveness with tears.

I am sorry, but it does not say that. What it says is that "he found no place for repentance, though he sought it carefully with tears." Repentance is very different from forgiveness. Repentance means a change of mind. The Revised Version reads: "he found no place for a change of mind in his father, though he sought it diligently with tears."

An Imaginary Discrepancy

Is there not a discrepancy between the statements of the twenty-sixth and the twenty-seventh verses of Genesis 46? In one verse the figures are 66 and in the other they are 70. Can you explain?

Yes, very easily, for the discrepancy is only imaginary. In verse 26 you have "the souls that came with Jacob into Egypt," and in verse 27 you have "all the souls of the house of Jacob which came into Egypt." You must add to the 66 who came with Jacob, those of his house whom he found already there, namely, Joseph and his two sons, and Jacob himself; which makes the total 70.

Illegitimate Children

There is a passage in Scripture that I do not understand. It mentions something about bastards not being able to enter the Kingdom of Heaven. I know that some mothers are unfortunate and they are good Christian mothers. Please explain this.

Deuteronomy 23:2 says: "A bastard shall not enter into the congregation of the Lord; even unto the tenth generation shall he not enter into the congregation of the Lord." This says nothing about entering the Kingdom of Heaven: It refers only to the congregation of the Lord in Israel under the law. Under the Gospel there is the gift of eternal life for whosoever will receive it. Incidentally, let me point out that one of the persons named in the genealogical table of Luke was born out of wedlock, namely Phares, son of Judah by Tamar (Gen. 38). This is the genealogy of Mary herself through her father Eli (printed Heli). In Matthew's genealogy of Joseph there is also the name of Bathsheba, who bore a child of David out of wedlock; but this child died, and Solomon was born of her after David had made her his wife (2 Sam. 11). Our Lord was not descended from Solomon but from another son of David named Nathan. (Compare Matt. 1:6,7 and Luke 3:31.) All this shows how grace has overleaped every obstacle. Praise God! "Whosoever will may come."

A Man After God's own Heart

Why did God call David call "a man after mine own heart" (Acts 13:22)?

Because David believed what God told him, and stood for Him when he had to stand alone among men. David was a great sinner, and God's heart was grieved by that, but when David's sin was called to his attention he did not seek to justify himself. He confessed his sin, and was freely forgiven, though God brought severe suffering upon him in discipline. "Whom the Lord loveth he chasteneth."

No Contradiction

Can you harmonize the two accounts in 2 Samuel of King Saul's daughter who was married to David and separated by King Saul? One account said she had no children unto her death; in a later chapter it said she bore five children.

I am sorry, but it is not exactly said that "she bore five children." It is true that in 2 Samuel 6:23 it is written that "Michal the daughter of Saul had no children unto the day of her death"; and that in 2 Samuel 21:8,9, it is written that King David took "the five sons of Michal the daughter of Saul, . . . and delivered them into the hands of the Gibeonites." But notice that in the eighth verse these "five sons of Michal" were only her adopted children, "whom she brought up for Adriel." Adriel was Michal's brother-in-law, being the husband of Michal's sister Merab (1 Sam. 18:19).

"Ye Are Gods"

Are men ever called gods in the Bible?

Yes. In Psalm 82:6, addressing the human judges and rulers, God says: "I have said, Ye are gods; and all of you are children of the most high." And, in John 10:31-36, when our Lord said, "I and my Father are one," the Jews threatened to stone Him, "for blasphemy; because that thou, being a man, makest thyself God" (31-33). And He in reply said: "Is it not written in your law, I said, Ye are gods? If he called them gods, unto whom the word of God came, and the scripture cannot be broken; say ye of him, whom the Father hath sanctified, and sent into the world, Thou blasphemest; because I said, I am the Son of God?" (34-36).

In verse 30 the word "are" is in the masculine gender—"we" (two persons) are; while the word "one" is neuter—one thing. That would signify that He and His Father are not one in person, but one in nature. This disposes of the teaching that there is only one person in the Godhead, and that the Son is inferior to the Father.

Those called gods in Psalm 82 are the judges or magistrates as the official representatives and commissioned agents of God. Our Lord's comparison of Himself with them was intended to show that the idea of a communication of the divine majesty to human nature was not foreign to the revelations of the Old Testament. But there is also a contrast between Him and these men "unto whom the word of God (merely) came." It is never recorded of our Lord that the Word of God came to Him, for He Himself was—and is—the Word of God. The Jews did not understand Him to claim to be a god in the sense of

Psalm 82, or they would not have threatened to stone Him; but God in the sense of Deity; and this claim He acknowledged, both here and in chapter 5.

Driving Out the Canaanites

How could a righteous God drive the Canaanitish nations out of their land before the children of Israel?

It was the very righteousness of God that compelled Him to do it. These nations had become so corrupt as to make it necessary for a just God to judge and destroy them. Read Leviticus 18, especially verses 24-30, and also Deuteronomy 12:29-32.

The Daysman

What did Job mean by a "daysman" (Job 9:33)?

The word has the same meaning as "mediator." The answer to Job's desire for a daysman is found in 1 Timothy 2:5,6.

Philemon and Onesimus

What is the meaning of the phrase, "in the flesh," in verse 16 of the Epistle to Philemon?

It must mean that Philemon and Onesimus were brothers in the physical sense, sons of the same parents. If this is what Paul meant to say, he could not have used Philemon's language. It is apparent that Philemon had enslaved his own brother, and Paul in the Epistle is urging him to set him free.

Ezra's Shame

Why was Ezra ashamed to ask the king's help, as stated in Ezra 8:22?

The reason is given in the verse Itself. "I was ashamed because we had spoken unto the king, saying, 'The hand of our God is upon all them for good that seek him; but his power and his wrath is against all them that forsake him.'" Ezra felt that, after having given such a testimony, he must act accordingly. And "so," as he says in verse 23, "we fasted and besought our God for this: and he was entreated of us." Ezra was glad for what the king had already done to further his expedition (Ezra 7:27,28); but to accept help willingly offered, and to ask for help, are two different things.

Nehemiah's Woe

How long did it take Nehemiah to get the wall around Jerusalem rebuilt?

Fifty-two days (Neh. 6:15), and it was a marvelous accomplishment. Of course, there was much to be done after the wall had been sufficiently "finished" to shut out the enemy, but to get even this done in less than eight weeks was an astonishing feat. It was only possible because Nehemiah was a great leader, and because "the people had a mind to work" (Neh. 4:6). The opposition was fivefold: (1) by ridicule (2:19; 4:1-6), (2) by anger (4:7-9), (3) by opposition of discouraged brethren (4:10-23), (4) by greed (5:1-19), and (5) by craft (6:1-14).

The Edomites

Of what nation is it said in Scripture that God hates it forever?

You are probably thinking of Edom, the people descended from Esau, Jacob's twin brother. Their land was called Edom, or Idumea. God never forgave Edom for refusing to allow Israel to pass through its land in the days of the exodus (Num. 20:14-21; Lam. 4:22; Jer. 49:7-22; Ezek. 25:12-14; 32:29,30; 35:1-15; 36:5; Joel 3:19; Amos 1:11,12).

The book of Obadiah is altogether occupied with the humiliation of Edom (vs. 1-9); the sin of Edom (10-14); and the judgment awaiting Edom (15-21). And, finally, we read in Malachi 1:4 that Edom is "the people against whom Jehovah hath indignation for ever."

The Name of Esther

What was Esther's original name, and why was it changed?

Her name was originally Hadassah, meaning "myrtle," and it was changed to Esther, which means star. She is a wonderful type of the Church of God, the King's bride, exalted from a lowly to a heavenly position. "He raiseth up the poor out of the dust, and lifteth up the beggar from the dunghill, to set them among princes, and to make them inherit the throne of glory" (1 Sam. 2:8).

Cain, Balaam and Core

Please explain the way of Cain, the error of Balaam and the gainsaying of Core, mentioned in the eleventh verse of the Epistle of Jude; also the way of Balaam (2 Peter 2:15) and the doctrine of Balaam (Rev. 2:14).

1. The way of Cain is the way of the religionist, who, like Cain, knows there is a God, but insists upon worshiping Him in self-will, setting aside blood redemption as God's appointed way of approach unto Him (Gen. 4:1-7).

2. Balaam was a false prophet who entered the employ of a heathen king and undertook to bring upon the nation of Israel the curse of God (Num. 22nd and 23rd chapters). His error was in supposing that since Israel was a sinful people, therefore a righteous God needed only to be reminded of their sinfulness to curse them. He was blind to the higher ethic of the cross which God saw in the future (Rev. 13:8), and by which God had found a way to be just and the justifier of His shining people (Rom. 3:26).

3. The way of Balaam is the way of those professed ministers of righteousness who commercialize their gifts and sell them to the highest bidder. These, like Balaam, are looking "for reward" (Jude 11), and love "the wages of unrighteousness" (2 Peter 2:15). The reward or wages may be money, as were Balaam's, or might be applause or promotion or popular favor. There are many of

these messengers of Satan masquerading as Christian ministers, "whose end shall be according to their works" (2 Cor. 11:13-15).

4. The doctrine of Balaam was his teaching the king of Moab to induce the children of Israel to intermarry with the heathen and to indulge in their heathen practices, including fornication. Having failed to curse God's people, he sought to rob them of His blessing through their failure to walk in a path of separation. Wherever there is intermarriage between the saved and the unsaved and wherever there is fellowship with the works of darkness, the doctrine of Balaam is having its effect. (See 2 Cor. 6:14 to 7:1.)

5. The gainsaying of Core (or Korah) is recorded in the sixteenth chapter of Numbers. It consisted in denying Moses' authority as God's appointed spokesman and leader, and usurping the office of the priesthood contrary to God's word. There is much of this kind of thing in our day and those guilty of it will likewise perish.

Did Lazarus Walk Out?

How did Lazarus come out of his tomb at Bethany? We have heard it objected that he could not have walked out, since he was bound in his grave clothes.

There is no record that he "walked out," and he was not told to walk out. The Lord cried saying, "Lazarus, come forth," and the Word says that "he that was dead came forth, bound hand and foot with grave clothes" (John 2:43,44).

The Magdalene

Why is Mary called the Magdalene? Does the word convey the idea that she was an impure, immoral woman?

Not at all. She was called the Magdalene because she came from Magdala. And there is no evidence that she was an unchaste woman. She had been delivered from demon possession (Mark 16:9), but that is no indication that she was immoral. It is altogether too bad that the word Magdalene should ever be applied to hospitals for fallen women. This practice may be due to confusing Mary of Magdala with the woman "which was a sinner" who anointed our Lord in the Pharisee's house (Luke 7:36), but this was by no means Mary of Magdala.

Man's Natural Clothing

Was man created naked? And was it originally intended that he should wear artificial clothing?

Of course, he was created naked, both the man and the woman; for in Genesis 2:25 it is written that "they were both naked, the man and his wife, and were not ashamed." But their original nakedness seems to have been different from the nakedness wrought by their sin, for in Genesis 3:7 it is written that "the eyes of them both were opened, and they knew that they were naked; and they sewed fig leaves together, and made themselves aprons." This seemed to avail so long as they were alone, but when they heard God's voice they ran from Him, and Adam said, "I heard thy voice in the garden, and I was afraid, because I was naked; and I hid myself." Then it was that by killing animals God provided "coats of skin, and clothed them" (Gen. 3:21); thus teaching in a figure that "without the shedding of blood there is no remission." It is probable that before his sin, man was clothed like God Himself, who coveres Himself with light as with a garment (Ps. 104:2), and that when he is fully redeemed from the fall, receiving a body like that of his Lord, he will again be thus arrayed in light (Rom. 8:23; 1 John 3:1-3).

David's Prayer for Restoration

For exactly what did David pray in Psalm 51:12? Was be praying for God to save him?

No, indeed. He was already a saved man, though he had fallen into grievous sin. His prayer was: "Restore unto me (not salvation, for this he already had, but) the joy of thy salvation." He had not lost his salvation, but he had lost his joy, and he was seeking its restoration.

Was Judas Ever Saved?

Please tell us whether Judas was ever saved?

He was never saved. He was a disciple and an apostle, but he was never born again. He was "a devil" (John 8:70,71), and when he died he went "to his own place" (Acts 1:25).

The Edomites

Who are the Edomites?

They are the descendants "of Esau who is Edom" (Gen. 36:1). Another form of the word is Idumea (Isa. 34:5,6; Ezek. 35:15; 36:5).

The Arab

Are the Arabs the descendants of Esau?

No. They come from Ishmael, the son of Abraham and Hagar.

From Dan to Beersheba

What do people mean by the expression, "from Dan to Beersheba"?

Dan was in the extreme north and Beersheba in the extreme south. So the expression signifies "from end to end," or "from one end to the other." A similar expression today would be "from coast to coast."

The Waters of Marah

Can you tell us what is meant by the incident at Marah described in Exodus 15:23-27?

The word Marah is the same as the word Mary and its meaning is "bitter" or "bitterness." The people of Israel were walking through the wilderness as they were led of God when they came upon Marah where the waters were bitter. When Moses cried unto God, Jehovah "showed him a tree, which when he had cast into the waters, the waters were made sweet." These bitter waters found in the path of God's leading may speak of the sufferings of God's people as they walk with Him in the way. The Lord Jesus Himself declared that in the world we should have tribulation. These tribulations are sometimes for chastening, but always they are for the purpose of training the people of God. The tree typifies the cross of Calvary, which when we cast it into the waters of our afflictions makes the water sweet. See Romans 5:3,4. The cross itself was made sweet unto the Lord Jesus because it was in the way of His Father's leading. See John 18:11.

Abraham and Lot

Was Lot a saved person?

Yes. In 2 Peter 2:7,8 Lot is spoken of twice as a "just" or "righteous" man, which means that he was justified by faith. The difference between Lot and Abraham was that Lot was not a *separated* man, while Abraham was. And it is to be noted that when Lot got into trouble on account of mixing with the world it was Abraham the separated man who had power to help. Compare Genesis 13:5-18; 14:1-16; 19:29. And it is so today. Power is with the man who is not only saved but who walks in a path of separation with God and from the world (2 Tim. 2:20,21). When the choice was presented to Lot he "chose him all the plain of Jordan," looking only to the present advantage. Abraham, on the other hand, "looked for a city which hath foundations" (Heb. 11:10), and "came and dwelt in the plain of Mamre, which is in Hebron" (Gen. 13:18). Mamre is a word which means "fatness." Hebron means "communion." Thus it is seen that these men are types, Lot of the worldly Christian, and Abraham of the spiritual Christian.

Immortality

Were Adam and Eve immortal before they had sinned?

Immortality is freedom from death. And since death entered through sin, and since therefore there would have been no death except for sin, it is clear that if Adam and Eve had never sinned they would never have died. See Romans 5:12.

David's Sin in Numbering the People

Will you please explain to us what was wrong in David numbering the people of Israel and Judah as recorded in 2 Samuel 24? How could it have been so wrong for the king to have a census taken to show the number of people in his kingdom?

The twenty-first chapter of 1 Chronicles is a parallel account of this same matter. But in the Chronicles account it says that "Satan stood up against Israel, and provoked David to number Israel," while in Samuel it reads that "the anger of Jehovah was kindled against Israel, and he moved David against them to say, Go, number Israel and Judah." The explanation of this seeming contradiction is that the idea came from Satan in the first place, and that David was activated by pride rather than by a desire to do the will of God. It is true that God also moved David to do it, but this was God's permissive will rather than His directive will. If a servant of God really wants to do something contrary to the plan of God, and wants to do it rather than to do the will of God, it is often possible that God will consent to it in order to show His servant by the outcome that it was not the best way. In both accounts you will see that Joab, the head of the army, sought to dissuade David from his purpose, but without success. It appears that David was seeking to ascertain his military strength, and was leaning upon the army rather than upon God.

At any rate the matter was a very serious thing from God's point of view, for it resulted in the death of 70,000 men in Israel. The lesson for us is that we ought to seek always God's directive will rather than His permissive will, because God's way is always better than our way.

The Dead Sea Basin

Can you tell us what is the estimated wealth of the chemical salts in the waters of the Dead Sea?

It is estimated that the potash, bromine and other chemical salts, deposited in the Dead Sea basin are worth more than all the other wealth of the world beside. The figures of the experts are staggering. They declare that the potential value of these deposits is more than twelve hundred billions of dollars. How thrilling it is to reflect that, while men for centuries considered the Dead Sea basin as the most worthless and godforsaken spot earth, God was using it as a safety deposit vault to make the land of Israel the richest territory in the world! Surely, His ways are not as our ways.

The Age of Accountability

When Jesus remained in the temple at the age of twelve years, did it indicate at what age a child's personal responsibility begins?

There is nothing of such indication in the record. The age of accountability doubtless varies in different children, but it is often reached before the age of twelve years.

The Apostles' Conversion

Had the disciples been converted before being called by Christ?

There is no evidence that the apostles (I suppose you refer to them in your word "disciples") had been converted before they were called by Christ. As a matter of fact, I doubt whether any of them were born again until Matthew 16:16, where Simon Peter made the great confession by which he became a child of God.

Jews and Israelites

Were all twelve apostles Jews?

Yes. It is true that only Judas the betrayer was of the tribe of Judah which was also the tribe to which our Lord belonged; but the word "Jew" does not come from the tribal name, but rather from the religious term "Judaism." There are today many who contend that the Jews and Israel are two different peoples, that the present-day British and other English-speaking peoples are Israel, and that through them the promises of universal blessing are to be fulfilled. But in the Scriptures all the tribes are often called Jews. Mordecai, who is called a Jew eight times in the book of Esther, was a Benjamite (Esther 2:5). In Isaiah 27:6 Israel is seen to include "them that come of Jacob," and through them the face of the world is to be filled with fruit. Zechariah 8:23 says that the time is coming when ten Gentiles shall lay hold upon the skirt of a Jew, saying, "We will go with you, for we know that God is with you." And Romans 11:25-27, to cite a New Testament instance, shows that the people now in blindness (the Jews) will remain in that blindness until the fullness of the Gentiles be come in (or, until the Church is completed), and then all Israel shall be saved as it is written."

Jerubbaal and Gideon

Who was Jerubbaal, and what does the name mean?

Jerubbaal was a symbolic name for Gideon (Judg. 8:35). The word means "Baal will contend," and the word Gideon comes from a root meaning to fell, as felling a tree. The name Gideon means "feller," that is, a warrior, one who cuts down, hews down, or destroys. And all this Gideon did as a faithful warrior of God.

Dionysius the Areopagite

Why is Dionysius called the Areopagite in Acts 17:34?

Mars' Hill was the Roman name for what the Greeks called Areopagus, meaning the Rock of Ares. Ares was the name of the Greek god of war, just as Mars was the god of war of the Romans. Dionysius, whose name means "a reveler," was probably a member of the court held on Mars' Hill, and therefore he is called the Areopagite.

Apostates

Can a saved person become an apostate?

A saved person cannot become an apostate. Apostates are in mind in 1 John 2:19. One commentator, in a footnote on the last clause of this verse, says: "This is a frequent idiom in the Greek, and is a strong way of saying that no apostates were Christians."

Cain's Name

Why did Eve name her first-born son "Cain" and what is the connection between that name and her remark in relation to it in Genesis 4:1: "I have gotten a man from the Lord"?

"Cain" means "acquisition," and the name was chosen because she had acquired or "gotten" her child. The remark of Eve to which you refer is more literally translated, as in the marginal rendering of the Authorized Version, "I have gotten a man, even the LORD." The Revised Version helps us still further in giving the name "Jehovah" in place of "the LORD." Whenever "LORD" appears in our English Old Testament spelled with capital letters throughout, it stands for this mysterious name Jehovah, whose meaning is "He who eternally is and who is coming." Eve fondly, though mistakenly, imagined that her firstborn son was really the Seed of the woman, the coming one, promised in Genesis 3:15. Therefore she said: "I have gotten a man, even Jehovah."

The Conquest of Jericho

Do you really believe that the walls of Jericho fell down flat because the children of Israel marched around those walls once a day for six days and then seven times on the seventh day, as recorded in the sixth chapter of Joshua?

I verily believe that the walls of Jericho fell down flat after the people of Israel had marched around the city once a day for six days and seven times on the seventh day, and after the priests had blown the trumpets, and the people had shouted as commanded by Joshua. I believe all that. Why should it be thought a thing incredible with you that God, even by such means, should cause the walls of a city to fall down flat?

There is a great significance in the story of the conquest of Jericho. The central teaching is that, by means esteemed foolish in the eyes of man, God accomplishes His results. It is even so with relation to the gospel of Christ, which is looked upon as a foolish thing. "For the preaching of the cross is to them that perish foolishness; but unto us which are saved it is the power of God. . . . Hath not God made foolish the wisdom of this world? For after that in the wisdom of God the world by wisdom knew not God, it pleased God by the foolishness of preaching to save them that believe. For the Jews require a sign, and the Greeks seek after wisdom: but we preach Christ crucified, unto the Jews a stumbling-block, and unto the Greeks foolishness; but unto them which are called, both Jews and Greeks, Christ the power of God, and the wisdom of God. Because the foolishness of God is wiser than men; and the weakness of God is stronger than men" (1 Cor. 1:18-25). The point is that the gospel, which the world considers to be foolishness, is the only means by which men can be saved from sin.

When I say "saved from sin" I am not now speaking of being saved from hell. Salvation includes deliverance from hell in the future, but salvation also delivers from sin here and now. And it is all done through that foolish thing called the gospel of Christ, which is ever "the power of God unto salvation to every one that believeth; to the Jew first, and also to the Greek" (Rom. 1:16,17).

Bruised Reeds and Smoking Flax

Please explain Matthew 12:20: "A bruised reed shall he not break,

and smoking flax shall he not quench, till he send forth judgment unto victory."

The context shows that when the Lord Jesus was threatened by His enemies, who "held a council against Him, how they might destroy Him" (verse 14), instead of destroying them, or even rebuking them, He "withdrew Himself from thence," charging those who followed Him not to make Him known: that the word might be fulfilled which was spoken in Isaiah 42:1-4: "Behold my servant (referring to Christ) . . . He shall not cry, nor lift up, nor cause his voice to be heard in the street. A bruised reed shall he not break, and the smoking flax shall he not quench: . . . He shall not fail nor be discouraged, till he have set judgment in the earth: and the isles shall wait for his law."

Israel was a broken reed, "whereon if a man lean, it will go into his hand, and pierce it" (Isa. 36:6); it could not be relied upon, and the time had not yet come to deal with it in judgment. Israel was like smoking flax, giving out an offensive odor, and yet the time had not come to deal with it in judgment. Therefore, He "withdrew himself from thence." In due time He who once came to save will return to judge and to subdue His enemies under His feet. In Isaiah 36:6—"Lo, thou trusteth in the staff of this broken reed, on Egypt; whereon if a man lean, it will go into his hand, and pierce it"—the Revisers have changed "broken" to "bruised."

Solar or Lunar

I heard a preacher say that the "years" of the fifth chapter of Genesis were lunar periods of a month, rather than solar periods of twelve months; and that Methuselah was really only 969 months old when he died, rather than 969 solar years. Is he right?

No. The absurdity of his contention will appear if you examine the chapter. For example, chapter 21 says that Methuselah's father "Enoch lived sixty and five years, and begat Methuselah." According to the lunar theory, therefore, Enoch became a father when he was less than six years old!

Bath-sheba's Father

In 2 Samuel 11:3 the father of Bath-sheba, David's wife, is called Eliam, and in 1 Chronicles 3:5 he is called Ammiel. Can you explain why the same man is called by different names?

You will notice that the two names have the same syllables except that the first and last syllables are transposed. Eliam is Ammiel backwards. They are only two forms of the same name. You will observe that the name of Bath-sheba occurs in another form (Bath-shua) in the second Scripture you cite.

Some Better Thing for Us

Please explain Hebrews 11:39,40.

The meaning of this passage is that the Old Testament saints are waiting eagerly for the day when our Lord shall come to earth again in glory, for it is not until then that they themselves will enter into the fullness of their own inheritance. This does not mean that they are not already present with the Lord, but it does mean that until the Son of God is glorified, and they are glorified with Him, they shall not have been "made perfect" (see Zech. 14:5; 2 Thess. 1:10; Jude 14).

The Herod Family

In the second chapter of Matthew, verse 19, we read, "But when Herod was dead, behold, an angel of the Lord appeared in a dream to Joseph in Egypt." And in the twentieth verse we read that Joseph was told to "Arise and take the young child and his mother and go into the land of Israel: for they are dead which sought the young child's life." Then in the twenty-third chapter of Luke, beginning at the seventh verse, we read: "And as soon as he knew that he belonged unto Herod's jurisdiction, he sent him to Herod, who himself also was at Jerusalem at the time." Then in the eighth verse it continues: "And when Herod saw Jesus, he was exceeding glad: for he was desirous to see Him of a long season, because he had heard many things of Him; and he hoped to have seen some miracle done by Him." What I want to know and what puzzles me is how can it be that Herod died when the Lord Jesus was a babe, and then had an interview with Jesus when Jesus had become a man 30 years after Herod was reputed to be dead.

The answer to your question is that there were several rulers named Herod. The king reigning at the time of our Lord's birth was Herod the Great, son of Antipater and an Idumean by descent. His son Archelaus succeeded him (Matt. 2:22). "Herod the tetrarch" of Matthew 14:1-12 was Herod Antipas, another son of Herod the Great. Still another son of Herod the Great was Herod Philip, tetrarch of Iturea and of the region of Trachonitis (Luke 3:1) The Herod of Acts 13 was Herod Agrippa I, a grandson of Herod the Great. And Herod Agrippa II of Acts 25 and 26 was a son of Herod Agrippa I, and therefore a grandson of Herod the Great.

The Prophecy of Caiaphas

Please give me some help on John 11:49-51; 18:14. Did Caiaphas obtain his knowledge from the Scriptures, as we have them? I have looked for references, but am unable to find any.

I think that the passages cited explain themselves. Caiaphas did not get his information from the Scriptures, but "being the high priest that same year" he prophesied as the Holy Spirit revealed His will to him.

Other Boats

What is the meaning of "there came other boats from Tiberias" (John 6:23)?

Tiberias was a town on the Sea of Galilee, which sea was also called the Lake of Tiberias. The town itself was the capital of Galilee for some time. It was from this town that the boats spoken of had come and had landed near the place where the miracle of feeding the five thousand had taken place, and it was in these boats that the people who sought the Lord Jesus came across to Capernaum seeking Him.

True and False Teachers

How may we distinguish between true and false teachers? I am familiar with the test laid down in 1 John 4:2,3, but I cannot seem to get much help from it. It seems to me that even the false teachers confess that Jesus Christ is come in the flesh. Please help me in this matter if you can.

The mystery will clear up if you will remember the true significance of the expression, "Jesus Christ." The word "Christ" is not really a name, but a title. It means the anointed one. And the question laid down in this test is as to whether the teacher who claims to come from God confesses that Jesus of Nazareth is the Christ of God come in flesh. The Christ of God (Luke 9:20) is described in such detail in the Word of God as to make it perfectly easy to recognize Him, and quite impossible to be deceived by any counterfeit of Him, if only one's eyes are open to the Word of God and subject to its authority.

What then must a teacher confess about Jesus of Nazareth? The answer is that he must confess that Jesus of Nazareth is the Christ of the Scriptures.

The Scriptures demand and declare that Christ is Himself God (John 1:1-3; Col. 1:13-18; Heb. 1:1-3, 6-13; compare Ps. 2:7; 2 Sam. 7:14; Ps. 104:4; 45:6,7; 102:25-27; 110:1). The Christ of God must become incarnate in a virgin's Son (Isa. 7:14; Matt. 1:18-25; John 1:14). The Christ of God must die on a cross as a substitutionary sacrifice for the sins of men, the Lamb of God which taketh away the sin of the world (Ps. 22; Isa. 53; John 1:29; 1 Cor. 15:3). The Christ of God must rise from the dead on the third day, having been delivered up for our offenses. He must be raised again for our justification (1 Cor. 15:4-8; Rom. 4:25). The Christ of God must ascend into heaven and sit on the right hand of God as our great High Priest ever living to make intercession for His people, and therefore able to save them to the uttermost, or to the end (Ps. 110:1; Heb. 7:25). The Christ of God who lives in heaven in His bodily capacity also lives now on earth in His people, Christ in us the hope of glory (Gal. 2:20; Col. 1:27). And, finally, the Christ of God must come again in like manner as He went into heaven (Acts 1:11).

Every spirit that confesses that Jesus of Nazareth is the Christ of God thus described in the Scriptures of God is himself a teacher come from God. And everyone who confesses not these things shows that he is not a teacher come from God, and against such we are warned in 2 Corinthians 11:13-15: "For such are false apostles, deceitful workers, transforming themselves into the apostles of Christ. And no marvel; for Satan himself is transformed into an angel of light. Therefore it is no great thing if his ministers also be transformed as the ministers of righteousness; whose end shall be according to their works."

The Stoning of Paul

Was Paul actually stoned to death and then raised from the dead at Lystra?

We are not fully informed. The record is given in Acts 14:19 where we read that Jews came from Antioch and Iconium to Lystra "who persuaded the people, and, having stoned Paul, dragged him out of the city, supposing that he was dead" (R.V.). Then we are told that as his disciples stood around about him mourning his death he rose up and went straight back into the city and stayed there overnight, departing on the morrow for Derbe.

When it is remembered that the Jews stoned to death those criminals judged worthy of death, and that they stoned them by raining down great rocks down upon them, it is almost impossible to doubt that Paul was actually stoned to death, and raised from the dead miraculously.

And yet if we believe, as seems very probable, that Paul is discussing his Lystra experience in 2 Corinthians 12:1-10 we must leave the question unanswered as to whether he actually died under the Lystra stoning, for he says he cannot tell whether or not he was in the body. Comparing the dates between Acts 14 and 2 Corinthians 12 you will find that just about "fourteen years" elapsed between them (see 2 Cor. 12:2). Whether the stoning was actually to death or not, it is certain his recovering so quickly and so fully was miraculous, and that the infirmity of the flesh, resulting from the experience, was given him only that he might not be ruined in his testimony by undue exaltation.

Peter's Martyrdom

Please tell us what our Lord meant by the mysterious words of John 21:18: "Verily, verily, I say unto thee, When thou wast young, thou girdedst thyself, and walkedst whither thou wouldest but when thou shalt be old, thou shalt stretch forth thy hands, and another shall gird thee, and carry thee whither thou wouldest not."

The words were addressed to Simon Peter and their meaning is explained in the verse 19: "This spake he, signifying by what death he should glorify God." That is to say, he was telling Peter that he must one day die by crucifixion, even as his Lord had already done, for it was the risen Lord who said this thing to his disciple. Peter was curious to know about his fellow apostle John, and as John stood by Peter seeing him, said to Jesus, "Lord, and what shall this man do?" That is to say, "Now that Thou hast told me how I am to die, tell me about John: how shall he die?" To this the Lord Jesus answered, "If I will that he tarry till I come, what is that to thee? follow thou me." This gave rise to a saying among the brethren that John should never die, but John himself is writing and says, "Jesus said not unto him, He shall not die; but, if I will that he tarry till I come, what is that to thee?"

While our Lord did not actually predict that John would live until his Lord's second coming, He did declare or imply that he might live until that time. And so John went on to the end of his life on earth with the possibility that the Lord

Jesus might come before he should die, while Peter went on with the sure anticipation of ending his life by crucifixion; and according to what seems to be reliable tradition Peter did die by crucifixion. But he was crucified with his head downward and his feet upward, since he felt so unworthy to die exactly as his Lord had died.

Our position today as disciples of Christ is precisely the same as that of John during his earthly lifetime. We cannot know that we shall not die, and neither can we know that we shall ever die at all, for it is possible for our Lord to come for His own at any moment of any day or any night and catch them away to meet Him in the air. "We shall not all sleep" (1 Cor. 15:51-54; compare 1 Thess. 4:13-18).

The Living Creatures

Were the four living creatures, called "beasts" in the Authorized Version, saved by the blood? If so why did they not have crowns with the rest of the redeemed?

The cherubim or living creatures were not saved by blood because they had never been lost. The pronoun "us" in Revelation 5:9 should be omitted. It has no place in the Greek text. The living creatures and the twenty-four elders join in the song, saying, "Thou art worthy to take the book and to open the seals thereof: for thou wast slain, and hast redeemed to God by thy blood out of every kindred, and tongue, and people, and nation," etc.

Cain's Wife

Who was Cain's wife?

The only possible answer to your question is that Cain's sister became his wife. In Genesis 5:3-5 we learn that Adam, who lived 930 years, begat daughters as well as sons. We do not have the names of these daughters, nor are we told how many there were, but, plainly, at least one of them had to become the wife of one of the sons in order that the race might be perpetuated.

Children and Sons

Could you explain the first part of Galatians 4, concerning sonship? Are not all Christians sons of God?

The contrast is between the status of Jewish believers before the death and resurrection of Christ, and that of all believers, whether from among Jews or Gentiles, afterwards. In the old dispensation, believers were in the position of minor children and under the Law, but in the new dispensation, believers—all of them—are in the position of full-grown sons, free from the Law, and in partnership and fellowship with the Father. The "elements of the world" (verse 3) are the Commandments of Sinai (compare verses 9 and 21 and Col. 2:20). The Law was an elementary "schoolmaster unto Christ," that they might be justified by faith. But after faith came they were delivered from the old schoolmaster, being no longer under Law, but under grace (Gal. 3:23-25; Rom. 6:14). In Galatians 3:26 the word "children" should read "sons." The whole matter is worked out in the fourth chapter.

Death of the Apostles

How did the apostles meet their death? Where can this information be found?

There is a tradition, apparently well founded, that all the apostles except John died a violent death, being put to death for their testimony. All the information available about that may be found in *The Encyclopedia Britannica*, or any other good Encyclopedia, in separate articles under the separate names of the apostles.

The Age of the Earth

Is the world many thousands of years old, as scientists are led to believe? If so, how may we account for the date of creation as B.C. 4004 in the Bible? I believe the Bible and should like to be able to explain this to one who believes only part of it.

The chronological dates found in our Bibles have no reference to the creation of the earth, but only to the creation of man. No one questions the antiquity of the material creation, but no one has brought forth any proof that the creation of Adam was further back than 4004 B.C. The date of Genesis 1:1 is unrevealed. The second verse tells of a replenishing of the earth following some great catastrophe between the first and second verses, which is not recorded.

Elisha and the "Innocent Children"

Last Sunday I listened to a very good sermon about the Shunammite woman, and in his preliminary remarks, the preacher said that doubt had risen in the minds of some regarding these stories concerning the doings of Elisha, as to whether they told of something that actually happened or not. The reason for this doubt was that inasmuch as Elisha's work was principally acts of mercy it seemed incredible that he should curse a group of innocent children and cause them to be torn to pieces by two bears. He said that he disliked to believe that anything like that could be true, but left it to his hearers to judge for themselves.

It seems to me that there is nothing in the story to indicate that it is allegory, but that it tells of something that actually happened.

I would appreciate it very much if I might have your views regarding the truth of the story and also the seeming cruelty of the act.

I believe God's Word as written and like to see the stand you take. May God bless you.

There is no reason whatever to doubt the historicity of the Bible record of Elisha. The things recorded there, as you put it, "actually happened." I am passing on to you the helpful comment of John Urquhart on the passage particularly referred to:

This event furnishes so convenient a weapon for those who desire to assault the Bible that we cannot be astonished that many have used it. There have been those who, quite apart from the use thus made of it by the foe, have found not a little perplexity in it. They have felt it to be quite opposed to the spirit of the New Testament. My readers are so familiar, not only with the objections, but also with the feelings to which I refer that I do not require to dwell upon them. But they may not have sufficiently considered a very obvious reply.

What is the spirit of the New Testament? They conceive of it possibly as an infinite patience—a spirit that can suffer but that cannot strike, that is always gentle, and never terrible. But what, then, of the swift and fearful judgment upon Ananias and Sapphira? What of Paul's address to the sorcerer Elymas: "O full of all subtilty and all mischief, thou child of the devil, thou enemy of all righteousness, wilt thou not cease to pervert the right ways of the Lord?" And what of the judgment upon him when he was immediately deprived of sight?

What, too, of the judgments threatened in the New Testament? It is surely needful that those who talk so confidently about the spirit of the New Testament should see to it that they are not substituting their own fancies for New Testament facts. Perhaps the reply is that they are referring specially to the spirit of Jesus. I know that the predictions were amply fulfilled that said He should not strive, nor cry, nor break the bruised reed, nor quench the smoking flax.

But what of His rebuke to Peter: "Get thee behind me, Satan," and of those fearful woes upon the Pharisees? And shall we find no place for those awful indications of coming judgment found in the parables in which the Lord has pictured to us His coming again? The notion entertained by some of the spirit of the New Testament is as opposed to New Testament statements as it is out of accord with God's dealings with Israel, with the nations, and with ourselves. He is a God of mercy, but He is also a God of judgment.

Let us now look at the facts and see whether even this tragic incident did not serve God and Israel's highest interests. It is unfortunate that our version should have given the translation "little children." The word used in the Hebrew answers to our word "lad," or "youth"; and, while sometimes used of mere children, is also applied to fully grown young men. The word "little," which appears in the description, plainly points out that these were not fully grown young men, but were "young lads."

Bethel had from the first been the seat of the revolt against God's law, and the spirit of revolt seems to have spread until even the youth of the city were filled with it. The tidings of the wonders on the east and on the west of Jordan—the ascent of Elijah, the endowment of Elisha with a double portion of his spirit, the parting of the waters of the Jordan, and the healing of the fountain at Jericho—had, no doubt, been carried over all that district. Indeed, there seems to be a reference to the ascension of Elijah in the taunt that is now flung at his successor. The word which occurs in verse 11 ("And Elijah went up by a whirlwind into heaven") is used in the lads' cry. They shout after this solitary man on whom is now resting the burden of Israel's sin and need—"Ascend, Baldhead! Ascend, Baldhead!"

Understood in this way it was a peculiarly daring and impious mockery of the sign which God had just given to them in common with the rest of Israel. Now, will those who have been troubled with what we may freely call the appalling severity of this judgment, ask themselves one question? If this scornful repudiation and mockery of God's ambassador had been passed over in silence, and if the example of Bethel had been followed all over the land, could Israel have escaped a corresponding judgment? Would not the land have rushed in its madness against the buckler of the Almighty?

In any case, Elisha's mission would have been a failure. A prophet, jeered at and hooted by the lads at the gate of a city, could not have effected much good within its walls. Looked at in this way there was both wisdom and mercy in the prompt action that nipped rebellion in the bud. The flood of impiety that might have covered the land was arrested. Its grave was dug in the judgment which fell so swiftly upon that tumultuous throng; and the heart of Israel, and of Bethel also, was awed as these "forty and two" were carried to the tomb, and as the tidings of their swift destruction sped from tribe to tribe.

Ham's Descendants

I desire an explanation of the inferiority of Ham's descendants. If, before the call of Abraham, humanity was one vast stream with neither Jew nor Gentile, how do Ham's descendants come to be inferior? Seeing that God Himself cursed no man, I really doubt if He would allow drunken Noah to pronounce a curse to ruin a man and his descendants for life.

I think it will not do for us to ascribe to a "drunken Noah" the wonderful program laid down in the book of Genesis. The prophecy has been too accurately fulfilled to allow for any such treatment of it. The tenth chapter of Genesis has been pronounced by able scholars as containing more important matters than many a bulky volume. The first five verses give us the names of the seven sons of Japheth and the descendants of two of them; the next, and by far the longest section, verses 6 to 20, informs us of the four sons of Ham and the nations which sprang from them, including the Canaanites; while the third and closing section is devoted to the five sons of Shem, with their posterity.

According to good authorities there is ground for believing that the words "Ham abi" (Ham the father of), had been omitted from the text preceding the word Canaan in the sentence which says, "God shall enlarge Japheth, and he shall dwell in the tents of Shem; and Canaan shall be his servant" (Gen. 9:27). With these words supplied it would read, "and Ham the father of Canaan shall be his servant." Dr. H. Grattan Guinness in an old work, entitled, *The Divine Program of the World's History*, reviews at length the history of the ancient races and sums up the matter as follows:

The Hamitic races lost all rule and empire twenty-five centuries ago; they now count for nothing among the powers of the world. The Semitic races were never greatly enlarged—never great conquerors, save for a short period in the Saracenic era. They have ruled the world by another weapon than the sword;

they rule it still, and will rule it forever—religiously. The Japhetic races are, and have for over 2,000 years been, supreme among the children of men. The round globe itself is the only measure of their enlargement. They influence even China and Japan and the vast expanses of Central Asia and Central Africa. The North Pole and the South alike are visited by them. They girdle the globe with submarine cables, cross its continents with their railways, and its oceans with their steamships, carry their commerce to its most distant shores, and force the unwilling heathen into friendly intercourse. Moreover, they dwell in the tents of Shem both spiritually and physically; they share by faith the blessings of Abraham's covenant, and they occupy and influence lands once occupied by Semitic peoples.

Is not all this fulfilled prophecy on the grandest of scales? The entire ethnological development of the posterity of Noah foreseen and foretold when as yet the patriarch himself still lived! Did he guess how all this prolonged future would turn out? Was it by chance he assigned these widely different destinies to the descendants of his three sons? How came he to make no mistake? If Moses puts these words into his lips, why did he delineate a future absolutely contrary to every indication of his times? Why did he not make Noah assign supremacy to Ham, seeing, as he did, Hamitic empires all around him? Why did he not assign enlargement to Shem, and, as he knew little of Japheth, put the servitude down to his account? It would have seemed to human foresight a much more likely outline of the future. But no. Moses had nothing to do with the prophecy save as an editor. Noah had nothing to do with it save as an utterer. God Himself was and must have been its Author; and the second father of the human race was and must have been one of the "holy men of old," who "spake as they were moved by the Holy Ghost."

Herod the Great

When did the Herod die who reigned when Christ was born?

The death of Herod the Great took place during the year of our Lord's birth, which according to our common chronology is 4 B.C.

Jephthah's Vow?

What was the meaning of Jephthah's vow?

The story of Jephthah's vow is recorded in Judges 11:30-40. It has been the subject of much discussion. We quote from John Urquhart:

Did Jephthah intend to offer a human sacrifice to God, and did he really slay and present his own child as a burnt offering? It is quite true that heathen rites had everywhere made the world familiar with such atrocities; and it is not to be wondered at that for the first eleven centuries of the Christian era both Jews and Gentiles should rush to the conclusion that Jephthah had considered himself bound by his oath to commit such an abomination. The Targum of Jonathan says, for example: "A man may not offer son or daughter for a burnt offering, as did Jephthah the Gileadite, and did not consult Phinehas the priest; and if he had consulted Phinehas the priest, he would have redeemed her." Similar references are found in early Christian writers. But the question is not how the Scripture has been interpreted, but rather how it ought to be interpreted, and when we read this passage with due care, we shall find it impossible, I think, to approve of the older interpretations.

Let us recall the facts. Israel had gone deeply into idolatry, but, taught by bitter experience, "they put away the strange gods from among them, and served the LORD" (10:16). Now let it be remembered that the law had emphatically expressed God's utter abhorrence of human sacrifices. "Thou shalt not do so unto the LORD thy God: for every abomination to the LORD, which he hateth, have they done unto their gods; for even their sons and their daughters they have burnt in the fire to their gods. What thing soever I command you, observe to do it: thou shalt not add thereto, nor diminish from it" (Deut. 12:31, 36). Is it credible, then, that at a time when Israel had returned in penitent grief and with eager cleansing of the land from heathen pollutions, Jephthah would have perpetrated such a crime? His daughter and her companions bewailed her virginity for the space of two months. During that time the tidings of the national hero's intention must have gone all over the land. Let me ask again, Is it conceivable that, even though Jephthah, under some mistaken notion as to the sacredness of his vow, had resolved to present his daughter as a burnt offering, Israel would have looked on in silence? Would a people eager to please God have suffered the deed to be done? The longer the matter is looked at in this light, the more impossible will it be to believe that such a sacrifice was offered.

But one passage, which has received too little attention, sweeps this notion entirely away. We read: "And it was a custom in Israel, that the daughters of Israel went yearly to lament the daughter of Jephthah the Gileadite four days in a year" (verses 39,40). The word rendered "lament" does not bear that meaning. It means on the contrary, "to praise," "to celebrate" (which is the translation in the Revised Version), or "commemorate." Four days a year the Israelitish maidens celebrated this incident in their nation's history. Is it credible that such a place would have been given to the praise and the celebration of one of the darkest deeds which man had ever perpetrated? Let us for the moment say with the critics that the people's thought was being only gradually purged from such terrible conceptions of what was pleasing to God; can we even then conceive that after ages would have labored to keep alive the recollection of such a fearful deed? Where, in that case, would be the onward development which critics would substitute for the Law and the Gospel? On the face of it, this annual celebration can only mean that Israel saw nothing wrong in Jephthah's offering, but found in it rather matter for high and sacred and long-continued national approval.

It is quite in keeping with this that there is not a trace of blood in the narrative. So much is this the case that writers speak of the Scripture "drawing a vail" over the transaction. But why should it draw a vail over this, when it tells the story so unreservedly? It is surely more natural to conclude that there was no vail to draw, and that there is not a trace of blood in the narrative for the simple reason that there was none in the transaction.

"But wherein, then, lay Jephthah's surrender and his daughter's self-sacrifice? To answer that question a word or two will suffice. The Law had provided for a case like this. In Leviticus 27:1-8 we read: "And the LORD spake unto Moses, saying, Speak unto the children of Israel, and say unto them, When a man shall make a singular vow, the persons shall be for the LORD by thy estimation. And thy estimation shall be of the male from twenty years old even unto sixty years old, even thy estimation shall be fifty shekels of silver, after the shekel of the sanctuary; and if it be a female, then thy estimation shall be thirty shekels," etc.

But there were, no doubt, cases in which redemption was not to be thought of, and this was one of them. Was there, then, any place for the devoted one in God's service? It will be remembered that Samuel was devoted before his birth; and, when Hannah came with the child to Eli, the high priest, she was apparently doing a quite customary thing. There was no question in her mind as to the child's being received for the service of the tabernacle. The offering of women for the same service was also a custom in Israel from the time the tabernacle was made till Israel's last temple was destroyed. In Exodus 38:8 we are told that Bezaleel "made the laver of brass, and the foot of it of brass, of the looking-glasses of the women assembling, which assembled at the door of the tabernacle of the congregation." The word translated "assembling" means "serving." It is applied in Numbers 4:23, and elsewhere, *to the service of the priests in the tabernacle*. The giving up of the mirrors by these women was an expression of their consecration. These were things they had no further use for. The elaborate dressing of the hair, and the adornment of the person, were for them things of a past to which they were not to return. That their service was spiritual, and not menial, we may gather from the reference to Anna, in Luke 2:37: She "departed not from the temple, but served *with fastings and prayers* night and day." Here also the word refers to sacred service, and is the New Testament equivalent for the word used in Numbers.

But, it may be asked, if this was all that Jephthah's vow brought down upon his daughter, how can we explain his grief? It will be observed that Jephthah's judgeship has several very peculiar features. There is no direct divine commission to deliver Israel. Jephthah is ambitious, and his ambition has all the intensity of a fire that has been damped down for a time, and then suddenly stirred. Wronged before his birth by others' sin, he suffered additional injury from his brethren. They refuse him any share in the family possessions, and drive him from his home. And now the elders of Gilead come and beg him to take the supreme command of the Israelitish forces. Jephthah does what no previous judge had done save Abimelech: he makes a bargain with his afflicted brethren. "And Jephthah said unto the elders of Gilead, If ye bring me home again to fight against the children of Ammon, and the LORD deliver them before me, shall I be your head? And the elders of Gilead said unto Jephthah, The LORD be witness between us, if we do not according to thy words. Then Jephthah went with the elders of Gilead, and the people made him head and captain over them: and Jephthah uttered all his words before the LORD in Mizpeh" (11:9-11).

This was plainly an attempt to found a royal house in Israel; and *the attempt was frustrated by the unforeseen result of his vow.* "And Jephthah came to Mizpeh unto his house, and, behold, his daughter came out to meet him with timbrels and with dances: and *she was his only child*; beside her he had neither son nor daughter. And it came to pass when he saw her, that he rent his clothes, and said, Alas, my daughter! thou hast brought me very low, and thou art one of them that trouble me: for I have opened my mouth unto the LORD, and I cannot go back" (verses 34,35).

The reader will note where the emphasis is put by the Scripture. "She was his only child; beside her he had neither son nor daughter." With her consecration to the tabernacle service, the hope with which Jephthah had been so busy in these last days was suddenly cut down to the ground. The hope of establishing a royal house that should put to shame the houses of the men who had wronged him was now a vain dream. His honors would perish with him.

If anything further were needed to show that this is the right reading of this incident, it would be found in the burden of his daughter's sorrow. She asks to be left alone for a couple of months—not that she may bid farewell to life and to all that makes it dear—but to bewail her "virginity." She sorrows over the extinction of her father's house, and his hope of a posterity that would wear his newly-acquired glory (*The New Biblical Guide*).

The Destruction of Jerusalem

In what period of Church history would you place the destruction of Jerusalem by Titus?

Jerusalem was destroyed by the Roman armies under Titus in the year A.D. 70. The beginning of the Church was in A.D. 30 with the descent of the Holy Spirit ten days after the ascension of our Lord. Thus the destruction of Jerusalem was 40 years after the birth of the Church.

Was Job Sinless?

In Job 1:8 the Lord says of Job: "There is none like him in the earth, a perfect and an upright man." Does the Lord mean that Job had no sin at all? And in Job 27:6, Job says: "My righteousness I hold fast, and will not let it go." Was Job self-righteous? If he was, did he have a right to be self-righteous? Some think it was all right for Job to be self-righteous, since he had no sin and was perfect and upright. I should like to have this explained.

Job was a wonderful man, but he was not sinless, "for there is no difference: for all have sinned, and come short of the glory of God" (Rom. 3:22,23). It is true that Job, in defending himself from the insinuations of his three friends, went pretty far in what you call self-righteousness. But when Jehovah appeared to him Job confessed, saying, "I have heard of thee by the hearing of the ear: but now mine eye seeth thee. Wherefore I abhor myself, and repent in dust and ashes" (Job 42:5,6).

Job's Prophecy

Please explain Job 19:25-27. Is Job here prophesying of the Second Coming of Christ and the bodily resurrection?

Yes. That is not to say that Job fully understood the matter: the prophets were often ignorant as to the true meaning of the messages they delivered (1 Peter 1:10-12). But certainly the Second Coming of Christ and the resurrection of the body are included in Job's prophecy.

Jonah

Did Jonah die in the belly of the fish (Jonah 1:17; 2:2)? Is there any word in the original translation to signify that he actually died? Is it not just a type of the death and burial of the Lord Jesus Christ? For Christ said, "As Jonas was three days and three nights in the whale's belly; so shall the Son of man be three days and three nights in the heart of the earth" (Matt. 12:40); and then in John 3:14,15, He points to the serpent in the wilderness as a type of Himself—"As Moses lifted up the serpent in the wilderness, even so must the Son of man be lifted up." Are these not figures, speaking to us of the death and burial of our Lord?

There is much difference of opinion concerning this matter of Jonah among enlightened Bible students. The word translated "hell" in Jonah 2:2 is *Sheol*; and this is the word employed in the Old Testament for the place where the dead go. It is the equivalent of Hades in the New Testament. There is no doubt about Jonah's experience being a type of the death and burial and resurrection of our Lord, and if Jonah really died, as I believe he did, and then was brought to life again, it would make the type all the more striking.

Unquestionably also, the serpent in the wilderness was a type, setting forth the saving power of Christ in His death on the cross.

Jonah as a Psalmist

Did Jonah write a Psalm while in the belly of the fish? and, if he did, where is it to be found in the Bible?

Jonah did not write a Psalm while in the fish's belly. His own statement of the matter is that he prayed unto Jehovah his God out of the fish's belly; and his prayer, written (presumably by him) after his deliverance, and which reads much like a Psalm, is recorded in the second chapter of the book bearing his name.

Jonah's Father

What was the name of Jonah's father? and what does it mean?

Jonah was the son of Amittai, according to 2 Kings 14:25 and Jonah 1:1. Amittai is Hebrew for "truth," or "truth-telling."

Jonah's Name

What is the meaning of Jonah's name?

Jonah is the Hebrew word for "dove." Jamieson, Fausset and Brown's Commentary suggests a likeness between the dove seeking rest when released from the ark of Noah and Jonah seeking rest when thrown overboard from the boat.

Joshua's Long Day

Will you kindly explain Joshua 10:12,13? It says the sun stood still. Does the sun move? Are we not taught that the earth moves around the sun?

It is supposed that the true meaning of Joshua 10:12,13 is, that the sun and moon "stood still" with reference to their relation to the earth. It is a fact admitted by astronomers that the sun and moon both move, although the sun does not move around the earth, as it seems to do. It is only that daylight was lengthened by the sun and earth maintaining for a longer time than usual the relative positions required for such a result.

Judas

Please give us your thought as to the reason (if this can be known) for the call of Judas.

The "reason for the call of Judas" is a question, I think, which is beyond our knowledge. No doubt God had a righteous reason for all that He did with reference to Judas, including, of course, his call, but, so far as I know, that reason is not revealed in Scripture, unless the revelation be in the words of our Lord recorded in John 13:18: "I speak not of you all: I know whom I have chosen: but that the scripture may be fulfilled, He that eateth bread with me hath lifted up his heel against me." Of course this answer does not go far enough to satisfy our questioning minds, but I know of nothing on the point which does go far enough.

Judas a Devil

Was Judas, one of the twelve, converted at any time?

Judas was never born again. He was always "the son of perdition." The Lord Jesus Himself called Judas a devil in John 6:70. The word is not "demon" but "devil" (*diabolos*). Apart from Satan, Judas is the only one to have this term applied to him in Scripture. The word so often translated "devils" should always be rendered "demons."

Judas and Peter

Why did Jesus not pray for Judas the same as He prayed for Peter after he fell? Could Judas ever have repented and have been forgiven as Peter was? Or was Judas a victim of prophecy in that someone had to be chosen to betray and sell the Lord Jesus, as the shadow of the cross had fallen aslant Eden's gate many years before? Why could not Judas have been saved, too?

Peter was a believer, but Judas was never a believer. Judas was all the time "the son of perdition" (John 17:12), and the Lord Jesus actually called him "a devil" (John 6:70,71). He was a free moral agent, but he chose of his own free will to reject the Son of God; and while it is true that through him the Lord Jesus was "delivered by the determinate counsel and foreknowledge of God," it is also true that "by wicked hands" He was betrayed and "crucified and slain" (Acts 2:23). There is without controversy great mystery in all this, but we may depend upon it that "the Judge of all the earth" has done right in it all (Gen. 18:25).

Death of Judas

Will you please reconcile Matthew 27:5 with Acts 1:18 with reference to the death of Judas?

If you will read the two verses together with their contexts, I think the difficulty will clear up: "And he cast down the pieces of silver in the temple and departed . . . And the chief priests took the silver pieces, and said, It is not lawful for to put them into the treasury, because it is the price of blood. And they took counsel, and bought with them the potter's field, to bury strangers in." Thus "this man purchased a field with the reward of iniquity." After departing from the temple Judas "went and hanged himself, and falling headlong, he burst asunder in the midst, and all his bowels gushed out. And it was known unto all the dwellers at Jerusalem; insomuch as that field is called in their proper tongue, Aceldama, that is to say, The field of blood. Wherefore that field was called, The field of blood, unto this day. Then was fulfilled that which was spoken by Jeremiah the prophet, saying, And they took the thirty pieces of silver, the price of him that was valued, whom they of the children of Israel did value; and gave them for the potter's field, as the Lord appointed me." Matthew 27:3-10 and Acts 1:18-20 include all that is contained in the two passages on the subject.

Did Lazarus Die Twice?

In your opinion did Lazarus suffer physical death a second time? In Hebrews 9:27 it is written that "it is appointed unto men once to die." I somehow feel that Lazarus was translated after the Lord's ascension. Do you think I am right?

Well, I myself "somehow feel" that you may be right, but I also "somehow feel" that you may be wrong. I wish I knew. It would seem that once is quite enough for any saved man to die, and I am indulging the hope that I may be among those who shall be excused from even that appointment (Heb. 9:27); but as to what happened to Lazarus, your opinion is as good as mine, and that means it is no good at all.

The Four Living Creatures

Who are the four living creatures in Revelation 4?

The living creatures of Revelation 4 (not "beasts" as in A.V.) are doubtless the same as in Ezekiel 1, and, as pointed out by Dr. Scofield, "are identical with the Cherubim. The subject is somewhat obscure, but from the position of the Cherubim at the gate of Eden, upon the cover of the Ark of the Covenant, and in Revelation 4, it is clearly gathered that they have to do with the vindication of the holiness of God as against the presumptuous pride of sinful man who, despite his sin, would 'put forth his hand, and take also of the tree of life' (Gen. 3:22-24). Upon the Ark of the Covenant, of one substance with the Mercy Seat, they saw the sprinkled blood which, in type, spoke of the perfect maintenance of the divine righteousness by the sacrifice of Christ (Ex. 25:17-20; Rom. 3:24-26, *notes*). The living creatures (or Cherubim) appear to be actual beings of the angelic order. Compare Isaiah 6:2, *note*. The Cherubim or living creatures are not identical with the Seraphim (Isa. 6:2-7). They appear to have to do with the holiness of God as outraged by *sin*; the Seraphim with *uncleanness* in the people of God. The passage in Ezekiel is highly figurative, but the effect was the revelation to the prophet of the Shekinah glory of the Lord. Such revelations are connected invariably with new blessing and service. Compare Exodus 3:2-10; Isaiah 6:1-10; Daniel 10:5-14; Revelation 1:12-19" (*Scofield Reference Bible*, page 840, *footnote* 1). It ought to be pointed out in this connection that in the song of Revelation 5:8-10, in which the living creatures join with the four and twenty elders, the pronoun "us" in verse 9 (A.V.) does not occur in the text. The living creatures are not among the redeemed. The R.V. has supplied the word "men" in the place of "us."

Lot's Wife

Whom does Lot's wife typify in Luke 17:32?

The context shows that she typifies those who start to flee from judgment but turn back and are overcome by it. This is exactly what Lot's wife did (Gen. 19:26). Lot himself was a justified believer, as shown by 2 Peter 2:7,8, and therefore his life was saved when Sodom was destroyed; but his wife was an unbeliever, and she went out of Sodom only a short distance, following "behind him." Her heart was really in Sodom all the time, and therefore the judgment overcame her.

Melchisedec

Please explain Nehemiah 7:1-3. Has the word "order of Melchisedec" any reference to the way it is used today in speaking of orders? Also, should we emphasize his being a type of Christ as to verse 3?

The word "order" used in connection with Melchisedec has nothing whatever to do with the use of the word in connection with present-day organizations often called *orders*. Our Lord is at the head of a new priesthood. The old priesthood was in the tribe of Levi. Jesus was descended, according to the flesh, from Judah; so the order of Aaron was displaced by the order of Melchisedec. Melchisedec is a wonderful type of Christ, and the type is unfolded in the opening verses of Hebrews 7, including, certainly, the third verse. It is held by some that Melchisedec was Christ Himself in one of His preincarnate manifestations. But this cannot be true, for if it were true it could not be said of Melchisedec that he was "*made like* unto the Son of God." He was not the Son of God himself, but he was "made like unto" Him.

Michael Is not Christ

Is Michael, mentioned in Daniel 10:21, the Lord Jesus?

No. In Jude 9 we read that "Michael the archangel, when contending with the devil he disputed about the body of Moses, durst not bring against him a railing accusation, but said, The Lord rebuke thee." Michael called upon the Lord to rebuke Satan, but Jesus is the Lord Himself. Thus Michael cannot be the Lord.

Who Is Michael?

Who is Michael, and where was the contention spoken of in Jude 9?

Michael is described in Jude as "the archangel," and in Daniel 12:1 as "the great prince which standeth for the children of thy (Daniel's) people"; that is, the people of Israel. The contention spoken of in Jude 9 was "about the body of Moses," and was therefore doubtless "in a valley in the land of Moab, over against Beth-peor" (Deut. 34:6).

Moses' Father-in-law

Who was really Moses' father-in-law, Raguel, Jethro or Hobab?

Here is one of the "difficulties of Scripture" which disappears when the light of the truth is thrown upon it. It is so with them all.

There is a very enlightening discussion of the problem of Moses' father-in-law in *The New Biblical Guide* by John Urquhart, volume 3, page 181, which I pass on to you:

The father-in-law of Moses is called in Exodus 2:18, Reuel, or more correctly Raguel. But in chapter 3:1, we read that "Moses kept the flock of Jethro his father-in-law." The same name is repeated in 4:18: "And Moses went and returned to Jethro his father-in-law." Now this might have given us trouble enough even if it had stood alone; but it does not stand alone. In Numbers 10:29, we read: "And Moses said unto Hobab, the son of Raguel the Midianite, Moses' father-in-law, We are journeying," etc. Here a third name is introduced. It is quite true that the phrase "Moses' father-in-law" *might* be understood as referring to Raguel the Midianite and not to Hobab. No one could say that we might not read the passage in that way. But that device would not help us much; for in Judges 4:11, we read that Heber the Kenite was "of the children of Hobab the father-in-law of Moses."

Here, then, is a glaring difficulty, and it was only to be expected that the most would be made of it. A great German critic (Eichhorn) thought there must have been two writers of Exodus, the one of whom believed that Raguel was Moses' father-in-law and the other who was equally confident that it was Jethro's daughter whom Moses had married. A very minor English critic (Wilson) thought that the German had not gone far enough. He wrote, "Three different writers gave varying accounts, and the compiler of the Pentateuch implicitly followed his original documents," because "not any single writer would throw such uncertainty about his subject." Nor were those who maintained that the Pentateuch was the work of Moses quite clear as to the explanation. It often happens so, and then our varying explanations make the difficulty still greater. The Jews had noticed the difference in the names long ago, but they held that they were only different names of the same person. Jethro, according to them, had seven names, so that the case might easily have been worse and yet have had a very simple explanation.

That solution, however, will hardly satisfy an English reader. He would ask for some proof, and would besides remember that, while Jethro takes his leave of Moses and returns to his own people, Hobab remains, and finally settles with the Israelites in Canaan. It is quite clear that we are dealing with persons and not with names merely. Others explained that the name was Raguel, and that "Jethro" was not a name but an official title, meaning "his excellency." This might have swept Jethro away, but Hobab still remained, and it was plain that that explanation helped as little as the other. And yet the solution was very simple. The trouble was caused not by the Bible but by its translators. The word rendered "father-in-law" is ***khothen***, which seems to have been applied to any relation by marriage. Kalisch makes the astounding statement: "this meaning of ***Khothen*** is, with certainty, not found in any passage of the Bible." That from a Rabbi, who, if he knew anything, ought to have known his Hebrew Bible, looks as if it settled the matter. But the reader will see what dependence is to be sometimes placed upon learning. In Genesis 19:12, we read that the angels said to Lot: "Hast thou here any besides? Son-in-law," etc.; and again in verse 14, "and Lot went out, and spake unto his sons-in-law, who married his daughters." The word in each case ***is the same that is applied to Jethro and Hobab***, and here, undoubtedly, it has the meaning of "son-in-law." But, more astonishing still, it is used in Exodus 4:25,26, in the sense of "husband." Zipporah exclaims: "a bloody husband art thou to me." It is quite true that the Jews have made two words out of one by supplying them with different vowel-points; but these vowel-points were not in use till several centuries after the beginning of the Christian era, and are only a Jewish comment. The word which Moses penned was in every case the same. He wrote each time the same three characters, in the same order, and like the corresponding word in Arabic and Syriac, it means any relation by marriage. Raguel was Moses' ***Khothen*** or ***Khathan***, because Moses had married his daughter. But to Jethro and to Hobab the same term equally applied because Moses had married their sister. In the same way Moses was the ***Khathan*** of Zipporah because he was her husband.

The Nicolaitanes

Kindly tell me who the Nicolaitanes are mentioned in Revelation 2:6?

The term is probably symbolic. It comes from *Nikos*, ruler or conqueror, and *laos*, the people. The Nicolaitanes then would be the original introducers of priestcraft into the churches. The whole Church is made up of an equal brotherhood of priests, but it has been divided into "clergy" and "laity," which is a grievous error, and "which thing," the risen Lord says, "I hate."

Noah, Daniel, and Job

In Ezekiel 14:14 Noah, Daniel, and Job are cited as typical righteous men. Why more than Moses, Joseph, Samuel, and others?

I take it that Noah, Daniel and Job are mentioned only as samples of a large company of men who might have been mentioned. But it did not please the Lord to mention the whole list all at once.

One Omitted Tribe

Why were the tribes of Joseph and Levi put into the list of Revelation 7 and Dan and Ephraim left out?

The tribe of Joseph is the same as the tribe of Ephraim. Joseph was Ephraim's father, and there were two half tribes in his family, namely, Ephraim and Manasseh; so Ephraim is not left out, but appears in the list under the name of Joseph.

Levi is included, because Levi was one of the twelve tribes.

The only tribe omitted is the tribe of Dan. Dan was the first of the tribes to apostasize. Please read Judges 17 and 18, and see how the tribe of Dan departed from God, departed from their own country, and set up a religion of their own, which was a system of idolatry. This may be the reason for Dan's exclusion from the list of the sealed remnant in Revelation 7.

The name "Dan" means "judge." If you will turn to Genesis 49 where we have Jacob's dying blessing bestowed upon his sons, you will find the promise in the 16th and 17th verses concerning Dan, that he "shall judge his people, as one of the tribes of Israel." So it appears that in the final manifestation of the kingdom the tribe of Dan will be restored to its place.

Was Paul Married?

Was the apostle Paul a married man?

It is evident that Paul was a widower. That he had been married appears from the fact that before his conversion he was a member of the Sanhedrin, voting as such for the condemnation and execution of the early Christians (Acts 26:10, R.V.), and to be a member of the Sanhedrin, as all agree, it was necessary to have a wife. That his wife had died in the meantime is shown by his words in 1 Corinthians 7:8, where he says "to the unmarried and widows, It is good for them if they abide even as I" (compare also 1 Cor. 9:5 and 15).

Paul's Jewish Vow

When Paul took the Jewish vow as recorded in Acts 21:18-26 was he not carrying out the spirit of 1 Corinthians 9:19-23?

Very likely that was his motive, but Acts 21:4 shows that Paul was forbidden to go to Jerusalem at all, and it is therefore evident that he was out of the Lord's will.

Paul's Stripes

Does not 2 Corinthians 11:24 mean that Paul was beaten five times with thirty-nine stripes each time? Or might it mean that he had four times received forty stripes, and a lesser number in the fifth beating? If he received thirty-nine stripes five times, can you tell me why he received each time one stripe short of the maximum number allowed in Deuteronomy 25:3?

I have no doubt that what Paul means to tell us is that he was beaten five times with thirty-nine stripes each time. And I suppose that thirty-nine stripes became the rule rather than forty in order always to avoid going beyond forty. That is to say, playing safe, so to speak, so that the legal number should not by any means be exceeded.

Peter

What did our Lord mean by His question to Peter, "Lovest thou me more than these?"

He meant, "Do you love me more than these other men love me?" Peter's backsliding began by his claiming just that (Matt. 26:33). His replies to the Lord's queries in John 21 showed that all his boastfulness was gone.

Peter and the Keys

When did Peter use the keys mentioned in Matthew 16:19? If he has not already used them, will he not use them when the Kingdom is ushered in?

He has already used them, and all of them. As the authorized spokesman for the risen Lord, he used the first key in Acts 2, when he declared that the door was open to the children of Israel; the second key in Acts 8, when he joined with John in laying hands upon the Samaritan believers, thus showing that the Samaritans (who were, strictly speaking, neither Jews nor Gentiles, but a hybrid mixture of both) were eligible; and the third in Acts 10, when he brought the first Gospel message to a Gentile audience, announcing that "WHOSOEVER believeth in him shall receive remission of sins." Since that time there has been no further use of keys. The door stands wide open for "whosoever will."

Peter's Denial

Do you believe the Bible teaches whether or not Peter was "born again" before his denial? Please explain Luke 22:32 in that light.

To me it is clear from Matthew 16:16 that Simon Peter was a born-again man when he fell into a backslidden state and denied his Lord. Through it all he never stopped believing that Jesus was the Christ the Son of God, for his Lord had prayed for Him that his faith fail not. From Luke 24:34 it appears that there was an interview between Simon Peter and his Lord early on the resurrection day. It was no doubt at that interview that Peter was restored to fellowship through confession, according to the method pointed out for backslidden children of God in 1 John 1:9.

The Threefold Question to Peter

Why did the Lord Jesus ask Peter three times, "Lovest thou me?" (John 21).

Probably because Peter's denial had been threefold: in order to bring about Peter's full restoration, the threefold open denial must be balanced by the threefold open confession. How precious it is to observe that the Lord never stopped until His servant's restoration to fellowship and service was complete, and He could say, "Feed my sheep!"

Peter the Rock

Please explain Matthew 16:18, "And I say also unto thee, That thou art Peter, and upon this rock I will build my church."

The storm of conflict raging about this passage largely turns upon the question as to what our Lord Jesus meant to signify by the word "rock." Peter is the English equivalent for the Greek word, "*petros*," meaning a stone; while "rock" is "*petra*" in the Greek. In the original text this distinction is made—"Thou art Petros, and upon this petra I will build my church."

The whole fabric of the Papacy rests upon the Roman interpretation of this passage, by which it is claimed—

First—That the rock was Peter himself. The Romanist commentators point out that our Lord spoke not Greek but Syriac or Aramaic, and that in the language employed by Him there is but one word for a stone and a rock, namely, "cepha." Thus the declaration would read, "Thou art Cepha, and upon this cepha I will build my church." They also claim

Second—That the fact that Peter is the rock upon which the Church is built, together with the further fact that to Peter were delivered the keys of the Kingdom of Heaven—that these facts establish the primacy of Peter among the Apostles. And the still further claim is made

Third—That the primacy of Peter has descended to his successors in office as Bishop of Rome. In short, that Peter was the first Pope and that all the Popes are fully authorized as his successors by the declaration of the Lord Jesus in Matthew 16.

Among the Protestant commentators there is no intelligible consensus. By some it is claimed that by the expression "this rock" is meant Christ Himself. It is suggested that perhaps the Lord Jesus, while speaking, laid His hand on His own breast (as when He said, "Destroy this temple," meaning the temple of His body John 2:19).

Others, by "this rock" understand Peter's confession of faith. By these it is pointed out that Peter's confession—"Thou art the Christ, the Son of the living God"—is the great truth upon which the Church rests; and that Christ had this in mind when He spoke to Peter, as if He had said, "This is that great truth upon which I will build my church."

Without assuming any knowledge beyond that of our brethren, and without any desire to be wise above what is written, let us seek to discover, as the Spirit of truth may be pleased to guide us, whatever God has revealed in the Scriptures, bearing upon the interpretation of this passage. Surely, it cannot be possible that God has left such important questions obscure and incapable of solution as are presented to us here. Remembering, then, that these things of the Spirit cannot be searched out by the natural man, and relying upon our divine Guide to lead us into the truth, let us examine the testimony of the Word of God as it relates to the portion before us.

The Church's One Foundation

First—We are not for a moment left in doubt as to the foundation of the Church. "Other foundation can no man lay than that which is laid, which is Jesus Christ" (1 Cor. 3:11). This is He of whom it is written in Isaiah 28:16 "Behold, I lay in Zion for a foundation a stone, a tried stone, a precious cornerstone of sure foundation." It was this same Peter, filled with the Holy Spirit, who, speaking of his ascended Lord, in Acts 4:11,12, said, "He is the stone, which was set at nought of you the builders, which was made the head of the corner. And in none other is there salvation: for neither is there any other name under heaven that is given among men, wherein we must be saved." And it was Peter again, who, in his First Epistle, referring to the passage from Isaiah, quoted above, wrote of the Lord Jesus, "Unto whom coming, a living stone, rejected indeed of men, but with God elect, precious, ye also, as living stones, are built up a spiritual house, to be a holy priesthood, to offer up spiritual sacrifices, acceptable to God through Jesus Christ. Because it is contained in Scripture, Behold, I lay in Zion a chief corner-stone, elect, precious: and he that believeth on him shall not be put to shame. For unto you therefore that believe is the preciousness: but for such as disbelieve, the stone which the builders rejected, the same was made the head of the corner; and a stone of stumbling, and a rock of offense" (1 Peter 2:4-8, R.V.). The rock is used as a symbol of Christ many times in the Scriptures, as, for example, in 1 Corinthians 10:4, and doubtless also in Matthew 7:24,25 and Luke 6:48. We may, therefore, count it settled that

"The Church's one Foundation
Is Jesus Christ, her Lord.
She is His new creation
By water and the Word.
From Heaven He came and sought her,
To be His holy Bride;
With His own blood He bought her,
And for her life He died."

Second—Nor is there any slightest question as to the Head of the Church.

God has raised His Son from the dead, and made Him to sit at His right hand in the heavenlies, far above all rule, and authority, and power, and dominion, and every name that is named, not only in this age, but also in that which is to come; and He has put all things in subjection under His feet, and given Him to be Head over all things to the Church, which is His body, the fullness of Him that fills all in all (Eph. 1:20-23). The Spirit of God declares unto us, in Ephesians 4:8-16, that the whole purpose of gifts in the Church is that we may grow up in all things into Him, who is the Head, even Christ; from whom all the body fitly framed and knit together, through that which every joint supplieth, according to the working in due measure of each several part, makes the increase of the body unto the building up of itself in love. That Christ is the Head of the Church is repeated in Ephesians 5:23 and Colossians 1:18, while in Colossians 2:18,19 we are warned against those teachers who fail to give Him that place.

Third—And yet, in spite of all that we have so far discovered, it still seems to be only fair and honest to conclude that when Jesus said, "Thou art a stone, and upon this rock I will build my church," He meant us to understand that by the rock, as well as the stone, He meant Peter himself. Any other conclusion makes our Lord's words, "Thou art Peter," to mean nothing and to have no connection with what follows.

Indeed, it seems very clear that if we had our Lord's words in the language in which He spoke them, we should find no difference between the word translated Peter and the word rendered rock. This at least is the view maintained by many of the private translators of the New Testament. Dr. Young's Bible Translation makes the disputed passage read, "Thou art a rock, and upon this rock I will build my assembly."

Wakefield reads it, "Thou art truly named Peter, and upon this very stone I will build my church."

George Campbell renders it, "Thou art named Rock, and on the rock I will build my church."

Taylor's New Testament has the word "Rock" in brackets, reading thus, "Thou art Peter [Rock], and upon this rock I will build my church."

The Emphatic Diaglott reads, "Thou art a rock, and on this rock I will build my church."

Samuel Sharpe also employs the brackets, reading, "Thou art Peter [or a rock], and on this rock I will build my church."

Andrews Norton shares the same view, for his translation reads, "You are, as I have named you, a rock, and on this rock I will build my church."

Charles Thomson is very emphatic, rendering these words, "Thou art named Peter (a rock), and upon this very rock I will build my church."

And the Twentieth Century New Testament reading is, "Your name is 'Peter'—a rock, and on this rock I will build my church."

This conclusion does not at all affect the former one that Christ is the Foundation of the Church. In Ephesians 2:20, the Church is represented as being built upon the foundation of the Apostles and Prophets, Christ Jesus Himself being the chief Corner-stone. In the description of the Bride, the

Lamb's Wife, in Revelation 21, it is written that the city wall has twelve foundations, and on them the twelve names of the twelve Apostles of the Lamb. Now Peter was the first of the Apostles of the Lamb who was gathered as a living stone unto Christ the great Living Stone. The building began, after Christ Himself, with Peter. He was the first stone to be laid upon the great underlying Foundation, which is Jesus Christ. Therefore, Jesus could say to Peter, as He did say, "Upon this rock I will build my church."

Even to this day, whenever an important building is to be erected, the first thing to be done, after the foundation is completed, is to lay what we call the corner-stone. This is not the kind of corner-stone the New Testament uses as a figure of Christ, for the corner-stone in that case supports the whole building. But the importance attached to the modern corner-stone consists in the fact that it is the first stone to be laid after the substructure is completed. Otherwise, it is no more important than the stones at the other corners, but because it is the very first stone in the superstructure we lay it with public ceremonies and give it a place of honor. In a sense, the whole building is built upon it, for the building begins with it. This is what Peter is in the Church. He is not and he never was a Pope. There is not a scrap of evidence that he was ever Bishop of Rome. He is a brother in a common brotherhood, though he was the first to enter that brotherhood. The Romanist premise does not lead to the Romanist conclusion.

Peter himself, by the Holy Spirit, has once and forever disposed of all the pretensions of the Papal hierarchy, falsely made in his name. Hear him as he speaks in 1 Peter 5:1-4: "The elders therefore among you I exhort, who am a fellow-elder, and a witness of the sufferings of Christ, who am also a partaker of the glory that shall be revealed. Tend the flock of God which is among you, exercising the oversight, not of constraint, but willingly, according to the will of God; nor yet for filthy lucre, but of a ready mind; neither as lording it over the charge allotted to you, but making yourselves examples to the flock. And when the chief Shepherd shall be manifested, ye shall receive the crown of glory that fadeth not away."

Fourth—As to Peter's successors, he has none. There is not the slightest ground here for the doctrine of Apostolic Succession. Christ has no Vicegerent on the earth and needs none, for He Himself is present with His Church—He never leaves her nor forsakes her. As for the priesthood in the Church, there can be no separate order of priests, for the Church is a royal priesthood; every believer is a priest having full access into the holy of holies, where God dwells (See Heb. 10:19-25).

Dean Alford, in his *Greek Testament for English Readers*, says:

The name Peter (not now first given, but prophetically bestowed by our Lord on His first interview with Simon, John 1:42), or Cephas, signifying a rock, the termination being only altered from Petra to Petros to suit the masculine appellation, denotes the personal position of this Apostle in the building of the Church of Christ. He was the first of those foundation stones (Rev. 21:14) on which the living Temple of God was built: this building itself beginning on the day of Pentecost by the laying of three thousand living stones on this very foundation.

That this is the simple and only interpretation of the words of our Lord, the whole usage of the New Testament shows: in which not doctrines nor confessions, but men, are uniformly the pillars and stones of the spiritual building. See 1 Peter 2:4-6; 1 Timothy 3:15 (where the pillar is not Timothy, but the congregation of the faithful) and note: Galatians 2:9; Ephesians 2:20; Revelation 3:12. And it is on Peter, as by divine revelation making this confession as thus under the influence of the Holy Ghost, as standing out before the Apostles in the strength of this faith, as himself founded on the one foundation, Jesus Christ, 1 Corinthians 3:11—that the Jewish portion of the Church was built, Acts 2 to 5, and the Gentile, Acts 10 and 11. After this last event, we hear little of him, but during this, the first building time, he is never lost sight of: see especially Acts 1:15; 2:14, 37; 3:12; 4:8; 5:15, 29; 9:34, 40; 10:25,26.

We may certainly exclaim with Bengel, "All this may be said with safety; for what has this to do with Rome?" Nothing can be further from any legitimate interpretation of this promise than the idea of a perpetual primacy in the successors of Peter; the very notion of succession is precluded by the form of the comparison, which concerns the person, and him only, so far as it involves a direct promise. In its other and general sense, as applying to all those living stones (Peter's own expression for members of Christ's Church) of whom the Church should be built, it implies, as Origen excellently comments on it, saying, that all this must be understood as said not only to Peter, as in the letter of the Gospel, but to every one who is such as Peter here showed himself, as the spirit of the Gospel teaches us.

The application of the promise to St. Peter has been elaborately impugned by Dr. Wordsworth. His zeal to appropriate the rock to Christ has somewhat overshot itself. In arguing that the term can apply to none but God, he will find it difficult surely to deny all reference to a rock in the name Peter. To me, it is equally difficult, nay, impossible, to deny all reference in "upon this rock," to the preceding word Peter. Let us keep to the plain, straightforward sense of Scripture, however that sense may have been misused by Rome. (Vol. 1, part 1, page 119.)

Philip's Message to Samaria

In Acts 8:12 we read that when the Samaritans "believed Philip preaching the things concerning the kingdom of God, and the name of Jesus Christ, they were baptized, both men and women." Just what did Philip preach?

He preached the same message as the Lord Jesus had preached to Nicodemus in John 3: "Except a man be born again, he cannot see the kingdom of God. For God sent not his Son into the world to condemn the world; but that the world through him might be saved. He that believeth on him is not condemned: but he that believeth not is condemned already, because he hath not believed in the name of the only begotten Son of God" (verses 3, 17,18). The Kingdom of God viewed here is the unseen Kingdom, which "cometh not with observation" (Luke 17:20-21). Believers are immediately translated into it when they believe and are born again; in Colossians 1:13 it is called the Kingdom of

God's dear Son, but that is identical with the Kingdom of God in its present unseen form. There is a time coming, however, when the Kingdom will be manifested, and then it will come with observation, and may be seen. "Then shall the righteous shine forth as the sun in the kingdom of their Father" (Matt. 13:43). It is for this manifestation of the sons of God that the whole creation is waiting in earnest expectation (Rom. 8:19).

The Roman Empire

What countries are now wholly or partly occupying the territory of the old Roman Empire?

There was included in the old Roman Empire the whole of North Africa, comprising Egypt, Morocco, etc.; Israel and vicinity; Turkey; Balkan States; Austria; Spain; Italy; France; part of the Netherlands; and England as far north as the Cheviot Hills.

Simon the Sorcerer

Is there any reason for believing that Simon, in Acts 8:18-24, was not a saved man?

Yes. Peter's declaration that Simon had "neither part nor lot in this matter" constitutes a very strong reason for believing that Simon's profession of faith was a false one.

The Antediluvian Sons of God

Who are the "sons of God" mentioned in Genesis 6:1-4?

The reference is to believers who at that time sinned against God by intermarriage with unbelievers. It is held by some that these "sons of God" were angels. But this teaching is contrary to that of our Lord in Matthew 22:30. It has always been a grievous sin among God's people to intermarry with His enemies, and against this we are expressly warned (2 Cor. 6:14 to 7:1).

Specks in the Universe

A postmillennial friend of mine put this question to me: "Why should we be so conceited as to think that our earth is so much more important than any other planet? We are nothing but mere specks in the universe anyhow." Perhaps you can help me.

"Specks in the universe" is right. The Word of God goes even further than your friend when it says: "Behold, the nations are as a drop of a bucket, and are counted as the small dust of the balance: behold, he taketh up the isles as a very little thing. . . . All nations before him are as nothing; and they are counted to him less than nothing and vanity" (Isa. 40:15-17).

And yet for some inexplicable reason, "God so loved the world, that he gave his only begotten Son that whosoever believeth in him should not perish, but have everlasting life" (John 3:16). Glory, Hallelujah, Amen!

Paul's Thorn in the Flesh

Can you give me any light as to what Paul's thorn in the flesh was? Some think it was an affliction of the eyes, others think that Paul realized that in his determination to reach the goal to which he was aiming Satan had turned loose the demons of Hell to buffet him. Would Galatians 6:17 have anything to do with this?

In Galatians 6:17 Paul says: "From henceforth let no man trouble me: for I bear in my body the marks of the Lord Jesus." The word "marks" represents the Greek word, *stigmata*, a word employed to describe a mark incised or punched upon the person of a slave for recognition of ownership. No doubt Paul used this word to refer to the scars of service which he bore upon his body as the result of the many sufferings he had endured. Of course, these might include the thorn in the flesh to which he refers. I am inclined to the belief that he alludes to an affliction of the eyes, resulting perhaps from his awful experience at Lystra where he was stoned and dragged out of the city and left for dead. This conclusion would seem to be logical from a careful study of Acts 14:19,20 and 2 Corinthians 12:1-9, both of which passages evidently refer to the same experience. The language of Galatians 4:13-15 may also be understood as tending to confirm this conclusion.

However, the question you raise is one that cannot be positively answered; it is one of the things that must wait "until the morning."

The Witch of Endor

Will you be kind enough to explain why God allowed Samuel to appear when Saul went to the witch of Endor? Some teachers claim he did not appear—it was only a representation, as the demons do in the present day. But the Bible distinctly says Samuel appeared. Then the witch herself seems not to have expected him—she was so badly frightened. Personally, this does not bother me very much, but whenever I talk with those who believe in spiritism, they always bring up this incident from the Bible. If you can give me a clear explanation, I would be very grateful.

It is true that there is much confusion among Bible teachers on this subject, but I must agree with you that the definite statements that Samuel appeared to the woman, and that he spoke to Saul time and again, force us to the conclusion that it was Samuel himself who appeared and not a representation of Samuel by a demon. It is also true, as you suggest, that the witch herself was badly frightened, because what had actually occurred was far beyond her powers. The keys of Hades are not in a witch's hands, but He who holds them in *His* hands did a new thing here and caused Samuel to appear and pronounce the doom of the apostate king. All this, however, gives no biblical warrant for spiritism (see Lev. 19:31; 20:6; Deut. 18:10-12).

The Cloud of Witnesses

Who are the cloud of witnesses of Hebrews 12:1?

They are the believers described in the preceding chapter. The word "witnesses" does not signify those who merely look on, though it may include that; but its true meaning is ***witness-bearers***, or those who give testimony. The imagery of the passage is probably that of the amphitheater where the great crowd looks on and sees the gladiators contesting in the arena. In order to get the full meaning, however, we must imagine the great crowd of onlookers made up of those who themselves had at some time in the past been in the arena. They therefore knew from experience what the contest really meant.

The Woman Who Was a Sinner

Was the woman "in the city, which was a sinner," who anointed the Lord Jesus in the Pharisee's house, as recorded in Luke 7:36-38, Mary of Bethany, or were there two anointings?

There were two anointings. The woman in Luke 7 is not Mary of Bethany. The anointing of Luke 7 took place in Galilee during the early part of our Lord's ministry, while the other anointing recorded in Matthew 26:6-13, Mark 14:3-9 and John 12:1-8, took place at Bethany in Judaea very shortly before the crucifixion. It is proper to observe here also that there is no ground for the widespread notion that the woman of Luke 7:37, "which was a sinner," was Mary of Magdala, out of whom the Lord Jesus cast seven demons. The woman of Luke 7:37 is not named, nor do we know anything of her except what is recorded in connection with her act of devotion in washing her Lord's feet with her tears and wiping them with the hairs of her head, and then kissing his feet and anointing them with the ointment.

Zacharias' Punishment for Unbelief

What happened to Zacharias, the priest, father of John the Baptist, for not believing the message of Gabriel? Is it true, as someone has told me, that he was made deaf as well as dumb?

Yes; he was dumb as well as deaf, for when his friends wanted to communicate with him at the end of the period of his dumbness, they "made signs" to ask him about his son's name (Luke 1:62).

MISCELLANEOUS

The Grammar of Genesis 1:1

Will you please explain the grammatical construction of the first verse of the Bible?

The first verse of Genesis 1 is most interesting from the standpoint of grammar. The Hebrew language has three numbers, instead of two as in English. There is the singular, indicating one person, place or thing; then the dual, for two persons, places or things; and then the plural, for three or more persons, places or things.

In Genesis 1:1 all these forms appear. The first word, translated God, is Elohim, a plural noun, thus intimating that in some way God is more than one, and even more than two; that He is at least threefold.

But the verb, "created," is a singular verb. Thus we have at the very threshold of divine inspiration an intimation of the trinity and also the unity of God.

The word for "earth" is singular. But the word for "heaven" is neither singular nor plural, but dual. This would indicate that the heaven of the original creation was twofold.

How, then, was it that when Paul was caught up into Paradise he found himself in "the third heaven," as related in 2 Corinthians 12? The answer is that Paradise had been removed from Hades at the ascension of the Lord Jesus, and had become the third heaven far above all other heavens, the place of God's throne. (See Ps. 68:18; Eph. 4:8-10.)

A Difficulty

May I ask you to explain the following seeming discrepancies, etc., so that I may be able to give a reasonable answer to unbelievers?

In Exodus 9:6 we read that ALL the cattle of Egypt died. In verses 20 and 21 of the same chapter the Egyptians are again seen as having cattle.

We are not informed as to how long an interval there may have been between verses 7 and 8. The Egyptians may have restocked with cattle during that interval by purchasing from the Israelites or the neighboring countries.

Death Better Than Life

In there any Scripture which reads as follows: "Weep and mourn at the birth and rejoice at the death"?

No, there is no such Scripture. The only Scripture I recall at all similar to this is Ecclesiastes 7:1,2, which says: "A good name is better than precious ointment; and the day of death than the day of one's birth. It is better to go to the house of mourning, than to go to the house of feasting; for that is the end of all men, and the living will lay it to his heart."

The book of Ecclesiastes gives the view of human life from "under the sun," and the above quotation shows that unless there were something beyond the horizon of human reasoning it would be better to die than to be born; better, indeed, not to have lived at all. (Compare 1 Cor. 15:19.)

Manna

What was manna, and why was it called by that name?

Manna was the food for the people of Israel which God sent down from heaven every day for 40 years, except on Saturday the sabbath, and enough was sent down on Friday to last over the weekend. It is described in Exodus 16:31 as being "like coriander seed, white; and the taste of it was like wafers made with honey." In Numbers 11:7,8 we read that "the manna was as coriander seed, and the color thereof as the color of bdellium. And the people went about, and gathered it, and ground it in mills, or beat it in a mortar, and baked it in pans, and made cakes of it: and the taste of it was as the taste of fresh oil."

The word "manna" means "What is it?" or, as Strong's Concordance defines it, the meaning is "a whatness." Manna is a type of Christ as "the bread of life" come down from heaven to die for the life of the world (John 6:35-51). Its very name, "What is it?" is suggestive of Him Who is in His own person a mystery.

In Exodus 16:14 it is called a "small" thing, which came upon the dew and was gathered morning by morning. The Lord Jesus is looked upon by the world as a small thing, having no form nor comeliness, and no beauty that men should desire Him (Isa. 53:2). In His humiliation He must be seen as our Savior, and then we must meditate upon Him, and feed upon Him in order to grow. Manna, however, as the bread of life, is only one of the many symbols of Christ as the believer's food. He is also symbolized by "the old corn of the land" (Josh. 5:11), the solid food of Hebrews 5:13,14, etc.

The Language of Daniel

I have heard that not all of the book of Daniel was written in Hebrew. Is that true?

Yes. Beginning with the fourth verse of the second chapter, and continuing to the end of the seventh chapter, Daniel was written in Aramaic, the ancient language of Syria, the vernacular of the people among whom Daniel lived at the time of the writing.

The Temple of Solomon

Is it true that the temple of Solomon was built without any noise? And if so, what is the typical significance of that fact?

According to 1 Kings 6, 7, the temple of Solomon "when it was in building, was built of stone made ready before it was brought thither; so that there was neither hammer nor axe nor any tool of iron heard in the house, while it was in building." The typical significance of this remarkable statement has to do with the work now going on of constructing the Church which is God's temple. This Church universal, made up of all those who are born again, is the body of Christ (Eph. 1:22,23) and the temple of God (Eph. 2:19-22).

This temple is graphically described in 1 Peter 2, where Christ Himself is set forth as the great foundation, and the children of God are stones in the building. These children of God have come to Christ, "as unto a living stone, disallowed indeed of men, but chosen of God, and precious," and they, "as lively stones, are built up a spiritual house, an holy priesthood, to offer up the spiritual sacrifices, acceptable to God by Jesus Christ" (verses 1-5).

Now all this work, as the work of Solomon's temple, is going on silently, and is proceeding to a glorious consummation, when Christ will present the Church to Himself, "a glorious church, not having spot, or wrinkle, or any such thing; but that it should be holy and without blemish" (Eph. 5:25-27).

The Ribband of Blue

What is the meaning of "the ribband of blue" in the fringe of the borders of the priests' garments, referred to in Numbers 15:38?

"Ribband" is the old style spelling for ribbon. Blue, in Scripture imagery, is the heavenly color, and the blue ribbon in the hem of the priests' garments signified that the servants of God are to be heavenly in their conduct and to walk in a path of separation with God.

Tires

Please explain Isaiah 3:18-26. I have heard this refers to automobile tires.

It has no such significance. The word "tires" in the passage refers to a crescent-shaped ornament worn by women on the head. In the Revised Version, in verse 18, instead of "their round tires like the moon," it reads, "the crescents."

Insurance

Have we any Scripture to justify us in carrying life insurance policies, or sick and accident policies?

It appears clear to me that 1 Timothy 5:8 covers the matter: "If any provide not for his own, and especially for those of his own house, he hath denied the faith, and is worse than an infidel." If we have those dependent upon us for support, we should do our utmost to provide for them, not only while we are here to help them, but also after we are gone, or are disabled and unable to care for them.

Zion

What does "Zion" mean?

The meaning of the word is "Sunny Mount." It is applied in Scripture (1) to one of the hills in the city of Jerusalem, the other being Moriah; (2) the whole city of Jerusalem; (3) the temple; (4) the hill on which the temple stood (usually called Moriah) as distinct from "the city of David"; (5) the religious system of Judaism; and (5) to heaven.

The Axe That Swam

Was the iron that floated (2 Kings. 6:5,6) the same material as we know today called "iron"?

I see no reason to doubt it.

A Universal Language

Is it promised in the Bible that there shall be a universal language?

Yes. In Zephaniah 3:8,9, it is written: "Therefore wait for me, saith Jehovah, until the day that I was up to the prey; for my determination is to gather the nations, that I may assemble the kingdoms, to pour upon them mine indignation, even all my fierce anger; for all the earth shall be devoured with the fire of my jealousy.

"For then will I turn to the peoples a pure language, that they may all call upon the name of Jehovah, to serve him with one consent" (R.V.).

The Lamentations of Jeremiah

Please tell us something about the book of Lamentations.

The full title of the book is "The Lamentations of Jeremiah." Jeremiah was preeminently the weeping prophet (Jer. 13:17), and in the five lamentations of this book he weeps continually for Israel, whom he loves and whose sins he hates. The book shows the undying love of Jehovah for His people whom He chastens. "Whom the Lord loveth he chasteneth" (Heb. 12:6). The book of Lamentations is highly poetical, being arranged in a series of acrostics, based upon the twenty-two letters of the Hebrew alphabet. The verses of each chapter begin with the letters of the alphabet in their order, the third chapter having three verses for each letter. See 1:22; 2:22; 3:66; 4:22; 5:22.

Plowshares and Swords

What does the Bible say about turning plowshares into swords or turning swords into plowshares?

In Joel 3 it is written, "Beat your plowshares into swords, and your pruning hooks into spears." The context (verses 9-16) shows that this refers to the judgments of the awful Day of the Lord, when the Son of Man shall return to the earth to subdue His enemies and set up His throne (Isa. 63:1-6; Rev.19:11-21).

In Isaiah 2:4 and Micah 4:3 the opposite picture is presented, pointing to the promise for the last days, when, after subduing His enemies, the Lord will bring in the promised peace. "And he shall judge among the nations, and shall rebuke many people: and they shall beat their swords into plowshares, and their spears into pruning hooks: nation shall not lift up sword against nation, neither shall they learn war any more" (Isa. 2:1-5; Mic. 4:1-3).

The Significance of Numbers

What is the significance of the number forty in God's creation of mankind in His Word?

Forty is the multiple of four and ten. Four is the earth number: the four winds and four quarters of the earth (Rev. 7:1; Dan. 7:2); Eden's four streams (Gen. 2:10; Ezek. 37:9, etc.); and ten is the governmental number: ten commandments; ten talents; ten cities in reward for ten pounds gained, etc. Forty symbolizes earthly governmental testing: the forty days of rain in the flood; Moses' forty years in Egypt and forty in Midian; forty days on the mount (Ex. 24:18), and a second forty days after Israel's sin in calf worship (Deut. 9:18, 25); forty years in the desert wanderings, resulting from the forty days' probation in the searching of Canaan; the forty days' warning to Nineveh (Jonah 3:4); the forty days of our Lord's temptation (testing) in the wilderness (Matt. 4:2), etc.

The Pyramids

Is it true that one of the pyramids in Egypt has great spiritual significance? We hear much discussion concerning it. Please tell us what the Scriptures teach about it.

It is true that there is widespread teaching concerning the spiritual significance of the great pyramids, and it is claimed by those who propagate this teaching that the pyramid is referred to in Isaiah 19:19,20, where it is written, "In that day shall there be an altar to Jehovah in the midst of the land of Egypt, and a pillar at the border thereof to Jehovah. And it shall be for a sign and for a witness unto Jehovah of hosts in the land of Egypt." I have read much concerning this matter, but am not at all satisfied that this Scripture is a reference to the great pyramids. There seems to be no real evidence that the pyramid was ever used as an altar or considered as such. Just what is the altar referred to we cannot tell. For my own part, I am satisfied that the Scriptures of the Old and New Testament are a quite sufficient revelation for our faith and guidance.

The Golden Rule

Is the doctrine of "the Golden Rule" found in the Bible? If so, where?

The words of the Lord Jesus in Matthew 7:12 are often referred to as the golden rule: "Therefore all things whatsoever ye would that men should do to you, do ye even so to them: for this is the law and the prophets." It is by no means a statement of the way of salvation. There is no other way of salvation but to receive the Lord Jesus Christ as one's own personal Savior and Lord. Those who do this are born again and receive the gift of God which is eternal life.

The Feast of Weeks

What was the feast of weeks in Israel?

The feast of weeks is described in Deuteronomy 16:9-12. It came between the passover and the feast of tabernacles, the former emphasizing the beginning, and the latter the consummation of God's dealings with Israel. The passover sets forth redemption through blood, which must be the beginning of all God's dealings with man. The feast of tabernacles pointed to the regathering of Israel into her own land and to the blessing of God in connection with the kingdom. Between these two feasts came the feast of weeks, occupying seven weeks, during which the people rejoiced in the blessing of God already experienced, and in the anticipation of future blessing. We today who have taken our place under the shelter of the shed blood of Christ are celebrating in antitype our feast of weeks. "Being justified by faith, we have peace with God through our Lord Jesus Christ: by whom also we have access by faith into this grace wherein we stand, and rejoice in hope of the glory of God" (Rom. 5:1,2).

Benedictions

I have heard that you taught that there are no benedictions in the Bible except for believers. Is this true?

Yes, it is true. There is no Scriptural ground for the universal custom of pronouncing benedictions upon all present in an assembly, without reference to whether they are believers or unbelievers. It is true that the New Testament benedictions often include the words "you all," but that is because they are found in Epistles addressed to the Church of God only. As a matter of fact, the New Testament carefully distinguishes between the friends of God and the enemies of God. In 1 Corinthians 16:22 It is written, "If any man love not the Lord Jesus Christ, let him be Anathema Maranatha," which means, "let him be accursed: our Lord cometh." Let not that man who is treading underfoot the Son of God, making the blood of the covenant an unholy thing, and doing despite to the Spirit of Grace—let not that man think that he may receive the blessing of God. The benedictions properly belong to those only "that love our Lord Jesus Christ in sincerity" (Eph. 6:24).

The Sword

If you find it convenient I should appreciate it if you would give your understanding of verses 36 and 38 of chapter 22 of Luke's Gospel. I am unable to harmonize the commandment to buy a sword with the tenor of the other Scriptures of the New Testament.

A sword might be useful and perhaps indispensable, to deal with fierce beasts in the way. It is not necessary to assume that our Lord advocated the use of the sword against men. As I write today I am in the heart of Central America, where almost every man one meets on the road, even in this time of peace, bears a machete, a big long knife, not for use against humans, but for various uses in field and forest.

Anathema Maranatha

What is the meaning of "Anathema Maranatha" in 1 Corinthians 16:22?

"Anathema" is "accursed," and "Maranatha" is a word of Chaldean origin meaning "Our Lord cometh." The sentence is a malediction pronounced upon our Lord's enemies. While it is a universal custom in our day for the preacher to "pronounce the benediction" upon all present, whether they are all the Lord's people or not, the custom is contrary to Scripture, whose benedictions are always confined to God's own people, and whose word for His enemies is a malediction, instead. Compare 1 Corinthians 16:22 with Ephesians 6:24.

Urim and Thummim

What is meant by "the Urim and Thummim" of Exodus 28:30?

The words mean "lights and perfection," and they are believed to be a name for the stones of the breastplate of the high priest. Or it may be that they were stones in addition to the stones of the breastplate. In Leviticus 8:8 we read that in clothing Aaron, Moses "put the breastplate upon him: also had put in the breastplate the Urim and the Thummim." In some mysterious way not fully revealed the Urim and the Thummim were used in Israel to ascertain the will of God (see Num. 27:21; Deut. 33:8; 1 Sam. 28:6; Ezra 2:63).

Care in Use of Words

Should Christians use the term "sacrament" or "Eucharist" in referring to the Lord's Supper; or should they speak of "the sabbath" or "Sunday"? or should they use the word "kingdom" as applied to the church?

In 2 Timothy 1:13 we are exhorted to "hold fast the form of sound words." "Sacrament" means an oath, and the Roman soldiers' oath on enlistment was so called. The Lord's Supper is in no sense a sacrament. "Eucharist" is not so bad, for it means thanksgiving, and the Supper is a feast of thanksgiving. "Sabbath" is a much misused word; the first day of the week should be called the Lord's day. And the Kingdom is not the church. The Church is made up, not of subjects to be ruled over in the coming Kingdom, but rather of co-rulers to be associated with Christ in reigning over the kingdom. By "the Church," of course, I mean only those persons who are really born again.

The Meaning of Apostasy

Does apostasy mean to change one's mind in some religious views, or rejecting Christ as one's Savior, or lowering His righteousness and raising our own?

It means none of these things. Apostasy differs from backsliding in that a true Christian may backslide, but an apostate proves by his apostasy that he never was really born again. Judas, who was never saved, was an apostate; Peter was a saved man who fell out of communion. The Christian who backslides loses his fellowship and joy and fruitfulness, though he does not lose his salvation, for salvation is the free gift of God, and includes eternal life and eternal security (John 5:24). An apostate is one who, after professing to believe the Gospel, turns away even from his profession. The apostate is described in 1 John 2:19: "They went out from us, but they were not of us; for if they had been of us, they would no doubt have continued with us: but they went out, that they might be made manifest that they were not all of us." Their going out from us is a matter of doctrine. Of course, they may go on calling themselves Christians, but no man is a Christian who denies the fundamental doctrines touching the Person and work of Christ. "Whosoever transgresseth, and abideth not in the doctrine of Christ, hath not God. He that abideth in the doctrine of Christ, he hath both the Father and the Son. If there come any unto you, and bring not this doctrine, receive him not into your house, neither bid him God speed: for he that biddeth him God speed is partaker of his evil deeds" (2 John 9-11).

The Apostasy of Today

Is the apostasy of today well established?

Yes, the apostasy is certainly well established. Whether it is yet fully developed I cannot say.

The Apostles' Creed

Why is there no mention made of the Lord's return in the Apostles' Creed? Do you not believe that the omission of this fact has helped to increase the doubt and unbelief in this teaching even among saints? Would you consider it correct to say that Satan was responsible for the omission?

But there is mention of the Lord's return in the Apostles' Creed. Does it not say, "From thence He shall come to judge the quick and the dead"? Of course, that is not an intelligent statement about our Lord's return, for it implies a general judgment, of which the Scriptures know nothing. It is a mistake to call it the Apostles' Creed, for the Apostles knew nothing about it and had nothing to do with it. The Creed is supposed to have originated about the end of the fourth century. The saints have no need to be confused, for they have the Bible which they can study for themselves, and it is so clear that the wayfaring man, though he be a fool, need not err therein.

Noah's Ark

Where can I find that Noah was 120 years building the ark?

The widespread belief that "the ark was a preparing" (1 Peter 3:20) during the period of 120 years is based upon Genesis 6:3, which says, "My Spirit shall not always strive with man, for that he also is flesh: yet his days shall be an hundred and twenty years." Since it was right after this that Noah was called of God and instructed concerning the ark (Gen. 6:13,14), the assumption is that it did actually take 120 years to build the ark, because the flood took place 120 years after that time.

Honey

Will you kindly tell me the meaning of Proverbs 25:27: "It is not good to eat much honey"?

The idea is that it is not good to eat too much honey. In the sixteenth verse of the same chapter we read: "Hast thou found honey? eat so much as is sufficient for thee, lest thou be filled therewith, and vomit it." Now read the twenty-seventh verse in full: "It is not good to eat much honey: so for men to search their own glory is not glory." Too much "sweet praise" is not good for us. The Revised Version reads: "It is not good to eat much honey: so for men to search out their own glory is grievous."

Honey was excluded from the burnt-offerings under the law of Moses: "No meat-offering, which ye shall bring unto Jehovah, shall be made with leaven: for ye shall burn no leaven, nor any honey, in any offering of Jehovah made by fire" (Lev. 2:11). Leaven is a type of corruption, and, therefore, of course, it would be excluded from any offering typifying the Lord Jesus Christ, in whom there was no corruption. And honey, which is merely natural sweetness, could no more symbolize His perfection than could leaven.

All this throws light upon the true meaning of Proverbs 25:27, which might be paraphrased to read: "It is not good to depend too much upon mere natural sweetness; so for men to search out their own glory is grievous."

Automobiles and Prophecy

Did Nahum in his prophecy (2:3,4) see our automobiles? I should like to have your comment on these verses.

I do not believe that there is any reference to automobiles and other motor-driven vehicles in Nahum 2:3,4. Even the fastest automobiles do not "run like the lightnings." The immediate reference is to the Assyrian invasion which was only about one hundred years after the prophecy was uttered. But I have no doubt that there is also reference to the ultimate destruction of Jerusalem in the end-time at the close of the period of the Great Tribulation.

Selah

What is the meaning of "Selah," frequently occurring in the Psalms?

It is believed to be a musical sign, similar to what is now called the "rest" sign. It has been variously defined as meaning "pause" or "meditate." One rather good suggestion is that it means "Think of that!"

Why Parables?

Why did Jesus employ parables in His teaching?

Jesus Himself gives us the clue in Mark 4:12. He did not begin to do so until His miracles were malignantly ascribed to Satanic agencies. His enemies saw His works, yet closed their eyes to their source and spiritual meaning. They heard His words, for He "spake as never man spake"; yet they were deaf to the life-giving message conveyed. They voluntarily refused to accept the Gospel and at length became morally incapable of doing so.

Carefulness in Soul Winning

Will you please explain Jude 23?

The teaching of Jude 23 is that we must have a care in the work of soul-winning, lest in putting men out of the fire we ourselves shall become tainted with their sins. The work of soul-winning is dangerous business, but it is a good business; for it is written, "He that winneth souls is wise," and "They that be wise shall shine as the brightest of the firmament; and they that turn many to righteousness as the stars forever and ever" (Prov. 11:30; Dan. 12:3).

Capital Punishment

I thought I once read this in the Bible: "If a man commit an offense, for which the penalty is to be stoned or hung, ye shall take him out at once and execute him, that fear shall sink into the heart of the evil and he turn from his evil." I forget the book and page, but I think it was in one of the books of Moses. Is such language in the Bible? And if so, when one commits a premeditated brutal crime, is it not wrong to beg for soft punishment, when the evil will not fear but continue in crime and the innocent suffer? Is not the death penalty given expressly for protection of society? And is not one who opposes the death penalty really an enemy of organized society?

Language similar to that quoted in your letter is found in Deuteronomy 13:10,11 and Ecclesiastes 8:11. Capital punishment is based upon God's covenant to Noah (Gen. 9:6) and it is also approved in the New Testament (Rom. 13:4). To set it aside on the plea of mercy is to flout God's authority as the Ruler of His universe—the righteous "Judge of all the earth" (Gen. 18:25).

Capital Punishment Pre-Christian

Should I as a Christian believe in capital punishment? Since the law was given to the Jews and we are not under the law, why should we observe their customs?

The law of capital punishment antedates the Jewish law by almost a thousand years. It is a part of the Noahic Covenant, and it still stands as written: "Whoso sheddeth man's blood, by man shall his blood be shed, for in the image of God made he man" (Gen. 9:6). It has never been abrogated nor modified in any way. It constitutes the distinctive feature of the covenant, establishing for the first time the institution of human government—"the government of man by man. The highest function of government is the judicial taking of life. All other governmental powers are implied in that" (Scofield). Capital punishment therefore is not only permissible, but it is obligatory upon every civil government. The state not only has a right to put a murderer to death, but it has no right to let him live. Capital punishment is an integral and inseparable part of God's charter of government.

The objection is often raised that capital punishment is unchristian. It would be more strictly true to say that it is pre-christian, for it was established of God nearly twenty-five hundred years before the Christian Church, and though for this reason it is not distinctly Christian, it is nevertheless distinctively and absolutely divine.

Bobbed Hair

What is the great objection to short hair for women? I honestly cannot find any Scripture against it, although I have looked up all the references given in my concordance. In my case there are several very real advantages in having my hair short, and I intend to keep it short unless you convince me that I, as a Christian, should let it grow.

You do not need to look up many passages on the subject of bobbed hair in order to find a conclusion as to what a Christian woman at the time of Christ ought to do. First Corinthians 11:15 should have settled it for any woman at that time who sought to do the will of God as revealed in His Word: "But if a woman have long hair, it is a glory to her: for her hair is given her for a covering." And in verse 6 of this chapter we are told that it is "a shame for a woman to be shorn or shaven." It seems clear to me that the regulations at this time concerning long hair for women and short hair for men were based upon God's plan that a man should not make himself look like a woman, nor a woman make herself look like a man. See Deuteronomy 22:5. The same principle can be applied today, if not the same regulations.

Suffering Among God's People

Why is it that there is so much suffering among the people of God?

I believe that your question may be answered conclusively by one verse of Scripture, namely, Colossians 1:24, where Paul speaking of himself says: "Who now rejoice in my sufferings for you, and fill up that which is behind of the afflictions of Christ in my flesh for his body's sake, which is the church." The Church which is the body of Christ is made up of all those and only those who are born again, and as they are born again, member by member, they are added to that body. So the body of Christ is brought into existence and unto completion by birth.

In the natural world birth is accompanied by suffering. It seems to be inevitable that in bringing her child into the world the mother must suffer. She risks her life and sometimes sacrifices it in order that her child may be born. Just so in some mysterious way the body of Christ must be brought to perfection and completion by suffering. God has warned us that in the world we will have tribulation, and this would not be and could not be without His permission. To us it is given in behalf of Christ not only to believe on Him, but also to suffer for His sake (Phil. 1:29). Let us humble ourselves therefore under the mighty hand of God, that He may exalt us in due time; casting all our care upon Him; for He cares for us. And let us assure our hearts that the God of all grace, who has called us unto His eternal glory by Christ Jesus, after that we have suffered a while, will make us perfect, establish, strengthen, and settle us (1 Peter 5:6-10). Let us always remember that however great the sufferings may be they are not worthy to be compared with the glory that shall be revealed toward us (Rom. 8:18)

Longevity Before the Flood

How long did men live before the flood?

The oldest of all was Methuselah, who lived 969 years; then in their order of longevity were Jared, 962 years; Noah, 950 years; Adam, 930 years; Seth, 912 years; Cainan, 910 years; Enos, 905 years; and Mahaleel, 895 years. See Genesis 5:4-32 and 9:29.

The Flood of Noah

Was the flood of Noah really universal, or was it confined to that part of the earth inhabited at the time? What is meant by "the great deep," whose fountains were "broken up"?

1. It is evident, from the record in Genesis 7: 19,20, that the flood was universal: "And the waters prevailed exceedingly upon the earth; and all the high hills, that were under the whole heaven, were covered. Fifteen cubits upward did the waters prevail; and the mountains were covered."

2. It is believed by many students that the earth before the flood was enclosed in a globe of vapor, which refracted the rays of the sun, giving practically equal light and heat all over the earth, making it as light and warm at the poles as at the equator; and that this great mass of vapor was the "great deep" referred to in Genesis 7:11 and 8:2. The vapor became condensed into water and this water was precipitated upon the earth, causing rain to fall "upon the earth forty days and forty nights" (Gen. 7:11,12).

From Genesis 2:5,6 it appears that in the primitive creation there was no rain, "for the Lord God had not caused it to rain upon the earth, but there went up a mist from the earth, and watered the whole face of the ground."

This precipitation would explain the origin of the rainbow (Gen. 9:13) for there could be no rainbow without rain. Also it would explain the rotation of the seasons, "cold and heat, summer and winter, and day and night" (Gen. 8:22), since, by the refraction of light and heat already spoken of, there would be no such rotation.

There are traditions of a universal flood in various parts of the world, including Assyria, Babylonia, Egypt, China, Africa, Persia, and among the Aztec and American Indians. But these so-called "corroborations" of the sacred record are not needed by the believer.

Capital Punishment

In capital punishment disapproved in the Bible?

No, indeed. Quite to the contrary, capital punishment is authorized by God Himself in the dispensation of human government committed to Noah and his descendants. In Genesis 9:5, according to the divine decree, "Whoso sheddeth man's blood, by man shall his blood be shed." This decree has never been abrogated or modified and is still in full force.

The Jewish New Year

Why do the Jews celebrate their new year in September instead of

January? And why do they place the creation of man 243 years later than the common reckoning?

According to the Jewish calendar the creation of man took place 3,760 years and three months before the commencement of the Christian era. But the year with them is lunisolar and, according as it is ordinary or embolismic, consists of 12 or 13 lunar months, each of which has 29 or 30 days. This makes the embolismic year 384 days, and the ordinary year 354 days. Of course, this would account for the difference between 3,760 years and 4,004 years, as we reckon it.

Prior to the exodus from Egypt the Hebrew year began in the autumn with the month Tisri, which was practically parallel with our September. A new year was established at the time of the exodus in obedience to the command of Exodus 12:1,2: "And Jehovah spake unto Moses and Aaron in the land of Egypt, saying, 'This month shall be unto you the beginning of months: it shall be the first month of the year to you.'" This was in the month Abib, or as it was later called, Nisan, and corresponded nearly to our April. Therefore, it comes about that the Hebrews have the sacred year, beginning in the spring, and the civil year, beginning in the fall (compare Ex. 23:16; 34:22).

The difference in the Hebrew chronology as placing the creation later than the ordinary Christian reckoning is due to the difference in the length of the Hebrew year as compared with our solar year.

Zealousy Affected

Please tell me what is meant by the mysterious words of Galatians 4:17,18: "They zealously affect you, but not well; yea, they would exclude you, that ye might affect them. But it is good to be zealously affected always in a good thing, and not only when I am present with you."

Your difficulty arises from the fact that words, especially in such a fluid language as our English, are often changed in their meaning as time goes on. Our Authorized Version is over 300 years old, and so it is wise to consult the Revised Version in such a case as this. I think you will find real help in so doing, for in the Revision it reads: "They zealously seek you in no good way; nay, they desire to shut you out, that ye may seek them. But it is good to be zealously sought in a good matter at all times, and not only when I am present with you." The reference is to the enemies of grace who sometimes profess zeal and affection toward God's children in order to influence them against the truth.

The Little Book

What is the "little book" mentioned in Revelation 10:8-11?

It consisted of the message revealed to John on Patmos, by which he was commissioned to prophesy, not "before" but "over" or "concerning (see R.V. text and margin) many peoples, and nations, and tongues, and kings" (verse 11). John's message was a message of woes and judgments, and in his belly it was bitter, but in his mouth it was sweet because it was the Word of God (compare Ezek. 2:8 to 3:3 and Jer. 25:15-26).

The Book and Tree of Life

Please explain the words of Revelation 22:19, "God shall take away his part out of the book of life." If this does not mean the loss of one's salvation, what does it mean?

It is a case of mistranslation. The Revisers have corrected it to read: "And if any man shall take away from the words of the book of this prophecy, God shall take away his part from the tree of life, and out of the holy city, which are written in this book." There is nothing in the Scriptures to show that a name once inscribed upon the book of life is ever erased.

The verse should be read in connection with verse 14, also in the Revision, where "do his commandments" is changed to "wash their robes." Literally, verse 14 reads: "Blessed (are) they that wash their robes, that they may have right to the tree of life, and that they should go in by the gates into the city."

The question of the eternal security of believers does not enter into the purview of these verses. Believers are those who have "washed their robes," and these will not add to or take away from the book. It is not to believers but rather to rebels that God addresses the terrible warning of verses 18 and 19. Though the world may lightly esteem the book of The Revelation of Jesus Christ, it is esteemed very highly by God, and He will not tolerate any tampering with it.

The Book of Life

Will you please explain Revelation 3:5: "I will not blot out his name out of the Book of Life"? I have heard it given as a proof that a Christian can sin away his salvation and be lost.

The words mean just what they say: "I will not blot out his name." It is only by inference that these words could be made to imply "that a Christian can sin away his salvation and be lost." Such inferences are misleading, and lead to no end of difficulty and confusion among God's dear people. If we take the statement just as it stands, we have a beautiful assurance of the believer's eternal security in Christ: his name will never be blotted out from the Book of Life. A somewhat similar passage is found in John 6:37: "Him that cometh to me I will in no wise cast out." The meaning of this is seen in what follows: "For I came down from heaven, not to do mine own will, but the will of him that sent me. And this is the Father's will which hath sent me, that of all which he hath given me I should lose nothing, but should raise it up again at the last day. And this is the will of him that sent me, that every one which seeth the Son, and believeth on him may have everlasting life: and I will raise him up at the last day" (38-40). The believer's security is not a matter of doubt if only the plain statements of the Word of God are read and believed.

Not Blotted Out

Is any one's name ever blotted out of the Book of Life? and if not,

why does our Lord say in Revelation 3:5: "He that overcometh, the same shall be clothed in white raiment; and I will not blot out his name out of the book of life"? Does this not imply the possibility of some names being blotted out from that book?

No, there is no such implication. Disfranchisement was a common method of punishment in olden times for those who came into conflict with the constituted authority. Such a man's name was blotted out from the register of citizens or voters. Let such an one know that there is one place where if his name is written it will not be blotted out.

Again, men were often put out of the synagogues for the name of the Lord. In John 9 the man who was born blind was excommunicated from the synagogue because of his testimony concerning the Lord Jesus. He said: "Since the world began was it not heard that any man opened the eyes of one that was born blind. If this man were not of God, he could do nothing." To which they answered and said unto him: "Thou wast altogether born in sins, and dost thou teach us? And they cast him out," that is, they excommunicated him. And when "Jesus heard that they had cast him out," He at once went looking for him, and "when he had found him," He ministered unto him and brought him into the full joy of fellowship with Himself.

His name had been blotted out of the membership roll of the synagogue, but his name should not be blotted out of the Book of Life. It may be that in these last days many of the children of God will find themselves in conflict with the ecclesiastical authorities. They may be cast out by those authorities, and their names blotted out from the membership roll of earthly churches, but let them be comforted by the words of Revelation 3:5: "He that overcometh, the same shall be clothed in white raiment; and I will NOT blot out his name out of THE BOOK OF LIFE, but I will confess his name before my Father, and before his angels."

The New Covenant

What is the meaning of the statement, "For this is my blood of the new testament (or covenant)," Matthew 26:28? To what covenant does it apply?

The New Covenant is clearly defined for us in Jeremiah 31:31-34, where, of course, its direct application is to Israel, and its fulfillment awaits a time yet future for the nation.

But the language of Jeremiah 31 is quoted in Hebrews 10:16,17, where it is shown by the context that we who have believed, whether Israelites or Gentiles, have entered into the blessing of the New Covenant based upon "the offering of the body of Jesus Christ once for all," by which "offering he hath perfected forever them that are sanctified" (verses 10 and 14).

The Days of Creation

Are the days of the Genesis Creation 24 hours long?

From Exodus 20:11 some believe that the days of Creation were 24-hour days. Since I was not there when it happened, I do not know for sure, but I certainly believe God could do the job in 24 hours if He so desired!

Cremation

Is there anything in the Scriptures against cremation? That is, for the believer? How do you feel about it personally?

I do not know any Scriptures touching this point. Therefore let every man be fully persuaded in his own mind. As to how I feel about it personally, I do not like the idea. But that, of course, has nothing to do with the case.

Cremation and Cemeteries

1. Is it right for a Christian to leave orders that after his death his body shall be cremated?

2. Is it right for a Christian who believes in and looks for the coming of the Lord to buy a lot in a cemetery and prepare a grave to be buried in?

1. I should not like to judge the point. Such orders are not often given by Christians, but rather by unbelievers who seem to be trying to avoid a resurrection. But it won't make any difference in either case. God knows how to bring them all forth, whether in the resurrection of life or in the resurrection of damnation.

2. This is another question which cannot be answered, Yes or No. Let each one be fully persuaded in his own mind. I like the philosophy of the little boy who said, "I am not looking for the undertaker but for the uppertaker." Keep looking up!

Daniel in the Lions' Den

I recently heard it expressed that while Daniel was in the lions' den, God took the lions' hunger from them, or stopped their hunger at that time. Is that the meaning of Daniel 6:22?

The language of Daniel 6:22 is: "My God hath sent his angel, and hath shut the lions' mouths, that they have not hurt me." As to whether the lions were hungry the record does not say. Of course it was perfectly easy for God to take away their hunger, or to leave their hunger with them and yet prevent them from hurting His servant. Nothing is impossible with God! But if the lions' hunger was removed, it certainly returned in a hurry when Daniel's enemies were cast into the den (see verse 24).

The Authenticity of Daniel

Will you please give proof of the authenticity of Daniel? It is said by some, as you doubtless know, that the book was written by an unknown writer as late as 100 B.C.

For answer to this query we pass on the following from the late Dr. W. G. Moorehead:

1. The book claims to have been written by Daniel. In the last six chapters

the author uses such phrases as, "I saw in the night visions"; "I, Daniel, alone saw the vision"; "I, Daniel, understood by books," etc. These chapters are inseparably bound up with the first six. The pertinent question is, Are these statements true? He would be reckless indeed who would impeach the author's veracity, or charge him with forgery.

2. Josephus affirms that Alexander the Great was shown the prophecies in Daniel concerning himself by the high priest Jaddua, and the conqueror was so delighted that he offered to confer any favor on the Jews. Alexander antedated Antiochus more than 150 years.

3. Daniel and his three companions are referred to in 1 Maccabees 2:49-60, in such a way as to lead us to believe the book was extant when this apocryphal writing was composed.

4. Ezekiel testifies both to the existence and character of Daniel, 14:14-20. In 28:3, there is a manifest allusion to Daniel's wisdom as a revealer of secrets, "a resolver of doubts." It seems clear that Ezekiel knew of the prophet's interpretation of Nebuchadnezzar's dream, and of the handwriting on the wall of Belshazzar's palace. This witness is all the more important because the two prophets were contemporaries, and no one doubts the authenticity of Ezekiel's book.

5. Our Lord sets his seal to the reality of Daniel's official character and the truth of his predictions, Matthew 24:15. Christ teaches that this prediction of Daniel still remained to be fulfilled when he uttered the memorable discourse, that is, more than a century and a half after the time of Antiochus.

6. The records of ancient Babylon as deciphered by archaeologists harmonize with the statements of the prophet. In many minute particulars Daniel has been vindicated by modern research. The words of M. Lenormant deserve serious attention: "The more the knowledge of the cuneiform texts advances, the more is felt the necessity to revise (correct) the too hasty condemnation of the book of Daniel by the German exegetical school" (*La Magie*, page 14).

Conditions of Discipleship

Explain Luke 14:26.

Dr. Scofield's footnote is as good an explanation as I know. He says: "All terms which define the emotions or affections are comparative. Natural affection is to be, as compared with the believer's devotedness to Christ, as if it were hate. See Matthew 12:47-50, where Christ illustrates this principle in His own person. But in the Lord the natural affections are sanctified and lifted to the level of the divine love (compare John 19:26,27; Eph. 5:25-28)."

Distinguishing the Dispensations

I should appreciate some explanation of Mark 10:29,30. Is the promise in verse 30 literally true? Especially as to the houses? No one would want a large number of houses. Just what does this mean?

It should be remembered that in the Synoptic Gospels, meaning Matthew, Mark and Luke, we are not yet on Church ground. Strictly speaking, the New

Testament does not begin with the opening of our Lord's ministry, but with His death and resurrection and the descent of the Holy Spirit (Luke 22:20). Thus it will appear that the words "now in this time" as seen in Mark do not refer to our time, but rather to the time of the coming Kingdom. The appointed path of the Christian "now in this time" is one of suffering and rejection (1 Peter 2:19-21).

The Seven Dispensations

What are the Seven Dispensations, and where does each one begin in Scripture?

(1) The Dispensation of Innocence, from the creation of man to his expulsion from Eden. (2) The Dispensation of Conscience, from the expulsion from the Garden to the Flood. (3) The Dispensation of Human Government, from the Flood, and still going on; will end at the Second Coming of Christ, when He, the Stone of Daniel 2, will smite the whole system of human government, destroying all human rule and authority, and taking to Himself His great power, reigning over the whole earth as King of kings and Lord of lords. (4) The Dispensation of Promise, beginning with the Abrahamic Covenant, which is still in force, and which is to be fully accomplished when Christ comes again to earth. (5) The Dispensation of Law, beginning with Sinai, and ending at the Cross of Calvary (Gal. 3:19-25). This was for Israel alone, and is "done away in Christ" (2 Cor. 3). (6) The Dispensation of Grace, beginning with the descent of the Holy Spirit in Acts 2, and going on to the Rapture of the true Church, which will be followed by the final apostasy and destruction of the professing Church. (7) The Dispensation of the Kingdom, beginning with the Second Advent of Christ, and continuing for a thousand years; this is the Millennium.

Conditions before Adam

Does Jeremiah 4:23-27 mean that there were people on the earth before it was destroyed in Genesis 1:2? Some say there were only angels on the earth, and that the judgment was only a judgment of angels; but in verse 25 it speaks of man. Surely someone had to be on the earth, or there would have been no cause for judgment.

The expression "without form and void" of verse 23 is identical with that of Genesis 1:2, and is evidently a description of the earth's condition resulting from a pre-Adamite judgment which overthrew the primal order, whatever that order may have been. The judgment comes between the first and second verses of the first chapter of Genesis. It is true that verse 25 in the passage you cite contains the word "man," but it hardly speaks of man, for it says, "I beheld, and, lo, there was no man." Dr. Scofield's footnote is enlightening in this connection: "Jeremiah 4:23-26, Isaiah 24:1 and 45:18 clearly indicate that the earth had undergone a cataclysmic change as the result of a divine judgment. The face of the earth bears everywhere the marks of such a catastrophe. There are no wanting intimations which connect it with a previous testing and fall of angels. See Ezekiel 28:12-15 and Isaiah 14:9-14, which certainly go beyond the Kings of Tyre and Babylon" (*Scofield Reference Bible*, page 3, footnote 3).

A Question of Expediency

Would it be Scriptural for some of our young people, including girls, to visit jails and hold services on Sunday afternoons? I understand these particular jails contain men only. Mother objects.

It might be difficult to show the Scripturalness or unScripturalness of it, except for that little sentence, "Mother objects." Mother probably has good grounds for her objection, and the words are still in the Book, "Children, obey your parents in the Lord: for this is right" (Eph. 6:1). And even if there were no objecting mother, it might still be wise in the circumstances for men only to go to these jails to minister to men. "All things are lawful, but not all things are expedient."

False Teaching

As God is sovereign, why are so many people permitted to be led astray by false teaching, also by errors in translations of the Bible? We know that the masses cannot translate from the original languages for themselves.

I should say that God as Sovereign has made ample provision for the safety of His own children, and that every one of His children is perfectly safe from false teachers and teaching, as shown in 1 John 2:20-27. Please read it over thoughtfully and carefully and see how gracious and kind God has been.

As to errors in Bible translations, every one is privileged to translate the Bible who cares to try it. But even at that point it is still true that God's Spirit, the Holy Spirit—the Anointing which we have from above—is our infallible Teacher, and will protect God's children from apostasy.

On the other hand, those who will not receive the love of the truth that they might be saved, God turns over to believe a lie. This is the principle of God's dealings. It is a fearful thing to fall into the hands of the living God and to trifle with His truth.

False Worship

Recently our Sunday school class discussed Leviticus, chapter 10, and our teacher insisted that Nadab and Abihu went down "straight to Hell" because of their sin. Although they were certainly chastened of the Lord because of their presumptuous disobedience, I do not see that there is anything in the chapter to warrant our asserting that they were damned. Their sin and consecration offerings had been accepted, and they had been anointed with both the blood and the oil. When I so argued, I was told in effect I was foolish enough to believe "once saved, always saved." I should be grateful for your opinion.

The record reads that "Nadab and Abihu the sons of Aaron, took either of them his censer, and put fire therein, and put incense thereon, and offered strange fire before Jehovah, which he commanded them not. And there went out fire from Jehovah, and devoured them, and they died before Jehovah" (Lev. 10:1,2). It seems to me that in verses 8 and 9 there is a strong implication that the two priests were intoxicated when they sinned at the altar. Dr. Scofield, in a footnote in his Reference Bible, says that "Fire 'from before the Lord' had kindled upon the altar of burnt-offering the fire which the care of the priests was to keep burning (Lev. 6:12). No commandment had yet been given (Lev. 16:12) how the incense should be kindled. The sin of Nadab and Abihu was in acting in the things of God without seeking the mind of God. It was 'will worship' (Col. 2:23), which often has 'a show of wisdom' 'and humility.' It typifies any use of carnal means to kindle the fire of devotion and praise."

There is a close parallel in the New Testament, where priests (for every Christian is a priest) were judged of God for disorderly and unworthy conduct at the Lord's Supper. For this cause many of them became weak and sickly, and many even died under the chastening hand of God. And yet they were not lost and they did not go down "straight to Hell"—they were not "condemned with the world" (1 Cor. 11:23-34, R.V.).

Fellowship with the Father

A child of God fell into sin likened unto David's. However, since that time confession has been made to God, and the blood of Christ accepted as the only remission for sin. But Satan continually accuses the soul for this gross transgression, hence robbing the heart of peace and joy. Will you please point out the way of peace for this distressed believer?

First, are you sure that in the beginning there was real conversion, and not merely a "professed conversion"? It frequently happens that in a professed conversion there is no real turning of the heart to God and therefore no regeneration. Let this troubled one examine himself whether he be in the faith. Let him give all diligence to make his calling and election sure. Then when that is settled, and if it is assured that he is really a child of God who has fallen into grievous sin, it follows that by that sin his fellowship with his Heavenly Father was cut off until that sin was fully and faithfully dealt with.

The Word is perfectly clear for such a case, "If we confess our sins, he is faithful and just to forgive us our sins, and to cleanse us from all unrighteousness" (1 John 1:9). The human heart is slow to believe all that God says, especially all He says about the blood of Christ. God assures us that "if we walk in the light, as he is in the light," that is, if we are frank and candid with Him, not trying to hide anything from Him, but dragging everything out into the light, judging ourselves in His sight, then "we have fellowship one with another, and the blood of Jesus Christ his Son cleanseth us from all sin" (1 John 1:7). Satan loves to attack us at this point, and our hearts are apt to listen to him rather than to God, but the Word is written in order that we should by it assure our hearts before Him. "For if our heart condemn us, God is greater than our heart, and knoweth all things" (1 John 3:20). The whole First Epistle of John should be carefully studied and believed by the backslidden child of God for his complete restoration.

Fully Persuaded

What is the meaning of "let every man be fully persuaded in his own mind"?

The exhortation to every man to "be fully persuaded in his own mind" means that each one of us for himself must study the Word of God until convinced as to what that Word teaches, and then having come to know what it teaches we must obey it. We all need to pray definitely for two things, namely, wisdom and grace. We need wisdom to know the will of God, and we need grace to do that will when we know it.

God's Permissive Will

A man was killed on the railroad. Was it God's will that he should be killed? Some say his time was up here on earth; others say it was not God's will that his life was crushed out. We know that God has power to prevent it.

Precisely so! And since God did not prevent it, therefore it was done by His permissive will. There is a vast difference between God's *directive* will and His *permissive* will. No one can know why God permits such a thing to occur as you have described; but that God has a good and righteous reason will not be doubted by any who have put their trust in Him.

Have All Heard the Gospel?

Have all the heathen at some time had a chance to accept the Lord?

There are many millions of people in the world who have never yet heard the Gospel. As a matter of fact, it is estimated that only one-third of the human race has had the Gospel preached to them, leaving two-thirds in ignorance of it.

Grace for Grace

Please explain the phrase "grace for grace" in John 1:16.

The whole verse is truly wonderful: "And of his fullness have all we received, and grace for grace." The Revisers' margin reads, "and grace upon grace." The meaning is "grace corresponding to grace." It is as a mirror reflects all the loveliness of a beautiful face; there is in the mirror a grace for every grace in the face there reflected. God has already bestowed upon His children the "fullness" of Christ, including a grace corresponding to each grace in Him who is "altogether lovely" (Song 5:16). We already have Christ in us, "the hope of glory" (Col. 1:27), and one day Christ will be fully formed in us (Gal. 4:19), and then the glory will be revealed, and "we shall be like him" (1 John 3:1-3). For this revealing of the sons of God the whole creation is eagerly awaiting (Rom. 8:19). "Then shall the righteous shine forth as the sun in the kingdom of their Father" (Matt. 13:43). Then shall we be presented without fault before the presence of His glory with exceeding joy (Jude 24). Hallelujah! What a Savior!

Greater Works than These

Will you please tell us what our Lord meant by the "greater works than these" in John 14:12?

Verses 12-14 should be read together: the greater works referred to were to be made possible because our Lord went to His Father, and whatsoever His believing people might then ask in His name, "that will I do, that the Father may be glorified in the Son. If ye shall ask any thing in my name, I will do it." To bring men to a saving faith in Christ is a far greater work than the so-called miracles (John 6:28,29; compare Prov. 11:30; Dan. 12:3). John Knox in Scotland and David Livingstone in Africa wrought far greater works than if they had turned water into wine or fed multitudes with a handful of food.

Hardening the Heart

Do not John 12:40, Romans 9:18 and Hebrews 3:13 plainly show that Christians may be hardened by sin?

No. Christians are not in mind in any of the Scriptures you cite, but rather unbelievers. I do not deny that Christians may be thus hardened; I only say that these Scriptures do not teach it. Even the "brethren" of Hebrews 3:12,13 are Hebrew brethren thus addressed by the Hebrew writer of the Epistle to the Hebrews.

The Book of Iddo

In 2 Chronicles 13:22 it speaks of the book of Iddo, or rather the story of the prophet Iddo; also in 2 Chronicles 12:15 of the book of Shemaiah. In several other places, reading the Bible through, I have come across different other books mentioned which do not seemingly appear in the Bible. Now, are they combined in some other book of the Bible, or what has become of them? Are they really a part of the Bible, or have they never been found?

No one can tell who the prophet Iddo was or what has become of the book of Iddo or of certain other books which are mentioned in the Bible but not included therein. It is supposed by some that Iddo's writings are included in the books of Chronicles. Tradition identifies Iddo with "the man of God" who denounced Jeroboam's calf altar at Bethel (1 Kings 13). The statement of 2 Chronicles 9:29 may have a bearing upon this point. Others believe that Iddo is the same as Oded, the father of Azariah (2 Chron. 15:1).

Immaculate Conception

What is the immaculate conception as taught by the Catholics?

I am quoting you a paragraph from the *Encyclopedia Britannica*, which gives the explanation of the immaculate conception as I have always understood it:

"The dogma of the immaculate conception of the Virgin Mary, as held by the church of Rome, is to the effect that 'the most blessed Virgin was, in view of the merits of Jesus Christ the Savior of the human race, by the singular grace and favor of Almighty God, from the first moment of her conception in the womb of her mother, preserved free from all taint of original sin.'"

Two Immutable Things

About two years ago I heard a Bible teacher say that Zacharias meant "God's oath," and that Mary meant "God remembered His oath." If this is true can you tell me in what language it is?

I think that you must have confused the name of Mary with that of Elisabeth, Zacharias' wife. Elisabeth is the Greek form of the Hebrew name Elisheba, and its meaning is: "the oath of God," or, "God's oath." The meaning of Mary is: "bitterness or rebelliousness." It is equivalent to Mara, the name adopted by Naomi upon her return to Bethlehem-Judah from Moab (Ruth 1:20). She said "Call me not Naomi (meaning, 'pleasant' or 'pleasantness'), call me Mara (meaning, 'bitter' or 'bitterness'): for the Almighty hath dealt very bitterly with me." The meaning of Zacharias' name is: "remembered by Jehovah." I have no doubt that these names are significant as used in Luke's first chapter. God had made promises concerning Israel and concerning Israel's Redeemer; and He had confirmed these promises "by an oath; that by two immutable things (His promise and His oath), in which it was impossible for God to lie, we might have a strong consolation, who have fled for refuge to lay hold upon the hope set before us: which hope we have as an anchor of the soul, both sure and steadfast, and which entereth into that within the veil; whither the forerunner is for us entered, even Jesus, made an high priest forever after the order of Melchisedec" (Heb. 6:17-20). So there was the oath of God, as indicated by Elisabeth's name; and in addition to the oath of God, there was God's memory. He certainly could not make a promise and then forget it. God remembered His promise and His oath, and all this is pointed out or intimated by the name of Zacharias, "remembered by Jehovah."

The Responsibility of Leadership

Are not the leaders of our denominations, who practice unscriptural things and teach the members of various churches wrongly, more responsible than the members?

Undoubtedly; and there is a long score for them to settle in the final check-up. The responsibility of leadership is very great.

The Marks of the Lord Jesus

Will you please explain the meaning of Galatians 6:17—"From henceforth let no man trouble me: for I bear in my body the marks of the Lord Jesus"?

The word for "marks" is *stigmata*, from which we derive our word "stigma." Paul was a veteran warrior of Christ, and in his body he bore the scars of battle, which, he reasoned, gave him the right to speak as a competent witness of the things he had been discussing.

It is quite apropos that in the mail bringing your letter, or about the same time, there came a letter from a daughter of the late Dr. Charles Frederick Sheldon, in which she related a remark made by her father in reply to somebody's suggestion that he would be satisfied even to sneak into Heaven through the back door. Dr. Sheldon answered, "Well, that would not satisfy me. When I enter Heaven I want to go in at the front door, with the bands playing and the flags flying, and bearing some scars gained in the good fight of faith down here."

The Mizpah Benediction

Would you advise the use of the Mizpah benediction in closing a meeting?

No. The so-called Mizpah benediction is not a benediction at all, but a *malediction*, as its reading, with context, will make clear. The record, in Genesis 31, shows that at the end of a bitter quarrel Jacob and Laban built a heap of stones between them. They gave it various names including *Jegarsahadutha* (Chaldee for "The Heap of Witness"), *Galeed* (Hebrew for "The Heap of Witness"), and *Mizpah* (meaning, "A Beacon," or "Watchtower"). Then said Laban to Jacob, "The LORD watch between me and thee, when we are absent one from another! . . . This heap be witness, and this pillar be witness, that I will not pass over this heap to thee, and that thou shalt not pass over this heap and this pillar unto me, for harm." It was equivalent to saying, "Let the Lord keep His eye on you when I can't! You keep on your side, and I'll keep on my side!" It is surely a queer kind of "benediction." Why not use a real benediction? There are plenty of them in the Bible.

Danger from the Moon

Please tell me what you understand the intent of the Spirit to be in the expression, "Nor the 'moon' by night" in Psalm 121:6. It is easy to see how the intense rays of the sun, in a hot country, might he held as a smiting to be avoided; but now unless, perhaps, the moon (which with the stars are ordained to rule the night) is meant to stand for the "terror by night" which in Psalm 91:5 the Spirit assures us shall not reach us, I should not know how to explain the last line of Psalm 121:6.

The following matter from Spurgeon's *Treasury of David* explains the effect of the moonlight in oriental countries:

Quoting from John Carne, in *Letters from the East*, published in 1826: "The effect of the moonlight on the eyes in this country is singularly injurious. . . . The moon here really strikes and affects the sight, when you sleep exposed to it, much more than the sun, a fact of which I had a very unpleasant proof one night, and took care to guard against it afterwards; indeed, the sight of a person who should sleep with his face exposed at night would soon be utterly impaired or destroyed."

A writer, signing himself "C.W.," in *The Biblical Treasury*, says: "In the cloudless skies of the east, where the moon shines with such exceeding clearness, its effects upon the human frame have been found most injurious. The inhabitants of these countries are most careful in taking precautionary measures before exposing themselves to its influence. Sleeping much in the open air, they are careful to cover well their heads and faces. It has been proved beyond a doubt that the moon smites as well as the sun, causing blindness for a time, and even distortion of the features. Sailors are well aware of this fact; and a naval officer relates that he has often, when sailing between the tropics, seen the commanders of vessels waken up young men who had fallen asleep in the moonlight. Indeed, he witnessed more than once the effects of a moonstroke, when the mouth was drawn on one side and the sight injured for a time. He was of opinion that, with long exposure, the mind might become seriously affected. It is supposed that patients suffering under fever and other illnesses are affected by this planet, and the natives of India constantly affirm that they will either get better or worse, according to her changes."

A Matter of Pronouns

Please explain why Paul changes his pronouns for example, in Colossians 2:13 he says, "And you, being dead in your sins and the uncircumcision of your flesh, hath he quickened together with him, having forgiven you all trespasses." And then in the very next verse he says "Blotting out the handwriting of ordinances that was against us, which was contrary to us, and took it out of the way, nailing it to his cross." Why this change?

The answer is that in verse 13, as indeed in the whole passage, including verses 10 to 13, he is referring to the Gentile Christians to whom he is writing; but when it comes to verse 14 he is referring to the Jews who alone had been under "the handwriting of ordinances," that is, the law of Moses. Paul himself was a Hebrew, and so he says, "Blotting out the handwriting of ordinances that was against us, which was contrary to us," which he could not have said of the Gentiles. In Romans 2:14 we are told twice that the Gentiles have not the law. In Romans 6:14 we are assured that sin shall not have dominion over us, for we are not under the law, but under grace. You will find the same change of pronouns in Paul's other writings; for example, in Galatians 3:23 he says: "But before faith came, we (that is, the Jews) were kept under the law . . . Wherefore the law was our (Israel's) schoolmaster to bring us unto Christ, that we might be justified by faith. But after that faith is come, we are no longer under a schoolmaster." And then in the next verse, referring to all Christians, Gentiles as well as Jews, he says: "For ye are all the children of God (sons of God, R.V.) by faith in Christ Jesus." And so on through the whole passage down to Galatians 4:7. These distinctions in pronouns are very important to observe throughout Paul's writings.

Numerics

In your "Simple Studies in The Revelation" you state that the numerical value of the name of Jesus is 888. How is this result arrived at? Also what is the numerical value of the name Christ?

In many languages there are numerical equivalents given to the letters of the alphabet. The idea is familiar to us in connection with the Roman numerals, in which I is used for 1, V for 5, X for 10, L for 50, C for 100, and so on. In the Greek alphabet the first letter, alpha, stands for 1, and each letter stands for a certain number, the last, omega, being valued at 800. The Greek letters in the name of Jesus are: iota, 10; eta, 8; sigma, 200; omicron, 70; upsilon, 400; and sigma, 200. The sum of these numbers is 888. Christos, the Greek form of Christ, foots up 1480, as follows: chi, 600; rho, 100; iota, 10; sigma, 200; tau, 300; omicron, 70; sigma, 200; total, 1480. Adding these two totals together gives us 2368 as the numerical value of Iesous Christos, or Jesus Christ.

Once Every Year

Did the high priest enter into the holy of holies more than once on the day of atonement?

Yes. For while Hebrews 9:7 says the high priest entered "once every year," the meaning is evident that he entered upon only one occasion or one day each year. Leviticus 16 gives the order of service for the day of atonement and it shows that the high priest went into the holy of holies once on behalf of himself and his family (verse 12), and again on behalf of the congregation (verse 15).

Nahum's Predictions

Does Nahum 2:3,4 refer to this present time before Jesus comes in the air, or does it come in the Great Tribulation, or has it already happened in the past?

It evidently refers to the terrors of the Great Tribulation. It is foolish to say it refers to present-day automobiles, which certainly do not "run like the lightnings."

The Passing Over of Sins Done Aforetime

How do you explain the statement of Acts 17:30: "the times of this ignorance God winked at"? In view of Ephesians 2:12, Romans 2:12 and Romans 1:18-20 it cannot refer to the salvation of the soul.

The words "winked at" should be translated as in the Revision, "overlooked." The teaching is the same as in Romans 3:25, where again the Revised Version is preferable, and where God is said to have set forth His Son "a propitiation, through faith, in his blood, to show his righteousness because of the passing over of the sins done aforetime, in the forbearance of God." The point is that Christ died for the redemption of transgressions which were under the first covenant (Heb. 9:15), that is, He died for the sins committed by men who lived before Calvary as well as for those committed by men who have lived since Calvary. Those who were saved in olden time were saved through faith in God's testimony, and to them was imputed the righteousness of God in Christ, and their sins were imputed to Christ, who bore them all in due time on Calvary's cross.

The Last Passover

Please explain Luke 22:14-18. Did our Lord eat the last Passover with His disciples on the night of His betrayal? Mark 14:18 would seem to indicate that He did. There are some who say that the Passover lamb was slain at the same hour that Christ died on the Cross. Did Jesus and His disciples eat the Passover before the day appointed, or what do these verses mean?

Our Lord ate the Passover with His disciples at the beginning of the Crucifixion day, which was Wednesday, the 14th of Abib. Remember that the Hebrew day began at 6 P.M. rather than midnight; so that Wednesday began at what we would now call six o'clock on Tuesday evening. It is doubtless true that the death of the Lamb of God on Calvary took place at the hour on Wednesday afternoon that the Passover lamb was killed in the Temple. Thus our Lord anticipated the killing of the Passover by several hours, in order that He might eat with His disciples before He suffered, which may explain the language of Luke 22:15; but it was nevertheless on the same day, since the day began at sunset the night before.

The Passover Minus the Lamb

Is there a lamb used now by the Jews in celebrating the Passover?

No. It would be contrary to the Word of God to do so except at the temple in Jerusalem; and since there is now no Jewish temple in Jerusalem, the Passover is celebrated without a sacrifice. Hosea 3:4 is now being fulfilled, and the 5th verse will be as surely and literally fulfilled in the future: "4 For the children of Israel shall abide many days without a king, and without a prince, and without a sacrifice, and without an image, and without an ephod, and without teraphim:

"5 Afterward shall the children of Israel return, and seek Jehovah their God, and David their king: and shall fear Jehovah and his goodness in the latter days."

Peace

"Peace I leave with you, my peace I give unto you" (John 14:27). What is the difference here in the "peace"? Does the former mean the peace that we have with God through regeneration, and the latter, that peace we have because of the indwelling of the Holy Spirit as a part of the fruit of the Spirit? Or are they the same in meaning? Please answer.

I am not sure that our Lord meant to speak of two kinds of peace in that part of the verse you have quoted. The contrast rather is indicated by the remainder of the sentence: "Not as the world giveth, give I unto you." In other words, the distinction He draws is indicated by the pronoun "my," *His* peace—the peace *He* gives—is not the kind of peace that the world gives.

Of course it is true, as we learn elsewhere, that there are different gradations in the peace which He gives us. There is the "peace *with* God" of Romans

5:1, which comes when we are born again and as a result of justification by faith; then there is the "peace *of* God, which passeth all understanding," together with the conscious presence of "the God of peace" Himself, which comes as the result of our being "careful for nothing," and "in everything by prayer and supplication with thanksgiving" letting our "requests be made known unto God" (Phil. 4:6,7, 9). All this is very wonderful, as is well known by those who have experienced it, and it is something of which the world knows nothing and can know nothing, for it all comes "through our Lord Jesus Christ."

Typical Meaning of Pentecost

Please explain the meaning of Leviticus 23:17.

Leviticus 23:17 points to Pentecost. The two wave-loaves are the Jews and Gentiles brought together in one body which is the Church. They were to be baked with leaven because believers have sin in them and are made acceptable only on account of the blood, which was always offered in connection with this Pentecostal feast. The words "they are the firstfruits unto the LORD" point to James 1:18, where we are said to be a kind of firstfruits unto Him.

The First Polygamist

What do you understand by Genesis 4:19-24, especially verses 23 and 24? Was Lamech the first polygamist?

I think it is quite true that Lamech was the first polygamist. The Revised Version has made some important changes in the translation of Genesis 4:23,24. In the Revision it reads: "And Lamech said unto his wives: Adah and Zillah, hear my voice; Ye wives of Lamech, hearken unto my speech: for I have slain a man for wounding me, and a young man for bruising me: if Cain shall be avenged sevenfold, truly Lamech seventy and sevenfold."

Let me call your attention to Dr. Scofield's comment in the margin of his Bible: "Cain had slain an unoffending man and yet was protected by Jehovah; how much more Lamech, who had slain in self-defense."

This seems to be the true meaning of the passage.

Polygamy

When was polygamy abolished among God's people? Is there any record in the Old Testament that the practice was wrong in God's sight?

I know of no exact point in the history of God's people where polygamy ceased to be practiced or was formally abolished. God did not forbid it to man, and in some cases, notably in the case of Jacob, He seemed to let His blessing rest upon it; the nation of Israel came from two wives, Leah and Rachel, and two concubines, Bilhah and Zilpah. In Deuteronomy 17:17, however, God uttered a warning against polygamy on the part of the future kings of Israel: the king must not "multiply wives to himself, that his heart turn not away." For his wholesale disobedience of this command Solomon brought much trouble upon himself and his people (1 Kings 11:1-4). In the New Testament the rule is plainly laid down that there must be no polygamy among God's people. The Bishop or Pastor, as well as the Deacon, in the Christian Church must be the husband of one wife only (1 Tim. 3:2-12; Titus 1:6), and the same restriction applies to all believers alike: "Let every man have his own wife, and let every woman have her own husband" (1 Cor. 7:2).

The Preaching to Them that Are Dead

Please explain 1 Peter 4:6, "For this cause was the gospel preached also to them that are dead, that they might be judged according to men in the flesh, but live according to God in the spirit."

You notice it doesn't say the men who *were* dead. It says it was preached to them that *are* dead. The meaning is that those who are now dead had the Gospel preached to them while they were yet living. The third chapter of 1 Peter has something on practically the same subject, verses 18,19 and 20: "For Christ also hath once suffered for sins, the just for the unjust, that he might bring us to God, being put to death in the flesh, but quickened by the Spirit: by which also he went and preached unto the spirits in prison; which sometimes were disobedient, when once the long-suffering of God waited in the days of Noah, while the ark was a preparing, wherein few, that is, eight souls were saved by water." The answer is that Christ went in His Spirit—the Spirit of Christ, the Spirit of God—the Holy Spirit, and preached through Noah in the days before the flood to those who now are spirits in prison. It does not mean that He has gone to them since they entered the prison and preached there to them. There is mystery about these passages, but this seems to be the true explanation.

The Place of Preeminence

Who cares more for the things of the Lord, a married or a single woman? Is it the same now as in Paul's time (1 Cor. 7:32-34)?

I am unable to answer your question. I know only that it is a very dangerous thing to put anyone, no matter how beloved, into the place of preeminence in one's heart and affections that belongs only to the Lord Himself.

Prizes

I regularly attend our church and Sunday school, and now they are putting prizes on for the best attendance through the year. I am not in favor of this, as I was brought up a strict Christian from childhood. This is the worst time in my life for prizes, plays, dances, and card playing in and around our church and home. What can be done about it?

It is rather difficult to answer your question without fuller information as to just what is involved in it. Sometimes it would seem to be legitimate to encourage regular attendance in the church or Sunday school by the presentation of a proper prize like a Bible or a good book or something of that kind. As for the plays and cards and vices which you speak of as around your church and home, of course these things are to be regretted. God is calling His people to a life of separation from the world and the things of the world.

May the Lord Himself guide you in these things that are concerning you so much!

A Personal Problem

I am requested to have you answer this question:

Should we succeed in persuading a young man to accept Jesus Christ as his Savior, and he is soundly converted, but there is no church of any denomination in his community that teaches the fundamental doctrines, what course should he take?

Let him find a church somewhere which is true to God's Word and put his membership in that church. Then let him keep in touch with the church he has joined, maintaining fellowship with it in prayer and giving, and attending its meetings as frequently as possible.

Many of God's children are facing this problem in these days of declension and darkness.

God's Eternal Purpose

Please give me your comments on Romans 8:28-30.

The three verses read as follows: "And we know that all things work together for good to them that love God, to them who are the called according to his purpose. For whom he did foreknow, he also did predestinate to be conformed to the image of his Son, that he might be the first-born among many brethren. Moreover whom he did predestinate, them he also called: and whom he called, them he also justified: and whom he justified them he also glorified."

In verse 28 "his purpose" is the great thing. Who can withstand the eternal purpose of God? If salvation were offered to the believer conditionally; if something were left to his faithfulness, or his obedience, or his prayerfulness, then, indeed, the case would be hopeless, for the history of man shows that, whenever he is put under a system of probation, he breaks down. The Law was such a system, and under it life was offered as a condition of obedience: "The man which *doeth* those things shall live by them"; but the Law proved an intolerable burden (Acts 15:10), a ministration of condemnation and a ministration of death (2 Cor. 3:7, 9).

In the Gospel all conditions are swept aside, and whosoever will may come. He is only to come, and God does all the rest. Let him come in all his vileness and weakness, and God will not so much as mention either his vileness or his weakness, but will just take him into His loving arms, and undertake for him, and thereafter see to it that all things work together for good unto him. This is His eternal purpose which He purposed before the world was, and of course, with such a salvation, based upon such a purpose, it cannot be otherwise than that all things shall work together for good unto the children of God.

The word "for," in verse 29, has the force of "because," and it introduces the reason for our assurance that all things are working together for our good.

He foreknew us; He also predestinated us to be conformed to the image of His Son, that He might be the first-born among many brethren; He also called us with an effectual calling; and He also justified us, and He has also glorified us. The past tense continues through the whole passage, although the glorification is yet future, for God is able to count things done even when they have not been done. Our glorification is according to His purpose, and nothing is to be suffered to thwart His purpose. Having been foreknown and predestinated and called and justified, we shall also be glorified.

No Rain before the Flood

How would you explain the "mist" spoken of in Genesis 2:6? Did this take the place of rain until the time of the covenant with Noah after the flood? Or, otherwise, what would explain the giving of the rainbow as a sign or token of His covenant?

It is obvious that before the flood of Noah there was no rain, and that therefore there had been no rainbow; for wherever there is rain with sunshine there must be a rainbow. There is strong evidence that before the flood the earth was surrounded, or enclosed, in a hollow sphere of vapor, which shielded the earth from the direct rays of the sun and refracted those rays in such a manner as to equalize, or nearly equalize, the heat and cold over the whole earth, making it nearly as warm at the poles as at the equator, and nearly as cold at the equator as at the poles. This hollow globe of vaporized water—"the waters which were above the firmament" (Gen. 1:7)—was perhaps "the great deep" which was "broken up" and precipitated upon the earth in the flood. There are intimations, too, in Scripture that this shield from the direct rays of the sun may be restored in connection with the Millennial glory, "and there shall be a pavilion for a shade in the day-time from the heat, and for a refuge and for a covert from storm and from rain" (Isa. 4:6, R.V.).

Origin of the Rainbow

What is the meaning of Genesis 9:13: "I do set my bow in the cloud"? Was this the origin of the rainbow?

Apparently so. A rainbow, as you of course know, is caused by the sun's rays passing through the rain and shining upon clouds. But until the flood "the LORD God had not caused it to rain upon the earth, . . . but there went up a mist from the earth, and watered the whole face of the ground" (Gen. 2:5,6). It is easy to see that to those who had never seen a rainstorm the effect might well be terrifying, and God pointed out the bow in the cloud as a sign of His covenant with man, including the promise that the earth should not again be destroyed by a flood (Gen. 9:12-17).

Human Reasoning or the Word of God, Which?

What would you tell a very intellectual friend who says there is no such thing as a real personal Devil, and who believes babies to be born pure and holy, without sin, and when they become bad it is because of their environment?

I should tell such "a very intellectual friend" to read his Bible. There is no more definite testimony in the Bible to the existence of a personal God than there is to the existence of "a real personal Devil."

And as for babies being born "pure and holy, without sin," that also is quite contrary to the teachings of the Word of God, which declares that we are all born in sin, and are by nature the children of wrath, even as others.

But there is really no profit in debating such questions with intellectual friends who depend upon their reasonings rather than upon the Word of God.

The Meaning of Reprobate

Please explain 2 Corinthians 13:5: "Examine yourselves, whether ye be in the faith; prove your own selves. Know ye not your own selves, how that Jesus Christ is in you, except ye be reprobates?"

The Revised Version has taken the "s" off the last word, making it read "reprobate." But what is the meaning of "reprobate"? The Greek word is *adokimos*, which is *dokimos* with the negative prefix. The meaning of *dokimos* is "acceptable," and it is translated "approved" in Romans 14:18; 16:10; 1 Corinthians 11:19; 2 Corinthians 10:18; 13:7; 2 Timothy 2:15. The same word is translated "tried" in James 1:12.

The negative form of the word, *adokimos*, is translated "castaway" in 1 Corinthians 9:27; "rejected" in Hebrews 6:8; and "reprobate" in Romans 1:28; 2 Timothy 3:8; Titus 1:16; 2 Corinthians 13:5-7.

The use of the word in 1 Corinthians 9:27, where it is translated "castaway" in the Authorized Version and "rejected" in the Revised Version, is in relation to *service*, and Paul is there speaking of his strong desire to avoid the Lord's disapproval of his service at the end of the road.

But in 2 Corinthians 13:5 it is a question as to the standing of these professing Christians in Corinth. Are they really Christians at all? Have they been born again? The Lord Jesus Christ indwells all who are truly born again, but there are many who profess to be His, and who are not truly born again, and will be found unacceptable, disapproved, rejected, when the test is applied. "Not every one that saith unto me, Lord, Lord, shall enter into the kingdom of heaven; but he that doeth the will of my Father which is in heaven. Many will say to me in that day, Lord, Lord, have we not prophesied in thy name? and in thy name have cast out demons? and in thy name done many wonderful works? And then will I profess unto them, I never knew you: depart from me, ye that work iniquity" (Matt. 7:21-23).

If the question arises as to what this "will of my Father which is in heaven" is, and how we are to do it, the answer is not difficult to find, for, "This is his commandment, That we should believe on the name of his Son Jesus Christ, and love one another, as he gave us commandment. And he that keepeth his commandments dwelleth in him, and he in him. And hereby we know that he abideth in us, by the Spirit which he hath given us" (1 John 3:23,24).

Reverence toward the Lord Jesus Christ

My pastor has repeatedly made the statement that it is extremely flippant and nothing short of sacrilege to say the words, "blessed

Jesus" or "dear Jesus" in one's prayers. His argument is that Christ in His high-priestly prayer, and in every other recorded prayer of His, said, "Father" or "Holy Father." Then, too, he says that we should not even use the word "Jesus" alone, as that is His human name.

As I was thinking about this, I tried to remember some of the prayers I had heard made by Bible scholars—prayers that lifted one into the very presence of God Himself, and I know that in many of those prayers I had heard the word "Jesus" or "blessed Jesus" used many times. I am not sure about it, but it seems that I have heard you use one or the other of those terms in some of your prayers. I may be mistaken, but anyway I thought I would ask you about it. I do think a great deal of my pastor, but his prayers always make me feel that God is a very, very far-off Being, a sort of Potentate set upon a pedestal, and so very, very much higher, and above us, and so all-powerful that we dare hardly even approach Him, and then only with the greatest fear. I do know that we should revere God with every atom of our being, and that He is holy and just and far, far above us in power. But He sent Jesus to the world to show us His love and to provide a new way to come to Him, so that we could come boldly and not be fearful of Him. Jesus ascended into Heaven in His glorified body and is seated there now as a Man, and it seems to me that we can talk with Him as "Jesus," as friend to friend, and feel very, very close to His heart. We are told that God talked with Moses as a man with his friend, and I think God called Abraham His friend, and if He did that in those very far-off days, it seems that now, in this age of grace, He would want us to come as a friend to a friend. What do you think about all this?

I think I know what your Pastor means, and I agree with him that there is such a thing as the wrong kind of familiarity with the name of our blessed Lord. It is well to remember that He is our Lord, and that as such we should worship and revere Him.

I do not think that you ever heard me addressing the Lord Jesus in prayer at all, for I am always careful to address my prayers to the Father in the name of the Lord Jesus, as we are taught in John 16:23,24. And, too, I try to be careful when I refer to our Lord Jesus at all to be reverent in such reference. I think perhaps that I should agree with your pastor pretty fully along that line.

But, on the other hand, I should disagree with him in his stand that "we should not even use the word 'Jesus' alone, as that is His human name," etc. The same argument is advanced by Sir Robert Anderson in his book entitled, *For His Name's Sake*. Of course, we all agree that we ought to be reverent. I confess that I have heard people speaking to Him in prayer and calling Him "dear Jesus" and "blessed Jesus," when my heart revolted at the apparent lightness of this. But He is called "Jesus" ten times in the first chapter of John alone, and this name is applied to Him by the Holy Spirit in the New Testament some hundreds of times doubtless, and of course no one will accuse the Holy Spirit of any lack of reverence toward our Lord Jesus Christ.

It is true that God talked with Abraham and Moses and called them His friends, but that is far different from Abraham or Moses talking to God and calling Him their Friend. It is written in the Word that the Lord Jesus is not ashamed to call us brethren. That is beautiful, but I should hesitate to address Him as my Brother. We often hear Him spoken of as our Elder Brother, and it is true that He is our Elder Brother, but I should rather have Him say it than say it myself.

I would suggest that you talk to your pastor about it. It may be that he and you are closer together in the matter than you think. I doubt very much that he thinks of God as "a very, very far-off Being, a sort of Potentate set upon a pedestal," etc. I think you misunderstand your pastor. Talk it over with him and see if you cannot get closer together than you may now imagine.

Righteousness

What is meant by the righteousness of God and the righteousness of Christ?

The righteousness of God, spoken of in connection with salvation, is that righteousness which is reckoned to the believer—"even the righteousness of God which is by faith of Jesus Christ unto all and upon all them that believe" (Rom. 1:17; 3:22). Christ Himself is righteousness, and is made righteousness unto all who put their trust in Him (1 Cor. 1:30; 2 Cor. 5:21).

The Old Testament Sacrifices

Will you explain why, in the Old Testament, so many offerings to God were required, as hundreds and thousands of bullocks and sheep? Did these offerings take away the sins of the offerers?

No, they did not (Heb. 10:4). But they were "a figure for the time present," pointing to the time when Christ should die for the sins of the world (Heb. 9:9, R.V.), including those who lived before that time as well as afterwards (Rom. 3:25; Heb. 9:15). Old Testament believers were saved by faith in the coming One, as we today are saved by faith in the One who has already come.

Saving Others with Fear

Will you please explain Jude 23?

The teaching of Jude 23 is that we must have a care in the work of soul-winning, lest in pulling men out of the fire we ourselves shall become tainted with their sins. The work of soul-winning is dangerous business, but it is a wise business; for it is written, "He that wins souls is wise," and "They that be wise shall shine as the brightness of the firmament; and they that turn many to righteousness as the stars forever and ever" (Prov. 11:30; Dan. 12:3).

Saving One's Life and Losing It

Please explain Luke 9:24: "For whosoever will save his life shall lose it: but whosoever will lose his life for my sake, the same shall save it."

Verse 25 is our Lord's comment on verse 24: "For what is a man advantaged, if he gain the whole world, and lose himself, or be cast away?" The man who devotes his time and attention exclusively to himself and to saving his own life is the man who, when he comes to depart from this world, will find that he has lost what he was trying to save. On the other hand, the man who lives the life of self-sacrifice, devoting himself to God, seeking first the Kingdom of God and His righteousness, and laying down his life for the benefit of others, is the man who, when he comes to the end of things here, will find that in losing his life he has really saved it.

The Continuing Seasons

Is there anything in the Bible to show that during the last days the summer and winter will be so much alike that it will be hard to distinguish between them? I have always understood that we would have the different seasons.

In the covenant with Noah is included the promise that "while the earth remaineth, seedtime and harvest, and cold and heat, and summer and winter, and day and night shall not cease" (Gen. 8:22). Yet, according to Zechariah 14:6,7, it appears that there will be certain wonderful physical changes in the end-time: for "it shall come to pass in that day, that the light shall not be clear, nor dark; but it shall be one day which shall be known to Jehovah, not day, nor night: but it shall come to pass, that at evening time it shall be light." Much poetic nonsense has been based upon this verse, whose obvious teaching is that in the time that is coming there will not be darkness during half of each day, but the light will continue through the twenty-four hours. There are indications in Scripture that in the time before the flood of Noah the seasons were far different from now: that the earth was surrounded by a shield, perhaps of mist or vapor, which protected it from the direct rays of the sun and by refraction distributed its light and heat more equally than now over the surface of the whole earth.

It may be that this enveloping shield or covering was what is described as "the great deep" which was "broken up," thus opening "the windows of heaven" and precipitating the flood of waters hitherto suspended over the earth. This would leave the earth unprotected from the direct rays of the sun, causing extreme heat at the equator and extreme cold at the poles, with all the suffering involved in such extremes. In the time before the flood "Jehovah God had not caused it to rain upon the earth, but there went up a mist from the earth, and watered the whole face of the ground" (Gen. 2:5,6).

The removal of the protecting shield at the time of the flood of Noah made it necessary thereafter to water the earth by means of rain. If this explanation is the right one, it would account for the rainbow (Gen. 9:13); for, of course, if there had been no rain before that time there could have been no rainbow. The restoration of the antediluvian shield or covert in the future is intimated by certain of the prophetic Scriptures, such as Isaiah 4:5,6, where it is promised that "Jehovah will create upon every dwelling place of Mount Zion, and upon her assemblies, a cloud and smoke by day, and the shining of a flaming fire by night: and there shall be a tabernacle for a shadow in the daytime from the heat, and for a place of refuge, and for a covert from storm and from rain" (see also Isa. 60:19,20).

Service from the Unsaved

Cannot an unbeliever render any service which God will accept?

An unsaved man cannot know God or obey God, or please God (John 3:3-6; Jer. 17:9; 1 Cor. 2:14; Rom. 8:7,8). So long as a man rejects the Lord Jesus Christ, the Father will have nothing to do with him, nor will He receive anything from him, whether service or money or any other gift. "He that despised Moses' law died without mercy under two or three witnesses: of how much sorer punishment, suppose ye, shall he be thought worthy, who hath trodden under foot the Son of God, and hath counted the blood of the covenant, wherewith he was sanctified, an unholy thing, and hath done despite unto the Spirit of grace?" (Heb. 10:28,29).

Serving the Lord at Home

Is it wrong, do you think, to have given up all service in the church, when such service seemed to have been blessed, to wait on a sick loved one at home, and in fact to give up everything but the home and its work? I just feel that I have neglected spiritual things, but perhaps the Lord desires me to take care of this aged one. I hope I have done right.

Your service at home may be the one way in which you may now please God. Pleasing Him is the great thing. You have only one person to please at a time, and only one thing to do. Our Lord, on the cross, committed His mother Mary to the care of His friend John; and it is believed, from probably reliable tradition, that until Mary's death John was never heard of in public ministry. There can be no doubt that in thus serving the Lord at home John was doing the one thing he could then do in real ministry. To be where He desires, doing the thing He desires, is the one thing worth while. "For we are his workmanship, created in Christ Jesus unto good works, which God hath before ordained that we should walk in them" (Eph. 2:10).

No More a Sin-Offering

Please explain the meaning of Hebrews 10:26,27.

It is characteristic of the Epistle to the Hebrews that it abounds in appeals to Hebrews, to whom the way of salvation had been revealed in the Gospel, urging them to obey the holy commandment delivered unto them, namely, to believe the Gospel and be saved. Of course, they were under temptation to remain in Judaism, at least so long as the temple was yet standing, and the bloody offerings continued. The writer of the Epistle, however, continually points out to them that the sin-offering in the temple had lost its value, by reason of the "one sacrifice for sins forever," which had been accomplished on Calvary. Hebrews 10 is a summing up of the whole matter. The blood of bulls and of goats was never able to take away sin (verses 1-4). In due time the Lamb of God had come to do God's will in the offering of Himself on the cross (verses 5-9). By this will of God thus done believers are "sanctified through the offering of the body of Jesus Christ once for all" (verse 10). The priest in the temple, going on with his interminable sacrifices, was accomplishing nothing; "but this man, after he had offered one sacrifice for sins forever, sat down on the right hand of God; from henceforth expecting till his enemies be made his footstool. For by one offering he hath perfected (that is, given perfect rest in the conscience) forever them that are sanctified" (verses 11-14). God's way of giving rest to the conscience is in keeping with the New Covenant promise in Jeremiah 31:33,34, according to which God does a new work in the believer's heart, writing in his heart and mind His laws; and as for their sins and iniquities, they have been purged by the blood of Jesus, and He will remember them no more (verses 15-17).

Now comes verse 18, which must be read in connection with verse 26: "Now where remission of these (forgiveness of sins) is, there is no more a sin-offering" (verse 18). Then follows the exhortation for the Hebrew who knows the way, to walk in it and enter into the holiest by the blood of Jesus (verses 19-25). The alternative is pointed out in verses 26 and 27. If the Hebrew, or any other for that matter, should "sin willfully after" he had "received the knowledge of the truth," that is, after he had come to know the way of salvation—if he sins willfully in refusing to walk in the way thus opened before him—there remains no more a sin-offering, "but a certain fearful looking for of judgment and fiery indignation, which shall devour the adversaries." In verses 28 to 31 a contrast is drawn between the man who despised Moses' Law and was stoned to death for thus despising it, and the man who despises the Son of God and treads Him under foot, and counts His blood as a common thing, and insults the Spirit of grace. There is nothing for him but vengeance, and "it is a fearful thing to fall into the hands of the living God."

Soul and Spirit

Please explain the difference between the soul and the spirit. I have a Scofield Bible, but reading the notes in Genesis and Thessalonians does not make it clear to me.

Your question is a difficult one, and I can hardly hope to help you if Dr. Scofield has failed to do so. Then, too, an exhaustive discussion of the subject is hardly possible here. Briefly, however, I will state my own position in the matter:

1. Man has a body. In this he is like all the creation of God throughout the animal and vegetable world. The brutes have living bodies, and so do the trees and plants.

2. Man has a soul. In this he is unlike the trees and plants, but he is like the lower animals. The soul is the seat of the emotions, the passions, the feelings, the desires, the likes and dislikes, the affections, and the will. All these things we have in common with the beasts.

3. Man has a spirit. In this he is unique among God's creatures. "The spirit of man is the candle of Jehovah" (Prov. 20:27), and it is this that is set aglow when man is born again; and then God's Spirit testifies with man's spirit that he is a child of God. God cannot be known by the body, nor by the soul, but only by the spirit. And even the human spirit is incapable of finding out anything about God or of knowing God except by revelation of the Spirit of God. "For what man knoweth the things of a man, save the spirit of man which is in him? even so the things of God knoweth no man, but the Spirit of God. Now we have received, not the spirit of the world, but the Spirit which is of God; that we might know the things that are freely given to us of God. . . . But the soulish (so the Greek) man receives not the things of the Spirit of God: for they are foolishness unto him: neither can he know them, because they are spiritually discerned. But he that is spiritual discerneth all things, yet he himself is discerned of no man" (1 Cor. 2:11-15).

The believer is spiritual only when he is ruled through his own spirit by the Spirit of God. If he is ruled by his body as dominated by his soul, he becomes a slave to his own affections, appetites, emotions, passions, and therefore is a willful, selfish man. The Word of God is extremely careful to distinguish: between things of the soul and of the spirit even judging "the thoughts and intents of the heart" as to whether such thoughts and intents are spiritual or soulish (Heb. 4:12). It declares that any wisdom which is not from above and therefore not from the Spirit of God, is "earthly, soulish, devilish" (James 3:15). It asserts that the false teachers of the end-time are "they who make separations, soulish, having not the Spirit" (Jude 19); and that having not the Spirit, they are "none of his" (Rom. 8:9). And, finally, it gives us the glorious assurance that when we get our resurrection bodies (1 Cor. 15:44) they will be no longer soulish ("natural" is incorrect here also), but spiritual: no longer dominated by selfishness and willfulness, but rather under the full and free control of the Spirit of God.

Do Beasts Have Souls?

Is it true that beasts have souls?

The Hebrew word for soul, *nephesh*, like the Greek *psuche*, implies self-conscious life, as distinguished from vegetables which have unconscious life. In this sense the beasts have "soul." But "soul" is not by any means identical with "spirit." Man has "spirit," which the beast does not have.

Spirits in Prison

Please explain 1 Peter 3:19.

I am passing on to you the answer of Dr. Scofield to a question proposed to him on this verse:

It is interpreted in three ways: (1) It is said that between Christ's crucifixion and resurrection He went into Hades and offered salvation through His cross to all the wicked dead; (2) that He preached in Hades declaratively—merely announcing the consummation of the predicted sacrifice to those who had rejected the promises during Old Testament times. The objection to the first interpretation is that the context of the verse limits the preaching to a particular class of sinners—those antediluvians who rejected Noah's gospel. Such favor to a special class of sinners who were warned for 120 years before the flood came is inconceivable. The objection to the second interpretation is that it puts Christ in the position of, so to speak, taunting the irredeemably lost—which is also inconceivable. He might have wept over them; He could never have exulted over them; (3) the third interpretation harmonizes the passage, the context, and the known character of the Redeemer. It is best stated in paraphrase. "Christ was quickened by the Spirit, by which Spirit in the days of Noah, while the ark was preparing, and the long-suffering of God waited, he preached to those who are now imprisoned spirits," awaiting the judgment.

This is as near to a satisfactory answer as any that I know. I suppose that for full light on the subject we must wait until the morning dawn.

Spiritual Filthiness

What is meant by the filthiness of the spirit in 2 Corinthians 7:1?

The answer is to be found in the whole passage, beginning with 6:14. Filthiness of the spirit is fellowship with that which is opposed to God. Satan is a spirit, and a great religious leader; and God's children are warned against that which is Satanic, particularly in the realm of religion. I believe that Masonry, with all its train of lodge-ism, is spiritual filthiness, because it is a Satanic unitarian religious system, opposed to God and His Christ. Beware of it.

Spoken by Jeremiah

Matthew 27:9,10 reads: "Then was fulfilled that which was spoken by Jeremiah the prophet, saying, And they took the thirty pieces of silver, the price of him that was valued, whom they of the children of Israel did value; and gave them for the potter's field, as the Lord appointed me." I cannot find this passage in Jeremiah, and the margin of my Bible gives the reference Zechariah 11:12,13. Does this make it appear that the Bible is not without error, and that 2 Timothy 3:16 is untrue?

The Syriac Version of Matthew, which is very ancient, omits the name of "Jeremiah" altogether and simply reads that "It was spoken by the prophet," not naming any. And therefore some have believed that the word "Jeremiah" has been added by some scribe in the New Testament text.

Others think that the whole volume of the prophets being in one book, with the prophecy of Jeremiah first in the old Hebrew arrangement, the reference was to the book which bore his name. The Jews used to say that "the spirit of Jeremiah was in Zechariah," and so they were as one prophet. Also, it has been suggested that the words were *spoken* by Jeremiah, but *written* by Zechariah. Or that Jeremiah himself was the author of the 9th, 10th and 11th chapters of Zechariah.

In any event it does not affect the truthfulness of the record. We shall find some day that every Word of God is pure.

Spoken, not Written

Is there a book called "The Lost Prophecy," referring to Matthew 2:23, "He shall be called a Nazarene"?

We have no knowledge of a book entitled, "The Lost Prophecy." It does not seem to me that there is such a mystery about the verse as many have suggested. It does not say that the prophets wrote, but only that they spoke, saying, "He shall be called a Nazarene." Doubtless the prophecy had been uttered by more than one prophet, else the plural noun, "prophets," would not be used. There can be no doubt that the Old Testament prophets see far more than they wrote, and this probably came down as an oral tradition rather than a part of a written document.

Suffering and Reigning

From 1 Timothy 2:11,12 it would appear that only those who suffer with Him shall reign with Him. Do not all Christians suffer in some degree, and are we not rewarded according to the amount of suffering we endure?

Yes, to both questions. According to 1 Corinthians 3:11-15 the believer's rewards are shown to depend upon the abiding character of his works as he builds upon the foundation, which is Jesus Christ. Of course, there is a very real relation between the believer's work and his suffering. No saved person can escape all suffering with Christ. In Revelation 2:26-28 authority over the nations is committed to the overcomer, and the overcomer in Scripture is described in Revelation 12:11: "And they overcame him by the blood of the Lamb, and by the word of their testimony; and they loved not their lives unto the death."

Suicide

I surely believe that if a person is born again he is saved and safe, but cannot see how a person could have time to repent while he is committing suicide, especially some kinds of suicide. People, when they suffer, often say that it would be so much better to be with the Lord, but Paul and Job and so many others did such great good while suffering on earth that I do not see how a person could commit suicide if he were born of God.

I think your confusion comes from a lack of understanding as to the solid foundation upon which the believer's security is resting. You say that you "cannot see how a person could have time to repent while he is committing suicide, especially some kinds of suicide." This remark leads me to suppose that you are under the impression that if a believer should fall into sin and then die before confessing the sin he would be lost. But the forgiveness referred to here is governmental or disciplinary forgiveness, and it does not touch the question of a believer's eternal salvation in any way whatever.

When a sinner believes on the Lord Jesus Christ and receives Him as his own personal Savior he is born again and comes into possession of eternal life;

and the teaching of Scripture is that this gift is really and truly "eternal." The believer is now a child of God. If he falls into sin after becoming a child of God, then his fellowship with the Father is interrupted until he confesses his sin and judges himself. When he thus confesses his sin and judges himself, forgiveness is held out to him and his fellowship with the Father is restored. But in case he should die before confessing his sin he would be taken at once into the Father's presence and live with Him there throughout eternity. "For if we would judge ourselves, we should not be judged. But when we are judged, we are chastened of the Lord, that we should not be condemned with the world" (1 Cor. 11:31,32).

Again—Suicide

I should like to have some information from the Scriptures regarding suicide. I have found nothing to advocate such a thing, nor anything against it. In this particular case the man made a profession of faith in the Lord Jesus Christ for a number of years, and I know he took an interest in the Lord's work. I believe that when a sinner accepts Christ Jesus the matter of salvation in settled.

I agree with you perfectly that salvation is the gift of God by grace through faith, and when once received it is forever.

I have no doubt that our loving Father will deal faithfully with His child. No one can tell why a person commits suicide. It is almost unthinkable that such a thing could be done when one is in one's right mind. But the Lord knows all about that, and whatever sin there is in it is included in the sins for which our Lord Jesus Christ died on Calvary.

On the other hand, of course, you never know whether a man is saved or not by the profession he makes. The Lord knows them who are His, but we do not. At any rate, we may depend upon it that the Judge of the whole earth will do right.

Why a Sword?

What is the meaning of Christ's words in Luke 22:36, "He that hath no sword, let him sell his garment, and buy one"?

We quote from Dean Alford in reply to this question. In discussing the much-controverted passage referred to in Luke, he says that its meaning appears to be, "to forewarn the Apostles of the outward dangers which will await them henceforward in their mission—unlike the time when He sent them forth without earthly appliances, upheld by His special providence, they must now make use of common resources for sustenance, yea, and even of the sword itself for defense. This they misunderstand, and point to the two swords which they have—for which they are rebuked . . . The sword of the Spirit (Olhausen and others) is wholly out of the question in interpreting this command. The saying is both a description to them of their altered situation with reference to the world without, and a declaration that self-defense and self-provision would henceforward be necessary. It forms a decisive testimony from the mouth of the Lord Himself, against the views of the Quakers and some other sects on these points. But He does not warrant aggression by Christians, nor, as some Roman Catholics would have it, spreading the Gospel by the sword."

On verse 37, Dean Alford says: "The connection is this: 'Your situation among men will be one of neglect and danger; for I myself (see Matt. 10:24,25) am about to be reckoned among transgressors.' By the very form of the expression it is evident that the sword alluded to could have no reference to *that night's danger*, or of *defending him from it.*" On verse 38, the Dean says: "Two of them were armed—either from excess of zeal to defend Him, excited by His announcement of His sufferings during the feast—or, perhaps, because they had brought their weapons from Galilee as protection by the way . . . They exhibit their swords, and supposing them to apply to that night. Our Lord breaks off the matter with *'It is enough'*—not *'They are sufficient';—but, 'It is well—we are sufficiently provided—it was not to this that my words referred.'* The rebuke is parallel with, though milder than, the one in Mark 8:17—as the misunderstanding was somewhat similar."

The Teacher's Responsibility

Will you kindly explain the meaning of James 3:1? Does it refer to the enmity of the world against anyone who in trying to do God's will?

No. It refers rather to the responsibility of the teacher. The 1911 Bible Translation reads: "My brethren, be not many teachers, knowing that we shall receive the severer judgment." There is a tremendous responsibility connected with the gift of teaching. It is the teacher's business to expound the Word of God, and woe be to the man who muddles his message and wrests the Scriptures! The judgment against him will be most severe.

The Study of Types

In his footnote for Exodus 25:1, Dr. Scofield, in discussing the authority for the types of Exodus, very scientifically lays down the Bible's proofs as to the verity of said typology, and then goes on most logically to state the two fundamental rules to be observed in determining just which person, event, ceremonial, etc., may be considered to be typical (in the Scripture sense of the word).

In Genesis 5 and 6, in discussing Enoch, Noah, the flood, the ark, Dr. Scofield distinctly speaks of them as respective types. While it is far beyond me to dispute our dear brother's word on this matter, seeing how exquisitely accurate he has shown himself to be in all his biblical analysis, I must confess that I cannot as yet understand why he did not consider these "types" as having the authority of "analogy, or spiritual congruity, merely," since I have not discovered any direct statements to the effect that in these instances we have evidence of typology and not simply analogy, etc.

I confess myself to be undoubtedly in error from the start, consid-

ering that I do not have time to examine thoroughly all the Scriptural bearings on the subject. For this reason, I have ventured to address you with regard to the matter as one who being thoroughly grounded in the harmony of Scripture cannot but lead an anxious child of God to see the light on these matters, notwithstanding their relative significance.

My own rule concerning types and typical study (and I think I am in agreement with Dr. Scofield) is this:

Any person or place or thing taken from the Old Testament and definitely employed in the New Testament in a typical sense is of course a type. There can be no question about that. But there are other types, as Dr. Scofield's notes intimate. He says: "All types not so authenticated must be recognized as having the authority of analogy, or spiritual congruity, merely." But you will observe that he speaks of these latter nevertheless as "types."

A rule I have always followed concerning types is this: I have insisted that no doctrine ought to be built on types alone, but that when the doctrine is established by the plain teaching of the Word of God, then it is beautiful and interesting and profitable to find the type in the Word of God which supports that doctrine.

In short, we may say there are two classes of types. First, those specifically authenticated by New Testament usage; and, second, those which while not so authenticated are yet so clear as to their "analogy, or spiritual congruity" as to be unmistakably intended for types.

Where it says in 1 Corinthians 10:11, "All these things happened unto them for types," it surely is not intended to limit the type to the things specifically mentioned in the chapter. The words, "all these things," constitute a general term, inclusive, as I understand it, of many other "things" not specifically mentioned in the chapter.

Unbelievers in Service

Should people who are not Christians sing Gospel hymns in public, that is, as solos or duets or special numbers? Can such be used by God for His glory?

The answer to the first question is No. For what is a person who is not a Christian? He is one who is treading under foot the Son of God, and counting the blood of the covenant an unholy thing, and doing despite unto the Spirit of grace (Heb. 10:29). How can he do anything that pleases God? He is a man in the flesh, and Romans 8:8 Paul says, "So then they that are in the flesh cannot please God." And then he goes on to say that the believer is not "in the flesh," but "in the Spirit."

The answer to the second question is that God is not limited, and therefore He can when He pleases use even such things to His glory. He can use a piece of dirty paper, if it happens to have the Gospel printed or written upon it, and if anyone reads and believes it he will surely be saved, despite the dirt on the paper. Thus an unsaved person might sing or even preach the Gospel, and anyone hearing it and believing it will be saved. But this does not mean that it is right to employ unbelieving singers or preachers, either paid or unpaid, to minister in holy things before God. It is wrong, and contrary to the Word of God.

Unbelievers Variously Described

Will you explain the difference between the children of disobedience, the children of wrath and the children of the devil (Eph. 2:2,3; 1 John 3:10); and also the ungodly and the sinner of 1 Peter 4:18? There must be a difference between these mentioned by Peter, because of the "and."

No; there is no difference. All five phrases are just different descriptions of unbelievers. They are all children of disobedience because they refuse to obey the Gospel; they are all children of wrath because the wrath of God rests upon them for this disobedience (John 3:36); they are all the children of the devil because they follow his desires (John 8:44); they are all ungodly because they refuse to conform to God's will for them; and they are all sinners because they have sinned and come short of the glory of God (Rom. 3:23). And we ourselves were by nature all these things: we were children of wrath as other. "BUT GOD!" Oh, what a glorious BUT is that! For the great love wherewith He loved us when we were DEAD, He saved us (Eph. 2:4). Who but God could love a dead thing and bring it to life? Hallelujah! What a Savior!

A Needed Warning

Will you kindly explain Galatians 4:17,18?

The Revised Version helps us here: "They zealously seek you in no good way; nay, they desire to shut you out, that ye may seek them. But it is good to be zealously sought in a good matter at all times, and not only when I am present with you." It is a needed warning against the enemies of grace, who sometimes profess great zeal and affection toward God's children in order to influence them against the truth.

Warning the Wicked

In Ezekiel 3:20 we read about a righteous man turning from his righteousness and committing iniquity. He shall die in his sins and his righteousness shall not be remembered. I always did believe, since I have been saved, that one who is born again will not be lost, but this verse has put a doubt in my mind. Please explain.

The context is important. Read the chapter, beginning with verse 17: "Son of man, I have made thee a watchman unto the house of Israel: therefore hear the word at my mouth, and give them warning from me. When I say unto the wicked, Thou shalt surely die; and thou givest him not warning, nor speakest to warn the wicked from his wicked way, to save his life; the same wicked man shall die in his iniquity; but his blood will I require at thine hand. Yet if thou warn the wicked, and he turn not from his wickedness, nor from his wicked way, he shall die in his iniquity; but thou hast delivered thy soul. Again, when a righteous man doth turn from his righteousness, and commit iniquity, and I lay a stumbling block before him, he shall die: because thou hast not given him warning, he shall die in his sin, and his righteousness which he hath done shall not be remembered; but his blood will I require at thine hand. Nevertheless if thou warn the righteous man, that the righteous sin not, and he doth not sin, he shall surely live, because he is warned; also thou hast delivered thy soul" (Ezek. 3:17-21).

You see, it was a preacher receiving his commission from God, being told what to preach. God is saying in effect, "You must preach what I tell you; and then, no matter what happens to the people, if you have preached faithfully what I tell you, you have delivered your soul." On the same principle Paul says in Acts 20:26,27: "Wherefore I take you to record this day, that I am pure from the blood of all men. For I have not shunned to declare unto you all the counsel of God." The life and death referred to in Ezekiel are not spiritual but physical. It is a matter of chastening, as in 1 Corinthians 11:30-32 and 1 John 5:16.

True Riches

Does the wealth of this world belong to God or to Satan? Is it God's will that some of His children should be poor?

"The earth is the LORD's, and the fullness thereof" (Ps. 24:1); "Behold, the heaven and the heaven of heavens is the LORD's thy God, the earth also, with all that therein is" (Deut. 10:14). He says: "Whatsoever is under the whole heaven is mine" (Job 41:11); "Every beast of the forest is mine, and the cattle upon a thousand hills. I know all the fowls of the mountains: and the wild beasts of the field are mine; . . . the world is mine, and the fullness thereof" (Ps. 60:10-12).

But, "hearken, my beloved brethren, Hath not God chosen the poor of this world rich in faith, and heirs of the kingdom which he hath promised to them that love him?" (James 2:5).

Riches are far more oftener a curse than a blessing, and poverty has done far more than riches to promote spiritual growth and health.

If you are saved you are rich indeed; and the multimillionaire who is unsaved is a poverty-stricken beggar compared with you.

Why Is Crime Permitted to Continue?

Will you please inform me as to how a just and loving God can sit in high Heaven and see the awful things that are being done these days, and not interfere?

Your question is not a new one. God's people have long faced it, and it is discussed frequently in the Word of God. There is much mystery connected with it, and we must wait for the solution of our problem until the morning comes without clouds, and shadows flee away. In Psalm 37:35,36 it is written: "I have seen the wicked in great power, and spreading himself like a green bay tree. Yet he passed away, and, lo, he was not: yea, I sought him, but he could not be found."

In Psalm 73 the same matter is discussed at great length. The Psalmist did not know what to say about it until he "went into the sanctuary of God; then understood" he "their end."

In some way not yet revealed to us, it would seem that the sufferings of this present time are necessary, and we are to remember that they are not worthy to be compared with the glory that is to be revealed. The proper attitude of faith is to wait on the Lord until the time of setting things right.

The Purpose of Parable Teaching

Why did the Lord Jesus teach in parables? Are parables and illustrations the same thing?

By no means. An illustration is given to ***reveal*** truth, but a parable is calculated to ***hide*** truth from those who have heard the truth and have refused to obey it. Read carefully Isaiah 6:9-13; 28:5-13; 53:1; Matthew 13:10-17; 4:10-12; Luke 8:9,10; John 12:35-41; Acts 28:25-28; Romans 11:25-27. (See also answer to question on "Inability to Believe, on page 81.)

The Peril of Perverting the Gospel

Please explain Galatians 1:8,9.

In this passage God's anathema is pronounce twice upon anyone preaching another gospel which is not another, thereby perverting "the gospel of Christ" (vs. 6,7). It is solemn language. "But though we, or an angel from heaven, preach any other gospel unto you than that which we have preached unto you, let him be accursed." As we said before, so say I now again, If any man preach any other gospel unto you than that ye have received, let him be accursed."

SUBJECT INDEX

A

Abaddon 62
Abomination of desolation, The 290
Abraham, Descendants of 309; Family of 309, 310; and Lot 319
Abraham's second family 481
According to His Purpose 210
Accountability, Age of 320
Adam, Before 55, 368
Adding to God's Words 12
Administration of the Ordinances 100
Adoption 80
Adornment, personal 206
Adultery, sin of 71
After the Great Tribulation 292
Age of Accountability 320
Age of the Earth 328
"All Israel" 137
Ambition, Christians and 200
Anathema Maranatha 357
Ancestry of our Lord— See *Genealogy*
Angels, fallen 64; nature of 64; of the churches 65; or men? 65
Annihilationism 153
Anointing of Christ's body 39
Anointings, Two, of our Lord 34
Antediluvian sons of God 348
Antichrist, The 274; Which Beast is? 287
Apollyon 62
Apostasy 321, 357; of today 358
Apostates 321
Apostles, Conversion of 320; Creed of 358; Death of 328
Apparent contradictions 17, 307
Appointed Portion 208
Appointed to die 148
Arab, The 318
Archangel, The 65
Ark, Noah's 358
Armageddon 291, 292
Assurance of salvation 82ff. See also *Eternal Security*
Astrology 251
At any moment 266
Atonement, The, and divine healing 243
Attaining the First Resurrection 280
Automobiles and prophecy 359
Avoiding offenses 206
Axe That Swam 354

B

Balaam 316
Baptism by fire 49
Baptism (Water) and circumsion 117; and the Lord's supper 114; and salvation 118; for the dead 121; Formula in 120; Greek words for 120; History of 117; of our Lord 121; of the Holy Spirit 46; No Salvation Through 118
Bathsheba, Father of 323
Beast, Mark of the 289
Beasts— See *Souls*
Beelzebub 62
Beersheba 318
Before Adam 55
Before and after the Great Tribulation 273ff.
Before the Rapture 274
Beginning of the New Testament 11
Belial 62
Believe, Inability to 81
Believer's Assurance 83
Believing and Understanding 222
Believing the Word 188
Bema, The 151
Bene, Israel 147
Benedictions 356, 374
Benjamin and Judah 141
Benjamin and Joseph 141
Bible, The, Whose Is? 15; and Baptism of the Holy Spirit 49; See also *Scriptures*
Binding of Satan, The 62
Birth, The Virgin, of our Lord 26, 32
Bishops 112
Blessing, Second 229
Blighted Fig Tree 143
Boats from Tiberias 324
Bobbed Hair 361
Body, Church both, Bride 98
Body, Satan's 61
Body, Vanity of 97; Discerning the 116
Book, A valuable 18; The Little, of Rev. 10 364; and Tree of Life 364; of Life 364; of Iddo 372
Books and the Book, The 305
Born Again, or from above 225
Born Dead, Case of Child 89
Born of Water and Spirit 225
Branches, Vine and 174
Bread, Children's 136
Brethren of our Lord 39
Bride, The— See *Church* 96ff.
Bride of Christ 98
British Israelism 251
Brother, Our Elder 29
Bruised reeds and smoking flax 232
Buchmanism 252— See *Oxford Movement*

C

Caiaphas, Prophecy of 324; Our Lord's reply to 34
Cain 316
Cain's name 321
Cain's wife 327
Calendar, The Jewish 145
Called and chosen 89
Canaanites, Driving out the 315
Canticles, The 10
Capital punishment 360, 362
Carcase, The, and eagles 293
Card-playing 207
Care in the use of words 357
Carefulness in soul-winning 360
Carnal Christians 207
Casting pearls before swine 308
Cast out, Not 83
Catholicism, Roman 249ff.
Cave, of Machpelah 209
Celibacy 249
Chance, No second 161
Child, Case of, Born Dead 89
Child Conductor, The 182
Children, of Joseph and Mary 31
Children and Sons, difference between 80, 327; how saved 88; Illegitimate 313; in the Kingdom 88; in the Rapture 88; Small, may they be saved? 87
Children's Bread, The 136; Crumbs 136; Salvation, Watch for your 88
Choir, Vested 101
Christ, Did He descend to Hell? 41; Finished work of 39; The Impeccability of 33; The Sinlessness of 33; After the Flesh 45; Reign of 301— See also *Jesus*;
Christ's Endless Kingdom 305
Christadelphianism 254
Christian: what is the? 87
Christian giving 106
Christians, and Ambition 200; and eating 214; and warfare 213; and worldliness 200; carnal 207; Christian stay-at-home 208; Science 254
Church, The, and Israel 60, 132; and the Tribulation 283; Discipline of 102; Institutional 110; Joining 101; of Christ 102; Ordinances of 114ff.; Raising money for 108; Selling books in 108; will it be divided in Heaven? 11; Women's Ministry in the 103
Church's Mission, The 96
Clergy and Laity 101
Clothing, Man's natural 317
Cloud of Witnesses, The 349
Coming, Second— See *Rapture*
Command, A Strange 34
Commanding God 238
Commandments, the Word 181
Commission, The Kingdom 275
Commission, The Great, in Mark 112; in Matthew 127
Complete Bible, A 10
Compromising with the World 202
Conception, The Immaculate 373
Conduct, Creed and 201
Conditions before Adam 369
Conditions of Discipleship 367
Confession and forgiveness 208; public 208
Conquest of Jericho 322
Conscience, an unsafe guide 210, 211
Consuming fire, A 21
Continue, If ye 80
Contradiction, No 314
Contradictions, Apparent 17
Conversion, Apostles 320
Converted, May small children be? 87
Convince a sinner, How to 184
Copyists' errors 17
Core 316
Cornelius 91
Cost of discipleship 207
Cousins, may they marry? 247
Covenant, Temporary 187
Created or evolved 57
Creation, A New 203; Days of 366; Firstborn of 25; God's perfect 55; The eternal 306
Creed and conduct 201
Cremation, why permitted to continue 396
Crisis of the World, The 217
Crowns— See *Rewards*
Crumbs, Children's 136
Crucifixion, Day of 191
Crucifixion and Resurrection Date 38
Cup, The, at Gethsemane 37

D

Dan to Beersheba 318
Danger from the moon 374
Daniel, Authenticity of book 352, 367; in the Lions' Den 366
Daniel's Seventy Weeks 285
Date setting 264
David, the tabernacle of 133
David, Throne of 296, 297, 298
David, Sure mercies of 298
David's prayer for restoration 318
David's sin in numbering the people 319
Day of Christ, of Lord, of God 294ff.; of the Lord 294; "That" 294
Daysman, The 315
"Days" of Dan. 12 287
Dead, Judgment of wicked 306
Dead Sea basin, The 320
Dead, Spiritually and physically 148
Dead, Child born 89; Preaching to 379
Death better than life 351; how abolished 148; in the millennium 304; of the apostles 328; the Second 159; to the law 180; Sought and not found 289; Soul after 159; Valley of the shadow of 153; Why Folks Die? 84
Debt to Israel 135
Decalogue 180— See also *Law and the Ten Commandments*

Definitions of Millennial Doctrines 261
Denominations 110
Departed, Consciousness and state of the 151
Desolation, Abomination of 290
Destruction of Flesh 103
Destruction of Jerusalem 339
Devil, The— See *Satan*
Did Christ Descend into Hell? 41
Die, Why Folks 184
Difference, Making a 206
Difficult to Determine 166
Dionysius the Areopagite 321
Dipping into Tithe 107
Disagreeing with Paul 99
Discipleship, Conditions of 367; Cost of 207
Discipline and eternal security 172
Discrepancy, An imaginary 313
Dispensation of the Gospel 125
Dispensations, Salvation and 77; distinguished 368; The Seven 368
Distinction with a difference, A 51
Distinguishing things that differ 294
Divine Healing, Is it in the Atonement? 243; May we Demand it? 244
Divine titles distinguished 20
Divisions in Psalm 119 14
Divorce 248
Dog and Hog 308
Double Sign 134
Drawings and desires of God 91
Drink, How to 203
Driving out the Canaanites 315

E

"Eagle" Saints, The 266
Eagles, The Carcase and the 293
Earth, Age of 328; Lifted up from 36
Eat, What may Christians 214
Ecclesiastes and immortality 162
Edomites, The 316, 318
Elder Brother, Our 29
Elders 112
Elders, The 272
Election and foreknowledge 221
Election and free grace 220
Election, God's Sovereignty 76
Elijah, How He Obtained Water 307
Elisha and the mocking children 328
"Eloi, Eloi, Lama Sabachthani" 39
Emmanuel 30
Enduring to the end 172
Equality of the priesthood, The 115
Eradication of the old nature 231— See also *Holiness* and *Sanctification*
Error, Sincerity in 95
Esau's tears 313
Escape, How shall we? 92
Esther 316
Eternal Creation 306
Eternal and everlasting 162; Life, Certainty of 167; Punishment 158
Eternal Security of the believer 165ff.; and Backsliding 165; and Discipline 164
Eternity—the word 161
Everlasting Father, The 28
Everlasting Habitations and Unrighteousness 195
Evolution 58; Scientists who discredit 57, 58
Excuse, Without 218
Expediency, a question of 369; Lawfulness and 205
Eye, The Needle's 87
Ezra's shame 315

F

Faith as a grain of mustard-seed 223; Living 222; Saving 222; The just shall live by 78
Fall of Man 66
False, teaching 369; worship 369
Fasting— See *Prayer and Fasting*
Fate of the lost at the Second Advent 293
Father, The Everlasting 28
Father, Who may call God 22
Fatherhood, Universal of God 22
Feast of Weeks 356
Fellowship with the Father 371
Fellowship, Way back to God's 84
Fig-tree, The blighted 143
Filthiness of the spirit 389
Finished work of Christ, The 39
Fire, A consuming 21; Lake of 150
Firstborn of creation 25
Flesh, Destruction of the 103; After the 45
Flood of Noah, The 362, 381
Forgiveness 167, 208
Feet Washing 122
Following, Responsibility of 211
Four Gospels, Why 11
"Four-square Gospel," The— See *Tongues*
Free from the Law 181
Frogs, The three 286
Fully persuaded 371
Fullness of the Gentiles, The 135
Future, concurrent events 288; generations 305; order of events in God's program 258

G

Gap Between Genesis 1:1 and 2 55
Genealogy of Jesus 5; Mary 29
Generation, This 132
Generations, Future 305
Genesis 1:1, Grammar of 351
Gentiles and the Law 183
Gentiles, The fullness of the 135
Gentiles, The times of 295
Ghost or Spirit 46
Gideon, Jerubbaal and 321
Gift of God, The 91
Gift of Tongues, The 54
Gifts from the Lost 103

Giving, Christian 106; Limit of 107
Glory, Knowledge of 300; millennial
"God is a Spirit" 23
God of gods 22
God Revealing Himself 8
God the Trinity 19, 20
God, Commanding 238; Drawings and Desires of 91; Gift of 91; How we shall see 155; the Rule and Righteousness of 23; The Son of— See *Jesus*; The unchangeable 22; and war 21; seeing 21; the Father 22; Without, and Hope 81
God's, name not mentioned 20; Perfect Creation 55; Sovereignty and man's responsibility 76, 220; will, How to know 209; "Gods many and lords many" 23
Gods, ye are 314
Golden rule, The 355
Gospel, the dispensation of 125; Have all heard 371; My 125; Paul's 125; What is it? 124; Why Four11
Gowned ministers and vested choirs 101
Grace, defined 186; falling from 186; for grace 85, 371; once in, always in 169
Grades of Offering 78
Grammar of Genesis 1:1 351
Grave, Hell and 149
Great, His Name Shall Be 23
Great Commission in Mark 112
"Greater works" 372
Greek New Testament, Why the 13
Growing into a Christian 226

H

Hades, past and present 148-149
Hair, Bobbed 361
Ham's descendants 330
Hardening the heart 372
Harlot, Rahab the 307
Harmony, Question of 151
Have All Heard the Gospel? 371
Head covering 103
Healed by His Stripes 245
Healing and the atonement 243; is it for this dispensation? 245; the sick 246; without saving 246
Hearing the trump 271
Heaven 154ff.; and Satan 61; a place 154; Assurance of being there 155; Catholics and 249; Gender in Heaven 156; Happiness in 154; Knowing each other there 156; New, and New Earth 156; No marriage in 157; Our loved ones there 156; Saved in 155; What it is like 154; Who will go there 155; Wives in 157— See also *Departed, State and Consciousness of the, and Hades*
Hebrew Feasts 132
Hebrew nation, The 131
Hell and the grave149
Hell, Did Christ descend into? 41
Hell, Reality of 158
Herod family, The 324
Herod the Great 331
Herod's Temple 144, 145
Hid Treasure and Pearl 197
His Name Shall Be Great 23
His Purpose, According to 210
His Wound Stripes 41
History of Baptism 117
Holiness 229; and perfection 229; and sinlessness 230— See also *Sanctification*
Holy Spirit— See *Spirit, Holy*
Honey 359
Hope, Without God and without 81; Our Present 265
Hoshea or Messiah 299
How Made to Believe? 223
How Many in the Rapture? 263
"How shall we escape?" 92
How to Convince a Sinner 184
How to Drink 203
How to Know God's Will 209
How to Tell 94
Human Reasoning or the Word of God? 382
Humiliation, Our Lord's Voluntary 25

I

Iddo, Book of 372
"If by any means" 278
"If ye continue" 80
Ignorance of Scriptures 12
Illegitimate children 313
Immaculate Conception 373
Immortality 162, 319
Immutable Things, Two 373
Impeccability of Christ 33
Imputation illustrated 67
Inability to believe 81
Insanity, The mysteries of 216
Insurance 353
Inspiration of Scriptures 7
Institutional Church, The 110
Intercession of Moses 238
International Bible Students' Assn.— See *Russellism*
Interpolation, An 17
Interpretation, Question of 14
Interpretation of Scripture 15
Israel, All 137; and the Church 60; and possession of the Land 133; Distinction between Judah and 138; Future Glory 147; in her own land 146; in travail 139; Lost tribes of 141; of God, The 142; Our debt to 135; Promises to 131; Restoration of 142, 143; The Remnant 140; Resurrection of 139; Special judgment for139; Special People 131— See also *Jews*
Israelites and Jews 142
Italicized words in the Bible 15
It is Possible 94

J

Jacob not a Jew 312
Jehovah's Witnesses— See *Russellism*
Jephthah's vow 331
Jeremiah, Spoken by 389; Lamentations of 354
Jericho, The conquest of 322
Jerubbaal and Gideon 321
Jerusalem, Destruction of 334; New 296
Jesus, Ancestry of 25— See also *Genealogy*; Reverence

toward 283; Temptation of 32
Jew and Gentile alike in blessing 143
Jew, Every 138
Jewish New Year, The 145, 363
Jewish sacrifices, Cessation of 143
Jews and Israelites 142, 321; and Jerusalem 144; Salvation of 139— See also *Israel*
Job's Prophecy 335
Joining the Church 101
Jonah as a type 335
Jonah as psalmist 335; the father of 335; meaning of his name 336
Joseph and Benjamin, types of Christ 141
Joseph and Mary's children 31
Joshua's long day 336
Judah, Israel and 138
Judah and Benjamin, Tribes of 141
Judah first 300
Judas Iscariot, a devil 336; and Peter 336; death of 337; reason for his call 336; son of perdition 336; never saved 318
Judge Not 212
Judgment of nations 296
Judgment of this world— See *Crisis*
Just persons 178
Just shall live by faith, The 78
Justifications, The Two 178

K

Keeping in the Love of God 213
Keys of the Kingdom 128
King or Lord? 29
Kingdom and Papacy 249; Commission, The 275; in a Picture 299; in mystery and manifestation 127; Keys of the 128; Laws of the 127; Offer of, to Jews 128
Knowing Christ after the flesh 45; Each Other in Heaven 156; our destination 164; When We Are Saved 163
Knowledge of the glory, The 300
Knowledge of time and place of salvation 83

L

Laity, Clergy and 101
Lake of fire, The 150
Lamb, Marriage Supper of the 273
Lamentations, Divisions in 14
Lamentations of Jeremiah, The 354
Land of the shadow of death 153
Language of Daniel 352
Language, A universal 354
Last Gentile Ruler 288
Law, The, and Gentiles 183; death to the 180; Free from 181— See also *Ten Commandments*
Lawfulness and expediency 205— See *Vegetarianism, Food*
Laying on of hands 52
Lazarus and Christ 194; Death of 337; Did he walk out 317; Rich Man and 152
Leaven, Meaning of 196
Led by the Holy Spirit 51
Left Behind, Those 216
Legalism and schism 110
Letter, The Spirit and 85
Life, Book of 364
"Lifted up from the earth" 34
Light, Christ as universal 217
Linen Clothes, Napkin 194
Literal or figurative interpretation 15
Living creatures, The four 327, 331
Living Faith 222
Longevity before the flood 362
Lord, Humiliation of the 25; His Voluntary Threefold Office 32; Is at Hand 277; Two Anointings of the 34
Lord's Brethren 39; Word to Caiaphas 34
Lord's Supper, The 114; and baptism 114; Use of wine 232
Lost, Gifts from 103
Lost Tribes of Israel 141
Lost, Why Men Are 86
Lot 319
Lot's wife 338
Love to God and man 186; of God; Keeping in the 213
Lucifer 62
Lunar 319

M

Machpelah, Cave of 405
Magdalene, The 317
Making a difference 206
Making His Grave with the Wicked 41
Mammon of unrighteousness— See *Steward*
Man 57; created or evolved? 57; Fall of 66; A Perfect 97
Manna 352
Man's Natural Clothing 317; Responsibilities 220
Many Called, but Few Chosen 89
Marah, The waters of 318
Mark of the Beast, The 289
Marks of the Lord Jesus, The 374
Marriage, Regulations as to 47ff.; and Divorce 247; Supper of the Lamb 273
Mary, Children of 31; Genealogy of 29
Masonry, a Unitarian organization 254
Matter of Pronouns, A 375
Meaning of Apostasy 357; Leaven 196; Reprobate 382
Melchisedec 338
Messiah and Christ 28
Michael the archangel 339
Mighty or Almighty 31
Millennial Condition 301
Millennial Dawnism— See *Russellism*
Millennial glory 300
Millennium, Bloody offerings in the 304; Conditions in 301; Death in 304; Our Lord's subjects in the 304; Our residence during the 303; Sin and death in 303ff.
Ministers, Gowned 101

Minister's Title, The 112
Mischievous Practice 265
Misconception, a popular 30
Mission, The Church's 96
Mizpah benediction 374
Modernism 255
Money, Raising, for the church 108
Moon, Danger from the 375
Moral obligations, Our 181
Mormonism 255
Moses, The body of 311; Was he virgin born? 310
Moses' disobedience 310, 311; parents 311; father-in-law 339; intercessory prayer 238
Murderers, Salvation for 92
Mystery of New Birth, The 82
Mystery of the Trinity 19
Mysteries of Insanity 216

N

Nahum's predictions 376
Nail in a sure place 45
Napkin and Linen Clothes 194
Nations, Judgment of 296
Nature Clothing, Man's 317
Nazarite vow, Our Lord's 36
Nearing the End 263
Needle's Eye, The 81
Nehemiah's woe 315
New Birth, Mystery of 82
New Covenant 365
New Creation, A 203
New Earth, The 296
New Heaven and New Earth, The 157
New Jerusalem 296
New Thought 256
New Year, The Jewish 363
Next thing, The 265
Nicolaitanes 340
No Contradiction 314
No Denominations in Heaven 156
No General Judgment 260
No Rain Before the Flood 381
No second chance 161
Noah, Daniel and Job 341; Descendants of 312
Noah's ark 358
Norm, The principle of the 13
Not Blotted Out 365
"Not cast out" 83
Not Changed but Abolished 187
Numbers, The significance of 355
Numerics 376

O

Obligations, Our Moral 181
Offenses, Avoiding 206
Offering, Grades of 78
Offering, One 227; No More a Sin, 387
Oil and wine in Rev. 6 293
Old Testament saints and the Bride 272
Omnipresence of the Holy Spirit 52
On what day did Jesus rise 42
"Once every year" 376
One Omitted Tribe 341
Onesimus 315
One taken and the other left 262
Ordained ministers and their functions 99
Order of events in prophecy 260
Order, Scriptural 114
Ordinance of the Red Heifer 209
Ordinances, administration of 100
Ordination of preachers 99
Origin of the Rainbow 381
Our appointed portion 208
Our Lord's, Brethren 39; Threefold Office 32; Voluntary Humiliation 25
Our present Hope 265
Oxford Group Movement 252

P

Papacy, The, Its Future 245
Parable teaching, The purpose of 195ff., 396
Parables, Why? 359
Paradise 150
Parallelisms in prophecy 271
Passover, The Last 377; minus the lamb 377
Pastors 112
Paul as a Pattern 271; Disagreeing with 99; the stoning of 326; : was he married? 341
Paul's fear of becoming a castaway 171; Jewish vow 341; stripes 342; thorn in the flesh 349
Peace 377
Pearl, Meaning of the 197
Pearls before Swine 308
Pentecost, Typical meaning of 378
Perdition, Son of 289, 336
Perfect, A, Man 97
Perfection, Holiness and 229
Peril of perverting the gospel, The 396
Peril of rejecting Christ, The 87
Personal Adornment 206; Problem 380
Personality of the Holy Spirit 48
Peter and the Keys 342; as the Rock 343; Denial of 342; The Threefold questioning of 342, 343
Peter's martyrdom 326
Petra, Refuge in 282
Philemon and Onesimus 315
Philip's Message to Samaria 347
Plowshares and swords 354
Polygamist, The first 378
Polygamy 378
Popular Misconception 30
Portion, Our Appointed 208
Pounds and Talents 196
Power of the air, The 61
Practice, A Mischievous 265
Pray, How to 240; How to in wartime 241; Who may 234, 240; Should little children? 241; Should the unsaved? 240
Prayer and Fasting 241, 242; Promise 239; Delay Is Not Denial 23; for the unsaved 237, 239; the Disciple's, called the Lord's Prayer 235; Moses' intercessory 238; Negative answers to 239; of faith 243; proper posture in, The 235; Successful 234; Unceasing 236
Praying for the Spirit 47
"Praying through" 237
Preacher's program, The 100

Preaching to the dead— See *Spirits in Prison*
Predestination 221— See *Election*
Pre-eminence, Place of 379
Pre-millennialism 262ff.
Presumptuous sins 67
Priesthood, Equality of 115
Principle of the norm, The 13
Problem, A personal 380
Prodigal Son, The 196
Professing Christians left behind 269
Prohibition 233
Promise, Prayer and 239
Pro-Millennialism 261
Promises to Israel 131
Pronouns, A matter of 375
Prophecy, U.S. in 286; and Automobiles 359; of Caiaphas 324
Prophetic parallelisms 271
Psalm 119, Divisions in 14
Punishment, Capital 360
Purgatory 149, 150
Purpose, God's eternal 210
Pyramids, The 355

Q

Question About Tongues 54
Question of Expediency, A 369
Question of Harmony 151
Question of Interpretation 14
Question of Time 30
Question of Trumpets 270

R

Rabble, The 311
Rahab the harlot 307
Rain before the flood 381
Rainbow, Origin of 381
Raising Money for the Church 108
Rapture, meaning of word 263; and second advent 263ff., 266, 267l; and the Great Tribulation 262, 273; Before the Great Tribulation 262; Imminent 262ff., 267; Interval between, and Revelation 267; Partial, not scriptural 263ff., 268; Preachers after 277; Pre-millennial 261ff.; Professing Christians left behind 269; Salvation after the 274; Who will have part in 263, 276
Raptured, Millennial position of those 261ff., 275
Reconciling Scripture 170
Redemption, Universal 82
Red Heifer, Ordinance of 209
Reformation and regeneration 226
Refuge in Petra 282
Regeneration: Born again, from above 226; Born of water and Spirit 226
Reign of Christ 301
Rejecting Christ, The peril of 87
Remnant, The Sealed 140; Present-time 140
Repentance and salvation 81
"Reprobate," meaning of 382
Responsibility of Following 211; of Leadership 373; of man 220
Resurrection of Christ 193, 194; and Life 261; body of believer 193; body of unbeliever 193, 281; no general 261; of Jewish nation 139, 279; of Lazarus 194; of saints 193; on what date 38; on what day 42
Resurrections, How many? 279
Revelation 12, Woman of 272
Reverence toward the Lord 383
Rewards, Salvation and 92, 93
Ribband of blue, The 353
Right to Pray 241
Righteousness of God and of Christ 384
Rightly Dividing the Word 267
Roman Catholic, Bible 17
Roman Empire, The 348
Rome and Russia 290
Rule and righteousness of God 23
Ruler, The last Gentile 288
Russellism 256-258
Russia and Rome in the End-time 290

S

Sabbath, The, and Lord's day 189; in the Millennium 189
Sacrifices, Old Testament 384
Saints Raised at Christ's Resurrection 193
Salvation, Adam's 92; and Rewards 92; and the dispensations 77; and Repentance 81; defined 76ff.; during the Great Tribulation 281; for murderers 92; in the Present time 79; of Unitarians and Roman Catholics 93; Working out your own 173
Samaria, The Holy Spirit at 50
Sanctification 227ff.; by contact 228; Instantaneous? 227; Progressive? 227
Satan and his body 61; delivered unto 60; his limitations 63; his personality and power 63; and Heaven 61; not omniscient 62; Sin and 67; the Church and Israel 60; to be bound 59, 62; Why study about him 59
Saved in Heaven 155
Saved and safe 173
Saved and sure of it 163
"Saved by his life" 90
Saved, Was Judas Ever? 318
Saved with difficulty 90
Saving one's life and losing it 384; others with fear 384
Schism, Legalism and 110
Scriptural Order 114
Scriptures, Ignorance of 12; of our Lord's time 16 — See also *Bible*
Sealed Remnant 140
Seasons, The continuing 385
Second blessing, The 229; chance, No 161
Seeking another's wealth 200
Selah 359
Selling Books in the Church 109
Separation 204
Septuagint, The 10
Service from the unsaved 386, 394

Serving the Lord at home 386
Setting of times and dates 264ff.
Seventy Weeks, The, of Daniel 285
Shall We Become Vegetarians? 215
Shame, Ezra's 315
Shiloh, Come 28
Sickness— See *Healing, Discipline*
Sign, Double 134
Significance of Numbers 355
Signs of the Lord's Coming 264
Simeon, Tribe of 140
Simon the Sorcerer 349
Sin and no Sin 71; Selfishness 70; Satan 67; Inbred 70; Presumptuous 67; righteousness and judgment 68; The Unpardonable 68, 69; of worry 215; unto Death 69; what it is; its cause 66ff.
Since or when 50
Sincerity in Error 95
Sinlessness 229— See also *Holiness*
Sinlessness of Christ 33
Sinner, A, how to convince 184
Sinning in Hell 150
"Six hundred threescore and six" 289
Solar and lunar years 323
Solomon, The temple of 144, 352
Some Better Thing for Us 323, 359
Son of Perdition, The 289
Sons, Children and 80
Soul and spirit 388; Sleeping 153
Soul Winning, Carefulness in 360
Souls of beasts 389
Sovereignty of God 76, 220— See also *Election, Predestination*
Spirit, Holy at Samaria, The 50; Baptism of 46; Blasphemy against 49, 52; Distinction With a Difference 51; Filled with 51; Ghost or Spirit 46; Grieving away the 52; Led by the 51; Omnipresence of 52; Personality of 48; Praying for 47; Striving with man 51; Tongues and the 54; Unity of the 53; Witness of 48
Spirit and the letter, The 85
Spiritism 258
Spirits in Prison 379, 389
Spiritual Filthiness 389
Spoken by Jeremiah 389
Spoken, not Written 390
Standing and State 204
Stay-at-Home Christians 214
Steward, The Unjust 195
Stoning of Paul, The 326
Strange command, A 34
Stripes, His Wound 41
Striving With Men, The Holy Spirit 51
Suffering among God's people 361
Suffering and Reigning 390
Suicide 391
Sun worship and Sunday worship 99
Supper, Lord's 114
Sure of Heaven 164
Sure Place, Nail in a 45
Swam, Axe That 354
Swine, Pearls Before 308
Sword, Use of 354, 356; Why the 392
Synoptics, The 12

T

Tabernacle of David 133
Talents, Pounds and 196
Tares, Wheat and 198
Teachers true and false 325
Temperance 232, 233
Temple of Herod 145; of Solomon 144, 352
Temples, The, of Zerubbabel and Herod 145
Temporary Covenant 187
Temptation of Jesus 32
Ten Virgins, Parable of 197
Theophanies, The 45
"This Generation" 132
"This is my body" 115
Thorn in the Flesh, Paul's 349
Those that look for Him 293
" Thou and thy house" 91
Time, A question of 30
Times of the Gentiles 295
Tires 353
Tithe, The 107; Dipping into the 107
Tongues and the Holy Spirit 54; as a sign 54
Touch, Mary forbidden to, the Risen Lord 44
Transition period 50
Travail, Israel in 139
Tribe, of Simeon 140
Tribulation, The Great 273ff., 281, 282; Salvation During 281; Years of 282
Tribulation and the Church 283; Before and after 274, 292; Length of 282; Out of the 282; Preachers in 282; Saints in 283
Trinity, The 19; and Unity 20; Mystery of 19
True riches 395
True and false teachers 325
Trump, The last 270
Trumpet and Trumpets 270
Trumpets and Revelation 270
Twenty-four Elders 272
Two Anointings of Our Lord 34
Two chapters alike 12
Two Justifications 178
Two immutable things 373
Two Witnesses 284
Types, Study of 378

U

Unbelievers described 394
Unceasing Prayer 236
Unequal yoke 204
Unevangelized world, The 218
Unitarianism 258
United States in prophecy, The 286
Unity 259; of God 20; of the body 97; of the Spirit defined 53
Universal Fatherhood and Brotherhood 259
Universal language 354
Universal Light 217
Universal Redemption 82, 259
Unjust Steward 195
Unrighteousness and Everlasting Habitations 195
Urim and Thummim 357

V

Valley and land of the shadow of death, The 153
Vegetarianism 215
Vested Choir 101
Vine, The, and the branches 174
Virgin birth, The 26, 32
Virgins, The Ten: meaning of 197
Voting for Christians 216

W

Walking in the flesh 94
War, God and 21
Warfare, Christian and 213
Warning the Wicked 295
Washing Feet 122
Watchfulness, Why exhortations to 269
Way Back to God's Fellowship 84
Wealth, Seeking Another's 200
What Day of the Week? 191
What Is Grace? 186
What May Christians Eat? 214
Wheat and Tares, Meaning of 198
When, Since or 50
Who Are They? 285
Who will be caught up? 268
Who will hear the shout? 269
Whose is the Bible? 15
Why a Sword? 392
Why folks die 184
Why Four Gospels 11
Why men are lost 86
Why Parables? 359
Why Should We Watch? 269
Why the Greek New Testament 13
Wicked dead, Judgment of 306
Wicked, Making His Grave With 41
Wine, Oil and 290; Our Lord's position as to 232
"With Me" 293
Without excuse 218
Witness of the Holy Spirit 48
Witnesses, Cloud of 349; The Two, of Rev. 11 284
Wives in Heaven? 157
Woman of Rev. 12, The 272; which was a Sinner, The 350
Woman's Ministry in the Church 103
Word, Believing the 188; of God 7; of God, Human Reasoning or 382
Words, Italicized 15; Care in the use of 357; of God, Adding to 12
Works, Greater Than These 372
World, Compromising with 202; Crisis of 217
Worldliness, Christians and 200
Worry, Sin of 215
Worship, False 369
Wound Stripes of the Lord 41

Y

"Ye are gods" 314
Years of the Tribulation 282
"Ye Think Ye Have" 172
Yoke, The unequal 204

Z

Zacaharias, Punishment for unbelief 350
Zealously affected 363
Zerubbabel, Temple of 144
Zion 353

SCRIPTURE INDEX

Genesis

1:1 20, 55, 328, 351
1:2 55, 368
1:7 381
1:14 217
1:24 57
1:26, 27 19
2:5, 6 362, 382, 386
2:6 381
2:10 355
2:16, 17 159
2:18 249
2:23, 24 97
2:24 98
2:25 317
3:1 64
3:4 162
3:7 317
3:15 26, 322
3:16 105
3:16, 17 66
3:20 92
3:21 318
3:22-24 338
4:1 321
4:1-7 316
4:19-24 378
5 393
5:3-5 327
5:4-32 362
6 393
6:1-4 348
6:2 65
6:3 51, 358
6:13, 14 358
7:7 312
7:11, 12 362
7:19, 20 362
8:2 362
8:22 362,385
9:1-6 213, 233
9:5 363
9:6 360
9:12-17 382
9:13 362, 381, 386
9:18, 19 312
9:27 330
9:29 362
10 312, 330
10:2 284
11:26-29 309, 310
11:31 310
12:4 310
12:5 57
13:5-18 319
13:18 319
14:1-16 319
14:18 305
15 178
15:6 178
15:13-16 146
17:9-14 311
17:17, 18 235
18:22, 23 235
18:25 337, 360
19:12, 14 340
19:26 218, 338
19:29 319
20:12 178, 309
21 323
22:9, 12 178
22:20-23 309
23:16-20 309
24:11-13 235
25:1-4 310
31:49 374
32:30 21
33:1,2 64
33:19 309
35:18 141
36:1 318
38 313
45:1-4 141
46:26, 27 313
49:10 298
49:16, 17 341
49:29-32 309
50:13 309

Exodus

2:18 339
3:1 339
3:2 64
3:2-10 338
4:18 339
4:24, 25 310, 311
4:25, 26 340
6:20 311
8:25, 26 202
8:27, 28 202
9:6-8, 20, 21 351
10:8-11 202
10:24-26 202
12 97, 98
12:1, 2 363
12:15-20 196
15:23-27 318
16:14 352
19:5, 6 197
20:8-11 109
20:11 366
23:16 132, 363
24:10, 11 45
24:18 355
25:1 393
25:17-20 338
25:40 157
28:30 357
29:37 228
30:29 228, 247
32:32, 33 238
34:22 363
38:8 333

Leviticus

2:11 196, 359
4:1, 12, 13 67
6:12 370
8:8 357
10 369
10:1, 2 67, 370
10:8, 9 370
11:1-8 215
12:1-8 30, 31
12:1-14 30
16:12 370
16:12, 15 376
18:1-30 247
18:24-30 315
19:2 230
19:31 349
20:6 349
20:10 71
22:14 67
23 132, 279
23:5 191
23:7, 8 191
23:9-14 44, 53
23:9-22 261
23:11 44
23:15-21 189
23:17 196, 378
23:24 271
26:18, 21, 24, 28 265
27:1-8 333
28:15-21 197

Numbers

4:23 333
6:3 36
6:4 36, 232
6:20 36
10:29 339
11:4-6 311, 312
11:7,8 352
14:20, 21 300
15:32-36 110
15:38 353
16 428
19 209
20:14-21 316
22 316
22:35-38 8
23 316
23:21 72
27:21 357

Deuteronomy

7:6-8 131
7:15 244
9:18-25 355

10:14 395
10:17 22
12:29-32 315
12:31, 36 332
13:10, 11 360
16:9-12 356
17:17 379
18:10-12 349
18:13 230
22:5 361
23:2 313
23:17, 18 303
24:1-4 248
25:3 342
27:6, 12 135
28 245
28:61 244
28:62-65 146
29:29 221, 264
30:1-3 146
30:1-9 310
32:8, 9 131
32:48-52 70
33:8 357
34:5, 6 311, 339

Joshua

5:11 352
7:6-9 235
7:16-26 70
10:12, 13 336
20:3-5 67
24:32 309

Judges

3:1, 2 214
4:11 339
7:2 300
8:35 321
10:16 332
11:9-11 333
11:30-40 331, 334
16:28 235
17 and 18 341

Ruth

1:20 373

1 Samuel

2:8 316
18:19 314
19:20-24 8
24:16 30
28:6 17, 357

2 Samuel

2:5 64
6:23 314
7:10 301
7:14 26, 325
7:18 235
11 313
11:3 323
21:8, 9 313
23:8 17
24 319

1 Kings

5:8, 9 144
6:7 144
7 352
7:16 124
8:61 230
10:1-3 6
11:1-4 379
11:29-32 141
12:17 141
12:20 141
12:21-23 141
13:1, 2 372
13:11-22 8
17:17 244
18:33-35 307
19:4 235

2 Kings

1:2 244
1:2-16 62
2:23-25 329
2:11 329
6:5, 6 354
8:8 244
14:25 335
16:6 312
18:5 307
20:2 235
23:25 307

1 Chronicles

3:5 25, 323
3:16 296
4:41-43 141
10:14 17
24 272

2 Chronicles

3:16 144
9:29 373
10:5, 12 192
11:12-14 141
12:15 372
13:22 372
15:1 373
15:9 141
16:9 52
16:12 244
20:7 178
21:15 244
34:6 141

Ezra

2:63 357
7:27, 28 315
8:22, 23 315
9:5, 6 235

Nehemiah

2:3, 4 235
2:19 316
4:1-6 315, 316
4:7-9 316
4:10-23 316
5:1-19 316
6:1-14 316
6:15 315
7:1-3 338
9:4, 5 235
9:13, 14 110

Esther

2:5 312, 321
4:16 192
5:1 192
1:5 67
1:6-12 59
1:8 334
1:9-12 61
2:4-6 61, 162
9:33 315
10:20-22 151
19:25-27 335
19:26 149, 160
27:6 334
33:19 244
39:27-30 293
41:11 395
42:5, 6 334

Psalms

2:5 283, 286
2:7 21, 26, 325
2:7-9 60
8:3 217
19:13 67
22 325
22:16 36
23:4 153
24:1 197, 395
34:20 98
37:20 159
37:35, 36 396
42:1-6 57
45 53, 198
45 6,7 425
45:11 29
45:14 272
50 260
51:4 74
51:6 208
51:12 318
60:10-12 395
65:4 155
68:18 152, 351
69:4 31
69:7-9, 21 31, 40
73 396
76:10 241
78:60-72 133, 134
82:6 21, 314
88:10 160
88:12 153
91:5 374
96:11-13 124
101:8 302
102:25, 26 157
102:25-27 325
104:2 318
104:4 325
104:14,15 232
107:9 232
110:1 325
111:9 112
115:17 160
119 14
119:105 198
121:6 374
133 53
135:4 197
144:1 214
145:20 159
146:4 159

Proverbs

11:22 308
11:30 195, 360, 372, 385
16:11 308
20:27 388
23:20 232
23:29-32 232
25:27 359
31:4-7 232

Ecclesiastes

1:1-4 162
3:19, 20 159
7:1, 2 352
8:11 360
9:5, 6, 10 159

Song of Solomon

5:16 372

Isaiah

2:4 354
2:10-22 284
3:18-26 353
4:5, 6 386
4:6 381
6 81
6:1-8 16
6:1-10 45, 338
6:2-7 338
6:9-13 396
7:14 325
8:19, 20 252
8:20 259
9 31
9:1, 2 153
9:6 28
9:6, 7 298
9:7 301
10:28-32 292
11:3-5 127
11:4 302
11:9 300
11:10, 11 299
11:12, 13 142, 301
14:9-11 160, 162
14:9-14 369
14:12-20 62
16:5 134
18:1 286
19:19, 20 355
21:27 103
22:25 44
22:15-25 44
24:1 369
27:6 131, 136, 197, 321
28:5-13 396
28:16 344
32:17 82
33:20-24 134
34:5, 6 318
34:11 55
35:4-10 124
35:8 94
36:6 323
38:18 150
40:15-17 348
41:8 178
42:1-4 323
43:19 282
45:11 238
45:18 55, 369
51:16 9
53 325
53:1 396
53:2 352
53:4 244
53:4, 5 245
53:5, 9 41
53:7 36
55:1, 2 232
55:8, 9 158
57:15 161, 208
60:19, 20 386
62 147
63:1-6 292, 354
63:3 293
65:17 157, 303
65:17-19 295
65:17-25 303
65:20 302, 304, 305
66:22 295
66:23 190

Jeremiah

1:9 9
4:23 55
4:23-27 368
13:17 354
17:9 386
22:24-30 25, 26, 33, 296, 299
22:30 298
23:5, 6 33, 298, 299
23:5-8 142, 146
24:1 296
25:15-26 364
25:11, 12 146
25:27-29 21
30:7 60, 286
31:31-34 135, 138, 149, 365, 387
31:33 48
32:37-41 135
49:7-22 316

Lamentations

1:22 354
2:22 354
3:66 354
4:22 316, 354
5:22 354

Ezekiel

1 338
2:8—3:3 364
3:17-21 395
14:14 341
14:14-20 367
20:33-38 137, 138, 139, 141
20:33-44 260
21:27 28
25:12-14 316
28:3 367
28:11-17 59
28:11-19 61
28:12-15 369
32:29, 30 316
33:11 159
35:15 316, 318
36:5 316, 318
36:25-27 226
36:34-36 142, 143
37 142
37:9 355
37:11-14 16
37:21-25 146
37:22 301
38 and 39 284, 290
39:25-28 143
43:21 304
47 142
48 142
48:1-7, 23-29 142

Daniel

2 368
2:35 287, 292
4:23, 33, 34 265
6:10 235
6:22 366
6:24 366
7 290, 291
7:2 355
7:13, 14 155
7:16 65
7:24 291
7:25 287
9:7 129
9:20-27 285
9:24-27 267, 282
9:27 284, 287
10:5-14 338
10:13 65
10:21 65
11:31 287, 291
11:37 288
12:1 65, 286, 339
12:1, 2 139
12:1-3 279
12:3 196, 360, 372, 385
12:4 287
12:7-13 287
12:11,12 287, 291

Hosea

2:1-23 310
2:14-23 141
3:4, 5 144, 377

Joel

2:31 295
3:9-16 354
3:19 316

Amos

1:11, 12 316
2:9 153
9:11-15 133, 134
9:13-15 143

Obadiah

1—9 316
10-14 316
15-21 316

Jonah

1:1 335
1:17—2:2 335
2:1 235
3:4 355

Micah

4:1-3 354, 355
5:2 26, 298
5:3 139

Nahum

2:3 294
2:3, 4 359

Habakkuk

1:12-17 78
2:2-4 78
2:1-15 78
2:14 300

Zephaniah

3:8, 9 354

Haggai

1:13 64
2:7 300

Zechariah

4:1-6 47, 198
6:1-6 28
8:13-23 147
8:20-23 143
8:23 251, 321
9, 10, 11 390
11:12, 13 390
12:7 300
12:10 272
14:2 290, 292
14:1-9, 16 143, 292, 295
14:4 224, 269, 292
14:5 292, 324
14:6, 7 385
14:16 190
14:21 136

Malachi

1:4 316
3:1 64
4:1 153
4:2 60
4:5 285

Matthew

1 299
1:1 297
1:1-16 26
1:5 307
1:6, 7 313
1:16 29
1:18-25 26, 30, 325
1:23 30
2:2 136
2:19, 20 324
2:22 324
2:23 30, 390
3:2 124, 301
3:15 121
3:16, 17 19
3:17 37
4:2 355
4:10-12 396
4:13-16 153
5:48 230
6:9-13 235
6:13 239
6:25-34 215
6:33 23
7:1 212
7:6 308
7:12 355
7:21-23 308, 383
7:22 64
7:24, 25 344
8:10 138
8:16,17 244
8:17 245
9:17 161
9:30 34
10:6 138, 161
10:16-23 172
10:22 172
10:24, 25 392
10:25 62
10:28 159
10:32 222
11:11, 12 11
11:21-26 34
11:23 149
11:25 9
12:20 322
12:22, 23 68
12:24 64
12:24-32 48, 52, 68
12:31, 32 69
12:33-37 69
12:40 191, 192, 335
12:46 39
12:47-50 207, 367
13:10-17 396
13:24-30 198
13:25, 38,39 55
13:33, 44-46 196, 197
13:43 348, 372
13:55, 56 31, 39
14:1-12 324
15:9 114
15:21-28 13, 136
15:24 161
15:26, 27 136, 137
16:6 196
16:16 320, 342
16:18 149, 343
16:19 53, 102, 128, 342
16:28 299
17 311
17:5 37
17:11 285
17:20 223
17:21 241
18:3 88
18:10 151
18:11 161
18:15-19 102
18:15-20 212
18:18 102, 129
19:4 57
19:8, 9 248
19:24 81
20:16 89
21:19 143
21:22 234
21:31, 32 307
22:14 89
22:23-33 156
22:30 156, 348
22:32 162
23:17-19 228, 247
24:13 172
24:14 113, 121, 124, 246, 265, 266, 275, 282, 283
24:15 285, 286, 290, 291, 367
24:19, 20 292
24:21 286
24:27-30 301
24:28 266, 293
24:29, 30 197, 273, 295
24:29-31 127, 267
24:32 142
24:32, 33 143
24:34 132, 133
24:36-44 267
24:40-42 262
24:48-51 276
25:1-13 197, 273
25:14-30 196, 276
25:31-46 260, 295, 296
25:31 124
25:34 128
25:41 64, 150, 159
25:41 64, 150, 159
25:46 161
26:26-13 35, 350
26:28 365
26:29 35, 232
26:33 342
26:38 36
26:39-42 37
26:40 198
26:64 34
27:3-10 337
27:9, 10 389
27:34 40
27:34-38 31
27:52, 53 193, 261
27:60 41
28:1 42, 187, 188, 191
28:18-20 113, 120, 127, 275

Mark

1:12, 13 61
2:22 161
3:22 48, 62
3:22-30 52
3:30 48, 52, 69
4:10-12 359
6:3 40
7:3, 4 171
7:18, 19 215
7:27, 28 136
8:15 196
8:17 392
8:22-26 34
8:31 192
9:1 299
9:11-13 285
9:29 241
9:38-48 159
9:42-48 149, 150, 258, 259
9:43-48 160, 162
10:6 57
10:29, 30 368
11:12-14 143
11:24-26 234
12:25 156
13:13 172
13:32-37 267, 269, 273
14:3 34, 35
14:3-9 35
14:18 377
14:58 192
16:15-18 112
16:16 119
16:18 246

Luke

1:19 65
1:26 65
1:31-33 26, 28, 29, 146, 298, 301
1:33 305
1:62 350
1:80 138

2:1-40 80
2:24 31, 79
2:37 333
2:39-41 31
3 22, 299
3:1 324
3:17 49
3:23 29, 297
3:23-38 25
3:31 313
4:22 297
5:30-32 307
6:38 108
6:48 344
7:24 64
7:36-38 35, 317, 350
7:36-50 34
7:37, 38 34
7:46 35
8:9, 10 396
8:56 33
9:2 245
9:3 245
9:20 28, 325
9:24, 25 385
9:27 299
9:62 173
10:1-12 248
10:14 89
10:15 149
10:17, 18 37
10:18 60, 61
10:27 186
11:13 47, 48
11:14-20 48
11:14-23 52
11:15-19 62
12:8 222
12:35, 36 198
13:6-9 143
14:3-9 350
14:16-24 207
14:26 207, 367
14:36 37
15 161, 196
15:1, 2 178
15:7 178
16 159, 257
16:1-9 195
16:8, 9 317
16:18 248
16:19-31 149, 150, 160, 162, 257
16:22-31 259
16:23 257
16:24 120
16:26 149, 150
17:6 223
17:20, 21 347
17:32 338
17:34-37 262
17:37 293
18:1 236
19:11 128
19:11-27 196
20:35 268
20:34-36 156
21:24 142, 144
21:28 124
21:34-36 267, 273
21:36 268
22:14-18 377
22:15 377
22:17 36
22:20 368
22:31, 32 61
22:32 342
22:36-38 245, 356, 392
22:42 37
23:34 239
23:43 149, 257
24:13-32 117
24:21 192
24:34 343
24:44 9, 17

John

1:1, 2 27
1:1-3 325
1:1-5 26
1:1-15 26
1:9 217
1:11, 12 222, 249
1:11-13 46, 48, 81, 82, 87
1:12, 13 165, 223
1:14 325
1:16 85, 371
1:18 21, 45
1:29 37, 218, 325
1:31 138
1:42 346
2:12 40
2:17 31, 40
2:18-22 193
2:19 81, 192, 343
2:20 145
2:21 31
2:43, 44 317
3:1-7 46
3:3 252, 347
3:3-7 49, 386
3:3-8 48, 54
3:5 118, 119, 225
3:6-8 310
3:10 138, 226
3:12 225
3:14 36
3:14, 15 335
3:14-16 36
3:15 162
3:15, 16 161
3:15, 16, 18, 36 165
3:16 162, 348
3:17 37, 347
3:18 82, 174, 185, 347
3:19 217
3:29 198
3:33 48, 225
3:36 162, 394
4:10-15 225
4:20-24 135
4:22 98, 131
4:42 37
5:17 39
5:18 167
5:22 64
5:24 162, 165, 174, 260, 358
5:28, 29 57
5:37-40 172
5:39 167, 172
5:39,40 82, 167
6:23 324
6:27 232
6:28, 29 372
6:35-56 352
6:37 84, 167
6:37-40 167, 364
6:39, 40 165
6:42 297
6:44 91
6:70 274, 336
6:70, 71 308, 337
7:3-5 31
7:5 39
7:37-39 203, 204, 209, 226
7:39 48
8:12 217
8:24 9
8:42-44 22
8:44 59, 394
8:56 160
8:70, 71 318
9 365
9:2, 3 246
9:31 234
10:17, 18 37
10:27, 28 69, 162
10:27-30 165, 168, 170, 174
10:28 162, 223
10:31-36 314
11:2 34
11:5, 6 236
11:25, 26 261, 271
11:26 160
11:33-44 194
11:49-51 324
11:49-52 8
12:1-8 34, 35, 350
12:25, 26 36
12:20-33 217, 218
12:25-33 36
12:31 60, 61, 68
12:32 36, 175, 217
12:33 36, 68
12:35-41 396
12:37-41 45
12:39 81
12:40 372
13:1-17 122
13:3-10 209
13:18 336
13:26 274
14:2 156
14:2-4 294
14:6 258
14:12-14 237, 240, 372
14:13, 14 234, 236
14:16 52
14:16,17 49
14:18 90
14:23 240
14:25,26 122
14:27 377
14:28 27
14:30 60
15:1 232
15:2 176
15:2, 6 174
15:7 234, 238, 240
15:10 213
15:10-12 74
15:25 31
16:3 68
16:7-11 185, 223
16:9 68
16:12, 13 122
16:12-15 49

16:13 47
16:19 102
16:23, 24 384
16:23-27 236, 237, 240
16:33 208, 283
17:3 162
17:4 39
17:9 237, 239
17:12 274, 289, 337
17:17 227
18:11 319
18:14 324
19:26, 27 208, 367
19:28-30 31, 40
19:31 191
19:31-37 98, 272
19:41, 42 41
20:7 194
20:8, 9 194
20:17 44
20:22, 23 49, 102
20:27 44
20:30, 31 12, 14, 81
21:15 342, 343
21:18-24 326

Acts

1:1 39
1:8 127
1:11 146, 325
1:14 40
1:15 347
1:16 9
1:18-20 337
1:25 150, 318
2 53, 277, 342, 347, 368
2:4 49
2:14, 37 347
2:20 295
2:23 337
2:25-27 150
1:27, 31 149, 150
2:27-34 149, 150
2:29-31 160
2:38 50, 119
2:38, 39 119, 129
2:39 129
3:12 347
4:8 347
4:11, 12 344
4:18-20 214
5:1-11 70
5:15, 29 347
6 99
7:2-4 310
7:51 52
7:59, 60 235
7:60 239
8 342
8:12 347
8:12-17 52, 53
8:14-17 50, 129
8:15-17 50
8:18-24 348
9:4, 5 235
9:34-40 347
10 103, 114, 342, 347
10:2-4 234
10:25,26 347
10:43 165
10:44-48 50, 117, 143
10:47, 48 113
11:14 91, 234
12:4 38
13 99, 324
13:22 313
13:33 26
14:15 33
14:19, 20 325, 349
14:22 208, 283
14:23 99
15:10 380
15:13-18 133
15:14 60, 135
15:14-17 146, 301
15:16 133
16:31 92, 165, 239
17:28 22
17:30 376
17:34 321
19 130
19:1-5 114
19:2 50
19:4, 5 113
20:24 124
20:26, 27 395
21:4 342
21:9 105
21:18-26 341
24:14 9
24:16 211
25 324
26 324
26:10 341
26:16-18 100
18:25-28 396

Romans

1:1 124
1:16 165
1:16, 17 322
1:17 78, 384
1:18-20 376
18:19, 20 218
1:20 218
1:28 382
2:1-16 143, 164, 218
2:6 143, 218
2:7 164
2:12 376
2:13-15 143
2:14 110, 180, 181, 182, 183, 187, 375
2:14, 15 180
2:25-27 143, 183
2:28, 29 142, 183
2:29 86
3:2 13
3:6 218
3:12 306
3:20 188
3:21-26 165
3:22 384
3:22, 23 82, 334
3:23 394
3:24-26 338, 376
3:25 78, 79, 85, 384
3:26 79, 91, 178, 316
4 165, 178, 222
4:2-4 178
4:5 178
4:5-8 72
4:9-12 143
4:12 142
4:13 296
4:15 73
4:16 186
4:25 83, 325
5:1 378
5:1, 2 300, 356
5:3, 4 319
5:8-10 90
5:10 90
5:12 319
5:12, 13 184
5:13 184
5:18, 19 82, 176
5:20 201
5:21 82
6:1-3 49, 201
6:2, 3 50
6:3 46, 48, 54
6:3, 4 117
6:11 201
6:11-13 47, 51
6:14 73, 80, 81, 82, 91, 159, 180, 181, 182, 187, 190, 205, 375
6:14, 15 201
7 278
7:1-4 187
7:6 86
7:7 188
7:16, 17 72
7:18 231
7:22-24 73, 74
7:23, 24 57
8 66, 188
8:1 17, 174
8:4 188
8:7, 8 386
8:8 103, 108, 394
8:8, 9 49, 230
8:8-11 48, 51
8:9 90, 198, 231, 388
8:12-14 94
8:15-18 220
8:16 48
8:16, 17 310
8:18 362
8:19 348, 372
8:23 80, 151, 244, 245, 318
8:26 240
8:28, 29 24, 210
8:28-30 221, 380
8:29 77
9, 10, 11 77
9:3 239
9:4, 5 272
9:18 372
10:3 73
10:8-10 165
10:9, 10 83, 222, 229, 249
10:12, 13 136
10:17 83
11:2 175
11:5 135, 140
11:6 175, 186
11:11-15 15
11:11-27 137
11:25 135
11:25-27 132, 136, 138, 139, 147, 175, 251, 321, 396
12:1 47, 51
12:1, 2 51, 79, 210, 229
13 213

13:1 233
13:1-7 21
13:4 360
13:11 280
13:15, 16 79
14:16 206
14:18 382
14:21 201, 205, 206, 207, 215
15:1 215
15:3 31
15:4 305
16:10 382
16:16 102

1 Corinthians

1:2 227
1:8 295
1:12 111
1:18-25 322
1:23, 24 36
1:30 229, 384
2:9-13 14
2:11 57
2:11-15 388
2:13 14
2:14, 15 14, 386
3:10-15 111
3:11 344, 347
3:11-15 93, 152, 170, 171, 207, 260, 390
3:15 206
3:16 47, 49, 229
4:2 126
4:5 212
5:1 247
5:1-5 169, 260
5:4, 5 102
5:5 60, 103, 246, 295
5:5-8 196
5:9-13 212
5:13 169
6:1-8 212
6:2, 3 276
6:3 64, 261
6:11 227
6:12 215
6:19 47, 51, 52, 198, 229
6:19, 20 48, 90, 197
7 249
7:2 379
7:5 242
7:8 341
7:8, 26 249
7:10-16 248
7:14, 15 228
7:14-16 247
7:32-34 379
7:39 247
8 206, 207, 215
8:5, 6 19
8:7 211
8:7, 12 211
8:13 205, 206, 207, 215
9:2 111
9:5 40
9:5, 15 341
9:19-23 341
9:24-27 93
9:27 170, 171, 382
10:4 344
10:11 393
10:13 63
10:20 22
10:23 205
10:23-29 200
10:24 200
10:31 207
10:32, 33 200
11 103, 104
11:1 200
11:5 105, 106
11:6, 15 361
11:16 102
11:17 115
11:17-34 170
11:19 382
11:20 115
11:23-34 370
11:24 97
11:25 11
11:26 114
11:26-32 170
11:27-32 70, 116
11:29 116
11:30 116, 175
11:30-32 69, 166, 207, 395
11:31, 32 93, 102, 170, 171, 174, 213, 260, 391
12:12, 13 49, 54, 229
12:13 46, 48
13:2 223
13:12 156, 267
14 54, 104
14:3 105
14:18, 22, 28 54
14:23-35 105
14:33 55
14:33-37 104, 105
15 155, 193
15:3 325
15:3, 4, 22, 23 159
15:4-8 325
15:19 352
15:20 193
15:20-23 261
15:20-24 44
15:22 176
15:23 44
15:24 128, 295, 301, 305
15:26 303
15:28 294, 305
15:29, 30 121
15:36, 37 281
15:44 388
15:47-50 57
15:51 148
15:51-54 261, 327
15:51-58 263
15:52 270, 271, 280
15:52, 53 149, 271
15:56, 57 74
16:2 106, 107
16:22 356, 357

2 Corinthians

1:14 295
1:21, 22 47, 48, 49, 54
2 169
2:1-4 149
2:5-7 260
2:5-11 103, 151
2:6-11 61
2:7-11 110, 170
3 182, 184, 189, 190, 368
3:1ff. 86, 111
3:3 182
3:6-9 86, 380
3:7-11 74, 109, 185, 187
3:11, 13 182
3:18 49, 86, 210
4:4 22, 60, 61, 124
4:7 198
4:16-18 246
5:1-8 155, 160
5:6-8 148, 150, 153, 162
5:8 164, 257, 258
5:9 200, 206, 260
5:10 93, 152, 260
5:14 37
5:14, 15 70
5:15 175
5:16 36, 45
5:17, 18 203
5:19-21 72, 260
5:21 66, 68, 384
6:5 242
6:9 215
6:14 204
6:14—7:1 247, 248, 255, 317, 348, 389
6:15 62
6:17 204
7:1 389
7:8-16 103
7:10 81
8:5 107, 108
8:5-12 107
8:8-12 107
8:9 79
8:12 107, 109
9:6, 8, 11 106
9:7 106, 108
10:1, 6-8 111
10:14 124
10:18 382
11:2 111, 198, 272
11:4 125
11:13 111
11:13-15 61, 317, 325
11:22 111
11:24 342
11:27 242
12:1-9 349
12:1-10 326
12:2 326
12:2-4 149, 150, 256, 257, 351
12:7 64, 155, 246
12:7-9 244
12:8, 9 239
13:5-7 382

Galatians

1:5 161
1:6 125
1:6-9 396
1:13, 14 278
1:18, 19 40
2:7 124
2:9 347
2:16-21 180
2:20 201, 325
3 165

3:13 245, 260
3:19 109, 182, 185
3:19-25 181, 368
3:19-29 189,
3:23-25 80, 187, 327
3:23 to 4:7 183ff., 375, 376
3:24 170, 182
3:24, 25 78, 80
3:25 109
3:25, 26 189
3:27 46, 48, 50, 54, 117, 118
3:28 60
4 327
4:5 80, 183
4:13-15 349
4:14 64
4:17, 18 363, 394
4:19 372
4:22-31 16, 225
4:26-29 310
5:1 181
5:4 186
5:6 179
5:8, 9 196
5:22, 23 47, 175
6:1 123
6:1, 2 213
6:2 74
6:6-8 108
6:14 181
6:17 349, 374

Ephesians

1:4 76, 77
1:5 77, 80
1:5, 11 221
1:7 236
1:13 49, 54
1:13, 14 47, 48, 54, 197
1:14 244
1:20-23 34, 345
1:22, 23 53, 60, 98, 135, 139, 272, 353
2:1-10 96, 165
2:2 60, 61
2:2-4 394
2:8 83, 91
2:8, 9 118
2:10 175, 387
2:12 136, 183, 376
2:14, 15 136
2:14-18 143
2:19-22 353
2:20 98, 345, 347
3:1-7 262
3:14 235
4:3, 13 53, 54, 60
4:4, 5 46
4:4-6 119
4:7-10 150
4:8 150, 193
4:8-10 148, 257, 351
4:8-16 345
4:10 154
4:12, 13 96
4:13 97
4:23 97
4:30 47, 48, 49, 52, 54
4:32 85, 236
5 97
5:8 179, 204
5:10-17 210
5:18 47, 49, 229, 232
5:18-21 48, 49
5:23 345
5:25, 26 97, 116, 226
5:25-27 119, 353
5:25-28 208, 367
5:25-31 98
5:25-33 98, 111, 272, 276
5:26 209
5:27 111
5:30 46, 97, 98, 112
5:31 97, 98
6 235
6:1 369
6:12 61, 211
6:15 124
6:18 238, 240
6:24 356, 357

Philippians

1:1 173
1:6 52, 295
1:6-10 295
1:19 173
1:21-23 160, 162
1:25, 26 173
1:29 361
2:5-11 27
2:7 25
2:12 175
2:16 295
3:2, 3 308
3:10, 11 278, 280
3:11 268
3:20, 21 281
4:1 93
4:6 234
4:6, 7 216
4:6, 7, 9 378
4:13 182

Colossians

1:9-12 210
1:13 347
1:13-18 325
1:15 25, 26
1:15-18 26
1:16, 17 27, 217
1:18 345
1:23 80
1:24 39, 361
1:27 325, 372
2:9 31, 155
2:9, 10 85
2:10-14 375
2:11, 12 117
2:12 117
2:13 236, 375
2:14-17 188
2:16 190
2:18 125
2:18, 19 345
2:20 327
2:23 370
3:1-4 165, 181
3:17 113

1 Thessalonians

1:4, 5 220
1:9, 10 98, 263, 267, 268, 269, 278, 283, 286, 293
2:14 102
2:19, 20 93
4:7 230
4:13-18 110, 148, 261, 263 267, 268, 285, 292, 327
4:16 266, 270, 280
4:16-18 60, 97, 271, 272, 295
4:17 263, 266, 269, 276, 292
5:2 295
5:9 49, 286
5:9, 10 263, 267, 280, 290
5:16-18 209
5:19 52
5:22, 23 51
5:23 227

2 Thessalonians

1:5 268
1:6-9 275
1:7-10 198, 273
1:9 161, 293
1:10 324
2:1-3 294
2:1-10 291
2:2 294, 295
2:3 112, 287, 289
2:3-8 274
2:4 102, 287, 291
2:7 51, 52, 277
2:8 161, 285
2:9-12 259

1 Timothy

1:5, 19 211
1:11 124
1:16 271
2 104
2:1 237, 239
2:1-4 237
2:4 91
2:5, 6 159, 315
2:6 257
2:7, 12, 13 16, 105
2:8 234
2:9 206
2:11-14 104, 390
3:2-12 379
3:6 59
3:9 211
3:15 347
4:1 254
4:1-3 249
4:1-5 215
4:2 211
4:4 205
4:10 37, 82, 176, 218
4:14 99
5:8 353
5:22 99
5:23 232
6:15, 16 28, 29, 32, 216

2 Timothy

1:3 211
1:6 99
1:10 148, 153
1:13 357
2:15 170, 382
2:19 198
2:20, 21 319
3:1-5 294
3:5 198

3:8 382
3:12 208
3:13 112
3:16 8, 181, 390
4:3 254
4:8 93, 280

Titus

1:6 379
1:15 211
1:16 382
3:5-7 210, 226

Philemon

16 67, 315
18 67

Hebrews

1:1 27
1:1-3 325
1:2 28, 310
1:3 9, 217
1:4 156
1:5 26
1:5, 6 64
1:6-13 325
2:3 92
2:9 37, 82, 176, 218
2:10 124
2:11-13 310
2:12 29
2:14 159
2:15 153
2:16 64
2:17, 18 25, 32
3:6 27
3:12-14 173, 372
3:14 80
4:12 388
4:15, 16 25, 32, 33
4:16 238
5:7 38
5:10 170
5:13, 14 352
6:4-6 170, 173
6:8 382
6:17-20 373
7:1-3 338
7:3 26, 28
7:9, 10 184
7:25 90, 325
8:2, 5 157
8:4, 5 144
9:7 376
9:9 384
9:11, 12 44
9:12-14 209
9:13, 14 209
9:14 211
9:15 78, 85, 377, 384
9:27 148, 337
9:28 273, 276, 280, 293
10:1-3, 11 144, 387
10:4 384
10:5 33, 387
10:8, 12 304
10:9,10 227
10:10 227, 229, 387
10:10-12 209
10:10-14 229, 366, 387
10:15 48
10:15, 16 387
10:16, 17 365, 387
10:18 387
10:19-25 346, 387
10:22 211
10:24, 25 214
10:26 166
10:26, 27 387
10:26-29 173
10:28, 29 386
10:28-31 387
10:29 82, 87, 103, 159, 165, 166, 394
10:29-31 21, 234, 241
10:37, 38 78
11:3 28
11:6 108, 234
11:10 319
11:31 307
11:35 280
11:39, 40 323
11:40 151, 263
12:1 349
12:1-11 93
12:6 174, 354
12:7 260
12:8 177
12:14 229
12:15 173
12:16, 17 313
12:18-24 181, 242
12:23 263
12:25-29 21
13:4 249
13:8 245
13:15, 16 79

James

1:12 93, 382
1:15 71
1:18 46, 48, 49, 119
2 222, 225, 226
2:5 396
2:14-17 224
2:14-26 178
3:1 392
3:15 388
4:7 68
5 137
5:14, 15 244, 245
5:16 167
5:17 33
5:19, 20 166

1 Peter

1:2 220, 221, 227
1:3-5 165, 280
1:4 244
1:10-12 335
1:18, 19 197
1:20 16
1:22, 23 225, 226
1:22-25 83
1:23 119
1:23-25 46, 48, 49
2:2 37
2:4 41
2:1-5 353
2:4-6 347
2:4-8 344
2:19-21 368
2:24, 25 245
3:1-4 206
3:9 220
3:15 10
3:16, 21 211
3:18-20 379
3:19 389
3:20 358
4:6 379
4:18 91, 394
5:1-4 346
5:1-5 112
5:4 93
5:6-10 362
5:7 216
5:8 59, 173

2 Peter

1:10 174
1:11 91
1:16-18 299
1:19 198
1:20 16
1:21 8, 9
2:1, 2 112, 254
2:4 64, 65, 261
2:7, 8 319, 338
2:15 316
2:20-22 87, 173
2:22 308
3:5, 6 55
3:5-13 157, 306
3:9 91
3:10 294, 295
3:10-13 295
3:15, 16 125
3:17 173

1 John

1:1-9 167, 211
1:7n 84, 209, 253, 305, 371
1:7-10 209
1:8 73
1:9 70, 84, 85, 196, 200, 208, 236, 260, 343, 370
2:1, 2 36, 82
2:2 36, 176, 218, 219
2:3-6 74
2:8 217
2:12 236
2:18, 19 167
2:18-27 47
2:19 321, 358
2:20-27 48, 49, 54, 94, 369
2:22, 23 258
3 227
3:1 208
3:1-3 265, 318, 372
3:2 227
3:4 188, 189
3:4-10 74
3:5 121
3:6 230
3:8 71
3:9 71-73, 230
3:10 394
3:14 83
3:20 371
3:23, 24 383
4:1 254
4:2, 3 182, 324
4:4 60
4:12, 18 45
5:1 223
5:1-13 165
5:2, 3 181, 182

5:4, 5 111
5:10 9, 48, 185
5:12 36
5:13 83, 164, 172, 223
5:14, 15 234, 238, 240
5:16 395
5:16, 17 69, 70

2 John

5 74
9-11 358

3 John

7 103

Jude

1 227
6 64, 261
8, 9 59, 311, 339
9 65
11 316
14 324
19 90, 388
21 213
22, 23 206
23 360, 385
24 47, 372
24, 25 227

Revelation

1:1 8
1:6 272
1:10 187
1:12-19 338
1:18 149
2 64
2:6 340
2:10 93
2:13 280
2:14 316
2:26-28 390
3 64
3:5 364, 365
3:7 45
3:8 280
3:10 239, 268, 280, 286
3:12 347
3:14 26
3:14-16 110, 197
3:20 34
4 337, 338
4:1 270
4:4 272
4:9, 10 161
5:6, 7 155
5:8 272
5:8-10 276, 338
5:9 327, 338
6:8 149
6:9-11 151, 155, 160, 162
6:15-17 293
7:1 355
7:1-8 282, 341
7:1-17 282
7:4 198
7:4-8 140
7:7 141, 283
7:9-14 124
7:9-17 151, 281, 282
7:14 277, 286
8:1-6 290
9:6 289
9:11 62
10:6 161
10:8-11 364
10:10 159
11:2 286
11:3 282, 286
11:3-12 284, 285
11:15 270
12:1-6, 13-17 60, 272
12:5 60, 97
12:6, 14 60, 282
12:7 65
12:9, 10 59, 61
12:11 111, 390
13 285, 286
13:1 288
13:1-4 60
13:1-8 291
13:2 274
13:5 287
13:7 283
13:8 85, 316
13:11 288
13:11-17 287
13:14-18 287
13:15 303
13:17 286
13:18 289
14:3, 4 198
14:6 124
14:13 160
15:1 267
16:1 267
16:13 287, 288
16:13, 14 286
16:14 284, 287
19 21, 292
19:11 262, 286, 295
19:11-16 267, 296
19:11-21 284, 295, 354
19:16 29
19:19 284
19:19, 20 161, 285, 287, 288
19:21 287, 303
20:1-3 62
20:1-10 301
20:3 303
20:4-6 261, 295, 296
20:5, 12-15 176
20:6, 12, 15 153
20:7 296
20:7-9 128, 284, 303
20:7-10 295
20:7-14 303
20:10 59, 60, 61, 64, 68, 158, 159, 161, 288, 301
20:11-13 57
20:11-15 151, 257, 261, 295, 296, 306
20:12 305
20:12, 13 160
20:13, 14 149, 150, 153
20:14, 15 41, 149, 150, 159, 167
21 97, 296, 346
21:1 295
21:1-4 303
21:2 133
21:8 167
21:9, 10 98
21:14 346
21:15 101
21:24-26 302
22:1 301, 305
22:4 151
22:11 150
22:14, 18, 19 13, 174, 364
22:17 133
22:19 173, 364
22:20 146